GENDER IMAGES

READINGS

FOR

COMPOSITION

GENDER IMAGES

READINGS

FOR

COMPOSITION

MELITA SCHAUM

CONNIE FLANAGAN
University of Michigan, Dearborn

HOUGHTON MIFFLIN COMPANY   Boston   Toronto
Dallas   Geneva, Illinois   Palo Alto   Princeton, New Jersey

Senior Sponsoring Editor: Carolyn Potts
Senior Developmental Editor: Lynn Walterick
Project Editor: Karen Parrish
Design Coordinator: Martha Drury
Production Coordinator: Renee LeVerrier
Manufacturing Coordinator: Priscilla Bailey
Marketing Manager: George Kane

Printed in the U.S.A.

Library of Congress Catalog Card Number: 91-71960

ISBN: 0-395-59489-8
  CDEFGHIJ-AH-99876543

ACKNOWLEDGMENTS

Anthony Astrachan. Anthony Astrachan, "Men and the New Economy," *M/r Magazine*, 1988, (Vol. 1, No. 1). Reprinted by permission of Georges Borchardt, Inc. for the Author. Copyright © 1988 by Anthony Astrachan.

Margaret Atwood. Margaret Atwood, "The Loneliness of the Military Historian," *Times Literary Supplement*, September 14–20, 1990, pp. 976. Reprinted by permission of Margaret Atwood, © 1990.

Eugene R. August. "Real Men Don't: Anti-Male Bias in English" from *The University of Dayton Review* 18 (Winter-Spring 1986–87). Copyright 1986 by Eugene R. August. Reprinted by permission.

Dave Barry. From DAVE BARRY'S GREATEST HITS by Dave Barry. Copyright © 1988 by Dave Barry. First published in the Miami Herald. Reprinted by permission of Crown Publishers, Inc.

Diane Barthel. Diane Barthel, "A Gentleman and a Consumer," *Putting on Appearances: Gender and Advertising* (Philadelphia: Temple University Press, 1988) pp. 169–183, 209–210. © 1988 by Temple University. Reprinted by permission of Temple University Press.

Acknowledgments are continued on pages 669–673, which constitute an extension of the coyright page.

CONTENTS

Contents

ANNOTATED CONTENTS

Slopping straight shots, eyes blotted, vanity-blown
In the expectation of glory: *she writes like man!*

At first the Crazy Lady appeared to be remarkably intelligent. She was
older than the rest of us, somewhere in her thirties (which was why we
thought of her as a Lady), with wild-tan hair, a noticeably breathing
bosom, eccentric gold-rimmed old-pensioner glasses, and a tooth-
crowded wild mouth that seemed to get wilder the more she talked.

I decided to be a writer not because I was a great reader as a child or
had any natural gift for language but because I wanted to speak the
truth as I saw it. . . . What is is my domain. What ought to be is the
business of politicians and preachers.

. . . in the Smithsonian Institution in Washington, D.C., there hangs a
quilt unlike any other in the world. In fanciful, inspired, and yet simple
and identifiable figures, it portrays the story of the Crucifixion. It is
considered rare, beyond price. . . . it was made by "an anonymous
Black Woman in Alabama, a hundred years ago."

"We'll be fine afterward. Just like we were before."
"What makes you think so?"
"That's the only thing that bothers us. It's the only thing that's
made us unhappy."

Comprehension is attained when the reader achieves a balance between empathy and judgment by maintaining a balance of detachment
and involvement.

And as soon as the old people said, "Poor Emily," the whispering began. "Do you suppose it's really so?" they said to one another. "Of
course it is. What else could . . ." This behind their hands; rustling of
craned silk and satin behind jalousies closed upon the sun of Sunday
afternoon as the thin, swift clop-clop-clop of the matched team passed:
"Poor Emily."

Not only is "A Rose for Emily" a supreme analysis of what men do to
women by making them ladies; it is also an exposure of how this act in
turn defines and recoils upon men.

13   Men Working   *532*

14   The Workplace Inside the Home   *563*

PREFACE

Gender is a topic that is relevant to both women and men. However, the few college anthologies now available on gender studies seem, on close inspection, to be overwhelmingly focused on women's issues, offering only a handful of token readings by and about men, despite a rich and growing body of work on masculinity and men's lives. Both women *and men* speak in *Gender Images: Readings for Composition*, and they do so from a variety of social and political viewpoints, from the outspokenly liberal to the more traditionally conservative. The seventy-five selections here offer individual perspectives on definitions of masculinity and femininity, women's and men's uses of language, sports and fairy tales, art and advertising, work and power, pornography and war.

Because gender is not a single area of study but encompasses and draws energy from a wide range of disciplines, these readings have been pulled from diverse fields to complement and challenge one another—history, politics, art, literature, popular culture, economics, psychology, sociology, and the sciences. The voices in the implied discussions among these fields are, desirably, quite varied, their conclusions still open, their arguments still debatable. Moreover, these voices articulate how extensively issues of gender are mediated by race and class, thereby challenging the assumption that when we speak of gender we speak of a constant or fixed entity.

On a technical level, the essays in *Gender Images* have all been selected as models of good writing and compelling analysis, presented through a variety of rhetorical methods. Students will find numerous prose styles and conventions represented, from scientific studies to humor, from personal narrative to political analysis, and from fables and poetry to polemic.

Above all, these writers share a strong intellectual commitment to their subjects, and their writing shows well-reasoned development of argument and clarity of expression. To help focus and contextualize these writings, we offer at the outset of each chapter a brief "Contexts" section. Questions at the end of each chapter, "Making Connections," urge students to think about ways in which essays within—as well as across—chapters play off each other, challenge or complement each others' positions, reinforce or call into question each others' findings. These questions encourage students to examine the fundamental assumptions behind a selection or selections and to respond thoughtfully through a range of discussion and writing assignments.

Our only regret in compiling this collection, and it was keenly felt, concerned the many fine essays we were not able to include because of the inevitable constraints of space. Many of these essays appear as references for further reading in the *Instructor's Resource Manual* that accompanies the text.

There, too, the instructor will find an introduction to critical thinking skills, summaries and suggestions for teaching the essays in *Gender Images*, and model course syllabi emphasizing particular themes.

The process of reading and thinking about these essays has been an exciting one for us, made even more stimulating by the many people who gave their time and energy in shaping this book. We wish to thank the reviewers who provided encouragement and insightful comments at each stage of the project: Valerie Balester, Texas A & M; Laurel Brodsley, UCLA; Patsy Callaghan, Central Washington University; Toni-Lee Capossela, Stonehill College; Margaret Ford, Houston Community College; Cheryl Glenn, Oregon State University; Susan Green, University of Oklahoma; Frank Hubbard, Marquette University; Carla Kaplan, Yale University; Rob Koelling, Northwest Community College; Eric Pankey, Washington University; Louise Z. Smith, University of Massachusetts, Boston; Molly Travis, Tulane University; and Irwin Weiser, Purdue University. Special thanks are due to Patsy Callaghan and Terry Martin of Central Washington University, who, with Judith Kleck of Central Washington University, wrote "The Readings: Issues and Strategies" section in the *Instructor's Resource Manual*, and to Patsy Callaghan for her incisive introduction to critical thinking in that manual.

Our thanks also to David Sosnowski, Bridget Weisse, and Heidi Schweingruber for assistance on the manuscript; to the good people at Shaman Drum Bookstore in Ann Arbor, Michigan; and to the Departments of Humanities and Behavioral Sciences at the University of Michigan, Dearborn, and the Center for Human Growth and Development at the University of Michigan, Ann Arbor, for research leaves and professional support. Above all, we owe thanks to the fine editorial and production staff at Houghton Mifflin, particularly our editor Karen Parrish, whose talent, diligence, grace, and good humor made the project a pleasure at every stage of the process. Finally, we would like to thank our friends, colleagues, and families who provided advice and encouragement throughout this project, particularly Abby Stewart, Toby Jayaratne, Jim Gruber, Kit Flanagan, and Les Gallay.

M. S.
C. F.

GENDER,
IMAGES AND ISSUES

A fifteen-year-old high-school sophomore in Ohio plans to become a surgeon. She is thinking of putting off marriage until her career is underway, and having children is something she doesn't feel strongly about one way or the other. Her dreams are to be professionally successful, make money, and own several cars.

A young girl in Zimbabwe, Africa, begins her day at 4:00 A.M. by fetching water from a well five miles from her home. From then until 9:00 at night she is busy preparing the family's meals, cleaning dishes, gathering food, and taking care of her younger brothers and sisters. Yet according to international economic definitions, she is considered unproductive, she "does not work."

In a suburban high-school classroom a lecturer is conducting a presentation on masculinity. In order to make a point, he jokingly suggests to a young male wrestler in the audience that, because the young man has streaks of pink in his shirt, he must be homosexual. Instead of laughing, the wrestler replies, "I'm going to kill you."

A child is in a movie theater on a Saturday afternoon, watching the Walt Disney movie *Cinderella*. Years later, she recalls the lessons she carried away from that film: that women are each others' enemies; that all women are alike.

A Vietnam veteran suffers from nightmares and anxiety attacks brought on by his memories of two years unloading body bags from the front. His psychoanalyst, who was passed up by the draft, finds he has trouble looking his client in the eye. He feels that by not serving in the war he himself is somehow inadequate, incomplete, less than a man.

What do these stories have in common? Although they come from the experiences of different people from very different backgrounds, they all point to how powerfully definitions of gender can affect our lives, choices, and identities. Whether we are young or old, men or women, and regardless of our race or class, gender is something we all have in common, although its manifestations are diverse and its implications span a wide spectrum. These stories, taken from the readings that follow, show the many different areas of our lives in which gender can be seen to operate—from images of fairy tales to images of war, from economics to politics to popular culture.

What do we mean when we use the word *gender?* Though the authors collected in this book approach gender from a variety of perspectives, they would all most likely agree that gender and sex are not the same thing. A person's sex—whether he or she is male or female—is a biological category and is determined genetically. Gender, on the other hand, refers to the social meanings of being a man or a woman. The opportunities one has, the choices one makes, the expectations others hold and even how one sees oneself are intimately linked to general societal attitudes about men and women.

Unlike biological sex, gender is constructed within a cultural and historical context. The norms and standards for masculinity and femininity can change over time or in different cultural settings. A 25-year-old woman living today in Chicago has quite likely been raised to think and feel about herself as a woman differently than her counterparts in New Delhi or Beijing. Moreover, these women are likely to have been taught different standards of femininity than their eighteenth- or nineteenth-century predecessors. The same variability applies to men and cultural norms of masculinity. The meaning of manhood may be quite different for a young Californian of the 1990s than it was for his Italian great-grandfather.

Attitudes about men's and women's roles in public life, family and child-rearing issues, concepts about race and class, notions of sexuality, and other factors all contribute to ideas about gender differences. In short, what it means to be male or female is determined by particular standards in a culture, which in turn shape the choices we make. Rather than being born with an understanding of the meaning of masculinity or femininity, we learn these standards over time, and many researchers believe that forming a gender identity is a lifelong process.

Images of the way society interprets gender surround us. From definitions of "the real man" or "the ideal woman," to standards of beauty in advertising, to the "proper" roles of husband and wife, gender images represent the culture's ideals. Whether or not one aspires to these ideals, they nonetheless influence the roles one will choose, the identity one develops, and the anxieties one must face. The boy who fights back tears on his first day at kindergarten may have never heard the word, but he is aware that he must play by the rules of gender if he is to be accepted by his peers. The teenager who feels too fat when she leafs through fashion magazines may not be able to define gender, but she understands at some level that gendered definitions of beauty set the standard by which she evaluates herself. When individuals or groups object to or attempt to change the dominant images of "masculinity" and "femininity," those images become issues, points of discussion and debate.

The authors whose voices you will hear in this book represent a broad spectrum of views in the ongoing debate about gender, as they consider its many personal, social, and political implications. We have structured the readings in this book to lead from some basic definitions of masculinity and femininity, into a look at how gender operates in a variety of fields like language, popular culture, advertising, the media, and the workplace, and finally into a consideration of the ways gender may play a part in a complex global phenomenon like war.

The authors in Part 1, "Defining Gender," examine how children become gendered members of society and discuss the strengths and limitations of various interpretations of masculinity and femininity. Can boys and girls be brought up free from gender differences, or is there an innate distinction between boys and girls that defies even the most "equal-opportunity" parenting? Are women in today's society still subject to discrimination on the basis of sex, or have advances in women's rights far outweighed social setbacks? How has the image of modern masculinity changed, and have visions of the "New Age Man" taken men too far in the direction of softness and sensitivity?

In Part 2, "Gender and Language," our focus turns to the power dynamics revealed in men's and women's uses of language—from conversation styles to literary accomplishment, listening skills to reading strategies. Chapters in this section on speaking, writing, and reading invite the reader to consider, among other things, whose voices are silenced and whose experiences are heard in culture.

Part 3, "Engendering Identity through Popular Culture," goes on to consider the place of two cultural phenomena, fairy tales and sports, as formative influences in the socialization of masculinity and femininity. What role does the image of the total athlete or the sports hero play in a boy's identity, or that of a beautiful princess in a girl's? How do these images translate into specific behaviors and pressures for both sexes? The authors in this section combine humor, personal anecdotes, and in-depth analysis to help us take a closer look at the powerful messages conveyed through popular culture.

We next examine the various ways that gender is packaged and sold as a product in society through the media, art and advertising, and pornography. The essays in Part 4, "Gendered Images as Commodity," ask us to think about how stereotypes are shaped and maintained by television and film, how perceptions of beauty and personal worth are constructed for us in art and advertising, and how an industry like pornography raises difficult questions about sexuality, civil liberties, and freedom of expression in society today.

We move into a consideration of "Gender and Work, Value, Power" in Part 5. This section explores the competing demands of paid work and family responsibilities, and asks us to reconsider how society's traditional definitions of "work" reveal implicit messages about gender roles and values. What are the changing meanings of work for both men and women, and how can we begin to evaluate the economics of the invisible "workplace inside the home"?

Finally, Part 6, "Gender and Culture: A Case Study," reflects on the complex connections between gender and war. Drawing together many of the themes and issues discussed in previous chapters, it offers the perspectives of soldiers, historians, journalists, and psychologists who are working to understand the meaning and impact of military action in Vietnam and the Persian Gulf.

Throughout this book you will be presented with the views of a wide range of people, from poets to politicians, scientists to factory workers, actors to political analysts, lawyers, comedians, art historians, and cultural critics. You will hear the voices of both men and women, of liberals and conservatives, of individuals advocating change and of those who are concerned that our culture might change too much. Some of these writers reinforce each others' views, some contradict or challenge each others' findings, but all share a commitment to their subject and a deep interest in the multiple ways gender affects our lives.

The aim of this book, however, is not just to have you listen in on this fascinating debate, but to invite you to join the discussion as well. To this end we have provided an opening section for each chapter, "Contexts," which gives a brief introduction to the selections that follow. Each chapter ends with a section titled "Making Connections," in which you are asked to think more deeply about the relationships among readings, to debate these views with your classmates, and to begin to formulate your own opinions on gender images and issues.

The topic of gender is one that has generated lively discussion, disagreement, and even heated exchange. Gender affects people on levels as personal as identity and intimate relationships and as public as the definition of work or the representation of war. Yet because it is such an integral part of who we are and how we interact with others it is easy to overlook its place in our lives. This book aims to bring the many facets of gender to light as issues for reflection and discussion. We hope that you will be inspired and challenged by these writers and compelled to respond with your own viewpoints and experiences. Indeed, your own knowledge and insight are your most valuable tools as you embark on this journey of reading, thinking, and writing.

DEFINING GENDER

1
BECOMING
GENDERED

C O N T E X T S

"Is it a boy or a girl?" is frequently the first question asked after the news of a baby's birth. The answer will determine, at least in part, how people will behave around the child and how they will interpret the child's behavior. Knowing whether one is in the presence of a boy or a girl can structure everything from expectations about the child's clothes ("pink for girls, blue for boys") to what is seen ("she's so pretty" or "he looks so strong") and heard ("she's *upset*" but "he's *angry*").

Sex is biologically determined. That is, whether we are male or female is determined by the chromosomes that we inherit. But our society gives meaning to these sexual assignments. The traits and behaviors that will be considered normal, the roles that will be encouraged, the opportunities made available to us as women or as men are issues of gender and are defined within the context of a particular cultural and historical period.

Gender, like other social categories, reduces the complexities of our world and provides us with norms for social interaction. As guidelines for acceptable male and female behavior, gender categories provide us with an orderly, comfortable way of acting in the world. They structure our thought and behavior so that we can quickly size up any given interpersonal or social situation. Who are the people we are meeting? How does their social status compare to our own? What should we expect of them, and how should we ourselves behave?

On the other hand, although gender categories give structure to our lives, they can be seen to restrict our behavior. They might prejudice our perceptions by encouraging us to think certain behaviors are inappropriate, unacceptable, even abnormal. The father who wants to rock his newborn but thinks it would be unmanly or the woman who keeps her opinions to herself because asserting them seems unfeminine are instances where enacting the rules of gender occur at the expense of personal development.

But gender categories are malleable, changeable. They can be redefined by individuals within a culture or by groups over time. Consider the last three generations in your own family. Chances are that roles today are different from what they were during your grandparents' era. In the same way that other cultural norms change, an activity perceived twenty years ago as unusual or even abnormal for one of the sexes may now seem perfectly normal.

During the past few decades especially there have been significant changes in our concepts of gender and the roles of women and men in society. But change is always difficult, and the debate over gender and change goes on. Some people argue that gender differences in roles and behaviors spring naturally from basic biological differences between women and men. Others contend that too much has been made of biological differences and that, contrary to Freud's dictum that "anatomy is destiny," concepts of gender are socially constructed and can, therefore, be modified over time.

The first two selections in this chapter present two sides of the debate between the biological and social conceptions of gender. Lois Gould's fantasy, "X: A Fabulous Child's Story," presents one aspect of the social argument. Her story about raising a child free of the restrictions of gender stereotypes illustrates how people rely on the knowledge of a child's sex as a kind of primary guide to their actions and reactions. In this story, it's the adults who are confused and alarmed at not knowing Baby X's sex, while X's classmates and friends find the absence of this knowledge liberating.

An argument for the biological basis of gender is provided in the next selection, Prudence Mackintosh's anecdotal "Masculine/Feminine." After many frustrated attempts to raise her sons free of gender stereotypes, the author contends that no amount of parental effort can overcome certain basic differences between girls and boys.

Our next essay, "Becoming Members of Society" by Holly Devor, discusses the socialization process in a more formal manner. Devor describes the development of gender identity as a lifelong process, one in which individual choice plays a part alongside the preferences and values of society and the specific pressures and suggestions of significant others (parents, friends, relatives, etc.). For Devor, people are not born gendered, but rather develop their gender identities through a complex series of social cues.

Finally, in her poem "The Stranger," Adrienne Rich imagines the human potential for androgyny, whereby an individual simultaneously possesses male and female characteristics. The speaker in Rich's poem tries to see, with a "visionary anger," beyond current gender categories to a future written "under the lids/of the newborn child." Rich's speaker seems to suggest that to envision such a future—a future free of gender restrictions—is to conceive of untold possibilities for human growth.

The authors in Chapter 1 agree that gender plays a critical role in human behavior and the structure of society. As they discuss this important topic, they raise a number of fundamental questions. Are we *born with* or do we *acquire* gendered traits and identities? How, and to what extent, does gender affect human interaction? Are gender categories helpful or harmful? We invite you to add your own views and experiences to the discussion that follows on the ways gender shapes human beings' personal and social development.

X: A FABULOUS CHILD'S STORY

◑

L O I S   G O U L D

Lois Gould is a writer and journalist whose articles
have appeared in numerous magazines and newspapers, including the *New York Times*. Her novels include
Such Good Friends (1970), *Necessary Objects* (1972), and
La Presidenta (1981). In this story she fantasizes about
a scientific "xperiment" in which the Jones family attempts to raise a *child* rather than a *boy* or a *girl*.

Once upon a time, a baby named X was born. This baby was named X so 1
that nobody could tell whether it was a boy or a girl. Its parents could tell,
of course, but they couldn't tell anybody else. They couldn't even tell Baby
X, at first.

You see, it was all part of a very important Secret Scientific Xperiment, 2
known officially as Project Baby X. The smartest scientists had set up this
Xperiment at a cost of Xactly 23 billion dollars and 72 cents, which might
seem like a lot for just one baby, even a very important Xperimental baby.
But when you remember the prices of things like strained carrots and stuffed
bunnies, and popcorn for the movies and booster shots for camp, let alone
28 shiny quarters from the tooth fairy, you begin to see how it adds up.

Also, long before Baby X was born, all those scientists had to be paid to 3
work out the details of the Xperiment, and to write the *Official Instruction
Manual* for Baby X's parents and, most important of all, to find the right set
of parents to bring up Baby X. These parents had to be selected very carefully.
Thousands of volunteers had to take thousands of tests and answer thousands
of tricky questions. Almost everybody failed because, it turned out, almost
everybody really wanted either a baby boy or a baby girl, and not Baby X at
all. Also, almost everybody was afraid that a Baby X would be a lot more
trouble than a boy or a girl. (They were probably right, the scientists admitted,
but Baby X needed parents who wouldn't *mind* the Xtra trouble.)

There were families with grandparents named Milton and Agatha, who 4
didn't see why the baby couldn't be named Milton or Agatha instead of X,
even if it *was* an X. There were families with aunts who insisted on knitting
tiny dresses and uncles who insisted on sending tiny baseball mitts. Worst of
all, there were families that already had other children who couldn't be trusted
to keep the secret. Certainly not if they knew the secret was worth 23 billion
dollars and 72 cents—and all you had to do was take one little peek at Baby
X in the bathtub to know if it was a boy or a girl.

But, finally, the scientists found the Joneses, who really wanted to raise 5
an X more than any other kind of baby—no matter how much trouble it
would be. Ms. and Mr. Jones had to promise they would take equal turns
caring for X, and feeding it, and singing it lullabies. And they had to promise
never to hire any baby-sitters. The government scientists knew perfectly well
that a baby-sitter would probably peek at X in the bathtub, too.

The day the Joneses brought their baby home, lots of friends and relatives 6
came over to see it. None of them knew about the secret Xperiment, though.
So the first thing they asked was what kind of a baby X was. When the Joneses
smiled and said, "It's an X!" nobody knew what to say. They couldn't say,
"Look at her cute little dimples!" And they couldn't say, "Look at his husky
little biceps!" And they couldn't even say just plain "kitchy-coo." In fact, they
all thought the Joneses were playing some kind of rude joke.

But, of course, the Joneses were not joking. "It's an X" was absolutely all 7
they would say. And that made the friends and relatives very angry. The
relatives all felt embarrassed about having an X in the family. "People will
think there's something wrong with it!" some of them whispered. "There *is*
something wrong with it!" others whispered back.

"Nonsense!" the Joneses told them all cheerfully. "What could possibly 8
be wrong with this perfectly adorable X?"

Nobody could answer that, except Baby X, who had just finished its bottle. 9
Baby X's answer was a loud, satisfied burp.

Clearly, nothing at all was wrong. Nevertheless, none of the relatives felt 10
comfortable about buying a present for a Baby X. The cousins who sent the
baby a tiny football helmet would not come and visit any more. And the
neighbors who sent a pink-flowered romper suit pulled their shades down
when the Joneses passed their house.

The *Official Instruction Manual* had warned the new parents that this 11
would happen, so they didn't fret about it. Besides, they were too busy with
Baby X and the hundreds of different Xercises for treating it properly.

Ms. and Mr. Jones had to be Xtra careful about how they played with 12
little X. They knew if they kept bouncing it up in the air and saying how
strong and *active* it was, they'd be treating it more like a boy than an X. But
if all they did was cuddle it and kiss it and tell it how *sweet* and *dainty* it was,
they'd be treating it more like a girl than an X.

On page 1,654 of the *Official Instruction Manual*, the scientists prescribed: 13
"plenty of bouncing and plenty of cuddling, *both*. X ought to be strong and
sweet and active. Forget about *dainty* altogether."

Meanwhile, the Joneses were worrying about other problems. Toys, for 14
instance. And clothes. On his first shopping trip, Mr. Jones told the store
clerk, "I need some clothes and toys for my new baby." The clerk smiled and
said, "Well, now, is it a boy or a girl?" "It's an X," Mr. Jones said, smiling
back. But the clerk got all red in the face and said huffily, "In *that* case, I'm
afraid I can't help you, sir." So Mr. Jones wandered helplessly up and down

the aisles trying to find what X needed. But everything in the store was piled up in sections marked "Boys" or "Girls." There were "Boys' Pajamas" and "Girls' Underwear" and "Boys' Fire Engines" and "Girls' Housekeeping Sets." Mr. Jones went home without buying anything for X. That night he and Ms. Jones consulted page 2,326 of the *Official Instruction Manual*. "Buy plenty of everything!" it said firmly.

So they bought plenty of sturdy blue pajamas in the Boys' Department 15 and cheerful flowered underwear in the Girls' Department. And they bought all kinds of toys. A boy doll that made pee-pee and cried, "Pa-pa." And a girl doll that talked in three languages and said, "I am the Pres-i-dent of Gen-er-al Mo-tors." They also bought a storybook about a brave princess who rescued a handsome prince from his ivory tower, and another one about a sister and brother who grew up to be a baseball star and a ballet star, and you had to guess which was which.

The head scientists of Project Baby X checked all their purchases and 16 told them to keep up the good work. They also reminded the Joneses to see page 4,629 of the *Manual*, where it said, "Never make Baby X feel *embarrassed* or *ashamed* about what it wants to play with. And if X gets dirty climbing rocks, never say 'Nice little Xes don't get dirty climbing rocks.'"

Likewise, it said, "If X falls down and cries, never say 'Brave little Xes 17 don't cry.' Because, of course, nice little Xes *do* get dirty, and brave little Xes *do* cry. No matter how dirty X gets, or how hard it cries, don't worry. It's all part of the Xperiment."

Whenever the Joneses pushed Baby X's stroller in the park, smiling 18 strangers would come over and coo: "Is that a boy or a girl?" The Joneses would smile back and say, "It's an X." The strangers would stop smiling then, and often snarl something nasty—as if the Joneses had snarled at *them*.

By the time X grew big enough to play with other children, the Joneses' 19 troubles had grown bigger, too. Once a little girl grabbed X's shovel in the sandbox, and zonked X on the head with it. "Now, now, Tracy," the little girl's mother began to scold, "little girls mustn't hit little . . ." and she turned to ask X, "Are you a little boy or a little girl, dear?"

Mr. Jones who was sitting near the sandbox, held his breath and crossed 20 his fingers.

X smiled politely at the lady, even though X's head had never been zonked 21 so hard in its life. "I'm a little X," X replied.

"You're a *what?*" the lady exclaimed angrily. "You're a little b-r-a-t, you 22 mean!"

"But little girls mustn't hit little Xes, either!" said X, retrieving the shovel 23 with another polite smile. "What good does hitting do, anyway?"

X's father, who was still holding his breath, finally let it out, uncrossed 24 his fingers, and grinned back at X.

And at their next secret Project Baby X meeting, the scientists grinned, 25 too. Baby X was doing fine.

But then it was time for X to start school. The Joneses were really worried 26
about this, because school was even more full of rules for boys and girls, and
there were no rules for Xes. The teacher would tell boys to form one line,
and girls to form another line. There would be boys' games and girls' games,
and boys' secrets and girls' secrets. The school library would have a list of
recommended books for girls, and a different list of recommended books for
boys. There would even be a bathroom marked BOYS and another one
marked GIRLS. Pretty soon boys and girls would hardly talk to each other.
What would happen to poor little X?

The Joneses spent weeks consulting their *Instruction Manual* (there were 27
249½ pages of advice under "First Day of School"), and attending urgent
special conferences with the smart scientists of Project Baby X.

The scientists had to make sure that X's mother had taught X how to 28
throw and catch a ball properly, and that X's father had been sure to teach X
what to serve at a doll's tea party. X had to know how to shoot marbles and
how to jump rope and, most of all, what to say when the Other Children
asked whether X was a Boy or a Girl.

Finally, X was ready. The Joneses helped X button on a nice new pair of 29
red-and-white checked overalls, and sharpened six pencils for X's nice new
pencilbox, and marked X's name clearly on all the books in its nice new
bookbag. X brushed its teeth and combed its hair, which just about covered
its ears, and remembered to put a napkin in its lunchbox.

The Joneses had asked X's teacher if the class could line up alphabetically, 30
instead of forming separate lines for boys and girls. And they had asked if X
could use the principal's bathroom, because it wasn't marked anything except
BATHROOM. X's teacher promised to take care of all those problems. But
nobody could help X with the biggest problem of all—Other Children.

Nobody in X's class had ever known an X before. What would they think? 31
How would X make friends?

You couldn't tell what X was by studying its clothes—overalls don't even 32
button right-to-left, like girls' clothes, or left-to-right, like boys' clothes. And
you couldn't guess whether X had a girl's short haircut or a boy's long haircut.
And it was very hard to tell by the games X liked to play. Either X played ball
very well for a girl, or else X played house very well for a boy.

Some of the children tried to find out by asking X tricky questions, like 33
"Who's your favorite sports star?" That was easy. X had two favorite sports
stars: a girl jockey named Robyn Smith and a boy archery champion named
Robin Hood. Then they asked, "What's your favorite TV program?" And
that was even easier. X's favorite TV program was "Lassie," which stars a girl
dog played by a boy dog.

When X said that its favorite toy was a doll, everyone decided that X 34
must be a girl. But then X said that the doll was really a robot, and that X
had computerized it, and that it was programmed to bake fudge brownies and
then clean up the kitchen. After X told them that, the other children gave up
guessing what X was. All they knew was they'd sure like to see X's doll.

After school, X wanted to play with the other children. "How about 35 shooting some baskets in the gym?" X asked the girls. But all they did was make faces and giggle behind X's back.

"How about weaving some baskets in the arts and crafts room?" X asked 36 the boys. But they all made faces and giggled behind X's back too.

That night, Ms. and Mr. Jones asked X how things had gone at school. 37 X told them sadly that the lessons were okay, but otherwise school was a terrible place for an X. It seemed as if Other Children would never want an X for a friend.

Once more, the Joneses reached for their *Instruction Manual.* Under 38 "Other Children," they found the following message: "What did you Xpect? *Other Children* have to obey all the silly boy-girl rules, because their parents taught them to. Lucky X—you don't have to stick to the rules at all! All you have to do is be yourself. P.S. We're not saying it'll be easy."

X liked being itself. But X cried a lot that night, partly because it felt 39 afraid. So X's father held X tight, and cuddled it, and couldn't help crying a little, too. And X's mother cheered them both up by reading an Xciting story about an enchanted prince called Sleeping Handsome, who woke up when Princess Charming kissed him.

The next morning, they all felt much better, and little X went back to 40 school with a brave smile and a clean pair of red-and-white checked overalls.

There was a seven-letter-word spelling bee in class that day. And a seven- 41 lap boys' relay race in the gym. And a seven-layer-cake baking contest in the girls' kitchen corner. X won the spelling bee. X also won the relay race. And X almost won the baking contest, except it forgot to light the oven. Which only proves that nobody's perfect.

One of the Other Children noticed something else, too. He said: "Win- 42 ning or losing doesn't seem to count to X. X seems to have fun being good at boys' skills *and* girls' skills."

"Come to think of it," said another one of the Other Children, "maybe 43 *X* is having twice as much fun as we are!"

So after school that day, the girl who beat X at the baking contest gave 44 X a big slice of her prizewinning cake. And the boy X beat in the relay race asked X to race him home.

From then on, some really funny things began to happen. Susie, who sat 45 next to X in class, suddenly refused to wear pink dresses to school any more. She insisted on wearing red-and-white checked overalls—just like X's. Overalls, she told her parents, were much better for climbing monkey bars.

Then Jim, the class football nut, started wheeling his little sister's doll 46 carriage around the football field. He'd put on his entire football uniform, except for the helmet. Then he'd put the helmet *in* the carriage, lovingly tucked under an old set of shoulder pads. Then he'd start jogging around the field, pushing the carriage and singing "Rock-a-bye Baby" to his football helmet. He told his family that X did the same thing, so it must be okay. After all X was now the team's star quarterback.

Susie's parents were horrified by her behavior, and Jim's parents were 47 worried sick about his. But the worst came when the twins, Joe and Peggy, decided to share everything with each other. Peggy used Joe's hockey skates, and his microscope, and took half his newspaper route. Joe used Peggy's needlepoint kit, and her cookbooks, and took two of her three baby-sitting jobs. Peggy started running the lawn mower, and Joe started running the vacuum cleaner.

Their parents weren't one bit pleased with Peggy's wonderful biology 48 experiments, or with Joe's terrific needlepoint pillows. They didn't care that Peggy mowed the lawn better, and that Joe vacuumed the carpet better. In fact, they were furious. It's all that little X's fault, they agreed. Just because X doesn't know what it is, or what it's supposed to be, it wants to get everybody *else* mixed up, too!

Peggy and Joe were forbidden to play with X any more. So was Susie, 49 and then Jim, and then *all* the Other Children. But it was too late; the Other Children stayed mixed up and happy and free, and refused to go back to the way they'd been before X.

Finally, Joe and Peggy's parents decided to call an emergency meeting of 50 the school's Parents' Association, to discuss "The X Problem." They sent a report to the principal stating that X was a "disruptive influence." They demanded immediate action. The Joneses, they said, should be *forced* to tell whether X was a boy or a girl. And then X should be *forced* to behave like whichever it was. If the Joneses refused to tell, the Parents' Association said, then X must take an Xamination. The school psychiatrist must Xamine it physically and mentally, and issue a full report. If X's test showed it was a boy, it would have to obey all the boys' rules. If it proved to be a girl, X would have to obey all the girls' rules.

And if X turned out to be some kind of mixed-up misfit, then X should 51 be Xpelled from the school. Immediately!

The principal was very upset. Disruptive influence? Mixed-up misfit? But 52 X was an Xcellent student. All the teachers said it was a delight to have X in their classes. X was president of the student council. X had won first prize in the talent show, and second prize in the art show, and honorable mention in the science fair, and six athletic events on field day, including the potato race.

Nevertheless, insisted the Parents' Association, X is a Problem Child. X is 53 the Biggest Problem Child we have ever seen!

So the principal reluctantly notified X's parents that numerous complaints 54 about X's behavior had come to the school's attention. And that after the psychiatrist's Xamination, the school would decide what to do about X.

The Joneses reported this at once to the scientists, who referred them to 55 page 85,759 of the *Instruction Manual*. "Sooner or later," it said, "X will have to be Xamined by a psychiatrist. This may be the only way any of us will know for sure whether X is mixed up—or whether everyone else is."

The night before X was to be Xamined, the Joneses tried not to let X see how worried they were. "What if . . . ?" Mr. Jones would say. And Ms. Jones would reply, "No use worrying." Then a few minutes later, Ms. Jones would say, "What if . . . ?" and Mr. Jones would reply, "No use worrying." 56

X just smiled at them both, and hugged them hard and didn't say much of anything. X was thinking. What if . . . ? And then X thought: No use worrying. 57

At Xactly 9 o'clock the next day, X reported to the school psychiatrist's office. The principal, along with a committee from the Parents' Association, X's teacher, X's classmates, and Ms. and Mr. Jones, waited in the hall outside. Nobody knew the details of the tests X was to be given, but everybody knew they'd be *very* hard, and that they'd reveal Xactly what everyone wanted to know about X, but were afraid to ask. 58

It was terribly quiet in the hall. Almost spooky. Once in a while, they would hear a strange noise inside the room. There were buzzes. And a beep or two. And several bells. An occasional light would flash under the door. The Joneses thought it was a white light, but the principal thought it was blue. Two or three children swore it was either yellow or green. And the Parents' Committee missed it completely. 59

Through it all, you could hear the psychiatrist's low voice, asking hundreds of questions, and X's higher voice, answering hundreds of answers. 60

The whole thing took so long that everyone knew it must be the most complete Xamination anyone had ever had to take. Poor X, the Joneses thought. Serves X right, the Parents' Committee thought. I wouldn't like to be in X's overalls right now, the children thought. 61

At last, the door opened. Everyone crowded around to hear the results. X didn't look any different; in fact, X was smiling. But the psychiatrist looked terrible. He look as if he was crying! "What happened?" everyone began shouting. Had X done something disgraceful? "I wouldn't be a bit surprised!" muttered Peggy and Joe's parents. "Did X flunk the *whole* test?" cried Susie's parents. "Or just the most important part?" yelled Jim's parents. 62

"Oh, dear," sighed Mr. Jones. 63

"Oh, dear," sighed Ms. Jones. 64

"*Sssh*," ssshed the principal. "The psychiatrist is trying to speak." 65

Wiping his eyes and clearing his throat, the psychiatrist began, in a hoarse whisper. "In my opinion," he whispered—you could tell he must be very upset—"in my opinion, young X here . . ." 66

"Yes? Yes?" shouted a parent impatiently. 67

"*Sssh!*" ssshed the principal. 68

"Young *Sssh* here, I mean young X," said the doctor, frowning, "is just about . . ." 69

"Just about *what?* Let's have it!" shouted another parent. 70

". . . just about the *least* mixed-up child I've ever Xamined!" said the psychiatrist. 71

"Yay for X!" yelled one of the children. And then the others began yelling, 72
too. Clapping and cheering and jumping up and down.

"*SSSH!*" SSShed the principal, but nobody did. 73

The Parents' Committee was angry and bewildered. How *could* X have 74
passed the whole Xamination? Didn't X have an *identity* problem? Wasn't X
mixed up at *all?* Wasn't X *any* kind of a misfit? How could it *not* be, when it
didn't even *know* what it was? And why was the psychiatrist crying?

Actually, he had stopped crying and was smiling politely through his 75
tears. "Don't you see?" he said. "I'm crying because it's wonderful! X has
absolutely no identity problem! X isn't one bit mixed up! As for being a
misfit—ridiculous! X knows perfectly well what it is! Don't you, X?" The
doctor winked, X winked back.

"But what *is* X?" shrieked Peggy and Joe's parents. "*We* still want to know 76
what it is!"

"Ah, yes," said the doctor, winking again. "Well, don't worry. You'll all 77
know one of these days. And you won't need me to tell you."

"What? What does he mean?" some of the parents grumbled suspiciously. 78

Susie and Peggy and Joe all answered at once. "He means that by the 79
time X's sex matters, it won't be a secret any more!"

With that, the doctor began to push through the crowd toward X's par- 80
ents. "How do you do," he said, somewhat stiffly. And then he reached out
to hug them both. "If I ever have an X of my own," he whispered, "I sure
hope you'll lend me your instruction manual."

Needless to say, the Joneses were very happy. The Project Baby X sci- 81
entists were rather pleased, too. So were Susie, Jim, Peggy, Joe, and all the
Other Children. The Parents' Association wasn't, but they had promised to
accept the psychiatrist's report, and not make any more trouble. They even
invited Ms. and Mr. Jones to become honorary members, which they did.

Later that day, all X's friends put on their red-and-white checked overalls 82
and went over to see X. They found X in the back yard, playing with a very
tiny baby that none of them had ever seen before. The baby was wearing very
tiny red-and-white checked overalls.

"How do you like our new baby?" X asked the Other Children proudly. 83

"It's got cute dimples," said Jim. 84

"It's got husky biceps, too," said Susie. 85

"What kind of baby is it?" asked Joe and Peggy. 86

X frowned at them. "Can't you tell?" Then X broke into a big, mischie- 87
vous grin. "*It's a Y!*"

MASCULINE/FEMININE

◑

PRUDENCE MACKINTOSH

Prudence Mackintosh is a writer and contributing editor of *Texas Monthly* magazine. This essay, a personal
account of her attempts to raise her three sons in a
gender-neutral fashion, appears in her collection,
Thundering Sneakers (1981). Her second collection of
essays, *Retreads*, was published in 1985.

I had every intention to raise liberated, nonviolent sons whose aggressive   1
tendencies would be mollified by a sensitivity and compassion that psychologists claim were denied their father's generation.

I did not buy guns or war toys (although Grandmother did). My boys   2
even had a secondhand baby doll until the garage sale last summer. I did buy
Marlo Thomas' *Free to Be You and Me* record, a collection of nonsexist songs,
stories, and poems, and I told them time and time again that it was okay to
cry and be scared sometimes. I overruled their father and insisted that first
grade was much too early for organized competitive soccer leagues. They
know that moms *and dads* do dishes and diapers. And although they use it
primarily for the convenient bathroom between the alley and the sandpile,
my boys know that the storeroom is now mother's office. In such an environment, surely they would grow up free of sex-role stereotypes. At the very least
wouldn't they pick up their own socks?

My friends with daughters were even more zealous. They named their   3
daughters strong, cool unisex names like Blakeney, Brett, Brook, Lindsay, and
Blair, names that lent themselves to corporate letterheads, not Tupperware
party invitations. These moms looked on Barbie with disdain and bought
trucks and science kits. They shunned frilly dresses for overalls. They sub-
scribed to Feminist Press and read stories called "My Mother the Mail Carrier" instead of "Sleeping Beauty." At the swimming pool one afternoon, I
watched a particularly fervent young mother, ironically clad in a string bikini,
encourage her daughter. "You're so strong, Blake! Kick hard, so you'll be the
strongest kid in this pool." When my boys splashed water in Blakeney's eyes
and she ran whimpering to her mother, this mom exhorted, "You go back in
that pool and shake your fist like this and say, 'You do that again and I'll bust
your lights out." A new generation of little girls, assertive and ambitious,
taking a backseat to no one?

It's a little early to assess the results of our efforts, but when my seven-   4
year-old son, Jack, comes home singing—to the tune of *"Frère Jacques"*—

"Farrah Fawcett, Farrah Fawcett, I love you" and five minutes later asks Drew, his five-year-old brother, if he'd like his nose to be a blood fountain, either we're backsliding or there's more to this sex-role learning than the home environment can handle.

I'm hearing similar laments from mothers of daughters. "She used to tell   5
everyone that she was going to grow up to be a lawyer just like Daddy," said one, "but she's hedging on that ambition ever since she learned that no one wears a blue fairy tutu in the courtroom." Another mother with two sons, a daughter, and a very successful career notes that, with no special encouragement, only her daughter keeps her room neat and loves to set the table and ceremoniously seat her parents. At a Little League game during the summer, fearful that this same young daughter might be absorbing the stereotype "boys play while girls watch," her parents readily assured her that she too could participate when she was eight years old. "Oh," she exclaimed with obvious delight, "I didn't know they had cheerleaders."

How does it happen? I have my own theories, but decided to do a little   6
reading to see if any of the "experts" agreed with me. I was also curious to find out what remedies they recommended. The books I read propose that sex roles are culturally induced. In simplistic terms, rid the schools, their friends, and the television of sexism, and your daughters will dump their dolls and head straight for the boardroom while your sons contemplate nursing careers. *Undoing Sex Stereotypes* by Marcia Guttentag and Helen Bray is an interesting study of efforts to overcome sexism in the classroom. After reading it, I visited my son's very traditional school and found it guilty of unabashedly perpetrating the myths that feminists abhor. Remember separate water fountains? And how, even if the line was shorter, no boy would be caught dead drinking from the girls' fountain and vice versa? That still happens. "You wouldn't want me to get cooties, would you, Mom?" my son says, defending the practice. What did I expect in a school where the principal still addresses his faculty, who range in age from 23 to 75, as "girls"?

Nevertheless, having been a schoolteacher myself, I am skeptical of neatly   7
programmed nonsexist curriculum packets like Guttentag and Bray's. But if you can wade through the jargon ("people of the opposite sex, hereafter referred to as POTOS"), some of the observations and exercises are certainly thought-provoking and revealing. In one exercise fifth-grade students were asked to list adjectives appropriate to describe women. The struggle some of the children had in shifting their attitudes about traditional male roles is illustrated in this paragraph written by a fifth-grade girl who was asked to write a story about a man using the adjectives she had listed to describe women:

> Once there was a boy who all his life was very *gentle*. He never hit anyone or started a fight and when some of his friends were not feeling well, he was *loving* and *kind* to them. When he got older he never changed. People started not liking him because he was *weak*, *petite*, and he wasn't like any of the other men—not strong or tough. Most of his life he sat alone thinking about why no one liked him. Then one day he went out and tried to act like the other

men. He joined a baseball team, but he was no good, he always got out. Then he decided to join the hockey team. He couldn't play good. He kept on breaking all the rules. So he quit the team and joined the soccer team. These men were *understanding* to him. He was really good at soccer, and was the best on the team. That year they won the championship and the rest of his life he was happy.

After reading this paragraph it occurred to me that this little girl's self-esteem and subsequent role in life would be enhanced by a teacher who spent less time on "nonsexist intervention projects" and more time on writing skills. But that, of course, is not what the study was meant to reveal. 8

The junior high curriculum suggested by *Undoing Sex Stereotypes* has some laudable consciousness-raising goals. For example, in teaching units called "Women's Roles in American History" and "The Socialization of Women and the Image of Women in the Media" teenagers are encouraged to critically examine television commercials, soap operas, and comic books. But am I a traitor to the cause if I object when the authors in another unit use *Romeo and Juliet* as a study of the status of women? Something is rotten in Verona when we have to consider Juliet's career possibilities and her problems with self-actualization. The conclusions of this project were lost on me; I quit reading when the author began to talk about ninth-graders who were "cognitively at a formal operational level." I don't even know what my "external sociopsychological situation" is. However, I think I did understand some of the conclusions reached by the kids: 9

> "Girls are smart."
> "If a woman ran a forklift where my father works, there would be a walkout."
> "Men cannot be pom-pom girls."

Eminently more readable, considering that both authors are educators of educators, is *How to Raise Independent and Professionally Successful Daughters*, by Drs. Rita and Kenneth Dunn. The underlying and, I think, questionable assumption in this book is that little boys have been reared correctly all along. Without direct parental intervention, according to the Dunns, daughters tend to absorb and reflect society's values. The Dunns paint a dark picture indeed for the parents who fail to channel their daughters toward professional success. The woman who remains at home with children while her husband is involved in the "real world" with an "absorbing and demanding day-to-day commitment that brings him into contact with new ideas, jobs, and people (attractive self-actualized females)" is sure to experience lowered IQ, according to the Dunns. They go on to predict the husband's inevitable affair and the subsequent divorce, which leaves the wife emotionally depressed and probably financially dependent on her parents. 10

Now I'm all for women developing competency and self-reliance, but the Dunns' glorification of the professional is excessive. Anyone who has worked longer than a year knows that eventually any job loses most of its glamour. 11

And the world is no less "real" at home. For that matter, mothers at home may be more "real" than bankers or lawyers. How is a corporate tax problem more real than my counseling with the maid whose boyfriend shot her in the leg? How can reading a balance sheet compare with comforting a five-year-old who holds his limp cat and wants to know why we have to lose the things we love? And on the contrary, it is my husband, the professional, who complains of lowered IQ. Though we wooed to Faulkner, my former ace English major turned trial lawyer now has time for only an occasional *Falconer* or Peter Benchley thriller. Certainly there is value in raising daughters to be financially self-supporting, but there is not much wisdom in teaching a daughter that she must achieve professional success or her marriage probably won't last.

In a chapter called "What to Do from Birth to Two," the authors instruct [12] parents to introduce dolls only if they represent adult figures or groups of figures. "Try not to give her her own 'baby.' A baby doll is acceptable only for dramatizing the familiar episodes she has actually experienced, like a visit to the doctor." If some unthinking person should give your daughter a baby doll, and she likes it, the Dunns recommend that you permit her to keep it without exhibiting any negative feelings, "but do not lapse into cuddling it or encouraging her to do so. Treat it as any other object and direct attention to other more beneficial toys." I wonder if the Dunns read an article by Anne Roiphe called "Can You Have Everything and Still Want Babies?" which appeared in *Vogue* a couple of years ago. Ms. Roiphe was deploring the extremes to which our liberation has brought us. "It is nice to have beautiful feet, it may be desirable to have small feet, but it is painful and abusive to bind feet. It is also a good thing for women to have independence, freedom and choice, movement, and opportunity; but I'm not so sure that the current push against mothering will not be another kind of binding of the soul. . . . As women we have thought so little of ourselves that when the troops came to liberate us we rushed into the streets leaving our most valuable attributes behind as if they belonged to the enemy."

The Dunns' book is thorough, taking parents step-by-step through the [13] elementary years and on to high school. Had I been raising daughters, however, I think I would have flunked out in the chapter "What to Do from Age Two to Five." In discussing development of vocabulary, the Doctors Dunn prohibit the use of nonsensical words for bodily functions. I'm sorry, Doctors, but I've experimented with this precise terminology and discovered that the child who yells "I have to defecate, Mom" across four grocery aisles is likely to be left in the store. A family without a few poo-poo jokes is no family at all.

These educators don't help me much in my efforts to liberate my sons. [14] And although I think little girls are getting a better deal with better athletic training and broader options, I believe we're kidding ourselves if we think we can raise our sons and daughters alike. Certain inborn traits seem to be immune to parental and cultural tampering. How can I explain why a little girl baby sits on a quilt in the park thoughtfully examining a blade of grass, while my baby William uproots grass by handfuls and eats it? Why does a mother of very bright and active daughters confide that until she went camping with another family of boys, she feared that my sons had a hyperactivity problem? I'm sure there are plenty of rowdy, noisy little girls, but I'm not just talking about rowdiness and noise. I'm talking about some sort of primal physicalness that causes the walls of my house to pulsate on rainy days. I'm talking about something inexplicable that makes my sons fall into a mad, scrambling, pull-your-ears-off-kick-your-teeth-in heap just before bedtime, when they're not even mad at each other. I mean something that causes them to climb the doorjamb with honey and peanut butter on their hands while giving me a synopsis of *Star Wars* that contains only five intelligible words: "And then this guy, he 'pssshhhhhhh.' And then this thing went 'vrongggggg.' But this little guy said, 'Nong-nee-nonh-nee.'" When Jack and Drew are not kicking a soccer ball or each other, they are kicking the chair legs, the cat, the baby's silver rattle, and, inadvertently, Baby William himself, whom they have affectionately dubbed "Tough Eddy." Staying put in a chair for the duration of a one-course meal is torturous for these boys. They compensate by never quite putting both feet under the table. They sit with one leg doubled under them while the other leg extends to one side. The upper half of the body appears committed to the task at hand—eating—but the lower extremities are poised to lunge should a more compelling distraction present itself. From this position, I have observed, one brother can trip a haughty dessert-eating sibling who is flaunting the fact he ate all his "sweaty little peas." Although we have civilized them to the point that they dutifully mumble, "May I be excused, please?" their abrupt departure from the table invariably overturns at least one chair or whatever milk remains. This sort of constant motion just doesn't lend itself to lessons in thoughtfulness and gentleness.

Despite my encouragement, my sons refuse to invite little girls to play anymore. Occasionally friends leave their small daughters with us while they run errands. I am always curious to see what these females will find of interest in my sons' roomful of Tonka trucks and soccer balls. One morning the boys suggested that the girls join them in playing Emergency with the big red fire trucks and ambulance. The girls were delighted and immediately designated the ambulance as theirs. The point of Emergency, as I have seen it played countless times with a gang of little boys, is to make as much noise with the siren as possible and to crash the trucks into each other or into the leg of a living-room chair before you reach your destination. 15

The girls had other ideas. I realized why they had selected the ambulance. It contained three dolls: a driver, a nurse, a sick man on the stretcher. My boys have used that ambulance many times, but the dolls were always secondary to the death-defying race with the fire trucks; they were usually just thrown in the back of the van as an afterthought. The girls took the dolls 16 out, stripped and re-dressed them tenderly, and made sure that they were seated in their appropriate places for the first rescue. Once the fire truck had been lifted off the man's leg, the girls required a box of Band-Aids and spent the next half hour making a bed for the patient and reassuring him that he was going to be all right. These little girls and my sons had seen the same NBC "Emergency" series, but the girls had apparently picked up on the show's nurturing aspects, while Jack and Drew were interested only in the equipment, the fast driving, and the sirens. . . .

Of course, I want my sons to grow up knowing that what's inside a 17 woman's head is more important than her appearance, but I'm sure they're getting mixed signals when I delay our departure for the swimming pool to put on lipstick. I also wonder what they make of their father, whose favorite aphorism is "beautiful women rule the world." I suppose what we want for these sons and the women they may marry someday is a sensitivity that enables them to be both flexible and at ease with their respective roles, so that marriage contracts are unnecessary. When my sons bring me the heads of two purple irises from the neighbor's yard and ask, "Are you really the most beautiful mama in the whole world like Daddy says, and did everyone want to marry you?" do you blame me if I keep on waffling?

BECOMING MEMBERS OF SOCIETY
Learning the Social Meanings of Gender

HOLLY DEVOR

Holly Devor teaches women's studies courses at Simon Fraser University in Burnaby, British Columbia. Her book *Gender Blending: Confronting the Limits of Duality* (1989), from which this selection is taken, examines the social construction of gender. It is based on interviews with fifteen women who lead lives that do not fit either of the socially proscribed roles of masculinity or femininity.

The Gendered Self

The task of learning to be properly gendered members of society only begins with the establishment of gender identity. Gender identities act as cognitive filtering devices guiding people to attend to and learn gender role behaviors appropriate to their statuses. Learning to behave in accordance with one's gender identity is a lifelong process. As we move through our lives, society demands different gender performances from us and rewards, tolerates, or punishes us differently for conformity to, or digression from, social norms. As children, and later adults, learn the rules of membership in society, they come to see themselves in terms they have learned from the people around them.

Children begin to settle into a gender identity between the age of eighteen months and two years.[1] By the age of two, children usually understand that they are members of a gender grouping and can correctly identify other members of their gender.[2] By age three they have a fairly firm and consistent concept of gender. Generally, it is not until children are five to seven years old that they become convinced that they are permanent members of their gender grouping.[3]

Researchers test the establishment, depth, and tenacity of gender identity through the use of language and the concepts mediated by language. The language systems used in populations studied by most researchers in this field conceptualize gender as binary and permanent. All persons are either male or female. All males are first boys and then men; all females are first girls and then women. People are believed to be unable to change genders without sex change surgery, and those who do change sex are considered to be both disturbed and exceedingly rare.

23

This is by no means the only way that gender is conceived in all cultures. 4
Many aboriginal cultures have more than two gender categories and accept
the idea that, under certain circumstances, gender may be changed without
changes being made to biological sex characteristics. Many North and South
American native peoples had a legitimate social category for persons who
wished to live according to the gender role of another sex. Such people were
sometimes revered, sometimes ignored, and occasionally scorned. Each culture had its own word to describe such persons, most commonly translated
into English as "berdache." Similar institutions and linguistic concepts have
also been recorded in early Siberian, Madagascan, and Polynesian societies,
as well as in medieval Europe.[4]

Very young children learn their culture's social definitions of gender and 5
gender identity at the same time that they learn what gender behaviors are
appropriate for them. But they only gradually come to understand the meaning of gender in the same way as the adults of their society do. Very young
children may learn the words which describe their gender and be able to
apply them to themselves appropriately, but their comprehension of their
meaning is often different from that used by adults. Five year olds, for example, may be able to accurately recognize their own gender and the genders
of the people around them, but they will often make such ascriptions on the
basis of role information, such as hair style, rather than physical attributes,
such as genitals, even when physical cues are clearly known to them. One
result of this level of understanding of gender is that children in this age
group often believe that people may change their gender with a change in
clothing, hair style, or activity.[5]

The characteristics most salient to young minds are the more culturally 6
specific qualities which grow out of gender role prescriptions. In one study,
young school age children, who were given dolls and asked to identify their
gender, overwhelmingly identified the gender of the dolls on the basis of
attributes such as hair length or clothing style, in spite of the fact that the
dolls were anatomically correct. Only 17 percent of the children identified
the dolls on the basis of their primary or secondary sex characteristics.[6] Children, five to seven years old, understand gender as a function of role rather
than as a function of anatomy. Their understanding is that gender (role) is
supposed to be stable but that it is possible to alter it at will. This demonstrates
that although the standard social definition of gender is based on genitalia,
this is not the way that young children first learn to distinguish gender. The
process of learning to think about gender in an adult fashion is one prerequisite to becoming a full member of society. Thus, as children grow older,
they learn to think of themselves and others in terms more like those used
by adults.

Children's developing concepts of themselves as individuals are necessar- 7
ily bound up in their need to understand the expectations of the society of
which they are a part. As they develop concepts of themselves as individuals,

they do so while observing themselves as reflected in the eyes of others. Children start to understand themselves as individuals separate from others during the years that they first acquire gender identities and gender roles. As they do so, they begin to understand that others see them and respond to them as particular people. In this way they develop concepts of themselves as individuals, as an "I" (a proactive subject) simultaneously with self-images of themselves as individuals, as a "me" (a member of society, a subjective object). Children learn that they are both as they see themselves and as others see them.[7]

To some extent, children initially acquire the values of the society around them almost indiscriminately. To the degree that children absorb the generalized standards of society into their personal concept of what is correct behavior, they can be said to hold within themselves the attitude of the "generalized other."[8] This "generalized other" functions as a sort of monitoring or measuring device with which individuals may judge their own actions against those of their generalized conceptions of how members of society are expected to act. In this way members of society have available to them a guide, or an internalized observer, to turn the more private "I" into the object of public scrutiny, the "me." In this way, people can monitor their own behavioral impulses and censor actions which might earn them social disapproval or scorn. The tension created by the constant interplay of the personal "I" and the social "me" is the creature known as the "self." 9

But not all others are of equal significance in our lives, and therefore not all others are of equal impact on the development of the self. Any person is available to become part of one's "generalized other," but certain individuals, by virtue of the sheer volume of time spent in interaction with someone, or by virtue of the nature of particular interactions, become more significant in the shaping of people's values. These "significant others" become prominent in the formation of one's self-image and one's ideals and goals. As such they carry disproportionate weight in one's personal "generalized other."[9] Thus, children's individualistic impulses are shaped into a socially acceptable form both by particular individuals and by a more generalized pressure to conformity exerted by innumerable faceless members of society. Gender identity is one of the most central portions of that developing sense of self.

Gender as a Cognitive Schema

The first important molders of children's concepts of social standards reside within the immediate family group, but very early in life children become exposed to the standards of others in a larger social context. Often the various people in children's lives give them conflicting or confusing messages as to the nature of social standards. Children are only able to make sense of such 10 variety according to their cognitive abilities and within the context of the experiences they have already had and the lessons they have already learned.

Certain ways of understanding social exchanges become more firmly established through repeated experience with them. These cognitive frameworks become more useful to children as they learn that they are the ways that many other people around them share. Different societies, or social groupings within societies, teach children and adults their own ways of recognizing and organizing knowledge. When members of societies share common ways of understanding the people, objects, and events of their lives, they use similar conceptual structures to organize their experience into cognitive bits which make sense to them, and which may be effectively communicated to others. Any conceptual structure that organizes social experience so that this sort of understanding and shared meaning can exist is called a cognitive schema.   11

Cognitive schemata are therefore basic to social organization and communication. They make it possible for persons to come to common understandings of shared experiences. Without socially accepted cognitive schemata, individuals who experienced the same events could place such diverse interpretations on their simultaneous experiences that it would be difficult to believe that they had all been at the same place at the same time.[10]   12

Most societies use sex and gender as a major cognitive schema for understanding the world around them.[11] People, objects, and abstract ideas are commonly classified as inherently female or male. The attributes, qualities, or objects actually associated with each class vary widely from society to society, but most do use gender as a most basic groundwork. Gender, then, becomes a nearly universally accepted early cognitive tool used by most children to help them understand the world. This means that children learn that gender is a legitimate way to classify the contents of the world and that others will readily understand them if they communicate through such a framework. Children also learn from those around them what to allocate to the categories of male and female, what elements of all things are considered to fall under the influence of the feminine principle, and which are classified as within the masculine sphere.   13

In North American society, the gender schema most widely in use is biologically deterministic. While there is some widespread belief and understanding that social factors have an influence on questions of gender, the dominant view remains that biological demands set the limits on the possible effects of social factors. In the script of the dominant gender schema, and in the parlance of the everyday world, the relationship between the main concepts is roughly as follows:[12] It is presumed that there are normally two, and only two, sexes, that all persons are either one sex or the other, and that no person may change sexes without extensive surgical intervention. Sex is believed to so strongly determine gender that these two classifications are com-   14 monly conflated to the extent that the terms are used interchangeably, and many people fail to see any conceptual difference between the two. Thus it is also believed that there are two, and only two, genders, and that individuals can effectively change genders only by also changing their sex. Gender roles are that part of the sex/gender bundle that may culturally vary within the constraints of biological imperatives. Gender roles, usually seen to be somewhat determined by social factors, are therefore thought to be less precisely tied to sex and gender than sex and gender are to each other.

Thus, sex is seen as wholly determining gender and largely determining gender role. The practices of gender roles are thought to be biologically constrained by the demands of one's biological sex/gender and socially defined by one's particular rearing within their gender (see Figure 1). 15

The specifics of the definitions of appropriate gender roles for members of each sex/gender class in North American societies vary mainly by age, race, regionality, socio-economic class, ethnicity, and by membership in sexually defined minority groups. Nonetheless, each sub-group generally subscribes to the main premises of the dominant gender schema and forms its particular definitions of appropriate gender roles from within those limitations. 16

In strongly sex-typed societies, or individuals, a gender schema tends to be a predominant mode of thought. In any given situation, there are always a number of cognitive frameworks one might use to understand the dynamics of that situation. Other major frameworks which might be used to understand situations involving human beings might revolve around race, social class, age, or physical size, but sex-typed individuals, and societies, tend to regard gender as one of the most significant factors in understanding themselves and the situations they find themselves in. 17

During the period in children's lives when they are first learning their gender identity and gender role, they also learn the definitions and usages of a gender schema. Children learn that they are girls or boys and that everyone else is either a girl or a boy. They learn that girls and boys are different by virtue of the different ways that they act and look, and that certain objects and ideas are associated with maleness and femaleness. As children assimilate the concepts and classifications of the gender schema of their social group, they learn to define themselves and those around them by its terms of reference. A process begins in young minds whereby it becomes not only 18

FIGURE I   Dominant Gender Schema

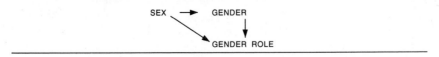

legitimate but also expedient to sift all experience through the mesh of a gender schema.[13]*

Children who are raised within a society which revolves around a gender   19
schema learn to embrace those aspects of the schema which apply to the
gender group that they have been assigned to. Because an element of our
gender schema is that there are two distinct, non-overlapping gender groups,
children also learn to reject those elements of their schema which do not
apply to themselves. But it is important that members of society do not so
thoroughly reject the gender lessons of the other gender that they become
unable to recognize its members and respond appropriately to their cues. As
gender schemata are highly complex and can be used to understand almost
any experience, children are engaged in this process with increasing sophistication as their cognitive abilities improve with age. . . .

Gender Role Behaviors and Attitudes

The clusters of social definitions used to identify persons by gender are   20
collectively known as femininity and masculinity. Masculine characteristics
are used to identify persons as males, while feminine ones are used as signifiers
for femaleness. People use femininity or masculinity to claim and communicate their membership in their assigned, or chosen, sex or gender. Others
recognize our sex or gender more on the basis of these characteristics than
on the basis of sex characteristics, which are usually largely covered by clothing in daily life.

These two clusters of attributes are most commonly seen as mirror images   21
of one another with masculinity usually characterized by dominance and
aggression, and femininity by passivity and submission. A more even-handed
description of the social qualities subsumed by femininity and masculinity
might be to label masculinity as generally concerned with egoistic dominance
and femininity as striving for cooperation or communion.[14] Characterizing
femininity and masculinity in such a way does not portray the two clusters of
characteristics as being in a hierarchical relationship to one another but rather
as being two different approaches to the same question, that question being
centrally concerned with the goals, means, and use of power. Such an alternative conception of gender roles captures the hierarchical and competitive
masculine thirst for power, which can, but need not, lead to aggression, and
the feminine quest for harmony and communal well-being, which can, but
need not, result in passivity and dependence.

---

* This essay is an edited version of a chapter from Devor's book. Footnotes after this point in
the text have been renumbered. [Editor's note]

Many activities and modes of expression are recognized by most members of society as feminine. Any of these can be, and often are, displayed by persons of either gender. In some cases, cross gender behaviors are ignored by observers, and therefore do not compromise the integrity of a person's gender display. In other cases, they are labeled as inappropriate gender role behaviors. Although these behaviors are closely linked to sexual status in the minds and experiences of most people, research shows that dominant persons of either gender tend to use influence tactics and verbal styles usually associated with men and masculinity, while subordinate persons, of either gender, tend to use those considered to be the province of women.[15] Thus it seems likely that many aspects of masculinity and femininity are the result, rather than the cause, of status inequalities.

Popular conceptions of femininity and masculinity instead revolve around hierarchical appraisals of the "natural" roles of males and females. Members of both genders are believed to share many of the same human characteristics, although in different relative proportions; both males and females are popularly thought to be able to do many of the same things, but most activities are divided into suitable and unsuitable categories for each gender class. Persons who perform the activities considered appropriate for another gender will be expected to perform them poorly; if they succeed adequately, or even well, at their endeavors, they may be rewarded with ridicule or scorn for blurring the gender dividing line.

The patriarchal gender schema currently in use in mainstream North American society reserves highly valued attributes for males and actively supports the high evaluation of any characteristics which might inadvertently become associated with maleness. The ideology which the schema grows out of postulates that the cultural superiority of males is a natural outgrowth of the innate predisposition of males toward aggression and dominance, which is assumed to flow inevitably from evolutionary and biological sources. Female attributes are likewise postulated to find their source in innate predispositions acquired in the evolution of the species. Feminine characteristics are thought to be intrinsic to the female facility for childbirth and breastfeeding. Hence, it is popularly believed that the social position of females is biologically mandated to be intertwined with the care of children and a "natural" dependency on men for the maintenance of mother-child units. Thus the goals of femininity and, by implication, of all biological females are presumed to revolve around heterosexuality and maternity.[16]

Femininity, according to this traditional formulation, "would result in warm and continued relationships with men, a sense of maternity, interest in caring for children, and the capacity to work productively and continuously in female occupations."[17] This recipe translates into a vast number of proscriptions and prescriptions. Warm and continued relations with men and an interest in maternity require that females be heterosexually oriented. A heterosexual orientation requires women to dress, move, speak, and act in ways

29

that men will find attractive. As patriarchy has reserved active expressions of power as a masculine attribute, femininity must be expressed through modes of dress, movement, speech, and action which communicate weakness, dependency, ineffectualness, availability for sexual or emotional service, and sensitivity to the needs of others.

Some, but not all, of these modes of interrelation also serve the demands   26
of maternity and many female job ghettos. In many cases, though, femininity is not particularly useful in maternity or employment. Both mothers and workers often need to be strong, independent, and effectual in order to do their jobs well. Thus femininity, as a role, is best suited to satisfying a masculine vision of heterosexual attractiveness.

Body postures and demeanors which communicate subordinate status and   27
vulnerability to trespass through a message of "no threat" make people appear to be feminine. They demonstrate subordination through a minimizing of spatial use: people appear feminine when they keep their arms closer to their bodies, their legs closer together, and their torsos and heads less vertical then do masculine-looking individuals. People also look feminine when they point their toes inward and use their hands in small or childlike gestures. Other people also tend to stand closer to people they see as feminine, often invading their personal space, while people who make frequent appeasement gestures, such as smiling, also give the appearance of femininity. Perhaps as an outgrowth of a subordinate status and the need to avoid conflict with more socially powerful people, women tend to excel over men at the ability to correctly interpret, and effectively display, nonverbal communication cues.[18]

Speech characterized by inflections, intonations, and phrases that convey   28
nonaggression and subordinate status also make a speaker appear more feminine. Subordinate speakers who use more polite expressions and ask more questions in conversation seem more feminine. Speech characterized by sounds of higher frequencies are often interpreted by listeners as feminine, childlike, and ineffectual.[19] Feminine styles of dress likewise display subordinate status through greater restriction of the free movement of the body, greater exposure of the bare skin, and an emphasis on sexual characteristics. The more gender distinct the dress, the more this is the case.

Masculinity, like femininity, can be demonstrated through a wide variety   29
of cues. Pleck has argued that it is commonly expressed in North American society through the attainment of some level of proficiency at some, or all, of the following four main attitudes of masculinity. Persons who display success and high status in their social group, who exhibit "a manly air of toughness, confidence, and self-reliance" and "the aura of aggression, violence, and daring," and who conscientiously avoid anything associated with femininity are seen as exuding masculinity.[20] These requirements reflect the patriarchal ideology that masculinity results from an excess of testosterone, the assumption being that androgens supply a natural impetus toward aggres-

sion, which in turn impels males toward achievement and success. This vision of masculinity also reflects the ideological stance that ideal maleness (masculinity) must remain untainted by female (feminine) pollutants.

Masculinity, then, requires of its actors that they organize themselves and their society in a hierarchical manner so as to be able to explicitly quantify the achievement of success. The achievement of high status in one's social group requires competitive and aggressive behavior from those who wish to obtain it. Competition which is motivated by a goal of individual achievement, or egoistic dominance, also requires of its participants a degree of emotional insensitivity to feelings of hurt and loss in defeated others, and a measure of emotional insularity to protect oneself from becoming vulnerable to manipulation by others. Such values lead those who subscribe to them to view feminine persons as "born losers" and to strive to eliminate any similarity to feminine people from their own personalities. In patriarchally organized societies, masculine values become the ideological structure of the society as a whole. Masculinity thus becomes "innately" valuable and femininity serves a contrapuntal function to delineate and magnify the hierarchical dominance of masculinity.

Body postures, speech patterns, and styles of dress which demonstrate and support the assumption of dominance and authority convey an impression of masculinity. Typical masculine body postures tend to be expansive and aggressive. People who hold their arms and hands in positions away from their bodies, and who stand, sit, or lie with their legs apart—thus maximizing the amount of space that they physically occupy—appear most physically masculine. Persons who communicate an air of authority or a readiness for aggression by standing erect and moving forcefully also tend to appear more masculine. Movements that are abrupt and stiff, communicating force and threat rather than flexibility and cooperation, make an actor look masculine. Masculinity can also be conveyed by stern or serious facial expressions that suggest minimal receptivity to the influence of others, a characteristic which is an important element in the attainment and maintenance of egoistic dominance.[21]

Speech and dress which likewise demonstrate or claim superior status are also seen as characteristically masculine behavior patterns. Masculine speech patterns display a tendency toward expansiveness similar to that found in masculine body postures. People who attempt to control the direction of conversations seem more masculine.[22] Those who tend to speak more loudly, use less polite and more assertive forms, and tend to interrupt the conversations of others more often also communicate masculinity to others. Styles of dress which emphasize the size of upper body musculature, allow freedom of movement, and encourage an illusion of physical power and a look of easy physicality all suggest masculinity. Such appearances of strength and readiness to action serve to create or enhance an aura of aggressiveness and intimidation

30

31

32

central to an appearance of masculinity. Expansive postures and gestures combine with these qualities to insinuate that a position of secure dominance is a masculine one.

Gender role characteristics reflect the ideological contentions underlying [33] the dominant gender schema in North American society. That schema leads us to believe that female and male behaviors are the result of socially directed hormonal instructions which specify that females will want to have children and will therefore find themselves relatively helpless and dependent on males for support and protection. The schema claims that males are innately aggressive and competitive and therefore will dominate over females. The social hegemony of this ideology ensures that we are all raised to practice gender roles which will confirm this vision of the nature of the sexes. Fortunately, our training to gender roles is neither complete nor uniform. As a result, it is possible to point to multitudinous exceptions to, and variations on, these themes. Biological evidence is equivocal about the source of gender roles,[23] psychological androgyny is a widely accepted concept.[24] It seems most likely that gender roles are the result of systematic power imbalances based on gender discrimination.[25]

Notes

1. Much research has been devoted to determining when gender identity becomes solidified in the sense that a child knows itself to be unequivocally either male or female. John Money and his colleagues have proposed eighteen months of age because it is difficult or impossible to change a child's gender identity once it has been established around the age of eighteen months. John Money and Anke A. Ehrhardt, *Man and Woman, Boy and Girl: The Differentiation and Dimorphism of Gender Identity from Conception to Maturity* (Baltimore: Johns Hopkins University Press, 1972), p. 243.

2. Mary Driver Leinbach and Beverly I. Fagot, "Acquisition of Gender Labels: A Test for Toddlers," *Sex Roles* 15 (1986), pp. 655–66.

3. Eleanor Maccoby, *Social Development: Psychological Growth in the Parent-Child Relationship* (New York: Harcourt Brace Jovanovich, 1980), pp. 225–29; Lawrence Kohlberg and Dorothy Z. Ullian, "Stages of the Development of Psychosexual Concepts and Attitudes," in *Sex Differences in Behavior*, ed. Richard Friedman et. al. (New York: John Wiley & Sons, 1974), p. 211.

4. See Susan Baker, "Biological Influences on Human Sex and Gender," in *Women: Sex and Sexuality*, ed. Catherine R. Stimpson and Ethel S. Person (Chicago: University of Chicago Press, 1980), p. 186; Evelyn Blackwood, "Sexuality and Gender in Certain Native American Tribes: The Case of Cross-Gender Females," *Signs* 10 (1984), pp. 27–42; Vern L. Bullough, "Transvestites in the Middle Ages," *American Journal of Sociology* 79 (1974), 1381–89; J. Cl. DuBois, "Transsexualisme et Anthropologie Culturelle," *Gynecologie Practique* 6 (1969), pp. 431–40; Donald C. Forgey, "The Institution of Berdache among the North American Plains Indians," *Journal of Sex Research* 11 (Feb. 1975), pp. 1–15; Walter L. Williams, *The Spirit and the Flesh: Sexual Diversity in American Indian Culture* (Boston: Beacon, 1986).

5. Maccoby, op. cit., p. 255.

6. Ibid., p. 227.

7. George Herbert Mead, "Self," in *The Social Psychology of George Herbert Mead*, ed. Anselm Strauss (Chicago: Phoenix Books, 1962, 1934), pp. 212–60.

8. G. H. Mead.

9. Hans Gerth and C. Wright Mills, *Character and Social Structure: The Psychology of Social Institutions* (New York: Harcourt Brace and World, 1953), p. 96.

10. Consider, for example, the different interpretations of symptoms of physical illness given by western medical practitioners and shamanistic peoples: invasion by bacteria or viruses, versus invasion by evil spirits.

11. Thomas S. Weisner, "Some Cross-Cultural Perspectives on Becoming Female," in *Being Female: Perspectives on Development*, ed. Claire B. Kopp and Martha Kirkpatrick (New York: The Plenum Press, 1979).

12. See Introduction for definitions of the terms "sex," "gender," "gender role."

13. Bem, "Gender Schema Theory: A Cognitive Account" and "Gender Schematic Theory and Its Implications."

14. Egoistic dominance is a striving for superior rewards for oneself or a competitive striving to reduce the rewards for one's competitors even if such action will not increase one's own rewards. Persons who are motivated by desires for egoistic dominance not only wish the best for themselves but also wish to diminish the advantages of others whom they may perceive as competing with them. See Maccoby, p. 217.

15. Judith Howard, Philip Blumstein, and Pepper Schwartz, "Sex, Power, and Influence Tactics in Intimate Relationships," *Journal of Personality and Social Psychology* 51 (1986), pp. 102–109; Peter Kollock, Philip Blumstein, and Pepper Schwartz, "Sex and Power in Interaction: Conversational Privileges and Duties," *American Sociological Review* 50 (1985), pp. 34–46.

16. Nancy Chodorow, *The Reproduction of Mothering* (Berkeley: University of California Press, 1978), p. 134.

17. Jon K. Meyer and John E. Hoopes, "The Gender Dysphoria Syndromes: A Position Statement on So-Called 'Transsexualism,'" *Plastic and Reconstructive Surgery* 54 (Oct. 1974), pp. 444–51.

18. Erving Goffman, *Gender Advertisements* (New York: Harper Colophon Books, 1976); Judith A. Hall, *Non-Verbal Sex Differences: Communication Accuracy and Expressive Style* (Baltimore: Johns Hopkins University Press, 1984); Nancy M. Henley, *Body Politics: Power, Sex and Non-Verbal Communication* (Englewood Cliffs, New Jersey: Prentice-Hall, 1979); Marianne Wex, *"Let's Take Back Our Space": "Female" and "Male" Body Language as a Result of Patriarchal Structures* (Berlin: Frauenliteraturverlag Hermine Fees, 1979).

19. Karen L. Adams, "Sexism and the English Language: The Linguistic Implications of Being a Woman," in *Women: A Feminist Perspective*, 3rd edition, ed. Jo Freeman (Palo Alto, Calif.: Mayfield, 1984), pp. 478–91; Hall, pp. 37, 130–37.

20. Joseph H. Pleck, *The Myth of Masculinity* (Cambridge, MA: The M.I.T. Press, 1981), p. 139.

21. Goffman, *Gender Advertisements*; Hall; Henley; Wex.

22. Adams; Hall, pp. 37, 130–37.

23. Holly Devor, *Gender Blending: Confronting the Limits of Duality* (Bloomington: Indiana University Press, 1989). See Chapter 1.

24. Ibid. See Chapter 2.

25. Howard, Blumstein, and Schwartz; Kollock, Blumstein, and Schwartz.

THE STRANGER

ADRIENNE RICH

Adrienne Rich is one of America's foremost poets and feminist theorists. "The Stranger" appears in her collection of poems *Diving Into the Wreck* (1973), for which she was co-winner of the National Book Award in 1974. She has published eleven volumes of poetry, including *The Will to Change* (1971), *The Dream of a Common Language* (1978), and *Your Native Land, Your Life* (1986).

Looking as I've looked before, straight down the heart
of the street to the river
walking the rivers of the avenues
feeling the shudder of the caves beneath the asphalt
watching the lights turn on in the towers
walking as I've walked before
like a man, like a woman, in the city
my visionary anger cleansing my sight
and the detailed perceptions of mercy
flowering from that anger

if I come into a room out of the sharp misty light
and hear them talking a dead language
if they ask me my identity
what can I say but
I am the androgyne
I am the living mind you fail to describe
in your dead language
the lost noun, the verb surviving
only in the infinitive
the letters of my name are written under the lids
of the newborn child

MAKING CONNECTIONS

1. An experiment like the one depicted in Lois Gould's fantasy has never been conducted. How possible would it be to raise a child in a "gender-free" fashion? Visit a toy store or the infant's section of a department store. Are there any gender themes or messages apparent in the organization of the departments? Do you find any gender-neutral items for sale? Write an essay to prospective parents describing your findings.

2. Watch several cartoon programs on Saturday morning television, and jot down your observations about the gender of the characters. How many females and males are depicted in the programs? What roles do they play? What do they do, say, wear, and care about? Do you believe that preschool boys and girls are influenced by the gender messages in these programs?

3. Fantasy has often been used to satirize social norms that, when looked at in a different light, are revealed to be oppressive or absurd. Some early nineteenth-century women writers, for instance, created amusing "utopias" in which gender roles for men and women were reversed. Try your own hand at fantasy writing. Write a short narrative about a world in which gender roles are reversed, eliminated, or carried to their extremes. Share your efforts with your classmates and discuss the aspects of gender you chose to focus on.

4. Prudence Mackintosh argues that there are certain innate differences between girls and boys that parents cannot influence. How does she convince the reader that her conclusion is valid? How would you evaluate her choice of experts? List the obstacles Mackintosh discusses. How many of these are caused by biology and how many by society? Would Mackintosh agree with the adage "boys will be boys"?

5. What was your own experience growing up male or female? In what ways did messages from your parents, teachers, or peers influence your sense of yourself as a boy or girl? Were these messages mainly traditional ones, or did your upbringing include opportunities and values that "broke the mold"? You might try interviewing your parents about their experiences raising you and any siblings you have, particularly if they are of the opposite sex. Were your parents' lessons and standards the same for each of you? Were their hopes and dreams similar? How do you think your upbringing might have shaped your sense of yourself as a man or woman today?

6. Write a short essay comparing the selections by Gould and Mackintosh. How would you characterize the narrator of each piece? How does each

author employ humor and devices such as exaggeration or sarcasm? Are they writing for similar or for different audiences? Which essay do you find more persuasive and why?

7. Early in her essay Holly Devor criticizes the notion that gender can be divided into just two categories. What evidence does she provide in the rest of the essay to support her criticism? Does she suggest an alternative concept of gender? Do you find her argument persuasive? This essay is part of a chapter from Devor's book, *Gender Blending: Confronting the Limits of Duality*. What can you infer about her thesis from this title?

8. How does Devor define "biological determinism"? Do you agree that biological determinism is the gender schema most widely used in North America? How does Devor define this gender schema and what does she mean when she says that this schema "conflates" sex and gender? Is it important to distinguish between sex and gender? Is Devor's argument persuasive? Where might it be made more so?

9. Who is "the stranger" in Adrienne Rich's poem? How does Rich show both the limitations of and the possibilities for the senses in defining what we see or hear? Whose language is Rich referring to in the phrase "your dead language"? How does this contrast with the writing "under the lids/of the newborn child"? What audience do you think Rich imagined for the poem?

10. Both Rich and Devor suggest that androgyny is a creative alternative to a binary concept of gender. Is androgyny an equally viable choice for men and women? What would an "androgynous" woman or man look or act like? What personal or social advantages would either gain or lose?

11. Choose three individuals of the same sex but from different generations in your family (i.e., your own, your parents', and your grandparents' generations). Write a short biographical sketch for the three people, using gender identity as a common theme. Consider each individual within the specific cultural and historical period in which he or she lived. In what ways were they representative of the men or women of their era? Were any of these individuals exceptions to the prevailing rules of gender for their time? When you compare these individuals, what conclusions can you draw about whether standards for gender change over time?

2
FEMININITY

C O N T E X T S

When you think of the word "feminine," what images come to mind? Different people may come up with different descriptions, but generally they will include such adjectives as soft, sweet, gentle, emotional, sensitive to others, vulnerable, passive, dependent. According to sociologist Talcott Parsons, femininity is associated with expressiveness and relationships, whereas masculinity is seen as more goal-directed. Another sociologist, Nancy Chodorow, has stated the distinction more succinctly: masculinity is associated with "doing," femininity with "being." The masculine image or ideal connotes action and things—going out for sports, fixing cars, making business deals, competing and winning in the outside world. The feminine ideal, on the other hand, is structured around relationships—caring for others, being sensitive and responding to others' needs.

Few people would disagree that such traits as nurturing or gentleness are positive attributes. These characteristics are essential to building and maintaining the bonds of personal relationships and, it can be argued, of society itself. However, if sensitivity to others means that a woman becomes overly accommodating, insecurity and dependence may become a part of her self-image. If nurturance begins to mean that a woman cares for the development of others at the expense of developing herself, she can easily lose her sense of autonomy and identity. Psychologist Phyllis Chesler has claimed that modern women face a dilemma: if they adhere closely to traditional definitions of femininity they risk stunting their own personal and emotional growth. Indeed, studies have shown that many of the very traits society associates with femininity are those that mental health professionals use to define unhealthy or immature adults. However, if women challenge feminine sterotypes too forcefully, they risk being rejected or criticized.

Our first author in this chapter, Susan Brownmiller, looks at the restrictions and dilemmas of "Femininity" in her own life. She traces how as a girl she learned the lessons of femininity from many sources: parents and relatives, books and magazines, toys and clothes labeled "appropriate" for girls. Brownmiller explores her growing exasperation with the limitations of the feminine ideal, the "rigid code of appearance and behavior defined by do's and don't-do's." Yet for Brownmiller, as for many women, the fear of "losing your femininity" still looms large, signalling both personal shortcomings and the loss of approval from others, particularly men. By making this claim, Brownmiller voices a complaint of women today, especially those achieving success in high-powered careers once considered available only to men. Women who are successful in professions that call for decisiveness, assertiveness, independence, and ambition risk being labeled "unfeminine" or feeling trapped by society's double messages.

But aren't women free to choose who they want to be regardless of the pressures of society? In our second essay, "What Do Women Want?: A Conservative Feminist Manifesto," Katherine Kersten takes issue with women who, she contends, blame the culture or the social system for personal choices and failures. Kersten challenges the position of feminists who feel that society still hinders women in the pursuit of their goals. She points out that significant changes in gender roles over the past few decades have allowed women to make major gains. In her view, rather than criticize "the system," women should be pleased that the system has made reforms possible. For Kersten, the key to success or failure lies in individual effort and ambition.

In her essay "Oppression," Marilyn Frye argues for a different view of women's situation. Frye encourages the reader to examine the barriers that restrict individuals in light of the larger social system in which they live. She argues that a focus on the individual alone can lead to a blindness about institutional injustice and the broader phenomenon of social oppression. Not only in the case of women, but for all members of groups restricted in society, Frye sees a danger in "blaming the victim" for inequities that exist within the system itself.

The authors in Chapter 2 provide very different assessments of femininity and of the feminist agenda. As you read these essays, think about your own experiences of and views on femininity. Is femininity a romantic concept that has become outdated, or is it an ideal that undergoes minor revisions to fit a particular historical period? Does the feminine standard impose any more restrictions on women's growth than the masculine ideal does on men's development? Have the battles for women's rights been won, or are there still gender inequities facing the women of today? Are the personal obstacles that individual women confront rooted in social structures, or is blaming "the system" a poor excuse for a lack of individual initiative?

FEMININITY

SUSAN BROWNMILLER

A journalist for more than twenty-five years, Susan
Brownmiller has been a reporter for *The Village Voice*
and a network newswriter for ABC. Her first book,
Against Our Will: Men, Women and Rape, published in
1975, was one of the first feminist studies of rape and
its consequences. This excerpt is taken from her national bestselling book, *Femininity*, published in 1984.

We had a game in our house called "setting the table" and I was Mother's [1]
helper. Forks to the left of the plate, knives and spoons to the right. Placing
the cutlery neatly, as I recall, was one of my first duties, and the event was
alive with meaning. When a knife or a fork dropped to the floor, that meant
a man was unexpectedly coming to dinner. A falling spoon announced the
surprise arrival of a female guest. No matter that these visitors never arrived
on cue, I had learned a rule of gender identification. Men were straight-
edged, sharply pronged and formidable, women were softly curved and held
the food in a rounded well. It made perfect sense, like the division of pink
and blue that I saw in babies, an orderly way of viewing the world. Daddy,
who was gone all day at work and who loved to putter at home with his pipe,
tobacco and tool chest, was knife and fork. Mommy and Grandma, with their
ample proportions and pots and pans, were grownup soup spoons, large and
capacious. And I was a teaspoon, small and slender, easy to hold and just right
for pudding, my favorite dessert.

Being good at what was expected of me was one of my earliest projects, [2]
for not only was I rewarded, as most children are, for doing things right, but
excellence gave pride and stability to my childhood existence. Girls were
different from boys, and the expression of that difference seemed mine to
make clear. Did my loving, anxious mother, who dressed me in white organdy
pinafores and Mary Janes and who cried hot tears when I got them dirty, give
me my first instruction? Of course. Did my doting aunts and uncles with their
gifts of pretty dolls and miniature tea sets add to my education? Of course.
But even without the appropriate toys and clothes, lessons in the art of being
feminine lay all around me and I absorbed them all: the fairy tales that were
read to me at night, the brightly colored advertisements I pored over in
magazines before I learned to decipher the words, the movies I saw, the comic
books I hoarded, the radio soap operas I happily followed whenever I had to

stay in bed with a cold. I loved being a little girl, or rather I loved being a fairy princess, for that was who I thought I was.

As I passed through a stormy adolescence to a stormy maturity, femininity increasingly became an exasperation, a brilliant, subtle esthetic that was bafflingly inconsistent at the same time that it was minutely, demandingly concrete, a rigid code of appearance and behavior defined by do's and don't-do's that went against my rebellious grain. Femininity was a challenge thrown down to the female sex, a challenge no proud, self-respecting young woman could afford to ignore, particularly one with enormous ambition that she nursed in secret, alternately feeding or starving its inchoate life in tremendous confusion. ₃

"Don't lose your femininity" and "Isn't it remarkable how she manages to retain her femininity?" had terrifying implications. They spoke of a bottom-line failure so irreversible that nothing else mattered. The pinball machine had registered "tilt," the game had been called. Disqualification was marked on the forehead of a woman whose femininity was lost. No records would be entered in her name, for she had destroyed her birthright in her wretched, ungainly effort to imitate a man. She walked in limbo, this hapless creature, and it occurred to me that one day I might see her when I looked in the mirror. If the danger was so palpable that warning notices were freely posted, wasn't it possible that the small bundle of resentments I carried around in secret might spill out and place the mark on my own forehead? Whatever quarrels with femininity I had I kept to myself; whatever handicaps femininity imposed, they were mine to deal with alone, for there was no women's movement to ask the tough questions, or to brazenly disregard the rules. ₄

Femininity, in essence, is a romantic sentiment, a nostalgic tradition of imposed limitations. Even as it hurries forward in the 1980s, putting on lipstick and high heels to appear well dressed, it trips on the ruffled petticoats and hoopskirts of an era gone by. Invariably and necessarily, femininity is something that women had more of in the past, not only in the historic past of prior generations, but in each woman's personal past as well—in the virginal innocence that is replaced by knowledge, in the dewy cheek that is coarsened by age, in the "inherent nature" that a woman seems to misplace so forgetfully whenever she steps out of bounds. Why should this be so? The XX chromosomal message has not been scrambled, the estrogen-dominated hormonal balance is generally as biology intended, the reproductive organs, whatever use one has made of them, are usually in place, the breasts of whatever size are most often where they should be. But clearly, biological femaleness is not enough. ₅

Femininity always demands more. It must constantly reassure its audience by a willing demonstration of difference, even when one does not exist in nature, or it must seize and embrace a natural variation and compose a rhapsodic symphony upon the notes. Suppose one doesn't care to, has other things on her mind, is clumsy or tone-deaf despite the best instruction and ₆

training? To fail at the feminine difference is to appear not to care about men, and to risk the loss of their attention and approval. To be insufficiently feminine is viewed as a failure in core sexual identity, or as a failure to care sufficiently about oneself, for a woman found wanting will be appraised (and will appraise herself) as mannish or neutered or simply unattractive, as men have defined these terms.

We are talking, admittedly, about an exquisite esthetic. Enormous plea- 7 sure can be extracted from feminine pursuits as a creative outlet or purely as relaxation; indeed, indulgence for the sake of fun, or art, or attention, is among femininity's great joys. But the chief attraction (and the central paradox, as well) is the competitive edge that femininity seems to promise in the unending struggle to survive, and perhaps to triumph. The world smiles favorably on the feminine woman: it extends little courtesies and minor privilege. Yet the nature of this competitive edge is ironic, at best, for one works at femininity by accepting restrictions, by limiting one's sights, by choosing an indirect route, by scattering concentration and not giving one's all as a man would to his own, certifiably masculine, interests. It does not require a great leap of imagination for a woman to understand the feminine principle as a grand collection of compromises, large and small, that she simply must make in order to render herself a successful woman. If she has difficulty in satisfying femininity's demands, if its illusions go against her grain, or if she is criticized for her shortcomings and imperfections, the more she will see femininity as a desperate strategy of appeasement, a strategy she may not have the wish or the courage to abandon, for failure looms in either direction.

It is fashionable in some quarters to describe the feminine and masculine 8 principles as polar ends of the human continuum, and to sagely profess that both polarities exist in all people. Sun and moon, yin and yang, soft and hard, active and passive, etcetera, may indeed be opposites, but a linear continuum does not illuminate the problem. (Femininity, in all its contrivances, is a very active endeavor.) What, then, is the basic distinction? The masculine principle is better understood as a driving ethos of superiority designed to inspire straightforward, confident success, while the feminine principle is composed of vulnerability, the need for protection, the formalities of compliance and the avoidance of conflict—in short, an appeal of dependence and good will that gives the masculine principle its romantic validity and its admiring applause.

Femininity pleases men because it makes them appear more masculine 9 by contrast; and, in truth, conferring an extra portion of unearned gender distinction on men, as unchallenged space in which to breathe freely and feel stronger, wiser, more competent, is femininity's special gift. One could say that masculinity is often an effort to please women, but masculinity is known to please by displays of mastery and competence while femininity pleases by suggesting that these concerns, except in small matters, are beyond its intent. Whimsy, unpredictability and patterns of thinking and behavior that are dominated by emotion, such as tearful expressions of sentiment and fear, are thought to be feminine precisely because they lie outside the established route to success.

If in the beginnings of history the feminine woman was defined by her physical dependency, her inability for reasons of reproductive biology to triumph over the forces of nature that were the tests of masculine strength and power, today she reflects both an economic and emotional dependency that is still considered "nature," romantic and attractive. After an unsettling fifteen years in which many basic assumptions about the sexes were challenged, the economic disparity did not disappear. Large numbers of women—those with small children, those left high and dry after a mid-life divorce—need financial support. But even those who earn their own living share a universal need for connectedness (call it love, if you wish). As unprecedented numbers of men abandon their sexual interest in women, others, sensing opportunity, choose to demonstrate their interest through variety and a change in partners. A sociological fact of the 1980s is that female competition for two scarce resources—men and jobs—is especially fierce.

So it is not surprising that we are currently witnessing a renewed interest in femininity and an unabashed indulgence in feminine pursuits. Femininity serves to reassure men that women need them and care about them enormously. By incorporating the decorative and the frivolous into its definition of style, femininity functions as an effective antidote to the unrelieved seriousness, the pressure of making one's way in a harsh, difficult world. In its mandate to avoid direct confrontation and to smooth over the fissures of conflict, femininity operates as a value system of niceness, a code of thoughtfulness and sensitivity that in modern society is sadly in short supply.

There is no reason to deny that indulgence in the art of feminine illusion can be reassuring to a woman, if she happens to be good at it. As sexuality undergoes some dizzying revisions, evidence that one is a woman "at heart" (the inquisitor's question) is not without worth. Since an answer of sorts may be furnished by piling on additional documentation, affirmation can arise from such identifiable but trivial feminine activities as buying a new eyeliner, experimenting with the latest shade of nail color, or bursting into tears at the outcome of a popular romance novel. Is there anything destructive in this? Time and cost factors, a deflection of energy and an absorption in fakery spring quickly to mind, and they need to be balanced, as in a ledger book, against the affirming advantage. . . .

WHAT DO WOMEN WANT?
A Conservative Feminist Manifesto

KATHERINE KERSTEN

Katherine Kersten, a spokesperson for conservative feminists, is a director of the Center of the American Experiment in Minneapolis, a public policy and educational organization. This essay first appeared in the Spring, 1991 issue of *Policy Review*.

Am I a feminist? Like many American women, I have been uncertain for years how to respond. This might seem odd, for as a professional woman, I owe an incalculable debt to those who battled to open the voting booths, the universities, and the boardrooms to women. I believe that men and women are one another's equals, and that both sexes must be free to develop their potential unhampered by preconceptions about their abilities. Moreover, I know from personal experience that in many of their endeavors women continue to face greater obstacles to their success than men do.

Yet despite these convictions, I find I have little in common with most of the women I know who call themselves feminists. Reduced to its essence, their feminism often seems a chip on the shoulder disguised as a philosophy; an excuse to blame others for personal failures; a misguided conviction that rage is the proper response to a society that—try as it might—can't seem to arrange things so that everyone "gets it all." I sometimes feel an outright antipathy to women's organizations that claim to have an inside track on my "interests" and "perspectives," and purport to speak for me in the public arena. These organizations seem ill-equipped to advance women's happiness, for all too often their leaders appear neither to understand nor to respect the majority of American women.

Debt to the West

What sets me apart from most contemporary feminists is that—more than anger at the injustices done to women in the past—I feel gratitude toward the social and political system that has made much-needed reform possible. I believe that American women will pay a heavy price if they allow feminists who do not feel such gratitude to lay claim to the moral authority of the feminist heritage, and to appropriate for themselves the right to set the feminist agenda.

Consequently, I propose an alternative to the feminism of the women's studies departments and "public interest" lobbies. I envision a self-consciously *conservative* feminism, inspired by what is best in our tradition, that can speak to women's concerns in both the private and public spheres. Such a feminism is based on three premises: first, that uniform standards of equality and justice must apply to both sexes; second, that women have historically suffered from injustice, and continue to do so today; and third, that the problems that confront women can best be addressed by building on—rather than repudiating—the ideals and institutions of Western culture.

The experiences of a lifetime—my studies, my brushes with sex discrimination and harassment, my work as a banker and attorney, and my career as a wife and mother—have convinced me that women need a philosophical framework that can help them make wise choices in their pursuit of happiness. I believe that a synthesis of conservative and feminist principles can most effectively sustain and inspire women in the post-Superwoman era. . . .

Feminism's Founding Principles

At the root of the American Founding is the notion of a universal human nature, which renders people everywhere more similar than different. This common humanity confers on all human beings certain natural and inalienable rights. In addition, it enables people of markedly different times and places to speak intelligibly to one another about questions of justice and virtue, of good and evil, and to enrich one another's understanding, despite the intervention of thousands of miles or thousands of years.

Yet, human nature, so noble in certain ways, is limited in its potential, as thinkers from James Madison to Thomas Sowell have reminded us. It is limited by passion and self-interest, by its finite capacity to gather and process information, and by its inability to realize its loftiest goals without provoking a host of unintended consequences. As a result of these limitations, and of human contingency on a natural world characterized by disease, disasters, and scarce resources, suffering and inequity are endemic to the human condition.

Perfect justice and equality, then, are beyond the grasp of any human society, present or future. However, justice and equality as *moral principles* must always animate the norms, institutions, and policies of a society that aspires to be good. As the political philosopher Charles Kesler has pointed out, conservatives differ from ideologues of both the Left and Right in according *prudence* a central role in determining how these principles can best be secured and honored in practice.

As Western, and specifically conservative, ideas about justice and equality have developed, a corollary line of thought has emerged. This is the tradition of classical feminism, which draws its inspiration from the Western belief in a universal human nature conferring inalienable rights on all who share it. Classical feminism holds that, because men and women participate equally in this nature, the application of uniform standards of justice and equality to both sexes is morally imperative. . . .

Equal Rights, Comparable Wrongs

Like other feminists, the conservative feminist sees the promotion of justice and equality as a primary goal of public policy. Yet she understands these principles quite differently than do most contemporary feminists. Specifically, the conservative feminist tends to see *individuals* as having rights to justice and equality, while other feminists tend to see *groups* as having such rights. 10

The conservative feminist understands justice in universal terms: she believes that its essence is fair treatment for *all* citizens. Justice requires that women have equal access to employment, education, housing, and credit, and—thanks to the civil rights legislation of the '60s and '70s—their rights to these things are now secure. But the conservative feminist believes that it is manifestly unjust to pass laws that create a privileged status for women, or that attempt to remedy past wrongs done to women by imposing wrongs or disadvantages upon men. 11

Road to Tyranny

The conservative feminist understands equality in universal terms as well. So long as men and women are governed by the same rules and judged by the same standards, she is satisfied that gender equality exists. Unlike most contemporary feminists, she does not leap to the conclusion that equality demands that the results of every social process be identical for men and women, viewed collectively. Indeed, she believes that attempts to enforce particular group results—for example, to require that a certain percentage of government contractors or college faculty be female—inevitably place great restraints on individual freedom of action. Moreover, like Friedrich von Hayek, the conservative feminist maintains that efforts to equalize *economic* results generally produce greater, and more dangerous, inequalities of *political* power among contending groups. She suspects, as Hayek did, that the goal of combining individual freedom and equality of group outcome is unattainable, and represents a hazardous first step on the road to tyranny. 12

In short, while most contemporary feminists advocate policies that maximize equivalence of condition among groups, the conservative feminist advocates policies that maximize individual freedom: the freedom of each citizen, male or female, to strive—and be rewarded—for personal excellence. 13

Her commitment to individual freedom determines her stance on many of the public policy issues dear to contemporary feminists' hearts, among them affirmative action, comparable worth, and sex discrimination and harassment.

Not surprisingly, the conservative feminist opposes affirmative action and group quotas as a vehicle for remedying past discrimination and imposing equality of condition. She endorses "special help" programs, like those that prepare women for traditionally male vocations such as engineering and the hard sciences. However, she insists that jobs and positions themselves be awarded solely on the basis of merit. She has little time for those who seek to whitewash quotas with appeals to "inclusiveness" or "diversity." While true diversity—diversity of interest, temperament, expertise, political orientation, and social background—may often be an asset, the conservative feminist sees little value in mere diversity of gender. 14

The Liberating Market

The conservative feminist believes that women are far better off under our current market-based pay system than they would be under a system based on the notion of "comparable worth." In our current system, wages fluctuate according to the market forces of supply and demand. But in a comparable-worth system, wages are set by bureaucracies that attempt to draw parallels between traditionally male and traditionally female occupations, in order to ensure that the wages paid for each are generally equivalent. 15

From the conservative feminist's perspective, to abandon the market's advantages and move toward a planned economy would be a serious mistake for women. Indeed, the conservative feminist knows that capitalism and the market, with their dynamism, flexibility, and appetite for innovation, are among the most powerful tools that women have in their quest for autonomy and prosperity. Capitalism, after all, got women off the farm and out of the house. It produced the typewriters and textile mills that made women's services essential for economic growth. By creating a veritable explosion of new technologies and opportunities, the capitalist system launched women's first tentative steps toward social equality and economic independence. 16

As historically marginalized Americans like Jews and Asians can attest, capitalism's "creative destruction" is one of history's greatest levellers. By rewarding "whatever works," rather than "the way it's always been done," capitalism slowly undermines ancient prejudices and restrictive stereotypes. Third World women deprived of the market's benefits have found little means of escaping the rigid roles that have constrained them for millennia. And while the planned economies of the Eastern bloc were born, like comparable worth, of egalitarian motives, they have failed to bring genuine equality or prosperity to anyone, least of all women. . . . 17

Callous Insensitivity

The conservative feminist believes that women who encounter sexual harass- 18
ment, in the form of persistent and unwelcome sexual advances on the job,
should have legal remedies. But she strongly condemns the current movement—particularly widespread on college campuses—to expand the definition
of sexual harassment as part of a campaign to impose "politically correct"
thinking. On many campuses, remarks that a woman might conceivably interpret as "offensive," "hostile," or even merely "insensitive" to her sex are
now prohibited and punished. For example, at the University of Minnesota,
where I attended law school, the policy manual on harassment forbids "callous
insensitivity to the experience of women," and warns that "sexual harassment
can be as blatant as rape or as subtle as a look." Not surprisingly, policies like
this are increasingly invoked in circumstances that have no sexual overtones,
but merely involve incidents that women find irritating or unpleasant.

Contemporary feminists' tendency to play fast and loose with the concept 19
of sexual harassment disturbs the conservative feminist for a variety of reasons.
It encourages women to relinquish responsibility for defending their ideas
and actions, and exhorts them to blame every intellectual challenge, every
disappointment, every awkward moment on male oppression or ill will. It
institutionalizes the view of woman as perpetual victim, as a helpless, hapless
creature unable to hold her own in the rough and tumble of social life without
special legal armor to protect her feelings. It taints campus life with a pervasive
atmosphere of group-based suspicion and hostility. And, ironically, it trivializes the suffering of women who encounter genuine sexual harassment. . . .

Private Solutions

The conservative feminist maintains that women have largely won their battle 20
for equality before the law. This does not mean that discrimination and
harassment are likely to disappear soon. It does mean that women now have
the tools they need to combat injustice of this sort, and that those who look
to government for more comprehensive solutions risk creating other, more
far-reaching problems. Reform is essential, however, in laws that affect family
life. Divorce and child support legislation, in particular, must be altered if
women and their children are to enjoy equal status with men.

But the conservative feminist is careful not to make the mistake of seeking 21
exclusively political solutions to problems that are essentially social and cultural in nature. She believes that changing individual behavior is the key to
reducing the ills that consign an increasing number of women to second-class
citizenship. She knows, of course, that passing laws can be easy, while influ-
encing behavior is notoriously difficult. Nevertheless, starting at home and
in her immediate community, she attempts to do just that.

Addressing herself to young people, the conservative feminist seeks to   22
define responsible behavior, and to articulate compelling arguments in its
favor. She urges social institutions—schools, churches, and community leaders—to join in this effort, and to stress in all their activities that public welfare
depends on private virtue. She believes that the environmental movement,
which has had a powerful effect on the imaginations of young people, provides
a useful model in this respect. For that movement shares many of the premises
that the conservative feminist wishes to promote: that citizenship entails
responsibilities, that the actions of every person affect the good of the whole,
that it is better to do what is right than what is convenient, and that careless
actions now may have unforeseen deleterious consequences down the road.

The conservative feminist also attempts to influence, or at least to blunt   23
the harmful effects of, the popular culture. She strives to convince parents of
the fact—well known to social philosophers from Plato to Jane Addams—
that young people's imaginations and moral reflexes are shaped as much by
the stories and images of the surrounding culture as by the formal lessons
taught in school. Children who spend their after-school hours watching MTV
rock stars demean scantily clad women are, in a sense being *educated* about
society's expectations regarding conduct toward women. The conservative
feminist lets entertainment executives and advertisers know how she feels
about their products, and she supports concerted action to convince them
that such products don't pay.

The conservative feminist attempts to provoke public scrutiny of the   24
consequences of feminist policies for the average American woman. She
makes clear the feminist leaders do harm every time they deride the traditional
family as the hung-up legacy of Ozzie and Harriet[1]; demand the adoption of
University of Beijing-style sexual harassment regulations; or burden the court
system with yet another costly and ill-conceived class-action suit. Her objective is to persuade foundations and public bodies to rethink the resources
they devote to the feminist establishment and to question the rhetoric and
worldview on which it is based.

Although she seeks to break their near-monopoly in the public policy   25
arena, the conservative feminist encourages feminist organizations to use their
resources and political clout in ways that truly benefit the majority of women.
If these organizations devoted themselves to reversing the popular culture's
degradation of women, for example, they might well do real good. And, if
public or student demand were loud enough, the women's studies programs
now firmly in the grip of academic feminists might be compelled to expand
their "oppression studies" curriculum to include useful investigations of "real

---

1. Ozzie and Harriet were the stars of *The Adventures of Ozzie and Harriet*, a popular television
series of the 1950s and 1960s that celebrated suburban middle-class life.

world" gender-related issues, like the causes and consequences of divorce and the realities of balancing a family and career.

Architect of Her Own Happiness

As she carries out the tasks she has set for herself, the conservative feminist cultivates an intellectual outlook quite distinct from that of most contemporary feminists. The word "victim" does not trip easily off her tongue. She regards adversity as an inevitable component of human life, rather than an aberration afflicting primarily her and her sex. When hard times come, she strives to face them with courage, dignity, and good humor—qualities often in short supply in the feminist camp. And when her own shortcomings lead to failure, she resists the temptation to blame a hostile "system."   26

The conservative feminist is the architect of her own happiness. She finds happiness in striving to fulfill her responsibilities, to cultivate wisdom, to develop her talents, and to pursue excellence in all her endeavors. The world being what it is, she knows that excellence must sometimes be its own reward. But no matter how unfair or frustrating others' behavior may be, she refuses to seek solace in a life of rage and self-pity. Rage and self-pity, she knows, are hallmarks of the weak, not of the strong.   27

At the heart of the conservative feminist's vision is her conception of a universal human nature. Believing that men and women share equally in this nature, she rejects the contemporary feminist view of life as a power struggle, in which self-oriented "interest groups" contend relentlessly for advantage. The conservative feminist knows that it is possible to identify transcendent *human* interests that can mediate between the sexes' competing claims and thereby illuminate a truly common good.   28

In everything she does, the conservative feminist's watchword is "balance." In her private life, she strives to balance her obligations to others with her quest for personal fulfillment. In her public life, she seeks to promote justice and equality, but also to safeguard individual freedom. Her boldness in pursuit of reform is tempered by her respect for fundamental social values and institutions, which embody the collective wisdom of generations who sought the good life as fervently as she. Prudent in her expectations, tireless in her quest for knowledge, she seeks to explore—and to advance—the conditions necessary for human happiness.   29

OPPRESSION

◑

MARILYN FRYE

Since completing her doctorate in philosophy at Cornell University, Marilyn Frye has written and taught extensively on the philosophical aspects of feminism. Her lectures in philosophy at Michigan State University provided the basis for her first book, *The Politics of Reality: Essays in Feminist Theory* (1983), where the essay "Oppression" appears.

It is a fundamental claim of feminism that women are oppressed. The word 'oppression' is a strong word. It repels and attracts. It is dangerous and dangerously fashionable and endangered. It is much misused, and sometimes not innocently.

The statement that women are oppressed is frequently met with the claim that men are oppressed too. We hear that oppressing is oppressive to those who oppress as well as to those they oppress. Some men cite as evidence of their oppression their much-advertised inability to cry. It is tough, we are told, to be masculine. When the stresses and frustrations of being a man are cited as evidence that oppressors are oppressed by their oppressing, the word 'oppression' is being stretched to meaninglessness; it is treated as though its scope includes any and all human experience of limitation or suffering, no matter the cause, degree or consequence. Once such usage has been put over on us, then if ever we deny that any person or group is oppressed, we seem to imply that we think they never suffer and have no feelings. We are accused of insensitivity; even of bigotry. For women, such accusation is particularly intimidating, since sensitivity is one of the few virtues that has been assigned to us. If we are found insensitive, we may fear we have no redeeming traits at all and perhaps are not real women. Thus are we silenced before we begin: the name of our situation drained of meaning and our guilt mechanisms tripped.

But this is nonsense. Human beings can be miserable without being oppressed, and it is perfectly consistent to deny that a person or group is oppressed without denying that they have feelings or that they suffer.

We need to think clearly about oppression, and there is much that mitigates against this. I do not want to undertake to prove that women are oppressed (or that men are not), but I want to make clear what is being said when we say it. We need this word, this concept, and we need it to be sharp and sure.

I

The root of the word 'oppression' is the element 'press'. *The press of the crowd;* ₅ *pressed into military service; to press a pair of pants; printing press; press the button.* Presses are used to mold things or flatten them or reduce them in bulk, sometimes to reduce them by squeezing out the gasses or liquids in them. Something pressed is something caught between or among forces and barriers which are so related to each other that jointly they restrain, restrict or prevent the thing's motion or mobility. Mold. Immobilize. Reduce.

The mundane experience of the oppressed provides another clue. One of ₆ the most characteristic and ubiquitous features of the world as experienced by oppressed people is the double bind—situations in which options are reduced to a very few and all of them expose one to penalty, censure or deprivation. For example, it is often a requirement upon oppressed people that we smile and be cheerful. If we comply, we signal our docility and our acquiescence in our situation. We need not, then, be taken note of. We acquiesce in being made invisible, in our occupying no space. We participate in our own erasure. On the other hand, anything but the sunniest countenance exposes us to being perceived as mean, bitter, angry or dangerous. This means, at the least, that we may be found "difficult" or unpleasant to work with, which is enough to cost one one's livelihood; at worst, being seen as mean, bitter, angry or dangerous has been known to result in rape, arrest, beating and murder. One can only choose to risk one's preferred form and rate of annihilation.

Another example: It is common in the United States that women, espe- ₇ cially younger women, are in a bind, where neither sexual activity nor sexual inactivity is all right. If she is heterosexually active, a woman is open to censure and punishment for being loose, unprincipled or a whore. The "punishment" comes in the form of criticism, snide and embarrassing remarks, being treated as an easy lay by men, scorn from her more restrained female friends. She may have to lie and hide her behavior from her parents. She must juggle the risks of unwanted pregnancy and dangerous contraceptives. On the other hand, if she refrains from heterosexual activity, she is fairly constantly harassed by men who try to persuade her into it and pressure her to "relax" and "let her hair down"; she is threatened with labels like "frigid," "uptight," "man-hater," "bitch" and "cocktease." The same parents who would be disapproving of her sexual activity may be worried by her inactivity because it suggests she is not or will not be popular, or is not sexually normal. She may be charged with lesbianism. If a woman is raped, then if she has been heterosexually active she is subject to the presumption that she liked it (since her activity is presumed to show that she likes sex), and if she has not been heterosexually active, she is subject to the presumption that she liked it (since she is sup-posedly "repressed and frustrated"). Both heterosexual activity and hetero-sexual nonactivity are likely to be taken as proof that you wanted to be raped, and hence, of course, weren't *really* raped at all. You can't win. You are caught in a bind, caught between systematically related pressures.

Women are caught like this, too, by networks of forces and barriers that expose one to penalty, loss or contempt whether one works outside the home or not, is on welfare or not, bears children or not, raises children or not, marries or not, stays married or not, is heterosexual, lesbian, both or neither. Economic necessity; confinement to racial and/or sexual job ghettos; sexual harassment; sex discrimination; pressures of competing expectations and judgments about *women, wives,* and *mothers* (in the society at large, in racial and ethnic subcultures and in one's own mind); dependence (full or partial) on husbands, parents or the state; commitment to political ideas; loyalties to racial or ethnic or other "minority" groups; the demands of self-respect and responsibilities to others. Each of these factors exists in complex tension with every other, penalizing or prohibiting all of the apparently available options. And nipping at one's heels, always, is the endless pack of little things. If one dresses one way, one is subject to the assumption that one is advertising one's sexual availability; if one dresses another way, one appears to "not care about onself" or to be "unfeminine." If one uses "strong language," one invites categorization as a whore or slut; if one does not, one invites categorization as a "lady"—one too delicately constituted to cope with robust speech or the realities to which it presumably refers.

The experience of oppressed people is that the living of one's life is confined and shaped by forces and barriers which are not accidental or occasional and hence avoidable, but are systematically related to each other in such a way as to catch one between and among them and restrict or penalize motion in any direction. It is the experience of being caged in: all avenues, in every direction, are blocked or booby trapped.

Cages. Consider a birdcage. If you look very closely at just one wire in the cage, you cannot see the other wires. If your conception of what is before you is determined by this myopic focus, you could look at that one wire, up and down the length of it, and be unable to see why a bird would not just fly around the wire any time it wanted to go somewhere. Furthermore, even if, one day at a time, you myopically inspected each wire, you still could not see why a bird would have trouble going past the wires to get anywhere. There is no physical property of any one wire, *nothing* that the closest scrutiny could discover, that will reveal how a bird could be inhibited or harmed by it except in the most accidental way. It is only when you step back, stop looking at the wires one by one, microscopically, and take a macroscopic view of the whole cage, that you can see why the bird does not go anywhere; and then you will see it in a moment. It will require no great subtlety of mental powers. It is perfectly *obvious* that the bird is surrounded by a network of systematically related barriers, no one of which would be the least hindrance to its flight, but which, by their relations to each other, are as confining as the solid walls of a dungeon.

It is now possible to grasp one of the reasons why oppression can be hard   11
to see and recognize: one can study the elements of an oppressive structure
with great care and some good will without seeing the structure as a whole,
and hence without seeing or being able to understand that one is looking at
a cage and that there are people there who are caged, whose motion and
mobility are restricted, whose lives are shaped and reduced.

The arresting of vision at a microscopic level yields such common con-   12
fusion as that about the male door-opening ritual. This ritual, which is remarkably widespread across classes and races, puzzles many people, some of
whom do and some of whom do not find it offensive. Look at the scene of
the two people approaching a door. The male steps slightly ahead and opens
the door. The male holds the door open while the female glides through.
Then the male goes through. The door closes after them. "Now how," one
innocently asks, "can those crazy womenslibbers say that is oppressive? The
guy *removed* a barrier to the lady's smooth and unruffled progress." But each
repetition of his ritual has a place in a pattern, in fact in several patterns. One
has to shift the level of one's perception in order to see the whole picture.

The door-opening pretends to be a helpful service, but the helpfulness   13
is false. This can be seen by noting that it will be done whether or not it
makes any practical sense. Infirm men and men burdened with packages will
open doors for able-bodied women who are free of physical burdens. Men
will impose themselves awkwardly and jostle everyone in order to get to the
door first. The act is not determined by convenience or grace. Furthermore,
these very numerous acts of unneeded or even noisome "help" occur in
counterpoint to a pattern of men not being helpful in many practical ways
in which women might welcome help. What *women* experience is a world in
which gallant princes charming commonly make a fuss about being helpful
and providing small services when help and services are of little or no use,
but in which there are rarely ingenious and adroit princes at hand when
substantial assistance is really wanted either in mundane affairs or in situations
of threat, assault or terror. There is no help with the (his) laundry; no help
typing a report at 4:00 a.m.; no help in mediating disputes among relatives or
children. There is nothing but advice that women should stay indoors after
dark, be chaperoned by a man, or when it comes down to it, "lie back and
enjoy it."

The gallant gestures have no practical meaning. Their meaning is sym-   14
bolic. The door-opening and similar services provided are services which
really are needed by people who are for one reason or another incapacitated—
unwell, burdened with parcels, etc. So the message is that women are incapable. The detachment of the acts from the concrete realities of what women
need and do not need is a vehicle for the message that women's actual needs
and interests are unimportant or irrelevant. Finally, these gestures imitate the
behavior of servants toward masters and thus mock women, who are in most
respects the servants and caretakers of men. The message of the false help-

fulness of male gallantry is female dependence, the invisibility or insignificance of women, and contempt for women.

One cannot see the meanings of these rituals if one's focus is riveted upon 15
the individual event in all its particularity, including the particularity of the
individual man's present conscious intentions and motives and the individual
woman's conscious perception of the event in the moment. It seems sometimes that people take a deliberately myopic view and fill their eyes with
things seen microscopically in order not to see macroscopically. At any rate,
whether it is deliberate or not, people can and do fail to see the oppression
of women because they fail to see macroscopically and hence fail to see the
various elements of the situation as systematically related in larger schemes.

As the cageness of the birdcage is a macroscopic phenomenon, the op- 16
pressiveness of the situations in which women live our various and different
lives is a macroscopic phenomenon. Neither can be *seen* from a microscopic
perspective. But when you look macroscopically you can see it—a network of
forces and barriers which are systematically related and which conspire to the
immobilization, reduction and molding of women and the lives we live.

II

The image of the cage helps convey one aspect of the systematic nature of 17
oppression. Another is the selection of occupants of the cages, and analysis
of this aspect also helps account for the invisibility of the oppression of
women.

It is as a woman (or as a Chicana/o or as a Black or Asian or lesbian) that 18
one is entrapped.

"Why can't I go to the park; you let Jimmy go!"
"Because it's not safe for girls."

"I want to be a secretary, not a seamstress; I don't want to learn to make
dresses."
"There's no work for negroes in that line; learn a skill where you can earn
your living."[1]

When you question why you are being blocked, why this barrier is in your
path, the answer has not to do with individual talent or merit, handicap or
failure; it has to do with your membership in some category understood as a
"natural" or "physical" category. The "inhabitant" of the "cage" is not an
individual but a group, all those of a certain category. If an individual is
oppressed, it is in virtue of being a member of a group or category of people

---

1. This example is derived from *Daddy Was A Number Runner*, by Louise Meriwether (Prentice-
Hall, Englewood Cliffs, New Jersey, 1970), p. 144.

that is systematically reduced, molded, immobilized. Thus, to recognize a person as oppressed, one has to see that individual *as* belonging to a group of a certain sort.

There are many things which can encourage or inhibit perception of someone's membership in the sort of group or category in question here. In particular, it seems reasonable to suppose that if one of the devices of restriction and definition of the group is that of physical confinement or segregation, the confinement and separation would encourage recognition of the group as a group. This in turn would encourage the macroscopic focus which enables one to recognize oppression and encourages the individuals' identification and solidarity with other individuals of the group or category. But physical confinement and segregation of the group as a group is not common to all oppressive structures, and when an oppressed group is geographically and demographically dispersed the perception of it as a group is inhibited. There may be little or nothing in the situations of the individuals encouraging the macroscopic focus which would reveal the unity of the structure bearing down on all members of that group.* 19

A great many people, female and male and of every race and class, simply do not believe that *woman* is a category of oppressed people, and I think that this is in part because they have been fooled by the dispersal and assimilation of women throughout and into the systems of class and race which organize men. Our simply being dispersed makes it difficult for women to have knowledge of each other and hence difficult to recognize the shape of our common cage. The dispersal and assimilation of women throughout economic classes and races also divides us against each other practically and economically and thus attaches *interest* to the inability to see: for some, jealousy of their benefits, and for some, resentment of the others' advantages. 20

To get past this, it helps to notice that in fact women of all races and classes *are* together in a ghetto of sorts. There is a women's place, a sector, which is inhabited by women of all classes and races, and it is not defined by geographical boundaries but by function. The function is the service of men and men's interests as men define them, which includes the bearing and rearing of children. The details of the service and the working conditions vary by race and class, for men of different races and classes have different interests, perceive their interests differently, and express their needs and demands in different rhetorics, dialects and languages. But there are also some constants. 21

Whether in lower, middle or upper-class home or work situations, women's service work always includes personal service (the work of maids, butlers, 22

* Coerced assimilation is in fact one of the *policies* available to an oppressing group in its effort to reduce and/or annihilate another group. This tactic is used by the U.S. government, for instance, on the American Indians.

cooks, personal secretaries),* sexual service (including provision for his genital sexual needs and bearing his children, but also including "being nice," "being attractive for him," etc.), and ego service (encouragement, support, praise, attention). Women's service work also is characterized everywhere by the fatal combination of responsibility and powerlessness: we are held responsible and we hold ourselves responsible for good outcomes for men and children in almost every respect though we have in almost no case power adequate to that project. The details of the subjective experience of this servitude are local. They vary with economic class and race and ethnic tradition as well as the personalities of the men in question. So also are the details of the forces which coerce our tolerance of this servitude particular to the different situations in which different women live and work.

All this is not to say that women do not have, assert and manage sometimes to satisfy our own interests, nor to deny that in some cases and in some respects women's independent interests do overlap with men's. But at every race/class level and even across race/class lines men do not serve women as women serve men. "Women's sphere" may be understood as the "service sector," taking the latter expression much more widely and deeply than is usual in discussions of the economy.

III

It seems to be the human condition that in one degree or another we all suffer frustration and limitation, all encounter unwelcome barriers, and all are damaged and hurt in various ways. Since we are a social species, almost all of our behavior and activities are structured by more than individual inclination and the conditions of the planet and its atmosphere. No human is free of social structures, nor (perhaps) would happiness consist in such freedom. Structure consists of boundaries, limits and barriers; in a structured whole, some motions and changes are possible, and others are not. If one is looking for an excuse to dilute the word 'oppression', one can use the fact of social structure as an excuse and say that everyone is oppressed. But if one would rather get clear about what oppression is not, one needs to sort out the sufferings, harms and limitations and figure out which are elements of oppression and which are not.

From what I have already said here, it is clear that if one wants to determine whether a particular suffering, harm or limitation is part of someone's being oppressed, one has to look at it *in context* in order to tell whether it is an element in an oppressive structure: one has to see if it is part of an

---

* At higher class levels women may not *do* all these kinds of work, but are generally still responsible for hiring and supervising those who do it. These services are still, in these cases, women's responsibility.

enclosing structure of forces and barriers which tends to the immobilization and reduction of a group or category of people. One has to look at how the barrier or force fits with others and to whose benefit or detriment it works. As soon as one looks at examples, it becomes obvious that not everything which frustrates or limits a person is oppressive, and not every harm or damage is due to or contributes to oppression.

If a rich white playboy who lives off income from his investments in   26
South African diamond mines should break a leg in a skiing accident at Aspen and wait in pain in a blizzard for hours before he is rescued, we may assume that in that period he suffers. But the suffering comes to an end; his leg is repaired by the best surgeon money can buy and he is soon recuperating in a lavish suite, sipping Chivas Regal. Nothing in this picture suggests a structure of barriers and forces. He is a member of several oppressor groups and does not suddenly become oppressed because he is injured and in pain. Even if the accident was caused by someone's malicious negligence, and hence someone can be blamed for it and morally faulted, that person still has not been an agent of oppression.

Consider also the restriction of having to drive one's vehicle on a certain   27
side of the road. There is no doubt that this restriction is almost unbearably frustrating at times, when one's lane is not moving and the other lane is clear. There are surely times, even, when abiding by this regulation would have harmful consequences. But the restriction is obviously wholesome for most of us most of the time. The restraint is imposed for our benefit, and does benefit us; its operation tends to encourage our *continued* motion, not to immobilize us. The limits imposed by traffic regulations are limits most of us would cheerfully impose on ourselves given that we knew others would follow them too. They are part of a structure which shapes our behavior, not to our reduction and immobilization, but rather to the protection of our continued ability to move and act as we will.

Another example: The boundaries of a racial ghetto in an American city   28
serve to some extent to keep white people from going in, as well as to keep ghetto dwellers from going out. A particular white citizen may be frustrated or feel deprived because s/he cannot stroll around there and enjoy the "exotic" aura of a "foreign" culture, or shop for bargains in the ghetto swap shops. In fact, the existence of the ghetto, of racial segregation, does deprive the white person of knowledge and harm her/his character by nurturing unwarranted feelings of superiority. But this does not make the white person in this situation a member of an oppressed race or a person oppressed because of her/ his race. One must look at the barrier. It limits the activities and the access of those on both sides of it (though to different degrees). But it is a product of the intention, planning and action of whites for the benefit of whites, to secure and maintain privileges that are available to whites generally, as members of the dominant and privileged group. Though the existence of the barrier has some bad consequences for whites, the barrier does not exist in

systematic relationship with other barriers and forces forming a structure oppressive to whites; quite the contrary. It is part of a structure which oppresses the ghetto dwellers and thereby (and by white intention) protects and furthers white interests as dominant white culture understands them. This barrier is not oppressive to whites, even though it is a barrier to whites.

Barriers have different meanings to those on opposite sides of them, even 29
though they are barriers to both. The physical walls of a prison no more dissolve to let an outsider in than to let an insider out, but for the insider they are confining and limiting while to the outsider they may mean protection from what s/he takes to be threats posed by insiders—freedom from harm or anxiety. A set of social and economic barriers and forces separating two groups may be felt, even painfully, by members of both groups and yet may mean confinement to one and liberty and enlargement of opportunity to the other.

The service sector of the wives/mommas/assistants/girls is almost exclu- 30
sively a woman-only sector; its boundaries not only enclose women but to a very great extent keep men out. Some men sometimes encounter this barrier and experience it as a restriction on their movements, their activities, their control or their choices of "lifestyle." Thinking they might like the simple nurturant life (which they may imagine to be quite free of stress, alienation and hard work), and feeling deprived since it seems closed to them, they thereupon announce the discovery that they are oppressed, too, by "sex roles." But that barrier is erected and maintained by men, for the benefit of men. It consists of cultural and economic forces and pressures in a culture and economy controlled by men in which, at every economic level and in all racial and ethnic subcultures, economy, tradition—and even ideologies of liberation— work to keep at least local culture and economy in male control.*

The boundary that sets apart women's sphere is maintained and promoted 31
by men generally for the benefit of men generally, and men generally do benefit from its existence, even the man who bumps into it and complains of the inconvenience. That barrier is protecting his classification and status as a male, as superior, as having a right to sexual access to a female or females. It protects a kind of citizenship which is superior to that of females of his class and race, his access to a wider range of better paying and higher status work, and his right to prefer unemployment to the degradation of doing lower status or "women's" work.

---

* Of course this is complicated by race and class. Machismo and "Black manhood" politics seem to help keep Latin or Black men in control of more cash than Latin or Black women control; but these politics seem to me also to ultimately help keep the larger economy in *white* male control.

If a person's life or activity is affected by some force or barrier that person [32] encounters, one may not conclude that the person is oppressed simply because the person encounters that barrier or force; nor simply because the encounter is unpleasant, frustrating or painful to that person at that time; nor simply because the existence of the barrier or force, or the processes which maintain or apply it, serve to deprive that person of something of value. One must look at the barrier or force and answer certain questions about it. Who constructs and maintains it? Whose interests are served by its existence? Is it part of a structure which tends to confine, reduce and immobilize some group? Is the individual a member of the confined group? Various forces, barriers and limitations a person may encounter or live with may be part of an oppressive structure or not, and if they are, that person may be on either the oppressed or the oppressor side of it. One cannot tell which by how loudly or how little the person complains.

IV

Many of the restrictions and limitations we live with are more or less inter- [33] nalized and self-monitored, and are part of our adaptations to the require- ments and expectations imposed by the needs and tastes and tyrannies of others. I have in mind such things as women's cramped postures and atten- uated strides and men's restraint of emotional self-expression (except for anger). Who gets what out of the practice of those disciplines, and who imposes what penalties for improper relaxations of them? What are the re- wards of this self-discipline?

Can men cry? Yes, in the company of women. If a man cannot cry, it is [34] in the company of men that he cannot cry. It is men, not women, who require this restraint; and men not only require it, they reward it. The man who maintains a steely or tough or laid-back demeanor (all are forms which suggest invulnerability) marks himself as a member of the male community and is esteemed by other men. Consequently, the maintenance of that demeanor contributes to the man's self-esteem. It is felt as good, and he can feel good about himself. The way this restriction fits into the structures of men's lives is as one of the socially required behaviors which, if carried off, contribute to their acceptance and respect by significant others and to their own self-esteem. It is to their benefit to practice this discipline.

Consider, by comparison, the discipline of women's cramped physical [35] postures and attenuated stride. This discipline can be relaxed in the company of women; it generally is at its most strenuous in the company of men.* Like

* Cf. *Let's Take Back Our Space: "Female" and "Male" Body Language as a Result of Patriarchal Structures*, by Marianne Wex (Frauenliteratureverlag Hermine Fees, West Germany, 1979), es- pecially p. 173. This remarkable book presents literally thousands of candid photographs of women and men, in public, seated, standing and lying down. It vividly demonstrates the very systematic differences in women's and men's postures and gestures.

men's emotional restraint, women's physical restraint is required by men. But unlike the case of men's emotional restraint, women's physical restraint is not rewarded. What do we get for it? Respect and esteem and acceptance? No. They mock us and parody our mincing steps. We look silly, incompetent, weak and generally contemptible. Our exercise of this discipline tends to low esteem and low self-esteem. It does not benefit us. It fits in a network of behaviors through which we constantly announce to others our membership in a lower caste and our unwillingness and/or inability to defend our bodily or moral integrity. It is degrading and part of a pattern of degradation.

Acceptable behavior for both groups, men and women, involves a required restraint that seems in itself silly and perhaps damaging. But the social effect is drastically different. The woman's restraint is part of a structure oppressive to women; the man's restraint is part of a structure oppressive to women.

V

One is marked for application of oppressive pressures by one's membership in some group or category. Much of one's suffering and frustration befalls one partly or largely because one is a member of that category. In the case at hand, it is the category, *woman*. Being a woman is a major factor in my not having a better job than I do; being a woman selects me as a likely victim of sexual assault or harassment; it is my being a woman that reduces the power of my anger to a proof of my insanity. If a woman has little or no economic or political power, or achieves little of what she wants to achieve, a major causal factor in this is that she is a woman. For any woman of any race or economic class, being a woman is significantly attached to whatever disadvantges and deprivations she suffers, be they great or small.

None of this is the case with respect to a person's being a man. Simply being a man is not what stands between him and a better job; whatever assaults and harassments he is subject to, being male is not what selects him for victimization; being male is not a factor which would make his anger impotent—quite the opposite. If a man has little or no material or political power, or achieves little of what he wants to achieve, his being male is no part of the explanation. Being male is something he has going *for* him, even if race or class or age or disability is going against him.

Women are oppressed, *as women*. Members of certain racial and/or economic groups and classes, both the males and the females, are oppressed *as members of those races and/or classes. But men are not oppressed *as men*.

. . . and isn't it strange that any of us should have been confused and mystified about such a simple thing?

MAKING CONNECTIONS

1. Brownmiller contends that "one works at femininity by accepting restrictions." Develop this point in your own essay by using Devor's description of gender schemata from Chapter 1. Do girls and women learn to incorporate the prohibitions they learn from society into their gender identity? Can you argue the same point for men? What differences, if any, are there between the "restrictions" placed on each sex?

2. Are there ways that femininity promotes personal confidence or builds self-esteem? What are some positive aspects of femininity that girls integrate into their gender identity? What opportunities or advantages might the feminine ideal allow for women? Do you agree or disagree with Brownmiller's views on the potential benefits of femininity?

3. What would Katherine Kersten's definition of "conservative feminism" be? On what points does she distinguish herself from the contemporary feminist movement? How does she attempt to convince the reader that she is a better spokesperson for women than other feminists? What phrases does she use to describe her opponents and what inferences does she make about their political positions? How does the title of her essay set the stage for her message?

4. How would Kersten respond to Brownmiller's assertion that despite some improvements in equality between the sexes, considerable economic disparities between men and women continue to exist? Construct a dialogue between Kersten and Brownmiller on the subject of unequal pay. What would each author claim are the causes of unequal pay? What solutions do you think each author might propose?

5. Kersten bases the conservative feminist agenda on the principle that all human beings share a common humanity and enjoy certain basic rights. Defend or critique her position that inherent flaws of human nature, not limitations of a social or political system, mean that "perfect justice and equality are beyond the grasp of any human society." Do you agree with her point that justice and equality, while important principles, should be secured in a "prudent" fashion?

6. Marilyn Frye states her purpose early in her essay: to be "sharp and sure" about the concept of oppression. Identify points in the essay where Frye uses definitions, synonyms, analogies, metaphors, and examples to achieve this objective. Is she successful? Develop your own position on the issue of oppression in a short essay. Are women oppressed as a group? Are men also oppressed? Can one really see the connections among specific instances of oppression by stepping back and looking at the bigger picture

as Frye suggests, or is each instance of oppression a unique and unrelated event?

7. What does Frye mean by the "double-binds" that oppressed people experience? Write an essay that gives examples of double-binds that might be experienced due to race, age, or social class. Have you experienced any yourself? What might be done to eliminate the circumstances that cause these double-binds?

8. What does Frye mean when she says that women's place is defined functionally? Do women's social positions and functions vary according to differences in their race, social class, or age? Are there universal beliefs about what constitutes "women's place"? What about "men's place"?

9. Frye and Brownmiller argue that women aid their own oppression by internalizing cultural messages, beliefs, and values about gender, that they, to borrow Frye's phrase, "participate in (their) own erasure." Is this statement more true of women than of men? Or does it apply to women in the past rather than to contemporary women? Write an essay that answers either of these questions. Draw on historical and/or contemporary examples to defend your position.

10. Write an essay comparing Kersten's and Frye's rhetorical strategies. In their introductions both authors make statements that are the antithesis of their own positions. What effect does this strategy have on you the reader? What devices do these authors use to convince the reader that their opponents are wrong? How would you characterize the tone of each essay? Do you think both authors are speaking to the same audience?

11. As a class project, research instances of the feminine ideal across cultures and/or throughout history. What differences in dress, behavior, or social roles do you find among "ideal" women in different societies or in past eras? What similarities are there among these various interpretations of "femininity"? Compare your findings to images of femininity you see in America today. What conclusions can you draw about the concept of femininity?

3
MASCULINITY

C O N T E X T S

Nearly three decades of research on sex role socialization suggests that, compared to girls, boys are socialized at an earlier age to accept narrower, more rigid definitions of their gender. Girls can wear pants, but boys wouldn't be caught dead in a dress. While fathers might brag fondly about their "tomboy" daughters, few would laugh, much less brag, about their sons acting like "sissies." If a boy acts like a girl he may be ridiculed or even rejected by his peers. The codes of behavior that define masculinity are strict and, as some critics have argued, unattainable. According to anthropologist Michael Gilmore, masculinity is a condition that is never completely achieved, that is always at risk, and that therefore must be constantly proven and re-proven throughout a man's life.

What is the impact of society's definition of manhood on the personal lives of men? Does masculinity offer power and privilege for those who conform to its rules, or is it a recipe for anxiety, a limitation to men's personal and emotional growth, even a health hazard for men as it makes them modern victims of stress, heart disease, and overwork? In the past 15 years the growing field of research called men's studies has begun to explore the meaning of masculinity in the experiences of individual men and as a force shaping the institutions and values of society. Its contributors include sociologists, psychologists, anthropologists, artists and political analysts, historians and critics of popular culture, along with the voices of ordinary men coming together to explore the impact of the masculine myth on their lives.

One such voice, among the many you will hear throughout this book, is that of poet and speaker Robert Bly who, in our opening essay, asks what it means to "be a man" today. As Bly points out in an excerpted chapter from his book *Iron John: A Book About Men*, the popular definition of masculinity has changed with historical conditions. According to Bly, the twentieth-century women's movement has played a powerful role in redefining men's sense of themselves by demanding that men be gentler, more thoughtful, "softer." But Bly contends that though modern men have learned a great deal about themselves from the women's movement, they haven't become freer or happier in the process. Drawing on the fairy tale "Iron John," Bly illustrates how men must reassert their masculine power, face their anxieties, free themselves from childhood attachments, and explore the possibilities for male validation in the world at large.

In our second essay, writer and men's activist Cooper Thompson presents another view of modern masculinity. In contrast to Bly's view that men have become too soft by trying to please women, Thompson claims that misogyny (the hatred of women) and homophobia (the fear and hatred of homosexuals) are at the heart of masculine socialization. He advocates "A New Vision of Masculinity" in which male and female traits would be valued equally. In such a world, Thompson contends, boys could experience genuine freedom from anxiety, because they would no longer need to guard vigilantly against being considered feminine.

In the final essay, "Men Loving Men: The Challenge of Gay Liberation," Gary Kinsman invites us to think about how personal life is fashioned to fit society's definitions of gender, sexuality, and relationships. He explores the history of sexuality to show how closely sexual norms are tied to historic, economic, and cultural conditions. "Sexual relations," he concludes, "are therefore changeable and are themselves the site of personal and social struggles." Given this new understanding of the variability of sexual meaning and identity, Kinsman argues that men today face two related challenges. First, they should re-examine the masculine stereotypes that limit them as human beings. Second, they need to question the more fundamental relationships of domination and subordination that permeate society.

Definitions of masculinity, like those of femininity, are specific to time and place. Though the authors in this chapter suggest that the time has come for our society to begin to form new definitions of masculinity, they disagree on the direction these new definitions should take. And though they agree that men should not be constrained by stereotypes, they offer different perspectives on which stereotypes to discard. Do boys grow up with excessive pressure to prove their toughness? If so, should they be encouraged to develop such qualities as empathy, warmth, and patience? Or have men devoted too much attention to their feminine qualities, becoming too soft and losing the essential fire of manhood? If so, how should men go about regaining their masculinity? The complexity of these questions suggests that there are no final answers and that there is ample room to add one's own voice and experience to the debate.

IRON JOHN

ROBERT BLY

Iron John: A Book About Men (1990) is the first full-length prose work by Robert Bly, a celebrated poet and translator who lectures widely on the subject of masculinity. Bly's poetry collections include *Silence in the Snowy Fields* (1962) and *Loving a Woman in Two Worlds* (1985). In 1968 he won the National Book Award for poetry for *The Light Around the Body*. Bly has translated into English the work of numerous poets, including Rainer Maria Rilke, Selma Lagerlof, and Tomas Tranströmer. This selection is an excerpt from Chapter 1 of *Iron John*, "The Pillow and the Key."

We talk a great deal about "the American man," as if there were some   1
constant quality that remained stable over decades, or even within a single
decade.

The men who live today have veered far away from the Saturnian, old-   2
man-minded farmer, proud of his introversion, who arrived in New England
in 1630, willing to sit through three services in an unheated church. In the
South, an expansive, motherbound cavalier developed, and neither of these
two "American men" resembled the greedy railroad entrepreneur that later
developed in the Northeast, nor the reckless I-will-do-without culture settlers
of the West.

Even in our own era the agreed-on model has changed dramatically.   3
During the fifties, for example, an American character appeared with some
consistency that became a model of manhood adopted by many men: the
Fifties male.

He got to work early, labored responsibly, supported his wife and chil-   4
dren, and admired discipline. Reagan is a sort of mummified version of this
dogged type. This sort of man didn't see women's souls well, but he appreciated their bodies; and his view of culture and America's part in it was boyish
and optimistic. Many of his qualities were strong and positive, but underneath
the charm and bluff there was, and there remains, much isolation, deprivation,
and passivity. Unless he has an enemy, he isn't sure that he is alive.

The Fifties man was supposed to like football, be aggressive, stick up for   5
the United States, never cry, and always provide. But receptive space or
intimate space was missing in this image of a man. The personality lacked
some sense of flow. The psyche lacked compassion in a way that encouraged

the unbalanced pursuit of the Vietnam war, just as, later, the lack of what we might call "garden" space inside Reagan's head led to his callousness and brutality toward the powerless in El Salvador, toward old people here, the unemployed, schoolchildren, and poor people in general.

The Fifties male had a clear vision of what a man was, and what male responsibilities were, but the isolation and one-sidedness of his vision were dangerous. 6

During the sixties, another sort of man appeared. The waste and violence of the Vietnam war made men question whether they knew what an adult male really was. If manhood meant Vietnam, did they want any part of it? Meanwhile, the feminist movement encouraged men to actually look at women, forcing them to become conscious of concerns and sufferings that the Fifties male labored to avoid. As men began to examine women's history and women's sensibility, some men began to notice what was called their *feminine* side and pay attention to it. This process continues to this day, and I would say that most contemporary men are involved in it in some way. 7

There's something wonderful about this development—I mean the practice of men welcoming their own "feminine" consciousness and nurturing it—this is important—and yet I have the sense that there is something wrong. The male in the past twenty years has become more thoughtful, more gentle. But by this process he has not become more free. He's a nice boy who pleases not only his mother but also the young woman he is living with. 8

In the seventies I began to see all over the country a phenomenon that we might call the "soft male." Sometimes even today when I look out at an audience, perhaps half the young males are what I'd call soft. They're lovely, valuable people—I like them—they're not interested in harming the earth or starting wars. There's a gentle attitude toward life in their whole being and style of living. 9

But many of these men are not happy. You quickly notice the lack of energy in them. They are life-preserving but not exactly life-giving. Ironically, you often see these men with strong women who positively radiate energy. 10

Here we have a finely tuned young man, ecologically superior to his father, sympathetic to the whole harmony of the universe, yet he himself has little vitality to offer. 11

The strong or life-giving women who graduated from the sixties, so to speak, or who have inherited an older spirit, played an important part in producing this life-preserving, but not life-giving, man. 12

I remember a bumper sticker during the sixties that read "WOMEN SAY YES TO MEN WHO SAY NO." We recognize that it took a lot of courage to resist the draft, go to jail, or move to Canada, just as it took courage to accept the draft and go to Vietnam. But the women of twenty years ago were definitely saying that they preferred the softer receptive male. 13

So the development of men was affected a little in this preference. Non-receptive maleness was equated with violence, and receptive maleness was rewarded. 14

Some energetic women, at that time and now in the nineties, chose and still choose soft men to be their lovers and, in a way, perhaps, to be their sons. The new distribution of "yang" energy among couples didn't happen by accident. Young men for various reasons wanted their harder women, and women began to desire softer men. It seemed like a nice arrangement for a while, but we've lived with it long enough now to see that it isn't working out.

I first learned about the anguish of "soft" men when they told their stories in early men's gatherings. In 1980, the Lama Community in New Mexico asked me to teach a conference for men only, their first, in which about forty men participated. Each day we concentrated on one Greek god and one old story, and then late in the afternoons we gathered to talk. When the younger men spoke it was not uncommon for them to be weeping within five minutes. The amount of grief and anguish in these younger men was astounding to me.

Part of their grief rose out of remoteness from their fathers, which they felt keenly, but partly, too, grief flowed from trouble in their marriages or relationships. They had learned to be receptive, but receptivity wasn't enough to carry their marriages through troubled times. In every relationship something *fierce* is needed once in a while: both the man and the woman need to have it. But at the point when it was needed, often the young man came up short. He was nurturing, but something else was required—for his relationship, and for his life.

The "soft" male was able to say, "I can feel your pain, and I consider your life as important as mine, and I will take care of you and comfort you." But he could not say what he wanted, and stick by it. *Resolve* of that kind was a different matter.

In *The Odyssey*, Hermes instructs Odysseus that when he approaches Circe, who stands for a certain kind of matriarchal energy, he is to lift or show his sword. In these early sessions it was difficult for many of the younger men to distinguish between showing the sword and hurting someone. One man, a kind of incarnation of certain spiritual attitudes of the sixties, a man who had actually lived in a tree for a year outside Santa Cruz, found himself unable to extend his arm when it held a sword. He had learned so well not to hurt anyone that he couldn't lift the steel, even to catch the light of the sun on it. But showing a sword doesn't necessarily mean fighting. It can also suggest a joyful decisiveness.

The journey many American men have taken into softness, or receptivity, or "development of the feminine side," has been an immensely valuable journey, but more travel lies ahead. No stage is the final stop.

Finding Iron John

One of the fairy tales that speak of a third possibility for men, a third mode, is a story called "Iron John" or "Iron Hans." Though it was first set down by the Grimm brothers around 1820, this story could be ten or twenty thousand years old.

As the story starts, we find out that something strange has been happening 22 in a remote area of the forest near the king's castle. When hunters go into this area, they disappear and never come back. Twenty others go after the first group and do not come back. In time, people begin to get the feeling that there's something weird in that part of the forest, and they "don't go there anymore."

One day an unknown hunter shows up at the castle and says, "What can 23 I do? Anything dangerous to do around here?"

The King says: "Well, I could mention the forest, but there's a problem. 24 The people who go out there don't come back. The return rate is not good."

"That's just the sort of thing I like," the young man says. So he goes into 25 the forest and, interestingly, he goes there *alone*, taking only his dog. The young man and his dog wander about in the forest and they go past a pond. Suddenly a hand reaches up from the water, grabs the dog, and pulls it down.

The young man doesn't respond by becoming hysterical. He merely says, 26 "This must be the place."

Fond as he is of his dog and reluctant as he is to abandon him, the hunter 27 goes back to the castle, rounds up three more men with buckets, and then comes back to the pond to bucket out the water. Anyone who's ever tried it will quickly note that such bucketing is very slow work.

In time, what they find, lying on the bottom of the pond, is a large man 28 covered with hair from head to foot. The hair is reddish—it looks a little like rusty iron. They take the man back to the castle, and imprison him. The King puts him in an iron cage in the courtyard, calls him "Iron John," and gives the key into the keeping of the Queen.

Let's stop the story here for a second. 29

When a contemporary man looks down into his psyche, he may, if con- 30 ditions are right, find under the water of his soul, lying in an area no one has visited for a long time, an ancient hairy man.

The mythological systems associate hair with the instinctive and the 31 sexual and the primitive. What I'm suggesting, then, is that every modern male has, lying at the bottom of his psyche, a large, primitive being covered with hair down to his feet. Making contact with this Wild Man is the step the Eighties male or the Nineties male has yet to take. That bucketing-out process has yet to begin in our contemporary culture.

As the story suggests very delicately, there's more than a little fear around 32 this hairy man, as there is around all change. When a man begins to develop the receptive side of himself and gets over his initial skittishness, he usually finds the experience to be wonderful. He gets to write poetry and go out and sit by the ocean, he doesn't have to be on top all the time in sex anymore, he becomes empathetic—it's a new, humming, surprising world.

But going down through water to touch the Wild Man at the bottom of   33
the pond is quite a different matter. The being who stands up is frightening,
and seems even more so now, when the corporations do so much work to
produce the sanitized, hairless, shallow man. When a man welcomes his
responsiveness, or what we sometimes call his internal woman, he often feels
warmer, more companionable, more alive. But when he approaches what I'll
call the "deep male," he feels risk. Welcoming the Hairy Man *is* scary and
risky, and it requires a different sort of courage. Contact with Iron John
requires a willingness to descend into the male psyche and accept what's dark
down there, including the *nourishing* dark.

For generations now, the industrial community has warned young busi-   34
nessmen to keep away from Iron John, and the Christian church is not too
fond of him either.

Freud, Jung, and Wilhelm Reich are three investigators who had the   35
courage to go down into the pond and to accept what they found there. The
job of contemporary men is to follow them down.

Some men have already done this work, and the Hairy Man has been   36
brought up from the pond in their psyches, and lives in the courtyard. "In
the courtyard" suggests that the individual or the culture has brought him
into a sunlit place where all can see him. That is itself some advance over
keeping the Hairy Man in a cellar, where many elements in every culture
want him to be. But, of course, in either place, he's still in a cage.

The Loss of the Golden Ball

Now back to the story.   37

One day the King's eight-year-old son is playing in the courtyard with   38
the golden ball he loves, and it rolls into the Wild Man's cage. If the young
boy wants the ball back, he's going to have to approach the Hairy Man and
ask him for it. But this is going to be a problem.

The golden ball reminds us of that unity of personality we had as chil-   39
dren—a kind of radiance, or wholeness, before we split into male and female,
rich and poor, bad and good. The ball is golden, as the sun is, and round.
Like the sun, it gives off a radiant energy from the inside.

We notice that the boy is eight. All of us, whether boys or girls, lose   40
something around the age of eight. If we still have the golden ball in kindergarten, we lose it in grade school. Whatever is still left we lose in high school.
In "The Frog Prince," the princess's ball fell into a well. Whether we are
male or female, once the golden ball is gone, we spend the rest of our lives
trying to get it back.

The first stage in retrieving the ball, I think, is to accept—firmly, defi-   41
nitely—that the ball has been lost. Freud said: "What a distressing contrast

there is between the radiant intelligence of the child and the feeble mentality of the average adult."

So where is the golden ball? Speaking metaphorically, we could say that 42 the sixties culture told men they would find their golden ball in sensitivity, receptivity, cooperation, and nonaggressiveness. But many men gave up all aggressiveness and still did not find the golden ball.

The Iron John story says that a man can't expect to find the golden ball 43 in the feminine realm, because that's not where the ball is. A bridegroom secretly asks his wife to give him back the golden ball. I think she'd give it to him if she could, because most women in my experience do not try to block men's growth. But she can't give it to him, because she doesn't have it. What's more, she's lost her own golden ball and can't find that either.

Oversimplifying, we could say that the Fifties male always wants a woman 44 to return his golden ball. The Sixties and Seventies man, with equal lack of success, asks his interior feminine to return it.

The Iron John story proposes that the golden ball lies within the magnetic 45 field of the Wild Man, which is a very hard concept for us to grasp. We have to accept the possibility that the true radiant energy in the male does not hide in, reside in, or wait for us in the feminine realm, nor in the macho/John Wayne realm, but in the magnetic field of the deep masculine. It is protected by the *instinctive* one who's underwater and who has been there we don't know how long.

In "The Frog Prince" it's the frog, the un-nice one, the one that everyone 46 says "Ick!" to, who brings the golden ball back. And in the Grimm brothers version the frog himself turns into the prince only when a hand throws him against the wall.

Most men want some nice person to bring the ball back, but the story 47 hints that we won't find the golden ball in the force field of an Asian guru or even the force field of gentle Jesus. Our story is not anti-Christian but pre-Christian by a thousand years or so, and its message is still true—getting the golden ball back is incompatible with certain kinds of conventional tameness and niceness.

The kind of wildness, or un-niceness, implied by the Wild Man image is 48 not the same as macho energy, which men already know enough about. Wild Man energy, by contrast, leads to forceful action undertaken, not with cruelty, but with resolve.

The Wild Man is not opposed to civilization; but he's not completely 49 contained by it either. The ethical superstructure of popular Christianity does not support the Wild Man, though there is some suggestion that Christ himself did. At the beginning of his ministry, a hairy John, after all, baptized him.

When it comes time for a young male to talk with the Wild Man he will 50 find the conversation quite distinct from a talk with a minister, a rabbi, or a guru. Conversing with the Wild Man is not talking about bliss or mind or spirit or "higher consciousness," but about something wet, dark, and low—what James Hillman would call "soul."

The first step amounts to approaching the cage and asking for the golden ball back. Some men are ready to take that step, while others haven't yet bucketed the water out of the pond—they haven't left the collective male identity and gone out into the unknown area alone, or gone with only their dog.

The story says that after the dog "goes down" one has to start to work with buckets. No giant is going to come along and suck out all the water for you: that magic stuff is not going to help. And a weekend at Esalen[1] won't do it. Acid or cocaine won't do it. The man has to do it bucket by bucket. This resembles the slow discipline of art: it's the work that Rembrandt did, that Picasso and Yeats and Rilke and Bach did. Bucket work implies much more discipline than most men realize.

The Wild Man, as the writer Keith Thompson mentioned to me, is not simply going to hand over the golden ball either. What kind of story would it be if the Wild Man said: "Well, okay, here's your ball"?

Jung remarked that all successful requests to the psyche involve deals. The psyche likes to make deals. If part of you, for example, is immensely lazy and doesn't want to do any work, a flat-out New Year's resolution won't do any good. The whole thing will go better if you say to the lazy part: "You let me work for an hour, then I'll let you be a slob for an hour—deal?" So in "Iron John," a deal is made: the Wild Man agrees to give the golden ball back if the boy opens the cage.

The boy, apparently frightened, runs off. He doesn't even answer. Isn't that what happens? We have been told so often by parents, ministers, grade-school teachers, and high-school principals that we should have nothing to do with the Wild Man that when he says "I'll return the ball if you let me out of the cage," we don't even reply.

Maybe ten years pass now. On "the second day" the man could be twenty-five. He goes back to the Wild Man and says, "Could I have my ball back?" The Wild Man says, "Yes, if you let me out of the cage."

Actually, just returning to the Wild Man a second time is a marvelous thing; some men never come back at all. The twenty-five-year-old man hears the sentence all right, but by now he has two Toyotas and a mortgage, maybe a wife and a child. How can he let the Wild Man out of the cage? A man usually walks away the second time also without saying a word.

Now ten more years pass. Let's say the man is now thirty-five . . . have you ever seen the look of dismay on the face of a thirty-five-year-old man?

51

52

53

54

55

56

57

58

1. The Esalen Institute, located on the Big Sur coast of California, is a hot-springs resort that offers seminars and group and individual therapy.

Feeling overworked, alienated, empty, he asks the Wild Man with full heart this time: "Could I have my golden ball back?"

"Yes," the Wild Man says, "If you let me out of my cage." 59

Now something marvelous happens in the story. The boy speaks to the 60 Wild Man, and continues the conversation. He says, "Even if I wanted to let you out, I couldn't, because I don't know where the key is."

That's so good. By the time we are thirty-five we don't know where the 61 key is. It isn't exactly that we have forgotten—we never knew where it was in the first place.

The story says that when the King locked up the Wild Man, "he gave 62 the key into the keeping of the Queen," but we were only about seven then, and in any case our father never told us what he had done with it. So where is the key?

I've heard audiences try to answer that one: 63

"It's around the boy's neck." 64

No. 65

"It's hidden in Iron John's cage." 66

No. 67

"It's inside the golden ball." 68

No. 69

"It's inside the castle . . . on a hook inside the Treasure Room." 70

No. 71

"It's in the Tower. It's on a hook high up on the wall!" 72

No. 73

The Wild Man replies, "The key is under your mother's pillow." 74

The key is not inside the ball, nor in the golden chest, nor in the safe 75 . . . the key is under our mother's pillow—just where Freud said it would be.

Getting the key back from under the mother's pillow is a troublesome 76 task. Freud, taking advice from a Greek play, says that a man should not skip over the mutual attraction between himself and his mother if he wants a long life. The mother's pillow, after all, lies in the bed near where she makes love to your father. Moreover, there's another implication attached to the pillow.

Michael Meade, the myth teller, once remarked to me that the pillow is 77 also the place where the mother stores all her expectations for you. She dreams: "My son the doctor." "My son the Jungian analyst." "My son the Wall Street genius." But very few mothers dream: "My son the Wild Man."

On the son's side, he isn't sure he wants to take the key. Simply transfer- 78 ring the key from the mother's to a guru's pillow won't help. Forgetting that the mother possesses it is a bad mistake. A mother's job is, after all, to civilize the boy, and so it is natural for her to keep the key. All families behave alike: on this planet, "The King gives the key into the keeping of the Queen."

Attacking the mother, confronting her, shouting at her, which some 79 Freudians are prone to urge on us, probably does not accomplish much—she may just smile and talk to you with her elbow on the pillow. Oedipus' conversations with Jocasta never did much good, nor did Hamlet's shouting.

A friend mentioned that it's wise to steal the key some day when your 80 mother and father are gone. "My father and mother are away today" implies a day when the head is free of parental inhibitions. That's the day to steal the key. Gioia Timpanelli, the writer and storyteller, remarked that, mythologically, the theft of the key belongs to the world of Hermes.

And the key has to be *stolen*. I recall talking to an audience of men and 81 women once about this problem of stealing the key. A young man, obviously well trained in New Age modes of operation, said, "Robert, I'm disturbed by this idea of stealing the key. Stealing isn't right. Couldn't a group of us just go to the mother and say, 'Mom, could I have the key back?'?"

His model was probably consensus, the way the staff at the health food 82 store settles things. I felt the souls of all the women in the room rise up in the air to kill him. Men like that are as dangerous to women as they are to men.

No mother worth her salt would give the key anyway. If a son can't steal 83 it, he doesn't deserve it.

"I want to let the Wild Man out!" 84

"Come over and give Mommy a kiss." 85

Mothers are intuitively aware of what would happen if he got the key: 86 they would lose their boys. The possessiveness that mothers typically exercise on sons—not to mention the possessiveness that fathers typically exercise on daughters—can never be underestimated.

The means of getting the key back varies with each man, but suffice it to 87 say that democratic or nonlinear approaches will not carry the day.

One rather stiff young man danced one night for about six hours, vig- 88 orously, and in the morning remarked, "I got some of the key back last night."

Another man regained the key when he acted like a whole-hearted Trick- 89 ster for the first time in his life, remaining fully conscious of the tricksterism. Another man stole the key when he confronted his family and refused to carry any longer the shame for the whole family.

We could spend days talking of how to steal the key in a practical way. 90 The story itself leaves everything open, and simply says, "One day he stole the key, brought it to the Wild Man's cage, and opened the lock. As he did so, he pinched one of his fingers." (That detail will become important in the next part of the story.) The Wild Man is then free at last, and it's clear that he will go back to his own forest, far from "the castle."

What Does the Boy Do?

At this point a number of things could happen. If the Wild Man returns to 91 his forest while the boy remains in the castle, the fundamental historical split in the psyche between primitive man and the civilized man would reestablish itself in the boy. The boy, on his side, could mourn the loss of the Wild Man forever. Or he could replace the key under the pillow before his parents got home, then say he knows nothing about the Wild Man's escape. After that subterfuge, he could become a corporate executive, a fundamentalist minister, a tenured professor, someone his parents could be proud of, who "has never seen the Wild Man."

We've all replaced the key many times and lied about it. Then the solitary hunter inside us has to enter into the woods once more with his body dog accompanying him, and then the dog gets pulled down again. We lose a lot of "dogs" that way. 92

We could also imagine a different scenario. The boy convinces, or imagines he could convince, the Wild Man to stay in the courtyard. If that happened, he and the Wild Man could carry on civilized conversations with each other in the tea garden, and this conversation would go on for years. But the story suggests that Iron John and the boy cannot be united—that is, cannot experience their initial union—in the castle courtyard. It's probably too close to the mother's pillow and the father's book of rules. 93

We recall that the boy in our story, when he spoke to the Wild Man, told him he didn't know where the key was. That's brave. Some men never address a sentence to the Wild Man. 94

When the boy opened the cage, the Wild Man started back to his forest. The boy in our story, or the thirty-five-year-old man in our mind—however you want to look at it—now does something marvelous. He speaks to the Wild Man once more and says, "Wait a minute! If my parents come home and find you gone, they will beat me." That sentence makes the heart sink, particularly if we know something about child-rearing practices that have prevailed for a long time in northern Europe. 95

As Alice Miller reminds us in her book *For Your Own Good*, child psychologists in nineteenth-century Germany warned parents especially about *exuberance*. Exuberance in a child is bad, and at the first sign of it, parents should be severe. Exuberance implies that the wild boy or girl is no longer locked up. Puritan parents in New England often punished children severely if they acted in a restless way during the long church services. 96

"If they come home and find you gone, they will beat me." 97

The Wild Man says, in effect, "That's good thinking. You'd better come with me." 98

So the Wild Man lifts the boy up on his shoulders and together they go off into the woods. That's decisive. We should all be so lucky. 99

As the boy leaves for the forest, he has to overcome, at least for the moment, his fear of wildness, irrationality, hairiness, intuition, emotion, the body, and nature. Iron John is not as primitive as the boy imagines, but the boy—or the mind—doesn't know that yet. 100

Still, the clean break with the mother and father, which the old initiators call for, now has taken place. Iron John says to the boy, "You'll never see your mother and father again. But I have treasures, more than you'll ever need." So that is that. . . . 101

A NEW VISION OF MASCULINITY

COOPER THOMPSON

Cooper Thompson is the coordinator of the Campaign to End Homophobia and is a regular contributor to *Changing Men*, a journal dedicated to examining fundamental changes in men's lives, and in which "A New Vision of Masculinity" first appeared in 1985. Thompson has conducted workshops on changing male socialization and has developed antisexist curricula for schools.

I was once asked by a teacher in a suburban high school to give a guest 1
presentation on male roles. She hoped that I might help her deal with four
boys who exercised extraordinary control over the other boys in the class.
Using ridicule and their status as physically imposing athletes, these four
wrestlers had succeeded in stifling the participation of the other boys, who
were reluctant to make comments in class discussions.

As a class we talked about the ways in which boys got status in that school 2
and how they got put-down by others. I was told that the most humiliating
putdown was being called a "fag." The list of behaviors which could elicit
ridicule filled two large chalkboards, and it was detailed and comprehensive;
I got the sense that a boy in this school had to conform to rigid, narrow
standards of masculinity to avoid being called a fag. I, too, felt this pressure
and became very conscious of my mannerisms in front of the group. Partly
from exasperation, I decided to test the seriousness of these assertions. Since
one of the four boys had some streaks of pink in his shirt, and since he had
told me that wearing pink was grounds for being called a fag, I told him that
I thought he was a fag. Instead of laughing, he said, "I'm going to kill you."

Such is the stereotypic definition of strength that is associated with mas- 3
culinity. But it is a very limited definition of strength, one based on dominance
and control and acquired through the humiliation and degradation of others.

Contrast this with a view of strength offered by Pam McAllister in her 4
introduction to *Reweaving the Web of Life*:

> The "Strength" card in my Tarot deck depicts, not a warrior going off to
> battle with his armor and his mighty sword, but a woman stroking a lion.
> The woman has not slain the lion nor maced it, not netted it, nor has she
> put on it a muzzle or a leash. And though the lion clearly has teeth and long
> sharp claws, the woman is not hiding, nor has she sought a protector, nor

has she grown muscles. She doesn't appear to be talking to the lion, nor flattering it, nor tossing it fresh meat to distract its hungry jaws.

The woman on the "Strength" card wears a flowing white dress and a 5 garland of flowers. With one hand she cups the lion's jaws, with the other she caresses its nose. The lion on the card has big yellow eyes and a long red tongue curling out of its mouth. One paw is lifted and the mane falls in thick red curls across its broad torso. The woman. The lion. Together they depict strength.

This image of strength stands in direct contrast to the strength embodied 6 in the actions of the four wrestlers. The collective strength of the woman and the lion is a strength unknown in a system of traditional male values. Other human qualities are equally foreign to a traditional conception of masculinity. In workshops I've offered on the male role stereotype, teachers and other school personnel easily generate lists of attitudes and behaviors which boys typically seem to not learn. Included in this list are being supportive and nurturant, accepting one's vulnerability and being able to ask for help, valuing women and "women's work," understanding and expressing emotions (except for anger), the ability to empathize with and empower other people, and learning to resolve conflict in non-aggressive, non-competitive ways.

Learning Violence

All of this should come as no surprise. Traditional definitions of masculinity 7 include attributes such as independence, pride, resiliency, self-control, and physical strength. This is precisely the image of the Marlboro man, and to some extent, these are desirable attributes for boys and girls. But masculinity goes beyond these qualities to stress competitiveness, toughness, aggressive-ness, and power. In this context, threats to one's status, however small, cannot be avoided or taken lightly. If a boy is called a fag, it means that he is perceived as weak or timid—and therefore not masculine enough for his peers. There is enormous pressure for him to fight back. Not being tough at these moments only proves the allegation.

Violence is learned not just as a way for boys to defend allegations that 8 they are feminized, but as an effective, appropriate way for them to normally behave. In "The Civic Advocacy of Violence" Wayne Ewing clearly states:

> I used to think that we simply tolerated and permitted male abusiveness in our society. I have now come to understand rather, that we *advocate* physical violence. Violence is presented as effective. Violence is taught as the normal, appropriate and necessary behavior of power and control. Analyses which interweave advocacy of male violence with "SuperBowl Culture" have never been refuted. Civic expectations—translated into professionalism, financial commitments, city planning for recreational space, the raising of male chil-dren for competitive sport, the corporate ethics of business ownership of

athletic teams, profiteering on entertainment—all result in the monument of the National Football League, symbol and reality at once of the advocacy of violence.

Ultimately, violence is the tool which maintains what I believe are the two most critical socializing forces in a boy's life: *homophobia*, the hatred of gay men (who are stereotyped as feminine) or those men believed to be gay, as well as the fear of being perceived as gay; and *misogyny*, the hatred of women. The two forces are targeted at different classes of victims, but they are really just the flip sides of the same coin. Homophobia is the hatred of feminine qualities in men while misogyny is the hatred of feminine qualities in women. The boy who is called a fag is the target of other boys' homophobia as well as the victim of his own homophobia. While the overt message is the absolute need to avoid being feminized, the implication is that females—and all that they traditionally represent—are contemptible. The United States Marines have a philosophy which conveniently combines homophobia and misogyny in the belief that "When you want to create a group of male killers, you kill 'the woman' in them." 9

The pressures of homophobia and misogyny in boys' lives have been poignantly demonstrated to me each time that I have repeated a simple yet provocative activity with students. I ask them to answer the question, "If you woke up tomorrow and discovered that you were the opposite sex from the one you are now, how would you and your life be different?" Girls consistently indicate that there are clear advantages to being a boy—from increased independence and career opportunities to decreased risks of physical and sexual assault—and eagerly answer the question. But boys often express disgust at this possibility and even refuse sometimes to answer the question. In her reports of a broadbased survey using this question, Alice Baumgartner reports the following responses as typical of boys: "If I were a girl, I'd be stupid and weak as a string;" "I would have to wear make-up, cook, be a mother, and yuckky stuff like that;" "I would have to hate snakes. Everything would be miserable;" "If I were a girl, I'd kill myself." 10

The Costs of Masculinity

The costs associated with a traditional view of masculinity are enormous, and the damage occurs at both personal and societal levels. The belief that a boy should be tough (aggressive, competitive, and daring) can create emotional pain for him. While a few boys experience short-term success for their toughness, there is little security in the long run. Instead, it leads to a series of challenges which few, if any, boys ultimately win. There is no security in being at the top when so many other boys are competing for the same status. Toughness also leads to increased chances of stress, physical injury, and even 11 early death. It is considered manly to take extreme physical risks and voluntarily engage in combative, hostile activities.

The flip side of toughness—nurturance—is not a quality perceived as masculine and thus not valued. Because of this boys and men experience a greater emotional distance from other people and fewer opportunities to participate in meaningful interpersonal relationships. Studies consistently show that fathers spend very small amounts of time interacting with their children. In addition, men report that they seldom have intimate relationships with other men, reflecting their homophobia. They are afraid of getting too close and don't know how to take down the walls that they have built between themselves.   12

As boys grow older and accept adult roles, the larger social costs of masculinity clearly emerge. Most women experience male resistance to an expansion of women's roles; one of the assumptions of traditional masculinity is the belief that women should be subordinate to men. The consequence is that men are often not willing to accept females as equal, competent partners in personal and professional settings. Whether the setting is a sexual relationship, the family, the streets, or the battlefield, men are continuously engaged in efforts to dominate. Statistics on child abuse consistently indicate that the vast majority of abusers are men, and that there is no "typical" abuser. Rape may be the fastest growing crime in the United States. And it is men, regardless of nationality, who provoke and sustain war. In short, traditional masculinity is life threatening.   13

New Socialization for Boys

Masculinity, like many other human traits, is determined by both biological and environmental factors. While some believe that biological factors are significant in shaping some masculine behavior, there is undeniable evidence that cultural and environmental factors are strong enough to override biological impulses. What is it, then, that we should be teaching boys about being a man in a modern world?   14

- Boys must learn to accept their vulnerability, learn to express a range of emotions such as fear and sadness, and learn to ask for help and support in appropriate situations.
- Boys must learn to be gentle, nurturant, cooperative, and communicative, and in particular, learn non-violent means of resolving conflicts.
- Boys must learn to accept those attitudes and behaviors which have traditionally been labeled feminine as necessary for full human development—thereby reducing homophobia and misogyny. This is tantamount to teaching boys to love other boys and girls.

Certain qualities like courage, physical strength, and independence, which are traditionally associated with masculinity, are indeed positive qual-   15 ities for males, provided that they are not manifested in obsessive ways nor used to exploit or dominate others. It is not necessary to completely disregard or unlearn what is traditionally called masculine. I believe, however, that the three areas above are crucial for developing a broader view of masculinity, one which is healthier for all life.

These three areas are equally crucial for reducing aggressive, violent   16
behavior among boys and men. Males must learn to cherish life for the sake of their *own* wholeness as human beings, not just *for* their children, friends, and lovers. If males were more nurturant, they would be less likely to hurt those they love.

Leonard Eron, writing in the *American Psychologist*, puts the issue of   17
unlearning aggression and learning nurturance in clear-cut terms:

> Socialization is crucial in determining levels of aggression. No matter how aggression is measured or observed, as a group males always score higher than females. But this is not true for all girls. There are some girls who seem to have been socialized like boys who are just as aggressive as boys. Just as some females can learn to be aggressive, so males can learn *not* to be aggressive. If we want to reduce the level of aggression in society, we should also discourage boys from aggression very early on in life and reward them too for other behaviors; in other words, we should socialize boys more like girls, and they should be encouraged to develop socially positive qualities such as tenderness, cooperation, and aesthetic appreciation. The level of individual aggression in society will be reduced only when male adolescents and young adults, as a result of socialization, subscribe to the same standards of behavior as have been traditionally encouraged for women.

Where will this change in socialization occur? In his first few years, much   18
of a boy's learning about masculinity comes from the influences of parents, siblings and images of masculinity such as those found on television. Massive efforts will be needed to make changes here. But at older ages, school curriculum and the school environment provide powerful reinforcing images of traditional masculinity. This reinforcement occurs through a variety of channels, including curriculum content, role modeling, and extracurricular activities, especially competitive sports.

School athletics are a microcosm of the socialization of male values.   19
While participation in competitive activities can be enjoyable and healthy, it too easily becomes a lesson in the need for toughness, invulnerability, and dominance. Athletes learn to ignore their own injuries and pain and instead try to injure and inflict pain on others in their attempts to win, regardless of the cost to themselves or their opponents. Yet the lessons learned in athletics are believed to be vital for full and complete masculine development, and as a model for problem-solving in other areas of life.

In addition to encouraging traditional male values, schools provide too   20
few experiences in nurturance, cooperation, negotiation, non-violent conflict resolution, and strategies for empathizing with and empowering others.

Schools should become places where boys have the opportunity to learn these skills; clearly, they won't learn them on the street, from peers, or on television.

Setting New Examples

Despite the pressure on men to display their masculinity in traditional ways, there are examples of men and boys who are changing. "Fathering" is one example of a positive change. In recent years, there has been a popular emphasis on child-care activities, with men becoming more involved in providing care to children, both professionally and as fathers. This is a clear shift from the more traditional view that child rearing should be delegated to women and is not an appropriate activity for men.   21

For all of the male resistance it has generated, the Women's Liberation Movement has at least provided a stimulus for some men to accept women as equal partners in most areas of life. These are the men who have chosen to learn and grow from women's experiences and together with women are creating new norms for relationships. Popular literature and research on male sex roles are expanding, reflecting a wider interest in masculinity. Weekly news magazines such as *Time* and *Newsweek* have run major stories on the "new masculinity," suggesting that positive changes are taking place in the home and in the workplace. Small groups of men scattered around the country have organized against pornography, battering and sexual assault. Finally, there is the National Organization for Changing Men which has a pro-feminist, pro-gay, pro-"new man" agenda, and its ranks are slowly growing.   22

In schools where I have worked with teachers, they report that years of efforts to enhance educational opportunities for girls have also had some positive effects on boys. The boys seem more tolerant of girls' participation in co-ed sports activities and in traditionally male shops and courses. They seem to have a greater respect for the accomplishments of women through women's contributions to literature and history. Among elementary school-aged males, the expression of vulnerable feelings is gaining acceptance. In general, however, there has been far too little attention paid to redirecting male role development.   23

Boys Will Be Boys

I think back to the four wrestlers and the stifling culture of masculinity in which they live. If schools were to radically alter this culture and substitute for it a new vision of masculinity, what would that look like? In this environment, boys would express a full range of behaviors and emotions without fear of being chastized. They would be permitted and encouraged to cry, to be afraid, to show joy, and to express love in a gentle fashion. Extreme concern   24 for career goals would be replaced by a consideration of one's need for recreation, health, and meaningful work. Older boys would be encouraged to tutor and play with younger students. Moreover, boys would receive as much recognition for artistic talents as they do for athletics, and, in general, they would value leisure-time, recreational activities as highly as competitive sports.

In a system where maleness and femaleness were equally valued, boys   25
might no longer feel that they have to "prove" themselves to other boys; they would simply accept the worth of each person and value those differences. Boys would realize that it is permissible to admit failure. In addition, they would seek out opportunities to learn from girls and women. Emotional support would become commonplace, and it would no longer be seen as just the role of the female to provide the support. Relationships between boys and girls would no longer be based on limited roles, but instead would become expressions of two individuals learning from and supporting one another. Relationships between boys would reflect their care for one another rather than their mutual fear and distrust.

Aggressive styles of resolving conflicts would be the exception rather than   26
the norm. Girls would feel welcome in activities dominated by boys, knowing that they were safe from the threat of being sexually harassed. Boys would no longer boast of beating up another boy or of how much they "got off" of a girl the night before. In fact, the boys would be as outraged as the girls at rape or other violent crimes in the community. Finally, boys would become active in efforts to stop nuclear proliferation and all other forms of military violence, following the examples set by activist women.

The development of a new conception of masculinity based on this vision   27
is an ambitious task, but one which is essential for the health and safety of both men and women. The survival of our society may rest on the degree to which we are able to teach men to cherish life.

MEN LOVING MEN:
The Challenge of Gay Liberation

GARY KINSMAN

In this essay from the collection *Beyond Patriarchy: Essays by Men on Pleasure, Power and Change* (1987), Gary Kinsman argues that the gay liberation movement poses fundamental questions about the role of masculinity in maintaining human oppression. A Canadian writer and activist for gay rights, Kinsman develops the ideas presented here in more detail in his book, *The Regulation of Desire: Sexuality in Canada* (1987).

The limits of "acceptable" masculinity are in part defined by comments like "What are you, a fag?"[1] As boys and men we have heard such expressions and the words "queer," "faggot," and "sissy" all our lives. These words encourage certain types of male behavior and serve to define, regulate, and limit our lives, whether we consider ourselves straight or gay. Depending on who is speaking and who is listening, they incite fear or hatred.

Even among many heterosexual men who have been influenced by feminism, the taboo against loving the same sex remains unchallenged. Lines like "I may be anti-sexist, but I am certainly not gay" can still be heard. These men may be questioning some aspects of male privilege, but in attempting to remake masculinity they have not questioned the institution of heterosexuality.[2] As a result their challenge to male privilege is partial and inadequate.

Gay men have often found much support in the "men's movement" or in groups of men against sexism. At the same time we have also seen our concerns as gay men marginalized and pushed aside and have often felt like outsiders. Joe Interrante expresses some of the reservations of gay men about the "men's movement" and its literature:

> As a gay man . . . I had suspicions about the heterocentrist bias of this work. It told me that my gayness existed "in addition to" my masculinity, whereas I found that it colored my entire experience of manhood. I distrusted a literature which claimed that gay men were just like heterosexual men except for what they did in bed.[3]

The literature of the men's movement has tended to produce an image of men that is white, middle-class, and heterosexual. As Ned Lyttleton has pointed out, "an analysis of masculinity that does not deal with the contradictions of power imbalances that exist between men themselves will be limited and biased, and its limits and biases will be concealed under the blanket of shared male privilege."[4] A series of masculinities becomes subsumed under one form of masculinity that becomes "masculinity." As a result, socially organized power relations among and between men based on sexuality, race, class, or age have been neglected. These power relations are major dividing lines between men that have to be addressed if progressive organizing among men is to encompass the needs and experiences of all men. The men's movement has reached a turning point.[5] It has to choose whether it is simply a movement for men's rights—defending men's rights to be human too—or whether it will deepen the challenge to an interlocked web of oppression: sexism, heterosexism, racism, and class exploitation. We have to choose between a vision of a world in which men are more sensitive and human but are still "real" men at the top of the social order, and a radically new vision that entails the transformation of masculinity and sexuality and the challenging of other forms of domination.

In developing this radical vision—radical in the sense of getting to the roots of the problem—the politics of gay liberation and the politics of lesbian feminism are important. So too are the experiences of those of us who have been made into outsiders, people labelled "faggot," "queer," or "dyke" who have reclaimed these stigmatized labels as ways of naming experiences of the world and as weapons of resistance to heterosexual hegemony. The struggle against the institutionalized social norm of heterosexuality opens up the door to other kinds of social and personal change. 5

Gay Liberation versus Heterosexual Privilege

In our society heterosexuality as an institutionalized norm has become an important means of social regulation, enforced by laws, police practices, family and social policies, schools, and the mass media. In its historical development heterosexuality is tied up with the institution of masculinity, which gives social and cultural meaning to biological male anatomy, associating it with masculinity, aggressiveness, and an "active" sexuality. "Real" men are intrinsically heterosexual; gay men, therefore, are not real men. 6

While gay men share with straight men the privilege of being in a dominant position in relation to women, we are at the same time in a subordinate position in the institution of heterosexuality. As a result, gay men's lives and experiences are not the same as those of heterosexual men. For instance, while we share with straight men the economic benefits of being men in a patriarchal society, we do not participate as regularly in the everyday interpersonal subordination of women in the realms of sexuality and violence. Although, like other men, we have more social opportunities, we are not accepted as open gays in corporate boardrooms or in many jobs, sports, and professions. We 7 can still be labeled "national security risks" and sick, deviant, or abnormal. Consequently, gay men experience a rupture between the presumably universal categories of heterosexual experience and their own particular experience of the world, a rupture that denies many of our experiences; for gay men exist in social situations that allow us to see aspects of life, desire, sexuality, and love that cannot be seen by heterosexual men.[6]

Gay men have had to question the institution of masculinity—which associates masculinity with heterosexuality—in our daily lives. We have experimented with and developed new ways of organizing our sexual lives and our love and support relations, of receiving and giving pleasure. Heterosexual men interested in seriously transforming the fabric of their lives have to stop seeing gay liberation as simply a separate issue for some men that has nothing to say to them. They should begin to ask what the experience of gay men can bring into view for them. As we break the silence and move beyond liberal tolerance toward gays and lesbians, we can begin to see how "queer baiting" and the social taboo against pleasure, sex, and love between men serves to keep all men in line, defining what proper masculinity is for us. Gay liberation suggests that heterosexuality is not the only natural form of sexuality but has instead been socially and culturally made the "normal" sexual practice and identity. As the Kinsey Institute studies suggested, the actual flux of human desire cannot be easily captured in rigid sexual categories. Many men who define themselves as straight have had sexual experiences with other men.[7] This has demonstrated the contradictions that can exist between our actual experiences and desires and the rigid social categories that are used to divide normal from deviant and that imply that any participation in homosexual activity automatically defines one as a homosexual.

Breaking the silence surrounding homosexuality requires challenging heterosexism and heterosexual privilege. Lesbian-feminist Charlotte Bunch once explained to heterosexual women that the best way to find out what heterosexual privilege is all about is to go about for a few days as an open lesbian:

> What makes heterosexuality work is heterosexual privilege—and if you don't have a sense of what privilege is, I suggest that you go home and announce to everybody that you know—a roommate, your family, the people you work with—everywhere that you go—that you're a queer. Try being a queer for a week.[8]

This statement could also be applied to the situation of straight men, and any heterosexual man can easily imagine the discomfort, ridicule, and fear he might experience, how his "coming out" would disrupt "normal" relations at work and with his family. Such experiences are the substance of gay oppression that make our lives different from those of straight men. Gay men in this heterosexist society are labeled with many terms of abuse. Young boys hurl the labels "queer," "fag," or "cocksucker" at each other before they know what the words mean. As we grow up we are denied images of men loving men and any models for our lives outside heterosexuality. In the United States, the age of consent varies from state to state, usually from sixteen to eighteen, although in some states all homosexual acts remain technically illegal. Under British law today, males under twenty-one are denied the right to have sexual relations with other boys and men. This was also true in Canada until 1988, when the offence of "gross indecency" was abolished and the age of consent for anal intercourse was lowered to 18, which is still higher than the age of consent for most heterosexual activities. Many members of the medical and psychiatric professions still practice psychological and social terrorism against us by trying to adjust us to fit the norm. We are excluded as open lesbians and gay men from most activities and institutions. When the mass media does cover us they use stereotypes or other means to show us to be sick, immoral, indecent, as some sort of social problem or social menace, or they trivialize us as silly and frivolous.[9] The police continue to raid our bookstores and seize our magazines. The mass media has fostered fear and hatred against gay men by associating all gay men with AIDS, especially through its early coverage of AIDS as the 'gay plague.' Such media stories shift and mold public opinion against us. On city streets we are often violently attacked by gangs of "queer-bashers." Most countries still deny lesbians and gay men their basic human and civil rights, leaving us open to arbitrary firings, evictions, and violence.

A variety of sexual laws are used to regulate and control gay men's sexual and community lives. Police in many cities have a policy of systematically entrapping and harassing gays. In recent years hundreds of men across North America have been arrested and often entrapped by the police in bath raids and in washrooms and parks. These campaigns—especially in small towns and cities—and the associated media attention have torn apart the lives of these men, many of whom define themselves as heterosexual and are married with families. 11

In fact, the society in which we have all grown up is so profoundly heterosexist that even many gays have internalized the social hatred against us in forms of "self-oppression."[10] This fear keeps many of us isolated and silent, hiding our sexuality. One of the first steps in combating this self-oppression is to reject this denial of our love and sexuality by affirming our existence and pride publically. Assertions that "gay is good" and affirmations of gay pride are the beginnings of our resistance to heterosexual hegemony on the individual and social levels. 12

The History of Sexuality

In addressing the matter of gay and lesbian oppression, we have to ask where this oppression has come from. How did heterosexuality come to be the dominant social relation? How did homosexuality come to be seen as a perverse outcast form of sexuality? If we can answer those questions, we can 13 begin to see how we could break down the institution of heterosexuality and its control over our lives.

As a result of numerous cross-cultural and historical studies that have demonstrated that there is no natural or normal sexuality, we can no longer see sex as simply natural or biologically given. Our biological, erotic, and sexual capabilities are only the precondition for the organization of the social and cultural forms of meaning and activity that compose human sexuality. Our biological capabilities are transformed and mediated culturally, producing sexuality as a social need and relation. As Gayle Rubin explained, each social system has its own "sex/gender system," which

> is the set of arrangements by which a society transforms biological sexuality into products of human activity, and in which these transformed sexual needs are satisfied.[11]

Recent historical studies have challenged the assumed natural categories of heterosexuality and homosexuality themselves.[12] Gay, lesbian, and feminist historians have expanded our understanding of sexual meaning and identity, contesting the dominant ways in which sexuality has been discussed and viewed in our society.[13] The dominant perspective for looking at sexuality is what has been called the "repression hypothesis," which assumes that there is a natural sexuality that is repressed to maintain social and moral order. Many leftists argue that sexuality is repressed by the ruling class—to maintain class society because of capitalism's need for the family and a docile work force. This interpretation was popularized in the writings and activities of Wilhelm Reich,[14] who called for the end of sexual repression through the liberation of natural sexuality, which was for him completely heterosexual. Variations of this repression theory, and its corresponding call for the liberation of natural sexuality, have inspired sexual liberationist politics, including much of the gay liberation movement, which sees homosexuality as a natural sexuality that simply needs to be released from social repression.

The experience by women of the male sexual (i.e., heterosexual) revolution of the sixties and seventies has led much of the feminist movement to a more complex understanding of sexuality than simple theories of sexual repression. Feminism has exposed the contradictions in a sexual revolution that increased women's ability to seek sexual satisfaction but only within male-dominated heterosexual relations. Feminism has also begun to explore how sexuality and social power are bound together and how sexuality has been socially organized in male-dominated forms in this society.[15] This view of sex opens up new possibilities for sexual politics—our sexual lives are no longer seen as divorced from human and social activity but as the results of human praxis (the unity of thought and activity). Sexual relations are therefore changeable and are themselves the site of personal and social struggles. We can then begin to question the natural appearance of such sexual categories as heterosexual and homosexual and to make visible the human activity that is involved in the making of sexuality. This opens up a struggle, not for the liberation of some inherent sexuality that just has to be freed from the bonds of capitalism or repressive laws, but for a much broader challenge to the ways our sexual lives are defined, regulated, and controlled. It opens up questions about the very making and remaking of sex, desire, and pleasure.

Enter the Homosexual

The historical emergence of the "homosexual" required a number of social preconditions, which can be summarized as three interrelated social processes: first, the rise of capitalist social relations, which created the necessary social spaces for the emergence of homosexual cultures;[16] second, the regime of sexuality that categorized and labeled homosexuality and sexual "deviations"; and third, the activities, cultural production, and resistance to the oppression of men in these same-sex desire-based cultures. [17]

The rise of capitalism in Europe between the fifteenth and nineteenth centuries separated the rural household economy from the new industrial economy and undermined the interdependent different-sex household economy. The working class was made, and made itself, in the context of this industrialization, urbanization, and commercialization. This separation of "work" from the household and the development of wage labor meant that it became possible for more men in the cities to live outside the family, earning a wage and living as boarders. Later they would be able to eat at restaurants or taverns and rent their own accommodation. This created the opportunities for some men to start organizing what would become, through a process of development and struggle, the beginnings of a homosexual culture, from the eighteenth century on.[17] [18]

A regime of sexuality has emerged as part of a series of social struggles over the last two centuries. The transition from feudalism to capitalism in the western countries meant a transition in the way kinship and sexual and class relations were organized. The new ruling class was no longer able to understand itself or organize its social life simply through the old feudal ties of blood or lineage.[18] New forms of family and state formation led to new forms of self-understanding, class consciousness, and notions of moral and social order. Sexuality emerged as an autonomous sphere separate from household production. A proper, respectable sexual and gender identity became an essential feature of the class unity of the bourgeoisie. This process is linked to the emergence of the ideology of individual identity. The regime of sexual definitions was first applied to the bodies of the bourgeoisie itself through its educational and medical systems and through the sexological knowledge that was generated by the new professional groups of doctors and psychiatrists and that served to draw a boundary between bourgeois respectability and the "bestial" sexual practices of the outcast poor and "lower orders." These norms [19] of sex and gender definition helped organize the relations of the bourgeois family and its sexual morality.

Later these same norms of sexual identity and morality were used against the urban working class and poor, who were considered a threat to social order by middle-class and state agencies. The working class both resisted this enforcement of social norms and at the same time adopted them as its own. The male-dominated "respectable" sections of the working class developed their own norms of family and sexual life that incorporated the socially dominant norms of masculinity, femininity, and reproductive heterosexuality. The uneven and at times contradictory development of sexual identity in different classes, genders, races, and nationalities is a subject that remains to be more fully explored. [20]

In the big cities sexuality becomes an object to be studied and a terrain for the expanding male-dominated fields of medicine, psychiatry, and sexology. Various forms of sexual behavior were categorized, classified, and ranked, with heterosexuality on the top and homosexuality and lesbianism near the bottom. The norm and the perversions were defined, separating normal and abnormal behavior. In this context sex in the ruling discourses became the truth of our being.[19] [21]

The heterosexual man was no longer simply carrying out the types of activities he had to carry out in the sexual division of labor, or the activities that would lead to the reproduction of the species; rather he had become someone with a particular erotic, sexual, and gender identity that linked his masculinity to an exclusively heterosexual way of life. The heterosexual and the homosexual emerged in relation to each other as part of the same historical and social process of struggle and negotiation. [22]

Men who engaged in sexual relations with other men in this emerging regime of sexuality (and who were affected by the ideology of individualism) began to organize their lives around their sexuality and to see themselves as separate and different from other men. They fought against campaigns by religious fundamentalists and the police who wished to curtail their activities.[20] In the last century, the emergence of sexology, increased police regulation of sexual behavior, and the passing of laws against sexual offenses combined with the development of these same-sex desire-based cultures to make the new social experience and social category of homosexuality. [23]

The term homosexual itself was not devised until 1869, when Károly Mária Benkert, a Hungarian, coined the term in an appeal to the government to keep its laws out of people's lives.[21] The category of homosexuality was originally elaborated by some homosexuals themselves, mostly professional men it seems, in order to name their "difference" and in order to protect themselves from police and legal prohibitions. The word was taken up by the various agencies of social regulation from the medical profession to the police and courts. Homosexuality was defined as an abnormality, a sickness, and a symptom of degeneracy. The efforts of medical and legal experts [24] were chiefly concerned with whether the disgusting breed of perverts could be physically identified for courts and whether they should be held legally responsible for their acts.[22]

An early Canadian reference—in 1898—to same-sex "perversion" among men by a Dr. Ezra Stafford (which refers to the work of Krafft-Ebing, one of the grandfathers of sexology) linked sex between men with prostitution in a theory of degeneracy. Stafford wrote that these things "may lead to the tragedy of our species."[23] This connection between homosexuality and prostitution as stigmatized social and sexual practices continued even to England's Wolfenden report of 1957, which linked these topics, and it continues to this day, in, for example, the use by the Canadian police of bawdy-house legislation, originally intended to deal with houses of female prostitutes, against gay men.

Simultaneously the needs of capitalism for a skilled labor force and a continuing supply of wage-laborers led to an emphasis on the heterosexual nuclear family. The rise of modern militarism and the scramble for colonies by the western powers led to demands for a larger and healthier supply of cannon fodder at the beginning of the twentieth century. An intensification of military discipline resulted in stiff prohibitions against homosexuality, which was seen as subversive of discipline and hierarchy in the armed forces. As a result, reproductive heterosexuality was reinforced for men, and motherhood further institutionalized for women.[24]

The category of the male homosexual emerged in sexology as an "invert" and was associated with some form of effeminacy and "gender inversion." A relation between gender dysfunction and abnormal sexuality was established:

> As defined by the ancient civil or canonical codes, sodomy was a category of forbidden acts. . . . The nineteenth century homosexual became a personage, a past, a case history, and a childhood, in addition to being a type of life, a life form, and a morphology, with an indiscreet anatomy and possibly a mysterious physiology. Nothing that went into his total composition was unaffected by his sexuality. . . . Homosexuality appeared as one of the forms of sexuality when it was transposed from the practice of sodomy onto a kind of interior androgyny, a hermaphrodism of the soul. The sodomite had been a temporary aberration; the homosexual was now a species.[25]

The categorization of "perverse" sexual types also provided a basis for resistance. Sexual categorization, as Foucault puts it,

> also made possible the formation of a "reverse" discourse: homosexuality began to speak on its own behalf, to demand that its legitimacy or "naturality" be acknowledged, often in the same vocabulary, using the same categories by which it was radically disqualified.[26]

Homosexuals themselves used this category to name their experiences, to articulate their differences and cultures, moving this category in a more progressive direction. There has been a century-long struggle over the meaning of homosexuality that has involved sexologists, the police, lawyers, psychiatrists, and homosexuals, a struggle that continues today. The regime of sexuality and the specification of different sexual categories in an attempt to buttress the emerging norm of heterosexuality has unwittingly also provided the basis for homosexual experiences, identities, and cultures. Through these experiences a series of new social and sexual needs, human capacities, and pleasures have been created among a group of men. This homosexual experience, along with the slightly later emergence of a distinct lesbian experience,[27] and the feminist movement have created the basis for contemporary challenges to the hegemony of heterosexuality.

Enter Gay Liberation and the Gay Community

Recent social changes in the western capitalist countries have put in question the patriarchal, gender, and sexual relations established during the last century. A prolonged crisis in sexual and gender relations and in the meaning of sexuality has occurred. The feminist and gay liberation movements, for example, have challenged the relegation of sexual relations and particularly "deviant" forms of sexuality to the socially defined private realm, subverting the public/private categories that have been used to regulate our sexual lives. The development of contraceptive and reproductive technologies has made it more and more possible to separate heterosexual pleasure and procreation, although the struggle continues about who will have access to, and control over, this technology. The expansion of consumer markets and advertising in the post-war period has led to an increasing drawing of sexuality and sexual images into the marketplace and the public realm.[28] This increasing public visibility of sexual images and sexual cultures has led to objections from those who would wish to reprivatize sexuality, in particular its "deviant" strains. And feminists have challenged the patriarchal values that are visible in much advertising and heterosexual male pornography.

The social ferment of the sixties—particularly the civil rights, black power, and feminist movements—combined with earlier forms of homosexual activism and the expansion of the gay commercial scene and culture to produce the gay liberation movement, which erupted in 1969 in the Stonewall Riot in New York City.[29] The movement developed a new, positive identity that has served as a basis for our resistance to heterosexual hegemony. The movement's most significant achievements were its contesting of the psychiatric definition of homosexuality as a mental illness and its creation of a culture and community that have transformed the lives of hundreds of thousands of men and women. As usual in a patriarchal society, many more opportunities have opened up for men than for women.

In a challenge to the "universality" of heterosexuality, gays have affirmed that gay is just as good as straight, calling on lesbians and gay men to affirm themselves and their sexualities. This has challenged the gender and social policies of the state, suggesting that sexual activity does not have to be solely for reproduction, but can also be for play, pleasure, love, and support, and questioning the very right of the state to regulate people's sexual lives. We have affirmed our right to sexual self-determination and control over our own bodies and sexuality and have affirmed this right for others as well.

The growth of a visible gay community and the emergence of gay streets and commercial areas in many big cities have led to a reaction from the police, conservative political parties, and the new right. These groups fear the breakdown of "traditional" sexual and family relations, which they associate with social and moral order, and see the challenge that gay liberation presents to heterosexual hegemony as a threat to the ways in which their lives and institutions are organized. They want lesbians and gay men out of public view and back in the closets, threatening our very existence as a public community. 33

In a sense the gay ghetto is both a playground and a potential concentration camp. While it provides people a place to meet and to explore and develop aspects of their lives and sexuality, it can also separate people from the rest of the population in a much larger closet that can be isolated and contained. The ghetto can tend to obscure the experiences gay men share with other men in their society. Locking people into the new categorization of gays as minority group or community may weaken the critique of sex and gender relations in society as a whole. As Altman explains, the "ethnic homosexual" has emerged, "the widespread recognition of a distinct cultural category which appears to be pressing for the same sort of 'equality,' in Western society as do ethnic minorities."[30] However, lesbians and gay men are not born into a minority group, but like heterosexuals assume a sexual identity through social and psychological processes.[31] Gays and lesbians are not only a minority group but also an oppressed and denied sexuality. The position that gays are simply a new minority group can deflect our challenges to the dominant way of life. 34

In challenging heterosexuality as the social norm gays have brought into question aspects of the institutions of masculinity and male privilege. Over the last decade images of gay men have shifted from the effeminacy of the "gender invert" to the new macho and clone looks that have dominated the gay men's community. This imagery challenges the previous stereotypes of homosexuals that associated our sexuality with gender nonconformity and has asserted that we can be both homosexual and "masculine" at the same time.[32] In defining ourselves as masculine we have had to make use of and transform the existing images of straight masculinity we find around us. These new images challenge heterosexual norms that associate "deviant" gender stereotypes with sexual "deviancy," for instance effeminacy with male homosexuality, but at the same time also tend to create new standards and stereotypes of what gay men are supposed to be like. These images and styles themselves continue to be imprisoned within the polarities of gender dichotomy. While gay men often believe we have freed ourselves from the social organization 35 of gender, what we have actually done is exchange "gender inversion" for a situation where homosexuality can be organized through "normal" gender identifications. This assertion of masculinized imagery can to some extent lead us away from the critique of the institution of masculinity and its effects in our lives and persuade us that gender is no longer a problem for gay men.

It is ironic that some forms of resistance to past ways in which we were 36 stigmatized can serve to accommodate us to aspects of the existing order of things. It is in this context that some of the challenges to masculinity and gender norms by straight men fighting against sexism will also be valuable to gay men. To be successful, gay liberation must challenge not only the institutionalization of heterosexuality as a social norm but also the institution of masculinity.

Gay Liberation and the Ruling Regime of Sex

Gay liberation has emerged from the contradictions within the ruling system 37 of sexual regulation and definition. It is fundamentally a struggle to transform the norms and definitions of sexual regulation. Gay liberation strives for the recognition of homosexuality as socially equal to the dominant social institution of heterosexuality. Yet as Weeks suggests,

> the strategic aim of the gay liberation movement must be not simply the validation of the rights of a minority within a heterosexual majority but the challenge to all the rigid categorizations of sexuality. . . . The struggle for sexual self-determination is a struggle in the end for control over our bodies. To establish this control we must escape from those ideologies and categorizations which imprison us within the existing order.[33]

The struggle to transform our sexual norms and to end the control of the 38 institution of heterosexuality over our lives holds out the possibility of beginning to disengage us from the ruling regime of sex and gender. As Foucault suggested, movements that have been called sexual liberation movements, including gay liberation, are

> movements that start with sexuality, with the apparatus of sexuality in the midst of which they are caught and which make it function to the limit; but, at the same time, they are in motion relative to it, disengaging themselves and surmounting them.[34]

The struggle for gay liberation can be seen as a process of transformation. 39 The assertion that gay is just as good as straight—which lies at the heart of gay liberation—is formally within the present regime of sexual categorization, for it still separates gay from straight as rigid categories and assigns value to sexuality, thus mirroring the limitations of the current sexual regime. However, the gay liberation movement operates both within *and* against this regime of sexual regulation. In asserting equal value for homosexuality and lesbianism, it begins to turn the ruling practices of sexual hierarchy on their head. Resistance begins within the present regime of sexual definitions, but it begins to shift the sexual boundaries that they have defined, opening up the possibility of transcending their limitations. By naming our specific experiences of the world, gay liberation provides the basis for a social and political struggle that can transform, defy, cut across, and break down the ruling regime of sex and gender.

The gay and lesbian communities, like other oppressed social groups, 40 oscillate between resistance and accommodation to oppression. This is a struggle on two closely interrelated fronts. First, the gay community itself needs to strengthen cultures of resistance by building on sexual and cultural traditions that question gender norms and the relegation of erotic life to the state-defined private sphere. This will involve challenging the internalization and reproduction of sexism, racism, ageism, and class divisions within the gay community, as well as building alliances with other social groups fighting these forms of domination. Secondly, it requires a struggle outside the gay and lesbian communities for the defense of a community under attack by the police, government, and media. A key part of this strategy would be campaigning for new social policies that uproot heterosexuality as *the* social norm.

Opening Up Erotic Choices for Everyone

In developing a radical perspective we need to draw on the insights of lesbian 41 feminism about the social power of heterosexuality and also on the historical perspectives provided by the new critical gay history, which reveals the social and historical process of the organization of heterosexual hegemony and the present system of sexual regulation more generally. These understandings create the basis for alliances between feminists, lesbians, gay liberationists, anti-sexist men, and other groups against the institution of heterosexuality, which lies at the root of the social oppression of women, lesbians, and gays. This alliance would contest the hegemony of heterosexuality in the legal system, state policies, in forms of family organization, and in the churches, unions, and other social bodies. The struggle would be for women, gays, and others to gain control over our bodies and sexuality and to begin to define our own eroticism and sexuality. A fundamental aspect of such an approach would be the elaboration and exploration of the experiences and visions of those of us living outside institutionalized heterosexuality.

Proposals for new and different ways of living (including collective and 42 nonsexist ways of rearing children) are particularly vital since the new right and moral conservatives in their various incarnations are taking advantage of people's fears about changes in family organization and sexual mores to campaign in support of patriarchal and heterosexist social norms. The defense of a male-dominated heterosexuality is not only central to the policies of the new right and moral conservatives regarding feminism and gay liberation, but is a central theme of their racial and class politics as well.[35] The progressive movement's failure to deal with people's real fears, concerns, and hopes regarding sexual and gender politics is an important reason why right-wing groups are able to gain support. Feminism, gay liberation, and all progressive movements will have to articulate a vision that will allow us to move forward beyond the confines of institutionalized heterosexuality.

Gay liberation enables heterosexual men who question heterosexism to contribute to this new social vision. The issues raised by gay liberation must be addressed by all men interested in fundamental change because heterosexism limits and restricts the lives of all men. This challenge will only be effective, however, if heterosexual privilege is challenged in daily life and in social institutions. This could help begin the long struggle to disentangle heterosexual desire from the confines of institutionalized masculinity and heterosexuality. Together we could begin to redefine and remake masculinity and sexuality. If sexuality is socially produced, then heterosexuality itself can be transformed and redefined and its pleasures and desires separated from the social relations of power and domination. Gay liberation can allow all men to challenge gender and sexual norms and redefine gender and sex for ourselves in alliance with feminism; it can allow all men to explore and create different forms of sexual pleasures in our lives. This redefining of masculinity and sexuality will also help destroy the anxieties and insecurities of many straight men who try so hard to be "real men." But the success of this undertaking depends on the ability to develop alternative visions and experiences that will help all people understand how their lives could be organized without heterosexuality as the institutionalized social norm. Such a goal is a radically transformed society in which everyone will be able to gain control of his or her own body, desires, and life.

Notes

Special thanks to Ned Lyttelton, Brian Conway, and Bob Gardner for comments on this paper. For more general comments on matters that pertain to topics addressed in this paper I am indebted to Varda Burstyn, Philip Corrigan, Bert Hansen, Michael Kaufman, Ian Lumsden, Dorothy E. Smith, George Smith, Mariana Valverde, and Lorna Weir.

1. See G. K. Lehne, "Homophobia Among Men," in Deborah David and Robert Brannon, *The Forty Nine Per Cent Majority* (Reading, Mass.: Addison-Wesley, 1976), 78.

2. On the notion of institutionalized heterosexuality see Charlotte Bunch," "Not For Lesbians Only," *Quest* 11, no. 2 (Fall 1975). Also see Adrienne Rich, "Compulsory Heterosexuality And Lesbian Existence," in Snitow, Stansell and Thompson, eds., *Powers of Desire: The Politics of Sexuality* (New York: Monthly Review Press, 1983): 177–205.

3. Joe Interrante, "Dancing Along the Precipice: The Men's Movement in the '80s," *Radical America* 15, no. 5 (September–October 1981): 54.

4. Ned Lyttelton, "Men's Liberation, Men Against Sexism and Major Dividing Lines," *Resources for Feminist Research* 12, no. 4 (December/January 1983/1984): 33. Several discussions with Ned Lyttelton were very useful in clarifying my ideas in this section and throughout this paper.

5. Interrante, op. cit., 54.

6. For further elaboration see my book, *The Regulation of Desire* (Montreal: Black Rose, 1987) and my article "'Homosexuality' Historically Reconsidered Challenges Heterosexual Hegemony," *Journal of Historical Sociology*, vol. 4, no. 2, June 1991, pp. 91–111.

7. See Kinsey, Pomeroy, and Martin, *Sexual Behavior in the Human Male* (Philadelphia: W. B. Saunders, 1948) and Mary McIntosh, "The Homosexual Role," in Plummer, ed., *The Making Of The Modern Homosexual* (London: Hutchinson, 1981), 38–43.

8. Bunch, "Not For Lesbians Only."

9. See Frank Pearce, "How to be Immoral and Ill, Pathetic and Dangerous all at the same time: Mass Media and the Homosexual," in Cohen and Young, eds., *The Manufacture of News: Deviance, Social Problems and the Mass Media* (London: Constable, 1973), 284–301.

10. See Andrew Hodges and David Hutter. *With Downcast Gays, Aspects of Homosexual Self-Oppression* (Toronto: Pink Triangle Press, 1977).

11. Gayle Rubin, "The Traffic In Women: Notes on the Political Economy of Sex," in Reiter, ed., *Towards An Anthropology Of Women* (New York: Monthly Review Press, 1975), 159. I prefer the use of sex and gender relations to sex/gender system since the notion of system tends to conflate questions of sexuality and gender and suggests that sex/gender relations are a separate system from other social relations rather than an integral aspect of them.

12. See Joe Interrante, "From Homosexual to Gay to ?: Recent Work in Gay History," in *Radical America* 15, no. 6 (November–December 1981); Martha Vicinus, "Sexuality and Power: A Review of Current Work in the History of Sexuality," *Feminist Studies* 8, no. 1 (Spring 1982): 133–56; and Robert A. Padgug, "Sexual Matters: On Conceptualizing Sexuality In History," *Radical History Review*, "Sexuality in History" Issue, no. 20 (Spring/Summer 1979): 3–23.

13. See for instance Michel Foucault, *The History of Sexuality* (New York: Vintage, 1980), vol. I. *An Introduction*: Jeffrey Weeks, *Sex, Politics and Society: The Regulation of Sexuality since 1800* (London: Hutchinson, 1981); and Jonathan Ned Katz, *Gay/Lesbian Almanac* (New York: Harper and Row, 1983). For recent feminist explorations of sexuality see Snitow, Stansell and Thompson, *Powers of Desire* (New York: Monthly Review, 1983); Carol Vance, ed., *Pleasure and Danger, Exploring Female Sexuality* (Boston: Routledge and Kegan Paul, 1984); Rosalind Coward, *Female Desire, Women's Sexuality Today* (London: Routledge and Kegan Paul, 1984); and Mariana Valverde, *Sex, Power and Pleasure* (Toronto: Women's Press, 1985).

14. See Wilhelm Reich, *The Sexual Revolution* (New York: Straus and Giroux, 1974) and Baxandall, ed., *Sex-Pol. Essays, 1929–1934, Wilhelm Reich* (New York: Vintage, 1972).

15. Unfortunately, over the last few years some anti-pornography feminists have suggested that sexuality is only a realm of danger for women, obscuring how it can also be a realm of pleasure. Some anti-porn feminists have been used by state agencies in attempts to clamp down sexually explicit material including sexual material for gay men and lesbians. See Vance, *Pleasure and Danger*; Varda Burstyn, ed., *Women Against Censorship* (Vancouver and Toronto: Douglas and McIntyre, 1985); and Varda Burstyn, "Anatomy of a Moral Panic" and Gary Kinsman, "The Porn Debate," *Fuse* 3, no. 1 (Summer 1984).

16. On this see the work of John D'Emilio, for instance his "Capitalism and Gay Identity," in Snitow, Stansell and Thompson, eds., *Powers of Desire*, 100–13, and his *Sexual Politics, Sexual Communities* (Chicago: University of Chicago Press, 1983).

17. See Randolph Trumbach, "London's Sodomites: Homosexual Behaviour and Western Culture in the 18th Century," *Journal of Social History*, Fall 1977, 1–33; Mary McIntosh, "The Homosexual Role," in Plummer, ed., *The Making of The Modern Homosexual*; Alan Bray, ' *no-*

sexuality in Renaissance England (London: Gay Men's Press, 1982); and Jeffrey Weeks, *Sex, Politics and Society.*

18. See Foucault, *The History of Sexuality*, vol. 1 and Kinsman, *The Regulation of Desire.*

19. This idea comes from the work of Foucault.

20. See Bray, *Homosexuality in Renaissance England* for the activities of the Society for the Reformation of Morals, which campaigned against same-sex desire-based networks in the early eighteenth century.

21. John Lauritsen and David Thorstad, *The Early Homosexual Rights Movement* (New York: Times Change Press, 1974), 6.

22. Arno Karlen, *Sexuality and Homosexuality* (New York: W. W. Norton, 1971), 185.

23. Ezra Hurlburt Stafford, "Perversion," the *Canadian Journal of Medicine and Surgery* 3, no. 4 (April 1898).

24. On this see Anna Davin. "Imperialism and Motherhood," *History Workshop*, no. 5 (Spring 1978).

25. Foucault, op. cit., 43.

26. Ibid., 101.

27. See Lillian Faderman, *Surpassing The Love Of Men* (New York: William Morrow, 1981); Christina Simmons, "Companionate Marriage and the Lesbian Threat," in *Frontiers* 4, no. 3 (Fall 1979); Martha Vicinus, "Sexuality and Power"; and Ann Ferguson, "Patriarchy, Sexual Identity, and the Sexual Revolution," *Signs* 7, no. 1 (Fall 1981): 158–72.

28. See Gary Kinsman, "Porn/Censor Wars And The Battlefields Of Sex," in *Issues of Censorship* (Toronto: A Space, 1985), 31–9.

29. See John D'Emilio, *Sexual Politics, Sexual Communities.*

30. Dennis Altman, "What Changed in the Seventies?," in Gay Left Collective, eds., *Homosexuality, Power and Politics* (London: Allison and Busby, 1980), 61.

31. One prejudice that is embodied in sexual legislation and social policies is the myth that lesbians and gay men are a special threat to young people and that gay men are "child molesters." Most studies show, on the contrary, tht more than 90 percent of sexual assaults on young people are committed by heterosexual men and often within the family or home. Breines and Gordon state that, "approximately 92 per cent of the victims are female and 97 percent of the assailants are males." See Wini Breines and Linda Gordon, "The New Scholarship on Family Violence," *Signs* 8, no. 3 (Spring 1983): 522. Also see Elizabeth Wilson, *What Is To Be Done About Violence Against Women* (London: Penguin, 1983), particularly 117–34. We have to eliminate special age restrictions on the right to participate in consensual lesbian and gay sex so that lesbian and gay young people can express their desires and instead challenge the principal source of violence against children and young people—the patriarchal family and straight-identified men. We have to propose changes in family relations and schooling and alternative social policies that would allow young people to take more control over their own lives, to get support in fighting unwanted sexual attention *and* be able to participate in consensual sexual activity.

32. See John Marshall, "Pansies, Perverts and Macho Men: Changing Conceptions of Male Homosexuality" and Greg Blachford, "Male Dominance In The Gay World," in Plummer, ed., *The Making of The Modern Homosexual*; and also Seymour Kleinberg's article elsewhere in this volume for a different approach.

33. Jeffrey Weeks, "Capitalism and the Organization of Sex," Gay Left Collective, eds., *Homosexuality, Power and Politics* 19–20.

34. Michel Foucault, "Power and Sex," *Telos*, no. 32 (Summer 1977): 152–61.

35. See Allen Hunter, "In the Wings, New Right Ideology and Organization," *Radical America* 15, no. 1–2 (Spring 1981): 127–38.

MAKING CONNECTIONS

1. How effective is Robert Bly's use of a fairy tale to discuss masculinity? What other rhetorical strategies does Bly use? You may want to consider the use of contrast, symbolism, anecdotes, and metaphors. Do Bly's apparent digressions help or hinder his argument? Who do you suppose is Bly's intended audience?

2. Bly states early in his essay that there is "something wonderful" and "something wrong" with the recent trend toward increased gentleness and thoughtfulness in men's development. Do you agree or disagree with his statement? Why? What qualities make up the character of the "Wild Man"? Are these qualities traditionally "masculine," "feminine," or neutral?

3. Bly contends that there has been a "new distribution of 'yang' [masculine] energy among couples" in recent years. Based on your experiences with men and women of your generation, write an essay assessing Bly's observation.

4. Although his essay focuses on the developmental direction for men in the 90s, can you make any inferences about the direction that Bly would like to see the 90s woman take? What is Bly's attitude toward the women's movement? How would each of the writers in Chapter 2 respond to Bly's thesis?

5. Compare and contrast Cooper Thompson's "new vision of masculinity" with Bly's. What are the "costs" that each author sees in the definition of masculinity that they reject? Choose either Thompson's or Bly's vision and discuss in your own essay ways that current male socialization—in families, schools, sports, Scouts, etc.—might have to change to foster that new definition of masculinity.

6. Write in essay form your own answer to the question that Thompson asks his students: "If you woke up tomorrow and discovered that you were the opposite sex from the one you are now, how would you and your life be different?"

7. Thompson contends that the use of ridicule is a common method for establishing a hierarchy of power among men. The high school class that he refers to made a long list of the behaviors that could elicit ridicule. As a class, make a list of such behaviors for high school boys and another for adult men. Does a comparison of the lists tell you anything about masculinity and male development? Are women also ridiculed for "stepping out of line"? What behaviors constitute women's "stepping out of line" in contrast to the list of behaviors you've compiled for men?

8. According to Thompson, homophobia and misogyny are the two critical forces in shaping male gender identity. How would Gary Kinsman respond to Thompson's assertion? What is your own opinion? Do you agree or disagree with Thompson that homophobia and misogyny are two sides of the same coin? Support your position with specific examples.

9. What does Kinsman mean by asserting that heterosexuality is socially constructed rather than naturally determined? Compare Kinsman's thesis to Devor's criticism of biological determinist thinking in Chapter 1. Write an essay either refuting or supporting Kinsman's argument. Do you believe that his meaning applies to women as well as men?

10. Write an imaginary conversation among Kinsman, Thompson, and Bly on the topic of violence and masculinity. Use specific phrases and statements from each author's essay to support the positions that you feel each would take.

11. What does Kinsman mean by "new possibilities for sexual politics"? Write an essay summarizing some of the "new possibilities" offered by the selections in the first three chapters. Consider Rich's poem (Chapter 1), the debate between Kersten and Frye (Chapter 2), and the different viewpoints on masculinity proposed by Bly and Cooper in this chapter.

12. As a group project, collect examples of how the masculine ideal is represented in such areas of popular culture as sports, music, or films. What are the key elements of the masculine ideal? Do you think that there is a wider range of acceptable male behavior today compared to the past? Compare and discuss your findings.

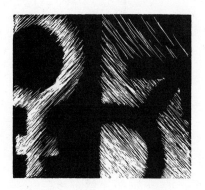

GENDER AND LANGUAGE

4
THE POLITICS OF SPEAKING

C O N T E X T S

Analyzing the language we use can seem as difficult and self-conscious as analyzing the air we breathe. As a medium, our language seems almost instinctive to us, intimate and individual, a direct extension of our personalities, feelings, and thoughts. Yet our patterns of speaking—and of being spoken about—carry deep-seated cultural assumptions about who we are and our place in society.

The study of language is challenging because language performs so many functions. On the one hand, language is private and personal, the means by which we express our identity. The ways we use language—our choice of words, the structure of our ideas, our styles of expression—reflect our individual histories and experiences. How we speak mirrors who we are.

But language also extends beyond us. The words we use existed before us, and we do not reinvent the rules of language each time we speak. Although we may add to or change language in our lifetime—by introducing slang, for instance, or coining a new high-tech term—its basic structures continue after we are gone. In this regard, we can see language as a kind of public property, or, in the words of one linguist, as "a public resource, like the water supply, that services a speech community and provides for the communication between individuals needed for social maintenance." Indeed, it can be argued that the words we inherit help shape the very ways we think and see the world.

Stereotypes about how women and men talk have been with us throughout history. The image of men as strong and silent or of women as talkative and illogical abound in jokes, proverbs, and literature and have even been reflected in the work of serious researchers. Otto Jespersen, an important linguist of the 1920s, sought to demonstrate woman's mental inferiority by way of her "inferior" use of language, arguing that the indirectness and imprecision of "women's expressions" act to pollute our public resource of language.

Can there be any truth to these stereotypes? Does the mere fact that we may believe them cause us to treat women and men differently as speakers? In the first essay in this chapter, Cheris Kramarae looks at modern folklore about women's styles of speaking. By analyzing the myth of "wishy-washy mommy talk"—the view of women's language as weak, illogical, and imprecise—Kramarae challenges the bias of researchers like Jespersen and shows how stereotypes about language are intimately linked to our cultural assumptions about women and men.

Other researchers have examined speech as a socialized behavior, something we learn along with other gendered ways of behaving. Scholars like Robin Lakoff (*Talking Like a Lady: Language and Woman's Place*, 1975) believe that just as little boys are encouraged to play aggressively and little girls urged toward more restrained activities, so too are boys allowed more "rough talk" and forceful expressions while girls are rewarded for being polite, quiet, and reserved in their ways of talking. This, however, presents a double bind as little girls grow into women and find themselves devalued for being unable to express themselves assertively or with precision.

Are women and men socialized to speak differently? The issue is one that Deborah Tannen, author of the recent book *You Just Don't Understand: Women and Men in Conversation* (1990), takes up in our second essay. In "Sex, Lies, and Conversation" Tannen examines the conversational styles of women and men in an attempt to understand the problems in communication between the sexes. To what extent are misunderstandings between the sexes due to different speaking styles and to men's and women's different uses of the spoken word? Tannen's findings shed light on the many subtle meanings of conversation as an interpersonal activity.

Poet Marge Piercy also offers a perspective on male-female misunderstanding. In her poem "You Don't Understand Me," she depicts the frustrations of an imagined conversation between a man and a woman. Next, Gloria Steinem looks at the broader picture of "The Politics of Talking in Groups" and reveals the power dynamics inherent in the spoken word. Issues such as who speaks and when, who introduces successful topics of discussion, and how points are raised and pursued reveal much about the gender and social position of speakers. Steinem offers some practical tips on becoming more aware of the strategies of group discussion.

In addition to the ways we as individuals speak, there are also assumptions about gender built into our language itself. Feminists have made inroads on changing certain sexisms implicit in our language, though the process of changing common speech takes time. Muriel Rukeyser's poem "Myth" addresses one usage that is still often taken for granted—using the generic term "man" to represent people of both sexes. Rukeyser has some fun with history to show how a thoughtless use of language might lead even a famous hero into dire and unexpected consequences. Finally, Eugene August offers a male point of view by arguing that men too can be seen as victims of sexism in language. In "Real Men Don't: Anti-Male Bias in English," he shows how men can be subject to equally limiting prejudices in the words we use to describe everything from parenthood to war, sexuality to crime.

Beyond their individual topics, the selections in this chapter invite broader questions about the nature of language and its role in culture. Does language merely reflect societal attitudes, or does it help construct and change them? What are the messages we send about power and authority in our modes of speech? Do certain patterns of talking and listening reflect power differences between women and men? Far from being something to take for granted, language and its uses are rich fields for study and debate. Moreover, they provide a foundation for thinking about the wider networks of cultural meaning which this book will take up in later chapters.

FOLK LINGUISTICS: WISHY-WASHY MOMMY TALK

CHERIS KRAMARAE

Cheris Kramarae is professor of speech communications at the University of Illinois at Champaign-Urbana and author of *Language and Power* (1984). She has also edited *The Voices and Words of Women and Men* (1981) and *Technology and Women's Voices: Keeping in Touch* (1988). The essay below was first published in 1974, in the popular journal *Psychology Today*.

Men and women speak a different language. According to popular belief, at least, the speech of women is weaker and less effective than the speech of men. Our culture has many jokes about both the quality of women's speech ("If my wife said what she thought, she'd be speechless") and its quantity ("Women need no eulogy, they speak for themselves"). Compared to male speech, the female form is supposed to be emotional, vague, euphemistic, sweetly proper, mindless, endless, high-pitched, and silly.

Such generalizations are not based on carefully controlled research. Although anthropologists have noticed sex-related differences in the languages of other cultures, there have been only a few quantitative studies of the way men and women differ in their use of English. Perhaps this is due to the fact that many researchers view women as peculiar human beings who stand outside the laws governing mankind (i.e., males).

A noted linguist who did devote some attention to sex differences in language had some unflattering things to say about the way women talk. In his 1922 book, *Language*, Otto Jespersen wrote an entire chapter on "The Woman." (There was no parallel chapter on "The Man.") Jespersen made many claims about women's speech, among them that women frequently leave sentences unfinished and that they are prone to jump from one idea to another when talking. These assertions rested on the author's own observations and examples drawn from literary works.

Until recently, Jespersen's chapter was one of the few published discussions of the topic. But with the emergence of the women's liberation movement, some social scientists and linguists have begun to speculate about how language helps maintain rigid sex role barriers. Most of these writers have derived hypotheses from their own intuitions as native speakers.

The Folklore of Female Language

In addition to the speculations of linguists, there is also a folk-linguistics of 5
women's speech, a body of folklore about female language that permeates
popular jokes and stories. These perceived differences do not necessarily
correspond to real ones, but they are important as indicators of cultural
attitudes and prejudices.

One way to study folk-linguistics is to examine comic art, which takes 6
much of its material from the relationships between the sexes, including how
they talk to each other. Social cartoons are especially useful, since their humor
depends on the exaggeration of popular stereotypes of human behavior. In a
recent study, I analyzed cartoons containing adult human speech, from three
consecutive months (13 issues) of *The New Yorker*, February 17 through May
12, 1973. I chose *The New Yorker* because it is a general-circulation magazine
with both male and female readers, and because many cartoonists and critics
consider it to be an innovator and leader in the field of social cartooning.

In order to check my own observations and judgments against those of 7
others, I asked 25 male and 25 female students at the University of Illinois to
help me identify some of the characteristics of women's and men's speech in
the cartoons. I gave each student a list of captions (but not the cartoons
themselves) from four consecutive issues, March 17 through April 7. I did
not identify the captions as coming from *The New Yorker*. I simply instructed
the students to indicate, for each one, whether they thought the words were
spoken by a male or female. At the end of the list there was room for
comments about what had guided the student's choices.

For most of the 49 captions, there was a clear consensus (at least 66 8
percent agreement) that the speaker in the cartoon was of a particular sex.
The male students were in unanimous or near-unanimous agreement on 14
captions, while females were in unanimous or near-unanimous agreement on
13.

The Silent Sex

A striking finding that emerged from my analysis was that women did not 9
speak in as many of the cartoons as did men. According to folk-linguistics,
women talk too much. But in the 156 cartoons in my sample, men speak 110
times, women only 44. In fact, the number for men goes up to 112 if we
assume that a commanding voice from the clouds is that of a masculine God,
and that a voice on the phone telling an elephant trainer to "Give him two
bottles of aspirin and call me in the morning" belongs to a male veterinarian.

There are several possible explanations for the relative silence of women 10
in these cartoons. Most cartoonists are men, and it may be that they depict

what they know best and consider most important, i.e., men and male activities. Some students suggested that men try harder to be funny and make more comic statements. Or perhaps the cartoons reflect real life, where men like to have the last, topping word.

Women in these cartoons not only speak less, they speak in fewer places. 11 Men speak in 38 different locations, including a courtroom, doctor's office, psychiatrist's office, police car, massage parlor, press conference, art museum, and floral shop. They are inside a home only 20 of the 110 (or 112) times they speak, excluding cocktail parties. Women, on the other hand, speak in only 16 different places, including the home, store, office, and airplane. They are at home on half the occasions when they talk, again excluding cocktail parties. In four of the 13 issues I looked at, women never spoke outside the home at all.

More important, men are in control of language wherever they happen 12 to be, but women, when they do leave home, often seem incapable of handling the language appropriate to the new location. Their speech then becomes the focus of humor. So we have a matron saying to a tight-lipped, barely patient stockbroker, "Now tell me, Mr. Hilbert, does Merrill Lynch think utilities are going to keep on being iffy?" And an enthusiastic woman at a cocktail party remarking to a man, "You have no idea how refreshing it is to meet someone raffish in West Hartford." And another woman inquiring of a book salesman, "Do you have any jolly fiction?" These cartoons are funny (subtly, in *The New Yorker* way) because in each case there is a word that does not quite belong, at least in that setting.

Politics and Pornography

The women and men who populate *The New Yorker* cartoons discuss different 13 topics. Men hold forth with authority on business, politics, legal matters, taxes, age, household expenses, electronic bugging, church collections, kissing, baseball, human relations, health, and—women's speech. Women discuss social life, books, food and drink, pornography, life's troubles, caring for a husband, social work, age, and life-style. Several of the students who rated the cartoon captions said they considered all statements about economics, business, or jobs to be male.

We have already seen what happens when a woman steps over these 14 boundaries and tries to discuss a topic like the stock market. In another cartoon, a woman who is listening with her husband to a TV news program and trying to keep up with current events complains, "I keep forgetting. Which is the good guy—Prince Souvanna Phouma or Prince Souphanouvong?" Forty of the 50 students rated this caption as female. A man with a similar question would probably drop the self-deprecating "I keep fogetting," and say something like, "Damn it! How are we supposed to remember which one is Souvanna Phouma and which is Souphanouvong?" This wording would put the blame for confusion on the owner of the difficult name, rather than the memory of the speaker.

In general, women in the cartoons speak less forcefully than men. For instance, they utter exclamations only five times when speaking to another adult, versus 27 times for men. Furthermore, exclamations seem to serve different functions for men and women. Males use them when they are angry or exasperated. A scowling boss yells into his intercom, "Miss Carter! Where's my input?" A husband says to his wife, "Damn it, Gertrude, Abe Beame isn't *supposed* to turn you on!" But women's exclamations are likely to convey enthusiasm, as when a woman who is admiring a picture says, "Aren't you lucky! Very few people have anything original that's nice." 15

Freedom to Swear

Since men do not have to be as mild as women, cartoonists let their male characters swear much more freely than their female characters. In *The New Yorker* cartoons, men use swear words (or exclamations with the word "God") 13 times. Women use them only twice, and on one of these occasions there is provocation. A woman says to her husband, who is pouring drinks at their bar, "My God, I mean is that really *all* you can say about me—I've stood the test of time?" Men curse for more trivial reasons. For example, a couple is dining in a restaurant, and the man says, "To hell with what the Sierra Club could do with the cost of a single F-111 fighter plane! Think of what *I* could do with the cost of a single F-111 fighter plane!" With the *hell*, the "masculine" topic, the emphatic *I*, and the exclamation mark, the speaker is clearly recognizable as a man. 16

Many of the student raters commented on the way profanity, and harsh language in general, distinguishes male from female speech. They echoed an observation made by Jespersen half a century ago, when he wrote that women feel an "instinctive shrinking from coarse and gross expressions." Not all modern women agree, however. When I showed Jespersen's remark to some women living in a college dormitory, the spontaneous reaction of several of them was "Shit!" 17

Another comment by some of the students in the study was that men use a simpler, more direct, more assertive type of language. They are blunt and to the point, whereas women tend to "flower up" their remarks. The caption ratings reflected this view. For example, all but two of the men and two of the women assigned "I'm probably old-fashioned, but I felt much more at home with the Forsytes than I do with the Louds," to a female speaker. One female rater explained, "Women are more likely to preempt their statements 18 with excuses for themselves, 'I may be old-fashioned, but—' . . . women are more concerned with a smooth emotional atmosphere." In contrast, men are perceived as self-assured and sometimes condescending. This came out in one of the cartoons, in which a woman complains to a man, "Can't you just say 'Scarlatti' instead of 'Scarlatti, of course'?"

Mommy Talk

Although the people of *The New Yorker* cartoons live in a world that is almost childless, there are some hints of what might be called mommy talk. For example, there is a cartoon portraying two men, one disgusted, the other puzzled, waiting in line for a public telephone. The woman using the phone gushes. "Yes, you are. You're my little snookums. Well, bye-bye for now, Sweetie Pie. Mommy's got to go . . . Hi. Was she wagging her tail?" [19]

Finally, according to folk-linguistics, certain adjectives, like "nice" and "pretty" are typical of female speech. In the cartoons, these words sometimes serve to identify a woman as a person with traditional ideas about women's role. At other times, they are the basis for a joke, as when a woman uses them while talking about a "masculine" topic. And occasionally, a man employs them to indicate a role reversal. Unfortunately, sex-linked vocabulary differences are difficult to quantify, but in general, the cartoons do reflect the usual beliefs about feminine adjectives. [20]

These and other findings demonstrate that stereotypical female speech is restricted and wishy-washy. The same picture emerges from other sources. For instance, the *New Seventeen Book of Etiquette and Young Living* contains a section on female speech entitled "Sweet Talk." It warns, "A pretty girl makes a good first impression with her looks, but if the sounds that come out of the pretty face are harsh, the effect is spoiled. She has to be easy on the ear as well as on the eyes." [21]

Mary Ellmann has described the stereotyped formlessness of women's language as it appears in the works of such male writers as James Joyce, Jean-Paul Sartre, Norman Mailer, and Ernest Hemingway; the Molly Blooms of literature have just let it all flow out. The same looseness of syntax is captured in a *Saturday Review* cartoon, where a miniskirted coed says to her male professor, "If we don't know how big the whole universe is, then I don't see how we could be sure how big anything in it is either, like the whole thing might not be any bigger than maybe an orange would be if it weren't in the universe, I mean, so I don't think we ought to get too uptight about any of it because it might be really sort of small and unimportant after all, and until we find out that everything isn't just some kind of specks and things, why maybe who needs it?" [22]

A few linguists have tried to pinpoint more precisely the devices women 23
use to weaken their words. Robin Lakoff has suggested that women use the
tag-question form for this purpose. Instead of a decisive statement, "That
house looks terrible," women are apt to use an indecisive form, "That house
looks terrible, doesn't it?" In this way, they ask for confirmation, and allow
themselves to be persuaded otherwise. Lakoff also believes women use intonation to turn answers into questions, thus communicating subordination and
uncertainty: "When will dinner be ready?" "Oh . . . around six o'clock . . . ?"

Is Folklore Fact?

Both folk-linguistics and the observations of professional linguists provide 24
useful clues to popular attitudes and are rich sources of hypotheses about
language. These hypotheses may or may not fit empirical data about the way
people actually talk. Unfortunately, there have been very few studies on sex-
related differences in actual speech. Some researchers have found that women
are more likely to use standard, "correct" grammar and pronunciation. Beyond that, we can make few generalizations.

Lately I have begun to explore the problem of perceived versus actual 25
differences. My work and the work of several others at the University of
Illinois indicates that while it is easy to write statements identifiable as feminine or masculine types, the sex-related cues in such statements appear relatively infrequently in the language of either sex.

In one recent study, I investigated whether men and women differ in 26
their use of modifiers. Lakoff and others have suggested that some adjectives,
like "adorable," "lovely," "divine," and "sweet," are peculiar to women; their
use by a man could damage his reputation. As I noted earlier, this feature of
women's speech showed up in some of *The New Yorker* cartoons. Women are
also said to use certain kinds of adverbs more often than men. Jespersen wrote
that women have a propensity for hyperbole, which leads them to tack *-ly*
onto adjectives, producing phrases like "awfully pretty" and "terribly nice." I
wanted to find out if women really do use more of these forms.

I was also interested in finding out if there is an absolute difference in 27
the number and variety of modifiers used by males and females. Opinion here
is divided. Jespersen felt that men have a more extensive vocabulary, and in
general take a greater interest in words. In fact, he advised people wanting to
learn a foreign tongue to read "many ladies' novels, because they will there
continually meet with just those everyday words and combinations which the
foreigner is above all in need of; what may be termed the indispensable small-
change of a language." If this is true, we might expect a greater variety of
descriptive words from men. However, another linguist, Dwight Bolinger,
claims that women use more adjectives than men.

Since this was an initial study, I limited my attention to *-ly* adverbs, and   28
prenominal adjectives (words that precede and modify nouns, such as "handsome" in "handsome man"). These particular kinds of modifiers, unlike others, are unambiguous and are easy to identify.

Inanimate Objects

I had 17 men and 17 women compose written descriptions of two black-and-   29
white photographs. Since some people have suggested that men are more
interested in inanimate objects than they are in people, and the reverse is true
for women, I used one photograph showing several people seated around a
table, and another showing a large building adorned with pillars and statues.
The subjects had 10 minutes in which to write their paragraphs.

I analyzed each paragraph by adding up the number of *-ly* adverbs and   30
prenominal adjectives, and comparing these numbers to the total number of
words used. I found none of the differences that are supposed to exist. Statistical analysis showed that women did not differ from men in either the
number or variety of *-ly* adverbs or prenominal adjectives they used. Although
men tended to use more words overall to describe the photographs, the
differences were not statistically significant. And there did not appear to be
any sex differences in the kinds of adjectives preferred.

Perhaps the differences are not in the number or variety of modifying   31
words, but in the way they are used. A sensitive person might be able to pick
up subtle cues that are not susceptible to statistical analysis. Since middle-
class women are supposed to be especially conscious of stylistic variation, I
enlisted the aid of 11 female students majoring in English to determine if the
sex of the writers could be deduced from internal cues. I gave them 10 typed
paragraphs, randomly selected from those written by the participants in the
first part of the study. Five had been written by women, five by men, all
described the photograph of a building. In only six of the 10 paragraphs was
a majority of the English majors able to identify the writer's sex. In all, there
were 59 correct guesses and 41 incorrect ones.

Interestingly, none of the English majors questioned the reasonableness   32
of trying to assign paragraphs to male or female authors, and they were all
able to give reasons for their choices. Most of these had to do with the number
and type of descriptive words used. In *incorrectly* ascribing to female authors
paragraphs that were actually written by males, some of the women explained
that the passages were graceful, sensitive, and contained a lot of detailed
description.

Many questions remain. A greater number of sex differences may exist in   33
spoken than in written language. Differences in written work might show up
under other circumstances. For example, an important factor may be whether
a woman is writing or speaking to another woman, to a man, or to a general

audience. Age and socioeconomic position may affect the writer's style. Since women are individuals, researchers must be careful not to make the error of simply grouping all women together.

Vacant Chambers of the Mind

Words, phrases, and sentence patterns are not inherently strong or weak. 34 They acquire these attributes only in a particular cultural context. If our society views female speech as inferior, it is because of the subordinate role assigned to women. Our culture is biased to interpret sex differences in favor of men.

For example, Jespersen reports an experiment in which male and female 35 subjects had to read a paragraph as quickly as possible, then write down as much as they could remember of it. Women were able to read the passage more quickly and recall more of what they had read. But they lost anyway. Jespersen paraphrases Havelock Ellis' ingenious explanation of the results: ". . . with the quick reader it is as though every statement were admitted immediately and without inspection to fill the vacant chambers of the mind, while with the slow reader every statement undergoes an instinctive process of cross-examination. . . ."

Thus, beliefs about sex-related language differences may be as important 36 as the actual differences. As long as women play a subordinate role, their speech will be stereotyped as separate and unequal.

SEX, LIES AND CONVERSATION
Why Is It So Hard for Men and Women to Talk to Each Other?

◑

DEBORAH TANNEN

Deborah Tannen is professor of linguistics at George-
town University and author of the recent book *You
Just Don't Understand: Women and Men in Conversation*
(1990). Tannen, who has also worked as a creative writing teacher, began publishing her linguistics research
in the early 1980s. The article below, which appeared
in the *Washington Post* in 1990, summarizes her findings about patterns of conversation between the sexes.

I was addressing a small gathering in a suburban Virginia living room—a 1
women's group that had invited men to join them. Throughout the evening,
one man had been particularly talkative, frequently offering ideas and anecdotes, while his wife sat silently beside him on the couch. Toward the end of
the evening, I commented that women frequently complain that their husbands don't talk to them. This man quickly concurred. He gestured toward
his wife and said, "She's the talker in our family." The room burst into
laughter; the man looked puzzled and hurt. "It's true," he explained. "When
I come home from work I have nothing to say. If she didn't keep the conversation going, we'd spend the whole evening in silence."

This episode crystallizes the irony that although American men tend to 2
talk more than women in public situations, they often talk less at home. And
this pattern is wreaking havoc with marriage.

The pattern was observed by political scientist Andrew Hacker in the late 3
'70s. Sociologist Catherine Kohler Riessman reports in her new book *Divorce
Talk* that most of the women she interviewed—but only a few of the men—
gave lack of communication as the reason for their divorces. Given the current
divorce rate of nearly 50 percent, that amounts to millions of cases in the
United States every year—a virtual epidemic of failed conversation.

In my own research, complaints from women about their husbands most 4
often focused not on tangible inequities such as having given up the chance
for a career to accompany a husband to his, or doing far more than their
share of daily life-support work like cleaning, cooking, social arrangements
and errands. Instead, they focused on communication: "He doesn't listen to

me," "He doesn't talk to me." I found, as Hacker observed years before, that most wives want their husbands to be, first and foremost, conversational partners, but few husbands share this expectation of their wives.

In short, the image that best represents the current crisis is the stereo-   5
typical cartoon scene of a man sitting at the breakfast table with a newspaper held up in front of his face, while a woman glares at the back of it, wanting to talk.

Linguistic Battle of the Sexes

How can women and men have such different impressions of communi-   6
cation in marriage? Why the widespread imbalance in their interests and expectations?

In the April issue of *American Psychologist*, Stanford University's Eleanor   7
Maccoby reports the results of her own and others' research showing that children's development is most influenced by the social structure of peer interactions. Boys and girls tend to play with children of their own gender, and their sex-separate groups have different organizational structures and interactive norms.

I believe these systematic differences in childhood socialization make talk   8
between women and men like cross-cultural communication, heir to all the attraction and pitfalls of that enticing but difficult enterprise. My research on men's and women's conversations uncovered patterns similar to those de-scribed for children's groups.

For women, as for girls, intimacy is the fabric of relationships, and talk   9
is the thread from which it is woven. Little girls create and maintain friend-ships by exchanging secrets; similarly, women regard conversation as the cornerstone of friendship. So a woman expects her husband to be a new and improved version of a best friend. What is important is not the individual subjects that are discussed but the sense of closeness, of a life shared, that emerges when people tell their thoughts, feelings, and impressions.

Bonds between boys can be as intense as girls', but they are based less on   10
talking, more on doing things together. Since they don't assume talk is the cement that binds a relationship, men don't know what kind of talk women want, and they don't miss it when it isn't there.

Boys' groups are larger, more inclusive, and more hierarchical, so boys   11
must struggle to avoid the subordinate position in the group. This may play a role in women's complaints that men don't listen to them. Some men really don't like to listen, because being the listener makes them feel one-down, like a child listening to adults or an employee to a boss.

But often when women tell men, "You aren't listening," and the men   12
protest, "I am," the men are right. The impression of not listening results from misalignments in the mechanics of conversation. The misalignment

begins as soon as a man and a woman take physical positions. This became clear when I studied videotapes made by psychologist Bruce Dorval of children and adults talking to their same-sex best friends. I found that at every age, the girls and women faced each other directly, their eyes anchored on each other's faces. At every age, the boys and men sat at angles to each other and looked elsewhere in the room, periodically glancing at each other. They were obviously attuned to each other, often mirroring each other's movements. But the tendency of men to face away can give women the impression they aren't listening even when they are. A young woman in college was frustrated: Whenever she told her boyfriend she wanted to talk to him, he would lie down on the floor, close his eyes, and put his arm over his face. This signaled to her, "He's taking a nap." But he insisted he was listening extra hard. Normally, he looks around the room, so he is easily distracted. Lying down and covering his eyes helped him concentrate on what she was saying.

Analogous to the physical alignment that women and men take in conversation is their topical alignment. The girls in my study tended to talk at length about one topic, but the boys tended to jump from topic to topic. The second-grade girls exchanged stories about people they knew. The second-grade boys teased, told jokes, noticed things in the room and talked about finding games to play. The sixth-grade girls talked about problems with a mutual friend. The sixth-grade boys talked about 55 different topics, none of which extended over more than a few turns.   13

Listening to Body Language

Switching topics is another habit that gives women the impression men aren't listening, especially if they switch to a topic about themselves. But the evidence of the 10th-grade boys in my study indicates otherwise. The 10th-grade boys sprawled across their chairs with bodies parallel and eyes straight ahead, rarely looking at each other. They looked as if they were riding in a car, staring out the windshield. But they were talking about their feelings. One boy was upset because a girl had told him he had a drinking problem, and the other was feeling alienated from all his friends.   14

Now, when a girl told a friend about a problem, the friend responded by asking probing questions and expressing agreement and understanding. But the boys dismissed each other's problems. Todd assured Richard that his drinking was "no big problem" because "sometimes you're funny when you're off your butt." And when Todd said he felt left out, Richard responded, "Why should you? You know more people than me."   15

Women perceive such responses as belittling and unsupportive. But the boys seemed satisfied with them. Whereas women reassure each other by implying, "You shouldn't feel bad because I've had similar experiences," men   16 do so by implying, "You shouldn't feel bad because your problems aren't so bad."

There are even simpler reasons for women's impression that men don't listen. Linguist Lynette Hirschman found that women make more listener-noise, such as "mhm," "uhuh," and "yeah," to show "I'm with you." Men, she found, more often give silent attention. Women who expect a stream of listener-noise interpret silent attention as no attention at all.

Women's conversational habits are as frustrating to men as men's are to women. Men who expect silent attention interpret a stream of listener-noise as overreaction or impatience. Also, when women talk to each other in a close, comfortable setting, they often overlap, finish each other's sentences and anticipate what the other is about to say. This practice, which I call "participatory listenership," is often perceived by men as interruption, intrusion and lack of attention.

A parallel difference caused a man to complain about his wife, "She just wants to talk about her own point of view. If I show her another view, she gets mad at me." When most women talk to each other, they assume a conversationalist's job is to express agreement and support. But many men see their conversational duty as pointing out the other side of an argument. This is heard as disloyalty by women, and refusal to offer the requisite support. It is not that women don't want to see other points of view, but that they prefer them phrased as suggestions and inquiries rather than as direct challenges.

In his book *Fighting for Life*, Walter Ong points out that men use "agonistic" or warlike, oppositional formats to do almost anything; thus discussion becomes debate, and conversation a competitive sport. In contrast, women see conversation as a ritual means of establishing rapport. If Jane tells a problem and June says she has a similar one, they walk away feeling closer to each other. But this attempt at establishing rapport can backfire when used with men. Men take too literally women's ritual "troubles talk," just as women mistake men's ritual challenges for real attack.

The Sounds of Silence

These differences begin to clarify why women and men have such different expectations about communication in marriage. For women, talk creates intimacy. Marriage is an orgy of closeness: you can tell your feelings and thoughts, and still be loved. Their greatest fear is being pushed away. But men live in a hierarchical world, where talk maintains independence and status. They are on guard to protect themselves from being put down and pushed around.

This explains the paradox of the talkative man who said of his silent wife, "She's the talker." In the public setting of a guest lecture, he felt challenged

116

to show his intelligence and display his understanding of the lecture. But at home, where he has nothing to prove and no one to defend against, he is free to remain silent. For his wife, being home means she is free from the worry that something she says might offend someone, or spark disagreement, or appear to be showing off; at home she is free to talk.

The communication problems that endanger marriage can't be fixed by mechanical engineering. They require a new conceptual framework about the role of talk in human relationships. Many of the psychological explanations that have become second nature may not be helpful, because they tend to blame either women (for not being assertive enough) or men (for not being in touch with their feelings). A sociolinguistic approach by which male-female conversation is seen as cross-cultural communication allows us to understand the problem and forge solutions without blaming either party. 23

Once the problem is understood, improvement comes naturally, as it did to the young woman and her boyfriend who seemed to go to sleep when she wanted to talk. Previously, she had accused him of not listening, and he had refused to change his behavior, since that would be admitting fault. But then she learned about and explained to him the differences in women's and men's habitual ways of aligning themselves in conversation. The next time she told him she wanted to talk, he began, as usual, by lying down and covering his eyes. When the familiar negative reaction bubbled up, she reassured herself that he really was listening. But then he sat up and looked at her. Thrilled, she asked why. He said, "You like me to look at you when we talk, so I'll try to do it." Once he saw their differences as cross-cultural rather than right and wrong, he independently altered his behavior. 24

Women who feel abandoned and deprived when their husbands won't listen to or report daily news may be happy to discover their husbands trying to adapt once they understand the place of small talk in women's relationships. But if their husbands don't adapt, the women may still be comforted that for men, this is not a failure of intimacy. Accepting the difference, the wives may look to their friends or family for that kind of talk. And husbands who can't provide it shouldn't feel their wives have made unreasonable demands. Some couples will still decide to divorce, but at least their decisions will be based on realistic expectations. 25

In these times of resurgent ethnic conflicts, the world desperately needs cross-cultural understanding. Like charity, successful cross-cultural communication should begin at home. 26

YOU DON'T UNDERSTAND ME

◐

MARGE PIERCY

Poet and novelist Marge Piercy's many writings explore the dynamics of gender in the modern world. Among her more famous novels are *Small Changes* (1973), *Women on the Edge of Time* (1976), *The High Cost of Living* (1978), and *Fly Away Home* (1984). Her collections of poetry include *Circles on the Water* (1982) and *Stone, Paper, Knife* (1983), from which the following poem is taken.

You don't understand me,

you gulp, a frog suddenly on my dinner
plate hopping through the buttered noodles
blinking cold eyes of reproach.

I can interpret the language of your hands
warm under calluses. Your body speaks into mine.
We are native users of the same jangling American.

A casual remark lets ants loose in your ears.
The wrong tone drips ice water on your nape.
Waiting I finger the bruise-colored why.

Look, I can't study you like the engine
of an old car coughing into silence on wet mornings.
Can't read the convolutions of your brain through the skull.

You want hieroglyphs at the corners of your squint decoded
in perfect silence that folds into your ribbed side,
a woman of soft accordion-pleated wool with healer's hands.

I don't understand you: you are not a book,
an argument, a theory. Speak to me.
I listen, and I speak back.

THE POLITICS OF TALKING IN GROUPS
How To Win the Game *and* Change the Rules

◐

GLORIA STEINEM

Since the 1960s, Gloria Steinem has been a leading voice in the women's movement in America. She is the founder of *Ms.* magazine and has lectured widely on the topic of women's rights. Her collection *Outrageous Acts and Everyday Rebellions* (1983), from which the following essay is taken, remains one of the seminal introductions to the spectrum of feminist concerns.

Once upon a time (that is, just a few years ago), psychologists believed that the way we chose to talk and communicate was largely a function of personality. If certain conversational styles and personality types turned out to be more common to one sex than the other (more abstract and aggressive talk for men, for instance; more personal and equivocal talk for women), then this was just another tribute to the influence of biology on personality. [1]

Consciously or otherwise, feminists challenged this assumption from the beginning. After all, many of us were encouraged by the idealism of the sixties to speak out on the injustices of war, as well as of race and class; yet even when we used exactly the same words and style as our male counterparts, we were less likely to be listened to or taken seriously. When we tried to talk about this and other experiences, the lack of listening got worse, with opposition and even ridicule just around the corner. Only women's own meetings and truth-telling began to confirm what we had thought each of us was alone in experiencing—and it was precisely those early consciousness-raising groups that began to develop a more cooperative, less combative style of talking; an alternative that many women have maintained and been strengthened by ever since. [2]

The problem is that this culturally different form has remained an almost totally female event. True, it has helped many, many women arrive at issues and strategies for public action, but as an influence on the culturally male style of public talking, it has remained almost as removed as its more domestic versions of the past. [3]

One reason for a Women's Movement delay in challenging existing styles of talking makes good feminist sense. Our first task was to change the words themselves; otherwise we were unlikely to be recognized in public dialogue [4] at all. We did not feel included (and usage studies showed that factually, we were not) in hundreds of such supposedly generic terms as "mankind" and "he," "manpower" and "statesman." Nor could we fail to see the racial parallels as being identified as "girls" at advanced ages, or with first names only, or by our personal connection (or lack of one) to a member of the dominant group. Furthermore, terms had to be invented for such nameless realities as "sexism," "sexual harassment," and "battered women"; as well as to replace such authoritarianisms as "population control" with "reproductive freedom"—and much more.

Hard as it was (and still is), this radical act of seizing the power to name 5 ourselves and our experience was easier than taking on the politics of conversation. Documenting society-wide patterns of talking required expensive research and surveys. Documenting the sexism in words, and even conjuring up alternatives, took only one courageous woman and a dictionary (for instance, the pioneering work of Alma Graham); a good economic reason why such works were among the first and best by feminist scholars.

In retrospect, the second cause for delay makes less feminist sense: the 6 long popularity of assertiveness training. Though most women needed to be more assertive (and even more aggressive, though that word was thought to be too controversial), many of these courses taught women how to play the game as it exists, not how to change the rules. Unlike the assault on sexist language, which demanded new behavior from men, too, assertiveness training pushed one-way change for women only, thus seeming to confirm masculine-style communication as the only adult or most effective model. Certainly, many individual women were helped—and many men were confronted with the educational experience of an assertive woman—but the larger impact was usually to flatter the existing masculine game of talk-politics with imitation.

Since then, however, a few feminist scholars have had the resources to 7 document conversational patterns of mixed- and single-sex groups, both here and in Europe. Traditional scholarship, influenced by feminism, has also begun to look at conversational style as a function of power and environment. If, for instance, employees pursue topics raised by their employers more than the reverse; older people feel free to interrupt younger ones; subordinates are more polite; yet women tend to share all those conversational habits of the less powerful, even across many lines of class and status—how accidental can that be?

Research still has a long way to go in neutralizing its masculine bias. 8 *Talking* is usually assumed to be the important and positive act, for instance, but *listening*, certainly a productive function, is the subject of almost no studies at all.

Nonetheless, there is now enough scholarship to document many of 9 women's group experiences and different styles; to point out some deficiencies of the masculine model of group talk in public and private life; and to give us some ideas on how to create a synthesis of both that could provide a much wider range of alternatives for women *and* for men.

I

Have you assumed the truth of the popular belief that women talk more than men— 10
and thus may prevail in social groups if nowhere else? If so, you're not alone. Researchers of sex differences in language started out with that assumption. So did many feminists, who often explained women's supposedly greater penchant for talking as a compensation for lack of power to act.

In fact, however, when the English feminist and scholar, Dale Spender, 11 surveyed studies of the quantity of talk for her recent book, *Man Made Language*, she concluded that "perhaps in more than any other research area, findings were in complete contradiction with the stereotype. . . . There has not been one study which provides evidence that women talk more than men, and there have been numerous studies which indicate that men talk more than women."

Her conclusion held true regardless of whether the study in question 12 asked individuals to talk into a tape recorder, with no group interaction; or compared men and women talking on television; or measured amounts of talk in mixed groups (even among male and female state legislators); or involved group discussions of a subject on which women might be expected to have more expertise. (Though competing with 32 female colleagues at a London workshop on sexism and education, for instance, the five men present still managed to talk more than 50 percent of the time.)

Some studies of male silence in heterosexual couples might seem to 13 counter these results among individuals or groups, but Spender's research supports their conclusion that a major portion of female talk in such one-to-one situations is devoted to drawing the man out, asking questions, introducing multiple subjects until one is accepted by him, or demonstrating interest in the subjects he introduces.

Clearly, silence from the dominant group is not necessarily the same as 14 listening. It can be a rejection of both the speaker and the vulnerability that might come from self-revelation. And talking by the subordinate group is not necessarily an evidence of power. Its motive can be a Scheherazade-like need to intrigue and thus survive.

In addition to their greater volume of talk, however, men interrupt 15 women more often, in groups as in couples, and with much less social punishment than vice versa. (Men also interrupt women more often than women interrupt each other.) Moreover, men are more likely to police the subject matter of conversation in mixed-sex groups. One study of working-class families showed that women might venture into such "masculine" topics as politics or sports, and men might join "feminine" discussions of domestic events,

121

but in both cases, it was the men who ridiculed or otherwise straightened out the nonconformers. (Even in that London workshop on sexism, the female participants' concrete experiences were suppressed in favor of the more abstract style of general conclusions on sexism that was preferred by the men.)

How did the myth of female talkativeness and conversational dominance 16 get started? Why has this supposed female ability been so accepted that many sociologists, and a few battered women themselves, have even accepted it as a justification of male violence against their lovers and wives?

The uncomfortable truth seems to be that women-who-talk have been 17 measured, not against the norms of men-who-talk, but against the expectation of female silence.

Indeed, women who accept and try to disprove the stereotype may pay 18 the highest price. In attempting to be the exceptions who do not "talk too much," we probably have been silencing ourselves. If so, measuring our behavior against real people and real studies should come as a relief; a confirmation of unspoken feelings. We are not crazy, for instance, if we feel that, when we finally do take the conversational floor in a group, we are out there in exposed verbal flight; like fearful soloists from the audience or chorus. We are not crazy to feel years of unspoken thoughts bottled up inside us, so that too many words come rushing into our heads and leave us feeling inadequate or frustrated.

Paradoxically, once we give up searching for approval by stifling our 19 thoughts—or by imitating the male norm of effective communicating—we often find it easier to simply say what needs to be said, and thus to earn approval. Losing self-consciousness allows us to focus on content.

As for women's skill as sensitive listeners (perhaps the real source of 20 "intuition"), we can bring it with us into the groups of our work and daily lives—if we affirm its value. Female culture has a great deal to contribute to the dominant one. Furthermore, women who talk equally, select subjects (and even interrupt occasionally) might survive longer if we took the reasonable attitude that we are helping men to be attentive, retentive listeners. After all, if more men gained such skills, they might have "intuition," too.

What are some practical steps toward achieving all this? Well, try tape- 21 recording a dinner-table conversation or group meeting (quietly, or in the guise of recording facts, so participants don't become self-conscious about their talk-politics); then play the tape back to the same group with the number of minutes talked, interruptions, and subject-introductions added up for each gender. Or give the same number of poker chips to each group participant, and require that one chip be given up each time that person speaks. Or go around the room once at the beginning of each meeting, consciousness-raising-style, with a question that each participant must answer personally, thus breaking the silence barrier. (It is said that the British Labour Party was born only after its warring factions spent an hour moving a large conference table into a small room. That one communal act helped break the isolation.)

If such methods require more advance planning or influence on the group 22 than you can muster, try some individual acts. Just talking about the results of studies on who-talks-more can produce some very healthy self-consciousness in both women and men. If one group member speaks rarely, try addressing more of your own remarks to her directly. On the other hand, if a man (or woman) is a domineering interrupter, try objecting directly, being inattentive, interrupting in return, or timing the minutes of his or her speech. If someone cuts you off, say quietly: "That's one"; then promise some conspicuous act when the interruptions get to three. Or keep score on "successful" topic introductions and add them up by gender.

If questions and comments following a lecture (even on feminism) come 23 mostly from men, stand up and say so. It may be a learning moment for everyone involved. In fact, the prevalence of male speakers has caused some feminist lecturers to take questions from women only, thus creating one public forum with a female priority.

To demonstrate the importance of listening as a positive act, try taking 24 notes on the content of female and male speakers; then giving a postmeeting quiz. Maybe you *won't* discover the usual: that men often remember what male speakers say better than they remember the words of women; and that women may remember male content better, too, but listen and retain the words of *both* sexes somewhat better than men do.

Most of all, check the talk-politics concealed in your own behavior. Does 25 your anxiety level go up (and your hostess instinct begin to nudge you) when women are talking and men are listening—but not the reverse? Men often seem to feel okay about "talking shop" for hours while women listen, for instance, but women seem able to "talk shop" (or even feminism) for only a short time before feeling anxious, apologizing, and trying to include the men. If you start to feel wrongly uncomfortable about making males listen, try this exercise: *keep on talking*—and encourage your sisters to do the same. You will be paying male speakers (and listeners) the honor of treating them as honestly as you would if they were women.

II

There is a popular conviction that women talk about themselves more than men do; 26 *hence the accusation of "gossip." Also that men prefer to talk to groups of men, and that the acceptance of women's topics is hampered by the style of their presenting. Do you act on these assumptions? Are they true or false?*

After recording the themes of single-sex and mixed conversational groups, 27 Elizabeth Aries found that men in all-male groups were more likely to talk about themselves, and to tell anecdotes that demonstrated superiority or aggressiveness. Women in all-female groups were less likely to talk about themselves (except to share an emotional reaction) and more likely to discuss human relationships.

Of course, "relationships" might fall under "gossip" in men's view. Male   28
conversation does seem more prone to impersonality and abstraction with even personal questions and anxieties disguised as generalities. (Feminist lecturers often comment, for instance, that women in the audience ask questions about problems in their own lives, while men are more likely to say something like: "How will feminism impact the American family?") Nonetheless, if a characteristic of "gossip" can be seen as self-aggrandizement through invoking the weaknesses of others, then many men may be more "gossipy" than many women; especially if one considers the tradition of sexual bragging.

Since subjects introduced by males in mixed groups are far more likely   29
to "succeed"—and, as Aries concluded, women in mixed groups are more likely to interact with men than with other women—it's not unreasonable to suppose that groups spend more time discussing the personal lives and interests of men participants than women.

Aries also documented the more cooperative, rotating style of talk and   30
leadership in women-only groups: the conscious or unconscious habit of "taking turns." Thus, women prefer talking in single-sex groups for the concrete advantages of both having a conversational turn and being listened to. On the other hand, she confirmed research that shows male-only groups to have more stable hierarchies, with the same one or several talkers dominating most of the time.

No wonder men prefer the variation and opportunity, as Aries points out,   31
of mixed-sex audiences with the seriousness of a male presence, but with more choice of styles (and, as Spender adds caustically, the assurance of at least some noncompetitive listeners).

Women's more gentle delivery, "feminine" choice of adjectives, attention   32
to grammar, and polite style have been greatly criticized. Linguist Robin Lakoff pioneered the exposure of "ladylike" speech as a double bind that is both required of little girls, and used as a reason why, as adults, they may not be seen as forceful or serious. (Even Lakoff seems to assume, however, that female speech is to be criticized as the deficient form, while male speech is the norm and can escape equal comment.) Arlie Hochschild also cites some survival techniques of racial minorities that women probably share: playing dumb and dissembling, for instance, and expressing frequent approval of others.

But with all this criticism of female speech patterns, justified or not, there   33
is also evidence that a rejection of the way a woman speaks is often a tactic to blame or dismiss her without dealing with the content of what she is saying.

For instance, how many women speakers have heard some version of: 34
"You have a good point—but you're just not making it effectively"? Or: "Your style is too aggressive/ladylike/loud/quiet"? It is with such paternalistic crit-

icisms that male politicians often dismiss the serious message of their female colleagues, or that husbands turn aside the content of arguments made by their wives.

There are two anomalies that give away this "helpful" criticism. First, it   35
is rarely used when the content of the woman's message is not challenging to male power. (How often are women criticized for being too aggressive or fierce in defense of their husbands and children?) Second, such criticism is rarely accompanied by real support; not even when the person doing the criticizing is supposed to be sympathetic, or is a subordinate. Women professors report criticism of their teaching style from young male students, for instance, and women political candidates say they often get critiques of their fund-raising techniques instead of cash.

Just as there is frequently a topic that men in a group find more com-   36
pelling than any that has been introduced by a woman, or a political issue that is "more important" than those of concern to women, so there is usually a better, more effective style than the one a woman happens to be using. Men *would* support us, we are told—if only we learned how to ask in the right way.

What can we do about these stereotypes and paternalisms? Well, keeping group   37
notes for one meeting or one week on the male/female ratio of gossip or self-aggrandizing stories could be eye-opening. Declaring a day's moratorium on words that end in "-tion" and on all abstractions might encourage men to state their personal beliefs, without disguising them as general conclusions.

Countering slippery generalities with a tangible example sometimes   38
works, too. When David Susskind and Germaine Greer were guests on the same television talk show, for instance, Susskind used general, pseudoscientific statements about women's monthly emotional changes as a subtle way of dealing with the challenges brought by this very intelligent woman. Greer simply turned politely to Susskind and asked, in substance: "Tell me, David. Can you tell if I'm menstruating right now or not?" The personal example wiped out any doubts raised by Susskind's generalities—as well as subduing his style for the rest of the show.

In an effort to break down masculine competitiveness and impersonality,   39
some men have been meeting in all-male consciousness-raising groups, learning how to communicate more openly among themselves. Many women are trying to be more honest and effective toward men by analyzing the barriers we ourselves maintain.

For instance: women's preference for talking to other women has a great   40
deal to do with the shorthand and easy understanding that shared experience provides, in contrast to the necessity of talking across a cultural divide. After all, the less powerful group usually knows the powerful one much better than vice versa. Just as blacks have to know whites in order to survive, women have often had to know men; yet the powerful group can afford to regard the less powerful as a mystery. Indeed, the idea of differentness and the Mysterious

Other may be necessary justifications for the power imbalance and the lack of empathy it requires. Women must live in two worlds, but men only have to live in one.

One result is that, even when the powerful group *wants* to listen, the 41 other may despair of talking: our experience is just too much trouble to explain. Recognizing this unequal knowledge encourages women to talk about ourselves to men; at least to match the time they spend talking about themselves to us. We cannot expect them to read our minds.

On criticisms of women's speaking style, role reversals might be enlight- 42 ening; for instance, asking a man to effectively argue his political point while speaking "like a lady." A woman candidate might also ask critics to write a speech in the style they think she should use. Finally, if you can't explain at the time why having your style condemned but your content ignored is so frustrating, try firing off a long and well-reasoned letter.

Of course, you can always respond in kind. There's a certain satisfaction 43 to saying, in the middle of a man's impassioned speech: "I suppose you have a point to make—but you're doing it badly. Now, if you just changed your language, your timing, and perhaps your suit. . . ."

III

Women's higher-pitched voices and men's lower ones are the result of physiology. 44 *Thus, women speakers will always have a problem: deep voices are just more pleasant and authoritative. Besides, female facial expressions and gestures don't have as much variation or force . . . and so on. These are inhibiting stereotypes. Are they inhibiting you?*

It's true that tone of voice is partly created by throat-construction and 45 the resonance of bones. Though a big area of male-female overlap exists in voice tone—as well as in our size, strength, and other physical attributes— we assume that most men will have a much deeper pitch than most women.

In fact, however, no one knows exactly how much of our speaking voices 46 may be imitative and culturally produced. In *Growing Up Free*, Letty Cottin Pogrebin notes a study of young boys before puberty: their voices lowered *even before physiological changes could account for it*, thus indicating an imitation of how males around them spoke. Dale Spender cites a study of males born deaf and unable to imitate sound: some of them never went through an adolescent voice change at all.

Whatever the mix of physiological and environmental factors, however, 47 the important point is that *acceptance* of vocal tone is definitely cultural and subject to change.

In Japan, for instance, a woman's traditionally high-pitched, soft tone is 48 considered a very important sexual attribute. (When asked in a public opinion poll what they found most attractive in women, the majority of Japanese men said "voice.") Though trained to use their upper registers, Japanese women, like many of their sisters around the world, may speak in lower tones when men are not present, and may even change their language as well. (Schoolgirls caused a scandal in Japan when their female-only conversations were taped, and they were found to be using masculine language forms among themselves.) Thus, Japanese men may find a high voice attractive, not for itself, but for its proof of conformity to a traditional role.

In the United States, some women also cultivate a high, childish, or 49 whispery voice (think of Marilyn Monroe) and are considered sexually attractive by men.

That style becomes a drawback, however, when women try for any adult 50 or powerful role. Female reporters were kept out of television and radio for years by the argument that their voices were too high, grating, or nonauthoritative to give the news credibly. Even now, their voices may be thought more suitable for human interest and "soft news," while men still announce "hard news" events. In the early days of television, women were allowed to report the weather—very sexily. When meteorology and maps became the vogue, however, most stations switched to men.

The rule seems to be that a woman's vocal tone, whatever it is, only 51 becomes a real issue when she has power, is taking "a man's job," or is saying what men don't want to hear. No one made much of Barbara Walters's lisp or voice, for instance, until she got a record-breaking million-dollar contract.

In the long run, however, men may suffer more from cultural restrictions 52 on tone of voice than women do.

Ruth Brend's study of male and female intonation patterns in the United 53 States, for instance, disclosed four contrastive levels used by women in normal speech, but only three levels used by men. This wasn't a result of physiology: men also had at least four levels available to them, but just chose to reject the highest one. Thus, women may speak publicly in both high and low tones with some degree of social acceptability, but men must use their lower tones only. It's okay to flatter masculinity with imitation, but rarely okay for men to imitate or sound like women. (Such upper-class exceptions as the female-impersonating shows put on by the Hasty Pudding Club at Harvard, or the very rich men of Bohemian Grove, seem to indicate that even ridicule of women requires security. It's much less likely to happen at the working-class level of bowling clubs and bars.)

As a result, men as a group pay the high price of loss of variety in their 54 speech, and an impaired ability to express diverse thoughts and emotions. The higher proportion of masculine monotones is also a penalty to the public ear.

Women are also allowed more variety of facial expression and gestures. 55 Not only may we use some cross-sex forms of nonverbal expression without social punishment, but physical expressiveness itself may be viewed as "feminine." Women can be vivacious. Men must be rocklike. Certainly, some emotive and expressive men are being imprisoned by that belief.

Of course, women's greater range of expression is also used to ridicule   56
females as emotionally unstable. That sad point is made by Nancy Henley in
Body Politics: Power, Sex, and Nonverbal Communication. "Women's facial expressivity," she explains, "has been allowed a wider range than men's, encompassing within the sex stereotype not only pleasant expressions, but negative
ones like crying." The ability to bring pain and unhappiness to a listener's
attention is important, but not always welcome.

Nonetheless, this wider range may also allow us to recognize more phys-   57
ical expression when we see it. Henley refers to a study showing that women
of all groups and black men usually do better than white men at identifying
nonverbal emotional clues. On the other hand, this greater sensitivity may
also be a survival skill of the less powerful.

As a group, women probably *do* need to focus and use emotional expres-   58
siveness better. But men are missing something, too. An end to any limitation
on full human abilities can be their long-term reward.

You can't change vocal chords (theirs or ours), but there are many remedial acts   59
and transforming tactics to try.

Tape-recording women together, then recording the same people in a   60
group with men, can let us know whether we're sending out geisha-like tonal
clues. Just listening to the irrefutable evidence of your own voice can be a
great revelation: many women may be using their cultural license to a wide
variety of intonations, but some are overcompensating for supposed emo-
tionalism by adopting a "reasonable" monotone. Men may also change under
pressure of such taped evidence as their dullness when talking with men, for
instance, versus their greater expressivity when talking to children.

To modify or expand what you hear is very possible. Many actors, female   61
and male, are living testimonials to how much and how quickly, with effort
and exercise, a vocal range can change.

Most important, remember that there is nothing *wrong* with voices that   62
"sound female," and no subject or emotion they cannot convey. That may be
difficult, especially if you are the only token or one of a few in a mostly male
group. (Women in law or business school report shock at hearing the sound
of their own voices, compared with so many males; a major obstacle to their
reciting in class.) But a head-turning response to the rare female voice in the
executive suite or assembly line is also a tribute to your importance as a
pioneer.

Facial and other nonverbal expressions can be understood much better,   63
individually or in groups, with the advent of home video recorders. (Although
the equipment is expensive, there are millions who also have access to it at
work, school, or community groups.) Probably, many men would also benefit
from a weekly session of charades; and many women should learn to trust in
public their lower vocal range, plus the body language they may now use only
when relaxed with other women.

If this whole area of sound and nonverbal communication seems minor   64
or obscure—to you or to others—just remind them and yourself of a lifetime

of overhearing friends and family on the phone. Can't you usually guess, without being told, whether a woman is talking to a man (or vice versa)? What does that difference say about power, the masks we adopt, and the social barriers to expression?

A feminist assault on the politics of talking—and listening—is a radical act. 65 It's a way of changing a cultural vessel in which both instant, personal change and long-term, anthropological transformation are carried.

Unlike the written word, or any other communication that can be di- 66 vorced from our presence, talking and listening don't allow us to hide behind a neutral page, image, sound, or even a genderless name. Its form demands that we be accepted and understood as our whole selves.

That's precisely what makes the change so difficult. And what makes its 67 importance so great.

MYTH

MURIEL RUKEYSER

Muriel Rukeyser's first book of poetry, *Theory of Flight*, was published in 1935, and from then until her death in 1980 she was a prolific poet, translator, biographer, and activist for social justice. Her early volumes of poetry, including *Beast in View* (1944) and *The Green Wave* (1948) dealt with the horrors of World War II, while her poetry of the 1950s, 1960s and 1970s responded to the violence of war in Korea and Vietnam. In the following poem she explores injustice of a different kind, turning the tables on history to make her point.

Long afterward, Oedipus, old and blinded, walked the
roads.   He smelled a familiar smell.   It was
the Sphinx.   Oedipus said, "I want to ask one question.
Why didn't I recognize my mother?"   "You gave the
wrong answer," said the Sphinx.   "But that was what
made everything possible," said Oedipus.   "No," she said.
"When I asked, What walks on four legs in the morning,
two at noon, and three in the evening, you answered,
Man.   You didn't say anything about woman."
"When you say Man," said Oedipus, "you include women
too. Everyone knows that."   She said, "That's what
you think."

REAL MEN DON'T: ANTI-MALE BIAS IN ENGLISH

◑

E U G E N E   R .   A U G U S T

A professor of English and a researcher in men's studies, Eugene August is author of *Men's Studies: A Selected
and Annotated Interdisciplinary Bibliography* (1985). His
earlier works include a book on racial tensions in
America and a study of the eighteenth-century philosopher and political economist John Stuart Mill. In the
following essay, August reverses the common assumption that sexism in language refers only to women and
shows how men too can be limited by what he sees as
an "anti-male bias" in language today.

Despite numerous studies of sex bias in language during the past fifteen   1
years, only rarely has anti-male bias been examined. In part, this neglect
occurs because many of these studies have been based upon assumptions
which are questionable at best and which at worst exhibit their own form of
sex bias. Whether explicitly or implicitly, many of these studies reduce human
history to a tale of male oppressors and female victims or rebels. In this view
of things, all societies become *patriarchal societies*, a familiar term used to
suggest that for centuries males have conspired to exploit and demean females.
Accordingly, it is alleged in many of these studies that men control language
and that they use it to define women and women's roles as inferior.

Despite the popularity of such a view, it has received scant support from   2
leading social scientists, including one of the giants of modern anthropology,
Margaret Mead. Anticipating current ideology, Mead in *Male and Female*
firmly rejected the notion of a "male conspiracy to keep women in their
place," arguing instead that

> the historical trend that listed women among the abused minorities . . .
> lingers on to obscure the issue and gives apparent point to the contention
> that this is a man-made world in which women have always been abused and
> must always fight for their rights.
>
> It takes considerable effort on the part of both men and women to
> reorient ourselves to thinking—when we think basically—that this is a world
> not made by men alone, in which women are unwilling and helpless dupes
> and fools or else powerful schemers hiding their power under their ruffled

petticoats, but a world made of mankind for human beings of both sexes. (298, 299–300)

The model described by Mead and other social scientists shows a world in which women and men have lived together throughout history in a symbiotic relationship, often mutually agreeing upon the definition of gender roles and the distribution of various powers and duties. 3

More importantly for the subject of bias in speech and writing, women— as well as men—have shaped language. As Walter J. Ong reminds us, 4

> Women talk and think as much as men do, and with few exceptions we all . . . learn to talk and think in the first instance largely from women, usually and predominantly our mothers. Our first tongue is called our "mother tongue" in English and in many other languages. . . . There are no father tongues. . . . (36)

Feminists like Dorothy Dinnerstein agree: "There seems no reason to doubt that the baby-tending sex contributed at least equally with the history-making one to the most fundamental of all human inventions: language" (22). Because gender roles and language are shaped by society in general—that is, by both men and women—anti-male bias in language is as possible as anti-female bias. 5

To say this, however, is emphatically not to blame women alone, or even primarily, for anti-male usage. If guilt must be assigned, it would have to be placed upon sexist people, both male and female, who use language to ma- nipulate gender role behavior and to create negative social attitudes towards males. But often it is difficult to point a finger of blame: except where prej- udiced gender stereotypes are deliberately fostered, most people evidently use sex-biased terminology without clearly understanding its import. In the long run, it is wiser to concentrate not on fixing blame, but on heightening public awareness of anti-male language and on discouraging its use. In par- ticular, teachers and writers need to become aware of and to question language which denigrates or stereotypes males. 6

In modern English, three kinds of anti-male usage are evident: first, gender-exclusive language which omits males from certain kinds of consid- eration; second, gender-restrictive language which attempts to restrict males to an accepted gender role, some aspects of which may be outmoded, bur- densome, or destructive; and third, negative stereotypes of males which are insulting, dehumanizing, and potentially dangerous. 7

Although gender-exclusive language which excludes females has often been studied, few students of language have noted usage which excludes males. Those academics, for example, who have protested *alumnus* and *alumni* as gender-exclusive terms to describe a university's male and female graduates have failed to notice that, by the same logic, *alma mater* (nourishing mother) is an equally gender-exclusive term to describe the university itself. Those who have protested *man* and *mankind* as generic terms have not begun to 8 question *mammal* as a term of biological classification, but by categorizing animals according to the female's ability to suckle the young through her mammary glands, *mammal* clearly omits the male of the species. Consequently, it is as suspect as generic *man*.

In general, gender-exclusive usage in English excludes males as parents and as victims. Until recently, the equating of *mother* with *parent* in the social sciences was notorious: a major sociological study published in 1958 with the title *The Changing American Parent* was based upon interviews with 582 mothers and no fathers (Roman and Haddad 87). Although no longer prevalent in the social sciences, the interchangeability of *mother* and *parent* is still common, except for *noncustodial parent* which is almost always a synonym for *father*. A recent ad for *Parents* magazine begins: "To be the best mother you can be, you want practical, reliable answers to the questions a mother must face." Despite the large number of men now seen pushing shopping carts, advertisers still insist that "Choosy mothers choose Jif" and "My Mom's a Butternut Mom." Frequently, children are regarded as belonging solely to the mother, as in phrases like *women and their children*. The idea of the mother as primary parent can be glimpsed in such expressions as *mother tongue, mother wit, mother lode, mother of invention*, and *mothering* as a synonym for *parenting*. 9

The male as victim is ignored in such familiar expressions as *innocent women and children*. In June 1985, when President Reagan rejected a bombing strike to counter terrorist activities, newspapers reported that the decision had been made to prevent "the deaths of many innocent women and children in strife-torn Lebanon" (Glass). Presumably strife-torn Lebanon contained no innocent men. Likewise, *rape victim* means females only, an assumption made explicit in the opening sentences of this newspaper article on rape: "Crime knows no gender. Yet, there is one offense that only women are prey to: rape" (Mougey). The thousands of males raped annually, in addition to the sexual assaults regularly inflicted upon males in prison, are here entirely overlooked. (That these males have been victimized mostly by other males does not disqualify them as victims of sexual violence, as some people assume.) Similarly, the term *wife and child abuse* conceals the existence of an estimated 282,000 husbands who are battered annually (O'Reilly et al. 23). According to many expressions in English, males are not parents and they are never victimized. 10

Unlike gender-exclusive language, gender-restrictive language is usually applied to males only, often to keep them within the confines of a socially prescribed gender role. When considering gender-restrictive language, one must keep in mind that—as Ruth E. Hartley has pointed out—the masculine gender role is enforced earlier and more harshly than the feminine role is (235). In addition, because the boy is often raised primarily by females in the virtual absence of close adult males, his grasp of what is required of him to *be a man* is often unsure. Likewise, prescriptions for male behavior are usually 11 given in the negative, leading to the "Real Men Don't" syndrome, a process which further confuses the boy. Such circumstances leave many males extremely vulnerable to language which questions their sense of masculinity.

Furthermore, during the past twenty years an increasing number of men and women have been arguing that aspects of our society's masculine gender role are emotionally constrictive, unnecessarily stressful, and potentially lethal. Rejecting "the myth of masculine privilege," psychologist Herb Goldberg reports in *The Hazards of Being Male* that "every critical statistic in the area of [early death], disease, suicide, crime, accidents, childhood emotional disorders, alcoholism, and drug addiction shows a disproportionately higher male rate" (5). But changes in the masculine role are so disturbing to so many people that the male who attempts to break out of familiar gender patterns often finds himself facing hostile opposition which can be readily and powerfully expressed in a formidable array of sex-biased terms. 12

To see how the process works, let us begin early in the male life cycle. A boy quickly learns that, while it is usually acceptable for girls to be *tomboys*, God forbid that he should be a *sissy*. In *Sexual Signatures: On Being a Man or a Woman* John Money and Patricia Tucker note: 13

> The current feminine stereotype in our culture is flexible enough to let a girl behave "boyishly" if she wants to without bringing her femininity into question, but any boy who exhibits "girlish" behavior is promptly suspected of being queer. There isn't even a word corresponding to "tomboy" to describe such a boy. "Sissy" perhaps comes closest, or "artistic" and "sensitive," but unlike "tomboy," such terms are burdened with unfavorable connotations. (72)

Lacking a favorable or even neutral term to describe the boy who is quiet, gentle, and emotional, the English language has long had a rich vocabulary to insult and ridicule such boys—*mama's boy, mollycoddle, milksop, muff, twit, softy, creampuff, pantywaist, weenie, Miss Nancy*, and so on. Although sometimes used playfully, the current popular *wimp* can be used to insult males from childhood right into adulthood.

Discussion of words like *sissy* as insults has been often one-sided: most commentators are content to argue that the female, not the male, is being insulted by such usage. "The implicit sexism" in such terms, writes one commentator, "disparages the woman, not the man" (Sorrels 87). Although the female is being slurred indirectly by these terms, a moment's reflection will show that the primary force of the insult is being directed against the male, specifically the male who cannot differentiate himself from the feminine. Ong argues in *Fighting for Life* that most societies place heavy pressure on males to differentiate themselves from females because the prevailing environment of human society is feminine (70–71). In English-speaking societies, terms like *sissy* and *weak sister*, which have been used by both females 14 and males, are usually perceived not as insults to females but as ridicule of males who have allegedly failed to differentiate themselves from the feminine.

Being *all boy* carries penalties, however: for one thing, it means being less   15 lovable. As the nursery rhyme tells children, little girls are made of "sugar and spice and all that's nice," while little boys are made of "frogs and snails and puppy-dogs' tails." Or, as an American version of the rhyme puts it:

> Girls are dandy,
> Made of candy—
> That's what little girls are made of.
> Boys are rotten,
> Made of cotton—
> That's what little boys are made of.
>
> *(Baring-Gould* 176n116)

When not enjoined to *be all boy*, our young lad will be urged to *be a big boy*,   16 *be a brave soldier*, and (the ultimate appeal) *be a man*. These expressions almost invariably mean that the boy is about to suffer something painful or humiliating. The variant—*take it like a man*—provides the clue. As Paul Theroux defines it, *be a man* means: "Be stupid, be unfeeling, obedient and soldierly, and stop thinking."

Following our boy further into the life cycle, we discover that in school   17 he will find himself in a cruel bind: girls his age will be biologically and socially more mature than he is, at least until around age eighteen. Until then, any ineptness in his social role will be castigated by a host of terms which are reserved almost entirely for males. "For all practical purposes," John Gordon remarks, "the word 'turkey' (or whatever the equivalent is now) can be translated as 'a boy spurned by influential girls' " (141). The equivalents of *turkey* are many: *jerk, nerd, clod, klutz, schmuck, dummy, goon, dork, square, dweeb, jackass, meathead, geek, zero, reject, goofball, drip*, and numerous others, including many obscene terms. Recently, a Michigan high school decided to do away with a scheduled "Nerd Day" after a fourteen-year-old male student, who apparently had been so harassed as a nerd by other students, committed suicide ("'Nerd' day"). In this case, the ability of language to devastate the emotionally vulnerable young male is powerfully and pathetically dramatized.

As our boy grows, he faces threats and taunts if he does not take risks or   18 endure pain to prove his manhood. *Coward*, for example, is a word applied almost exclusively to males in our society, as are its numerous variants— *chicken, chickenshit, yellow, yellow-bellied, lily-livered, weak-kneed, spineless, squirrelly, fraidy cat, gutless wonder, weakling, butterfly, jellyfish*, and so on. If our young man walks away from a stupid quarrel or prefers to settle differences more rationally than with a swift jab to the jaw, the English language is richly supplied with these and other expressions to call his masculinity into question.

Chief among the other expressions that question masculinity is a lengthy 19
list of homophobic terms such as *queer, pansy, fag, faggot, queen, queeny, pervert, bugger, deviant, fairy, tinkerbell, puss, priss, flamer, feller, sweet, precious, fruit, sodomite,* and numerous others, many obscene. For many people, *gay* is an all-purpose word of ridicule and condemnation. Once again, although homosexuals are being insulted by these terms, the primary target is more often the heterosexual male who fails or refuses to live up to someone else's idea of masculinity. In "Homophobia Among Men" Gregory Lehne explains, "Homophobia is used as a technique of social control . . . to enforce the norms of male sex-role behavior. . . . [H]omosexuality is not the real threat, the real threat is change in the male sex-role" (77).

Nowhere is this threat more apparent than in challenges to our society's 20
male-only military obligation. When a young man and a young woman reach the age of eighteen, both may register to vote; only the young man is required by law to register for military service. For the next decade at least, he must stand ready to be called into military service and even into combat duty in wars, "police actions," "peace-keeping missions," and "rescue missions," often initiated by legally dubious means. Should he resist this obligation, he may be called a *draft dodger, deserter, peacenik, traitor, shirker, slacker, malingerer,* and similar terms. Should he declare himself a conscientious objector, he may be labeled a *conchy* or any of the variants of *coward.*

In his relationships with women, he will find that the age of equality has 21
not yet arrived. Usually, he will be expected to take the initiative, do the driving, pick up the tab, and in general show a deferential respect for women that is a left-over from the chivalric code. Should he behave in an *ungentle-manly* fashion, a host of words—which are applied almost always to males alone—can be used to tell him so: *louse, rat, creep, sleaze, scum, stain, worm, fink, heel, stinker, animal, savage, bounder, cad, wolf, gigolo, womanizer, Don Juan, pig, rotter, boor,* and so on.

In sexual matters he will usually be expected to take the initiative and to 22
perform. If he does not, he will be labeled *impotent.* This word, writes Goldberg, "is clearly sexist because it implies a standard of acceptable masculine sexual performance that makes a man abnormal if he can't live up to it" (*New Male* 248). Metaphorically, *impotent* can be used to demean any male whose efforts in any area are deemed unacceptable. Even if our young man succeeds at his sexual performance, the sex manuals are ready to warn him that if he reaches orgasm before a specified time he is guilty of *premature ejaculation.*

When our young man marries, he will be required by law and social 23
custom to support his wife and children. Should he not succeed as breadwinner or should he relax in his efforts, the language offers numerous terms to revile him: *loser, deadbeat, bum, freeloader, leech, parasite, goldbrick, sponge, mooch, ne'er-do-well, good for nothing,* and so on. If women in our society have been

regarded as sex objects, men have been regarded as success objects, that is, judged by their ability to provide a standard of living. The title of a recent book—*How to Marry a Winner*—reveals immediately that the intended audience is female (Collier).

When he becomes a father, our young man will discover that he is a second-class parent, as the traditional interchangeability of *mother* and *parent* indicates. The law has been particularly obtuse in recognizing fathers as parents, as evidenced by the awarding of child custody to mothers in ninety percent of divorce cases. In 1975 a father's petition for custody of his four-year-old son was denied because, as the family court judge said, "Fathers don't make good mothers" (qtd. in Levine 21). The judge apparently never considered whether *fathers* make good *parents*.

And so it goes throughout our young man's life: if he deviates from society's gender role norm, he will be penalized and he will hear about it.

The final form of anti-male bias to be considered here is negative stereotyping. Sometimes this stereotyping is indirectly embedded in the language, sometimes it resides in people's assumptions about males and shapes their response to seemingly neutral words, and sometimes it is overtly created for political reasons. It is one thing to say that some aspects of the traditional masculine gender role are limiting and hurtful; it is quite another to gratuitously suspect males in general of being criminal and evil or to denounce them in wholesale fashion as oppressors, exploiters, and rapists. In *The New Male* Goldberg writes, "Men may very well be the last remaining subgroup in our society that can be blatantly, negatively and vilely stereotyped with little objection or resistance" (103). As our language demonstrates, such sexist stereotyping, whether unintentional or deliberate, is not only familiar but fashionable.

In English, crime and evil are usually attributed to the male. As an experiment I have compiled lists of nouns which I read to my composition students, asking them to check whether the words suggest "primarily females," "primarily males," or "could be either." Nearly all the words for lawbreakers suggest males rather than females to most students. These words include *murderer, swindler, crook, criminal, burglar, thief, gangster, mobster, hood, hitman, killer, pickpocket, mugger,* and *terrorist*. Accounting for this phenomenon is not always easy. *Hitman* may obviously suggest "primarily males," and the *-er* in *murderer* may do the same, especially if it reminds students of the word's feminine form, *murderess*. Likewise, students may be aware that most murders are committed by males. Other words—like *criminal* and *thief*—are more clearly gender-neutral in form, and it is less clear why they should be so closely linked with "primarily males." Although the dynamics of the association may be unclear, English usage somehow conveys a subtle suggestion that males are to be regarded as guilty in matters of law-breaking.

This hint of male guilt extends to a term like *suspect*. When the person's gender is unknown, the suspect is usually presumed to be a male. For example,

24

25

26

27

28

137

even before a definite suspect had been identified, the perpetrator of the 1980–1981 Atlanta child murders was popularly known as *The Man*. When a male and female are suspected of a crime, the male is usually presumed the guilty party. In a recent murder case, when two suspects—Debra Brown and Alton Coleman—were apprehended, police discovered *Brown's* fingerprint in a victim's car and interpreted this as evidence of *Coleman's* guilt. As the Associated Press reported:

> Authorities say for the first time they have evidence linking Alton Coleman with the death of an Indianapolis man.
>
> A fingerprint found in the car of Eugene Scott has been identified as that of Debra Brown, Coleman's traveling companion . . ." ("Police").

Nowhere does the article suggest that Brown's fingerprint found in the victim's car linked Brown with the death: the male suspect was presumed the guilty party, while the female was only a "traveling companion." Even after Brown had been convicted of two murders, the Associated Press was still describing her as "the accused accomplice of convicted killer Alton Coleman" ("Indiana").

In some cases, this presumption of male guilt extends to crimes in which   29
males are not the principal offenders. As noted earlier, a term like *wife and child abuse* ignores battered husbands, but it does more: it suggests that males alone abuse children. In reality most child abuse is committed by mothers (Straus, Gelles, Steinmetz 71). Despite this fact, a 1978 study of child abuse bears the title *Sins of the Fathers* (Inglis).

The term *rape* creates special problems. While the majority of rapes are   30
committed by males and the number of female rape victims outdistances the number of male rape victims, it is widely assumed—as evidenced by the newspaper article cited above—that rape is a crime committed only by males in which only females are victims. Consequently, the word *rape* is often used as a brush to tar all males. In *Against Our Will* Susan Brownmiller writes: "From prehistoric times to the present, I believe, rape . . . is nothing more or less than a conscious process of intimidation by which *all men* keep *all women* in a state of fear" (15; italics in original). Making the point explicitly, Marilyn French states, "All men are rapists and that's all they are" (qtd. in Jennes 33). Given this kind of smear tactic, *rape* can be used metaphorically to indict males alone and to exonerate females, as in this sentence: "The rape of nature—and the ecological disaster it presages—is part and parcel of a dominating masculinity gone out of control" (Hoch 137). The statement neatly blames males alone even when the damage to the environment has been caused in part by females like Anne Gorsuch Burford and Rita Lavelle.

Not only crimes but vices of all sorts have been typically attributed to   31
males. As Muriel R. Schulz points out, "The synonyms for *inebriate* . . . seem to be coded primarily 'male': for example, *boozer, drunkard, tippler, toper, swiller, tosspot, guzzler, barfly, drunk, lush, boozehound, souse, tank, stew, rummy*, and

bum" (126). Likewise, someone may be *drunk as a lord* but never *drunk as a lady*.

Sex bias or sexism itself is widely held to be a male-only fault. When 32 *sexism* is defined as "contempt for women"—as if there were no such thing as contempt for men—the definition of *sexism* is itself sexist (Bardwick 34).

Part of the reason for this masculinization of evil may be that in the 33 Western world the source of evil has long been depicted in male terms. In the Bible the Evil One is consistently referred to as *he*, whether the reference is to the serpent in the Garden of Eden, Satan as Adversary in Job, Lucifer and Beelzebub in the gospels, Jesus' tempter in the desert, or the dragon in Revelations. *Beelzebub*, incidentally, is often translated as *lord of the flies*, a term designating the demon as masculine. So masculine is the word *devil* that the female prefix is needed, as in *she-devil*, to make a feminine noun of it. The masculinization of evil is so unconsciously accepted that writers often attest to it even while attempting to deny it, as in this passage:

> From the very beginning, the Judeo-Christian tradition has linked women and evil. When second-century theologians struggled to explain the Devil's origins, they surmised that Satan and his various devils had once been angels. (Gerzon 224)

If the Judeo-Christian tradition has linked women and evil so closely, why is the writer using the masculine pronoun *his* to refer to Satan, the source of evil according to that tradition? Critics of sex-bias in religious language seldom notice or mention its masculinization of evil: of those objecting to *God the Father* as sexist, no one—to my knowledge—has suggested that designating Satan as the *Father of Lies* is equally sexist. Few theologians talk about Satan and her legions.

The tendency to blame nearly everything on men has climaxed in recent 34 times with the popularity of such terms as *patriarchy*, *patriarchal society*, and *male-dominated society*. More political than descriptive, these terms are rapidly becoming meaningless, used as all-purpose smear words to conjure up images of male oppressors and female victims. They are a linguistic sleight of hand which obscures the point that, as Mead has observed (299–300), societies are largely created by both sexes for both sexes. By using a swift reference to *patriarchal structures* or *patriarchal attitudes*, a writer can absolve females of all blame for society's flaws while fixing the onus solely on males. The give-away of this ploy can be detected when *patriarchy* and its related terms are never used in a positive or neutral context, but are always used to assign blame to males alone.

Wholesale denunciations of males as oppressors, exploiters, rapists, Na- 35 zis, and slave-drivers have become all too familiar during the past fifteen years. Too often the academic community, rather than opposing this sexism, has been encouraging it. All too many scholars and teachers have hopped the male-bashing bandwagon to disseminate what John Gordon calls "the myth of the monstrous male." With increasing frequency, this academically fashionable sexism can also be heard echoing from our students. "A white upper-middle-class straight male should seriously consider another college," declares a midwestern college student in *The New York Times Selective Guide to Colleges.* "You [the white male] are the bane of the world. . . . Ten generations of social ills can and will be strapped upon your shoulders" (qtd. in Fiske 12). It would be comforting to dismiss this student's compound of misinformation, sexism, racism, and self-righteousness as an extreme example, but similar yahooisms go unchallenged almost everywhere in modern academia.

Surely it is time for men and women of good will to reject and protest such bigotry. For teachers and writers, the first task is to recognize and condemn forms of anti-male bias in language, whether they are used to exclude males from equal consideration with females, to reinforce restrictive aspects of the masculine gender role, or to stereotype males callously. For whether males are told that *fathers don't make good mothers,* that *real men don't cry,* or that *all men are rapists,* the results are potentially dangerous: like any other group, males can be subtly shaped into what society keeps telling them they are. In *Why Men Are the Way They Are* Warren Farrell puts the matter succinctly: "The more we make men the enemy, the more they will have to behave like the enemy" (357). 36

Works Cited

Bardwick, Judith. *In Transition: How Feminism, Sexual Liberation, and the Search for Self-Fulfillment Have Altered Our Lives.* NY: Holt, 1979.

Baring-Gould, William S., and Ceil Baring-Gould. *The Annotated Mother Goose Nursery Rhymes Old and New, Arranged and Explained.* NY: Clarkson N. Potter, 1962.

Brownmiller, Susan. *Against Our Will: Men, Women and Rape.* NY: Simon, 1975.

Collier, Phyllis K. *How to Marry a Winner.* Englewood Cliffs, NJ: Prentice, 1982.

Dinnerstein, Dorothy. *The Mermaid and the Minotaur: Sexual Arrangements and Human Malaise.* NY: Harper, 1976.

Farrell, Warren. *Why Men Are the Way They Are: The Male-Female Dynamic.* NY: McGraw-Hill, 1986.

Fiske, Edward B. *The New York Times Selective Guide to Colleges.* NY: Times Books, 1982.

Gerzon, Mark. *A Choice of Heroes: The Changing Faces of American Manhood.* Boston: Houghton, 1982.

Glass, Andrew J. "President wants to unleash military power, but cannot." *Dayton Daily News* 18 June 1985: 1.

Goldberg, Herb. *The Hazards of Being Male: Surviving the Myth of Masculine Privilege.* 1976. NY: NAL, 1977.

———. *The New Male: From Self-Destruction to Self-Care.* 1979. NY: NAL, 1980.

Gordon, John. *The Myth of the Monstrous Male, and Other Feminist Fables.* NY: Playboy P, 1982.

Hartley, Ruth E. "Sex-Role Pressures and the Socialization of the Male Child." *The Forty-Nine Percent Majority: The Male Sex Role.* Ed. Deborah S. David and Robert Brannon. Reading, MA: Addison-Wesley, 1976. 235–44.

Hoch, Paul. *White Hero, Black Beast: Racism, Sexism and the Mask of Masculinity*. London: Pluto P, 1979.

"Indiana jury finds Brown guilty of murder, molesting." *Dayton Daily News* 18 May 1986: 7A.

Inglis, Ruth. *Sins of the Fathers: A Study of the Physical and Emotional Abuse of Children*. NY: St. Martin's, 1978.

Jennes, Gail. "All Men Are Rapists." *People* 20 Feb. 1978: 33–34.

Lehne, Gregory. "Homophobia Among Men." *The Forty-Nine Percent Majority: The Male Sex Role*. Ed. Deborah S. David and Robert Brannon. Reading, MA: Addison-Wesley, 1976. 66–88.

Levine, James A. *Who Will Raise the Children? New Options for Fathers (and Mothers)*. Philadelphia: Lippincott, 1976.

Mead, Margaret. *Male and Female: A Study of the Sexes in a Changing World*. NY: Morrow, 1949, 1967.

Money, John, and Patricia Tucker. *Sexual Signatures: On Being a Man or a Woman*. Boston: Little, 1975.

Mougey, Kate. "An act of confiscation: Rape." *Kettering-Oakwood* [OH] *Times* 4 Feb. 1981: 1b.

"'Nerd' day gets a boot after suicide." *Dayton Daily News* 24 Jan. 1986: 38.

Ong, Walter J. *Fighting for Life: Contest, Sexuality, and Consciousness*. Ithaca, NY: Cornell UP, 1981.

O'Reilly, Jane, et al. "Wife-Beating: The Silent Crime." *Time* 5 Sept. 1983: 23–4, 26.

"Police: Print links Coleman, death." *Dayton Daily News* 31 Aug. 1984: 26.

Roman, Mel, and William Haddad. *The Disposable Parent: The Case for Joint Custody*. 1978. NY: Penguin, 1979.

Schulz, Muriel R. "Is the English Language Anybody's Enemy?" *Speaking of Words: A Language Reader*. Ed. James MacKillop and Donna Woolfolk Cross. 3rd ed. NY: Holt, 1986. 125–27.

Sorrels, Bobbye D. *The Nonsexist Communicator: Solving the Problems of Gender and Awkwardness in Modern English*. Englewood Cliffs, NJ: Prentice, 1983.

Straus, Murray A., Richard J. Gelles, and Suzanne K. Steinmetz. *Behind Closed Doors: Violence in the American Family*. 1980. Garden City, NY: Doubleday, 1981.

Theroux, Paul. "The Male Myth." *New York Times Magazine* 27 Nov. 1983: 116.

MAKING CONNECTIONS

1. Speaking can be seen as a type of behavior. Demonstrate how behavioral qualities associated with "masculinity" and "femininity" discussed in Part I, "Defining Gender," are reflected in expectations and prejudices about how women and men use language. Some essays in Chapter 4 show how such expectations limit women's styles of talking. How might they also limit men's access to and use of language?

2. How accurate are Kramarae's findings in her study of cartoon captions? In your own experience, does the folklore about "mommy talk" still exist? If so, where do we find it, and how influential do you think it is in our perception of women as speakers? Is there such a thing as "daddy talk" as well? Try rewriting a brief article or piece of prose in "wishy-washy mommy talk." What happens to the subject matter of the piece?

3. Do you perceive any sex-related differences in language use today? Are there "appropriate" and "inappropriate" ways for women and men to express themselves? Make a list of as many slang expressions as you can think of. Does the list include expressions we only expect to hear from men or women? Is swearing still gendered? Do you find different adjectives used to describe men's and women's looks or behavior? Compare your findings with those of your classmates.

4. Tannen suggests that men are frequently socialized to see conversation as a kind of conflict or competition, while women learn to see conversation as rapport. Explore Tannen's view in light of your own experience, as well as in your perception of broader spheres of conversation. Do you see instances of conversation-as-conflict in the wider world, such as in business, law, or politics? Are there any instances where society is moving toward what Gloria Steinem calls a "more cooperative, less combative style of talking" in the professional or public sphere? How accurate is it to see these as "gendered" styles of communication?

5. Tannen sees communication differences between men and women as a problem of "cross cultural understanding." Agree or disagree with this analogy. How can men and women be seen as belonging to different "cultures"? Do any other essays in this chapter or previous chapters suggest or shed light on this division as well? Could a heightened sensitivity to male/female conversation differences help us in becoming more perceptive to the communication styles of other cultures or races? If so, how? If not, where does the comparison break down?

6. Take a close look at Piercy's poem, "You Don't Understand Me." Is the speaker male or female? At what point can you tell? What images in the

poem seem to be gender-specific images, and how does Piercy use them to express her point? You might try writing your own poem about misunderstanding. It could be between a man and a woman, between someone old and someone young, or between two people of different cultures or economic groups. Try to use imagery to convey the feelings and frustrations of miscommunication.

7. Test Steinem's points about the patterns of men and women talking in groups. Tape record one or a number of group conversations (a class discussion, gathering of friends, or club meeting). Then analyze the patterns you find according to Steinem's suggestions. Do you perceive indications of gender in the speech patterns you've recorded, or do the speakers seem to listen and respond equally? Do different situations create different results? Discuss your findings.

8. Explain Steinem's distinction between "playing the game as it exists" and "changing the rules" of conversation. Which do you feel is more important—to try matching one's skills to current standards or to revise those standards when they seem unfair or out of balance? What are the obstacles to either approach? How might the same division between "playing the game" and "changing the rules" apply to other areas of behavior and experience, such as work, school, relationships, or even personal appearance?

9. Does using the masculine pronoun "he" to represent any person constitute a form of sexism in language? What assumptions does it reflect and/or perpetuate? You might look for a passage of writing which uses the "neutral" masculine pronoun and switch it to the feminine. What happens to the meaning of the passage? Discuss your results.

10. What are the advantages and disadvantages in changing the titles of professions to make them gender-neutral—for instance, from "mailman" to "postal carrier," "stewardess" to "flight attendant," "chairman" to "chairperson" or "chair"? Write an argument for or against such changes in our vocabularies. Can we really change attitudes just by changing words?

11. Using August's essay as a guide, make a list comparing how men and women are limited by sexisms in language. Then select one area—such as the words used to describe parenthood, or terms of insult, or the vocabulary of sexuality—and write an essay which supports or challenges August's claim that men are as oppressed by sex bias in language as women. Is August's concept of oppression the same as Marilyn Frye's (Chapter 2)? What are your own definitions of the terms "oppression," "sexism" and "bias" as related to language use? Clarify your terms and, like August, try to use numerous examples to support your argument.

12. Taken together, the essays in this chapter seem to suggest that there exist contradictory stereotypes of men and women as speakers. How can women be seen as talkative ("yakkers") despite studies that show women speak far less often in public? How can the image of men as inexpressive ("strong and silent") coexist with their influence on group discussion and their public image as authoritative speakers? Write an essay that tries to explain how these contradictory images might coexist.

5
WRITING:
WOMEN FINDING VOICES

C O N T E X T S

> In talking about "English literature," and more espe-
> cially in arranging courses of study in literature, there
> is usually a silent assumption that we know, at least
> roughly speaking, who the important writers are and
> what texts are representative of major developments in
> literary history. These writers and texts constitute what
> is often referred to as "the canon"—that is, the essen-
> tial core of an entity which we call "English literature."

This quote from Ruth Sherry's book, *Studying Women's Writing* (1988),
describes the unspoken belief that English literature is somehow a stable
entity. We assume that writers and texts are judged to be "the best" or the
most "representative" by how well they survive the test of time or by some
universal, permanent criterion of excellence. But, in fact, the worth of individual texts and writers has been the subject of debate and dramatic change
throughout the centuries, and standards of literary merit have never been
obvious. As Sherry points out, even the reputation of Shakespeare, today
considered our "greatest writer," was in question during certain eras, and
many writers who were esteemed in the past are now unknown.

Who makes the decisions about which writers are important, which texts
are the "best," which viewpoints will survive? Sherry describes how scholars

re-examining the canon—particularly those interested in the literary voices of minorities and women—have argued that the shape of the canon is determined by the values of whichever group is most powerful in society. In the case of English literature, Sherry states, that group has been white, middle-to-upper class, and male. The result is that works that represent the opinions and experiences of this group will make up the lion's share of the canon and, according to these scholars, the voices of less powerful groups like ethnic minorities, the lower classes, and women will be underrepresented. This chapter looks at how women are struggling to re-assert their creative value and overcome the social, economic, and historic obstacles which have excluded women writers from the mainstream of literature.

Dale Spender opens this chapter with an examination of how prejudices about women as speakers influence their reception as writers. In "Language Studies: From the Spoken to the Written Word" she claims that women's writing is frequently denied a fair hearing, not only by male members of the literary establishment, but sometimes by women themselves who have internalized stereotypes about the low value of women's expression. Carolyn Kizer approaches this same topic poetically in our next selection. A segment of her long poem "Pro Femina" surveys women's literary history with a critical eye to both the failures and the ongoing struggle of women seeking their place in the canon.

Even today, discrimination against women as voices in culture continues. In her insightful and humorous narratives, excerpted from "We Are the Crazy Lady and Other Feisty Feminist Fables," fiction writer Cynthia Ozick describes some of the techniques and tactics of discrimination that still keep women writers "in their place." Her stories reveal much about the ways society renders some of its members invisible and can apply equally well to the experience of any group that is silenced in our culture.

What of women whose identities fall into more than one devalued group? In "Lesbian and Writer: Making the Real Visible," Jane Rule writes about the struggle to be heard as a writer without being categorized solely by her sexual preference. Next, Alice Walker focuses on the situation of African-American women who have long fought to keep their creative heritage alive in the face of enormous odds: the double prejudice against both race and sex. Her famous essay, "In Search of Our Mothers' Gardens," celebrates the spirit with which black women continue to find an identity and a voice to enrich and diversify our culture.

Throughout this chapter you will hear many reflections on the nature and meaning of writing. While the selections focus mainly on literary writing, they raise issues pertinent to all uses of the written word—issues about writing and power, writing and identity, the writer's freedom, the relationship between writing and reality, even writing as a kind of work subject to the same demands and discriminations as any other form of paid labor. Our assessment of the value of a given piece of writing is not just aesthetic, but has very real consequences for which voices carry weight in our culture and whose stories will be heard.

LANGUAGE STUDIES
From the Spoken to the Written Word

DALE SPENDER

Much of Dale Spender's work has been to reintroduce the voices of women writers and thinkers who have been ignored by our culture. Among her many books on literature, language, and culture are *Man Made Language* (1980) and *Mothers of the Novel: 100 Good Women Writers Before Jane Austen* (1986). The following essay is excerpted from her recent book *The Writing or the Sex? Or: Why You Don't Have to Read Women's Writing to Know It's No Good* (1989).

Despite the protests of women over the centuries—Elizabeth Cady Stanton among them[1]—twenty years ago it was still widely and unwaveringly accepted that women were *the talkative sex*. Women were the empty vessels that made the most sound, according to such eminent linguists as Otto Jespersen: Without one shred of supportive evidence, he insisted that women were linguistically incompetent and went so far as to argue that women had a debilitating effect on the language (1922: p. 246). It was partly because male linguists presented such a long list of women's language sins (sins that women were supposed to have committed) that I became so interested in documenting some of the dynamics of women's talk: Well can I remember some of my own initial and tentative ventures into the tape-recording arena.

I elected then to study the interactions between women and men and my method was to make tapes of their conversations in a variety of "natural" and "controlled" contexts. My goal was simple: To analyse the taped interactions and to establish any differences between the sexes in patterns of speech. But after weeks—indeed months—of making tapes and listening to them with the aim of identifying the characteristics of women's speech and the differences in the speech of men, I began to suspect that as a linguistic researcher, I was a distinct failure. Although I had hours of tapes of conversations between women and men it did not seem to me that I had enough data from women

---

1. See Elizabeth Cady Stanton *et al.* 1881, Vol. 1, p. 110, for the steps she took at women's conventions to ensure that the few men present did not dominate the conversation.

to draw any conclusions. At that stage I thought there was a limit to the information that could be gleaned from women's encouraging expressions—such as "Really," "Goodness me," "And then?" etc. Later I came to regard these as supportive/eliciting comments which kept (men's) conversations going: But at the time I saw them as non-data and I almost despaired of ever being able to record sufficient sustained speech to identify any possible features specific to women.

Of course it took some time for me to appreciate that the salient characteristic of women's talk in conversation with men was *silence;* this was an understanding I did not reach unaided. As an unquestioning believer in the received wisdom that women were exceedingly garrulous, I just kept on trying to make more tapes of more woman-talk, before Cheris Kramarae suggested that perhaps the problem was not my research procedures, but the speech conventions of a male-dominated society.   3

So I stopped dwelling on my own ostensible failure to obtain data and rephrased my questions about the language of women and men. Not just about why women talked so little in the presence of men, but why in the face of such overwhelming evidence to the contrary, we could continue to believe that women were the talkative sex?   4

Again it was Cheris Kramarae who found the key to the contradiction of women's silence—and loquaciousness. She suggested that "Perhaps a talkative women is one who does talk as much as a man" (Cheris Kramer, 1975: p. 47).   5

From this shift in perspective came a new set of insights—and explanations.   6

Within language studies it has now been established that over the centuries women have been enjoined by men to be silent. Sophocles might not have started it, but when he suggested that "silence gives the proper grace to women," he made a contribution to the image of a good woman as a silent woman in the western tradition. And once it is realised that silence is an attitude that men desire in women, there is no longer any apparent contradiction between the infrequency of women's utterances and the insistence that they talk too much. Quite simply, if a woman is expected to be quiet then any woman who opens her mouth can be accused of being talkative.   7

But if for me—all those years ago—this insight into women's language eliminated some of the inconsistencies in my research, it also introduced a whole new range of problems. (And one new inconsistency emerged: that of trying to *articulate* women's *silence,* a problem which plagues all who work in this area.) One of the consequences of my discovery that women talked so little, when I had assumed they talked so much, was that I became a committed non-believer. Never since have I trusted linguistic authorities or the supposed evidence of my senses. Assured and reassured by countless women and men that they have a fair share of the conversation, I have remained completely unconvinced and have gone on to make my own tapes, develop my own records, and to count for myself the space allocated to women. Not terribly   8 rigorous as research activity goes, but richly rewarding and revealing. The discrepancy between people's perceptions (my own included) and empirical reality has become a cornerstone in much of my research.

And I never cease to be amazed at the extent to which our reality is predicated on the premises with which we begin; or the extent to which measurement is in the eye of the beholder—or the ear of the listener.　　9

So when a few years ago I was challenged by some assertive women at a meeting where I suggested that women did not enjoy the same rights or opportunities to talk as did men, I again got out the tape recorder to check— not on women in general, but on particular women who took pride in their talking achievements with men.　　10

Within a university context I made twenty tapes of academic feminists in conversation with an assortment of academic men. I set up the concealed tape recorder, and only after the conversation concluded did I introduce myself, indicate the existence of the tape recorder, and seek permission to simply count the number of minutes taken by each speaker. Four men considered their conversations private so I erased the tapes and this left me with sixteen samples (of varying length). In each case, before counting the minutes taken by each sex, I asked just one question: *Do you think you had a fair share of the conversation?* All the women said yes, one declaring that she had had more than her share; twelve men said yes; and four said no.　　11

When I analysed these tapes I found that fourteen feminists who believed that they had had a *fair* share of the conversation, spoke between 8% and 38% of the time. In this group were two of the men who were of the opinion that they had *not* had a fair share and they spoke for 75% and 67% of the time respectively. Two of the women did slightly better, with one achieving 40% of the conversation time and the other 42%. Both of the men in these interactions had stated that they had not enjoyed a fair share. Given that 60% and 58% do not feel like a fair share to men, the question of course arises as to what they think they are entitled to. And what do women think is their fair share of the conversation cake? The woman who thought that she had received more than her fair share spoke for 35% of the time.　　12

While some of the women involved were incredulous when confronted with these results (and wherever possible I took the precaution of checking the tape in the presence of the speakers) I was not at all surprised by these statistics. I have always used my own life as a source for research and it seems to me that in general a woman is allowed up to about one third of the conversation time in interactions with male peers. Beyond this point, *both women and men* are likely to perceive the contribution of the woman as domineering.　　13

In my own case I have found it difficult—and impossible—to discover what happens if women aim, not for what feels like a *fair* share, but for *half* the conversation time. Difficult because a woman has to break every rule in the polite conversation book if she tries to talk for half the time: It *feels* unfair,　　14 rude, and objectionably overbearing. For me it has also been impossible to talk for 50% of the time because no man has stayed "conversing" with me for the mandatory three minutes—the time I set for the minimal unit of interaction. The highest score I have ever attained (in conversation with a male colleague) was 44% and this was accompanied by angry assertions on his part that I was "impossible," "unreasonable," and that I "didn't listen to a word that was being said." At the time—before the tape had been analysed—I felt he was probably right.

Of course there are some contexts in which women are the authority figures and where it is possible for them to talk for more than 50% of the time without necessarily feeling any guilt.[2] I have many tapes of myself talking to male students and in these circumstances my language behaviour is similar to that of many men talking to women. I am the authority, I set the terms, I do most of the talking, interrupting, and legislating of experience. 15

No doubt a comparable pattern would also emerge were tapes to be made of Mrs. Thatcher addressing her all-male cabinet. And what this implies is that it is not the sex, but the power and authority which determines the right to talk: It is interesting that so many men still possess such power and authority *vis-à-vis* women. 16

It is not just a simple *reversal*, however, when women have the power to talk, and men find it in their own interest to listen. For unlike women, men do not use the small amount of talking time they have available to encourage the talk of an authoritative woman. Male behaviour in this context is in line with other patterns of power, for students do not ordinarily encourage the authority figure—the teacher—to speak, and patients do not generally make supportive comments to doctors, designed to "draw them out." It seems that the phenomenon of the eliciting utterance—"Did you really?", "Do go on", "And then?", "How interesting" etc.—is confined to women talking to men and is noted primarily in its absence: Women who do not use such devices are invariably seen as rude or revolting as linguist Pamela Fishman (1977) has suggested. 17

Because there is such a vast difference between what people believe to be happening in conversations, and what the tape recorder reveals, it has taken some time to discredit—and discard—many of these language myths. That so many open-minded and perspicacious women can continue to think that they are enjoying a fair share of the conversation when they get to talk for about one third of the time is an indication of the power of unwritten social codes to determine perception. That so many astute and aware women can continue to think that they do not modify their behaviour with the entry of 18

2. I have no tapes of white women talking to black men and no means of hypothesising about the nexus of gender and ethnicity.

151

a man to their conversation is evidence of the extent to which human beings can be oblivious to some of their own actions and their implications.

But far from being discouraged by this "discrepancy," I find it quite an exciting challenge. One of the difficulties—and the delights—of undertaking research in this area is in identifying the various "codes" that play such a crucial role in daily life but that can rarely be articulated and are often fervently denied. [19]

So teachers will insist that they spend as much time with the girls as the boys, parents will assert that they treat their daughters and their sons precisely the same, and literary critics will argue that sex and gender have absolutely nothing to do with their literary evaluations. Yet all these individuals who are so convinced that they do *not* discriminate can readily be shown to be operating a sexual double standard. No sophisticated research project is required to demonstrate that teachers (feminists included!) spend more time with boys than with girls (even—or especially—if boys are the minority). Parents can be shown to operate totally different codes of behaviour in relation to their daughters and their sons, and literary critics can certainly be shown to utilise a sexual double standard, despite their protests to the contrary. [20]

That there can be such a *gap* between belief and behaviour is not (necessarily) because people are trying to conceal sexist (or racist) actions: On the contrary they can genuinely feel that there is nothing problematic about their behaviour and that they are performing in a perfectly honourable manner— even as they engage in the most blatantly discriminatory practices. Because they don't *feel* as though they are doing the wrong thing, because they don't feel as though they are operating a double standard, they can classify their conduct as reasonable—even right. And while ever discrimination is presented as something dreadful people do, as distinct from the *routine* practice of *all* members of the society, we can expect this discrepancy between belief and behaviour to continue. [21]

The fundamental importance of gender as a factor in daily life is not often appreciated. While everyone who has ever tried will know how difficult—impossible?—it is to talk to a baby of unknown sex, the implications of this situation are rarely spelled out. For in order to know what to say and how to say it—what stance to assume, what tone to adopt, what information to impart—it is necessary to know the sex of the conversation partner, even when it is a baby! The embarrassment can be acute if one gets "caught out" making conversation on the basis of the wrong sex: The speaker who finds that the supposed girl is really a boy is distressed, and not just because it is a case of mistaken identity but because the wrong thing may have been said, in the wrong form. Everything from body posture to vocabulary and volume can be governed by considerations of gender which is why it can be disorienting and confusing when the sex of the conversation partner is not known: The speaker simply does not know how to relate to the audience, or where to begin. [22]

From birth the two sexes are treated very differently: They are addressed   23
in different ways, provided with different information and expectations, and
evaluated according to very different criteria. And so different are these sexual
standards that even when females and males do the *same* thing, completely
different constructions can be placed upon their actions. As Muriel Schulz
(1975) has pointed out, spinsters and bachelors may both be unmarried adults
but references made to the two categories cannot involve a comparison of
like with like: There is a substantial difference between an old woman—and
an old man. Even between a woman—and a man.

The double standard permeates just about every facet of language behav-   24
iour so that it is extremely difficult trying to work out what knowledge is to
be "trusted." When women can be held to talk too much when they talk less
than a man, while men can still be regarded as the strong silent type, even
when they do most of the talking, the way through the language and gender
mine field is not always clear. When a woman who gives her opinion can be
categorised as rude, pushy, aggressive and bitchy, while a man who gives his
opinion can be rated as masterful, forceful, authoritative—and revealing leadership qualities—the need for guidelines about reliable evidence becomes
obvious.

Nowhere is this more clearly demonstrable than in the case of transcript   25
evaluations (where the sex of the speaker cannot be identified from the voice).
Again and again I have asked people to rate transcripts and the very same
speech can be rated as positive or negative, depending on the presumed sex
of the speaker. When I have indicated, for example, that a lengthy expression
of opinion is the pronouncement of a man, it has invariably been rated as
impressive, thoughtful, informative, and useful: the same speech, when attributed to a woman has been dismissed as rambling, irrational, tedious, and
(once)—"a waste of words."

Such a sexually discriminating response should not be all that surprising: 26
As Cheris Kramarae found as early as 1977, English speakers of *both sexes*,
believe that men's speech is forceful, efficient, blunt, authoritative, serious,
sparing, and masterful, while that of women is considered weak, trivial, ineffectual, hesitant, hyperpolite, euphemistic—and is often marked by gossip
and gibberish. And when women and men believe that this is the way that
women and men talk, they are predisposed to find such characteristics when
asked to assess the spoken—or the written word—of women and men.

One of the classic studies of the extent to which measurement exists in   27
the mind of the beholder was conducted in 1974 by Philip Goldberg. Using
professional literature from six fields (encompassing both traditionally masculine and feminine areas), he compiled two sets of booklets in which "the
same article bore a male name in one set of booklets, a female name in the
other" (p. 39). He then asked women students to rate the contributions of
the writers.

Of course they rated the male author John T. McKay as superior to Joan   28
T. McKay across the various areas. "Of all nine questions," comments Philip
Goldberg, "regardless of the author's occupational field, the girls [*sic*] consistently found an article more valuable—and its author more competent—when
the article bore a male name. Though the articles themselves were exactly
the same, the girls felt that those written by the John T. McKays were
definitely more impressive and reflected more glory on their authors than did
the mediocre offerings of the Joan T. McKays" (pp. 40–41).

Interestingly, Philip Goldberg confined his study to women. He seems   29
to think that the important point of his exercise was to demonstrate that
women are biased against women: "Women," he says, "seem to think men
are better at everything." But, of course, it isn't only women who believe this;
the whole society, men included, believe it too. This is what the sexual double
standard is all about. This is why it can be stated with a degree of certainty
that it is not the talking or the writing, but the sex, which can determine the
worth of a particular contribution.

That men can base their judgements on women's sex, as distinct from   30
women's performance, is a thesis that has been more recently and fully sub-
stantiated by Bernice Lott: "Findings generally support the hypothesis," she
says "that the typical responses (of men, primarily) to a competent woman
include prejudice, stereotyped beliefs, and overt or subtle discrimination"
(1985: p. 43): and she goes on to summarise the research results in this area:

> Goldberg (1968) using only women participants found that the same article
> was judged to be more valuable, and the author more competent, if authored
> by a man than a woman. Since then, college students of both genders have
> been shown to: select women for a managerial position less than men (Cann,
> Siegfried and Pearce, 1981; Rosen and Jerdee, 1974) and reject women even
> more sharply if the position is highly demanding (Rosen and Jerdee, 1974);
> rate men instructors (not their own) in a generally more favourable way than
> women (Denmark, 1979); evaluate men instructors as more intelligent and
> motivating than equally presented women teachers (Bernard, Keefauver, Els-
> worth and Naylor, 1981); rate men instructors as more powerful and effective
> (Kaschak, 1981) and prefer to take a course from a man (Lombardo and
> Tocci, 1979); rate a female applicant for an insurance agent's job as less
> suitable for the job than a similarly high-scoring man (Heneman, 1977); hire
> a man over a woman judged equally suitable for a department store job and
> try harder to persuade a man than a woman to stay with the firm (Gutek and
> Stevens, 1979); be more willing to recommend hiring a man than a woman
> for a sales management traineeship and at a higher salary (Dipboye, Arvey
> and Terpstra, 1977); and give more favorable evaluations to male than female
> applicants for a newswriting job on such attributes as professional compe-
> tence, predicted job success, value of a word sample, dedication to journalism,
> and writing style (Etaugh and Kasley, 1981). In some of the above studies
> bias against women was greater on the part of men than of women respon-
> dents *(Bernice Lott, 1985: p. 47).*

And there is every reason to believe that the same value judgements 31 operate in the world of letters. Such findings have enormous implications for literary studies, and for the assessments and judgements which are at the core of the entire literary profession and its practices.

That literary critics have not looked to some fields of social science to 32 provide insights on their own evaluative practices says more about their intellectual insulation than—in this instance—the absence of reliable information. For there is a great deal of evidence available from a wide variety of sources which suggests that no member of society can be value-free in relation to gender. Numerous studies in a range of disciplines suggest that like the women in Philip Goldberg's sample, teachers, examiners, editors—and referees of academic journals, not to mention literary critics—predictably provide different evaluations on the basis of perceived sex. Even within the field of literary criticism itself there is sufficient data available for the critics to be informed that works are rated differently according to sex.

Real-life situations as distinct from experiments, the cases of Charlotte 33 Brontë, Emily Brontë, and Elizabeth Gaskell nonetheless provide convincing documentation on the way the sex of the writer influences the assessment of even the most eminent and respected scholars and critics. The double standard in literary evaluation was blatantly exposed when on the publication of *Jane Eyre* by Currer Bell it was decreed that such a novel was a remarkable achievement if written by a man. But the same work was considered a disgrace if written by a woman (see Margot Peters, 1977: p. 205).

And Emily Brontë fared little better: Carol Ohmann (1986) has traced 34 the response to the first edition of *Wuthering Heights* when Ellis Bell was assumed to be male, and contrasted it with the reaction to the second edition when it was known that Emily Brontë was the author:

> There are not so many reviews of the second edition of *Wuthering Heights*. But there are enough, I think, to show that once the work of Ellis Bell was identified as the work of a woman, critical responses to it changed. Where the novel had been called again and again "original" in 1847 and 1848, the review in the *Athenaeum* in 1850 began by firmly placing it in a familiar class, and that class was not in the central line of literature. The review in the *Athenaeum* began by categorising *Wuthering Heights* as a work of "female genius and authorship". The reviewer was really not surprised to learn that *Jane Eyre* and its "sister-novels" were all written by women . . ."
>
> It is on Emily Brontë's life that the review spends most of its 2,000 words. References to *Wuthering Heights* are late and few and then it is grouped not only with *Jane Eyre* but also with *Agnes Grey*. All three are "characteristic tales"—characteristic of the Bell, that is to say the Brontë sisters, and, more generally, of tales women write. A single sentence is given to *Wuthering Heights* alone: "To those whose experience of men and manners is neither extensive nor various, the construction of a self-consistent monster is easier than the delineation of an imperfect or inconsistent reality . . ." The review ends there, repeating still another time its classification of the novel.

Wuthering Heights . . . is a "more than unusually interesting contribution to the history of female authorship in England." *(Carol Ohmann, 1986: p. 72)*

In emphasising that the work is the product of a woman's pen, and in lumping together "the sisters" in an undifferentiated mass, the reviewer in the *Athenaeum* engages in the classic "put down": to suggest that the experience of the woman writer is inevitably limited by her sex and that for her the less demanding course of action is preferable, is to make the typical value judgement about women which has persisted for centuries (see for example Dale Spender, 1982(a), *Women of Ideas—And What Men Have Done to Them*). 35

I wouldn't want to give this particular *Athenaeum* reviewer too much attention—after all, it's a pretty silly assessment which is being made. However, I would want to point out that the reviewer is but one of scores of critics who have indulged in making comparably silly assertions and yet have been taken seriously. 36

And the question which arises in these circumstances is—why do critics not monitor their own practices? Why is there no established forum for debate on the way in which gender—or ethnicity—influences the judgement of literary professionals? Why no courses in the academy on the reasons that Mary Ann Evans chose the pen name of a man, or on the dramatic shift in the response to Elizabeth Gaskell's novel of social protest when it was known the author was female? (Dale Spender, 1985: p. 207). Why no courses on the views, values, and vagaries of the men who have decreed society's literary standards? I am sure there would be no shortage of students for courses on the prejudices of the profession—on the habits of editors, publishers, reviewers, literary judges, and academics. 37

The means by which the written word gets accepted for publication, and for promotion, review, validation, and inclusion in the literary curriculum to become part of the cultural heritage, would have to be one of the most underresearched and least-taught areas of intellectual endeavour. And this cannot be because the process is unimportant: The production of the printed word in our society—and the role that *gatekeepers* play in it—is centrally significant and should be open to investigation. But currently, it seems that a policy of "no questions asked" is being employed in the world of letters. This in itself is cause for concern. 38

Of course one reason that there is not more research undertaken in this critical area (and one reason the research that has been done is not always widely known) is that the findings can have educational and social as well as literary implications. Measurement of the judgement of assessors can make a mockery of much of our sacred marking system on which a meritocracy depends: Were society to lose faith in the efficacy of marking—in exams and entrance qualifications, in appointments and degrees—chaos could quickly ensue. 39

For what has emerged, particularly in the educational realm, is that it is 40 not just that the *same* contribution can be accorded a different mark or status on the basis of perceived sex, but that the same status and mark can be granted different weightings on the basis of sex.

It borders on the astonishing, but it can be shown that in the study of 41 English, for example, when girls and boys get the same mark, teachers (and students) can invest it with systematically different meanings. Girls can have their performance denigrated on the grounds that it was only conformity and conventional correctness which was responsible for their "good" marks, while the boys—*who have been given the same grade*—are assumed to have attained their marks by virtue of their genuine *intellectual* ability.

Instances have been documented where girls have been awarded higher 42 marks than boys, but the teachers—like the women students in Philip Goldberg's study—will continue to insist that the boys are brighter and that the girls lack creativity. Like those of us who maintain the mindset that women are talkative, despite the dramatic evidence to the contrary, teachers can be committed to the premise that boys are brighter and proceed to substantiate their belief regardless of the data they are confronted with.

The existence of such entrenched bias in educational contexts has serious 43 ramifications, not the least of which is that girls are being robbed of their intellectuality and creativity as Katherine Clarricoates (1978) has so uncompromisingly pointed out. And there are of course no grounds for assuming that this theft of women's creativity is being confined to the classroom. Comparable practices are to be found across social, political, and business institutions. And their presence can be readily documented in the literary studies curriculum: The "marks" and status given to Emily Brontë and Elizabeth Gaskell once their sex was known are essentially the same as the marks and status given to the girls Katherine Clarricoates observed in school.

One finding that emerges from linguistic and educational research on the 44 importance of gender in perceptions is that all members of society learn the rules for the construction of reality—in this case that "men are better." While there are varying degrees of commitment to this principle (my own exacted unwillingly), no one can be completely free from such distortions and some who insist on their purity (as some critics are prone to do), simply proclaim their ignorance.

Not even knowledge about the sexual double standard and its operation 45 guarantees immunity. Whenever I include my own responses in my own research, in spite of the compensatory adjustments that I make, I too continue to rate John McKay as (marginally) superior to Joan McKay. I too need to know the sex of my conversation partner before I know what to say and how to say it. I can still think that I have had more than my fair share of the conversation when I have spoken for approximately one third of the time, and my tape recorder continues to inform me that I modify my language behaviour when a man enters the conversation. I defer to men, I develop their conversation topics at the expense of my own, and sometimes knowingly, but sometimes not, I behave (according to my own criteria) as a bit of a wimp!

In a classroom I can still give disproportionate attention to males and be far more concerned about not hurting men's feelings. To my eternal shame I continue to be ultra-sensitive to the male response when I deliver "fierce feminist" lectures to a mixed audience. And to this day I expect more from women than I do from men across a whole range of areas. To declare otherwise would be to defy the evidence of my tape recorder and my written responses. While it might feel as though this time I really am taking a *half* share in the conversation, that I really am treating my students equally, that I really am operating a single rather than a double sexual standard, empirical evidence belies my beliefs. There seems to be no way of avoiding this dilemma: To be a member of this society is to use its "rules" even when they encode offensive forms of sexual discrimination. 46

Which is why I laugh (or cry!) when members of the literary profession persist with their claims that their judgement is never clouded by issues of gender. Terrible that so many of them should be so arrogant, but worse that they should be so assiduously ignorant and disregard the implications of so much relevant research. If it were not so awful it could be extremely amusing to detect the eminent literary academics and critics running for the cover of "certainties" rather than confronting and examining the biases and limitations of their own processes of assessment. But instead of coming to terms with the *subjective* nature of their activities (which has connotations of "soft data" and the feminine), many male academics have scrambled to stake their claim to "hard data" and are—in the opinion of Elaine Showalter (1986)—trying to establish a second and more scientifically prestigious form of literary criticism: 47

> The new sciences of the text based on linguistics, computers, genetic struc-
> turalism, deconstructionism, neoformalism and deformalism, affective stylis-
> tics and psychoaesthetics, have offered literary critics the opportunity to
> demonstrate that the work they do is as manly and aggressive as nuclear
> physics—not intuitive, expressive and feminine, but strenuous, rigorous, im-
> personal and virile. *(Elaine Showalter, 1986: p. 140)*

This is not to suggest that such activities should be outlawed. However it is to suggest—as Elaine Showalter does—that these activities are a long way from reading books. And if the object of the exercise is to read books— to enjoy them and reflect upon them, to discuss their meanings and speculate on the worlds they create—then many of these new "sciences of the text" have little or nothing to offer. As simplified symbolic systems which allow for finite meanings—for certainties and proof—they need not be concerned with the richness, complexity, and infinite variations of the written word. The new sciences can steer clear of the challenges provided by the more open-ended questions of interpretation and appreciation. 48

But where the object of the exercise *is* to read books and to discuss the intellectual, philosophical, and pleasurable responses that they afford, then an appropriate frame of reference is called for, one which can take account of meaning, of language and its oppressive and liberating uses. And this is where research on the spoken word can be relevant and helpful. 49

At one level, of course, it is absurd that the studies of the spoken and written language should ever have been split and that they should have for so long been separated, but when some of the findings that have emerged in the context of language and gender studies are listed and linked with some of the issues in "lit-crit," the parallels between the two can be observed readily. 50

For example, when men today dominate the conversation and determine the agenda, they are behaving in much the same manner as the literary men who, over the centuries, have insisted that their words warrant more space in the canon and that their concerns are the significant and universal ones. And just as men have protected and perpetuated their primacy with the assertion that women talk too much, so have the men of letters protested when they have perceived women trespassing in what they have decreed is male literary territory. Although when it comes to publication rates, review space, and curriculum representation—and the status stakes—women have nothing like a half share in resources and recognition, there are literary men who can continue to carp that women are getting more than their share. Just as women talkers are confined to about one third of the conversation space, so too are women writers allocated only a small percentage of space in the literary curriculum. While there may be those who insist that there are too many women studied these days, that they are swamping the men writers—and *lowering the standards*—women don't ever seem to exceed 10% of the writers represented in mainstream literature courses. They were never more than 7% when Elaine Showalter (1974) conducted her study in 1970, they were 7% when Jean Mullen conducted hers in 1972, and between 5% and 8% when Joanna Russ (1984) conducted hers in 1977. And there is evidence which suggests there is a "backlash" against women writers and that things are getting better rather than worse. There are universities in Australia and England, for example, where there are courses on nineteenth-century poets and twentieth-century writers where not one woman is included on the reading list! 51

To assume that "progress" has been made since the startling studies of the seventies made the inequities of women's literary representation quite clear, is to be gravely misled. It isn't necessarily any easier now for women to attain a *half* share in any linguistic framework. Women who want to contribute equally with men in conversation have to be committed and courageous. A veritable battery of insults is available to intimidate them, to undermine their confidence, and ensure their withdrawal. "Domineering," "aggressive," "rude," "bitchy," and "disagreeable" are but some of the terms designed to 52 end women's spoken participation, and they have their parallels in the counsel and criticism—commented on in greater length later—that men have directed towards literary women.

When today men repeatedly interrupt women in conversation—and si-   53 lence them—they are replicating a pattern that for hundreds of years has characterised the response to women's written words. Both Tillie Olsen (1980) and Adrienne Rich (1980) have stated unequivocally that the history of women and their literature is the history of interruption—and silence:

> The entire history for women's struggle for self determination has been muffled in silence over and over. One serious cultural obstacle encountered by any feminist writer is that each feminist work has tended to be received as if it emerged from nowhere; as if each of us had lived, thought and worked without any historical past or contextual present. This is one of the ways in which women's work and thinking has been made to seem sporadic, errant, orphaned of any tradition of its own. *(Adrienne Rich, 1980: p. 11)*

The conditions under which women write are not dissimilar to the con-   54 ditions under which women talk: They can attend to their own needs only *after* they have met some of the physical and psychological needs of men. Tillie Olsen (1980) has movingly attested to the way in which women are required to do the "shitwork" in the home, and the extent to which marriage and motherhood curtail women's opportunities to write. Pamela Fishman (1977) in her classic study of mixed sex talk has shown how women are required to do the "shitwork" in conversation—to do all the routine and invisible chores which keep conversations going and which, of course, put women in the position of developing men's talk and topics at the expense of their own. All those helpful touches—the clean shirts and the supportive comments—the "emotional management" as women put their energy into making men feel comfortable.

This is a phenomenon that many women have written about—Virginia   55 Woolf among them. Because it has been widely recognised within women's literary history that women's words are being judged by men (and that it doesn't pay to antagonise them) extensive constraints have been placed upon women's work which have no counterparts among men:

> No male writer has written primarily or even largely for women, or with the sense of women's criticism as a consideration when he chooses his materials, his themes, his language. But to a lesser or greater extent every woman writer has written for men, even when, like Virginia Woolf, she was supposed to be addressing women. *(Adrienne Rich, 1980: pp. 37–38)*

Virginia Woolf was herself aware of this "influence" in her writing: She   56 gave it substance in her references to the "Angel in the House," the figure "who used to come between me and my paper when I was writing" and who used to "seduce" her by whispering—

Be sympathetic, be tender; flatter; deceive, use all the arts and wiles of our sex. Never let anyone guess that you have a mind of your own. Above all, be pure! *(Virginia Woolf, 1972: p. 285)*

It has been widely accepted among women that certain forms must be 57 followed if they are to get a hearing from men. With the spoken word and the written word women have tried to be polite, pure—and *supportive*—on the premise that they would be heard and heeded. But unfortunately the double standard can also give rise to the double bind with the result that women who practise politeness may get just as negative a reception as women who are "rude and disagreeable." Peter Trudgill (1975) is just one of the linguists who has suggested that it is because women speak more politely than men that their voice lacks authority.

So women are damned if they do and damned if they don't: Damned if 58 they are assertive (and talk like men), and damned if they are supportive— "hesitant"—and polite, and talk like women!

The similarities with the written word are obvious: Women are damned 59 for writing like women ("domestic dramas and tragedies at tea parties"), and they are damned for writing like men—when, of course, it is known that women are the authors.

When I was doing my own research on language and sex, I was often 60 perplexed by the way in which women's talk was categorised as "gossip"[3] (and dismissed) frequently without a hearing. To satisfy my own curiosity, I did a content analysis of women's talk and compared it with men's talk on a number of occasions. When I realised that women could be talking philosophically about the rearing of the next generation while men were revealing a partisan preference for particular football teams—*and that the women's talk was dismissed as gossip while the men's was held to be more important and interesting*—I concluded that the values being ascribed were based on the sex and not the talk. The only sensible statement that I could make on the basis of my comparison was that when men "gossip" it is called something different.

The same thesis applies to the written word as well and has a distinct 61 counterpart in the novel. Again, I have often been perplexed by the way women writers are undifferentiated and seen to write, en masse, the lowly form of romantic fiction. From Jane Austen to Barbara Cartland—and despite all the dramatic diversity in between—there is the implication that *all* women's writing is romance, in much the same way as all women's talk is gossip.

And a content analysis of the writing cannot possibly support such a 62 classification scheme. Look at the domestic melodramas of Thomas Hardy, at the romances of D. H. Lawrence. Clearly when men write romance it's

3. *A Feminist Dictionary* (Cheris Kramarae and Paula Treichler, 1985) defines "gossip"—"a woman's female friend invited to be present at a birth . . ." (p. 179)

called something different. It is the sex and not the *writing* that is responsible for such judgement.

Not surprisingly a long list could be compiled of the similarities in the treatment of women's spoken and written language in a male-dominated society. The overview contained here is not intended to be exhaustive but it is meant to make some of the connections and to state the case for looking at sex and gender as a central factor in literary judgement. However, no summary, no matter how brief, could be adequate if it did not include mention of the appropriation of women's words by men.

Few women could be unaware of the way in which their words can be "ignored" only to be taken up by men, minutes, sometimes even seconds, later, and accorded approval. So common is this practice that it has become "a joke" among multitudes of women. Numerous versions abound of "That's a good suggestion Miss Jones, we'll wait for a man to make it," and it points to the phenomenon whereby men readily avail themselves of the resources of women—without acknowledgement.

Pamela Fishman (1977) has declared that women are supposed to be good at the art of conversation—and that for women, the art of conversation is getting men to talk. At the crux of her somewhat facetious explanation for sexual inequalities in interaction is the far-reaching premise that women's linguistic resources are supposed to be put at the service of men. That women have no linguistic rights of their own, no linguistic autonomy; that their contribution is justified only in so far as it affords ideas, opportunities, encouragement, support for the linguistic achievements of men is one insight that her study provides.

And the same premise can be transferred to the written word where women's efforts have frequently—one might go so far as to say ordinarily— been used by men to enhance their own records of performance.

Not that this habit has been confined to language: There are now numerous studies in the history of music and art that provide a very simple explanation for the presumed absence of women in these fields. According to Joanna Russ (1984), with whom I completely concur, one of the reasons that there have been few "great" women musicians and artists is that their work has been attributed to or appropriated by men (pp. 50–51). Cynthia Fuchs Epstein has described the literary arrangements:

> I have begun to collect gracious acknowledgements to wives which indicate the intellectual contribution of the wife to a piece of work, but which do not give professional credit to her. An early example is the acknowledgement of Gabriel Kolko . . . in *Wealth and Power in America* (Praeger, paperback edition, 1967) which states: 'To my wife, Joyce, I owe a debt that mere words cannot express. This book is in every sense a joint enterprise and the first in a series of critical studies on which we're presently engaged' (p. xi) . . . the wife did not appear as co-author or junior author. (*Cynthia Fuchs Epstein, 1976: pp. 193–194*)

This is just another variation on the theme of "That's a good idea Miss 68
Jones, we'll wait until it's put forward by a man"; it is the means whereby the
work of many women is taken over by men. And it is a practice about which
few great male writers have felt much guilt. The assumption that women's
resources are available to men and that women's creativity is but the raw
material waiting to be wrought into artistic shape by gifted men is one which
is prevalent in literary circles—and one which demands serious and systematic
attention. It is not too much to assert that there have been eminent literary
men who have not only *stolen* women's words but who have seen nothing
problematic about the practice because they have believed they were only
taking what they were entitled to! This form of language acquisition is the
focus of the final chapter of this volume—"Polish, Plagiarism, and Plain
Theft."

But much of the discussion in this chapter has been based on the premise 69
that men have *first* read the words of women before they have found them
wanting. This too is the premise of much feminist literary criticism which
challenges the exclusion of women from the canon. While this is part of the
picture, it is not the whole picture. Just as Cheris Kramarae (1977) found
there are stereotypes of women's and men's language which mean people
don't actually have to listen to women and men speaking to know that the
women are "pathetic" and the men are "masterful," so too (as Philip Goldberg,
1974, pointed out) are stereotypical judgements being made about the written
word of women. It is my contention that the population in general and male
literary critics in particular entertain a negative image of women and their
words, to the extent that it is widely believed that you don't have to read
women's writing to know it's no good!

Kate Wilhelm (1975) has summed up what many women know—"My 70
first husband never read a word I wrote. . . . He knew it was all trivial." (p. 22)

To challenge literary men on the grounds that they do not give women 71
a fair hearing is one thing, to charge them with giving women no hearing at
all is quite another. Yet when the words of women do not even qualify for a
reading and an evaluation then the evidence that it is the sex and not the
writing which is being judged is incontrovertible. It is because women have
been dismissed as *women*, and then as writers, that it has become necessary to
call to account the judgement of literary men.

References

Bernard, M. E., L. W. Keefauver, G. Elsworth, and F. D. Naylor. 1981. "Sex role behavior and
gender in teacher-student evaluations." *Journal of Educational Psychology* 73:681–96.

Cann, A., W. D. Siegfried, and L. Pearce (1981). "Forced attention to specific applicant qualifications: Impact of physical attractiveness and sex of applicant biases." *Personal Psychology* 34:67–
76.

Clarricoates, Katherine (1978). "'Dinosaurs in the Classroom': A re-examination of some aspects of the hidden curriculum in primary schools." *Women's Studies International Quarterly* 1 no. 4:353–64.

Denmark, F. L. (1979). "The outspoken woman: can she win?" Paper presented at the New York Academy of Sciences, New York City.

Dipboye, R. L., R. D. Arvey and J. E. Terpstra (1977). "Sex and physical attractiveness of raters and applicants as determinants of resume evaluations." *Journal of Applied Psychology* 66:288–294.

Epstein, Cynthia Fuchs (1976). "Sex role stereotyping; occupations and social exchange." *Women's Studies* (3), 190:193–194.

Etaugh, C. and H. C. Kasley (1981). "Evaluating Competence: effects of sex, marital status and parental status." *Psychology of Women Quarterly* 6:196–203.

Fishman, Pamela (1977). "Interactional Shitwork." *Heresies: A Feminist Publication on Arts and Politics*, no. 2 (May): 99–101.

Goldberg, Philip (1974). "Are Women Prejudiced Against Women?" In *And Jill Came Tumbling After: Sexism in American Education*, eds. J. Stacey, S. Bereaud and J. Daniels, 37–42. New York: Dell Publishing.

Gutek, B. A. and D. A. Stevens (1979). "Effects of sex of subject, sex of stimulus use, and androgyny level on evaluations in work situations which evoke sex-role stereotype." *Journal of Vocational Behavior* 14:23–32.

Heneman, H. G. (1977). "Impact of test information and applicant sex on applicant evaluations in a selection simulation." *Journal of Applied Psychology* 62:524–526.

Jespersen, Otto (1922). *Language: Its Nature, Development and Origin*, London: Allen & Unwin.

Kaschak, E. (1981). "Another look at sex-bias in students' evaluations of professions: Do winners get the recognition they have been given?" *Psychology of Women Quarterly* 5:767–772.

Kramarae, Cheris and Paula Treichler (1985). *A Feminist Dictionary*, London: Pandora Press.

Kramer, Cheris (1975). "Women's Speech: Separate but Unequal." In *Language and Sex: Difference and Dominance*, eds. Barrie Thorne and Nancy Henley, 43–56. Rowley, Mass: Newbury House.

Kramer, Cheris (1977 April/June). "Perceptions of Female and Male Speech." *Language and Speech* 20, no. 2:151–161.

Lombardo, J. P. and M. E. Tocci (1979). "Attribution of positive and negative characteristics of instructors as a function of attractiveness and sex of instructor and sex of subject." *Perceptual and Motor Skills* 48:491–494.

Lott, Bernice (1985). "The devaluation of women's competence." *Journal of Social Issues* 41, no. 4:43–69.

Ohmann, Carol (1986). "Emily Brontë in the Hands of Male Critics." In *Feminist Literary Theory: A Reader*, eds. Mary Eagleton, 71–74. Oxford: Basil Blackwell.

Olsen, Tillie (1980). *Silences*, London: Virago.

Peters, Margot (1977). *Unquiet Soul: A Biography of Charlotte Bronte*, London: Futura.

Rich, Adrienne (1979/1980). *On Lies, Secrets and Silence: Selected Prose 1966–1978*, New York: W. W. Norton and London: Virago.

Rosen, B. and T. H. Jerdee (1974). "Effects of applicants' sex and difficulty of job on evaluation of candidates for managerial positions." *Journal of Applied Psychology* 59:511–512.

Russ, Joanna (1984). *How to Suppress Women's Writing*, London: The Women's Press.

Schultz, Muriel (1975). "The Semantic Derogation of Women." In *Language and Sex: Difference and Dominance*, eds. Barrie Thorne and Nancy Henley, 64–75. Rowley, Mass: Newbury House.

Showalter, Elaine (1974). "Women in the Literary Curriculum" (1970). In *And Jill Came Tumbling After*, eds. Judith Stacey, Susan Bereaud and Joan Daniels, 317–325. New York: Dell.

Showalter, Elaine (1986). "Introduction: The Feminist Critical Revolution." In *The New Feminist Criticism*, ed. Elaine Showalter, 3–17. London: Virago.

Spender, Dale (1982). *Women of Ideas—And What Men Have Done to Them*, London: Routledge & Kegan Paul.

Spender, Dale (1985). *For the Record: The Making and Meaning of Feminist Knowledge*, London: The Women's Press.

Trudgill, Peter (1975). "Sex Covert Prestige and Linguistic Change in the Urban British English of Norwich." In *Language and Sex: Difference and Dominance*, eds. Barrie Thorne and Nancy Henley, 88–104. Rowley, Mass: Newbury House.

Wilhelm, Kate (1975, April 3). "Women Writers: A Letter from Kate Wilhelm." *The Witch and the Chameleon*, 21–22.

Woolf, Virginia (1972). "Professions for Women." In *Collected Essays of Virginia Woolf*, Vol. 2, ed. Leonard Woolf, 284–289. London: Chatto and Windus.

PRO FEMINA

CAROLYN KIZER

Carolyn Kizer has been "in the racket" of writing since the 1940s as a poet, translator, creative writing teacher, and founding editor of the acclaimed journal *Poetry Northwest*. She has also served as director of literary programs for the National Endowment for the Arts. Among her volumes of poetry are *Knock Upon Silence* (1965), *Midnight Was My Cry* (1971), and *Yin* (1984). Her long poem "Pro Femina," meaning "for the woman," from which the following selection was excerpted, was written between 1963 and 1965, in the early days of the women's liberation movement.

Three

I will speak about women of letters, for I'm in the racket,
Our biggest successes to date? Old maids to a woman.
And our saddest conspicuous failures? The married spinsters
On loan to the husbands they treated like surrogate fathers.
Think of that crew of self-pitiers, not-very-distant,
Who carried the torch for themselves and got first-degree burns,
Or the sad sonneteers, toast-and-teasdales we loved at thirteen;
Middle-aged virgins seducing the puerile anthologists
Through lust-of-the-mind; barbiturate-drenched Camilles
With continuous periods, murmuring softly on sofas
When poetry wasn't a craft but a sickly effluvium,
The air thick with incense, musk, and emotional blackmail.

I suppose they reacted from an earlier womanly modesty
When too many girls were scabs to their stricken sisterhood,
Impugning our sex to stay in good with the men,
Commencing their insecure bluster. How they must have swaggered
When women themselves indorsed their own inferiority!
Vestals, vassals and vessels, rolled into several,
They took notes in rolling syllabics, in careful journals,
Aiming to please a posterity that despises them.
But we'll always have traitors who swear that a woman surrenders
Her Supreme Function, by equating Art with aggression

And failure with Femininity. Still, it's just as unfair
To equate Art with Femininity, like a prettily-packaged commodity
When we are the custodians of the world's best-kept secret:
Merely the private lives of one-half of humanity.

But even with masculine dominance, we mares and mistresses
Produced some sleek saboteuses, making their cracks
Which the porridge-brained males of the day were too thick to
  perceive,
Mistaking young hornets for perfectly harmless bumblebees.
Being thought innocuous rouses some women to frenzy;
They try to be ugly by aping the ways of the men
And succeed. Swearing, sucking cigars and scorching the bedspread,
Slopping straight shots, eyes blotted, vanity-blown
In the expectation of glory: *she writes like a man!*
This drives other women mad in a mist of chiffon
(one poetess draped her gauze over red flannels, a practical feminist).

But we're emerging from all that, more or less,
Except for some lady-like laggards and Quarterly priestesses
Who flog men for fun, and kick women to maim competition.
Now, if we struggle abnormally, we may almost seem normal;
If we submerge our self-pity in disciplined industry;
If we stand up and be hated, and swear not to sleep with editors;
If we regard ourselves formally, respecting our true limitations
Without making an unseemly show of trying to unfreeze our assets;
Keeping our heads and our pride while remaining unmarried;
And if wedded, kill guilt in its tracks when we stack up the dishes
And defect to the typewriter. And if mothers, believe in the luck of
  our children,
Whom we forbid to devour us, whom we shall not devour,
And the luck of our husbands and lovers, who keep free women.

WE ARE THE CRAZY LADY AND OTHER FEISTY FEMINIST FABLES

◑

C Y N T H I A   O Z I C K

In addition to imaginative writings like the following "fables," first published in 1972, Cynthia Ozick is widely known as a fiction writer, poet, reviewer, and essayist dealing with the issues of women and creativity. Her essays on literary criticism include such works as *Art and Ardor* (1983) and *Metaphor and Memory* (1989). Ozick's topic is frequently the blindness of the literary world in focusing more on an author's sex than on her literary skill, initiative, or accomplishment.

I: The Crazy Lady Double

A long, long time ago, in another century—1951, in fact—when you, dear young readers, were most likely still in your nuclear-family playpen (where, if female, you cuddled a ragbaby to your potential titties, or, if male, let down virile drool over your plastic bulldozer), the Famous Critic told me never, never to use a parenthesis in the very first sentence. This was in a graduate English seminar at a celebrated university. To get into this seminar, you had to submit to a grilling wherein you renounced all former allegiance to the then-current literary religion, New Criticism, which considered that only the text existed, not the world. I passed the interview by lying—cunningly, and against my real convictions, I said that probably the world *did* exist—and walked triumphantly into the seminar room.   1

There were four big tables arranged in a square, with everyone's feet sticking out into the open middle of the square. You could tell who was nervous, and how much, by watching the pairs of feet twist around each other. The Great Man presided awesomely from the high bar of the square. His head was a majestic granite-gray, like a centurion in command; he *looked* famous. His clean shoes twitched only slightly, and only when he was angry.   2

It turned out he was angry at me a lot of the time. He was angry because he thought me a disrupter, a rioter, a provocateur, and a fool; also crazy. And this was twenty years ago, before these things were *de rigueur* in the universities. Everything was very quiet in those days: there were only the Cold War and Korea and Joe McCarthy and the Old Old Nixon, and the only revolutionaries around were in Henry James's *The Princess Casamassima*.   3

Habit governed the seminar. Where you sat the first day was where you   4
settled forever. So, to avoid the stigmatization of the ghetto, I was careful not
to sit next to the other woman in the class: the Crazy Lady.

At first the Crazy Lady appeared to be remarkably intelligent. She was   5
older than the rest of us, somewhere in her thirties (which was why we thought
of her as a Lady), with wild-tan hair, a noticeably breathing bosom, eccentric
gold-rimmed old-pensioner glasses, and a tooth-crowded wild mouth that
seemed to get wilder the more she talked. She talked like a motorcycle, fast
and urgent. Everything she said was almost brilliant, only not actually on
point, and frenetic with hostility. She was tough and negative. She volunteered
a lot and she stood up and wobbled with rage, pulling at her hair and mouth.
She fought the Great Man point for point, piecemeal and wholesale, mixing
up queerly-angled literary insights with all sorts of private and public fury.
After the first meetings he was fed up with her. The rest of us accepted that
she probably wasn't all there, but in a room where everyone was on the make
for recognition—you talked to save your life, and the only way to save your
life was to be the smartest one that day—she was a nuisance, a distraction, a
pain in the ass. The class became a bunch of Good Germans, determinedly
indifferent onlookers to a vindictive match between the Critic and the Crazy
Lady, until finally he subdued her by shutting his eyes, and, when that didn't
always work, by cutting her dead and lecturing right across the sound of her
strong, strange voice.

All this was before R. D. Laing had invented the superiority of madness,   6
of course, and, cowards all, no one liked the thought of being tarred with the
Crazy Lady's brush. Ignored by the boss, in the middle of everything she
would suddenly begin to mutter to herself. She mentioned certain institutions
she'd been in, and said we all belonged there. The people who sat on either
side of her shifted chairs. If the Great Man ostracized the Crazy Lady, we
had to do it too. But one day the Crazy Lady came in late and sat down in
the seat next to mine, and stayed there the rest of the semester.

Then an odd thing happened. There, right next to me, was the noisy   7
Crazy Lady, tall, with that sticky-out sighing chest of hers, orangey curls
dripping over her nose, snuffling furiously for attention. And there was I, a
brownish runt, a dozen years younger and flatter and shyer than the Crazy
Lady, in no way her twin, physically or psychologically. In those days I was
bone-skinny, small, sallow and myopic, and so scared I could trigger diarrhea
at one glance from the Great Man. All this stress on looks is important: the
Crazy Lady and I had our separate bodies, our separate brains. We handed
in our separate papers.

But the Great Man never turned toward me, never at all, and if ambition   8
broke feverishly through shyness so that I dared to push an idea audibly out
of me, he shut his eyes when I put up my hand. This went on for a long time.
I never got to speak, and I began to have the depressing feeling that he hated
me. It was no small thing to be hated by the man who had written the most

impressive criticism of the century. What in hell was going on? I was in trouble; like everyone else in that demented contest I wanted to excel. Then, one slow afternoon, wearily, the Great Man let his eyes fall on me. He called me by name, but it was not my name—it was the Crazy Lady's. The next week the papers came back—and there, right at the top of mine, in the Great Man's own handwriting, was a rebuke to the Crazy Lady for starting an essay with a parenthesis in the first sentence, a habit he took to be a continuing sign of that unruly and unfocused mentality so often exhibited in class. And then a Singular Revelation crept coldly through me: because the Crazy Lady and I sat side by side, because we were a connected blur of Woman, the Famous Critic, master of ultimate distinctions, couldn't tell us apart. The Crazy Lady and I! He couldn't tell us apart! It didn't matter that the Crazy Lady was crazy! *He couldn't tell us apart!*

Moral 1: *All cats are gray at night, all darkies look alike.* 9

Moral 2: Even among intellectual humanists, every woman has a *Doppelgänger*—every other woman. 10

II: The Lecture, 1

I was invited by a women's group to be guest speaker at a Book-Author 11
Luncheon. The women themselves had not really chosen me: the speaker had been selected by a male leader and imposed on them. The plan was that I would autograph copies of my book, eat a good meal and then lecture. The woman in charge of the programming telephoned to ask me what my topic would be. This was a matter of some concern, since they had never had a woman author before, and no one knew how the idea would be received. I offered as my subject "The Contemporary Poem."

When the day came, everything went as scheduled—the autographing, 12
the food, the welcoming addresses. Then it was time to go to the lectern. I aimed at the microphone and began to speak of poetry. A peculiar rustling sound flew up from the audience. All the women were lifting their programs to the light, like hundreds of wings. Confused murmurs ran along the walls. Something was awry; I began to feel very uncomfortable. Then I took up the program. It read: "Topic: The Contemporary Home."

Moral: Even our ears practice the caste system. 13

III: The Lecture, 2

I was in another country, the only woman at a philosophical seminar lasting 14
three days. On the third day I was to read a paper. I had accepted the invitation with a certain foreknowledge. I knew, for instance, that I could not dare to be the equal of any other speaker. To be an equal would be to be less. I

understood that mine had to be the most original and powerful paper of all. I had no choice; I had to toil beyond my most extreme possibilities. This was not ambition, but only fear of disgrace.

For the first two days, I was invisible. When I spoke, people tapped impatiently waiting for the interruption to end. No one took either my presence or my words seriously. At meals, I sat with my colleagues' wives. 15

The third day arrived, and I read my paper. It was successful beyond my remotest imaginings. I was interviewed, and my remarks appeared in newspapers in a language I could not understand. The Foreign Minister invited me to his home. I hobnobbed with famous poets. 16

Now my colleagues noticed me. But they did not notice me as a colleague. They teased and kissed me. I had become their mascot. 17

Moral: There is no route out of caste which does not instantly lead back to it. 18

IV: Propaganda

For many years I had noticed that no book of poetry by a woman was reviewed without reference to the poet's sex. The curious thing was that, in the two decades of my scrutiny, there were *no exceptions* whatever. It did not matter whether the reviewer was a man or woman: in every case the question of the "feminine sensibility" of the poet was at the center of the reviewer's response. The maleness of male poets, on the other hand, hardly ever seemed to matter. 19

Determined to ridicule this convention, I wrote a tract, a piece of purely tendentious mockery, in the form of a short story. I called it "Virility." 20

The plot was, briefly, as follows: A very bad poet, lustful for fame, is despised for his pitiful lucubrations and remains unpublished. But luckily, he comes into possession of a cache of letters written by his elderly spinster aunt, who lives an obscure and secluded working-class life in a remote corner of England. The letters contain a large number of remarkable poems; the aunt, it turns out, is a genius. The bad poet publishes his find under his own name, and instantly attains world-wide adulation. Under the title *Virility*, the poems become immediate classics. They are translated into dozens of languages and are praised and revered for their unmistakably masculine qualities: their strength, passion, wisdom, energy, boldness, brutality, worldliness, robustness, authenticity, sensuality, compassion. A big, handsome, sweating man, the poet swaggers from country to country, courted everywhere, pursued by admirers, yet respected by the most demanding critics. 21

Meanwhile, the old aunt dies; the supply of genius runs out. Bravely and contritely the poor poet confesses his ruse, and in a burst of honesty publishes the last batch under the real poet's name; the book is entitled *Flowers from Liverpool*. But the poems are at once found negligible and dismissed: "Thin feminine art," say the reviews, "a lovely girlish voice." And: "Limited one- 22 dimensional vision." "Choked with female inwardness." "The fine womanly intuition of a competent poetess." The poems are utterly forgotten.

I included this fable in a collection of short stories. In every review the [23] salvo went unnoticed. Not one reviewer recognized that the story was a sly tract. Not one reviewer saw the smirk or the point. There was one delicious comment, though. "I have some reservations," a man in Washington, D.C., wrote, "about the credibility of some of her male characters when they are chosen as narrators."

Moral: In saying what is obvious, never choose cunning. Yelling works [24] better. . . .

LESBIAN AND WRITER
Making the Real Visible

JANE RULE

Jane Rule is perhaps best known for her novel *Desert of the Heart* (1985), on which the 1986 feature film "Desert Hearts" was based. The movie startled audiences by depicting a love affair between two women, showing in Rule's words, what is "not heroic or saintly but *real*" about people's lives and choices. Some of her many other novels are *This Is Not For You* (1970), *Against the Season* (1971), *The Young in One Another's Arms* (1977), and *Contract with the World* (1980). Rule is also the author of *Lesbian Images* (1975) and other writings about lesbianism and literature.

I am a politically involved lesbian, and I am a writer. I do not see the two as mutually exclusive; neither do I see them as inextricably bound together. Yet one of those two conflicting views is held by most people who read my work. The editors of *Chatelaine*,[1] for instance, would as soon their readers weren't reminded that the writer of the Harry and Anna stories, affectionately and humorously concerned with family life, is also the author of *Lesbian Images*. Most critics of my novels, on the other hand, use my sexuality to measure all my characters. Those who are lesbian are naturally the most persuasive. My male characters are considered weak. Even for those not so crudely tempted, I am judged as remarkably fair to all my characters when one considers that I am, after all, a lesbian. For critics who are themselves gay, I am held politically accountable for every less-than-perfect gay character and I am warned that I will lose a large part of my audience if I insist on including heterosexual characters in my work. And in the academy, I am dismissed as a marginal writer not because some of my characters share my sexuality but because I am a lesbian, therefore somehow mysteriously disqualified from presenting a vision of central value.

Kind, straight friends have argued that, if I weren't so visibly a lesbian, my work wouldn't be so often distorted and dismissed. But short of denying

1. General interest magazine based in Toronto.

my sexuality, there is little I can do. It is not I but the interviewer or reviewer who is more interested in the fact that I am a lesbian than in the fact that I am a writer. My only positive choice under the circumstance is to use the media to make educational points about my sexuality.

Many people in the gay movement do not understand why I don't use my work as I am often willing to use myself for propaganda. Though one heterosexual critic did call *Lesbian Images* a piece of propaganda because in it I make my own bias quite clear, even that book does not satisfy the homosexual propagandists who would have me not waste time on politically incorrect lesbian writers like Radclyffe Hall, May Sarton, Maureen Duffy—in fact, nearly all the writers I studied in depth, but concentrate only on my most radical contemporaries, who are writing experimental erotica and separatist utopias.

I decided to be a writer not because I was a great reader as a child or had any natural gift for language but because I wanted to speak the truth as I saw it. To understand and share that understanding has been my preoccupation since I was in my teens. No political or moral ideal can supercede my commitment to portray people as they really are. What is is my domain. What ought to be is the business of politicians and preachers.

It is still a popular heterosexual belief that all homosexuals are at least sick and probably depraved, and they should, therefore, be, if not incarcerated in mental hospitals and jails, at least invisible. It is the conviction of many gay militants that all homosexuals are victims and martyrs who must become heroically visible so that everyone will have to face the fact that education, industry, the law, medicine, and the government would all come to a grinding halt without the homosexuals who are the backbone of all our institutions: "Even Eleanor Roosevelt . . ." that argument can begin or end. The truth of experience lies elsewhere.

For offering a balanced view of society, I'm sure I know a disproportionate number of homosexuals, as I know a disproportionate number of artists, white people, Canadians. One of the truths about all of us is that we live in disproportionate groups. That is why novels tend to be full of Jews or Blacks or soldiers or Englishmen or heterosexuals. Very few tend to be full of homosexuals because, until recently, homosexuals didn't live in social groups except in some places in Europe. My first two novels, *Desert of the Heart* and *This Is Not For You*, though they are about lesbian relationships, are not full of lesbians. I was writing about what was ardent, dangerous and secret, which is what lesbian experience still is for a great number of people. In my third novel, *Against the Season*, which was the beginning of my preoccupation with groups of people rather than with one or two main characters, out of about a dozen characters two are lesbian. There are a gay male and a lesbian in my fourth novel, *The Young in One Another's Arms*, out of a cast of about ten. Three and a half of eight characters are homosexual in my latest novel, *Contract with the World*. In all of my novels my gay characters move in an essentially heterosexual world as most gay people do. Though some of them are closeted in that world, some punished and defeated by it, they are all visible to the reader who is confronted with who they are and how they feel.

In a rare and beautiful comment about a character in *Contract with the World*, Leo Simpson says, "When Allen is arrested on some kind of homosexual charge, he has become so real that the laws of society immediately seem barbarous. Comfortable prejudices look like a tyranny of fear, which is of course part of what Rule's novel wants to say." 7

Yes, exactly, not heroic or saintly but *real*, and it is *part* of what I want to say. But in this book I am basically concerned with six or eight people, each of whom deals with barbarous law and comfortable prejudice, not always to do with homosexuality or even sexuality. What gathers the characters into one book is their involvement with art in a provincial city far from any cultural centre. To be an artist in this country is very difficult. To deal with the pain and doubt and wonder of such aspirations is my chief preoccupation in this book. My characters are neither necessarily greatly talented nor superior in vision simply because they are artists. They all have to face the fact that, except for the few greatest, artists are considered failures. A great many, very gifted or not, can't stand such a climate. In this they share something of the strain it is to be homosexual in a homophobic culture. 8

I owe to my own art all the honesty and insight I have, not simply about homosexuals and artists, both of which I happen to be, but about the whole range of my experience as a member of a family, a community, a country. I don't write Harry and Anna stories to cater to *Chatelaine*'s heterosexual readers though I like the cheques well enough when they come in. (No one could eat writing for *Christopher Street*,[2] and I still give most of my short fiction away.) I write them out of affection for those men and women, like my own parents, who care for and love and enjoy their children and because I, too, have cared for and loved and enjoyed children. There are heterosexual men and women in all my work because there are heterosexual men and women in my life and world, to whom I owe much of my understanding. 9

A blind writer once said to me, "You're the only writer I know who includes characters who happen to be physically handicapped. In most fiction, if they are there at all, it's *because* they're handicapped." That for me is the real distinction between what I write and propaganda. I am trying to make the real visible. People "happen to be" a lot of things about which there are cultural phobias. I have never found either safety or comfort in a blind heart, as a way to work or live. 10

As a lesbian, I believe it is important to stand up and be counted, to insist on the dignity and joy loving another woman is for me. If that gets in the 11

2. Lesbian and gay literary magazine based in New York.

way of people's reading my books, I have finally to see that it is their problem and not mine. As a writer, I must be free to say what is in all the diversity I can command. I regret the distorting prejudices that surround me, whether they affect homosexuals or men or the physically handicapped, and I can't alone defeat them. They will not defeat me, either as a lesbian or a writer.

IN SEARCH OF OUR MOTHERS' GARDENS

◐

ALICE WALKER

Many people recognize Alice Walker by the film "The Color Purple," which was based on her 1982 novel about the life of a young black woman in the rural south. Her other novels about racism and the African American experience include *The Third Life of Grange Copeland* (1970), *In Love and Trouble* (1973), and *Meridian* (1976). Her nonfiction writings, including this essay from her 1983 collection *In Search of Our Mothers' Gardens: Womanist Prose,* explore the situation of women in our culture and celebrate the achievements and resiliency of women in history.

I described her own nature and temperament. Told how they needed a larger life for their expression. . . . I pointed out that in lieu of proper channels, her emotions had overflowed into paths that dissipated them. I talked, beautifully I thought, about an art that would be born, an art that would open the way for women the likes of her. I asked her to hope, and build up an inner life against the coming of that day. . . . I sang, with a strange quiver in my voice, a promise song.   —*Jean Toomer, "Avey," Cane*

The poet speaking to a prostitute who falls asleep while he's talking—   1

When the poet Jean Toomer walked through the South in the early   2
twenties, he discovered a curious thing: black women whose spirituality was so intense, so deep, so *unconscious*, that they were themselves unaware of the richness they held. They stumbled blindly through their lives: creatures so abused and mutilated in body, so dimmed and confused by pain, that they considered themselves unworthy even of hope. In the selfless abstractions their bodies became to the men who used them, they became more than "sexual objects," more even than mere women: they became "Saints." Instead of being perceived as whole persons, their bodies became shrines: what was thought to be their minds became temples suitable for worship. These crazy Saints stared out at the world, wildly, like lunatics—or quietly, like suicides; and the "God" that was in their gaze was as mute as a great stone.

Who were these Saints? These crazy, loony, pitiful women?   3
Some of them, without a doubt, were our mothers and grandmothers.   4

In the still heat of the post-Reconstruction South, this is how they seemed 5
to Jean Toomer: exquisite butterflies trapped in an evil honey, toiling away
their lives in an era, a century, that did not acknowledge them, except as "the
mule of the world." They dreamed dreams that no one knew—not even
themselves, in any coherent fashion—and saw visions no one could understand. They wandered or sat about the countryside crooning lullabies to
ghosts, and drawing the mother of Christ in charcoal on courthouse walls.

They forced their minds to desert their bodies and their striving spirits 6
sought to rise, like frail whirlwinds from the hard red clay. And when those
frail whirlwinds fell, in scattered particles, upon the ground, no one mourned.
Instead, men lit candles to celebrate the emptiness that remained, as people
do who enter a beautiful but vacant space to resurrect a God.

Our mothers and grandmothers, some of them: moving to music not yet 7
written. And they waited.

They waited for a day when the unknown thing that was in them would 8
be made known; but guessed, somehow in their darkness, that on the day of
their revelation they would be long dead. Therefore to Toomer they walked,
and even ran, in slow motion. For they were going nowhere immediate, and
the future was not yet within their grasp. And men took our mothers and
grandmothers, "but got no pleasure from it." So complex was their passion
and their calm.

To Toomer, they lay vacant and fallow as autumn fields, with harvest time 9
never in sight: and he saw them enter loveless marriages, without joy; and
become prostitutes, without resistance; and become mothers of children,
without fulfillment.

For these grandmothers and mothers of ours were not Saints, but Artists; 10
driven to a numb and bleeding madness by the springs of creativity in them
for which there was no release. They were Creators, who lived lives of spiritual
waste, because they were so rich in spirituality—which is the basis of Art—
that the strain of enduring their unused and unwanted talent drove them
insane. Throwing away this spirituality was their pathetic attempt to lighten
the soul to a weight their work-worn, sexually abused bodies could bear.

What did it mean for a black woman to be an artist in our grandmothers' 11
time? In our great-grandmothers' day? It is a question with an answer cruel
enough to stop the blood.

Did you have a genius of a great-great-grandmother who died under 12
some ignorant and depraved white overseer's lash? Or was she required to
bake biscuits for a lazy backwater tramp, when she cried out in her soul to
paint watercolors of sunsets, or the rain falling on the green and peaceful
pasturelands? Or was her body broken and forced to bear children (who were
more often than not sold away from her)—eight, ten, fifteen, twenty children—when her one joy was the thought of modeling heroic figures of re-
bellion, in stone or clay?

How was the creativity of the black woman kept alive, year after year and 13
century after century, when for most of the years black people have been in

America, it was a punishable crime for a black person to read or write? And the freedom to paint, to sculpt, to expand the mind with action did not exist. Consider, if you can bear to imagine it, what might have been the result if singing, too, had been forbidden by law. Listen to the voices of Bessie Smith, Billie Holiday, Nina Simone, Roberta Flack, and Aretha Franklin, among others, and imagine those voices muzzled for life. Then you may begin to comprehend the lives of our "crazy," "Sainted" mothers and grandmothers. The agony of the lives of women who might have been Poets, Novelists, Essayists, and Short-Story Writers (over a period of centuries), who died with their real gifts stifled within them.

And, if this were the end of the story, we would have cause to cry out in my paraphrase of Okot p'Bitek's great poem: 14

> O, my clanswomen
> Let us all cry together!
> Come,
> Let us mourn the death of our mother,
> The death of a Queen
> The ash that was produced
> By a great fire!
> O, this homestead is utterly dead
> Close the gates
> With *lacari* thorns,
> For our mother
> The creator of the Stool is lost!
> And all the young women
> Have perished in the wilderness!

But this is not the end of the story, for all the young women—our mothers and grandmothers, *ourselves*—have not perished in the wilderness. And if we ask ourselves why, and search for and find the answer, we will know beyond all efforts to erase it from our minds, just exactly who, and of what, we black American women are. 15

One example, perhaps the most pathetic, most misunderstood one, can provide a backdrop for our mothers' work: Phillis Wheatley, a slave in the 1700s. 16

Virginia Woolf, in her book *A Room of One's Own*, wrote that in order for a woman to write fiction she must have two things, certainly: a room of her own (with key and lock) and enough money to support herself. 17

What then are we to make of Phillis Wheatley, a slave, who owned not even herself? This sickly, frail black girl who required a servant of her own at times—her health was so precarious—and who, had she been white, would have been easily considered the intellectual superior of all the women and most of the men in the society of her day. 18

Virginia Woolf wrote further, speaking of course not of our Phillis, that "any woman born with a great gift in the sixteenth century [insert "eighteenth 19

179

century," insert "black woman," insert "born or made a slave"] would certainly have gone crazed, shot herself, or ended her days in some lonely cottage outside the village, half witch, half wizard [insert "Saint"], feared and mocked at. For it needs little skill and psychology to be sure that a highly gifted girl who had tried to use her gift for poetry would have been so thwarted and hindered by contrary instincts [add "chains, guns, the lash, the ownership of one's body by someone else, submission to an alien religion"], that she must have lost her health and sanity to a certainty."

The key words, as they relate to Phillis, are "contrary instincts." For when we read the poetry of Phillis Wheatley—as when we read the novels of Nella Larsen or the oddly false-sounding autobiography of that freest of all black women writers, Zora Hurston—evidence of "contrary instincts" is everywhere. Her loyalties were completely divided, as was, without question, her mind. 20

But how could this be otherwise? Captured at seven, a slave of wealthy, doting whites who instilled in her the "savagery" of the Africa they "rescued" her from . . . one wonders if she was even able to remember her homeland as she had known it, or as it really was. 21

Yet, because she did try to use her gift for poetry in a world that made her a slave, she was "so thwarted and hindered by . . . contrary instincts, that she . . . lost her health. . . ." In the last years of her brief life, burdened not only with the need to express her gift but also with a penniless, friendless "freedom" and several small children for whom she was forced to do strenuous work to feed, she lost her health, certainly. Suffering from malnutrition and neglect and who knows what mental agonies, Phillis Wheatley died. 22

So torn by "contrary instincts" was black, kidnapped, enslaved Phillis that her description of "the Goddess"—as she poetically called the Liberty she did not have—is ironically, cruelly humorous. And, in fact, has held Phillis up to ridicule for more than a century. It is usually read prior to hanging Phillis's memory as that of a fool. She wrote: 23

> The Goddess comes, she moves divinely fair,
> Olive and laurel binds her *golden* hair.
> Wherever shines this native of the skies,
> Unnumber'd charms and recent graces rise. [My italics]

It is obvious that Phillis, the slave, combed the "Goddess's" hair every morning; prior, perhaps, to bringing in the milk, or fixing her mistress's lunch. She took her imagery from the one thing she saw elevated above all others. 24

With the benefit of hindsight we ask, "How could she?" 25

But at last, Phillis, we understand. No more snickering when your stiff, struggling, ambivalent lines are forced on us. We know now that you were not an idiot or a traitor; only a sickly little black girl, snatched from your home and country and made a slave; a woman who still struggled to sing the 26 song that was your gift, although in a land of barbarians who praised you for your bewildered tongue. It is not so much what you sang, as that you kept alive, in so many of our ancestors, *the notion of song.*

Black women are called, in the folklore that so aptly identifies one's status in society, "the *mule* of the world," because we have been handed the burdens that everyone else—*everyone* else—refused to carry. We have also been called "Matriarchs," "Superwomen," and "Mean and Evil Bitches." Not to mention "Castraters" and "Sapphire's Mama." When we have pleaded for understanding, our character has been distorted; when we have asked for simple caring, we have been handed empty inspirational appellations, then stuck in the farthest corner. When we have asked for love, we have been given children. In short, even our plainer gifts, our labors of fidelity and love, have been knocked down our throats. To be an artist and a black woman, even today, lowers our status in many respects, rather than raises it: and yet, artists we will be. 27

Therefore we must fearlessly pull out of ourselves and look at and identify with our lives the living creativity some of our great-grandmothers were not allowed to know. I stress *some* of them because it is well known that the majority of our great-grandmothers knew, even without "knowing" it, the reality of their spirituality, even if they didn't recognize it beyond what happened in the singing at church—and they never had any intention of giving it up. 28

How they did it—those millions of black women who were not Phillis Wheatley, or Lucy Terry or Frances Harper or Zora Hurston or Nella Larsen or Bessie Smith; or Elizabeth Catlett, or Katherine Dunham, either—brings me to the title of this essay, "In Search of Our Mothers' Gardens," which is a personal account that is yet shared, in its theme and its meaning, by all of us. I found, while thinking about the far-reaching world of the creative black woman, that often the truest answer to a question that really matters can be found very close. 29

In the late 1920s my mother ran away from home to marry my father. Marriage, if not running away, was expected of seventeen-year-old girls. By the time she was twenty, she had two children and was pregnant with a third. Five children later, I was born. And this is how I came to know my mother: she seemed a large, soft, loving-eyed woman who was rarely impatient in our home. Her quick, violent temper was on view only a few times a year, when she battled with the white landlord who had the misfortune to suggest to her that her children did not need to go to school. 30

She made all the clothes we wore, even my brothers' overalls. She made all the towels and sheets we used. She spent the summers canning vegetables 31 and fruits. She spent the winter evenings making quilts enough to cover all our beds.

During the "working" day, she labored beside—not behind—my father in the fields. Her day began before sunup, and did not end until late at night. There was never a moment for her to sit down, undisturbed, to unravel her own private thoughts; never a time free from interruption—by work or the noisy inquiries of her many children. And yet, it is to my mother—and all our mothers who were not famous—that I went in search of the secret of what has fed that muzzled and often mutilated, but vibrant, creative spirit that the black woman has inherited, and that pops out in wild and unlikely places to this day. 32

But when, you will ask, did my overworked mother have time to know or care about feeding the creative spirit? 33

The answer is so simple that many of us have spent years discovering it. We have constantly looked high, when we should have looked high—and low. 34

For example: in the Smithsonian Institution in Washington, D.C., there hangs a quilt unlike any other in the world. In fanciful, inspired, and yet simple and identifiable figures, it portrays the story of the Crucifixion. It is considered rare, beyond price. Though it follows no known pattern of quilt-making, and though it is made of bits and pieces of worthless rags, it is obviously the work of a person of powerful imagination and deep spiritual feeling. Below this quilt I saw a note that says it was made by "an anonymous Black woman in Alabama, a hundred years ago." 35

If we could locate this "anonymous" black woman from Alabama, she would turn out to be one of our grandmothers—an artist who left her mark in the only materials she could afford, and in the only medium her position in society allowed her to use. 36

As Virginia Woolf wrote further, in *A Room of One's Own*: 37

> Yet genius of a sort must have existed among women as it must have existed among the working class. [Change this to "slaves" and "the wives and daughters of sharecroppers."] Now and again an Emily Brontë or a Robert Burns [change this to "a Zora Hurston or a Richard Wright"] blazes out and proves its presence. But certainly it never got itself on to paper. When, however, one reads of a witch being ducked, of a woman possessed by devils [or "Saint-hood"], of a wise woman selling herbs [our root workers], or even a very remarkable man who had a mother, then I think we are on the track of a lost novelist, a suppressed poet, of some mute and inglorious Jane Austen. . . . Indeed, I would venture to guess that Anon, who wrote so many poems without signing them, was often a woman. . . .

And so our mothers and grandmothers have, more often than not anonymously, handed on the creative spark, the seed of the flower they themselves never hoped to see: or like a sealed letter they could not plainly read. 38

And so it is, certainly, with my own mother. Unlike "Ma" Rainey's songs, which retained their creator's name even while blasting forth from Bessie 39

Smith's mouth, no song or poem will bear my mother's name. Yet so many of the stories that I write, that we all write, are my mother's stories. Only recently did I fully realize this: that through years of listening to my mother's stories of her life, I have absorbed not only the stories themselves, but something of the manner in which she spoke, something of the urgency that involves the knowledge that her stories—like her life—must be recorded. It is probably for this reason that so much of what I have written is about characters whose counterparts in real life are so much older than I am.

But the telling of these stories, which came from my mother's lips as 40 naturally as breathing, was not the only way my mother showed herself as an artist. For stories, too, were subject to being distracted, to dying without conclusion. Dinners must be started, and cotton must be gathered before the big rains. The artist that was and is my mother showed itself to me only after many years. This is what I finally noticed:

Like Mem, a character in *The Third Life of Grange Copeland*, my mother 41 adorned with flowers whatever shabby house we were forced to live in. And not just your typical straggly country stand of zinnias, either. She planted ambitious gardens—and still does—with over fifty different varieties of plants that bloom profusely from early March until late November. Before she left home for the fields, she watered her flowers, chopped up the grass, and laid out new beds. When she returned from the fields she might divide clumps of bulbs, dig a cold pit, uproot and replant roses, or prune branches from her taller bushes or trees—until night came and it was too dark to see.

Whatever she planted grew as if by magic, and her fame as a grower of 42 flowers spread over three counties. Because of her creativity with her flowers, even my memories of poverty are seen through a screen of blooms—sunflowers, petunias, roses, dahlias, forsythia, spirea, delphiniums, verbena . . . and on and on.

And I remember people coming to my mother's yard to be given cuttings 43 from her flowers; I hear again the praise showered on her because whatever rocky soil she landed on, she turned into a garden. A garden so brilliant with colors, so original in its design, so magnificent with life and creativity, that to this day people drive by our house in Georgia—perfect strangers and imperfect strangers—and ask to stand or walk among my mother's art.

I notice that it is only when my mother is working in her flowers that 44 she is radiant, almost to the point of being invisible—except as Creator: hand and eye. She is involved in work her soul must have. Ordering the universe in the image of her personal conception of Beauty.

Her face, as she prepares the Art that is her gift, is a legacy of respect 45 she leaves to me, for all that illuminates and cherishes life. She has handed down respect for the possibilities—and the will to grasp them.

For her, so hindered and intruded upon in so many ways, being an artist 46 has still been a daily part of her life. This ability to hold on, even in very simple ways, is work black women have done for a very long time.

This poem is not enough, but it is something, for the woman who literally   47
covered the holes in our walls with sunflowers:

> They were women then
> My mama's generation
> Husky of voice—Stout of
> Step
> With fists as well as
> Hands
> How they battered down
> Doors
> And ironed
> Starched white
> Shirts
> How they led
> Armies
> Headragged Generals
> Across mined
> Fields
> Booby-trapped
> Kitchens
> To discover books
> Desks
> A place for us
> How they knew what we
> *Must* know
> Without knowing a page
> Of it
> Themselves.

Guided by my heritage of a love of beauty and a respect for strength—   48
in search of my mother's garden, I found my own.

And perhaps in Africa over two hundred years ago, there was just such a   49
mother; perhaps she painted vivid and daring decorations in oranges and
yellows and greens on the walls of her hut; perhaps she sang—in a voice like
Roberta Flack's—*sweetly* over the compounds of her village; perhaps she wove
the most stunning mats or told the most ingenious stories of all the village
storytellers. Perhaps she was herself a poet—though only her daughter's name
is signed to the poems that we know.

Perhaps Phillis Wheatley's mother was also an artist.   50

Perhaps in more than Phillis Wheatley's biological life is her mother's   51
signature made clear.

MAKING CONNECTIONS

1. A large part of your college studies involves using your own writing skills to express yourself, refine your ideas, demonstrate your knowledge. What is your own relationship to writing and identity? Do you see writing as something that constrains you? Gives you access to power? Works to express or repress you? How is your identity shaped by your writing and in what ways can your identity shape your writing? How do you, or would you, write "as a man," "as a woman," or in a "gender-free" fashion?

2. Using Spender's essay and any essays from Chapter 4 you find appropriate, write your own essay discussing how prejudices about women's writing are tied into prejudices about gender and speaking. Make use of the readings you select for quotations and references, but try to construct your own stance on this topic, either by agreeing with or challenging these authors' conclusions.

3. Compare and contrast Kizer, Walker, and Ozick on the problems women writers faced and continue to face. Can you divide these problems into categories? How does the focus of each piece differ from the others, and in what aspects are they similar? How would Walker respond to Kizer's history of women writers, for instance? Or how might Ozick's fables compare with Walker's anecdotes as illustrations of women's marginalization? How effective is the genre each writer selected—poetry, fables, essay—in conveying her point?

4. In the style of Ozick, try writing one or two of your own "fables" to match the morals of her stories. Do any of your own experiences parallel hers? How might these stories shed light on the situations of other groups discriminated against in society? Can you draw any conclusions about the techniques and tactics of discrimination?

5. Rule's essay suggests the power of language—particularly of the written word—in shaping our ideas of reality. How does writing influence our view of what is real, through such channels as the media, classroom curricula, and literature? What is the relationship of literature to reality? Couldn't you argue that fiction is by definition "unreal," not tied into reality at all? Take a position and give examples supporting your point.

6. Compare and contrast Rule and Walker on the ways in which their "marginalized" identities (being lesbian, being black) are incorporated into their writing. In what ways can one's background or lifestyle be a handicap or a source of power and vision? How does each author address her audience in an attempt to inform, convince, or challenge them? Who do you think the imagined audience is for each essayist?

7. Discuss the tone of Alice Walker's essay and the images and style she uses to convey her points. What is her attitude toward the black women of the past, the "crazy, loony, pitiful women" she refers to? Explain her distinction between "Saints" and "Artists." Why was black women's involuntary "sainthood" a burden and a chain? In the end, how would you describe her relationship to her heritage?

8. In a personal narrative, compare your own heritage to Walker's. Discuss the gifts and struggles passed on to you either in your family or because of your race, class or sex—perhaps without your being fully aware of them. How might you draw on them to find your own identity and strength?

9. Write an essay on the writer's need for freedom. What kinds of freedom are important to pursue creative activity? Have women historically been denied such freedoms? If so, how might they work practically to reclaim them?

10. Rich's poem "The Stranger" in Chapter 1 makes a subtle connection between anger and clear vision. The issue of anger underlies many of this chapter's readings as well, whether explicitly or implicitly. What might be the positive uses of anger in addressing the history of discrimination against women writers? What are the "taboos" against anger, particularly for women, and what are the benefits and drawbacks of touching on anger to bring about new visions? Write an essay on anger, insight, and change that addresses these concerns.

11. Does language merely reflect social realities or does it have the power to create, perpetuate or change our attitudes? Select any two essays from this chapter, or one essay from this chapter and one from Chapter 4, and compare the ways language is seen to operate in each.

12. One source of social inequality lies in designating one way of being as "the best" and devaluing its opposite. In the case of gender, "masculine" qualities (such as assertiveness, independence, abstract logic) have traditionally been considered "the best," and "feminine" qualities (gentleness, nurturance, personal feeling) seen as "secondary." Select two or more essays from this chapter and show how they undermine that division, either by erasing it or by re-valuing a "feminine" mode of being.

6
READING: HOW
READERS MAKE
MEANING

C O N T E X T S

What happens when we read? How do readers make meaning out of texts? How can different readers come up with different, sometimes even contradictory interpretations of the same poem, story, or play? And can those readings all be valid, or is there a "right" and a "wrong" interpretation of any given text?

In school, we are usually trained to look for "the right answer," and our impulse to find it is strong, whether the field is mathematics or literature. If there is one solution to an equation, there must also be one "solution" to a poem or play—right? It is as if the meaning were somehow "out there," concealed in the poem or play, like a gift that must be unwrapped in a specific way. If we could all learn to unwrap the right way, we would all come to the same gift—the "right interpretation."

A recent school of literary criticism called "reader-response" challenges the view that there is only one fixed meaning that can be found *in* the text. Instead, meaning is something that happens *between* the text and the reader, a dynamic meeting of two forces. Rather than looking exclusively at the poem or play for understanding, reader-response criticism focuses on the "experience" of reading and on the reading process itself—what readers do and how they do it.

The process of reading is never a settled thing. On the one hand is the text, which is itself full of ambiguities, questions, possibilities—else why would we have to work to understand it, to "make" meaning out of it? On the other hand is the reader, who is even less of a known entity, bringing a unique and changeable attitude and background to every act of reading. Each reader will experience the text in an original way since meaning is only constructed in the active interchange between the two.

But what part does gender play in all this? The essays in this chapter address that question from several perspectives. Gender can be seen as part of what we bring to our acts of reading and thinking, not because of biological differences (though researchers are still arguing questions about hormones and the brain) but because our experiences as men and women make up a large part of how we see the world, the life experiences which help us understand or identify with a text. That understanding can take the form of how open we are to another point of view, how well we "listen" to what a poem or story has to say. In "Gender and Reading," Elizabeth Flynn suggests that women readers might be more open "listeners" to texts because they are socialized to be more receptive than aggressive in language use. Thus, the same qualities that are sometimes seen to undermine women's power as public speakers (Chapter 4) might account for what Flynn perceives to be their greater sensitivity and judgement as readers.

Gender can also play a role in the points we choose to focus on while reading a text, elements that we respond to or that ring true in our experience. Judith Fetterley's essay, "A Rose for 'A Rose for Emily'," offers a new reading of an old story from a feminist point of view, showing how the aspects we choose to highlight in our interpretations can lead to a very different understanding of the same text. Her book *The Resisting Reader: A Feminist Approach to American Fiction*, from which our selection is taken, provides numerous examples of how a new perspective can "resist" and change past views of literature.

But if the possibilities for interaction between reader and text are endless, is *everything* we say valid? Robert Crosman takes up this problem in the final essay, "How Readers Make Meaning," in which he constructs his own experiment in reader-response criticism. Although reading can be seen as an individual interchange between text and reader, meaning does still rely on certain conventions. Just as with spoken language, reading is not only personal but social as well. Making sense of a text is not a purely subjective, arbitrary act; the process relies also on a common understanding about language, a communal set of beliefs about what words say. Though this set of beliefs may itself be the subject of debate and may change over time, it allows us as readers to speak with one another, to compare and evaluate interpretations, to communicate views. Meaning is both private and public; we exist not only as individual readers but as members of a "reading community," which also guides our understanding.

We have included in this chapter two of the short stories the essayists use in their analyses—Ernest Hemingway's "Hills Like White Elephants" and William Faulkner's "A Rose for Emily." By reading these stories you can supply your own interpretations along with those discussed in the essays. We invite you to bring your knowledge and assumptions to bear on this chapter—in short, to *read*.

HILLS LIKE WHITE ELEPHANTS

◐

ERNEST HEMINGWAY

A key figure in modern American literature, Ernest Hemingway is most often studied for his novels *The Sun Also Rises* (1926), *A Farewell to Arms* (1929), *For Whom the Bell Tolls* (1940), and *The Old Man and the Sea* (1952), but many of his short stories are widely anthologized as well. The following brief story, written in 1927, is often used as an example of Hemingway's subtle skill with dialogue. Here, a seemingly ordinary quarrel between a woman and a man reveals much about their characters, their relationship, and their lives. Hemingway's many years as an expatriate writer in France and Spain make up the backdrop of this tale.

The hills across the valley of the Ebro[1] were long and white. On this side there was no shade and no trees and the station was between two lines of rails in the sun. Close against the side of the station there was the warm shadow of the building and a curtain, made of strings of bamboo beads, hung across the open door into the bar, to keep out flies. The American and the girl with him sat at a table in the shade, outside the building. It was very hot and the express from Barcelona would come in forty minutes. It stopped at this junction for two minutes and went on to Madrid.

"What should we drink?" the girl asked. She had taken off her hat and put it on the table.

"It's pretty hot," the man said.

"Let's drink beer."

"Dos cervezas," the man said into the curtain.

"Big ones?" a woman asked from the doorway.

"Yes. Two big ones."

The woman brought two glasses of beer and two felt pads. She put the felt pads and the beer glasses on the table and looked at the man and the girl. The girl was looking off at the line of hills. They were white in the sun and the country was brown and dry.

"They look like white elephants," she said.

---

1. A river in northern Spain.

"I've never seen one," the man drank his beer. 10

"No, you wouldn't have." 11

"I might have," the man said. "Just because you say I wouldn't have 12
doesn't prove anything."

The girl looked at the bead curtain. "They've painted something on it," 13
she said. "What does it say?"

"Anis del Toro. It's a drink." 14

"Could we try it?" 15

The man called "Listen" through the curtain. The woman came out from 16
the bar.

"Four reales."[2] 17

"We want two Anis del Toro." 18

"With water?" 19

"Do you want it with water?" 20

"I don't know," the girl said. "Is it good with water?" 21

"It's all right." 22

"You want them with water?" asked the woman. 23

"Yes, with water." 24

"It tastes like licorice," the girl said and put the glass down. 25

"That's the way with everything." 26

"Yes," said the girl. "Everything tastes of licorice. Especially all the things 27
you've waited so long for, like absinthe."

"Oh, cut it out." 28

"You started it," the girl said. "I was being amused. I was having a fine 29
time."

"Well, let's try and have a fine time." 30

"All right. I was trying. I said the mountains looked like white elephants. 31
Wasn't that bright?"

"That was bright." 32

"I wanted to try this new drink. That's all we do, isn't it—look at things 33
and try new drinks?"

"I guess so." 34

The girl looked across at the hills. 35

"They're lovely hills," she said. "They don't really look like white ele- 36
phants. I just meant the coloring of their skin through the trees."

"Should we have another drink?" 37

"All right." 38

The warm wind blew the bead curtain against the table. 39

"The beer's nice and cool," the man said. 40

"It's lovely," the girl said. 41

2. Spanish currency.

"It's really an awfully simple operation, Jig," the man said. "It's not really an operation at all." 42

The girl looked at the ground the table legs rested on. 43

"I know you wouldn't mind it, Jig. It's really not anything. It's just to let the air in." 44

The girl did not say anything. 45

"I'll go with you and I'll stay with you all the time. They just let the air in and then it's all perfectly natural." 46

"Then what will we do afterward?" 47

"We'll be fine afterward. Just like we were before." 48

"What makes you think so?" 49

"That's the only thing that bothers us. It's the only thing that's made us unhappy." 50

The girl looked at the bead curtain, put her hand out and took hold of two of the strings of beads. 51

"And you think then we'll be all right and be happy." 52

"I know we will. You don't have to be afraid. I've known lots of people that have done it." 53

"So have I," said the girl. "And afterward they were all so happy." 54

"Well," the man said, "if you don't want to you don't have to. I wouldn't have you do it if you didn't want to. But I know it's perfectly simple." 55

"And you really want to?" 56

"I think it's the best thing to do. But I don't want you to do it if you don't really want to." 57

"And if I do it you'll be happy and things will be like they were and you'll love me?" 58

"I love you now. You know I love you." 59

"I know. But if I do it, then it will be nice again if I say things are like white elephants, and you'll like it?" 60

"I'll love it. I love it now but I just can't think about it. You know how I get when I worry." 61

"If I do it you won't ever worry?" 62

"I won't worry about that because it's perfectly simple." 63

"Then I'll do it. Because I don't care about me." 64

"What do you mean?" 65

"I don't care about me." 66

"Well, I care about you." 67

"Oh, yes. But I don't care about me. And I'll do it and then everything will be fine." 68

"I don't want you to do it if you feel that way." 69

The girl stood up and walked to the end of the station. Across, on the other side, were fields of grain and trees along the banks of the Ebro. Far away, beyond the river, were mountains. The shadow of a cloud moved across the field of grain and she saw the river through the trees. 70

"And we could have all this," she said. "And we could have everything 71
and every day we make it more impossible."

"What did you say?" 72

"I said we could have everything." 73

"We can have everything." 74

"No, we can't." 75

"We can have the whole world." 76

"No, we can't." 77

"We can go everywhere." 78

"No, we can't. It isn't ours any more." 79

"It's ours." 80

"No, it isn't. And once they take it away, you never get it back." 81

"But they haven't taken it away." 82

"We'll wait and see." 83

"Come on back in the shade," he said. "You mustn't feel that way." 84

"I don't feel any way," the girl said. "I just know things." 85

"I don't want you to do anything that you don't want to do—" 86

"Nor that isn't good for me," she said. "I know. Could we have another 87
beer?"

"All right. But you've got to realize—" 88

"I realize," the girl said. "Can't we maybe stop talking?" 89

They sat down at the table and the girl looked across at the hills on the 90
dry side of the valley and the man looked at her and at the table.

"You've got to realize," he said, "that I don't want you to do it if you 91
don't want to. I'm perfectly willing to go through with it if it means anything
to you."

"Doesn't it mean anything to you? We could get along." 92

"Of course it does. But I don't want anybody but you. I don't want any 93
one else. And I know it's perfectly simple."

"Yes, you know it's perfectly simple." 94

"It's all right for you to say that, but I do know it." 95

"Would you do something for me now?" 96

"I'd do anything for you." 97

"Would you please please please please please please please stop talking?" 98

He did not say anything but looked at the bags against the wall of the 99
station. There were labels on them from all the hotels where they had spent
nights.

"But I don't want you to," he said, "I don't care anything about it." 100

"I'll scream," the girl said. 101

The woman came out through the curtains with two glasses of beer and 102
put them down on the damp felt pads. "The train comes in five minutes," she
said.

"What did she say?" asked the girl. 103

"That the train is coming in five minutes." 104

The girl smiled brightly at the woman, to thank her. 105

"I'd better take the bags over to the other side of the station," the man 106
said. She smiled at him.

"All right. Then come back and we'll finish the beer." 107

He picked up the two heavy bags and carried them around the station to 108
the other tracks. He looked up the tracks but could not see the train. Coming
back, he walked through the barroom, where people waiting for the train
were drinking. He drank an Anis at the bar and looked at the people. They
were all waiting reasonably for the train. He went out through the bead
curtain. She was sitting at the table and smiled at him.

"Do you feel better?" he asked. 109

"I feel fine," she said. "There's nothing wrong with me. I feel fine." 110

GENDER AND READING

◑

ELIZABETH A. FLYNN

Elizabeth Flynn is a leading researcher on issues of gender and the process of reading. She is author of numerous scholarly essays and editor of the critical collection *Gender and Reading* (1986), of which the following piece is the title essay. Here, she examines the responses of male and female college freshmen to three stories, including Ernest Hemingway's "Hills Like White Elephants," in order to study how gender might influence our performance as readers.

Recent scholarship on the relationship between gender and reading has arisen primarily from two different sources: reading research that examines the behavior of elementary and high school students, and feminist literary criticism that analyzes literary texts from a reader-oriented perspective. Reading researchers have contributed empirical data on gender-related similarities and differences among developing readers, and feminist literary critics have contributed descriptive studies of the ways in which texts shape responses along gender lines. We know very little, though, about the reading patterns of relatively mature male and female readers. In an attempt to extend the studies of reading researchers to include college-age students and to bring an empirical orientation to the reader-oriented work of feminist critics, I conducted an exploratory study designed to examine the interpretive strategies of college freshmen in their responses to three frequently anthologized short stories, James Joyce's "Araby," Ernest Hemingway's "Hills Like White Elephants," and Virginia Woolf's "Kew Gardens." The twenty-six women and twenty-six men who comprised my sample were enrolled in a freshman composition course taught at Michigan Technological University in 1980. Students in seven sections of composition wrote responses to the stories during three different class sessions. They were told that a wide range of responses was possible, including summarizing the stories, analyzing them, or relating them to their own experiences. (See the Appendix for a description of the course, the students, and the assignments.)

My analysis of the data was informed by a conception of the reading process which assumes that reading involves a confrontation between self and "other." The self, the reader, encounters the "other," the text, and the nature of that confrontation depends on the background of the reader as well as on

1

2

the text. Text and reader are necessarily foreign to each other in some ways, and so the exchange between them involves an imbalance, what Wolfgang Iser calls "asymmetry" or "contingency." Georges Poulet emphasizes this imbalance in his description of the reading process. He writes, "Since every thought must have a subject to think it, this thought, which is alien to me and yet in me, must also have a subject which is alien to me. It all happens, then, as though reading were the act by which a thought managed to bestow itself within me with a subject not myself."[1] The reader allows the foreign object to "bestow itself" within his or her mind, and so self and other coexist, for a time.

What Poulet does not emphasize is that the coexistence of reader and   3
text can take a number of different forms. The reader can resist the alien thought or subject and so remain essentially unchanged by the reading experience. In this case the reader dominates the text. Or the reader can allow the alien thought to become such a powerful presence that the self is replaced by the other and so is effaced. In this case the text dominates the reader. Either the reader resists the text and so deprives it of its force, or the text overpowers the reader and so eliminates the reader's powers of discernment. A third possibility, however, is that self and other, reader and text, interact in such a way that the reader learns from the experience without losing critical distance; reader and text interact with a degree of mutuality. Foreignness is reduced, though not eliminated. Self and other remain distinct and so create a kind of dialogue.[2]

The dominant pole is characterized by detachment, observation from a   4
distance. The reader imposes a previously established structure on the text and in so doing silences it. Memory dominates over experience, past over present. Readers who dominate texts become complacent or bored because the possibility for learning has been greatly reduced. Judgment is based on previously established norms rather than on empathetic engagement with and critical evaluation of the new material encountered. The reader absents the text. A response to Joyce's "Araby" illustrates this strategy of domination. The student wrote enthusiastically about his encounter with the text, but there is

---

1. Wolfgang Iser, *The Act of Reading: A Theory of Aesthetic Response* (Baltimore: Johns Hopkins University Press, 1978), p. 167; Georges Poulet, "Criticism and the Experience of Interiority," trans. Catherine and Richard Macksey, in *Reader-Response Criticism: From Formalism to Post-Structuralism*, ed. Jane P. Tompkins (Baltimore: Johns Hopkins University Press, 1980), p. 44. [Au.] See Iser, p. 1219. [Ed.]

2. These categories were also suggested by Tzvetan Todorov's discussion of the Spanish conquest of the Indians in his course "The Conquest of America," taught at the School of Criticism and Theory, Northwestern University, June/July 1981. Professor Todorov argued that individual Spaniards assimilated Indian culture into their own and in so doing destroyed it, identified so strongly with Indian culture that they lost their European identity, or engaged in dialogical interaction with the Indians. [Au.]

little evidence that a pattern of meaning was created as a result of that encounter.

> The beauty that one comes away with from reading "Araby" is the feeling. When I read this story I could almost say I was there. I was able to relate some of my past experiences with what James Joyce used for setting. The general feeling of the street, and the buildings gazing at one another are all related to past experiences. I am able to say that, "Hey, I was on a street just like that." And when I can put my personal experience to work the story becomes loaded with color.
>
> The adjectives that are used throughout the story are very descriptive. The garden was not just a garden, but it was a wild garden. I am able to picture a wild garden; however, a wild garden may be one thing to you and another to me, but it makes no difference to the net effect.[3]

The student's positive attitude toward the reading experience suggests that subsequent readings of the story will result in meaningful interaction. This first reading, however, has not moved the student very far beyond himself. The text activated his imagination, and so he remembered streets and gardens from his own past. He has not yet put those images to use in comprehending the story, however. He makes no reference to the plot of "Araby" or even to its protagonist.

The submissive pole, in contrast, is characterized by too much involvement. The reader is entangled in the events of the story and is unable to step back, to observe with a critical eye. Instead of boredom the reader experiences anxiety. The text is overwhelming, unwilling to yield a consistent pattern of meaning. A response to "Araby" written by another student illustrates this submissive stance.

> "Araby" is another story that has great inner meaning. Each paragraph has some meaning; for example, the first paragraph has some deep inner meaning about what the houses represent. The second paragraph is the same way, in the deep meaning sense, but talks about some dead priest's home and what was found in the back yard. And every paragraph in between, right up to the last one, has something to be interpreted. I would start to interpret them if I could, but I can't make much sense out of the whole thing.
>
> In describing the story, it starts out with a street description of some old homes. The story then goes to some boys playing in the street, and then to a specific boy and what is happening to him as he, apparently, falls in love with a neighbor girl. The narrator tells about all the little things the boy is doing when falling in love like gazing under the window blind until she comes out and walking behind her when she is walking to school. And then his first time talking to her.

---

3. Distracting errors in punctuation and spelling have been corrected in this and other response statements. [Au.]

This student was so close to the textual details that he could make no sense of them; he brought little of his past experiences to bear on the text and so could gain no critical distance from it. He summarized the plot of the story in hope that some meaning would emerge. For him the text is a reservoir of hidden meanings rather than a system of signs to be acted on. Like the author of the previous response, this student will no doubt interact with the text more meaningfully in subsequent readings of the story. Right now, however, he is so overwhelmed by the text that he is unable to assign meaning to it.

These two responses are potentially interactive but are so far from revealing meaningful engagement with the text that they represent minimal communication. Productive interaction involves the active participation of the reader in the construction of meaning. Readers formulate hypotheses as they encounter the signs of the text, and those hypotheses are constantly being altered as new information is processed. Iser in *The Act of Reading* explains the process as follows: "The reader's communication with the text is a dynamic process of self-correction, as he formulates signifieds which he must then continually modify" (p. 67). As the reader's perspective shifts, so do the signs in the text, so that they are constantly taking on different patterns of significance. The reader's energies are expended attempting to find a consistent pattern of meaning from among the seemingly incompatible stimuli, and meaning is finally achieved only when tensions are resolved. Iser calls this resolution a closed gestalt. Signs no longer appear unrelated or contradictory but, rather, form a meaningful whole. 6

Within the category of interaction, then, we have levels of engagement with the text. A reader may be at an early stage of the interactive process and so unable to resolve the conflicting patterns that phantasmagorically emerge and recede during the act of reading. Characters, images, events, take on importance and then shrink into insignificance as the reader gropes toward meaning. Evaluations of textual details shift until the reader reconciles conflicting elements and achieves a balance between detachment and involvement. 7

Productive interaction, then, necessitates the stance of a detached observer who is empathetic but who does not identify with the characters or the situation depicted in a literary work. Comprehension is attained when the reader achieves a balance between empathy and judgment by maintaining a balance of detachment and involvement. Too much detachment often results in too much judgment and hence in domination of the text; too much involvement often results in too much sympathy and hence in domination by the text. However, when the reader is able to integrate past experience with the experience created by the text through critical evaluation of the interwoven signs encountered in the process of reading, comprehension is achieved and learning takes place. Iser describes the effect of productive interaction as follows: 8

The new experience emerges from the restructuring of the one we have stored, and this restructuring is what gives the new experience its form. But what actually happens during this process can again only be experienced when past feelings, views, and values have been evoked and then made to merge with the new experience. The old conditions the form of the new, and the new selectively restructures the old. The reader's reception of the text is not based on identifying two different experiences (old versus new), but on the interaction between the two. (p. 132)

Past and present are synthesized into a new experience. The reader is transformed, renewed.

The following response statement reveals features of the interactive process. The discussion of "Araby" is clearly an initial reaction, but it nevertheless suggests that the student achieved a balance of detachment and involvement in reading the story. 9

> "Araby" by James Joyce is a very complicated story for as short as it is. He uses many symbols in this story. Religion is mentioned several times and through his use of this, it seems that the boy in the story imagines himself to be a crusader. He has a very high opinion of himself. When Mangan's sister asks him to buy her something at the bazaar he feels as if he is on a crusade for her. Joyce mentions a chalice and speaks of prayers and praises all concerned with this girl. The boy in the story treats the girl as an idol or a god. I think he fears touching her not only because he admires her so but also because it will make her appear more human. She might not appear so glorious in his eyes.
>
> The boy places entirely too much importance on going to the bazaar. He can hardly wait until Saturday comes and when it does he is even more impatient waiting for his uncle. It's like he's living his life to do this one thing, buy the girl something at the bazaar (Araby). When he gets to Araby he rushes in and soon realizes everything is above his price range. He becomes angry and disappointed, realizing that all along he had been fooling himself. He was too filled with self-importance and his sense of purpose to realize what might happen.

This student interacted with the text in the sense that she not only described the plot of the story, she also assessed the character of the boy and evaluated his behavior. She took the stance of an understanding and yet detached observer who seemed to understand what motivated the boy's behavior yet did not judge him overharshly. Like the narrator of the story—the young man who reflected on his childhood experiences—the student observed the boy from a distance and so came to understand him and hence to understand the text. She created a consistent pattern of meaning and resolved the tension between the unselfconscious and deluded young boy and the more knowing, more judgmental narrator.

My analysis of the responses to "Araby," "Hills Like White Elephants," 10 and "Kew Gardens" revealed, not surprisingly, that the preponderance of responses by both women and men were submissive. Because students were encountering the stories for the first time, they had difficulty stepping back from the texts in order to interpret them. Response statements contained attempts at interaction with the stories—partial explanations of characters or events, questions, tentative hypotheses. But they also contained expressions of frustration, uncertainty, puzzlement. Most students struggled to move from entanglement in the text to interaction with it. They wanted to comprehend the stories but had not yet been successful in doing so. A response written by a woman student is typical of the majority of the responses in the sample.

> This story ["Araby"] left me in the fog. Even though I read it over and over it still seems like I missed something in it.
>
> It starts off describing a street then it tells of a house. In this house lives a boy and his aunt and uncle. The author goes on and tells you about the street the children play on and also about the girl the boy likes.
>
> The boy sort of worships her; he never talks to her, he just admires her from a distance. One day she finally does talk to him. He was so shocked he didn't know what he said to her. She asked him if he was going to Araby (bazaar). He said he would try to go, and if he did he'd bring something back for her.
>
> When he got home he asked if he could go. His aunt and uncle said yes (in a way, but they really didn't give their final approval). So the day of the bazaar he waited all day for his uncle (work?), who didn't get home until late; finally when he did get home his uncle said he could go.
>
> At the end he goes to the bazaar and the English girl asked if she could help him in a rude manner.
>
> All I know is that he was Irish Catholic.

The reliance on plot summary, the expression of frustration, and the uncertainty are characteristic of statements written by students who have not yet arrived at a satisfying interpretation of a text. Actions are related but not evaluated. Events are retold but not deciphered.

On the periphery of these seemingly amorphous and indistinguishable 11 responses to the three short stories, though, were statements that revealed distinct patterns of response along gender lines. Some differences between the responses of some women and men students did emerge. A pattern of dominance was evident in some of the men's responses, especially in statements based on "Araby" and "Hills Like White Elephants," but no such pattern was evident in responses written by women. Also, more women than men were able to resolve the tensions in the stories and form a consistent pattern of meaning.

Differences between the men's and women's statements were most pro- 12 nounced in "Araby." The predicament of a young boy losing his sense of perspective because of his infatuation with his friend's older sister seemed to evoke extremes of rejection or identification in some of the men students, responses that interfered with their understanding of the story.

With the exception of the dominant response quoted before and the response of a male student who effaced the text by fragmenting it into disconnected examples of metaphoric personification, the male students who displayed a tendency toward domination of the text did so because they judged characters without empathizing with them or because they detached themselves from the emotional content of the text. One male student, for instance, rejected the text in its entirety and in so doing dominated it.   13

> This story seemed to be about a deranged person that is in love with a degradable woman. The author seems to fill in the story with descriptive words, because he realizes the events of the story are boring.
>
> The story was written in such a way that no one would know what was happening, so that he could be thought of as a good writer. . . . In this case, since no one knows what he's talking about many ideas about what is hidden in the story will be made up and therefore he will be thought of as a good writer (even though he thought of B.S. in the first place).

This student's way of dealing with the difficulty of the text was to dismiss it. The response is characteristically dominant in that it defends one-way projection as an appropriate reading strategy and thereby renders the text voiceless.

Four other male students were overly judgmental in their treatment of Mangan's sister, a response that distracted them from a central concern of the story, the boy's solipsistic infatuation. Three male students saw the girl as manipulating the boy for her own ends. One described the boy as having been "used" by the girl. Another described the girl as "just using him." Another remarked that the girl was "just playing him along." The fourth male student described the girl as "ignoring" the boy and equated her with the woman at the bazaar who was abrupt with him. The student wrote, "He had been ignored by the lady in the booth just like he had been ignored by the girl he was in love with, or were they the same people?"   14

The dominant reader is often a detached reader; the text is not engaged, and so the reader feels little empathy for the central characters. In three of the responses written by male students, the protagonist was treated with detachment, and so his experience was kept at a safe distance. One male student called the protagonist a "little guy"; another described the events portrayed in the story as "some guy's fantasy"; still another endowed the narrator with the name "Jack" and referred to him as a "young kid." If the boy is simply a "little guy," then his experiences are insignificant, and the conflict described in the story need not be taken seriously. The tone of the response statement written by the student who named the protagonist "Jack" is complacent, matter-of-fact.   15

> This is a story about a young kid who is in love with his friend's sister. The boy and his friend love to tease his sister by hiding in the shadows at night when she would call her brother in for tea.
>
> Jack was madly in love with this girl and went totally out of his way just to see her but not speak to her. He used to peep out the window and watch for her to leave for school and would chase after her. He would always walk behind her until it came time to part in different ways and then he would speed up and pass her.
>
> Jack would never hardly speak to her until she spoke to him first. She asked him if he was going to the bazaar Araby because it was going to be excellent. He went completely out of his way to see Araby because he said if he went he would bring her something.
>
> He was at the bazaar and was looking for something to buy her but this crabby lady drove him away and that made him very mad.

The response trivializes the boy's situation. The student's account suggests that the boy's frustration is externally induced, and it omits mention of the discovery the boy makes about himself.

These dominant responses suggest that these male readers were uncomfortable with "Araby," either because they found it too difficult or because its focus on male infatuation disturbed them. These responses account for fewer than half of the men's responses, however. An even greater number of male students had difficulty comprehending the story because they were too involved in the text, sometimes because they identified with the protagonist too strongly and were unable to distance themselves from him. These submissive responses almost always revealed an inability on the part of the reader to deal with the ending of the story. The conclusion of "Araby" brings together the narrator's perspective and the young boy's perspective so that the reader will recognize the extent to which the boy's fantasies isolated him from his family and peers. Very few male students responded to the resonating finale, though, often because they were unable to recognize the boy's limitations. [16]

A few male students expressed dissatisfaction with the ending of the story. [17] One wrote, "In judging this story, I really didn't think it was very good. I didn't like the way the author ended the story." Another responded, "The story just ended." A third suggested changing the ending to a happier one. The one male student who gave a fairly full account of the conclusion nevertheless failed to recognize the significance of the boy's judgment upon himself, partially because he identified with the boy too strongly. His response reads:

> James Joyce uses imagery and symbolism to illustrate the feelings which a young boy goes through when he is infatuated with a girl. Joyce says that the boy would sleep at her door waiting to see her. He would follow her to school thinking about her as he walked behind her. "Her name was like a summons to all his foolish blood."
>
> The young boy's feelings were not understood by the older generation who were callous to his words. They considered the bazaar to be a small happening, when it was actually a big event in the boy's eyes.

The boy finally does arrive at the bazaar but does not find things as he wanted them to be. He is shaken from the fantasy world by the absence of the girl. This anguish he feels because of the loss of the fantasy world is illustrated by the symbolistic sentence, "Gazing up into the darkness I saw myself as a creature driven and derided by vanity, and my eyes burned with anguish and anger." The protective coating was lifted and the bright light shown into his unprepared eyes causing them to burn and redden.

Joyce tells the story of a young boy's growing up through these imaginative symbols and images. These images tell the story in a vivid, alive manner.

The student clearly identified with the boy's experience and sympathized with him. He also recognized that the boy is "shaken from his fantasy world" and that the experience at the bazaar removes him of his "protective coating." His focus on the girl's absence, however, interfered with his comprehension of the boy's final judgment on himself. According to this student's account, the boy's epiphany results from a feeling of loss rather than a recognition of his own self-delusion.

That other male students identified with the boy is evident in their response statements. One, for instance, wrote, "It was easy to relate to the narrator's boyish infatuation with an older girl, since I can recall having similar experiences." His identification was not accompanied by comprehension of the story, however. He admitted, "I couldn't grasp the central thought in the story." Since a resolution of the tensions in "Araby" necessitates some understanding of the ending of the story and thus some detachment from the boy's situation, such close identification no doubt interfered with the student's ability to create a consistent pattern of meaning. Four other male students mentioned that they could relate to the boy's experience, and they, too, had difficulty interpreting the story. Only two women students mentioned that they could relate to the boy's experience. Their responses suggest that their identification with the boy was also a distraction, though not to the extent that it was for the men. Both mentioned that the boy felt anger or humiliation at the end of the story, but neither gave a full explanation for the boy's feelings. [18]

The women students in the sample were, for the most part, better able to achieve a balance between detachment and involvement in reading "Araby." No women students judged Mangan's sister overharshly, and none referred to the protagonist as a "little guy" or a "young kid." Many recognized the boy's limitations and yet regarded his experience as significant. And although the majority of responses by women students were submissive in that they revealed entanglement in the text, eleven women were successful in making sense of the story, usually because they came to a satisfying interpretation of its ending. One female student wrote, "After being tempted many times the boy finally realizes that he cannot survive in the world of vanity, and that he must return to the real world. The world that is filled with illusions that people put forward to make everything look nicer." Another woman observed, "He realized here that he had been driven there by his vain love for this girl [19] as stated in the last paragraph." Another accounted for the ending as follows: "I think he had come to realize how foolishly he had acted. This realization embarrassed him, so he turned it to anger at himself." Another female student described the boy's unsuccessful visit to the bazaar and concluded, "He gave up and left; thinking of himself as a person driven by vanity." Another wrote, "In the end, I think he realizes how foolish his feelings have been. In the darkness of the bazaar, he sees things in a new way. He realizes he just has a crush on this girl and she will never feel anything for him." Most of these accounts employ the word *vanity* and make specific reference to the last line of the text.

The concerns in "Hills Like White Elephants" are quite different from those of "Araby," and yet the students' responses followed a pattern similar to that found in the responses to Joyce's story. Some men dominated the text, though this strategy was not evident in the responses of the women. The majority of responses were submissive, but more women students were able to resolve the tensions in the story than were men students. Once again, men students were often closer to the extremes of domination or submission, and the women were often closer to the interactive center. [20]

"Hills Like White Elephants" focuses on a conversation between an American man and a young woman called Jig as they await a train that will take them to Madrid, where Jig will have an abortion. The conversation is tense because Jig is being pressured into going through with the operation yet is resistant because she feels the child would bring some stability and meaning to the couple's relationship. The conflict is resolved through the young woman's denial of her feelings and the man's assertion of his will. This is a story, then, about female vulnerability and defeat. The imagery suggests that the woman's position is life-affirming and that renewal is possible only through her victory over the man. The ending of the story, though, suggests that she is powerless to change the nature of the relationship. [21]

Surprisingly, only one student, a male, was overly judgmental in his reaction to the story. We might expect that college freshmen would be moralistic in their responses to an unmarried couple contemplating an abortion. He wrote, "In the story the man wants the girl to get an abortion. This man seems to know an awful lot about the operation so it must not be the first time he did it to a girl. The fact that he had so many hotel tags on his luggage indicates that he has only one thing on his mind." Other indications of domination by male students suggested rejection of the text because of its difficulty, or detachment from it rather than harsh judgment of the characters. The male student who found the protagonists of "Araby" to be "deranged" and "degradable" also rejected "Hills Like White Elephants," but his response suggests that he was bothered not by the immorality of the protagonists but by the difficulty of the text. [22]

The story stank. It was boring and didn't end with any main idea. It ended like a dream; it exists and has a hidden reason for happening. The hidden reason isn't worth finding out because it is small in comparison to the time it takes to search for it. A dream is enjoyable, but after being known it is thrown in the trash and forgotten forever.

This student seems once again to be reacting so strongly because he was unable to comprehend the text. He didn't understand the ending of the story, and he experienced the text as dreamlike because it seemed to defy coherent analysis. The student emphasized the imbalance between the value of the message contained in the story and the amount of energy required to extract that message. Perhaps he did not understand the nature of the conflict well enough to come to some evaluation of it. 23

Another dominant response by another male student also emphasized the difficulty of the story. He wrote: 24

My impression of the story was that it wasn't a story at all. It was just a short conversation between two people. The story consisted of just a couple of pages filled with quotes.

Another reason I didn't like it was it left the reader blind. The story just starts right up and doesn't tell anything about who the people are or about what is going on. I had to read through the story a couple of times just to figure out what they were talking about. Nothing was said right out in the open about getting an abortion.

All I have to say [is] it was short and different.

This student, too, rejected the story because he could not understand it. The text, for him, was "just a couple of pages filled with quotes."

The student who referred to the narrator of "Araby" as "Jack" and who detached himself from the boy's plight responded in a similar way to "Hills Like White Elephants." Once again he revealed an inability to empathize with the protagonists, and once again he trivialized the conflict being described. In the concluding paragraph of his response he wrote, "Finally after a lot of nagging she asked if he would do anything for her and he said yes. She then gave him the pretty please bit with a dozen pleases and asked him to quit bugging her and finish his drink." The student's use of slang expressions suggests that he did not take the interchange between the two seriously. 25

The male students, on the whole, revealed less self-involvement in "Hills Like White Elephants" than they did in "Araby." Fewer felt the need to dominate it, and there is less evidence of identification with the male protagonist. None of the male students, understandably, indicated that they had had a comparable experience to the one described in the story. They nevertheless had difficulty resolving its seemingly discordant elements, often because they were unable to make connections between the setting and the conversation between the man and the young woman. 26

Five of the twenty-six men in the sample discussed the relationship be-   27
tween setting and theme in analyzing the story. The remaining male students
either ignored the setting or expressed frustration in attempting to interpret
it. One male student wrote, "The 'Hills Like White Elephants' could find
little meaning in my interpretation of the story. I know that this symbol holds
the key to the understanding of the conflict in the story but my imagination
didn't quite cut through the story so I could see the meaning." Another
responded, "I'm having a hard time trying to figure out what the hills represent." These male students, and numerous female students as well, were
unable to recognize that the setting establishes a dichotomy between fertility
and infertility, which provides an indirect commentary on the man's desire
for the abortion and the woman's reluctance to go through with it, so the
students were unable to recognize the significance of the man's defeat of the
woman at the end of the story. The effect of this inability to make sense of
the ending was an inability to evaluate the conversation between the man and
the woman and so to recognize that the woman has been defeated. One male
student, for instance, accounted for the ending as follows: "She says she's fine.
She seems to be scared because of the unwanted operation. The heat and
tension have caused them to argue. When the entire event is over, the relationship will be much better." Another male student said, "The story just
seems to be about two people who travel a lot, are in love, and are now
troubled with a pregnancy." In neither response is there an evaluation of the
respective positions of the two protagonists. The students are too close to the
events of the story to see that two different approaches to life are being
displayed and judged.

One male student successfully integrated setting and characterization in   28
his response.

> Hemingway's "Hills Like White Elephants" relates the conversation between
> an American couple in Spain as they await a train to ride to the city for an
> abortion operation. The girl is hesitant about having the abortion, and com-
> ments on various aspects of their present surroundings and their past rela-
> tionship to convey this to the man. She sees the cool white hills, trees, and
> river across the valley as symbolizing the beauty and meaning a child could
> bring to their life, whereas the treeless landscape, the rail station, and the
> bar equate with the barren, transient life they have known to this point.
>
> The man loves the girl, but tries to convince her that their life is happiest
> when they are alone together; the prospect of a child has brought unhappi-
> ness. He does not want to assume fatherhood and its responsibilities; he does
> not want to share her.

Another male student made reference to the sterility/fertility dichotomy   29
in the setting and concluded, "The girl gazes longingly at the hills almost as
if she wishes she was surrounded by this fertile, rather than the dry, sterile
area." His response statement made no reference, however, to the conflict

between the two characters or to the man's final domination. One male student saw a connection between the phrase "hills like white elephants" and an abortion, since a "white elephant" refers to something gotten rid of, as does an abortion. He also wrote, "The part of the skin of the hills may have something to do with the skin of the child after the abortion." Neither association, however, led him toward a satisfying interpretation of the story, and he concluded his response with a digression: "Something that just occurred to me is that the sun was shining brightly on the hills, giving them an appearance of being white. Could this possibly have meant the son of God shining down on the dead child and taking its soul to heaven? The white being the brilliance of Jesus on the child?" Another male student made a connection between the white hills and the abortion but did not use the insight to evaluate the characters or their conflict, but found instead that "the story is trying to make us aware of the complex problem and feelings about abortion." This student concluded that "the argument between the two main characters is unresolved at the end of the story." Another male student referred to a different aspect of the setting, the train station, and decided, "The significance of the train station is that this whole ordeal can be carried right out of their lives afterwards and forgotten. The easy way out!" This account minimizes the significance of the resonating decision made at the end and implies that the choice will have few emotional ramifications.

These responses are typical of other submissive responses by male students in that they demonstrate a lack of critical distance. Often the male students in the sample portrayed the conflict as an argument between two equals which remains unresolved at the end of the story. Or the men's responses indicated that they were unaware of the man's domination or the woman's powerlessness. The women's responses were also predominantly submissive and also demonstrated a lack of critical distance. More women than men related setting to theme, however, and more women seemed able to gain enough distance from the two characters to judge their situation. [30]

Although we might expect that women students would react to "Hills Like White Elephants" the way some men reacted to "Araby"—by identifying with the same-sex protagonist and thereby losing critical perspective—this tendency was present but not pronounced in the response statements. A woman student who digressed in her response about the problems of "pregnancy before marriage" and who mentioned the example of a close friend who consulted her for advice did not come to a very precise critical assessment of the couple. She wrote, "Something had changed their lives. They were no longer happy; they had fallen into a rut." And another woman student who projected onto Jig her own delight in the purity and innocence of babies made no reference to the conflict between the two characters and said nothing of Jig's defeat at the end of the story. In both cases, it would seem, a preoccupation with the pregnancy distracted the students from the central focus of the story, the interaction between the characters. [31]

More frequently, however, sympathy for Jig was accompanied by discern- 32 ment of the limitations of the two characters. One woman student, for instance, empathized with the female character and yet revealed an awareness of her weakness.

> Ernest Hemingway's "Hills Like White Elephants" is a unique story. In it, there is a conflict going on between what may be man and wife or may be two lovers. The story takes place in a train station located near a river with mountains in the background. The mountains are a representative of the conflict. The girl believes that together they can have everything; however he disagrees. The actual conflict in the story is whether she should have an abortion or not. She is unsure but is willing to do it because of her love. He wants her to have the abortion because all he needs is her.
>
> This story could have been written today. Abortion often causes conflicts. The men like represented in the story don't always realize the many side effects which the woman experiences. They try to say that there are none, physical or mental, but there are. In the story, the girl doesn't care much about herself. She cares more for her lover/husband.
>
> Typically, in the end, the male's dominant views have come through. She agrees to have the abortion, and says that there is nothing wrong. Unfortunately this relationship will probably end because conflicts are not resolved. To have a meaningful relationship, they must be more open.

Although the student clearly sympathized with the female character, she was able to gain enough distance to see that Jig is incapable of asserting herself and of making her wishes known. The student was also aware of the man's domination of the woman and of the lack of communication between the two. And unlike a number of students who made no evaluation of the positions of the two characters, this student recognized that Jig's defeat is unfortunate. Another woman student was even more emphatic in her assessment of the two characters. She observed, "The woman is childlike and submissive wanting what the man wants and on the whole the relationship suggests shallowness and a sense of being naive (especially the woman seems to be naive)." A third woman student expressed a similar attitude. She wrote, "I get the distinct feeling that the girl is young and doesn't have too much mind of her own. She is very undecided in her decision of keeping the baby or not. The man is pressuring her to have the operation and gives reasons for it."

Other women students used the setting as a touchstone for evaluating 33 the characters in the story. One woman, for instance, saw the couple's discussion of the hills as a commentary on their approaches to life. She responded, "When the girl says the hills are like white elephants, the man says he never saw a white elephant. This seems to be saying that the man has no imagination. He just goes through life drinking beer and talking." Another woman took Jig's attitude toward the hills to be a reflection of her attitude toward her child.

> During the course of the story her feelings change about the child. She states that the hills no longer remind her of white elephants, which leads you to

believe that she is no longer sure about the abortion. It is obvious that the man is pressuring her to get the operation because he says that he will love her more if she gets it. She is torn both ways because she wants the baby, but if she keeps it she'll probably lose the man; and in order to keep the man she must give up the baby.

Another student mentioned Jig's looking across the field and seeing a cloud drift past. This gesture, and Jig's comment, "And we could have everything and every day we make it more impossible," revealed to the student that Jig wants to have the child and that the man's resistance to her desire is a reflection of his unwillingness to take on the responsibilities of fatherhood. Another woman student discussed Jig's confusion in terms of the title of the story. She said, "In my opinion the girl didn't know what to do at first so the baby was the white elephant but toward the end it seems she felt the operation was the white elephant. But she was still all confused not knowing which way to go." Another woman student used the setting to determine the author's attitude toward the abortion. She said, "The sombre tone and lifeless setting help to convey the type of operation. For example, the countryside is described as treeless and extremely hot. From this we can infer that the operation was not a pleasant one, but rather sad and unwanted. This idea is supported even more by the tone of the conversation." Two other women students used the setting to decipher character and theme. One thought Jig's reference to the hills looking like white elephants revealed her preoccupation with her unborn child. Another interpreted her comment that the hills look like skin to mean "although they look perfect and pure on the surface, there is something beneath the skin, some substance. This is how she imagines her relationship is: perhaps once clean and pure on the top, but underneath it all there seems to be nothing to bind them together."

The responses to "Kew Gardens" did not follow the pattern of the responses to the other two stories in that there was little evidence of domination of the text. Although both men and women students had difficulty comprehending the story, their frustrations did not take the form of aggression. It was as if the text, which deals explicitly with the rejuvenating powers of nature, had had the effect on the students that the garden had on the individuals who passed through it: it soothed and calmed otherwise anxious souls. The male student who found both "Araby" and "Hills Like White Elephants" to be boring and meaningless seemed to be pacified by "Kew Gardens." 34

The story was slow-moving, about a park. The people in the park were all going about their business while the insects were going about theirs, in their own world. It was like going to a park and resting on the ground, relaxing and seeing an ant just walking on the ground. The park itself was completely peaceful to you, and you see the ant and he seems without a worry, but then you remember he is in his own world and doesn't even know you exist.

Instead of resisting the text, the student placed himself within it. Domination became acceptance. Other male students who rejected or resisted the other stories seemed to be similarly drawn into the world of "Kew Gardens." The student who trivialized both "Araby" and "Hills Like White Elephants" took the events in "Kew Gardens" much more seriously. The student who reduced "Araby" to a series of unrelated figures of speech made an attempt to interpret "Kew Gardens" by identifying a common characteristic of the people who passed through the garden, their tendency to reflect on their past.

The preponderance of responses to "Kew Gardens" like the responses to 35 the other two stories, were submissive in that students had difficulty stepping back from the events of the story and finding a pattern of meaning. Responses included unassimilated plot summaries, hypotheses about the meaning of the text which accounted for only a fragment of the textual details, and expressions of frustration or confusion. As in the responses to the other two stories, however, more women were able to evaluate the disparate elements in the text and shape them into a meaningful pattern, one that involved empathetic judgment. Four male students and nine female students formulated statements that revealed a consistent pattern of meaning. The women's responses, however, tended to be more sharply focused.

One male student interpreted the story as follows: 36

> In the short story, "Kew Gardens," Virginia Woolf contrasts the unity and orderliness of nature with the apparent aimlessness of humanity. She describes the beauty of a flower bed, with all the different colored flowers joining together to produce a sense of unity and purpose, and then describes various persons as they stroll through the garden, each with his or her own thoughts and meaningless actions.
> Virginia Woolf shows how humans are wrapped up in their own world. We hurry about, busily attending to our own seemingly important affairs, and show little thought or concern for others around us. Instead of unity we practice individuality. We see, but we are blind to anyone and anything around us that does not directly benefit us.

Three other male students recognized that Woolf contrasts the human order with the natural order. One student wrote, "Woolf seems to be telling us that nature is actually a controlling force on man, not the other way around as usually is thought." Another wrote, "The human values weren't worth much compared to the easy-going life found in the garden. Descriptions of the people were vague and they all seemed to fade away into the hot atmosphere. This seemed to show they were fading away from nature back to the world of work." Another student wrote, "Through the detailed description of nature, the author relates nature's ingredients to human experiences. It seems throughout the essay that these human experiences are just another breeze, meaning that although many have gone by, many more are to come, and that many of these experiences aren't as important as the people think they are."

Nine women students expressed similar themes, often focusing, however, more sharply on the limitations of the people described in the story. One student wrote: "We listen to the human voices and see how ridiculous the conversations are. If the garden is left in silence it seems to live. But as soon as some person starts talking the garden is silent. The snail doesn't move. The voices cause everything to freeze. Once the people are gone the garden comes to life." Another observed, "It seems the author, Virginia Woolf, feels that nature is above mankind in the story. She gives the insects the ability to think and to possess goals. The humans walk about aimlessly and searching for something. What they are searching for I get the feeling they don't really know." Another wrote:

> Now the people themselves seemed to have influence over what takes place in (the) garden, but it was as if the garden had some sort of control over their past lives. It was as if the garden seemed to hide important mistakes that the people who came through the garden had made. The lives of the people seemed to change after they left the garden, almost as if they had just reached a turning point in their lives. It seems as if the flowers and the insects are an audience for the players: the players being all of the people that come into the garden, and they all seem to be putting an act on for each other.

These four male students and nine female students focused on the constancy of nature in contrast with the inconstancy of humanity. The women students, however, were more critical of the characters in the story: their conversations are "ridiculous"; they are searching for something but do not know what; the people are "putting on an act" for each other. Other responses by women students also indicated critical detachment. One woman wrote, "The garden, which all the people pass, is a symbol of nature's stability. The people who pass represent the unpredictable human race. The first couple that passes shows how people are never really satisfied with what they have. The small family seemed disjointed and unhappy. When the disoriented old man went by, the reader was aware of the kind of self-destruction one can induce." Another wrote, "Man's separation is shown through the disjointed conversation of the characters. They all have their own thoughts and show little concern for anyone else's thoughts. This is true of all three groups that pass the flower bed." Another wrote, "The people didn't seem to really relate to their surroundings; instead they allowed their thoughts to take them elsewhere. They chose to dive into the past and just leave the garden behind."

The conclusions that can be drawn from the analysis of the responses to the three stories must necessarily be tentative because of the size and nature of the sample. In order to make conclusive assertions about the relationship between gender and reading we need to look at a large number of response statements, at the responses of women and men readers from a variety of backgrounds, and at responses to numerous kinds of texts at various stages in the reading process. The study does suggest, however, that male students sometimes react to disturbing stories by rejecting them or by dominating them, a strategy, it seems, that women do not often employ. The study also suggests that women more often arrive at meaningful interpretations of stories because they more frequently break free of the submissive entanglement in a text and evaluate characters and events with critical detachment. My own informal observations of student readers bear out these contentions. I have noticed, for instance, that some male students react unempathetically to literature about vulnerable women characters such as Sylvia Plath's *The Bell Jar* and Margaret Atwood's *Surfacing*, and judge the protagonists "insane" or "crazy." I have also observed that women are often receptive to texts in that they attempt to understand them before making a judgment on them.

If further research supports my central contention, then we may find that women are considerably more confident and competent readers than they are speakers. Research on the relationship between gender and speaking indicates that men are assertive speakers who dominate conversations but that women are hesitant and deferential in speaking to others. Robin Lakoff in *Language and Woman's Place*, for instance, argues that women are tentative and cautious in their speech; men are authoritative, coercive. She observed that men more frequently use forceful intensifiers such as the superlative *very*, whereas women use less forceful intensifiers such as *so* and *such*. She also found that women tend to use questions when declaratives would be more appropriate and to use modals and hedges to express uncertainty more than men do.[4]

Pamela Fishman's research essentially supports Lakoff's contention that women lack power in speech settings. In order to determine how women and men interact in conversation, Fishman placed tape recorders in the homes of three couples and then analyzed their topics of conversation. Fishman found that men dominated the conversations, either by ignoring topics initiated by their partner or by developing topics they themselves initiated. Fishman writes:

> We have seen that, at least among intimates in their homes, women raise many more topics than men. They do so because their topics often fail. They fail because the men don't work interactionally to develop them, whereas the women usually do work at developing topics raised by men. Thus, the definition of what are appropriate or inappropriate topics for a conversation are the man's choice. What part of the world a couple orients to is in his control, not hers. Men control topics as much, if not more, by veto as by a positive effort.[5]

4. Robin Lakoff, *Language and Woman's Place* (New York: Harper and Row, 1975), pp. 142–43. [Au.]

5. Pamela Fishman, "What Do Couples Talk About When They're Alone?" in *Women's Language*

Reading is a silent, private activity and so perhaps affords women a degree 42 of protection not present when they speak. Quite possibly the hedging and tentativeness of women's speech are transformed into useful interpretive strategies—receptivity and yet critical assessment of the text—in the act of reading. A willingness to listen, a sensitivity to emotional nuance, an ability to empathize with and yet judge, may be disadvantages in speech but advantages in reading. We may come to discover that women have interpretive powers that have not been sufficiently appreciated.

Appendix

The twenty-six women and twenty-six men were enrolled in one of the seven 43 sections of freshman composition taught by two male colleagues and myself in the spring quarter, 1980. Students wrote responses to the three stories during the first twenty minutes of the first class period in which the story was to be discussed. This structure insured that responses would be relatively free of the influence of the instructor or other classmates. Eleven women and eleven men in the sample who were enrolled in sections taught by one of the instructors read "Hills Like White Elephants" during week two, "Kew Gardens" during week three, and "Araby" during week ten of a ten-week quarter. The remaining fifteen women and fifteen men studied "Hills Like White Elephants" in week five, "Araby" in week eight, and "Kew Gardens" in week nine. Students knew that response statements would count toward their grade (responses to nine stories would constitute 15 percent of their grade) and that they would receive full credit if their responses indicated they had read the stories carefully. Instructors provided little feedback on the responses, and students did not know their statements would be used for research purposes until the end of the term.

Students had the benefit of study questions that followed each story in 44 the Norton anthology. They sometimes made reference to the questions in their responses, especially in discussing "Hills Like White Elephants," since a questions indicated to them that Jig and the man were discussing an abortion.

Students who comprised the sample were fairly representative of the 45 1979–80 freshman class as a whole. The women in the sample had a mean score of 20.5 on their ACT composite score, compared to a mean score of 21.7 for all freshman women at Michigan Tech who entered the university in 1979. The men in the sample had a mean score of 19.04 on the English ACT, compared to a mean score for all freshman men at Michigan Tech of 19.8

---

and Style, ed. Douglass Butturff and Edmund L. Epstein (Akron, Ohio: E. L. Epstein, 1978), p. 21. [Au.]

(Mean scores for the sample were based on ACT scores of only 24 women and 24 men, as scores were not available for two women and two men.) These scores indicate that both in the sample and in the freshman class as a whole, women had somewhat higher verbal abilities, at least as measured by the ACT. Students in the sample were representative of Michigan Tech freshmen in other ways, as well. All but two men and one woman were 18 or 19 years old. Twenty-four of the twenty-six men were majoring in a field related to science, engineering, or math; the remaining two were majoring in business administration. Eighteen of the women were majoring in a field related to science, engineering, or math; the remaining eight were majoring in nursing (three), business administration (four), or social sciences (one). None of the students was majoring in humanities.

The selection of students was complicated by the fact that Michigan Tech 46 is a predominantly male institution: in 1979–80, men outnumbered women 4 to 1. The ratio of men to women in the 1979–80 freshman class was 3 to 1, but the ratio in the seven sections of composition which served as a source for the sample was even higher (3.5 to 1), since a number of women students generally place into honors sections. I had originally intended to include forty women and forty men in the sample, but found I had responses to the three stories from only twenty-six women after I eliminated students not taking the course in sequence. The twenty-six men were selected from the data pool at random.

A ROSE FOR EMILY

WILLIAM FAULKNER

Southern writer William Faulkner's many novels include *The Sound and the Fury* (1929), *Light in August* (1932), *Go Down, Moses* (1942), and *Intruder in the Dust* (1948). In 1950 he was awarded the Nobel Prize for Literature and the National Book Award for his collected short stories. In the following story, written in 1930, Faulkner demonstrates his mastery of literary techniques by using tone and suspense to create a startling tale of the post-Civil War South.

I

When Miss Emily Grierson died, our whole town went to her funeral: the ¹ men through a sort of respectful affection for a fallen monument, the women mostly out of curiosity to see the inside of her house, which no one save an old manservant—a combined gardener and cook—had seen in at least ten years.

It was a big, squarish frame house that had once been white, decorated ² with cupolas and spires and scrolled balconies in the heavily lightsome style of the seventies, set on what had once been our most select street. But garages and cotton gins had encroached and obliterated even the august names of that neighborhood; only Miss Emily's house was left, lifting its stubborn and coquettish decay above the cotton wagons and the gasoline pumps—an eyesore among eyesores. And now Miss Emily had gone to join the representatives of those august names where they lay in the cedar-bemused cemetery among the ranked and anonymous graves of Union and Confederate soldiers who fell at the battle of Jefferson.

Alive, Miss Emily had been a tradition, a duty, and a care; a sort of ³ hereditary obligation upon the town, dating from that day in 1894 when Colonel Sartoris, the mayor—he who fathered the edict that no Negro woman should appear on the streets without an apron—remitted her taxes, the dispensation dating from the death of her father on into perpetuity. Not that Miss Emily would have accepted charity. Colonel Sartoris invented an involved tale to the effect that Miss Emily's father had loaned money to the town, which the town, as a matter of business, preferred this way of repaying. Only a man of Colonel Sartoris' generation and thought could have invented it, and only a woman could have believed it.

When the next generation, with its more modern ideas, became mayors 4
and aldermen, this arrangement created some little dissatisfaction. On the
first of the year they mailed her a tax notice. February came, and there was
no reply. They wrote her a formal letter, asking her to call at the sheriff's
office at her convenience. A week later the mayor wrote her himself, offering
to call or to send his car for her, and received in reply a note on paper of an
archaic shape, in a thin, flowing calligraphy in faded ink, to the effect that
she no longer went out at all. The tax notice was also enclosed, without
comment.

They called a special meeting of the Board of Aldermen. A deputation 5
waited upon her, knocked at the door through which no visitor had passed
since she ceased giving china-painting lessons eight or ten years earlier. They
were admitted by the old Negro into a dim hall from which a stairway
mounted into still more shadow. It smelled of dust and disuse—a close, dank
smell. The Negro led them into the parlor. It was furnished in heavy, leather-
covered furniture. When the Negro opened the blinds of one window, a faint
dust rose sluggishly about their thighs, spinning with slow motes in the single
sun-ray. On a tarnished gilt easel before the fireplace stood a crayon portrait
of Miss Emily's father.

They rose when she entered—a small, fat woman in black, with a thin 6
gold chain descending to her waist and vanishing into her belt, leaning on an
ebony cane with a tarnished gold head. Her skeleton was small and spare;
perhaps that was why what would have been merely plumpness in another
was obesity in her. She looked bloated, like a body long submerged in motionless water, and of that pallid hue. Her eyes, lost in the fatty ridges of her
face, looked like two small pieces of coal pressed into a lump of dough as
they moved from one face to another while the visitors stated their errand.

She did not ask them to sit. She just stood in the door and listened quietly 7
until the spokesman came to a stumbling halt. Then they could hear the
invisible watch ticking at the end of the gold chain.

Her voice was dry and cold. "I have no taxes in Jefferson. Colonel Sartoris 8
explained it to me. Perhaps one of you can gain access to the city records and
satisfy yourselves."

"But we have. We are the city authorities, Miss Emily. Didn't you get a 9
notice from the sheriff, signed by him?"

"I received a paper, yes," Miss Emily said. "Perhaps he considers himself 10
the sheriff. . . . I have no taxes in Jefferson."

"But there is nothing on the books to show that, you see. We must go 11
by the—"

"See Colonel Sartoris. I have no taxes in Jefferson." 12

"But, Miss Emily—" 13

"See Colonel Sartoris." (Colonel Sartoris had been dead almost ten years.) 14
"I have no taxes in Jefferson. Tobe!" The Negro appeared. "Show these
gentlemen out."

II

So she vanquished them, horse and foot, just as she had vanquished their 15 fathers thirty years before about the smell. That was two years after her father's death and a short time after her sweetheart—the one we believed would marry her—had deserted her. After her father's death she went out very little; after her sweetheart went away, people hardly saw her at all. A few of the ladies had the temerity to call, but were not received, and the only sign of life about the place was the Negro man—a young man then—going in and out with a market basket.

"Just as if a man—any man—could keep a kitchen properly," the ladies 16 said; so they were not surprised when the smell developed. It was another link between the gross, teeming world and the high and mighty Griersons.

A neighbor, a woman, complained to the mayor, Judge Stevens, eighty 17 years old.

"But what will you have me do about it, madam?" he said. 18

"Why, send her word to stop it," the woman said. "Isn't there a law?" 19

"I'm sure that won't be necessary," Judge Stevens said. "It's probably just 20 a snake or a rat that nigger of hers killed in the yard. I'll speak to him about it."

The next day he received two more complaints, one from a man who 21 came in diffident deprecation. "We really must do something about it, Judge. I'd be the last one in the world to bother Miss Emily, but we've got to do something." That night the Board of Aldermen met—three gray-beards and one younger man, a member of the rising generation.

"It's simple enough," he said. "Send her word to have her place cleaned 22 up. Give her a certain time to do it in, and if she don't . . ."

"Dammit, sir," Judge Stevens said, "will you accuse a lady to her face of 23 smelling bad?"

So the next night, after midnight, four men crossed Miss Emily's lawn 24 and slunk about the house like burglars, sniffing along the base of the brick-work and at the cellar openings while one of them performed a regular sowing motion with his hand out of a sack slung from his shoulder. They broke open the cellar door and sprinkled lime there, and in all the outbuildings. As they recrossed the lawn, a window that had been dark was lighted and Miss Emily sat in it, the light behind her, and her upright torso motionless as that of an idol. They crept quietly across the lawn and into the shadow of the locusts that lined the street. After a week or two the smell went away.

That was when people had begun to feel really sorry for her. People in 25 our town, remembering how old lady Wyatt, her great-aunt, had gone com-pletely crazy at last, believed that the Griersons held themselves a little too high for what they really were. None of the young men were quite good enough for Miss Emily and such. We had long thought of them as a tableau; Miss Emily a slender figure in white in the background, her father a spraddled silhouette in the foreground, his back to her and clutching a horsewhip, the two of them framed by the back-flung front door. So when she got to be thirty and was still single, we were not pleased exactly, but vindicated; even with insanity in the family she wouldn't have turned down all of her chances if they had really materialized.

When her father died, it got about that the house was all that was left to her; and in a way, people were glad. At last they could pity Miss Emily. Being left alone, and a pauper, she had become humanized. Now she too would know the old thrill and the old despair of a penny more or less. 26

The day after his death all the ladies prepared to call at the house and offer condolence and aid, as is our custom. Miss Emily met them at the door, dressed as usual and with no trace of grief on her face. She told them that her father was not dead. She did that for three days, with the ministers calling on her, and the doctors, trying to persuade her to let them dispose of the body. Just as they were about to resort to law and force, she broke down, and they buried her father quickly. 27

We did not say she was crazy then. We believed she had to do that. We remembered all the young men her father had driven away, and we knew that with nothing left, she would have to cling to that which had robbed her, as people will. 28

III

She was sick for a long time. When we saw her again, her hair was cut short, making her look like a girl, with a vague resemblance to those angels in colored church windows—sort of tragic and serene. 29

The town had just let the contracts for paving the sidewalks, and in the summer after her father's death they began to work. The construction company came with niggers and mules and machinery, and a foreman named Homer Barron, a Yankee—a big, dark, ready man, with a big voice and eyes lighter than his face. The little boys would follow in groups to hear him cuss the niggers, and the niggers singing in time to the rise and fall of picks. Pretty soon he knew everybody in town. Whenever you heard a lot of laughing anywhere about the square, Homer Barron would be in the center of the group. Presently we began to see him and Miss Emily on Sunday afternoons driving in the yellow-wheeled buggy and the matched team of bays from the livery stable. 30

At first we were glad that Miss Emily would have an interest, because the ladies all said, "Of course a Grierson would not think seriously of a Northerner, a day laborer." But there were still others, older people, who said that even grief could not cause a real lady to forget *noblesse oblige*[1]—without calling 31

1. Upper class obligations.

it *noblesse oblige*. They just said, "Poor Emily. Her kinsfolk should come to her." She had some kin in Alabama; but years ago her father had fallen out with them over the estate of old lady Wyatt, the crazy woman, and there was no communication between the two families. They had not even been represented at the funeral.

And as soon as the old people said, "Poor Emily," the whispering began.   32
"Do you suppose it's really so?" they said to one another. "Of course it is. What else could . . ." This behind their hands; rustling of craned silk and satin behind jalousies closed upon the sun of Sunday afternoon as the thin, swift clop-clop-clop of the matched team passed: "Poor Emily."

She carried her head high enough—even when we believed that she was   33
fallen. It was as if she demanded more than ever the recognition of her dignity as the last Grierson; as if it had wanted that touch of earthiness to reaffirm her imperviousness. Like when she bought the rat poison, the arsenic. That was over a year after they had begun to say "Poor Emily," and while the two female cousins were visiting her.

"I want some poison," she said to the druggist. She was over thirty then,   34
still a slight woman, though thinner than usual, with cold, haughty black eyes in a face the flesh of which was strained across the temples and about the eyesockets as you imagine a lighthouse-keeper's face ought to look. "I want some poison," she said.

"Yes, Miss Emily. What kind? For rats and such? I'd recom—"   35
"I want the best you have. I don't care what kind."   36
The druggist named several. "They'll kill anything up to an elephant.   37
But what you want is—"
"Arsenic," Miss Emily said. "Is that a good one?"   38
"Is . . . arsenic? Yes ma'am. But what you want—"   39
"I want arsenic."   40
The druggist looked down at her. She looked back at him, erect, her face   41
like a strained flag. "Why, of course," the druggist said. "If that's what you want. But the law requires you to tell what you are going to use it for."

Miss Emily just stared at him, her head tilted back in order to look him   42
eye for eye, until he looked away and went and got the arsenic and wrapped it up. The Negro delivery boy brought her the package; the druggist didn't come back. When she opened the package at home there was written on the box, under the skull and bones: "For rats."

IV

So the next day we all said, "She will kill herself"; and we said it would be   43
the best thing. When she had first begun to be seen with Homer Barron, we had said, "She will marry him." Then we said, "She will persuade him yet," because Homer himself had remarked—he liked men, and it was known that he drank with the younger men in the Elk's Club—that he was not a marrying

man. Later we said, "Poor Emily," behind the jalousies as they passed on Sunday afternoon in the glittering buggy, Miss Emily with her head high and Homer Barron with his hat cocked and a cigar in his teeth, reins and whip in a yellow glove.

Then some of the ladies began to say that it was a disgrace to the town 44 and a bad example to the young people. The men did not want to interfere, but at last the ladies forced the Baptist minister—Miss Emily's people were Episcopal—to call upon her. He would never divulge what happened during that interview, but he refused to go back again. The next Sunday they again drove about the streets, and the following day the minister's wife wrote to Miss Emily's relations in Alabama.

So she had blood-kin under her roof again and we sat back to watch 45 developments. At first nothing happened. Then we were sure that they were to be married. We learned that Miss Emily had been to the jeweler's and ordered a man's toilet set in silver, with the letters H. B. on each piece. Two days later we learned that she had bought a complete outfit of men's clothing, including a nightshirt, and we said, "They are married." We were really glad. We were glad because the two female cousins were even more Grierson than Miss Emily had ever been.

So we were not surprised when Homer Barron—the streets had been 46 finished some time since—was gone. We were a little disappointed that there was not a public blowing-off, but we believed that he had gone on to prepare for Miss Emily's coming, or to give her a chance to get rid of the cousins. (By that time it was a cabal, and we were all Miss Emily's allies to help circumvent the cousins.) Sure enough, after another week they departed. And, as we had expected all along, within three days Homer Barron was back in town. A neighbor saw the Negro man admit him at the kitchen door at dusk one evening.

And that was the last we saw of Homer Barron. And of Miss Emily for 47 some time. The Negro man went in and out with the market basket, but the front door remained closed. Now and then we would see her at a window for a moment, as the men did that night when they sprinkled the lime, but for almost six months she did not appear on the streets. Then we knew that this was to be expected too; as if that quality of her father which had thwarted her woman's life so many times had been too virulent and too furious to die.

When we next saw Miss Emily, she had grown fat and her hair was turning 48 gray. During the next few years it grew grayer and grayer until it attained an even pepper-and-salt iron-gray, when it ceased turning. Up to the day of her death at seventy-four it was still that vigorous iron-gray, like the hair of an active man.

From that time on her front door remained closed, save for a period of 49 six or seven years, when she was about forty, during which she gave lessons in china-painting. She fitted up a studio in one of the downstairs rooms, where the daughters and granddaughters of Colonel Sartoris' contemporaries were sent to her with the same regularity and in the same spirit that they were sent on Sundays with a twenty-five cent piece for the collection plate. Meanwhile her taxes had been remitted.

Then the newer generation became the backbone and the spirit of the town, and the painting pupils grew up and fell away and did not send their children to her with boxes of color and tedious brushes and pictures cut from the ladies' magazines. The front door closed upon the last one and remained closed for good. When the town got free postal delivery Miss Emily alone refused to let them fasten the metal numbers above her door and attach a mailbox to it. She would not listen to them. `50`

Daily, monthly, yearly we watched the Negro grow grayer and more stooped, going in and out with the market basket. Each December we sent her a tax notice, which would be returned by the post office a week later, unclaimed. Now and then we would see her in one of the downstairs windows—she had evidently shut up the top floor of the house—like the carven torso of an idol in a niche, looking or not looking at us, we could never tell which. Thus she passed from generation to generation—dear, inescapable, impervious, tranquil, and perverse. `51`

And so she died. Fell ill in the house filled with dust and shadows, with only a doddering Negro man to wait on her. We did not even know she was sick; we had long since given up trying to get any information from the Negro. He talked to no one, probably not even to her, for his voice had grown harsh and rusty, as from disuse. `52`

She died in one of the downstairs rooms, in a heavy walnut bed with a curtain, her gray head propped on a pillow yellow and moldy with age and lack of sunlight. `53`

V

The Negro met the first of the ladies at the front door and let them in, with their hushed, sibilant voices and their quick, curious glances, and then he disappeared. He walked right through the house and out the back and was not seen again. `54`

The two female cousins came at once. They held the funeral on the second day, with the town coming to look at Miss Emily beneath a mass of bought flowers, with the crayon face of her father musing profoundly above the bier and the ladies sibilant and macabre; and the very old men—some in their brushed Confederate uniforms—on the porch and the lawn, talking of Miss Emily as if she had been a contemporary of theirs, believing that they had danced with her and courted her perhaps, confusing time with its mathematical progression, as the old do, to whom all the past is not a diminishing road, but, instead, a huge meadow which no winter ever quite touches, divided from them now by the narrow bottleneck of the most recent decade of years. `55`

Already we knew that there was one room in that region above stairs 56
which no one had seen in forty years, and which would have to be forced.
They waited until Miss Emily was decently in the ground before they opened
it.

The violence of breaking down the door seemed to fill this room with 57
pervading dust. A thin, acrid pall as of the tomb seemed to lie everywhere
upon this room decked and furnished as for a bridal: upon the valance curtains
of faded rose color, upon the rose-shaded lights, upon the dressing table,
upon the delicate array of crystal and the man's toilet things backed with
tarnished silver, silver so tarnished that the monogram was obscured. Among
them lay a collar and tie, as if they had just been removed, which, lifted, left
upon the surface a pale crescent in the dust. Upon a chair hung the suit,
carefully folded; beneath it the two mute shoes and the discarded socks.

The man himself lay in the bed. 58

For a long while we just stood there, looking down at the profound and 59
fleshless grin. The body had apparently once lain in the attitude of an embrace, but now the long sleep that outlasts love, that conquers even the
grimace of love, had cuckolded him. What was left of him, rotted beneath
what was left of the nightshirt, had become inextricable from the bed in which
he lay; and upon him and upon the pillow beside him lay that even coating
of the patient and biding dust.

Then we noticed that in the second pillow was the indentation of a head. 60
One of us lifted something from it, and leaning forward, that faint and invisible dust dry and acrid in the nostrils, we saw a long strand of iron-gray hair.

A ROSE FOR "A ROSE FOR EMILY"

JUDITH FETTERLEY

Literary critic Judith Fetterley demonstrates how a shift in focus can yield revealing new interpretations of a story like Faulkner's. This essay is taken from Fetterley's landmark collection, *The Resisting Reader: A Feminist Approach to American Fiction* (1978), which examines a number of literary works from a feminist point of view. Fetterley is also editor of a collection of writings by nineteenth-century women titled *Provisions: A Reader From 19th-Century American Women* (1985). She is currently Professor of English at the State University of New York at Albany.

In "A Rose for Emily" the grotesque reality implicit in Aylmer's idealization of Georgiana becomes explicit.[1] Justifying Faulkner's use of the grotesque has been a major concern of critics who have written on the story. If, however, one approaches "A Rose for Emily" from a feminist perspective, one notices that the grotesque aspects of the story are a result of its violation of the expectations generated by the conventions of sexual politics. The ending shocks us not simply by its hint of necrophilia; more shocking is the fact that it is a woman who provides the hint. It is one thing for Poe to spend his nights in the tomb of Annabel Lee and another thing for Miss Emily Grierson to deposit a strand of iron-gray hair on the pillow beside the rotted corpse of Homer Barron. Further, we do not expect to discover that a woman has murdered a man. The conventions of sexual politics have familiarized us with the image of Georgiana nobly accepting death at her husband's hand. To reverse this "natural" pattern inevitably produces the grotesque.

Faulkner, however, is not interested in invoking the kind of grotesque which is the consequence of reversing the clichés of sexism for the sake of a cheap thrill; that is left to writers like Mickey Spillane. (Indeed, Spillane's ready willingness to capitalize on the shock value provided by the image of woman as killer in *I, the Jury* suggests, by contrast, how little such a sexist

---

1. In an earlier chapter of her book, Fetterley analyzes Hawthorne's "The Birthmark," a story that deals with Aylmer, a man of science, who attempts to remove a birthmark from his beautiful wife Georgiana's cheek, thereby killing her.

223

gambit is Faulkner's intent.) Rather, Faulkner invokes the grotesque in order to illuminate and define the true nature of the conventions on which it depends. "A Rose for Emily" is a story not of a conflict between the South and the North or between the old order and the new; it is a story of the patriarchy North and South, new and old, and of the sexual conflict within it. As Faulkner himself has implied, it is a story of a woman victimized and betrayed by the system of sexual politics, who nevertheless has discovered, within the structures that victimize her, sources of power for herself. If "The Birthmark" is the story of how to murder your wife and get away with it, "A Rose for Emily" is the story of how to murder your gentleman caller and get away with it. Faulkner's story is an analysis of how men's attitudes toward women turn back upon themselves; it is a demonstration of the thesis that it is impossible to oppress without in turn being oppressed, it is impossible to kill without creating the conditions for your own murder. "A Rose for Emily" is the story of a *lady* and of her revenge for that grotesque identity.

"When Miss Emily Grierson died, our whole town went to her funeral." The public and communal nature of Emily's funeral, a festival that brings the town together, clarifying its social relationships and revitalizing its sense of the past, indicates her central role in Jefferson. Alive, Emily is town property and the subject of shared speculation; dead, she is town history and the subject of legend. It is her value as a symbol, however ambivalent, of something that is of central significance to the identity of Jefferson and to the meaning of its history that compels the narrator to assume a communal voice to tell her story. For Emily, like Georgiana, is a man-made object, a cultural artifact, and what she is reflects and defines the culture that has produced her.   3

The history the narrator relates to us reveals Jefferson's continuous emotional involvement with Emily. Indeed, though she shuts herself up in a house which she rarely leaves and which no one enters, her furious isolation is in direct proportion to the town's obsession with her. Like Georgiana, she is the object of incessant attention; her every act is immediately consumed by the town for gossip and seized on to justify their interference in her affairs. Her private life becomes a public document that the town folk feel free to interpret at will, and they are alternately curious, jealous, spiteful, pitying, partisan, proud, disapproving, admiring, and vindicated. Her funeral is not simply a communal ceremony; it is also the climax of their invasion of her private life and the logical extension of their voyeuristic attitude toward her. Despite the narrator's demurral, getting inside Emily's house is the all-consuming desire of the town's population, both male and female; while the men may wait a little longer, their motive is still prurient curiosity: "Already we knew that there was one room in that region above stairs which no one had seen in forty years, and which would have to be forced. They waited until Miss Emily was decently in the ground before they opened it."   4

In a context in which the overtones of violation and invasion are so palpable, the word "decently" has that ironic ring which gives the game away.   5

When the men finally do break down the door, they find that Emily has satisfied their prurience with a vengeance and in doing so has created for them a mirror image of themselves. The true nature of Emily's relation to Jefferson is contained in the analogies between what those who break open that room see in it and what has brought them there to see it. The perverse, violent, and grotesque aspects of the sight of Homer Barron's rotted corpse in a room decked out for a bridal and now faded and covered in dust reflects back to them the perverseness of their own prurient interest in Emily, the violence implicit in their continued invasions of her life, and the grotesqueness of the symbolic artifact they have made of her—their monument, their idol, their lady. Thus, the figure that Jefferson places at the center of its legendary history does indeed contain the clue to the meaning of that history—a history which began long before Emily's funeral and long before Homer Barron's disappearance or appearance and long before Colonel Sartoris' fathering of edicts and remittances. It is recorded in that emblem which lies at the heart of the town's memory and at the heart of patriarchal culture: "We had long thought of them as a tableau, Miss Emily a slender figure in white in the background, her father a spraddled silhouette in the foreground, his back to her and clutching a horsewhip, the two of them framed by the back-flung front door."

The importance of Emily's father in shaping the quality of her life is insistent throughout the story. Even in her death the force of his presence is felt; above her dead body sits "the crayon face of her father musing profoundly," symbolic of the degree to which he has dominated and shadowed her life, "as if that quality of her father which had thwarted her woman's life so many times had been too virulent and too furious to die." The violence of this consuming relationship is made explicit in the imagery of the tableau. Although the violence is apparently directed outward—the upraised horsewhip against the would-be suitor—the real object of it is the woman-daughter, forced into the background and dominated by the phallic figure of the spraddled father whose back is turned on her and who prevents her from getting out at the same time that he prevents them from getting in. Like Georgiana's spatial confinement in "The Birthmark," Emily's is a metaphor for her psychic confinement: her identity is determined by the constructs of her father's mind, and she can no more escape from his creation of her as "a slender figure in white" than she can escape his house.

What is true for Emily in relation to her father is equally true for her in relation to Jefferson: her status as a lady is a cage from which she cannot escape. To them she is always *Miss* Emily; she is never referred to and never thought of as otherwise. In omitting her title from his, Faulkner emphasizes the point that the real violence done to Emily is in making her a "Miss"; the omission is one of his roses for her. Because she is *Miss* Emily *Grierson*, Emily's father dresses her in white, places her in the background, and drives away her suitors. Because she is Miss Emily Grierson, the town invests her with that communal significance which makes her the object of their obsession and the subject of their incessant scrutiny. And because she is a lady, the town is able to impose a particular code of behavior on her ("But there were still others, older people, who said that even grief could not cause a real lady to forget *noblesse oblige*") and to see in her failure to live up to that code an excuse for interfering in her life. As a lady, Emily is venerated, but veneration results in the more telling emotions of envy and spite: "It was another link between the gross, teeming world and the high and mighty Griersons"; "People . . . believed that the Griersons held themselves a little too high for what they really were." The violence implicit in the desire to see the monument fall and reveal itself for clay suggests the violence inherent in the original impulse to venerate.

The violence behind veneration is emphasized through another telling 8 emblem in the story. Emily's position as an hereditary obligation upon the town dates from "that day in 1894 when Colonel Sartoris, the mayor—he who fathered the edict that no Negro woman should appear on the streets without an apron on—remitted her taxes, the dispensation dating from the death of her father on into perpetuity." The conjunction of these two actions in the same syntactic unit is crucial, for it insists on their essential similarity. It indicates that the impulse to exempt is analogous to the desire to restrict, and that what appears to be a kindness or an act of veneration is in fact an insult. Sartoris' remission of Emily's taxes is a public declaration of the fact that a lady is not considered to be, and hence not allowed or enabled to be, economically independent (consider, in this connection, Emily's lessons in china painting; they are a latter-day version of Sartoris' "charity" and a brilliant image of Emily's economic uselessness). His act is a public statement of the fact that a lady, if she is to survive, must have either husband or father, and that, because Emily has neither, the town must assume responsibility for her. The remission of taxes that defines Emily's status dates from the death of her father, and she is handed over from one patron to the next, the town instead of husband taking on the role of father. Indeed, the use of the word "fathered" in describing Sartoris' behavior as mayor underlines the fact that his chivalric attitude toward Emily is simply a subtler and more dishonest version of her father's horsewhip.

The narrator is the last of the patriarchs who take upon themselves the 9 burden of defining Emily's life, and his violence toward her is the most subtle of all. His tone of incantatory reminiscence and nostalgic veneration seems free of the taint of horsewhip and edict. Yet a thoroughgoing contempt for the "ladies" who spy and pry and gossip out of their petty jealousy and curiosity is one of the clearest strands in the narrator's consciousness. Emily is exempted from the general indictment because she is a *real* lady—that is, eccentric, slightly crazy, obsolete, a "stubborn and coquettish decay," absurd but indulged; "dear, inescapable, impervious, tranquil, and perverse"; indeed, anything and everything but human.

Not only does "A Rose for Emily" expose the violence done to a woman by making her a lady; it also explores the particular form of power the victim gains from this position and can use on those who enact this violence. "A Rose for Emily" is concerned with the consequences of violence for both the violated and the violators. One of the most striking aspects of the story is the disparity between Miss Emily Grierson and the Emily to whom Faulkner gives his rose in ironic imitation of the chivalric behavior the story exposes. The form of Faulkner's title establishes a camaraderie between author and protagonist and signals that a distinction must be made between the story Faulkner is telling and the story the narrator is telling. This distinction is of major importance because it suggests, of course, that the narrator, looking through a patriarchal lens, does not see Emily at all but rather a figment of his own imagination created in conjunction with the cumulative imagination of the town. Like Ellison's invisible man, nobody sees *Emily*. And because nobody sees *her*, she can literally get away with murder. Emily is characterized by her ability to understand and utilize the power that accrues to her from the fact that men do not see her but rather their concept of her: "'I have no taxes in Jefferson. Colonel Sartoris explained it to me. . . . Tobe! . . . Show these gentlemen out.'" Relying on the conventional assumptions about ladies who are expected to be neither reasonable nor in touch with reality, Emily presents an impregnable front that vanquishes the men "horse and foot, just as she had vanquished their fathers thirty years before." In spite of their "modern" ideas, this new generation, when faced with Miss Emily, are as much bound by the code of gentlemanly behavior as their fathers were ("They rose when she entered"). This code gives Emily a power that renders the gentlemen unable to function in a situation in which a lady neither sits down herself nor asks them to. They are brought to a "stumbling halt" and can do nothing when confronted with her refusal to engage in rational discourse. Their only recourse in the face of such eccentricity is to engage in behavior unbecoming to gentlemen, and Emily can count on their continuing to see themselves as gentlemen and her as a lady and on their returning a verdict of helpless noninterference.

It is in relation to Emily's disposal of Homer Barron, however, that Faulkner demonstrates most clearly the power of conventional assumptions about the nature of ladies to blind the town to what is going on and to allow Emily to murder with impunity. When Emily buys the poison, it never occurs to anyone that she intends to use it on Homer, so strong is the presumption that ladies when jilted commit suicide, not murder. And when her house begins to smell, the women blame it on the eccentricity of having a man servant rather than a woman, "as if a man—any man—could keep a kitchen properly." And then they hint that her eccentricity may have shaded over into madness, "remembering how old lady Wyatt, her great aunt, had gone completely crazy at last." The presumption of madness, that preeminently female response to bereavement, can be used to explain away much in the behavior of ladies whose activities seem a bit odd.

But even more pointed is what happens when the men try not to explain but to do something about the smell: "'Dammit, sir,' Judge Stevens said, 'will you accuse a lady to her face of smelling bad?'" But if a lady cannot be told that she smells, then the cause of the smell cannot be discovered and so her crime is "perfect." Clearly, the assumptions behind the Judge's outraged retort go beyond the myth that ladies are out of touch with reality. His outburst insists that it is the responsibility of gentlemen to make them so. Ladies must not be confronted with facts; they must be shielded from all that is unpleasant. Thus Colonel Sartoris remits Emily's taxes with a palpably absurd story, designed to protect her from an awareness of her poverty and her dependence on charity, and to protect him from having to confront her with it. And thus Judge Stevens will not confront Emily with the fact that her house stinks, though she is living in it and can hardly be unaware of the odor. Committed as they are to the myth that ladies and bad smells cannot coexist, these gentlemen insulate themselves from reality. And by defining a lady as a sub-human and hence sublegal entity, they have created a situation their laws can't touch. They have made it possible for Emily to be extra-legal: "'Why, of course,' the druggist said, 'If that's what you want. But the law requires you to tell what you are going to use it for.' Miss Emily just stared at him, her head tilted back in order to look him eye for eye, until he looked away and went and got the arsenic and wrapped it up." And, finally, they have created a situation in which they become the criminals: "So the next night, after midnight, four men crossed Miss Emily's lawn and slunk about the house like burglars." Above them, "her upright torso motionless as that of an idol," sits Emily, observing them act out their charade of chivalry. As they leave, she confronts them with the reality they are trying to protect her from: she turns on the light so that they may see her watching them. One can only wonder at the fact, and regret, that she didn't call the sheriff and have them arrested for trespassing. [12]

Not only is "A Rose for Emily" a supreme analysis of what men do to women by making them ladies; it is also an exposure of how this act in turn defines and recoils upon men. This is the significance of the dynamic that Faulkner establishes between Emily and Jefferson. And it is equally the point of the dynamic implied between the tableau of Emily and her father and the tableau which greets the men who break down the door of that room in the region above the stairs. When the would-be "suitors" finally get into her father's house, they discover the consequences of his oppression of her, for the violence contained in the rotted corpse of Homer Barron is the mirror image of the violence represented in the tableau, the back-flung front door flung back with a vengeance. Having been consumed by her father, Emily in turn feeds off Homer Barron, becoming, after his death, suspiciously fat. Or, to put it another way, it is as if, after her father's death, she has reversed his [13] act of incorporating her by incorporating and becoming him, metamorphosed from the slender figure in white to the obese figure in black whose hair is "a vigorous iron-gray, like the hair of an active man." She has taken into herself the violence in him which thwarted her and has reenacted it upon Homer Barron.

That final encounter, however, is not simply an image of the reciprocity of violence. Its power of definition also derives from its grotesqueness, which makes finally explicit the grotesqueness that has been latent in the description of Emily throughout the story: "Her skeleton was small and spare; perhaps that was why what would have been merely plumpness in another was obesity in her. She looked bloated, like a body long submerged in motionless water, and of that pallid hue. Her eyes, lost in the fatty ridges of her face, looked like two small pieces of coal pressed into a lump of dough." The impact of this description depends on the contrast it establishes between Emily's reality as a fat, bloated figure in black and the conventional image of a lady— expectations that are fostered in the town by its emblematic memory of Emily as a slender figure in white and in us by the narrator's town of romantic invocation and by the passage itself. Were she not expected to look so different, were her skeleton not small and spare, Emily would not be so grotesque. Thus, the focus is on the grotesqueness that results when stereotypes are imposed upon reality. And the implication of this focus is that the real grotesque is the stereotype itself. If Emily is both lady and grotesque, then the syllogism must be completed thus: the idea of a lady is grotesque. So Emily is metaphor and mirror for the town of Jefferson; and when, at the end, the town folk finally discover who and what she is, they have in fact encountered who and what they are. [14]

Despite similarities of focus and vision, "A Rose for Emily" is more implicitly feminist than "The Birthmark." For one thing, Faulkner does not have Hawthorne's compulsive ambivalence; one is not invited to misread "A Rose for Emily" as one is invited to misread "The Birthmark." Thus, the interpretation of "The Birthmark" that sees it as a story of misguided idealism, despite its massive oversights, nevertheless *works;* while the efforts to read "A Rose for Emily" as a parable of the relations between North and South, or as a conflict between an old order and a new, or as a story about the human relation to Time, don't work because the attempt to make Emily representative of such concepts stumbles over the fact that woman's condition is not the "human" condition. To understand Emily's experience requires a primary awareness of the fact that she is a woman. [15]

But, more important, Faulkner provides us with an image of retaliation. Unlike Georgiana, Emily does not simply acquiesce; she prefers to murder rather than to die. In this respect she is a welcome change from the image of woman as willing victim that fills the pages of our literature, and whose other face is the ineffective fulminations of Dame Van Winkle. Nevertheless, [16]

Emily's action is still reaction. "A Rose for Emily" exposes the poverty of a situation in which turnabout is the only possibility and in which one's acts are neither self-generated nor self-determined but are simply a response to and a reflection of forces outside oneself. Though Emily may be proud, strong, and indomitable, her murder of Homer Barron is finally an indication of the severely limited nature of the power women can wrest from the system that oppresses them. Aylmer's murder of Georgiana is an indication of men's absolute power over women; it is an act performed in the complete security of his ability to legitimize it as a noble and human pursuit. Emily's act has no such context. It is possible only because it can be kept secret; and it can be kept secret only at the cost of exploiting her image as a lady. Furthermore, Aylmer murders Georgiana in order to get rid of her; Emily murders Homer Barron in order to have him.

Patriarchal culture is based to a considerable extent on the argument that men and women are made for each other and on the conviction that "masculinity" and "femininity" are the natural reflection of that divinely ordained complement. Yet, if one reads "The Birthmark" and "A Rose for Emily" as analyses of the consequences of a massive differentiation of everything according to sex, one sees that in reality a sexist culture is one in which men and women are not simply incompatible but murderously so. Aylmer murders Georgiana because he must at any cost get rid of woman; Emily murders Homer Barron because she must at any cost get a man. The two stories define the disparity between cultural myth and cultural reality, and they suggest that in this disparity is the ultimate grotesque.

17

HOW READERS MAKE MEANING

ROBERT CROSMAN

Reader-response critic Robert Crosman tackles the
difficult question of how readers can come up with
different yet equally valid interpretations of one text.
Here, he examines two very distinct responses to William Faulkner's "A Rose for Emily." This essay first
appeared in the scholarly journal *College Literature* in
1982. Crosman is also author of a work on the seven-
teenth-century English poet John Milton titled *Reading Paradise Lost* (1980).

For a number of years now I have been arguing that readers make the
meanings of literary texts, and that accordingly there is no such thing as "right
reading." Such a conclusion troubles most students of literature, and raises a
host of questions, some of which—like "By what authority can I tell a student
his interpretation is wrong?" or "How then can English be called a discipline?"—are questions of campus politics that are, theoretically at least, very
easily answered. The problem for us is to answer the much more complex
question of *how* readers make meaning: under what impulses or constraints,
following what conventions or strategies? Beyond this lies a second thorny
question: are different readers' results all equally valid?[1]

I want to try answering these general questions by looking at a specific
text—William Faulkner's short story "A Rose for Emily"—and two antithetical interpretations of it. My contention is that although these interpretations
contradict each other, both are valid. How this can be, it will be my task to
explain. The two readers are myself and one of the students in a course called
"Responses to Literature" that I taught at Trinity College in 1976. Our
procedure was to read a text, and then immediately to write in our journals
about our thoughts, feelings, and fantasies during and after reading. Here
first is my journal entry, warts and all, exactly as I wrote it:

> This is a story I had never actually read, though I had heard of it, read
> something about it, and in particular knew its ending, which kept me from
> feeling the pure shock that the reader must feel who knows nothing of what
> is coming. Even so I felt a shock, and reacted with an audible cry of mingled
> loathing and pleasure at the final and most shocking discovery: that Emily
> has slept with this cadaver for forty years. The loathing is easy enough to

explain: the problem is to explain the pleasure. But before trying, let me record other parts of my "response."

I found my mind wandering as I read this story; there were paragraphs I had to reread several times. For one reason or another I was "uninvolved" with the story, perhaps a product of the circumstances under which I read it, but possibly also a response to the story itself. There are various reasons why I might tonight shun wrestling with a "serious" story, but perhaps I also shrank from the "horror" I knew was coming. Perhaps the story of a woman killing her faithless lover is not one I particularly want to hear. I've known about this story for years, yet had no urge to read it, perhaps because I knew what it contained.

She kills him. What do I care about him?—he's hardly in the story at all. But I noticed the repeated differentiation at the story's beginning between men and women, and the put-downs of women. The story seemed to be setting me up for some attitude toward women, and even though I noticed this, I did take the attitude: women are mean, ill-willed, and therefore (though not men's equals) menacing. Miss Emily is menacing. But at first she seems grotesque and stupid: her house smells bad; she's fat, with a dead look; she faces down the fathers [i.e. the aldermen] by (apparently) missing their point. Only gradually do I see the force of her will, that just because she doesn't go out or *do* anything doesn't mean that she isn't in control.

The scene with the rat-poison is crucial here: Miss Emily got her way, and the fact that her way is inscrutable, though surely menacing (arsenic), only makes it worse. The whole feeling of the story is of a mystery, something to do with male-female relationships, as well as time, perhaps, but a mystery one doesn't entirely want solved. Perhaps because I knew what was coming my mind wandered, putting even further distance between myself and the disgusting (but fascinating) revelation of the "bedroom" scene at the end. But the distancing is there in the story itself. The time-lags, the mysteriousness, the indirection, all put barriers between you and the story's subject.

So this is what I'd say at first reading, anyway. As far as response goes, mine is a considerable *fear* of the discovery I know is waiting, the sex-and-death thing, though there is a *fascination*, too. As far as the story's technique goes, I think it sets up shields of various sorts, that hide the ultimate truth, yet that have chinks that give us inklings, and the effect of secrets-not-entirely-hidden, of horrible-premonitions-defended-against, is what I'd guess is the technique that seems to arouse my feelings.

Now let me admit, right off, that this isn't an "unmediated" response to Faulkner's story. It was written not during but immediately after reading the story, by a relatively sophisticated, self-conscious reader, who also had some foreknowledge of the story's shocking climax. Most of all, it is a *written account* of a response, and so subject to all kinds of misrepresentation on my part *as I wrote it*. Also it was written by someone who has had considerable exposure to psychotherapy, and who therefore is somewhat at ease when expressing a taboo pleasure at contemplating necrophilia, an activity that is widely considered (and no doubt really is) loathsome to engage in.

Nonetheless, all this said, my response should give comfort to literary   4
Freudians. For what I saw in "A Rose for Emily" was pretty certainly a "primal
scene." Both my fear and my interest, my loathing and pleasure, derived, at
least in part, from remembered childish speculation as to what went on in
the parental bedroom. The structure of the story's plot is to set up a dark and
impenetrable mystery—what is troubling Emily?—and to penetrate deeper
and deeper into her past in hopes of getting an answer. Formally the pleasure
is derived from solving the mystery, but the solution is a shocking one. My
unconscious *knew* all along that nothing good went on behind a locked bedroom door, but now it has proof, and has won a victory over my conscious
mind, which assured me it was none of my business. My conscious mind,
meanwhile, has to content itself with solving a puzzle, with the self-evident
reflection that after all Emily and Homer aren't Mom and Dad, and that,
anyway, "it's only a story."

Beyond the illicit pleasure of letting a taboo thought become momentarily   5
conscious, there was more bad news for my conscious mind in my response
to "A Rose for Emily," for it turns out that my unconscious is a nasty little
sexist, as I dutifully though rather reluctantly reported in my journal: "women
are mean, ill-willed, men's inferiors, and menacing." I don't approve of such
feelings, or consciously agree with them—some of my best friends are
women—but they are *there* lying in wait for me when I read Faulkner. My
shocked response to the imagined scene of Emily bedding down with Homer
Barron's decomposing body, and my related interest at male/female antagonism and conflict in the story are only the beginnings of an interpretation, of
course, but any class I would teach, or essay I would write on the story would
feature such interests prominently.

In sharp contrast to my response was that of my student, Stacy. Since her   6
notebook remained in her possession, I will summarize from memory her
entry on "A Rose for Emily." Surprisingly, Stacy did not mention the terrible
denouement of the story—the discovery of Homer Barron's remains in Emily's bed. On questioning, she said that Emily's poisoning of Homer remained
shadowy and hypothetical in her mind, and she had completely missed the
implication of the strand of Emily's hair found on the pillow next to the
corpse. Instead, Stacy had written a rather poetic reverie about her *grandmother*, of whom she was strongly reminded by Emily. The grandmother
lived, Stacy wrote, shut away in a house full of relics and mementos of the
past. Events of long ago, and people long dead, were more real to her than
the world of the present, but Stacy found very positive things in her grandmother, and (by implication) in Emily as well: endurance, faith, love. She
even identified the frail, pretty woman with Faulkner's picture of Emily when
young: "a slender figure in white."

The contrast between our two reactions to the story was striking, and   7
cause for discussion in class. In a more conventional course, I might have
been tearing my hair over a student who so "missed the point" of the story

as to ignore in her interpretation the terrifying climax of Emily's story, and who did not even notice the grisly implications of that strand of iron-gray hair on the pillow beside Homer Barron. But what I found myself doing, instead, was to go back over the story and see how much of its meaning *I* had missed, how much there was in Faulkner's picture of Emily that *was* attractive, noble, tragic. Deprived of all normal suitors by a domineering father, she had clung to that father, even in death; deprived of her father, she had found a suitor outside the limits of respectability for a woman of her class and background; threatened with his loss as well she found a way to keep him, and then she remained true to him all the days of her life. Certainly it is hard entirely to like a Juliet who poisons her Romeo, yet remember that this is an extraordinarily evasive, indirect story, in which the reader can easily overlook unwanted implications. No poisoning actually occurs in its pages; the deed is left for the reader to infer. Stacy found it easy to ignore, and when confronted with it, accepted it as a qualification, but not a refutation of her admiration for Emily: just as I was able to modify my interpretation of the story without giving up my spontaneous horror, so Stacy could acknowledge the horror, without surrendering her view of Emily as embodying positive values.

What happened between Stacy and me is a perfectly familiar event in the lives of all of us: we communicated our differing interpretations to each other and both learned from the exchange. I wasn't right and she wrong, nor vice versa. Nor did we emerge from the exchange with identical interpretations of the story: Emily will doubtless never be as noble a character for me as she is for Stacy. Nonetheless, each of us improved his or her sense of understanding the story by sharing it with the other. Similarly, I can imagine no essay that I might read on "A Rose for Emily" that would leave my sense of the story entirely unchanged, nor any essay that would completely obliterate my old sense of the story. Meaning, as David Bleich has so eloquently argued, is constituted by individual readers as response, and is then negotiated by them into group knowledge. Readers, first individually and then collectively, make meaning. 8

Now what, we might want to ask, must Faulkner's text be like, if Stacy's interpretation and mine are both "right"—both defensible, that is, under the laws of logic and evidence? The obvious answer is that the text must be ambiguous. Indeed we have already seen its ambiguity with reference to Emily's own character. A figure of pathos as a young girl under her father's thumb, she develops in later years into a formidable figure herself. Victimized first by her father and then by Homer Barron, she turns the tables and becomes a victimizer; but even in this latter role she is ambiguous—the villainous-heroic resolver of an impossible situation. Even physically our imaginations must hover between the picture of Emily as a slender, girlish, angelic creature, and that of the older Emily: "She looked bloated, like a body long submerged in motionless water, and of that palid hue." To complicate matters still further, the advanced-age description occurs earlier in the story. 9

The ambiguities of Emily's character are echoed in those of the other 10
people portrayed in the story. The fact is that, like Emily, all characters in
this story are seen through such a veil of vagueness, of mysteriousness, of
innuendo pointing in no clearly defined direction, that whatever stance a
reader takes toward any of the characters is conjecture based on little real
information.

Equally vague and contradictory are the subjects and themes that we find 11
in the story. Take the issue that spoke to me most at first reading: the man/
woman polarity. The narrator (although typically given no name, age, sex, or
other distinguishing characteristic) begins in the first sentence to distinguish
between the sexes:

> When Miss Emily Grierson died, our whole town went to her funeral: the
> men through a sort of respectful affection for a fallen monument, the women
> mostly out of curiosity to see the inside of her house. . . .

In contrast to women, men seem high-minded here, capable of a gallantry
echoed in Judge Stevens' refusal to force Emily to clean her house: "'Dammit,
sir,' Judge Stevens said, 'will you accuse a lady to her face of smelling bad?'"
When Emily begins her "affair" with Homer Barron (the exact nature of
which is, to put it mildly, unclear) it is "the ladies" who try to meddle, while
"the men did not want to interfere." Struggle is certainly there between men
and women, but my initial interpretation of the story as "bad woman destroys
good man" suppresses a good deal of evidence that it is the men, father and
lover, who are ultimately responsible for Emily's pitiful condition. If she later
turns the tables on them and wins a series of victories, isn't this an instance
of the underdog triumphing? Emily's "victories" are, in any case, utterly
grotesque (she succeeds in buying arsenic from the reluctant druggist, she
succeeds in "keeping" her faithless lover) and could as easily be called *moral
defeats*. If there is a battle of the sexes in "A Rose for Emily," the reader must
decide who wins.

Other polarities are equally ambiguous. The story sets up tensions—or 12
allows tensions to be felt—between age and youth, parent and child, black
and white, individual and group, North and South, past and present, love and
hate, and perhaps most of all between life and death. The picture (not actually
in the story, but imperatively implied by it in my experience) of "bloated"
corpselike Emily lying with her decomposing lover is as vivid an image of
death-in-life as I know: Emily already dead in a sense, Homer still alive to
her (despite the stink, the "fleshless grin"). Which one of them is deader?
Which one would you rather be? Nowhere in literature do I remember the
line between death and life so definitively rubbed out.

Indeed, I find it tempting to picture Faulkner's story as a series of wid- 13
ening concentric rings, with the dead/alive lovers at their center. As we move
outward, we reach progressively wider polarities: the family (Emily/Father),
the community (individual/group; men/women; older/younger generations),

the nation (North/South: "And now Miss Emily had gone to join the representatives of those august names where they lay in the cedar-bemused cemetery among the ranked and anonymous graves of Union and Confederate soldiers who fell at the battle of Jefferson"), and the universe (past/present; life/death). "What is true at the center," the story seems to say, "is equally true at every wider circumference." But what (I ask) is true at the center? Those lovers on their bed seem to be a hieroglyph of some profound truth about life, death, time—about *everything*, in fact. But any attempt to pin it down, to state its meaning, excludes other equally possible interpretations—which doesn't mean that we shouldn't interpret, but only that we should have some humility about the status of our results.

Finally, with respect to the story's technique, we find the same sort of ambiguities. I mentioned in my original journal entry the extraordinary indirection with which the story is told. The narrator is anything but omniscient, reporting only what is common knowledge in Jefferson, and even then withholding foreknowledge of earlier events—such as the cause of the bad smell emanating from Emily's house in the months following Homer's disappearance—until the right moment comes to spring it on the reader. 14

The narrator is himself a "reader" of Emily's story, trying to put together from fragments a complete picture, trying to find the meaning of her life in its impact upon an audience, the citizens of Jefferson, of which he is a member. He disregards chronology, working generally backward from recent events to ever-earlier ones, as if seeking their explanation in a receding past that never throws quite enough light. Displaced chronology and the narrator's carefully limited point of view are two sources of the story's murkiness, which leaves us constantly guessing about events—What caused the smell? Why did Emily buy arsenic? What happened to Homer? Yet the narrator can be wonderfully, or cruelly, explicit too in his handling of details. 15

To read Faulkner's story, then, is to negotiate a series of oppositions that the text itself has left unresolved. We feel compelled to resolve its ambiguities, but however we do so, some of the evidence will have to be ignored. Small wonder if Stacy and I each constructed our interpretations out of different bits of this conflicting, shifting, and incomplete mass of evidence, each of us ignoring what didn't fit. 16

It is often argued, when this point is reached, that the text in question is in a special (though daily widening) category of texts whose meaning is, in effect, "everything is ambiguous." Modern critics—New Critical, Structuralist, semiotic, deconstructive—are fond of finding this message everywhere they look. I confess a fondness for it myself, yet I remember that at first "A Rose for Emily" had a definite meaning for me; that only second, more "mature" thoughts softened it into a structure of irresolvable ambiguities. I am not convinced, in other words, that ambiguity is the *meaning* of Faulkner's story. I think, rather, that it is the *nature* of this text to be ambiguous, and that meaning is what the reader makes, by choosing among its paired, antith- 17 etical elements. I hope to have demonstrated this contention with respect to "A Rose for Emily." I cannot hope to prove here, but do affirm my belief that all literary texts are by nature ambiguous, and that the reader makes their meaning.

In his extensive inquiry into the psychology of reading, *5 Readers Reading*, Norman Holland asks what is the nature of a text, and then shrugs his shoulders:

> A reader reads something, certainly, but if one cannot separate his "subjec-tive" response from its "objective" basis, there seems no way to find out what that "something" is in any impersonal sense. It is visible only in the psycho-logical processes the reader creates in himself by means of the literary work. (p. 40)[2]

Certainly Holland has a point: it is impossible to discover a situation in which a text can be observed without an observer (a reader) being present. Yet it is well to remember that this predicament is shared by all the sciences, even by particle physics, which nonetheless goes on finding leptons and quarks, the sub-subatomic particles of matter. Moreover, if it is impossible to describe the *text* with certainty, that same limitation applies, in spades, to describing with certainty the reader's "psychological processes"—approximation and plausibility are the most we can hope for in either enterprise.

Holland writes as if a solitary reader confronted a solitary text in a void, equipped only by the internal psychological processes described by Freud. This is for Holland a fruitful hypothesis; yet, from another, equally sound, point of view, the individual reader is a member of a society, a product of a lifetime of education whose substance is the learning of conventions shared by other members of society. The very language in which the literary text is written is the product not of his own psyche but of a human community ongoing over millennia. It seems clear that the individual reader reads, in part at least, according to conventions, strategies, and expectations that he has learned from other human beings and that he shares with them.

Remember, for example, that though Stacy and I interpreted Emily in antithetical ways, we both shared a reading strategy: call it reading-for-char-acter. It would seem that the text could accordingly be described as embodying the "character-reading code," put there by Faulkner, who knew the code as well as anyone. This is the approach of the relatively new discipline of Se-miotics, whose goal is to specify all the codes operating in a text and thus to read "scientifically." In practice, though, the name and nature of the codes are variable with the critic and the work, and the codes become so numerous and so redundant that instead of achieving with their help a specific meaning we are left, once again, contemplating the universal aesthetic message of ambiguity.

We are on firmer ground, I think, when we think of the "codes" as in the reader, not in the text, and call them "reading conventions" or "reading strategies." Stacy and I (and many others) read "A Rose for Emily" as a portrait of its heroine's character, but that's not *all* we read it as, and other readers will apply entirely different strategies: the Marxist will read for (and find) representations of a decaying class-structure and social victimization, a deconstructionist will read it as a self-consuming artifact, allegorizing readers of all sorts will read for all sorts of symbols, a Structuralist will read for structures; and in no case (except perhaps by majority-rule) can we exclude any of these strategies from validity, though some will interest us more than others.

But if the "codes" are in the reader, what is in the text? I suggest that when we look closely at texts what we find are not "codes"—consistent, coherent, smoothly concatenated—but a jumble of "features" or "elements." The maddening thing is that these elements seem to spring into being only when a reader is present—that is, when a reading strategy is being applied. The reader's freedom is limited both by the elements in the story, and by the codes he has learned from his culture, but since he *is* free to select which codes he applies, which elements he constitutes, he is in practice no more constrained by them than putting on a pair of sneakers compels me to run. What he *is* forced to do is to apply *some* strategy, look at *some* elements of the text (since that, after all, is what reading is) and in so doing he joins a community of which all other readers, and the author himself are members— he enters, that is, a dialogue, all of whose voices speak within him, all of whose roles he plays.

It is my conclusion—a tentative conclusion, as always, such issues are never definitively settled—that since literary texts are richly ambiguous, individual readers do resolve those ambiguities, fill in the hermeneutic gaps, with their own individual psychological makeups, their own "identity themes," to borrow Holland's phrase. But reader and text do not exist in a void. Rather, they are framed by a vast series of linguistic, literary, and cultural conventions of interpretation, some of which, at least, readers cannot help knowing and using, since that is what "reading" is. These conventions, or codes, are *so* numerous, however, and so mutually contradictory, that the individual reader still exercises considerable freedom in the way he interprets, merely by his choice and emphasis among the conventions.

Reading is *both* a solitary *and* a communal enterprise; we read *both* for self-discovery *and* to learn about the world; and we go on learning, after we have read a text, by sharing our interpretation with others, and by letting their interpretations enrich our own.

I won't pretend that disagreements, even violent disagreements, can't occur. Many of them are due to the pernicious belief in "right reading": the idea that if you and I disagree, one of us is wrong, and it better not be me! But disagreements can also result from real moral or political differences. Even here, though, negotiation and compromise may be a more useful approach than the verbal equivalent of war, however stimulating and entertaining a quarrel may be.

Still, it helps to remember that these disagreements are not epistemological but political, whether on or off the campus. I had only to *offer* my interpretation of "A Rose for Emily" for Stacy to change hers, but if she had resisted mine completely, I would still have listened to hers and learned from it, confident that sooner or later she would follow my example. Telling her that she was "wrong" would have been not only unhelpful but untrue. Her interpretation was *not* wrong; it was merely partial, incomplete, and *all* interpretations are incomplete. Literary study *is* a discipline not because it gives *certain* answers—no field of inquiry does that—but because it is eternally in the business of developing procedures for assembling evidence and answering questions about an area of human experience that human beings collectively judge to be important and worthy of inquiry. Literary theory, I submit, is nothing more nor less than the study, with regard to literary texts, of how readers make meaning.

Notes

1. "How Readers Make Meaning" is a sequel to my earlier article, ("Do Readers Make Meaning?") printed in *The Reader in the Text: Essays on Audience and Interpretation*, ed. Susan R. Suleiman and Inge Crosman (Princeton: Princeton University Press, 1980), 149–64. "How Readers" was delivered in an earlier form to the Theories of Reading Conference sponsored by the Society for Critical Exchange and Indiana University and held in Bloomington on 28–30 September 1981.

   Those acquainted with "reader-response" theories will recognize, throughout my essay, bits and pieces of the ideas and methods of Norman Holland, David Bleich, Wolfgang Iser, Jonathan Culler, and Stanley Fish, and of Structuralism ("binary opposition"), Semiotics ("codes"), and deconstruction (Derrida: "the reader writes the text"). Those for whom these names and slogans are not household words will find a useful, 23-page bibliography by Inge Crosman in Suleiman and Crosman. More on these matters will also be found in my essay "The Twilight of Critical Authority," *Annals of Scholarship* 1, no. 1 (Winter, 1980) and in the first chapter of my book *Reading Paradise Lost* (Bloomington: Indiana University Press, 1980).

2. [Holland, 5 *Readers Reading* (New Haven: Yale University Press, 1975).]

MAKING CONNECTIONS

1. Write your own interpretation of "Hills Like White Elephants." As a class, or in small groups, compare your interpretations of the story. Do you find any differences similar to the results of Flynn's study? Do you find differences that can be explained in other ways than through gender?

2. Is there anything in the stories by Hemingway and Faulkner that indicate they were written by men? Analyze their styles, uses of language, characters, and point of view. Are there clues to the gender of the authors in the ways they write? You might try comparing a sample of prose passages by male writers with passages by female writers. What differences appear, and can those differences be attributed to gender or are they purely matters of individual style? What are the implications of trying to identify "male" and "female" writing styles?

3. Construct an outline of Flynn's essay. Essentially, the essay documents an experiment. What is her hypothesis? How does she define her terms? How representative are her subjects, and are there other factors besides gender that may have influenced their responses? If so, could these factors also be related to gender? How does Flynn explain and qualify her conclusions? What further research does she suggest?

4. How do the very qualities that make women seem "insecure" as speakers help make them more "competent" readers in Flynn's view? Can you draw any conclusions about the ability to listen well in conversation and the ability to read well? Might this explain why literature and the arts have traditionally been seen as more "feminine" areas of study? If so, why are most of the writers and artists studied in the field still male?

5. Discuss the use of the narrator in Faulkner's "A Rose for Emily." Is the narrator male or female? How does the narrative tone help to include or distance us as readers, and why? How does it create suspense and surprise? What are the narrator's feelings about Miss Emily, and do we share them as readers?

6. Fetterley describes Emily's sheltered life as a kind of violence done to women. Do you agree or disagree that women's being more "sheltered" than men constitutes a kind of oppression? Give examples from your own experience or from previous readings to support or challenge Fetterley's position. How might the essayists in Chapter 2 respond to this issue?

7. Fetterley calls Faulkner's story "feminist." Referring to her discussion in paragraph 15, explain what she means by the term "feminist." How does Fetterley's view of feminism compare with Kersten's (Chapter 2)? How

would Kersten, as a "conservative feminist," respond to Fetterley's reading of the story and her views on the oppression of women it portrays?

8. Analyze the fairness of Crosman's comparison between his own reading of "A Rose for Emily" and that of Stacy, his student. Do you feel that both are presented as valid readings of the story? What issues might be raised by the fact that Stacy is a student and Crosman the professor? Does his choice of participants for this study help or hinder the essay's argument?

9. What does Crosman mean by "ambiguities" in a text? In your view, is ambiguity a positive or negative quality of Faulkner's story and of literature in general? How does Crosman suggest we overcome the "jumble of 'features' or 'elements'" that make up texts? Would Crosman's view of reading work if applied to all your college classes? Why or why not?

10. Suppose women and men simply "are" different readers, writers, and speakers. Is difference positive or negative? Does it affirm identity or invite oppression and inequality? If men and women are different users of language, should we work to emphasize and celebrate our differences or attempt to erase differences altogether? Why not simply divide society and recognize a clear "women's culture" and "men's culture," complete with different educations, media services, literary canons? What would a world like this look like? What would the benefits or drawbacks be? Are there elements of our society that already look like this?

11. List all the uses of communication you find in Part II, "Gender and Language" (e.g., to assert power, to nurture and validate, to express oneself). What is the relative importance of these functions in society? Are there any overlaps or contradictions? (When, for instance, might "expressing oneself" mean an access to power, and when might it mean vulnerability or weakness?) What conclusions can you draw about the role of gender in language or the role of language in shaping gender?

Engendering Identity Through Popular Culture

7
IMAGES OF
WOMEN:
FAIRY TALES

C O N T E X T S

Fairy tales are among the most pervasive cultural artifacts throughout the world. They have been with us for centuries and exist with remarkable similarity across all languages and cultures. For instance, researchers have discovered over 500 versions of the Cinderella story, spanning from Europe to Africa to the Middle East and reaching back as far as ancient China. Like myths, fairy tales seem to be a basic part of our collective humanity, and their memorable lessons about good and evil, society and the individual have influenced generations of the world's children.

Bruno Bettelheim, in his book *The Uses of Enchantment: The Meaning and Importance of Fairy Tales*, suggests that fairy stories retain such power through the ages and around the world because they speak to our basic desires, fears, and questions about life. On the one hand, they address the issues of individual development: How do we learn to overcome life's obstacles and our own fears and slay the dragon, win the princess, achieve the rewards of adulthood? On the other hand, fairy tales also convey powerful lessons about social life, teaching us the values and expectations by which we will be judged as successful or unsuccessful members of the community. As such, fairy tales "speak simultaneously to all levels of the human personality, communicating in a manner which reaches the uneducated mind of the child as well as that of the sophisticated adult" (pp. 5–6).

Recently, researchers and writers, both male and female, have begun to question the social values that fairy tales convey, particularly their representation of gender differences and the messages they send about the development and social place of girls and women. If one of fairy tales' most important lessons about human development is learning to use one's skills—courage, strength, intelligence—to overcome life's trials and grow into adult independence, it is notable that girls in these tales seldom demonstrate initiative or action, but rather wait passively to be saved, whether by a prince's kiss or a hero's brave exploits. Indeed, rather than winning the prize herself, more often than not the girl is herself the "prize" or object to be won.

This is not to say that boys aren't also represented in these tales, or that fairy tales are only formative for girls. Indeed, all children learn about the self and society from the stories they hear, and many other aspects of culture are conveyed through fairy tales as well. The readings in this chapter reflect just one facet of a fascinating field of study: the ways in which popular culture helps create our sense of ourselves and the world.

In the first essay in this chapter, "'Some Day My Prince Will Come': Female Acculturation through the Fairy Tale," Marcia Lieberman examines the multiple lessons fairy tales teach little girls. The importance of being beautiful, for instance, is a pervasive premise for girls in fairy tales, conveying the message that being "fairest of them all" is essential to women's success. In addition, girls are enjoined to be passive: they must wait to be chosen, and being chosen itself constitutes their ultimate reward. The idea of marriage as the major "happy ending" for women also dominates these tales and is usually linked with becoming wealthy, the only means of social mobility for the girls. Throughout, Lieberman unveils the images of helplessness and power in these tales that act to reinforce unequal patterns in society.

Many of these themes recur in the other selections that follow, all of which offer imaginative and revealing meditations on fairy tale motifs. In "The Archaeology of a Marriage," Maxine Kumin looks at the nature of illusion by imagining the married life of Sleeping Beauty and Prince Charming in middle age. Fantasy and reality blend in her poem, raising questions about our ideals in love and in life and taking that daring step beyond the "happily ever after" of the tales. Louise Bernikow's personal essay, "Cinderella: Saturday Afternoon at the Movies," reflects on the enmity and competition between women exemplified in such tales. To what extent are women set up to be distrustful antagonists in the contest to win a place in the glamorous world of men? And how can women overcome the social messages about competition that keep them divided and apart? Sara Maitland examines a different aspect of the Cinderella story by telling "The Wicked Stepmother's Tale." In her eye-opening new perspective on the story we come to explore the complex relationship between mothers and daughters and the ways women can either hinder or help each other to grow.

One of the most chilling outcomes of fairy tales' portrayal of women is taken up by Susan Brownmiller in "Victims: The Setting," an excerpt from her book *Against Our Will: Men, Women and Rape*. Here, she illustrates the ways a tale like "Little Red Riding Hood" reinforces the notion of the female as "prey," a message which works together with other cultural sanctions to "train women to be victims" of sexual violence in our society. Finally, fiction writer Angela Carter reverses the story of Red Riding Hood in a startling tale of cunning and passion, "The Company of Wolves." In this provocative story we examine the power of women reclaiming their sexuality via Carter's memorable red-capped heroine, a modern girl who knows full well "she's nobody's meat."

Together, the writers in this chapter illustrate the importance of understanding the pervasive cultural messages we receive, even as children, through the stories we hear. These powerful lessons remain with us into adulthood, shaping our behaviors, our images of self, our perception of our place in the world. By reflecting on and transforming the stories, these writers show that we can challenge old myths that no longer serve us and construct new visions that celebrate the development of all members of society.

'SOME DAY MY PRINCE WILL COME'
Female Acculturation through the Fairy Tale

◑

MARCIA K. LIEBERMAN

This analysis of women's roles by Marcia Lieberman was first published in *Don't Bet on the Prince* (1986), a collection of writings by psychologists, artists, and cultural critics on the fairy tale in North America and England. Here, she examines the lessons about women's place in society taught by such classic fairy tales as "Sleeping Beauty," "Cinderella," and "Snow White," and sheds light on the messages of female powerlessness and passivity these stories convey.

In a review of children's stories for a Christmas issue of the *New York Review of Books*, Alison Lurie praised traditional fairy and folk tales as

> one of the few sorts of classic children's literature of which a radical feminist would approve . . . These stories suggest a society in which women are as competent and active as men, at every age and in every class. Gretel, not Hansel, defeats the Witch; and for every clever youngest son there is a youngest daughter equally resourceful. The contrast is greatest in maturity, where women are often more powerful than men. Real help for the hero or heroine comes most frequently from a fairy godmother or wise woman, and real trouble from a witch or wicked stepmother . . . To prepare children for women's liberation, therefore, and to protect them against Future Shock, you had better buy at least one collection of fairy tales . . .[1]

Radical feminists, apparently, bought neither Ms. Lurie's ideas nor the collections of fairy tales. It is hard to see how children could be 'prepared' for women's liberation by reading fairy tales; an analysis of those fairy tales that children actually read indicates instead that they serve to acculturate women to traditional social roles.

Ms. Lurie has now repeated her argument in a recent article, in which she objects to the opinion that feminists actually have of such stories as 'Cinderella' and 'Snow White':

> It is true that some of the tales we know best, those that have been popularized by Disney, have this sort of heroine. But from the point of view of European folklore they are a very unrepresentative selection. They reflect the taste of the refined literary men who edited the first popular collections

247

of fairy tales for children during the Victorian era. Andrew Lang, for instance, chose the tales in his *Blue Fairy Book* (first published in 1889) from among literally thousands known to him as a folklorist; and he chose them . . . partly for their moral lesson. Folk tales recorded in the field by scholars are full of everything Lang leaves out: sex, death, low humor, and female initiative.

In the other more recent collections of tales—as well as in Lang's later collections—there are more active heroines . . .[2]

No one would disagree with Ms. Lurie that Andrew Lang was very selective in choosing his tales, but to a feminist who wishes to understand the acculturation of women, this is beside the point. Only the best-known stories, those that everyone has read or heard, indeed, those that Disney has popularized, have affected masses of children in our culture. Cinderella, the Sleeping Beauty, and Snow White are mythic figures who have replaced the old Greek and Norse gods, goddesses, and heroes for most children. The 'folk tales recorded in the field by scholars,' to which Ms. Lurie refers, or even Andrew Lang's later collections, are so relatively unknown that they cannot seriously be considered in a study of the meaning of fairy tales to women. 3

In this light, *The Blue Fairy Book* is a very fruitful book to analyze, for it contains many of the most famous stories, and has perhaps been the best-known and hence most influential collection of tales. It was compiled by Andrew Lang and first published by Longman's Green, and Co. in London in 1889. It was followed by *The Red Fairy Book*, and then the *Green*, and then by many others, the *Yellow*, the *Brown*, the *Rose*, the *Violet*, etc. In the preface to *The Green Fairy Book*, in 1892, Lang noted that the stories were made not only to amuse children, but also to teach them. He pointed out that many of the stories have a moral, although, he wrote, 'we think more as we read them of the diversion than of the lesson.'[3] The distinction that Lang drew between diversions and lessons is misleading, for children do not categorize their reading as diverting or instructive, but as interesting or boring. If we are concerned, then, about what our children are being taught, we must pay particular attention to those stories that are so beguiling that children think more as they read them 'of the diversion than of the lesson'; perhaps literature is suggestive in direct proportion to its ability to divert. We know that children are socialized or culturally conditioned by movies, television programs, and the stories they read or hear, and we have begun to wonder at the influence that children's stories and entertainments had upon us, though we cannot now measure the extent of that influence. 4

Generations of children have read the popular fairy books, and in doing so may have absorbed far more from them than merely the outlines of the various stories. What is the precise effect that the story of 'Snow-White and the Seven Dwarfs' has upon a child? Not only do children find out what happens to the various princes and princesses, wood-cutters, witches, and 5 children of their favorite tales, but they also learn behavioral and associational patterns, value systems, and how to predict the consequences of specific acts or circumstances. Among other things, these tales present a picture of sexual roles, behavior, and psychology, and a way of predicting outcome or fate according to sex, which is important because of the intense interest that children take in 'endings'; they always want to know how things will 'turn out.' A close examination of the treatment of girls and women in fairy tales reveals certain patterns which are keenly interesting not only in themselves, but also as material which has undoubtedly played a major contribution in forming the sexual role concept of children, and in suggesting to them the limitations that are imposed by sex upon a person's chances of success in various endeavors. It is now being questioned whether those traits that have been characterized as feminine have a biological or a cultural basis: discarding the assumptions of the past, we are asking what is inherent in our nature, and what has become ours through the gentle but forcible process of acculturation. Many feminists accept nothing as a 'given' about the nature of female personality; nearly all the work on that vast subject is yet to be done. In considering the possibility that gender has a cultural character and origin we need to examine the primary channels of acculturation. Millions of women must surely have formed their psycho-sexual self-concepts, and their ideas of what they could or could not accomplish, what sort of behavior would be rewarded, and of the nature of reward itself, in part from their favorite fairy tales. These stories have been made the repositories of the dreams, hopes, and fantasies of generations of girls. An analysis of the women in *The Blue Fairy Book* presents a picture that does not accord with Ms. Lurie's hypothesis.

Certain premises and patterns emerge at once, of which only the stereotyped figure of the wicked step-mother has received much general notice. The beauty contest is a constant and primary device in many of the stories. Where there are several daughters in a family, or several unrelated girls in a story, the prettiest is invariably singled out and designated for reward, or first for punishment and later for reward. Beautiful girls are never ignored; they may be oppressed at first by wicked figures, as the jealous Queen persecutes Snow White, but ultimately they are chosen for reward. Two fundamental conventions are associated here: the special destiny of the youngest child when there are several children in a family (this holds true for youngest brothers as well as for youngest sisters, as long as the siblings are of the same sex), and the focus on beauty as a girl's most valuable asset, perhaps her only valuable asset. Good-temper and meekness are so regularly associated with beauty, and ill-temper with ugliness, that this in itself must influence children's expectations. The most famous example of this associational pattern occurs in 'Cinderella,' with the opposition of the ugly, cruel, bad-tempered older sisters to the younger, beautiful, sweet Cinderella, but in *The Blue Fairy Book* it also occurs in many other stories, such as 'Beauty and the Beast' and 'Toads

6

and Diamonds.' Even when there is no series of sisters (in 'Snow-White and Rose-Red' both girls are beautiful and sweet) the beautiful single daughter is nearly always noted for her docility, gentleness and good temper.

This pattern, and the concomitant one of reward distribution, probably acts to promote jealousy and divisiveness among girls. The stories reflect an intensely competitive spirit: they are frequently about contests, for which there can be only one winner because there is only one prize. Girls win the prize if they are the fairest of them all; boys win if they are bold, active, and lucky. If a child identifies with the beauty, she may learn to be suspicious of ugly girls, who are portrayed as cruel, sly, and unscrupulous in these stories; if she identifies with the plain girls, she may learn to be suspicious and jealous of pretty girls, beauty being a gift of fate, not something that can be attained. There are no examples of a crossed-pattern, that is, of plain but good-tempered girls. It is a psychological truth that as children, and as women, girls fear homeliness (even attractive girls are frequently convinced that they are plain), and this fear is a major source of anxiety, diffidence, and convictions of inadequacy and inferiority among women. It is probably also a source of envy and discord among them. Girls may be predisposed to imagine that there is a link between the lovable face and the lovable character, and to fear, if plain themselves, that they will also prove to be unpleasant, thus using the patterns to set up self-fulfilling prophecies. 7

The immediate and predictable result of being beautiful is being chosen, this word having profound importance to a girl. The beautiful girl does not have to *do* anything to merit being chosen; she does not have to show pluck, resourcefulness, or wit; she is chosen because she is beautiful. Prince Hyacinth chooses the Dear Little Princess for his bride from among the portraits of many princesses that are shown to him because she is the prettiest; the bear chooses the beautiful youngest daughter in 'East of the Sun & West of the Moon'; at least twenty kings compete to win Bellissima in 'The Yellow Dwarf'; the prince who penetrates the jungle of thorns and briars to find the Sleeping Beauty does so because he had heard about her loveliness; Cinderella instantly captivates her prince during a ball that amounts to a beauty contest; the old king in 'The White Cat' says he will designate as his heir whichever of his sons brings home the loveliest princess, thereby creating a beauty contest as a hurdle to inheriting his crown; the prince in 'The Water-Lily or The Gold-Spinners' rescues and marries the youngest and fairest of the three enslaved maidens; the King falls in love with Goldilocks because of her beauty; the enchanted sheep dies for love of the beautiful Miranda in 'The Wonderful Sheep'; Prince Darling pursues Celia because she is beautiful; the young king in 'Trusty John' demands the Princess of the Golden Roof for her beauty, and so on. This is a principal factor contributing to the passivity of most of the females in these stories (even those few heroines who are given some sort of active role are usually passive in another part of the story). Since the heroines are chosen for their beauty (*en soi*), not for anything they do (*pour* 8 *soi*), they seem to exist passively until they are seen by the hero, or described to him. They wait, are chosen, and are rewarded.

Marriage is the fulcrum and major event of nearly every fairy tale; it is the reward for girls, or sometimes their punishment. (This is almost equally true for boys, although the boy who wins the hand of the princess gets power as well as a pretty wife, because the princess is often part of a package deal including half or all of a kingdom.) While it would be futile and anachronistic to suppose that these tales could or should have depicted alternate options or rewards for heroines or heroes, we must still observe that marriage dominates them, and note what they show as leading to marriage, and as resulting from it. Poor boys play an active role in winning kingdoms and princesses; Espen Cinderlad, the despised and youngest of the three brothers in so many Norwegian folk tales, wins the Princess on the Glass Hill by riding up a veritable hill of glass. Poor girls are chosen by princes because they have been seen by them.

Marriage is associated with getting rich: it will be seen that the reward basis in fairy and folk tales is overwhelmingly mercenary. Good, poor, and pretty girls always win rich and handsome princes, never merely handsome, good, but poor men. (If the heroine or hero is already rich, she or he may marry someone of equal rank and wealth, as in 'The White Cat,' 'Trusty John,' 'The Sleeping Beauty,' etc.; if poor, she or he marries someone richer.) Since girls are chosen for their beauty, it is easy for a child to infer that beauty leads to wealth, that being chosen means getting rich. Beauty has an obviously commercial advantage even in stories in which marriage appears to be a punishment rather than a reward: 'Bluebeard,' in which the suitor is wealthy though ugly, and the stories in which a girl is wooed by a beast, such as 'Beauty and the Beast,' 'East of the Sun & West of the Moon,' and 'The Black Bull of Norroway.'

The bear in 'East of the Sun & West of the Moon' promises to enrich the whole family of a poor husbandman if they will give him the beautiful youngest daughter. Although the girl at first refuses to go, her beauty is seen as the family's sole asset, and she is sold, like a commodity, to the bear (the family does not know that he is a prince under an enchantment). 'Beauty and the Beast' is similar to this part of 'East of the Sun,' and the Snow-White of 'Snow-White and Rose-Red' also becomes rich upon marrying an enchanted prince who had been a bear.[4] Cinderella may be the best-known story of this type.

Apart from the princesses who are served out as prizes in competitions (to the lad who can ride up a glass hill, or slay a giant, or answer three riddles, or bring back some rarity), won by lucky fellows like Espen Cinderlad, a few girls in *The Blue Fairy Book* find themselves chosen as brides for mercantile reasons, such as the girl in 'Toads and Diamonds' who was rewarded by a fairy so that flowers and jewels dropped from her mouth whenever she spoke. In 'Rumpelstiltzkin,' the little dwarf helps the poor miller's daughter to spin straw into gold for three successive nights, so that the King thinks to himself, "'She's only a miller's daughter, it's true . . . but I couldn't find a richer wife if I were to search the whole world over'", consequently making her his queen.[5] The system of rewards in fairy tales, then, equates these three factors: being beautiful, being chosen, and getting rich.

Alison Lurie suggests that perhaps fairy tales are the first real women's literature, that they are literally old wives' tales: 'throughout Europe . . . the story-tellers from whom the Grimm Brothers and their followers heard them were most often women; in some areas they were all women.'[6] She wonders if the stories do not reflect a matriarchal society in which women held power, and she mentions Gretel as an example of an active, resourceful young heroine (I will set aside the problem of the power of older women for the moment.) An examination of the best-known stories shows that active resourceful girls are in fact rare; most of the heroines are passive, submissive, and helpless. In the story of 'Hansel and Gretel' it is true that Gretel pushes the witch into the oven; Hansel is locked up in the stable, where the witch has been fattening him. At the beginning of the story, however, when the children overhear their parents' plan to lose them in the forest, we read that 'Gretel wept bitterly and spoke to Hansel: "Now it's all up with us." "No, no, Gretel," said Hansel, "don't fret yourself, I'll be able to find a way of escape, no fear.'" (p. 251) It is Hansel who devises the plan of gathering pebbles and dropping them on the path as they are led into the forest. 'Later in the dark forest, Gretel began to cry, and said: "How are we ever to get out of the wood?" But Hansel comforted her. "Wait a bit," he said, "till the moon is up, and then we'll find our way sure enough." And when the full moon had risen he took his sister by the hand and followed the pebbles, which shone like new threepenny bits, and showed them the path.' (p. 252)

After they get home, they overhear their parents scheming to lose them again. Gretel weeps again, and again Hansel consoles her. Gretel does perform the decisive action at the end, but for the first half of the story she is the frightened little sister, looking to her brother for comfort and help.

Even so, Gretel is one of the most active of the girls, but her company is small. The heroines of the very similar 'East of the Sun' and 'The Black Bull of Norroway' are initially passive, but then undertake difficult quests when they lose their men. The heroine of 'East of the Sun' succumbs to curiosity (the common trap for women: this story is derived from the myth of Cupid and Psyche), and attempts to look at her bear-lover during the night, and the second heroine forgets to remain motionless while her bull-lover fights with the devil (good girls sit still). The lovers disappear when their commands are broken. The girls travel to the ends of the earth seeking them, but they cannot make themselves seen or recognized by their men until the last moment. The Master-maid, in a story whose conclusion resembles these other two, is concealed in a backroom of a giant's house. A prince, looking for adventure, comes to serve the giant, who gives him tasks that are impossible to accomplish. The Master-maid knows the giant's secrets and tells the prince how to do the impossible chores. She knows what to do, but does not act herself. When the giant tells her to kill the prince, she helps the prince to run away, escaping with him. Without her advice the escape would be impossible, yet apparently she had never attempted to run away herself, but had been waiting in the back room for a prince-escort to show up.

Most of the heroines in *The Blue Fairy Book*, however, are entirely passive, [16] submissive, and helpless. This is most obviously true of the Sleeping Beauty, who lies asleep, in the ultimate state of passivity, waiting for a brave prince to awaken and save her. (She is like the Snow-White of 'Snow-White and the Seven Dwarfs,' who lies in a death-like sleep, her beauty being visible through her glass coffin, until a prince comes along and falls in love with her.) When the prince does penetrate the tangle of thorns and brambles, enters the castle, finds her chamber, and awakens her, the princess opens her eyes and says, "'Is it you, my Prince? You have waited a long while.'" (p. 59) This is not the end of the story, although it is the most famous part. The Sleeping Beauty, who was, while enchanted, the archetype of the passive, waiting beauty, retains this character in the second part, when she is awake. She marries the prince, and has two children who look savory to her mother-in-law, an Ogress with a taste for human flesh. While her son is away on a hunting trip the Ogress Queen orders the cook to kill and serve for dinner first one child and then the other. The cook hides the children, serving first a roast lamb and then a kid, instead. When the Ogress demands that her daughter-in-law be killed next, the cook tells her the Queen-mother's orders. The young Queen folds up at once: "'Do it; do it" (said she, stretching out her neck). "Execute your orders, and then I shall go and see my children . . . whom I so much and so tenderly loved."' (p. 62) The compassionate cook, however, decides to hide her too, and the young King returns in time to save them all from the Ogress' wrath and impending disaster.

Cinderella plays as passive a role in her story. After leaving her slipper at [17] the ball she has nothing more to do but stay home and wait. The prince has commanded that the slipper be carried to every house in the kingdom, and that it be tried on the foot of every woman. Cinderella can remain quietly at home; the prince's servant will come to her house and will discover her identity. Cinderella's male counterpart, Espen Cinderlad, the hero of a great many Norwegian folk tales, plays a very different role. Although he is the youngest of the three brothers, as Cinderella is the youngest sister, he is a Cinderlad by choice. His brothers may ridicule and despise him, but no one forces him to sit by the fire and poke in the ashes all day; he elects to do so. All the while, he knows that he is the cleverest of the three, and eventually he leaves the fireside and wins a princess and half a kingdom by undertaking some adventure or winning a contest.

The Princess on the Glass Hill is the prototype of female passivity. The [18] whole story is in the title; the Princess has been perched somehow on top of

253

a glass hill, and thus made virtually inaccessible. There she sits, a waiting prize for whatever man can ride a horse up the glassy slope. So many of the heroines of fairy stories, including the well-known Rapunzel, are locked up in towers, locked into a magic sleep, imprisoned by giants, or otherwise enslaved, and waiting to be rescued by a passing prince, that the helpless, imprisoned maiden is the quintessential heroine of the fairy tale.

In the interesting story of 'The Goose-Girl,' an old Queen sends off her beautiful daughter, accompanied by a maid, to be married to a distant prince. The Queen gives her daughter a rag stained with three drops of her own blood. During the journey the maid brusquely refuses to bring the Princess a drink of water, saying "'I don't mean to be your servant any longer.'" The intimidated Princess only murmurs, "'Oh! heaven, what am I to do?'" (p. 266) This continues, the maid growing ruder, the Princess meeker, until she loses the rag, whereupon the maid rejoices, knowing that she now has full power over the girl, 'for in losing the drops of blood the Princess had become weak and powerless.' (p. 268) The maid commands the Princess to change clothes and horses with her, and never to speak to anyone about what has happened. The possession of the rag had assured the Princess' social status; without it she becomes *déclassée*, and while her behavior was no less meek and docile before losing the rag than afterwards, there is no formal role reversal until she loses it. Upon their arrival the maid presents herself as the Prince's bride, while the Princess is given the job of goose-girl. At length, due solely to the intervention of others, the secret is discovered, the maid killed, and the goose-girl married to the Prince.

The heroine of 'Felicia and the Pot of Pinks' is equally submissive to ill-treatment. After their father's death, her brother forbids her to sit on his chairs:

> Felicia, who was very gentle, said nothing, but stood up crying quietly; while Bruno, for that was her brother's name, sat comfortably by the fire. Presently, when suppertime came, Bruno had a delicious egg, and he threw the shell to Felicia, saying: 'There, that is all I can give you; if you don't like it, go out and catch frogs; there are plenty of them in the marsh close by.' Felicia did not answer but she cried more bitterly than ever, and went away to her own little room. (p. 148)

The underlying associational pattern of these stories links the figures of the victimized girl and the interesting girl; it is always the interesting girl, the special girl, who is in trouble. It needs to be asked whether a child's absorption of the associational patterns found in these myths and legends may not sensitize the personality, rendering it susceptible to melodramatic self-conceptions and expectations. Because victimized girls like Felicia, the Goose-girl, and Cinderella are invariably rescued and rewarded, indeed glorified, children learn that suffering goodness can afford to remain meek, and need not and perhaps should not strive to defend itself, for if it did so perhaps the fairy godmother would not turn up for once, to set things right at the end. More-over, the special thrill of persecution, bordering at once upon self-pity and self-righteousness, would have to be surrendered. Submissive, meek, passive female behavior is suggested and rewarded by the action of these stories.

Many of the girls are not merely passive, however; they are frequently   22
victims and even martyrs as well. The Cinderella story is not simply a rags-to-riches tale. Cinderella is no Horatio Alger; her name is partly synonymous with female martyrdom. Her ugly older sisters, who are jealous of her beauty, keep her dressed in rags and hidden at home. They order her to do all the meanest housework. Cinderella bears this ill-treatment meekly: she is the patient sufferer, an object of pity. When the older sisters go off to the ball she bursts into tears; it is only the sound of her weeping that arouses her fairy godmother. Ultimately, her loneliness and her suffering are sentimentalized and become an integral part of the glamor. 'Cinderella' and the other stories of this type show children that the girl who is singled out for rejection and bad treatment, and who submits to her lot, weeping but never running away, has a special compensatory destiny awaiting her. One of the pleasures pro-vided by these stories is that the child-reader is free to indulge in pity, to be sorry for the heroine. The girl in tears is invariably the heroine; that is one of the ways the child can identify the heroine, for no one mistakenly feels sorry for the ugly older sisters, or for any of the villains or villainesses. When these characters suffer, they are only receiving their 'just deserts.' The child who dreams of being a Cinderella dreams perforce not only of being chosen and elevated by a prince, but also of being a glamorous sufferer or victim. What these stories convey is that women in distress are interesting. Fairy stories provide children with a concentrated early introduction to the arche-type of the suffering heroine, who is currently alive (though not so well) under the name of Jenny Cavilleri.*

The girl who marries Blue Beard is a prime example of the helpless   23
damsel-victim, desperately waiting for a rescuer. She knows that her husband will not hesitate to murder her, because she has seen the corpses of his other murdered wives in the forbidden closet. The enraged Blue Beard announces that he will cut off her head; he gives her fifteen minutes to say her prayers, after which he bellows for her so loudly that the house trembles:

> The distressed wife came down, and threw herself at his feet, all in tears, with her hair about her shoulders.
>
> 'This signifies nothing,' said Blue Beard: 'you must die': then, taking hold of her hair with one hand, and lifting up the sword with the other, he was going to take off her head. The poor lady, turning about to him, and

---

* The female protagonist in Erich Segal's novel *Love Story*.

looking at him with dying eyes, desired him to afford her one little moment to recollect herself.

    'No, no,' said he, 'recommend thyself to God,' and was just about to strike. . . . (p. 295)

'At this very instant,' as the story continues, her brothers rush in and save her.   24

It is worth noticing that the one Greek legend that Lang included in *The Blue Fairy Book* is the Perseus story, which Lang entitled 'The Terrible Head.'   25 It features two utterly helpless women, the first being Danae, who is put into a chest with her infant son, Perseus, and thrown out to sea, to drown or starve or drift away. Fortunately the chest comes to land, and Danae and her baby are saved. At the conclusion of the story, as the grown-up Perseus is flying home with the Gorgon's head, he looks down and sees 'a beautiful girl chained to a stake at the high-water mark of the sea. The girl was so frightened or so tired that she was only prevented from falling by the iron chain about her waist, and there she hung, as if she were dead.' (p. 190) Perseus learns that she has been left there as a sacrifice to a sea-monster, he cuts her free, kills the monster, and carries her off as his bride.

Few other rescues are as dramatic as that of Blue Beard's wife or of   26 Andromeda, but the device of the rescue itself is constantly used. The sexes of the rescuer and the person in danger are almost as constantly predictable, men come along to rescue women who are in danger of death, or are enslaved, imprisoned, abused, or plunged into an enchanted sleep which resembles death. Two well-known stories that were not included in *The Blue Fairy Book*, 'Snow-White and the Seven Dwarfs' and 'Rapunzel,' are notable examples of this type: Snow-White is saved from a sleep which everyone assumes is death by the arrival of a handsome prince; Rapunzel, locked up in a tower by a cruel witch, is found and initially rescued by her prince.

Whatever the condition of younger women in fairy tales, Alison Lurie   27 claims that the older women in the tales are often more active and powerful than men. It is true that some older women in fairy tales have power, but of what kind? In order to understand the meaning of women's power in fairy tales, we must examine the nature, the value, and the use of their power.

There are only a few powerful good women in *The Blue Fairy Book*, and   28 they are nearly all fairies: the tiny, jolly, ugly old fairy in 'Prince Hyacinth,' the stately fairies in 'Prince Darling,' 'Toads and Diamonds,' and 'Felicia,' and of course Cinderella's fairy godmother. They are rarely on the scene; they only appear in order to save young people in distress, and then they're off again. These good fairies have gender only in a technical sense; to children, they probably appear as women only in the sense that dwarfs and wizards appear as men. They are not human beings, they are asexual, and many of them are old. They are not examples of powerful women with whom children can identify as role models; they do not provide meaningful alternatives to the stereotype of the younger, passive heroine. A girl may hope to become a princess, but can she ever become a fairy?

Powerful, bad, older women appear to outnumber powerful, good ones. A certain number of these are also not fully human; they are fairies, witches, trolls, or Ogresses. It is generally implied that such females are wicked because of their race: thus the young king in 'The Sleeping Beauty' fears his mother while he loves her, 'for she was of the race of the Ogres, and the King (his father) would never have married her had it not been for her vast riches; it was even whispered about the Court that she had Ogreish inclinations, and that, whenever she saw little children passing by, she had all the difficulty in the world to avoid falling upon them.' (p. 60) Either extra-human race or extreme ugliness is often associated with female wickedness, and in such a way as to suggest that they explain the wickedness. The evil Fairy of the Desert in 'The Yellow Dwarf' is described as a 'tall old woman, whose ugliness was even more surprising than her extreme old age.' (p. 39) The sheep-king in 'The Wonderful Sheep' tells Miranda that he was transformed into a sheep by a fairy '"whom I had known as long as I could remember, and whose ugliness had always horrified me."' (p. 223) The bear-prince in 'East of the Sun' is under a spell cast by a troll-hag, and the fairy who considers herself slighted by the Sleeping Beauty's parents is described as being old: the original illustration for Lang's book shows her to be an ugly old crone, whereas the other fairies are young and lovely. 29

In the case of wicked but human women, it is also implied that being ill-favored is corollary to being ill-natured, as with Cinderella's step-mother and step-sisters. Cinderella is pretty and sweet, like her dead mother. The step-mother is proud and haughty, and her two daughters by her former husband are like her, so that their ill-temper appears to be genetic, or at least trans-mitted by the mother. The circumstances in 'Toads and Diamonds' are similar: the old widow has two daughters, of whom the eldest resembles her mother 'in face and humour. . . . They were both so disagreeable and so proud that there was no living with them. The youngest, who was the very picture of her father for courtesy and sweetness of temper, was withal one of the most beautiful girls ever seen.' (p. 274) 30

Powerful good women are nearly always fairies, and they are remote: they come only when desperately needed. Whether human or extra-human, those women who are either partially or thoroughly evil are generally shown as active, ambitious, strong-willed and, most often, ugly. They are jealous of any woman more beautiful than they, which is not surprising in view of the power deriving from beauty in fairy tales. In 'Cinderella' the domineering step-mother and step-sisters contrast with the passive heroine. The odious step-mother wants power, and successfully makes her will prevail in the house; we are told that Cinderella bore her ill-treatment patiently, 'and dared not tell her father, who would have rattled her off; for his wife governed him entirely.' The wicked maid in 'The Goose-Girl' is not described as being 31 either fair or ugly (except that the Princess appears to be fairer than the maid at the end), but like the other female villains she is jealous of beauty and greedy for wealth. She decides to usurp the Princess' place, and being evil she is also strong and determined, and initially successful. Being powerful is mainly associated with being unwomanly.

The moral value of activity thus becomes sex-linked.[7] The boy who sets out to seek his fortune, like Dick Whittington, Jack the Giant-Killer, or Espen Cinderlad, is a stock figure and, provided that he has a kind heart, is assured of success. What is praiseworthy in males, however, is rejected in females; the counterpart of the energetic, aspiring boy is the scheming, ambitious woman. Some heroines show a kind of strength in their ability to endure, but they do not actively seek to change their lot. (The only exceptions to this rule are in the stories that appear to derive from the myth of Cupid and Psyche: 'East of the Sun' and 'The Black Bull of Norroway,' in which the heroines seek their lost lovers. We may speculate whether the pre-Christian origin of these stories diminishes the stress placed on female passivity and acceptance, but this is purely conjectural.) We can remark that these stories reflect a bias against the active, ambitious, 'pushy' woman, and have probably also served to instill this bias in young readers. They establish a dichotomy between those women who are gentle, passive, and fair, and those who are active, wicked, and ugly. Women who are powerful and good are never human; those women who are human, and who have power or seek it, are nearly always portrayed as repulsive.

While character depiction in fairy tales is, to be sure, meagre, and we can usually group characters according to temperamental type (beautiful and sweet, or ugly and evil), there are a couple of girls who are not portrayed as being either perfectly admirable or as wicked. The princesses in 'The Yellow Dwarf,' 'Goldilocks,' and 'Trusty John' are described as being spoiled, vain, and willful: the problem is that they refuse to marry anyone. The Queen in 'The Yellow Dwarf' expostulates with her daughter:

> 'Bellissima,' she said, 'I do wish you would not be so proud. What makes you despise all these nice kings? I wish you to marry one of them, and you do not try to please me.'
>
> 'I am so happy,' Bellissima answered: 'do leave me in peace, madam. I don't want to care for anyone.'
>
> 'But you would be very happy with any of these princes,' said the Queen, 'and I shall be very angry if you fall in love with anyone who is not worthy of you.'
>
> But the Princess thought so much of herself that she did not consider any one of her lovers clever or handsome enough for her; and her mother, who was getting really angry at her determination not to be married, began to wish that she had not allowed her to have her own way so much. (p. 31)

Princess Goldilocks similarly refuses to consider marriage, although she is not as adamant as Bellissima. The princess in the Grimms' story, 'King

Thrushbeard,' which is not included in this collection, behaves like Bellissima; her angry father declares that he will give her to the very next comer, whatever his rank: the next man to enter the castle being a beggar, the king marries his daughter to him. This princess suffers poverty with her beggar-husband, until he reveals himself as one of the suitor kings she had rejected. Bellissima is punished more severely; indeed, her story is remarkable because it is one of the rare examples outside of H. C. Andersen of a story with a sad ending. Because Bellissima had refused to marry, she is forced by a train of circumstances to promise to marry the ugly Yellow Dwarf. She tries to avoid this fate by consenting to wed one of her suitors at last, but the dwarf intervenes at the wedding. Ultimately the dwarf kills the suitor, whom Bellissima had come to love, and she dies of a broken heart. A kind mermaid transforms the ill-fated lovers into two palm trees.

These princesses are portrayed as reprehensible because they refuse to marry; hence, they are considered 'stuck-up,' as children would say. The alternate construction, that they wished to preserve their freedom and their identity, is denied or disallowed (although Bellissima had said to her mother, '"I am so happy, do leave me in peace, madam"'). There is a sense of triumph when a willful princess submits or is forced to submit to a husband. [35]

The Blue Fairy Book is filled with weddings, but it shows little of married life. It contains thirty stories in which marriage is a component, but eighteen of these stories literally end with the wedding. Most of the other twelve show so little of the marital life of the hero or heroine that technically they too may be said to end with marriage. Only a few of the stories show any part of the married life of young people, or even of old ones. The Sleeping Beauty is a totally passive wife and mother, and Blue Beard's wife, like the Sleeping Beauty, depends on a man to rescue her. Whereas the Sleeping Beauty is menaced by her mother-in-law who, being an Ogress, is only half-human, Blue Beard's wife is endangered by *being* the wife of her ferocious husband. (Her error may be ascribed to her having an independent sense of curiosity, or to rash disobedience.) This widely-known story established a potent myth in which a helpless woman violates her husband's arbitrary command and then is subject to his savage, implacable fury. It is fully the counterpoise of the other stock marital situation containing a scheming, overbearing wife and a timid, hen-pecked husband, as in 'Cinderella'; moreover, whereas the domineering wife is always implicitly regarded as abhorrent, the helpless, threatened, passive wife is uncritically viewed and thus implicitly approved of. As Andromeda, Blue Beard's wife, or the imperiled Pauline, her function is to provide us with a couple of thrills of a more or less sadistic tincture. [36]

The other peculiar aspect of the depiction of marriage in these stories is that nearly all the young heroes and heroines are the children of widows or widowers; only five of the thirty-seven stories in the book contain a set of parents: these include 'The Sleeping Beauty,' in which the parents leave the castle when the hundred-year enchantment begins, and the two similar tales [37] of 'Little Thumb' and 'Hansel and Gretel,' in both of which the parents decide to get rid of their children because they are too poor to feed them. (In 'Little Thumb' the husband persuades his reluctant wife, and in 'Hansel and Gretel' the wife persuades her reluctant husband.) Cinderella has two parents, but the only one who plays a part in the story is her step-mother. In general, the young people of these stories are described as having only one parent, or none. Although marriage is such a constant event in the stories, and is central to their reward system, few marriages are indeed shown in fairy tales. Like the White Queen's rule, there's jam tomorrow and jam yesterday, but never jam today. The stories can be described as being preoccupied with marriage without portraying it; as a real condition, it's nearly always off-stage.

In effect, these stories focus upon courtship, which is magnified into the most important and exciting part of a girl's life, brief though courtship is, because it is the part of her life in which she most counts as a person herself. After marriage she ceases to be wooed, her consent is no longer sought, she derives her status from her husband, and her personal identity is thus snuffed out. When fairy tales show courtship as exciting, and conclude with marriage, and the vague statement that 'they lived happily ever after,' children may develop a deep-seated desire always to be courted, since marriage is literally the end of the story. [38]

The controversy about what is biologically determined and what is learned has just begun. These are the questions now being asked, and not yet answered: to what extent is passivity a biological attribute of females; to what extent is it culturally determined. Perhaps it will be argued that these stories show archetypal female behavior, but one may wonder to what extent they reflect female attributes, or to what extent they serve as training manuals for girls? If one argued that the characteristically passive behavior of female characters in fairy stories is a reflection of an attribute inherent in female personality, would one also argue, as consistency would require, that the mercantile reward system of fairy stories reflects values that are inherent in human nature? We must consider the possibility that the classical attributes of 'femininity' found in these stories are in fact imprinted in children and reinforced by the stories themselves. Analyses of the influence of the most popular children's literature may give us an insight into some of the origins of psycho-sexual identity. [39]

Notes

1. Alison Lurie, 'Fairy Tale Liberation,' *The New York Review of Books*, December 17, 1970, p. 42.

2. Lurie, 'Witches and Fairies: Fitzgerald to Updike,' *The New York Review of Books*, 2 December, 1971, p. 6.

3. Andrew Lang, ed., *The Green Fairy Book* (New York: McGraw-Hill, 1966), pp. ix–xi.

4. In these stories, the girl who marries a beast must agree to accept and love a beast as a husband; the girl must give herself to a beast in order to get a man. When she is willing to do this, he can shed his frightening, rough appearance and show his gentler form, demonstrating the softening agency of women (as in the story of Jane Eyre and Mr. Rochester). These heroines have an agentive role, insofar as they are responsible for the literal reformation of the male.

5. Lang, ed., *The Blue Fairy Book* (New York: McGraw-Hill, 1966), p. 98. All quotations are from this edition.

6. Lurie, 'Fairy Tale Liberation,' *loc. cit.*

7. Ruth Kelso's *Doctrine for the Lady of the Renaissance* (Urbana: University of Illinois Press, 1956) demonstrates that 'the moral ideal for the lady is essentially Christian . . . as that for the gentleman is essentially pagan. For him the ideal is self-expansion and realization. . . . For the lady the direct opposite is prescribed. The eminently Christian virtues of chastity, humility, piety, and patience under suffering and wrong, are the necessary virtues.' (p. 36)

THE ARCHAEOLOGY OF A MARRIAGE

MAXINE KUMIN

A noted poet, novelist, and teacher of creative writing at such universities as Princeton and Columbia, Kumin won the Pulitzer Prize in 1973 for her collection of poetry *Up Country*. She has written numerous volumes of poetry, from the 1961 collection *Halfway* to *Our Ground Time Here Will Be Brief* (1982), in addition to five novels, three children's books, and a collection of essays titled *To Make a Prairie* (1979).

When Sleeping Beauty wakes up
she is almost fifty years old.
Time to start planning her retirement cottage.
The Prince in sneakers stands thwacking
his squash racquet. He plays
three nights a week at his club,
it gets the heart action up.
What *he* wants in the cottage
is a sauna and an extra-firm Beauty-
rest mattress, which *she* sees as an exquisite
sarcasm directed against her long slumber.
Was it *her* fault he took so long
to hack his way through the brambles?
Why didn't he carry a chainsaw
like any sensible woodsman?
Why, for that matter, should any
twentieth-century woman
have to lie down at the prick of
a spindle etcetera etcetera
and he is stung to reply
in kind and soon they are at it.

If only they could go back to
the simplest beginnings. She
remembers especially a snapshot
of herself in a checked gingham outfit.
He is wearing his Navy dress whites.

She remembers the illicit weekend
in El Paso, twenty years before
illicit weekends came out of the closet.
Just before Hiroshima
just before Nagasaki
they nervously straddled the border
he an ensign on a forged three-day pass
she a technical virgin from Boston.
What he remembers is vaster:
something about his whole future
compressed to a stolen weekend.
He was to be shipped out tomorrow
for the massive land intervention.
He was to have stormed Japan.
Then, merely thinking of dying
gave him a noble erection.

Now, thanatopsis is calmer,
the first ripe berry on the stem,
a loss leader luring his greedy
hands deeper into the thicket
than he has ever been.
Deeper than he cares to be.
At the sight of the castle, however,
he recovers his wits and backtracks
meanwhile picking. Soon his bucket
is heavier etcetera than ever
and he is older etcetera
and still no spell has been recast
back at Planned Acres Cottage.
Each day he goes forth to gather
small fruits. Each evening she stands
over the stewpot skimming
the acid foam from the jam
expecting to work things out
awaiting, you might say, a unicorn
her head stuffed full of old notions
and the slotted spoon in her hand.

CINDERELLA
Saturday Afternoon at the Movies

LOUISE BERNIKOW

Louise Bernikow's insightful personal essays about women's culture have been collected into her book *Among Women* (1980), which deals with friendship, women's psychology, and the bonds between women. The following essay, taken from that collection, looks at the way the story of Cinderella sets women against each other in competition to find a place in the powerful world of men.

No, Cinderella, said the stepmother,
you have no clothes and cannot dance.
That's the way with stepmothers.

(Anne Sexton, "Cinderella")

Turn and peep, turn and peep,
No blood is in the shoe,
The shoe is not too small for her,
The true bride rides with you.

(*Grimms'* Cinderella)

I begin with a memory of movies and mother, a dark theatre and a Saturday afternoon. In a miasma of Walt Disney images, Bambi burning and Snow White asleep, the most memorable is "Cinderella." I carry her story with me for the rest of my life. It is a story about women alone together and they are each other's enemies. This is more powerful as a lesson than the ball, the Prince or the glass slipper. The echoes of "Cinderella" in other fairy tales, in myth and literature, are about how awful women are to each other. The girl onscreen, as I squirm in my seat, needs to be saved. A man will come and save her. Some day my Prince will come. Women will not save her; they will thwart her. There is a magical fairy godmother who does help her, but this, for me, has no relation to life, for the fairy is not real and the bad women are. The magical good fairy is a saccharine fluff.

There are two worlds in the Cinderella cartoon, one of women, one of men. The women are close by and hostile, the men distant and glittering.

Stepsisters and stepmother are three in one, a female battalion allied against Cinderella. The daughters are just like their mother. All women are alike. Lines of connection, energy fields, attach sisters to mother, leaving Cinderella in exile from the female community at home.

Father is far off. On film, neither he nor the Prince has much character. Father is her only tie, her actual blood tie, but the connection does her no good. Daddy is King in this world; I cannot keep Daddy and King apart in my memory. My own father was as far off, as full of authority, as surrounded by heraldry, the trumpets of fantasy, to me, to my mother. King Daddy. 3

The Prince is rich and handsome. Rich matters more than handsome. The girl among the cinders, dressed in rags, will escape—I am on her side, I want her to escape, get away from the cinders and the awful women—because the Prince will lift her out. The world of the Prince is the world of the ball, music, fine clothes and good feeling. Were everything to be right at home, were the women to be good to one another and have fun together, it would not be sufficient. The object is the ball, the Prince, the big house, the servants. Class mobility is at stake. Aspiration is being titillated. 4

To win the Prince, to be saved, requires being pretty. All the women care about this. Being pretty is the ticket and because Cinderella is pretty, the stepmother and stepsisters want to keep her out of the running. There is no other enterprise. Cinderella does not turn up her nose and hide in a corner reading a book. Being pretty, getting to the ball, winning the Prince is the common ground among the women. What we have in common is what keeps us apart. 5

Cinderella must be lonely. Why, I wonder, doesn't she have a friend? Why doesn't she go to school? Why doesn't her father tell the awful women to stop? A hurt and lonely girl, with only a prince to provide another kind of feeling. Why doesn't she run away? Why can't the situation be changed? It is as though the house they live in is the only world, there is no other landscape. Women are always in the house, being awful to each other. 6

Magic. Cinderella has a fairy godmother who likes her and wants her to be happy. She gives the girl beautiful clothes. She doesn't have to instruct Cinderella or give her advice about how to waltz or how to lift her skirt or even give her directions to the palace. Only the clothes and the accoutrements—and a prohibition about coming home at midnight. A powerful woman who wants Cinderella to be pretty and successful in the social world. I know, at whatever age it is that I watch this story unfold, that the mother beside me is not the woman on the screen. Her feelings on such matters are, at best, mixed up. She is not so powerful. 7

I am stirred and confused by the contrast between bad and good women and the way it all seems to revolve around the issue of being pretty. Some women are hostile and thwarting, others enabling and powerful. The stepmother hates Cinderella's prettiness; the fairy godmother adorns it. I look sideways at my mother, trying to decide which kind of woman she is, where 8 she stands on the business of pretty. Often, she braids my hair and settles me into polka dot, parades me before my beaming father. It is good to be pretty. Yet, onscreen, it is bad to be pretty—Cinderella is punished for it. In the enterprise of pretty, other women are your allies and your enemies. They are not disinterested. The heat around the issue of pretty, the urgency and intensity of it, is located among the women, not the men, at whom it is supposedly aimed. Luckily, we move on to the ball and the lost slipper.

This is one of the oldest and most often-told stories, varying significantly 9 from one version to another, one country to another, one period to another. What appears on movie theatre screens or television on Saturday afternoons comes from as far away as China, as long ago as four hundred years. Each teller, each culture along the way, retained some archetypal patterns and transformed others, emphasized some parts of the story, eradicated others. Disney took his version of Cinderella from one written down by a Frenchman named Perrault in the seventeenth century. Perrault's is a "civilized" version, cleaned up, dressed up and given several pointed "lessons" on top of the original material.

Many of the details about fashionability that we now associate with the 10 story come from Perrault. His has the atmosphere of Coco Chanel's dressing rooms, is modern and glamorous. He concocted a froufrou, aimed at an aristocratic audience and airily decorated with things French. He named one of the sisters Charlotte and set the action in a world of full-length looking glasses and inlaid floors. He invented a couturière called Mademoiselle de Poche to create costumes for the ball, linens and ruffles, velvet suits and headdresses. Disney dropped the French touches.

Perrault's story is set in a world of women with their eyes on men. Even 11 before the King's ball is announced, the stepmother and stepsisters are preoccupied with how they look. They are obsessed with their mirrors, straining to see what men would see. Once the ball is on the horizon, they starve themselves for days so that their shapes shall be, when laced into Mademoiselle de Poche's creations, as extremely slender as those in our own fashion magazines. The ball—and the prospects it implies—intensifies the hostility toward Cinderella. They have been envious. Now, they must keep the pretty girl out of competition. Most of the action of Perrault's story is taken up with the business of the ball.

Cinderella is a sniveling, self-pitying girl. Forbidden to go to the ball, 12 she does not object but, instead, dutifully helps her stepsisters adorn themselves. She has no will, initiates no action. Then, magically, the fairy godmother appears. She comes from nowhere, summoned, we suppose, by Cinderella's wishes. Unlike the fairy godmother in other versions of the story, Perrault's and Disney's character has no connection to anything real, has no meaning, except to enable Cinderella to overcome the opposition of the women in her home, wear beautiful clothes and get to the ball. Cinderella stammers, unable to say what she wants—for she is passive, suffering and good, which comes across as relatively unconscious. The fairy divines Cinderella's desire and equips her with pumpkin/coach, mice/horses, rats/coachmen, lizards/footmen, clothes and dancing shoes. She adds the famous prohibition that Cinderella return by midnight or everything will be undone.

These details of the fairy godmother's magic—the pumpkin, image of All 13 Hallows' Eve; midnight, the witching hour; mice, rats and lizards originated with Perrault. They are specific reminders of an actual and ancient female magic, witchcraft. Since Perrault wrote his story in the seventeenth century, it is not surprising to find echoes of this magic, which was enormously real to Perrault's audience.

Thousands had been burned at the stake for practicing witchcraft, most 14 of them women. A witch was a woman with enormous power, a woman who might change the natural world. She was "uncivilized" and in opposition to the world of the King, the court, polite society. She had to be controlled. Perrault's story attempts to control the elements of witchcraft just as various kings' governments had, in the not too recent past, controlled what they believed to be an epidemic of witchcraft. Perrault controls female power by trivializing it. The witchcraft in this story is innocent, ridiculous, silly and playful. It is meant to entertain children.

The prohibition that Cinderella return by midnight is also related to 15 witchcraft. She must avoid the witching hour, with its overtones of sexual abandon. The fairy godmother acts in this capacity in a way that is familiar to mothers and daughters—she controls the girl, warns her against darkness, uses her authority to enforce restraint, prevent excess, particularly excess associated with the ball, the world of men, sexuality.

Cinderella's dancing shoes are glass slippers. Perrault mistranslated the 16 fur slipper in the version that came to him, substituting *verre* for *vire* and coming up glass. No pendant came along to correct the mistake, for the glass slipper is immensely appropriate to the story in its modern form and the values it embodies. Call it dainty or fragile, the slipper is quintessentially the stereotype of femininity. I wonder how Cinderella danced in it.

The rags-to-riches moment holds people's imaginations long after the 17 details of the story have disappeared. It appeals to everyone's desire for magic, for change that comes without effort, for speedy escape from a bad place— bad feelings. We all want to go to the ball, want life to be full of good feeling and feeling good. But Cinderella's transformation points to a particular and limited kind of good feeling—from ugly to beautiful, raggedy to glamorous. The object of her transformation is not actually pleasure (she does not then walk around her house feeling better) but transportation to the ball with all the right equipment for captivating the Prince.

Transformed, Cinderella goes to the ball, which is the larger world, the 18 kingdom ruled by kings and fathers. The stepmother has no power in that world and does not even appear. This part of the story focuses on men, who are good to Cinderella as forcefully as women have been bad to her. Perrault embellishes Cinderella's appearance in a way that would have been congenial to the French court. In fact, she seems to have gone to the French court. The story is suffused with perfume and "fashionability." The Prince is taken with Cinderella and gives her some candy—"citrons and oranges," according to the text. How French. She, forever good, shares the candy with her stepsisters, who do not, of course, know who she is.

Cinderella has a wonderful time. As readers, hearers, watchers, we have a wonderful time along with her. More than the music and the dancing, the aura of sensual pleasure, everyone's good time comes from the idea that Cinderella is a "knockout." This is exciting. Perrault's word for what happens is that the people are *étonnés*, which means stunned. Cinderella is a show-stopper, so "dazzling" that "the King himself, old as he was, could not help watching her." He remarks on this to his Queen, whose reactions we are not told. Being "stunning" is being powerful. This is the way women have impact, the story tells us. This is female power in the world outside the home, in contrast to her former powerlessness, which was within the home, which was another country. This tells me why women spend so much time trying to turn themselves into knockouts—because, in Cinderella and in other stories, it *works*.

Presumably, Cinderella's giddiness over her own triumph at the ball makes her forget her godmother's command and almost miss her midnight deadline. Lest we lose the idea that all men adore Cinderella, Perrault adds a courtier at the end of the story, as the search for the missing Cinderella is carried out, and has him, too, say how attractive Cinderella is. She fulfills, then, the masculine idea of what is beautiful in a woman. She is the woman men want women to be.

Cinderella flees at midnight and loses her shoe. Perrault plays this part down, but Disney has a visual festival with the glinting glass slipper on the staircase and the trumpet-accompanied quest to find its owner. Perrault's Prince sends a messenger to find the shoe's owner, which puts the action at some distance, but Disney gives us a prince in all his splendor.

Cinderella is a heroine and in the world of fairy tales what the heroine wins is marriage to the Prince. Like any classic romance, wafted by perfume and fancy clothes, the young girl is lifted from a lowly powerless situation (from loneliness and depression, too) by a powerful man. He has no character, not even a handsome face, but simply represents the things that princes represent, the power of the kingdom.

Opposition to achieving this triumph comes from the women in the house; help comes from daydream and fantasy. The only proper activity for women to engage in is primping. What is expected of them is that they wait "in the right way" to be discovered. Cinderella obeys the rules. Her reward is to be claimed by the Prince. The lesson of Cinderella in these versions is that a girl who knows and keeps her place will be rewarded with male favor.

Like a saint, she shows neither anger nor resentment toward the women who treated her so badly. In fact, she takes her stepsisters along to the castle, where she marries each off to a nobleman. Now everyone will be happy. Now there will be no conflict, no envy, no degradation. If each woman has a prince or nobleman, she will be content and the soft humming of satisfaction will fill the air. Women otherwise cannot be alone together. 24

This is the sort of story that poisoned Madame Bovary's imagination. In Flaubert's novel, a woman married to a country doctor, with aspirations for a larger life, goes to a ball where a princely character pays her some attention. The ball and the Prince, seen by Emma Bovary as possibilities for changing everyday life, haunted her uneasy sleep. The ball was over. Wait as she might for its return, for a second invitation, all she got was a false prince—a lover who did not lift her from the ordinariness of her life—and then despair. 25

The romance depends on aspiration. The Prince must be able to give the heroine something she cannot get for herself or from other women. He must represent a valuable and scarce commodity, for the women must believe there is only one, not enough to go around, and must set themselves to keeping other women from getting it. In "Cinderella," like other fairy tales and other romances, the world of the Prince represents both actual and psychological riches. 26

Perrault's Cinderella is the daughter of a gentleman, turned into a peasant within the household. She has been declassed by female interlopers, reduced to the status of servant, for she belongs to her father's class only precariously. One of the ways women exercise their power, the story tells us, is by degrading other women. Cinderella will be saved from her female-inflicted degradation first by another female, the fairy godmother, who puts her on the road to her ultimate salvation. At the end of the story, she is restored to her class position, or, better, raised to an even higher position by the Prince. 27

Her fall from class is represented not only by her tattered clothes, but by the work she is forced to do. She is the household "drudge" and housework is the image of her degradation. Her work has no value in the story; it is the invisible, repetitious labor that keeps things going and makes it possible for the sisters and stepmother to devote themselves to *their* work, which is indolence on the one hand and trying to be beautiful for men on the other. Historically, indolence has been revered as the mark of a lady. What is "feminine" and "ladylike" is far removed from the world of work. Or the world of self-satisfying work. A man prides himself on having a wife who does not work; it increases his value in the eyes of other men; it means he provides well; it enforces conventional bourgeois "masculinity." A lady has long fingernails; neither the typewriter nor the kitchen floor has cracked them. She has porcelain skin; neither the rough outdoors nor perspiration has cracked that. Out of the same set of values comes the famous glass slipper. 28

The stepmother's class position is as precarious as Cinderella's is. The story does not tell, but we can imagine that whether she was married before 29 to a poorer man or one equally a gentleman, her status and security are now tied to the man she has married and the ones she can arrange for her daughters. History, experience, and literature are full of landless propertyless women trying to secure marriage to stand as a bulwark against poverty, displacement and exile, both actual and psychological. The actual situation bears emphasis. The economic reality behind the fairy tale and the competition among the women for the favor of the Prince is a world in which women have no financial lives of their own. They cannot own businesses or inherit property. The kingdom is not theirs. In order to survive, a woman must have a husband. It is in the interests of her daughters' future—and her own—that the stepmother works to prevent competition from Cinderella. She is not evil. Within the confines of her world and the value systems of that world, she is quite nice to her own daughters, only cruel to Cinderella.

Still, the stepmother is an archetypal figure in fairy tales, always a 30 thwarter, often a destroyer of children. Psychologists, and Bruno Bettelheim in particular, have a psychological explanation for this. The "bad" stepmother, Bettelheim points out, usually coexists with the "good" mother, representing two aspects of a real mother as experienced by a child. The stepmother is shaped by the child's unacceptable anger against her own mother. But there are real facts of life at work in these stepmother stories, too, especially as they describe what can happen among women at home. To a man's second wife, the daughter of the first marriage is a constant reminder of the first wife. The second wife is continually confronted with that memory and with the understanding that wives are replaceable, as they frequently and actually *were* in a world where women died young in childbirth, and men remarried, moved on.

A woman marries a man who has a daughter and comes to his household, 31 where the daughter's strongest connection is to her father; the stepmother's strongest connection is to the husband. The Eternal Triangle appears, husband/father at the center, mediating the relationship, stepmother and daughter as antagonists, competing for the husband/father's attention and whatever he may represent. Anxious, each in her own way and equally displaced, they face each other with enmity. The masculine imagination takes prideful pleasure in the story, placing, as it does, husband/father at center stage, making him King, arbiter of a world of women. . . .

I am writing an essay about Cinderella, spending mornings at the type- 32 writer, afternoons in libraries, interpreting information on index cards of various colors and sheets of yellow paper. I discover something bizarre woven in the story as we now know it: that the story took root in ancient China. The remnants of that culture, especially of the ancient practice of footbinding, are in the story, in the value of the small foot, in the use of the shoe to represent the potential bride. I see, then, the historical truth behind the terrible moment at the end of "Cinderella."

The Prince brings the slipper to the house of Cinderella's father. First 33 one stepsister, then the other attempts to slip her foot into it, but each foot is too large. The first stepsister's toe is too large. The stepmother hands her daughter a knife and says, "Cut off the toe. When you are Queen you won't have to walk anymore." The second stepsister's heel is too large and her mother repeats the gesture and the advice.

Mutilation. Blood in the shoe, blood on the knife, blood on the floor and unbearable pain, borne, covered, masked by the smile. It is too familiar, frightening in its familiarity. The mother tells the daughter to mutilate herself in the interests of winning the Prince. She will not have to walk. Again, indolence enshrined. As mothers, in fact, did in China until the twentieth century—among the upper classes as unquestioned custom and among peasants as great sacrifice and gamble. 34

It began when the girl was between five and seven years old. The bandages were so tight, the girl might scream. Her mother pulled them tighter and might have tried to soothe her. Tighter. At night, in agony, the girl loosens them. She is punished, her hands tied to a post to prevent unlacing. The bones crack. The pain is constant. Tighter. She cannot walk. Tighter. By her adolescence, the girl has learned to bind her feet herself and the pain has lessened. She has, as a reward, special shoes, embroidered and decorated, for her tiny feet. 35

I translate the actual foot-binding, the ritual interaction of mother and daughter, to metaphor. A black mother straightens her daughter's hair with a hot iron, singeing the scalp, pulling and tugging. The daughter screams. My mother buys me a girdle when I am fifteen years old because she doesn't like the jiggle. She slaps my face when I begin to menstruate, telling me later that it is an ancient Russian custom and she does not know its origin. I sleep with buttons taped to my cheeks to make dimples and with hard metallic curlers in my hair. Tighter. I hold myself tighter, as my mother has taught me to do. 36

Is the impulse to cripple a girl peculiar to China between the eleventh and twentieth centuries? The lotus foot was the size of a doll's and the woman could not walk without support. Her foot was four inches long and two inches wide. A doll. A girl-child. Crippled, indolent and bound. This is what it meant to be beautiful. And desired. This women did and do to each other. 37

Pain in the foot is pain in every part of the body. A mother is about to bind her daughter's feet. She knows the pain in her own memory. She says: "A daughter's pretty legs are achieved through the shedding of tears." 38

This women did to each other.
This women do.
Or refuse to do.
. . . .

THE WICKED STEPMOTHER'S TALE

◐

SARA MAITLAND

What if Cinderella needed to be saved, not from her life of hard work, but from her own passivity? Fiction writer Sara Maitland re-tells the story of Cinderella from the stepmother's point of view, in this narrative from the collection *Tales I Tell My Mother* (1987). Maitland is author of a number of books ranging from novels to works of theology, short stories to biography. She has also written television screenplays.

The wife of a rich man fell sick and as she felt that her end was drawing near, she called her only daughter to her bedside and said, 'Dear Child, be good and pious, and then the good God will always protect you, and I will look down from heaven and be near you.' Thereupon she closed her eyes and departed. Every day the maiden went out to her mother's grave and wept, and she remained pious and good. When winter came the snow spread a white sheet over the grave and by the time the spring sun had drawn it off again the man had taken another wife . . .

Now began a bad time for the poor step-child . . . They took her pretty clothes away, put an old grey bedgown on her and gave her wooden shoes . . . She had to do hard work from morning to night, get up before daybreak, carry water, light fires, cook and wash . . . In the evening when she had worked until she was weary she had no bed to go to, but had to sleep by the hearth in the cinders. And as on that account she always looked dusty and dirty, they called her Cinderella.

You know the rest I expect. Almost everyone does.

I'm not exactly looking for self-justification. There's this thing going on at the moment where women tell all the old stories again and turn them inside-out and back-to-front—so the characters you always thought were the goodies turn out to be the baddies, and vice versa, and a whole lot of guilt is laid to rest: or that at least is the theory. I'm not sure myself that the guilt isn't just passed on to the next person, *intacta* so to speak. Certainly I want to carry and cope with my own guilt, because I want to carry and cope with my own virtue and I really don't see that you can have one without the other. Anyway it would be hard to find a version of this story where I would come out a shiny new-style heroine: no true version anyway. All I want to say is that it's more complicated, more complex, than it's told, and the reasons why it's told the way it is are complex too.

But I'm not willing to be a victim. I was not innocent, and I have grown out of innocence now and even out of wanting to be thought innocent. Living is a harsh business, as no one warned us when we were young and carefree under the apple bough, and I feel the weight of that ancient harshness and I want to embrace it, and not opt for some washed-out asceptic, hand wringing, Disneyland garbage. (Though come to think of it he went none-too-easy on stepmothers did he? Snow White scared the socks off me the first time I saw the film—and partly of course because I recognised myself. But I digress.) 2

Look. It was like this. Or rather it was more like this, or parts of it were like this, or this is one part of it. 3

She was dead pretty in a Pears Soap sort of way, and, honestly, terribly sweet and good. At first all I wanted her to do was concentrate. Concentration is the key to power. You have to concentrate on what is real. Concentration is not good or bad necessarily, but it is powerful. Enough power to change the world, that's all I wanted. (I was younger then, of course; but actually they're starving and killing whales and forests and each other out there; shutting your eyes and pretending they're not doesn't change anything. It does matter.) And what she was not was powerful. She wouldn't look out for herself. She was so sweet and so hopeful; so full of faith and forgiveness and love. You have to touch anger somewhere, rage even; you have to spit and roar and bite and scream and know it before you can be safe. And she never bloody would. 4

When I first married her father I thought she was so lovely, so good and so sad. And so like her mother. I knew her mother very well, you see; we grew up together. I loved her mother. Really. With so much hope and fondness and awareness of her worth. But—and I don't know how to explain this without sounding like an embittered old bitch which I probably am—she was too good. Too giving. She gave herself away, indiscriminately. She didn't even give herself as a precious gift. She gave herself away as though she wasn't worth hanging on to. Generous to a fault, they said when she was young, but no one acted as though it were a fault, so she never learned. 'Free with Kellogg's Cornflakes' was her motto. She equated loving with suffering I thought at one time, but that wasn't right, it was worse, she equated loving with being; as though she did not exist unless she was denying her existence. I mean, he was not a bad bloke her husband, indeed I'm married to him myself, and I like him and we have good times together, but he wasn't worth it—no one is—not what she gave him, which was her whole self with no price tag on. 5

And it was just the same with that child. Yes, yes one can understand: she had difficulty getting pregnant actually, she had difficulties carrying those babies to term too. Even I can guess how that might hurt. But her little girl was her great reward for suffering, and at the same time was also her handle on a whole new world of self-giving. And yes, of course she looked so lovely, who could have resisted her, propped up in her bed with that tiny lovely child 6 sucking, sucking, sucking; the mother who denied her little one nothing, the good mother, the one we all longed for, pouring herself out into the child. Well, I'll tell you, I've done it too, it is hell caring for a tiny daughter, I know. Everything, everything drags you into hell; the fact that you love and desire her, the fact that she's so needy and vulnerable, the fact that she never leaves you alone until your dreams are smashed in little piles and shabby with neglect, the fact that pleasure and guilt come so precisely together, as so seldom happens, working towards the same end and sucking your very self-hood out of you. It is a perilous time for a woman, that nursing of a daughter, and you can only survive it if you cling to yourself with a fierce and passionate love, *and* you back that up with a trained and militant lust for justice *and* you scream to the people around you to meet your needs and desires *and* you do not let them off, *and* when all is said and done you sit back and laugh at yourself with a well timed and not unmalicious irony. Well she could not, of course she could not, so she did not survive. She was never angry, she never asked, she took resignation—that tragic so-called virtue—as a ninth-rate alternative to reality and never even realised she had been short-changed.

So when I first married my husband I only meant to tease her a little, to rile her, to make her fight back. I couldn't bear it, that she was so like her mother and would go the same way. My girls were more like me, less agreeable to have about the house, but tough as old boots and capable of getting what they needed and not worrying too much about what they wanted or oughted, so to speak. I didn't have to worry about them. I just could not believe the sweetness of that little girl and her wide-eyed belief that I would be happy and love her if she would just deny herself and follow me. So of course I exploited her a bit, pushed and tested it, if you understand, because I couldn't believe it. Then I just wanted her to *see*, to see that life is not all sweetness and light, that people are not automatically to be trusted, that fairy-god-mothers are unreliable and damned thin on the ground, and that even the most silvery of princes soon go out hunting and fighting and drinking and whoring, and don't give one tuppeny ha'penny curse more for you than you give for yourself. Well she could have looked at her father and known. He hardly proved himself to be the great romantic lover of all time, even at an age when that would have been appropriate, never mind later. He had replaced darling Mummy with me, after all, and pretty damned quick too, and so long as he was getting his end off and his supper on the table he wasn't going to exert himself on her behalf, as I pointed out to her, by no means kindly.

(And, I should like to add, I still don't understand about that. I couldn't believe how little the bastard finally cared when it came to the point. Perhaps he was bored to tears by goodness, perhaps he was too lazy. He was a sentimental old fart about her of course, his eyes could fill with nostalgic tears every time he looked at her and thought of her dead mother; but he never *did* anything; or even asked me to stop doing anything. She never asked, and he never had eyes to see, or energy or . . . God knows what went on his head about her and as far as I'm concerned God's welcome. She loved him and trusted him and served him and he never even bloody noticed. Which sort of makes my point actually because he would never treat me like that, and yet he and I get on very well now; like each other and have good times in bed and out of it. Of course I'd never have let him tell me how to behave, but he might have tried, at least just once.)

Anyway, no, she would not see. She would not blame her father. She would not blame her mother, not even for dying, which is the ultimate outrage from someone you love. And she would not blame me. She just smiled and accepted, smiled and invented castles in the air to which someone, though not herself, would come and take her one day, smiled and loved me. No matter what I did to her, she just smiled. 9

So, yes, in the end I was cruel. I don't know how to explain it and I do not attempt to justify it. Her wetness *infuriated* me. I could not shake her good will, her hopefulness, her capacity to love and love such a pointless and even dangerous object. I could not make her hate me. Not even for a moment. I could not make her hate me. And I cannot explain what that frustration did to me. I hated her insane dog-like devotion where it was so undeserved. She treated me as her mother had treated him. I think I hated her stupidity most of all. I can hear myself almost blaming her for my belly deep madness; I don't want to do that; I don't want to get into blaming the victim and she was my victim. I was older than her, and stronger than her, and had more power than her; and there was no excuse. No excuse, I thought the first time I ever hit her, but there was an excuse and it was my wild need, and it escalated. 10

So in the end—and yes I have examined all the motives and reasons why one woman should be cruel to another and I do not find them explanatory— so in the end I was cruel to her. I goaded and humiliated and pushed and bullied her. I used all my powers, my superior strength, my superior age, my superior intelligence against her. I beat her, in the end, systematically and severely; but more than that I used her and worked her and denied her pleasures and gave her pain. I violated her space, her dignity, her integrity, her privacy, even her humanity and perhaps her physical safety. There was an insane urge in me, not simply to hurt her, but to have her admit that I had hurt her. I would lie awake at night appalled, and scald myself with contempt, with anger and with self-disgust, but I had only to see her in the morning for my temper to rise and I would start again, start again at her with an unrea- sonable savagery that seemed to upset me more than it upset her. Picking, picking and pecking, endlessly. She tried my patience as no one else had ever done and finally I gave up the struggle and threw it away and entered into the horrible game with all my considerable capacity for concentration. 11

And nothing worked. I could not make her angry. I could not make her hate me. I could not stop her loving me with a depth and a generosity and a 12 forgiveness that were the final blow. Nothing moved her to more than a simper. Nothing penetrated the fantasies and day-dreams with which her head was stuffed so full I'm surprised she didn't slur her consonants. She was locked into perpetual passivity and gratitude and love. Even when she was beaten she covered her bruises to protect me; even when she was hungry she would not take food from my cupboards to feed herself; even when I mocked her she smiled at me tenderly.

All I wanted was for her to grow up, to grow up and realise that life was not a bed of roses and that she had to take some responsibility for her own life, to take some action on her own behalf, instead of waiting and waiting and waiting for something or someone to come shining out of the dark and force safety on her as I forced pain. What Someone? Another like her father who had done nothing, nothing whatever, to help her and never would? Another like him whom she could love generously and hopelessly and serve touchingly and givingly until weariness and pain killed her too. I couldn't stand it. Even when I beat her, even as I beat her, she loved me, she just loved and smiled and hoped and waited, day-dreamed and night-dreamed, and waited and waited and waited. She was untouchable and infantile. I couldn't save her and I couldn't damage her. God knows, I tried. 13

Now of course it's just an ancient habit. It has lost its sharp edges, lost the passion in both of us to see it out in conflict, between dream and reality, between hope and cynicism. There is a great weariness in me, and I cannot summon up the fire of conviction. I do not concentrate any more, I do not have enough concentration, enough energy, enough power. Perhaps she has won, because she drained that out of me years and years ago. Sometimes I despair, which wastes still more concentration. We plod on together, because we always have. Sweetly she keeps at it, smile, smile, dream, hope, wait, love, forgive, smile, smile, bloody smile. Tiredly, I keep at it too: 'Sweep that grate.' 'Tidy your room.' 'Do your homework.' 'What can you see in that nerd.' 'Take out those damn ear-phones and pay attention.' 'Life doesn't come free, you have to work on it.' 'Wake up, hurry up, stop day-dreaming, no you can't, yes you must, get a move on, don't be so stupid.' And 'You're not going to the Ball, or party, or disco, or over your Nan's, dressed like *that*.' 14

She calls it nagging. 15

She calls me Mummy. 16

VICTIMS
The Setting

SUSAN BROWNMILLER

Susan Brownmiller has worked as a journalist and net-work television newswriter for over twenty years. Her articles have appeared in the *New York Times Magazine*, *Esquire, Vogue, Mademoiselle*, and other publications. The following excerpt is taken from her landmark book, *Against Our Will: Men, Women and Rape* (1975), chosen by the *New York Times Book Review* as one of the Outstanding Books of the Year. In this excerpt, Brownmiller takes a candid look at the underlying messages of the "Little Red Riding Hood" myth.

Women are trained to be rape victims. To simply learn the word "rape" is to take instruction in the power relationship between males and females. To talk about rape, even with nervous laughter, is to acknowledge a woman's special victim status. We hear the whispers when we are children: *girls get raped.* Not boys. The message becomes clear. Rape has something to do with our sex. Rape is something awful that happens to females: it is the dark at the top of the stairs, the undefinable abyss that is just around the corner, and unless we watch our step it might become our destiny.

Rape seeps into our childhood consciousness by imperceptible degrees. Even before we learn to read we have become indoctrinated into a victim mentality. Fairy tales are full of a vague dread, a catastrophe that seems to befall only little girls. Sweet, feminine Little Red Riding Hood is off to visit her dear old grandmother in the woods. The wolf lurks in the shadows, contemplating a tender morsel. Red Riding Hood and her grandmother, we learn, are equally defenseless before the male wolf's strength and cunning. His big eyes, his big hands, his big teeth—"The better to see you, to catch you, to eat you, my dear." The wolf swallows both females with no sign of a struggle. But enter the huntsman—he will right this egregious wrong. The kindly huntsman's strength and cunning are superior to the wolf's. With the twist of a knife Red Riding Hood and her grandmother are rescued from inside the wolf's stomach. "Oh, it was so dark in there," Red Riding Hood whimpers. "I will never again wander off into the forest as long as I live . . ."

Red Riding Hood is a parable of rape. There are frightening male figures abroad in the woods—we call them wolves, among other names—and females are helpless before them. Better stick close to the path, better not be adventurous. If you are lucky, a *good, friendly* male may be able to save you from certain disaster. ("Funny, every man I meet wants to protect me," says Mae West. "I can't figure out what from.") In the fairy-tale code book, Jack may kill giants but Little Red Riding Hood must look to a kindly huntsman for protection. Those who doubt that the tale of Red Riding Hood contains this subliminal message should consider how well Peter fared when he met his wolf, or even better, the survival tactics of the Three Little (male) Pigs. Who's Afraid of the Big Bad Wolf? Not *they*.

The utter passivity of Red Riding Hood in the teeth of the wolf is outdone by Sleeping Beauty, who lay immobile for one hundred years before she was awakened by the kiss of the prince. As a lesson in female sexuality, Sleeping Beauty's message is clear. The beauteous princess remains unresponsive until Mr. Right comes along. The prince is the only one who can awaken the princess. She cannot manage this feat by herself. Her role is to be beautiful and passive. Snow White in her glass coffin also remains immobile until her prince appears. Cinderella, too, needs a prince to extricate her from her miserable environment. Thus is female sexuality defined. Beautiful passivity. Wait, just wait, Prince Charming will soon be by; and if it is not Prince Charming but the Big Bad Wolf who stands at the door, then proper feminine behavior still commands you to stay immobile. The wolf is bigger and stronger than you are. Why try to fight back? But don't you worry, little girl. We have strong and kindly huntsmen patrolling these woods.

THE COMPANY OF WOLVES

ANGELA CARTER

In this rewriting of "Little Red Riding Hood," taken from her collection *The Bloody Chamber* (1979), British fiction writer Angela Carter illustrates the power of female sexuality, a topic which has informed her many novels and stories from the 1960s to the present. Her novels include *The Magic Toyshop* (1968) and *Nights at the Circus* (1984). She has edited *The Old Wives' Fairy Book* (1990) and written a scholarly study of images of women in the writings of the Marquis de Sade titled *The Sadeian Woman and the Ideology of Pornography* (1978).

One beast and only one howls in the woods by night.

The wolf is carnivore incarnate and he's as cunning as he is ferocious; once he's had a taste of flesh, then nothing else will do.

At night, the eyes of wolves shine like candle flames, yellowish, reddish, but that is because the pupils of their eyes fatten on darkness and catch the light from your lantern to flash it back to you—red for danger; if a wolf's eyes reflect only moonlight, then they gleam a cold and unnatural green, a mineral, a piercing color. If the benighted traveler spies those luminous, terrible sequins stitched suddenly on the black thickets, then he knows he must run, if fear has not struck him stock-still.

But those eyes are all you will be able to glimpse of the forest assassins as they cluster invisibly round your smell of meat as you go through the wood unwisely late. They will be like shadows, they will be like wraiths, gray members of a congregation of nightmare. Hark! his long, wavering howl . . . an aria of fear made audible.

The wolfsong is the sound of the rending you will suffer, in itself a murdering.

It is winter and cold weather. In this region of mountain and forest, there is now nothing for the wolves to eat. Goats and sheep are locked up in the byre, the deer departed for the remaining pasturage on the southern slopes— wolves grow lean and famished. There is so little flesh on them that you could count the starveling ribs through their pelts, if they gave you time before they pounced. Those slavering jaws; the lolling tongue; the rime of saliva on the grizzled chops—of all the teeming perils of the night and the forest, ghosts, hobgoblins, ogres that grill babies upon gridirons, witches that fatten their captives in cages for cannibal tables, the wolf is worst, for he cannot listen to reason.

You are always in danger in the forest, where no people are. Step between 7 the portals of the great pines where the shaggy branches tangle about you, trapping the unwary traveler in nets as if the vegetation itself were in a plot with the wolves who live there, as though the wicked trees go fishing on behalf of their friends—step between the gateposts of the forest with the greatest trepidation and infinite precautions, for if you stray from the path for one instant, the wolves will eat you. They are gray as famine, they are as unkind as plague.

The grave-eyed children of the sparse villages always carry knives with 8 them when they go out to tend the little flocks of goats that provide the homesteads with acrid milk and rank, maggoty cheeses. Their knives are half as big as they are; the blades are sharpened daily.

But the wolves have ways of arriving at your own hearthside. We try and 9 try but sometimes we cannot keep them out. There is no winter's night the cottager does not fear to see a lean, gray, famished snout questing under the door, and there was a woman once bitten in her own kitchen as she was straining the macaroni.

Fear and flee the wolf; for worst of all, the wolf may be more than he 10 seems.

There was a hunter once, near here, that trapped a wolf in a pit. This 11 wolf had massacred the sheep and goats; eaten up a mad old man who used to live by himself in a hut halfway up the mountain and sing to Jesus all day; pounced on a girl looking after the sheep, but she made such a commotion that men came with rifles and scared him away and tried to track him into the forest but he was cunning and easily gave them the slip. So this hunter dug a pit and put a duck in it, for bait, all alive-oh; and he covered the pit with straw smeared with wolf dung. Quack, quack! went the duck, and a wolf came slinking out of the forest, a big one, a heavy one, he weighed as much as a grown man and the straw gave way beneath him—into the pit he tumbled. The hunter jumped down after him, slit his throat, cut off all his paws for a trophy.

And then no wolf at all lay in front of the hunter but the bloody trunk 12 of a man, headless, footless, dying, dead.

A witch from up the valley once turned an entire wedding party into 13 wolves because the groom had settled on another girl. She used to order them to visit her, at night, from spite, and they would sit and howl around her cottage for her, serenading her with their misery.

Not so very long ago, a young woman in our village married a man who 14 vanished clean away on her wedding night. The bed was made with new sheets and the bride lay down in it; the groom said he was going out to relieve himself, insisted on it, for the sake of decency, and she drew the coverlet up to her chin and she lay there. And she waited and she waited and then she waited again—surely he's been gone a long time? Until she jumps up in bed and shrieks to hear a howling, coming on the wind from the forest.

That long-drawn, wavering howl has, for all its fearful resonance, some 15 inherent sadness in it, as if the beasts would love to be less beastly if only they knew how and never cease to mourn their own condition. There is a vast melancholy in the canticles of the wolves, melancholy infinite as the forest, endless as these long nights of winter, and yet that ghastly sadness, that mourning for their own, irremediable appetites, can never move the heart, for not one phrase in it hints at the possibility of redemption; grace could not come to the wolf from its own despair, only through some external mediator, so that, sometimes, the beast will look as if he half welcomes the knife that dispatches him.

The young woman's brothers searched the outhouses and the haystacks 16 but never found any remains, so the sensible girl dried her eyes and found herself another husband, not too shy to piss into a pot, who spent the nights indoors. She gave him a pair of bonny babies and all went right as a trivet until, one freezing night, the night of the solstice, the hinge of the year when things do not fit together as well as they should, the longest night, her first good man came home again.

A great thump on the door announced him as she was stirring the soup 17 for the father of her children and she knew him the moment she lifted the latch to him although it was years since she'd worn black for him and now he was in rags and his hair hung down his back and never saw a comb, alive with lice.

"Here I am again, missis," he said. "Get me my bowl of cabbage and be 18 quick about it."

Then her second husband came in with wood for the fire and when the 19 first one saw she'd slept with another man and, worse, clapped his red eyes on her little children, who'd crept into the kitchen to see what all the din was about, he shouted: "I wish I were a wolf again, to teach this whore a lesson!" So a wolf he instantly became and tore off the eldest boy's left foot before he was chopped up with the hatchet they used for chopping logs. But when the wolf lay bleeding and gasping its last, the pelt peeled off again and he was just as he had been, years ago, when he ran away from his marriage bed, so that she wept and her second husband beat her.

They say there's an ointment the Devil gives you that turns you into a 20 wolf the minute you rub it on. Or that he was born feet first and had a wolf for his father and his torso is a man's but his legs and genitals are a wolf's. And he has a wolf's heart.

Seven years is a werewolf's natural span, but if you burn his human 21 clothing you condemn him to wolfishness for the rest of his life, so old wives hereabouts think it some protection to throw a hat or an apron at the were-wolf, as if clothes made the man. Yet by the eyes, those phosphorescent eyes, you know him in all his shapes; the eyes alone unchanged by metamorphosis.

Before he can become a wolf, the lycanthrope strips stark naked. If you spy a naked man among the pines, you must run as if the Devil were after you. 22

It is midwinter and the robin, the friend of man, sits on the handle of the gardener's spade and sings. It is the worst time in all the year for wolves, but this strong-minded child insists she will go off through the wood. She is quite sure the wild beasts cannot harm her although, well-warned, she lays a carving knife in the basket her mother has packed with cheeses. There is a bottle of harsh liquor distilled from brambles; a batch of flat oat cakes baked on the hearthstone; a pot or two of jam. The flaxen-haired girl will take these deli-cious gifts to a reclusive grandmother so old the burden of her years is crushing her to death. Granny lives two hours' trudge through the winter woods; the child wraps herself up in her thick shawl, draws it over her head. She steps into her stout wooden shoes; she is dressed and ready and it is Christmas Eve. The malign door of the solstice still swings upon its hinges, but she has been too much loved ever to feel scared. 23

Children do not stay young for long in this savage country. There are no toys for them to play with, so they work hard and grow wise, but this one, so pretty and the youngest of her family, a little latecomer, had been indulged by her mother and the grandmother who'd knitted her the red shawl that, today, has the ominous if brilliant look of blood on snow. Her breasts have just begun to swell; her hair is like lint, so fair it hardly makes a shadow on her pale forehead; her cheeks are an emblematic scarlet and white and she has just started her woman's bleeding, the clock inside her that will strike, henceforward, once a month. 24

She stands and moves within the invisible pentacle of her own virginity. She is an unbroken egg; she is a sealed vessel; she has inside her a magic space the entrance to which is shut tight with a plug of membrane; she is a closed system; she does not know how to shiver. She has her knife and she is afraid of nothing. 25

Her father might forbid her, if he were home, but he is away in the forest, gathering wood, and her mother cannot deny her. 26

The forest closed upon her like a pair of jaws. 27

There is always something to look at in the forest, even in the middle of winter—the huddled mounds of birds, succumbed to the lethargy of the season, heaped on the creaking boughs and too forlorn to sing; the bright frills of the winter fungi on the blotched trunks of the trees; the cuneiform slots of rabbits and deer, the herringbone tracks of the birds, a hare as lean 28 as a rasher of bacon streaking across the path where the thin sunlight dapples the russet brakes of last year's bracken.

When she heard the freezing howl of a distant wolf, her practiced hand sprang to the handle of her knife, but she saw no sign of a wolf at all, nor of a naked man, neither, but then she heard a clattering among the brushwood and there sprang onto the path a fully clothed one, a very handsome young one, in the green coat and wide-awake hat of a hunter, laden with carcasses of game birds. She had her hand on her knife at the first rustle of twigs, but he laughed with a flash of white teeth when he saw her and made her a comic yet flattering little bow; she'd never seen such a fine fellow before, not among the rustic clowns of her native village. So on they went together, through the thickening light of the afternoon. 29

Soon they were laughing and joking like old friends. When he offered to carry her basket, she gave it to him although her knife was in it because he told her his rifle would protect them. As the day darkened, it began to snow again; she felt the first flakes settle on her eyelashes, but now there was only half a mile to go and there would be a fire, and hot tea, and a welcome, a warm one, surely, for the dashing huntsman as well as for herself. 30

This young man had a remarkable object in his pocket. It was a compass. She looked at the little round glass face in the palm of his hand and watched the wavering needle with a vague wonder. He assured her this compass had taken him safely through the wood on his hunting trip because the needle always told him with perfect accuracy where the north was. She did not believe it; she knew she should never leave the path on the way through the wood or else she would be lost instantly. He laughed at her again; gleaming trails of spittle clung to his teeth. He said if he plunged off the path into the forest that surrounded them, he could guarantee to arrive at her grandmother's house a good quarter of an hour before she did, plotting his way through the undergrowth with his compass, while she trudged the long way, along the winding path. 31

I don't believe you. Besides, aren't you afraid of the wolves? 32

He only tapped the gleaming butt of his rifle and grinned. 33

Is it a bet? he asked her. Shall we make a game of it? What will you give me if I get to your grandmother's house before you? 34

What would you like? she asked disingenuously. 35

A kiss. 36

Commonplaces of a rustic seduction; she lowered her eyes and blushed. 37

He went through the undergrowth and took her basket with him, but she forgot to be afraid of the beasts, although now the moon was rising, for she wanted to dawdle on her way to make sure the handsome gentleman would win his wager. 38

Grandmother's house stood by itself a little way out of the village. The freshly falling snow blew in eddies about the kitchen garden and the young 39 man stepped delicately up the snowy path to the door as if he were reluctant to get his feet wet, swinging his bundle of game and the girl's basket and humming a little tune to himself.

There is a faint trace of blood on his chin; he has been snacking on his catch. 40

He rapped upon the panels with his knuckles. 41

Aged and frail, granny is three-quarters succumbed to the mortality the ache in her bones promises her and almost ready to give in entirely. A boy came out from the village to build up her hearth for the night an hour ago and the kitchen crackles with busy firelight. She has her Bible for company; she is a pious old woman. She is propped up on several pillows in the bed set into the wall peasant fashion, wrapped up in the patchwork quilt she made before she was married, more years ago than she cares to remember. Two china spaniels with liver-colored blotches on their coats and black noses sit on either side of the fireplace. There is a bright rug of woven rags on the pantiles. The grandfather clock ticks away her eroding time. 42

We keep the wolves outside by living well. 43

He rapped upon the panels with his hairy knuckles. 44

It is your granddaughter, he mimicked in a high soprano. 45

Lift up the latch and walk in, my darling. 46

You can tell them by their eyes, eyes of a beast of prey, nocturnal, devastating eyes as red as a wound; you can hurl your Bible at him and your apron after, granny; you thought that was a sure prophylactic against these infernal vermin. . . . Now call on Christ and his mother and all the angels in heaven to protect you, but it won't do you any good. 47

His feral muzzle is sharp as a knife; he drops his golden burden of gnawed pheasant on the table and puts down your dear girl's basket, too. Oh, my God, what have you done with her? 48

Off with his disguise, that coat of forest-colored cloth, the hat with the feather tucked into the ribbon; his matted hair streams down his white shirt and she can see the lice moving in it. The sticks in the hearth shift and hiss; night and the forest has come into the kitchen with darkness tangled in its hair. 49

He strips off his shirt. His skin is the color and texture of vellum: A crisp stripe of hair runs down his belly, his nipples are ripe and dark as poison fruit, but he's so thin you could count the ribs under his skin if only he gave you the time. He strips off his trousers and she can see how hairy his legs are. His genitals, huge. Ah! huge. 50

The last thing the old lady saw in all this world was a young man, eyes like cinders, naked as a stone, approaching her bed. 51

The wolf is carnivore incarnate. 52

When he had finished with her, he licked his chops and quickly dressed himself again, until he was just as he had been when he came through her 53 door. He burned the inedible hair in the fireplace and wrapped the bones up in a napkin that he hid away under the bed in the wooden chest in which he found a clean pair of sheets. These he carefully put on the bed instead of the telltale stained ones he stowed away in the laundry basket. He plumped up the pillows and shook out the patchwork quilt, he picked up the Bible from the floor, closed it and laid it on the table. All was as it had been before except that grandmother was gone. The sticks twitched in the grate, the clock ticked and the young man sat patiently, deceitfully beside the bed in granny's night-cap.

Rat-a-tap-tap. 54

Who's there, he quavers in granny's antique falsetto. 55

Only your granddaughter. 56

So she came in, bringing with her a flurry of snow that melted in tears 57 on the tiles, and perhaps she was a little disappointed to see only her grand-mother sitting beside the fire. But then he flung off the blanket and sprang to the door, pressing his back against it so that she could not get out again.

The girl looked round the room and saw there was not even the inden- 58 tation of a head on the smooth cheek of the pillow and how, for the first time she'd seen it so, the Bible lay closed on the table. The tick of the clock cracked like a whip. She wanted her knife from her basket but she did not dare reach for it because his eyes were fixed upon her—huge eyes that now seemed to shine with a unique, interior light, eyes the size of saucers, saucers full of Greek fire, diabolic phosphorescence.

What big eyes you have. 59

All the better to see you with. 60

No trace at all of the old woman except for a tuft of white hair that had 61 caught in the bark of an unburned log. When the girl saw that, she knew she was in danger of death.

Where is my grandmother? 62

There's nobody here but we two, my darling. 63

Now a great howling rose up all around them, near, very near, as close 64 as the kitchen garden, the howling of a multitude of wolves; she knew the worst wolves are hairy on the inside and she shivered, in spite of the scarlet shawl she pulled more closely round herself as if it could protect her, although it was as red as the blood she must spill.

Who has come to sing us carols? she said. 65

Those are the voices of my brothers, darling; I love the company of 66 wolves. Look out of the window and you'll see them.

Snow half-caked the lattice and she opened it to look into the garden. It 67 was a white night of moon and snow; the blizzard whirled round the gaunt, gray beasts who squatted on their haunches among the rows of winter cab-bage, pointing their sharp snouts to the moon and howling as if their hearts would break. Ten wolves; twenty wolves—so many wolves she could not count them, howling in concert as if demented or deranged. Their eyes reflected the light from the kitchen and shone like a hundred candles.

It is very cold, poor things, she said; no wonder they howl so.   68

She closed the window on the wolves' threnody and took off her scarlet   69 shawl, the color of poppies, the color of sacrifices, the color of her menses, and since her fear did her no good, she ceased to be afraid.

What shall I do with my shawl?   70

Throw it on the fire, dear one. You won't need it again.   71

She bundled up her shawl and threw it on the blaze, which instantly   72 consumed it. Then she drew her blouse over her head; her small breasts gleamed as if the snow had invaded the room.

What shall I do with my blouse?   73

Into the fire with it, too, my pet.   74

The thin muslin went flaring up the chimney like a magic bird and now   75 off came her skirt, her woolen stockings, her shoes, and onto the fire they went, too, and were gone for good. The firelight shone through the edges of her skin; now she was clothed only in her untouched integument of flesh. Thus dazzling, naked, she combed out her hair with her fingers; her hair looked white as the snow outside. Then went directly to the man with red eyes in whose unkempt mane the lice moved; she stood up on tiptoe and unbuttoned the collar of his shirt.

What big arms you have.   76

All the better to hug you with.   77

Every wolf in the world now howled a prothalamion outside the window   78 as she freely gave the kiss she owed him.

What big teeth you have!   79

She saw how his jaw began to slaver and the room was full of the clamor   80 of the forest's *Liebestod*,[1] but the wise child never flinched, even when he answered:

All the better to eat you with.   81

The girl burst out laughing; she knew she was nobody's meat. She laughed   82 at him full in the face, she ripped off his shirt for him and flung it into the fire, in the fiery wake of her own discarded clothing. The flames danced like dead souls on Walpurgisnacht and the old bones under the bed set up a terrible clattering, but she did not pay them any heed.

Carnivore incarnate, only immaculate flesh appeases him.   83

She will lay his fearful head on her lap and she will pick out the lice from   84 his pelt and perhaps she will put the lice into her mouth and eat them, as he will bid her, as she would do in a savage marriage ceremony.

---

1. The title of the finale of Richard Wagner's opera *Tristan und Isolde*, a story of two ill-fated lovers. *Liebestod* loosely means "death in love."

The blizzard will die down. 85

The blizzard died down, leaving the mountains as randomly covered with 86
snow as if a blind woman had thrown a sheet over them, the upper branches
of the forest pines limed, creaking, swollen with the fall.

Snowlight, moonlight, a confusion of pawprints. 87

All silent, all still. 88

Midnight; and the clock strikes. It is Christmas Day, the werewolves' 89
birthday; the door of the solstice stands wide open; let them all sink through.

See! Sweet and sound she sleeps in granny's bed, between the paws of 90
the tender wolf.

MAKING CONNECTIONS

1. What is the nature of fantasy? Is it a harmless escape from reality, a reflection of reality, or a force that can shape reality in some way? Why are fairy tales so powerful, and why have the same stories lasted for so many generations? You might explore your library's holdings in fantasy and fairy tales. Are fairy tales a subject for anthropology, psychology, literature or some other discipline? What are the similarities and differences among the approaches you find?

2. Compare your own knowledge of fairy tales with Lieberman's analysis. Can you think of any in which women are depicted as strong without being wicked? What about "Goldilocks and the Three Bears," or "Beauty and the Beast"? Which elements fit Lieberman's findings, and which diverge? Try comparing one of Grimms' original tales, or a tale from the Tatterhood collection of stories, with a contemporary "Walt-Disneyfied" version. What aspects of the story have been changed for modern American consumption? What impact do these changes have on the ways gender is portrayed?

3. Fairy tales deal with broad motifs like "the rescue," being chosen, or the reward of marriage. Can you identify instances in adult culture where these themes continue to be reinforced? What are some of the motifs in Harlequin romances, soap operas, or women's magazines? Does the concept "Some Day My Prince Will Come" play any part in your own thinking? Write an essay that traces one of these motifs in culture today. Feel free to include visual evidence like magazine advertisements or art to illustrate your points.

4. How does Kumin blend details of real life and fantasy in her poem? Where do these elements seem to clash, and why? What role do you think fantasy plays in a relationship like marriage? In real life, does a fantasy like Sleeping Beauty give us an ideal to strive for, or does it necessarily set us up for disillusion? What do you think Kumin's view would be?

5. Explain Bernikow's phrase about women: "What we have in common is what keeps us apart." Can you think of instances in which this holds true in everyday life? How might women's being "kept apart" work against their recognizing the limitations of the roles society wants them to play?

6. Both Bernikow and Maitland deal with mothers as an influence on their daughters' lives. How can mothers resist or perpetuate what both authors see as society's oppression of women? How are Bernikow's thoughts about Chinese footbinding relevant? How does Maitland explode the image of

the "perfect" mother in her story? Why is this important? As a writing exercise, compose a letter from a mother to a daughter—or from a father to a daughter—which tries to explain difficult choices in raising a young woman today.

7. Brownmiller suggests that culture "trains" women to be victims. Try making a list of all of the cautions you can think of that society has for women, such as not walking alone after dark, not going to bars alone, not listing your full name in the telephone directory if you live alone, etc. How many of these are you familiar with and which do you practice? Do you see these as "natural" proscriptions for all people, or are there some that exist for women but seldom apply to men? Do you think our acceptance of these cautions helps "train" women to be victims or, if they are ignored, make it easier to blame the victim instead of the criminal? What connections can you make between Brownmiller's piece and Marilyn Frye's essay "Oppression" in Chapter 2?

8. How would you characterize Carter's heroine? Is she weak? Strong? Both? Are there any aspects of her personality or behavior that seemed at first to be weak but that turned out to be strong? Were any stereotypes about women shaken up by this tale? How would you paraphrase Carter's message in the story?

9. Try re-writing your own fairy tale, giving women more power or more compassion for each other. What would "Hansel and Gretel" look like if Gretel befriended the witch? What if Cinderella enjoyed her work and started a national cinder franchise? Be as innovative as you like—this is fantasy!

10. Select one or more essayists from Chapter 5 on women's writing. How would these authors respond to Maitland or Carter or Kumin as writers using the power of language to express or shape women's reality? Write an imaginary review of one of the selections in Chapter 7 by one of the essayists in Chapter 5. Try to capture the spirit of the "reviewer" you select.

11. Compare and contrast the images of women in fairy tales with the images of men that little boys receive in these stories. What is the difference between the hero and the heroine in fairy tales? What lessons about growing up and finding a place in the world are conveyed for boys, and are there any limitations in those lessons as well? You might construct this as a class or group project, with each member selecting one classic fairy tale to analyze and discuss, then comparing your views.

8
IMAGES OF MEN:
SPORTS

C   O   N   T   E   X   T   S

The ritual of Monday Night Football, the image of the locker room, jokes about sports "widows" exasperated by their husbands' obsession with Playoffs and World Series—all point to the popular folklore that sports are the domain of men. Boys grow up playing sports, learning sports legends and scores, finding heroes and role models among the celebrity-athletes of football, basketball, or wrestling. For a majority of men the attraction of sports continues into adulthood, on the playing field or in the living room, as they follow intently their favorite teams, analyze and discuss players and performances, look forward with excitement to major sporting events. Professional athletics, particularly men's sports, are a multibillion dollar industry in our society, and the rhetoric of sports—performance, competition, scoring, winning—permeates many areas of life from education to business, sexuality to war. While women, too, have become increasingly active in the domain of sports, both as spectators and participants, this chapter looks primarily at the images of men and masculinity conveyed in the language, history, and folklore of athletics.

Because sports are so basic to our culture, and particularly to men's socialization, it is a fascinating field to analyze for the values it embodies and the messages it conveys about gender, equality, and society. Writers have studied its myriad aspects: its past and present role in society, sports as a business, the images and ideology that surround its publicity, the structure of games themselves, the power of athletic metaphors in life. No one chapter of a collection could cover all the facets of this cultural phenomenon, but the essays that follow attempt at least to open a few of these issues for your reflection.

In "Why Sports is a Drag," humorist Dave Barry opens the chapter with a comic look at the masculine domain of sports, from the sonorous pronouncements of Howard Cosell to the human drama of neighborhood softball to his ultimate test of gender—the 1960 World Series. Next, Bruce Kidd takes a more serious look at "Sports and Masculinity." He examines the history of events like the Olympics and traces the image of sport as a "masculinizing" activity, designed by and for men alone. What are the tactics, motives, and psychology behind gender discrimination in sports, and what are the consequences for men and women when healthy competition crosses the line into aggression and injustice? Kidd argues eloquently, not for abolishing sports, but for transforming them in concrete ways to reflect more humane, less repressive practices both on the playing field and off.

Whereas Kidd offers a male perspective on the social impact of athletics, Joyce Carol Oates turns a woman's eye onto the predominantly masculine sport of boxing in an attempt to understand and capture its balance of artistry and violence, sensuality and pain. These excerpts from her book *On Boxing* explore the subtleties of sport as human expression—the drama of contest, the perfection of physical strength and instinct, the rituals that make boxing as symbolic and unified as a symphony or a play. With imagination and acuity, Oates ventures into the deeper connections between athletics and masculinity as revealed in its images, its language, and its art.

In our next essay, Don Sabo shifts the focus of attention onto men's sexuality, specifically the ways in which the rhetoric and imagery of competitive sports help construct "The Myth of the Sexual Athlete." For Sabo, the emphasis on performance, aggression, emotional repression, and hypermasculinity in sports can easily spill over into men's sexual lives, creating what he terms "sexual schizophrenia"—the uneasy tension in men between wanting intimacy and openness in relationships, yet being driven by the aggressive, performance-oriented model of "the sexual athlete." The result is an unfair and limiting cultural message for men, a trap that hinders their experience and restricts their sexuality in self-defeating ways.

Finally, Mike Messner offers a perspective on race, class, and athletics in his essay "Sports and Inequality." Rather than accept the myth of the playing field as a democratic, neutral arena for competition, Messner sees numerous reflections of our stratified society in the meaning of American sports. He documents the ways in which professional athletics reinforce racism and re-produce dangerous social injustices. At the same time, however, Messner shows how on an individual level sports can help overcome the barriers of race and class and transcend the limits of prejudice.

Common to all the essays in this chapter is a belief in the value, beauty, and excitement of sports—qualities that these writers find central to the full expression of athletics in our culture. At the same time, these essayists show a keen awareness of the way sports can mirror negative aspects of society and shape individual identities in what are sometimes limiting ways. Our pleasure in sports does not need to diminish because we understand its influence on us. Instead, by examining its inherent problems and acting to change them, we can reclaim those qualities that make sport an exhilarating and expansive activity.

WHY SPORTS IS A DRAG

DAVE BARRY

Winner of the Pulitzer Prize for Commentary, humorist Dave Barry has written numerous satires of our life and times, including *Babies and Other Hazards of Sex* (1984), *Claw Your Way to the Top* (1986), and *Homes and Other Black Holes* (1988). He currently lives in Florida and writes for the *Miami Herald*. The piece that follows was taken from his collection *Dave Barry's Greatest Hits*, published in 1988.

Mankind's yearning to engage in sports is older than recorded history, dating back to the time, millions of years ago, when the first primitive man picked up a crude club and a round rock, tossed the rock into the air, and whomped the club into the sloping forehead of the first primitive umpire. What inner force drove this first athlete? Your guess is as good as mine. Better, probably, because you haven't had four beers. All I know is, whatever the reason, Mankind is still nuts about sports. As Howard Cosell, who may not be the most likable person in the world but is certainly one of the most obnoxious, put it: "In terms of Mankind and sports, blah blah blah blah the 1954 Brooklyn Dodgers."

Notice that Howard and I both use the term "Mankind." Womankind really isn't into sports in the same way. I realize things have changed since my high-school days, when sports were considered unfeminine and your average girls' gym class consisted of six girls in those gym outfits colored Digestive Enzyme Green running around waving field-hockey sticks and squealing, and 127 girls on the sidelines in civilian clothing, claiming it was That Time of the Month. I realize that today you have a number of top female athletes such as Martina Navratilova who can run like deer and bench-press Chevrolet pickup trucks. But to be brutally frank, women as a group have a long way to go before they reach the level of intensity and dedication to sports that enables men to be such incredible jerks about it.

If you don't believe me, go to your local racquetball club and observe the difference between the way men and women play. Where I play, the women tend to gather on the court in groups of random sizes—sometimes three, sometimes five, as if it were a Jane Fonda workout—and the way they play is, one of them will hit the ball at the wall and the rest of them will admire the shot and compliment her quite sincerely, and then they all sort of relax, as if they're thinking, well, thank goodness *that's* over with, and they always seem very surprised when the ball comes *back*. If one of them has the presence of mind to take another swing, and if she actually hits the ball, everybody is *very* complimentary. If she misses it, the others all tell her what a *good* try she made, really, then they all laugh and act very relieved because they know they have some time to talk before the ball comes bouncing off that darned *wall* again.

Meanwhile, over in the next court, you will have two males wearing various knee braces and wrist bands and special leatheroid racquetball gloves, hurling themselves into the walls like musk oxen on Dexedrine, and after every single point one or both of them will yell "S—!" in the self-reproving tone of voice you might use if you had just accidentally shot your grandmother. American men tend to take their sports seriously, much more seriously than they take family matters or Asia.

This is why it's usually a mistake for men and women to play on teams together. I sometimes play in a coed slow-pitch softball league, where the rules say you have to have two women on the field. The teams always have one of the women play catcher, because in slow-pitch softball the batters hit just about every pitch, so it wouldn't really hurt you much if you had a deceased person at catcher. Our team usually puts the other woman at second base, where the maximum possible number of males can get there on short notice to help out in case of emergency. As far as I can tell, our second basewoman is a pretty good baseball player, better than I am anyway, but there's no way to know for sure because if the ball gets anywhere near her, a male comes barging over from, say, right field, to deal with it. She's been on the team for three seasons now, but the males still don't trust her. They know that if she had to choose between catching a fly ball and saving an infant's life, deep in her soul, she would probably elect to save the infant's life, without even considering whether there were men on base.

This difference in attitude between men and women carries over to the area of talking about sports, especially sporting events that took place long ago. Take the 1960 World Series. If we were to look at it objectively, we would have to agree that the outcome of the 1960 World Series no longer matters. You could make a fairly strong case that it didn't really matter in 1960. Women know this, which is why you almost never hear them mention the 1960 World Series, whereas you take virtually any male over age 35 and even if he can't remember which of his children has diabetes, he can remember exactly how Pirates shortstop Bill Mazeroski hit the ninth-inning home run that beat the Yankees, and he will take every available opportunity to discuss it at length with other males.

See that? Out there in Readerland, you females just read right through that last sentence, nodding in agreement, but you males leaped from your chairs and shouted: "Mazeroski wasn't a SHORTSTOP! Mazeroski played SECOND BASE!" Every male in America has millions of perfectly good brain cells devoted to information like this. We can't help it. We have no perspective. I have a friend named Buzz, a successful businessman and the most rational person you ever want to meet, and the high point of his entire life is the time he got Stan Albeck, the coach of the New Jersey Nets, to look directly at him during a professional basketball game and make a very personal remark rhyming with "duck shoe." I should explain that Buzz and I have season tickets to the Philadelphia 76ers, so naturally we hate the Nets a great deal. It was a great honor when Albeck singled Buzz out of the crowd for recognition. The rest of us males congratulated Buzz as if he'd won the Nobel Prize for Physics.

It's silly, really this male lack of perspective, and it can lead to unnecessary tragedy, such as soccer-riot deaths and the University of Texas. What is even more tragic is that women are losing perspective, too. Even as you read these words, women are writing vicious letters to the editor, expressing great fury at me for suggesting they don't take their racquetball seriously. Soon they will be droning on about the importance of relief pitching.

SPORTS AND MASCULINITY

BRUCE KIDD

Canadian Olympic athlete Bruce Kidd looks at the history of sports and the ideology of professional athletics in this 1987 essay. Kidd currently teaches physical education at the University of Toronto and has authored several books on the politics of sport and athletes' rights, including *The Political Economy of Sport* (1979), *Athletes' Rights in Canada* (1982) co-authored with Mary Eberts, and *The Death of Hockey* (1972) co-authored with John Macfarlane.

"Ideology is like B.O.," a wag once said. "You never smell your own." That's   1
certainly true for men in sports. Most of us grew up playing sports, dreaming about starring in them, and making lifelong friends through them. Many of us still play them as adults, and we follow them endlessly, admiring and analyzing the performances of our favorites, discussing them with friends and workmates in the daily rituals of coffee and the pub, scheduling our lives around the calendar of the major sports events. Some of us actively encourage our children in them, driving them to the rink or park, helping with coaching and officiating. Yet men have rarely subjected our engagement in sports to the systematic questioning we focus on work, life and love, and other forms of cultural expression—literature and the visual and performing arts. Because they are so engrossing and so familiar, we assume that they have always been played, and that they have been unaffected by history or politics. Even when an Olympic boycott forces us to admit some connection between the structures and conflicts of a society and its sports, our personal experience leads us to protest that the activity itself is innocent of partisanship or prejudice and beneficial to all. Yet an outpouring of feminist scholarship now compels us to revise the popular image and explore the ways in which men have created sports to celebrate and buttress patriarchal (and class) power. Such an examination is not without its terrors, for it requires us to question radically something that many of us have found to be joyous and validating. But it is essential if we are to understand fully what it means "to be a man" and to promote human liberation.

The purpose of this article is to contribute to this necessary analysis by   2
synthesizing the revisionist scholarship and then discussing its implications for men. I will argue that the games we play were created by males for males

without taking the needs and experiences of females into account in any way. I will also argue that rather than being an "innocent" pastime, modern sports reinforce the sexual division of labor, thereby perpetuating the great inequality between the sexes and contributing to the exploitation and repression of both males and females. I do not advocate the abolition of sports, for they can strengthen people of both sexes in beneficial, exhilarating ways. But I will contend that they should be transformed and, to this end, I will suggest some practical steps.

The "Naturalness" of Sports

My starting point is the insight of social history that sports as we know them today are not the universal, transhistorical physical activity they are commonly thought to be, played in much the same way by all peoples in all periods of human history. They are, rather, a group of activities developed under the specific social conditions of rapidly industrializing nineteenth-century Britain and spread to the rest of the world through emigration, emulation, and imperialism. Although modern sports are popularly equated to the athletic events of the ancient Olympic Games, scholars now argue that the differences between the Olympic contests of antiquity and those of our own era significantly outweigh the similarities and that we must seek to understand each of these competitions in its own terms.[1]

The classical games also celebrated class and patriarchal power, but few of us would have recognized in them what we call sport. By modern standards, they were extremely violent. The combative events, which were the most popular spectacles, were conducted with little regard for safety or fairness. There were no weight categories to equalize strength and size, no rounds, and no ring. Bouts were essentially fights to the finish, which is not surprising when you consider that these competitions began as preparations for war. Victory alone brought glory; defeat brought undying shame. Although the Greeks had the technology to measure records in the running, jumping, and throwing events, they rarely did so: performance for itself—pursuing the personal best despite one's placing—was meaningless to them. In fact, champions tried to intimidate their opponents so that they would withdraw and the victor could boast that he had won without having to compete. There were no team events, because competitors did not want to share the glory of victory. No competitor would have congratulated an opponent for a fairly fought or outstanding triumph. Today's handshake would have seemed an act of cowardice to them.[2] Nor were those fiercely competitive games common to all cultures living along the Mediterranean in that period. In fact, anthropologists have established that only warlike peoples have used their leisure for combative events.[3]

Sports as "Male Practice"

Armed with this insight about the social specificity of the various forms of physical activity, we can begin to take a closer look at our own. Pierre de Coubertin did not revive the Olympics, as he liked to claim: he appropriated and recast the symbols of the ancient games for his own purpose, which was to combat the decadence and militarism of *fin-de-siècle* Europe by inculcating in young men the qualities he admired in English rugby and cricket.[4] These sports had their origins in the rural folk games of the late middle ages. In the mid- to late-nineteenth century, they were fashioned into the first modern sports—characterized by standard rules, a bureaucratic structure, the over-emphasis on setting records and the concept of fair play—by middle- and upper-class males in the increasingly bourgeois institutions of the public school, the university, and the private club.[5] Innovators, organizers, and creative publicists like Coubertin, consciously regarded sports as educational, preparing boys and young men for careers in business, government, colonial administration, and the military by instilling physical and mental toughness, obedience to authority, and loyalty to the "team."[6] When working-class males began to take them up too, some groups refused to accommodate them: at the Royal Henley Regatta, for example, working-class oarsmen were excluded by definition until 1933.[7] Most groups, however, eventually adopted the strategy of "rational recreation," incorporating workers as players and spectators, under strict middle-class leadership, as a means of fostering respect for the established order and reducing class tensions.[8] In the sports contested in Coubertin's Olympics, the tactic most frequently employed to regulate class relations was the amateur code. As the sociologist Richard Gruneau has written, sports "mobilize middle class bias" to this day.[9]

Education or socialization through sport was consciously understood to be "masculinizing." At the outset of Thomas Hughes's *Tom Brown's Schooldays*, the romanticization of the all-male Rugby School under Thomas Arnold, Squire Brown ponders what advice to give his son who is departing for Rugby:

> Shall I tell him to mind his work, and say he's sent to school to make himself a good scholar? Well, but he isn't sent to school for that—at any rate, not for that mainly. I don't care a straw for Greek particles, or the digamma; no more does his mother. What is he sent to school for? Well, partly because he wanted so to go. If he'll only turn out a brave, helpful, truthtelling Englishman, and a gentleman, and a Christian, that's all I want.[10]

Then in the course of six years of rugby, cricket, cross-country running, and impromptu fist fighting, young Brown acquires courage and stamina, ingenuity, close friendships, and leadership, attributes traditionally associated with maleness by the dominant class. Hughes's bestseller persuaded schoolmasters and youth leaders throughout the English-speaking world to encourage sports as a "toughener" for their male charges and inspired Coubertin to develop the ideology of the modern Olympics. Working-class men also imbued sports with notions of masculinity.[11] The most popular nineteenth-century games and contests—football, hockey, lacrosse, track and field, and boxing—were termed "the manly sports." Although they have now lost the epithet, they continue to be encouraged for the same reason.

To be sure, there have been differences in the values emphasized by sports and in the approaches different participants may take to a single sport. Soccer and rugby have always encouraged more spontaneous creativity than North American football. The Montreal Canadiens have never practiced the "beat-'em-in-the-alley" tactics of their traditional rivals, the Toronto Maple Leafs. These differences should be read in part as contributions to a continuing debate about which aspects of masculinity are most attractive. When Charles Dickens championed boxing in the pages of *The Pickwick Papers* against the contemporary prohibition, he was not endorsing brutality, but a more scientific, humane, and democratic method for men to settle their disputes than the duel.[12] When Wayne Gretzky skated away from a fight in a playoff game several years ago, he made it clear he was rejecting the dominant code of "masculinity" in North American hockey—which emphasizes defending your "honor" by dropping your stick and gloves to fight—in favor of the intelligence of staying out of the penalty box.[13] The frequent vehemence of these debates only serves to underline the importance of sports as signifiers of "masculinity."

Sports as Male Preserves

The men who developed and promoted sports in the nineteenth and twentieth centuries were careful to ensure that only males were masculinized in this way. They kept sports as male preserves by actively discouraging females from participating. They denied them adequate facilities and programs, ridiculed their attempts, and threatened them with the specter of ill health and "race suicide." Male doctors and physical educators argued that humans had only a finite quantity of energy, which in the case of women was needed for reproduction, an energy drain "which would make the stroke oar of the University crew falter." If women used up their energy in vigorous athletic activity, went the argument, they would not only be undermining their own health, but the future of the white race. Working-class men generally shared these prejudices and contributed to the exclusionary practices. Thus sports helped to strengthen and extend male bonds between classes. Many girls and women were also deterred from taking part in sports by economic and social conditions—long hours of domestic labor, differential and generally less adequate diets, and restrictive dress.[14]

Women persisted, however. During the 1920s and 1970s especially, girls and women engaged in competitive sports in growing numbers. But males have continued to exclude them from their own games and contests, requiring them to play on women's teams with inferior resources.[15] Despite the examples

299

from agriculture, industry, and sports of women performing arduous "men's tasks," many persist in the belief that a distinct female biology prevents women from competing in the male realm. (The argument falsely assumes that all men are the same in size, strength, and fitness, and that all women are uniformly inferior. In the reality many so blithely ignore, there is a tremendous range in male and female size, strength, fitness, and so on. For most of the population, including trained athletes, those ranges overlap.)[16] Organizers have also tried to confine females to those sports believed to enhance traditional "femininity," such as swimming, tennis, and gymnastics, and to devise "girls' rules" to discourage the ambitious and aggressive play expected of boys and men.[17] Women athletes have also faced inordinate pressure to conform to the heterosexual expectations of most men.[18]

Sports as Patriarchal Ideology

One legacy of this pattern of development is the well-known inequalities that continue to plague females seeking sporting opportunities and careers. In North America, despite a decade of "progress," males still have more than twice the opportunities and public resources available for sport. There is little evidence that the men who control sport are genuinely committed to redressing the balance. In the Olympic Games, there are still more than twice as many events for men as for women.[19] But if we were to conclude that the problem is simply one of allocation, we would be missing the most important insight of the feminist critique. The effect of sports is also to perpetuate patriarchy by reinforcing the sexual division of labor. By giving males exciting opportunities, preaching that the qualities they learn from them are "masculine," and preventing girls and women from learning in the same situations, sports confirm the prejudice that males are a breed apart. By encouraging us to spend our most creative and engrossing moments as children and our favorite forms of recreation as adults in the company of other males, they condition us to trust each other much more than women. By publicly celebrating the dramatic achievements of the best males, while marginalizing females as cheerleaders and spectators, they validate the male claim to the most important positions in society. Abby Hoffman, a four-time Canadian Olympian and now Director-General of Sport Canada, has written:

> The overall place of women in the labor force is in the lower-paying and sedentary occupations. There are of course many reasons for this, but certainly arguments about the physical inferiority of women learned and repeated through sport help buttress a system where women become stenographers, typists, retail salespersons, telephone operators, etc., and men become truck drivers, carpenters, labourers, construction workers, and workers in a host of manual trades which involve a modicum of physical capacity.[20]

10

Sports contribute to the underdevelopment of the female majority of the population and the undervaluing of those traditionally "feminine" skills of nurturing and emotional maintenance essential to human survival and growth.

I believe these relationships are understood by sportsmen as well. In nineteenth-century Canada and the United States, men introduced sports to public-school boys and the adolescent members of organizations such as the YMCA to combat the feminization of teaching.[21] British sociologists Kevin Sheard and Eric Dunning have suggested a direct relationship between the development of the boorish, sexist subculture of rugby—the public moonings, songs of male sexual conquest of women, and exaggerated drinking—and first-wave feminism:

> The historical conjuncture represented by the simultaneous rise of rugby football and the suffragette movement within the upper and middle classes may have been of some significance with respect to the emergence of the specific pattern of socially tolerated taboo breaking. For women were increasingly becoming a threat to men, and men responded by developing rugby football as a male preserve in which they could bolster up their threatened masculinity and at the same time mock, objectify, and vilify women, the principal source of the threat.[22]

We are witnessing a similar conjuncture today. In Toronto, where there is a strong women's movement, the city fathers have just given final approval to a new domed stadium, to be built on prime public land and subsidized by municipal and provincial grants. The architect calls it "a secular cathedral." I suggest it be called the Men's Cultural Center. It is being developed by an almost exclusively male board of a provincial crown corporation. Its primary tenants will be the local franchises of the commercial baseball and football cartels, the Blue Jays and the Argonauts, which stage male team games for largely male audiences. The other major beneficiaries will be the public and private media corporations, which sell the predominantly male audiences to the sponsoring advertisers.[23] There is no doubt the stadium is popular, among both men and women. It will be a great improvement over the existing stadium, increasing the pleasure derived from watching gifted athletes. But at the ideological level, especially in the absence of comparable opportunities for female athletes, coaches, managers, and sports impresarios, it will celebrate male privilege, displaying male prowess while leaving the gendered nature of sport unchallenged. Women as well as men are capable of difficult, dramatic, and pleasing feats of grace, agility, strength, and teamwork, but we will never know this from this stadium. They will be either rendered invisible or exploited as sex objects (cheerleaders) along the sidelines. Males who identify with the athletes on the field are also basking in the privilege that sports bring them and in the "symbolic annihilation"[24] of women. If a city were to devote twenty-five acres of prime downtown real estate and at least $85 million of public funds to a stadium in which only Anglo-Saxons could play, there would be howls of protest, but in the matter of sex, most of us take such favoritism for granted. Needless to say, there are other forces at work—in Toronto's case, the deal was initiated by land developers and the holding company of the brewery that owns the baseball team—but it is more than a coincidence that during the period of second-wave feminism, male political leaders and business and media executives have worked hard to place the male-only sports on a more commodious and visible stage, while women's crisis centers go underfunded. The stadium will even look like a Men's Cultural Center. Standing at the foot of the world's tallest freestanding telecommunications tower, it will be a gigantic Claes Oldenberg–like sculpture of the male genitals.

Men's Fears

The Australian social biologist Ken Dyer has shown that women's records in the measurable sports like track and field and swimming are now being broken significantly faster than men's records in the same events and has concluded that lack of opportunity—not biology—is the primary reason why female performances have always lagged behind those of males. Projecting his findings into the future, he suggests that if opportunities for women can be equalized, in most sports the best females will eventually be able to compete on a par with the best males.[25] Imagine a woman winning the open 100 meters at the Olympics or playing in the National Hockey League! Performances once considered impossible are now common in virtually every sport, but most men balk at Dyer's suggestion. It's not only that they don't believe it could happen, but it frightens them. They fear that the character of sport would change if women played with men. "You have to play softer with women," a softball official testified to the Ontario Human Rights Commission to explain why he felt integrated competition, even when the female players had been chosen for their ability, would reduce the satisfaction for males.[26] But although it is unspoken, I believe they also fear the profound social and psychological changes that might result if women were understood to be fully competent in the special domain of men. At present in Ontario, the 500,000-male-strong Ontario Hockey Association has refused to allow a thirteen-year-old girl to play on one of its teams, although she won a place on the team in a competitive tryout. The OHA has gone to court three times in an effort to stop her, and it continues to block her participation while the matter will be heard one more time by the Ontario Human Rights Commission.[27] Is one thirteen-year-old female player, or even two hundred female players, going to topple the male hockey leadership, or drastically alter the values of this century-old sport? Hardly. There must be something deeper.

In part, what they fear is the disorientation of the male psyche. As Nancy Chodorow has argued in *The Reproduction of Mothering*,[28] boys develop their identity by differentiating themselves from their mothers. Since most child rearing has been done by women, the primary interaction for young males has been with women, with the result that they have great difficulty in identifying with their fathers. So, Chodorow says, in developing a "masculine" identity, males are essentially learning to differentiate themselves from their mothers and from women in general. They rehearse and strengthen this "positional" masculinity in activities that accentuate male-female differences and stigmatize those characteristics generally associated with women. Although Chodorow does not discuss sports, it is clear that they were developed—and serve—that very purpose in the industrial capitalist societies with which we are most familiar. It was certainly my experience growing up in Toronto in the 1940s and 1950s. I played sports endlessly as a child. I gobbled up the rules, skills, strategies, and lore, none of which seemed to interest my mother, her friends, or the girls of my own age on the street. Certainly we rarely included them. I also learned to accept (rather than question) physical pain, to deny anxiety and anger, and to be aggressive in ways that were clearly valued as "manly." I realize now that I gained an enormous sense of my own power when I could respond to challenges in this way, for it meant I was not "like a girl." In fact, sometimes I teased my mother and sister to tears to confirm that I had succeeded in being different from them. Yet it shows how shaky such positional identity can be, because when I put myself into the emotional state I remember from that period, I realize that I would have been devastated if a girl had played on any of the teams I was so proud to belong to. It would have proclaimed to the world that I was inadequate. At the deepest psychological levels, the blurring of sex roles undermines not only the male-privileging sexual division of labor, but the very process by which males raised within sexually segregated sports have gained personal confidence and social validation.

There are other possible disruptions as well. Men also fear the loss of traditional nurturing that might result if women learned through sports (and other predominantly male activities) to be as hard and unyielding as males. This helps explain why so many men are still determined to keep sports a male sanctuary, why in the quintessentially masculine sport of boxing many jurisdictions still prohibit women from competing at all, even against other women. It also helps us understand the psychological weight of the pressures on female athletes to be "feminine." To be sure, many women share these fears and support the status quo. As Dorothy Dinnerstein points out, males and females actively collaborate to maintain the existing gender arrangements: "nostalgia for the familiar is a feeling that has . . . been mobilized in opposition to social change."[29] But the price of such collaboration is high.

A Men's Problem

Most observers consider the inequalities and power dynamics I have described to be a "women's problem," but I would argue that the patriarchal nature of modern sports has harmed men, too. By encouraging and reinforcing a positional identity, sports have led us to limit our options as humans, to deny feelings and to disparage—and therefore not to learn—the interpersonal skills associated with females. By teaching us a form of strength and assertiveness disconnected from emotional understanding and the skills of emotional support, they have encouraged us to ignore our own inner feelings and those of others. Through sports, men learn to cooperate with, care for, and love other men, in a myriad of rewarding ways, but they rarely learn to be intimate with each other or emotionally honest. On the contrary, the only way many of us express fondness for other men is by teasing or mock fighting (the private version of what has become a public form of tribute—the roast). As other authors in this volume point out, anything more openly affectionate would be suspect.

Chodorow and Dinnerstein argue that the development of positional 16 identity has also contributed to the process by which males value abstract achievement—which in sport has meant victory and records. Because they elevate external goals over intrinsic ones, sports have encouraged those who become athletes to treat their bodies as instruments and to submit to physical and psychological injury and to inflict it on others. The active repression of pain is an everyday part of the sports world: "no pain, no gain" is a common slogan, but it has ruined the careers of countless athletes and left many permanently crippled. There are also psychological scars: the constant emphasis on external goals such as winning and being chosen for an international team is highly pathological and leaves many forever stunted and unable to define their own goals. At the same time, sports label those who cannot meet the ever higher standards of performance expected of athletes as "failures."[30]

I am particularly concerned about the effect of sports on our relations 17 with other men. The Australian sociologist Bob Connell suggests that sports instruct men in two aspects of power: the development of force ("the irresistible occupation of space") and skill ("the ability to operate on the objects within that space, including other humans").[31] The rules of football (all codes), basketball, boxing, hockey, and other sports where territorial control is important almost literally conform to this definition. They encourage athletes to treat each other as enemies to be intimidated and brutalized, when in reality they are co-players without whom the rewards of playing cannot be obtained. This is the other side of "that sweet spot in time," or "walking tall," the exhilaration of doing it right in sport. Thomas Tutko, the noted American sports psychologist, likes to say that "to be a champion, you have to be the meanest Son-of-a-Bitch in the valley."[32] Certainly I felt this when I was a successful middle-distance runner. I developed the sense that I owned every race, and I instinctively resented—without ever really thinking about it—any attempt by other runners to try for the lead. "How dare they!" I'd hear my inner self say, as I surged to beat back their challenge. I also revelled in the psychological warfare that is endemic in sports and loved to probe a competitor's personality and to devise tactics to intimidate him. But as productive as aggressiveness and competitiveness were when it came to winning races, they are enormous barriers to the development and maintenance of close relationships. I've spent the past twenty years trying to bring them under control. Other athletes I know say the same.

Toward More Humane Sporting Practices

There are no magic solutions to the problems I have described. They are [18] deeply rooted in long-established patterns of child rearing and human interaction and are perpetuated by powerful economic and political interests. We cannot dismiss or abolish sports, as some on the left have suggested, nor should we want to. They can help all humans acquire self-mastery in pleasurable, healthy and popular skills and rituals. Such opportunities are particularly important in societies like our own where work is more and more automated and alienating. Sports can also provide easily understood popular dramas in ways that strengthen the sense of community and confirm some of the most widely shared human values. Hockey may be a puberty rite for Canadian boys, but it is also a celebration of the creativity, energy, and elan of the human spirit in the depths of winter, the season of death. The contradictions of modern sports can sometimes undermine the very privilege they enshrine. In their claim to be democratic, sports organizations provide the arguments—though less frequently opportunities—for the disadvantaged to demonstrate their right to a better future. In the Olympic Games, for example, the universalist aspirations of the ruling International Olympic Committee (IOC) have paved the way for athletes from the poorest and smallest national communities to compete, even when they have had little chance at medals. In turn, the overwhelming presence of the Third World nations—there are now 161 national Olympic committees—has persuaded the elitist IOC, which is dominated by Western European countries, to support the international struggle against apartheid and racism and to begin a program of technical assistance to the have-not nations.

The liberation of sports from patriarchal (and class and Western) struc- [19] tures of domination will be a long and complex process. It will have to be undertaken in conjunction with similar efforts in other areas of everyday life. The outcome—how humans will play sports in a more egalitarian, less oppressive age—will largely depend upon those broader struggles, because as we have seen, forms of physical activity, including sport, are determined by history. But that should not dissuade us.

We can start by actively questioning the pervasive masculinist bias in the [20] sports world. The language is rife with words that unconsciously reinforce the male preserve: "jock," the popular term for athlete; "tomboy" to describe any bright, active girl who likes physical activity and is good at sports; "suck" and "sissy" to condemn anyone who betrays anxiety or fear—all remind us that sports were designed to harden males. We should challenge those words the way the civil rights movement did with "nigger" and "boy" and the women's movement has done with "mankind" and "girl." We need to develop substitutes (such as "athlete" for "jock") and then campaign to remove the offending terms from use. In some cases, it will be necessary to change the practices as well. Although we will always admire physical courage, we do ourselves a disservice if we continue uncritically to condemn the expression of pain and uneasiness that is usually associated with being a "sissy."

We should challenge the gross sexism of that inner sanctuary of patriarchy, the locker and shower room. Allen Sack, an American sociologist who played on the 1966 Notre Dame championship football team, has said that in many ways football is a training ground for rape. In the game, players learn to control the field and to dominate other players, and in the dressing room they endlessly fantasize and celebrate the male sexual conquest of women.[33] It takes a different kind of courage to contest the explicit, omnipresent misogyny of the locker room. Much of what is said is often exuberantly rich in humor. Yet it contributes to our own repression, as well as to the exploitation of women. If you contest it, you'll get anger and denial—"it's just a joke; I'm not a chauvinist!"—but it does cause a person to reconsider. 21

We can also help to redefine the rules and values of sports to make them more inviting to everybody. Physical educators, coaches, and community groups of both sexes have amended rules to make games safer and more genuinely educational. In Canada, parents, players, teachers, and government leaders have contributed to the effort to eliminate the gratuitous violence of ice hockey. In my neighborhood, a community softball league, to reduce collisions between players, has added a second first base (immediately adjacent to the original base, but in foul territory) and has eliminated the necessity of tagging the runner at home. These changes often require tradeoffs—I was sorry to see the softballers discourage the slide—but by doing so they subtly reduced the premium on physical dominance. (When I was nine, I was taught to throw a cross-body block at second, third, and home. "There's $10 on every bag," our coach would tell us, "and if you don't get it, he will.") These experiments, especially when they result from open discussion about the purpose of sports, should be encouraged. To opponents who appeal to "tradition," we can point out that the rules of games have been continually changed for other reasons, so why not make them more humane? 22

We should also struggle to change the tendency to see sports as battles. Competitions are viewed as zero-sum contests, and athletes are encouraged to treat each other as enemies. Military metaphors abound: quarterbacks "throw the long bomb"; teams, "whip," "punish," "roll over," and "savage" each other. This imagery is hardly coincidental: in many societies competitive physical activity has been closely associated with military training. But instead, I suggest we consider sports to be glorious improvisations, dialectical play, or 23 collective theatre where athletes are part antagonist, part partner. We can still applaud the winner, but not at the expense of other members of the cast. Such alternative descriptions fit the private experiences of many athletes. I realize now that while I defined them as combats, some of my best races came when other runners "helped with the work" of pace-setting, and challenged me with novel tactics. In the most intrinsically rewarding races, this reciprocal process of "let me lead the way" went on and on and invariably all of us were urged on to outstanding performances. Many other athletes have made the same point. Bill Russell of the Boston Celtics, one of the greatest basketball players of all time, has written:

> Every so often a Celtic game would heat up so that it became more than a physical or even a mental game, and would be magical. That feeling is difficult to describe, and I certainly never talked about it when I was playing. When it happened I could feel my play rise to a new level. That feeling would surround not only me, and the other Celtics, but also the players on the other team, and even the referees. To me, the key was that *both* teams had to be playing at their peaks, and they had to be competitive. The Celtics could not do it alone. . . .
>
> Sometimes the feeling would last all the way to the end of the game, and when that happened I never cared who won. I can honestly say that those few times were the only ones when I did *not* care. I don't mean that I was a good sport about it—I did not care who had won. If we lost, I'd still be as free as a sky hawk. But I had to keep quiet about it.[34]

If confident champions have "to keep quiet," what about the less gifted? We should strive to help all athletes understand their experiences this way.

There are powerful forces that structure games as contests and fuel the tremendous exhilaration of triumph. In North America, the mass media and governments have monopolized the interpretation of athletic performance, and the participants' voice has been distorted, if not silenced. But other cultural performers—painters, dancers, actors, film makers—and their audiences have begun to contest the corporate media's interpretation of their work, and sportspersons could well learn from their example. A sports culture that de-emphasized winning in favor of exploring artistry and skill and the creative interaction of "rival" athletes would be much less repressive.

Finally, we should actively support those feminists who are struggling to combat sexism and inequality in sports. In this, we should take our lead from advocacy groups, like the Canadian Association for the Advancement of Women and Sport (the "and Sport" rather than "in Sport" was a conscious recognition that it will not be enough just to increase the number of opportunities), that represent females on the front lines of these issues and have developed strategies and tactics from the experience. Here, too, the most useful work we can do will be with men. It will be necessary to assure males who resist integration on the basis of ability that we are strong enough to survive an "invasion" of outstanding female athletes. We can help defend

307

affirmative action and hiring programs planned to help sports women over-come the historic inequalities they face; we can support protections for the existing all-female programs and the scarce resources and opportunities they enjoy. The most difficult task will be to persuade other men that sex-divided sports are not only a "women's problem," but in dialectical interaction, harm us as well. Once that is understood, the essential redesigning of sports can really begin.

Notes

An earlier version of this article appears in the *Queen's Quarterly* 94, no. 1 (spring 1987).

1. Norbert Elias, "The Genesis of Sport as a Sociological Problem," in Eric Dunning, ed., *The Sociology of Sport* (Toronto: University of Toronto, 1972), 85–115.

2. M. I. Finlay and H. W. Pleket, *The Olympic Games: The First Thousand Years* (London: Chatto and Windus, 1976), and David Young, *The Myth of Greek Amateur Athletics* (Chicago: Ares, 1985).

3. R. G. Sipes, "War, Sports, and Aggression," *American Anthropologist* 75 (1973): 64–86.

4. John MacAloon, *This Great Symbol: Pierre de Coubertin and the Origins of the Modern Olympic Games* (Chicago: University of Chicago, 1981).

5. Hugh Cunningham, *Leisure in the Industrial Revolution* (London: Croom Helm, 1980); Eric Dunning and Kevin Sheard, *Barbarians, Gentlemen and Players* (New York: New York University, 1979); and Allen Guttman, *From Ritual to Record* (New York: Columbia, 1978).

6. J. A. Mangan, *Athleticism in the Victorian and Edwardian Public School* (Cambridge: Cambridge University Press, 1981).

7. Lincoln Allison, "Batsman and Bowler: the Key Relationship of Victorian England," *Journal of Sport History* 7, no. 2 (1980): 5–20.

8. Peter Bailey, *Leisure and Class in Victorian England* (Toronto: University of Toronto, 1978), and Morris Mott, "One Solution to the Urban Crisis: Manly Sports and Winnipeggers, 1900–1914," *Urban History Review* 12, no. 2 (1983): 57–70.

9. Richard Gruneau, *Class, Sports and Social Development* (Amherst: University of Massachusetts, 1983), 91–135

10. Thomas Hughes, *Tom Brown's Schooldays* (London: Macmillan, 1979), 60–1; first published in 1867.

11. See, for example, Bryan Palmer, *A Culture in Conflict* (Montreal and Kingston: McGill-Queen's University Press, 1979), 35–70.

12. James Marlow, "Popular Culture, Pugilism, and Pickwick," *Journal of Popular Culture* 15, no. 4 (1982).

13. Bruce Kidd, "Skating Away from a Fight: Canadian Sport, Culture, and Personal Respon-sibility," in William Baker and James Rog, eds., *Sports and the Humanities* (Orono: University of Maine at Orono, 1983), 41–54.

14. Paul Atkinson, "Fitness, Feminism, and Schooling," in Sara Delamont and Lorna Duffin, eds., *The Nineteenth Century Woman: Her Physical and Cultural World* (London: Croom Helm, 1978), and Helen Lenskyj, *Out of Bounds: Women, Sports, and Sexuality* (Toronto: Women's Press, 1986). The quotation is from London medical professor Henry Maudsley, quoted by Atkinson, p. 103.

15. Ann M. Hall and Dorothy Richardson, *Fair Ball* (Ottawa: Canadian Advisory Council on the Status of Women, 1982), and Mary Boutilier and Lucinda San Giovanni, *The Sporting Woman* (Champagne, Ill.: Human Kinetics, 1983).

16. Ruth Hubbard, Mary Sue Henifin, and Barbara Fried, *Biological Woman: The Convenient Myth* (Cambridge: Schenkman, 1982), and Lynda Birke, *Women, Feminism and Biology* (Brighton: Harvester, 1986).

17. Many women contributed to the development of "girls' rules." Paul Atkinson, Helen Lenskyj, and others have argued that in part this was a tactically necessary defense against male control of women's institutions, that without them girls and women would not have been allowed to play at all, and that they were a creative attempt to avoid some of the most brutalizing features of male sport. Nevertheless, they confined most females interested in sports to a ghetto of inequality and left the existing stereotypes about female frailty unchallenged.

18. Dorothy Kidd, "Getting Physical: Compulsory Heterosexuality in Sport," *Canadian Woman Studies* 4, no. 3 (1983): 62–5.

19. See, for example, John Sopinka, *Can I Play? Report of the Task Force on Equality in Athletics* (Toronto: Ontario Ministry of Labour 1983 and 1984), vols. 1 and 2. The Canadian sports minister Otto Jelinek has admitted that despite a twelve-year federal effort to increase women's opportunities, very little change has occurred. "My belief is that there hasn't been a commitment to promote the women's program," he said. See "Ottawa Aiming to Get More Girls Involved in Sport," the *Globe and Mail*, 7 Oct. 1986.

20. Abby Hoffman, "Towards Equality for Women in Sport—a Canadian Perspective," *Momentum* 4, no. 2 (1979): 3.

21. Joseph Kett, *Rites of Passage* (New York: Basic, 1977); Leila Mitchell McKee, "'Nature's Medicine': The Physical Education and Outdoor Recreation Programs in Toronto Volunteer Youth Groups," in Bruce Kidd, ed., *Proceedings of the 5th Canadian Symposium on the History of Sport and Physical Education* (Toronto: School of Physical and Health Education, 1982), 128–39, and David MacLeod, *Building Character in the American Boy* (Madison: University of Wisconsin, 1983).

22. Kevin Sheard and Eric Dunning, "The Rugby Football Club as a Male Preserve," *International Review of Sports Sociology* 3–4 (1973): 12.

23. Sut Jhally, "The Spectacle of Accumulation: Material and Cultural Factors in the Evolution of the Sports/Media Complex," *The Insurgent Sociologist* 12, no. 3 (1984): 41–57.

24. Boutilier and San Giovanni, *The Sporting Woman*, 185–218.

25. K. F. Dyer, *Challenging the Men* (New York: University of Queensland, 1982). For a critical feminist review, see Cathy Bray, *Canadian Woman Studies* 4, no. 3 (1983): 92–3.

26. *Re Ontario Softball Association and Bannerman* (1978), 21 O.R. (2d) 395 (H.C.J.–Div. Ct.).

27. The player, Justine Blainey, was successful in having the Ontario Court of Appeal declare that section 19(2) of the Ontario Human Rights Code, which had allowed sports bodies to discriminate on the basis of sex, was in violation of the Charter of Rights and Freedoms and therefore invalid. But the court would not declare that the OHA's refusal to allow Blainey to play was a violation of the code as amended by that decision. Blainey is therefore seeking such a ruling from the OHRC. See Bruce Kidd, "Ontario Legalizes Discrimination," *Canadian Woman Studies* 4, no. 3 (1984): 41–3, and Justine Blainey v. Ontario Hockey Association and Ontario Human Rights Commission, 17 April 1986, unreported (Ont. C.A. #630/85).

28. Chodorow, *The Reproduction of Mothering* (Berkeley: University of California, 1978).

29. Dinnerstein, *The Mermaid and the Minotaur* (New York: Harper, 1976), 229.

30. Dorcus Susan Butt, *Psychology of Sport* (Toronto: Van Nostrand Reinhold, 1976), and Terry Orlick and Cal Botterill, *Every Kid Can Win* (Chicago: Nelson Hall, 1974).

31. R. W. Connell, "Men's Bodies," in *Which Way Is Up?* (Sydney: George Allen and Unwin, 1983), 18.

32. Thomas A. Tutko and H. Bruns, *Winning Is Everything and Other American Myths* (New York: Macmillan, 1976).

33. Quoted by Varda Burstyn, "Play, Performance and Power—the Men," CBC Radio "Ideas," 2 Oct. 1986. The script is available from CBC Transcripts.

34. Bill Russell and Taylor Branch, *Second Wind: The Memories of an Opinionated Man* (New York: Random House, 1979).

ON BOXING

JOYCE CAROL OATES

One of our most prolific modern writers, Oates has published over fifty books including novels, short stories, essays, and poems. Among her novels are *Do With Me What You Will* (1973), *Unholy Loves* (1979), and *A Bloodsmoor Romance* (1982), and her short stories have been collected in such volumes as *Marriages and Infidelities* (1972) and *The Goddess and Other Women* (1974). Her volumes of poetry are *Women in Love, and Other Poems* (1968) and *Women Whose Lives Are Food, Men Whose Lives Are Money* (1978), and she has also written numerous critical essays and reviews. Her book *On Boxing*, which examines the many facets of this sport, was published in 1987.

Why are you a boxer, Irish featherweight champion Barry McGuigan was asked. He said: "I can't be a poet. I can't tell stories . . .

Each boxing match is a story—a unique and highly condensed drama without words. Even when nothing sensational happens: then the drama is "merely" psychological. Boxers are there to establish an absolute experience, a public accounting of the outermost limits of their beings; they will know, as few of us can know of ourselves, what physical and psychic power they possess—of how much, or how little, they are capable. To enter the ring near-naked and to risk one's life is to make of one's audience voyeurs of a kind: boxing is so intimate. It is to ease out of sanity's consciousness and into another, difficult to name. It is to risk, and sometimes to realize, the agony of which *agon* (Greek, "contest") is the root. 1

In the boxing ring there are two principal players, overseen by a shadowy third. The ceremonial ringing of the bell is a summoning to full wakefulness for both boxers and spectators. It sets into motion, too, the authority of Time. 2

The boxers will bring to the fight everything that is themselves, and everything will be exposed—including secrets about themselves they cannot fully realize. The physical self, the maleness, one might say, underlying the "self." There are boxers possessed of such remarkable intuition, such uncanny 3 prescience, one would think they were somehow recalling their fights, not fighting them as we watch. There are boxers who perform skillfully, but mechanically, who cannot improvise in response to another's alteration of strategy; there are boxers performing at the peak of their talent who come to realize, mid-fight, that it will not be enough; there are boxers—including great champions—whose careers end abruptly, and irrevocably, as we watch. There has been at least one boxer possessed of an extraordinary and disquieting awareness not only of his opponent's every move and anticipated move but of the audience's keenest shifts in mood as well, for which he seems to have felt personally responsible—Cassius Clay/Muhammad Ali, of course. "The Sweet Science of Bruising" celebrates the physicality of men even as it dramatizes the limitations, sometimes tragic, more often poignant, of the physical. Though male spectators identify with boxers no boxer behaves like a "normal" man when he is in the ring and no combination of blows is "natural." All is style.

Every talent must unfold itself in fighting. So Nietzsche speaks of the Hellenic past, the history of the "contest"—athletic, and otherwise—by which Greek youths were educated into Greek citizenry. Without the ferocity of competition, without, even, "envy, jealousy, and ambition" in the contest, the Hellenic city, like the Hellenic man, degenerated. If death is a risk, death is also the prize—for the winning athlete.   4

In the boxing ring, even in our greatly humanized times, death is always a possibility—which is why some of us prefer to watch films or tapes of fights already past, already defined as history. Or, in some instances, art. (Though to prepare for writing this mosaic-like essay I saw tapes of two infamous "death" fights of recent times: the Lupe Pintor–Johnny Owen bantamweight match of 1982, and the Ray Mancini–Duk Koo-Kim lightweight match of the same year. In both instances the boxers died as a consequence of their astonishing resilience and apparent indefatigability—their "heart," as it's known in boxing circles.) Most of the time, however, death in the ring is extremely unlikely; a statistically rare possibility like your possible death tomorrow morning in an automobile accident or in next month's headlined airline disaster or in a freak accident involving a fall on the stairs or in the bathtub, a skull fracture, subarachnoid hemorrhage. Spectators at "death" fights often claim afterward that what happened simply seemed to happen—unpredictably, in a sense accidentally. Only in retrospect does death appear to have been inevitable.   5

If a boxing match is a story it is an always wayward story, one in which anything can happen. And in a matter of seconds. Split seconds! (Muhammad Ali boasted that he could throw a punch faster than the eye could follow, and he may have been right.) In no other sport can so much take place in so brief a period of time, and so irrevocably.   6

Because a boxing match is a story without words, this doesn't mean that it has no text or no language, that it is somehow "brute," "primitive," "inar-   7 ticulate," only that the text is improvised in action; the language a dialogue between the boxers of the most refined sort (one might say, as much neuro-logical as psychological: a dialogue of split-second reflexes) in a joint response to the mysterious will of the audience which is always that the fight be a worthy one so that the crude paraphernalia of the setting—ring, lights, ropes, stained canvas, the staring onlookers themselves—be erased, forgotten. (As in the theater or the church, settings are erased by way, ideally, of transcendent action.) Ringside announcers give to the wordless spectacle a narrative unity, yet boxing as performance is more clearly akin to dance or music than narrative.

To turn from an ordinary preliminary match to a "Fight of the Century" like those between Joe Louis and Billy Conn, Joe Frazier and Muhammad Ali, Marvin Hagler and Thomas Hearns is to turn from listening or half-listening to a guitar being idly plucked to hearing Bach's *Well-Tempered Clavier* perfectly executed, and that too is part of the story's mystery: so much happens so swiftly and with such heart-stopping subtlety you cannot absorb it except to know that something profound is happening and it is happening in a place beyond words. . . .

I hate to say it, but it's true—I only like it better when pain comes.
(Frank "The Animal" Fletcher, former
middleweight contender)

Years ago in the early 1950s when my father first took me to a Golden Gloves boxing tournament in Buffalo, New York, I asked him why the boys wanted to fight one another, why they were willing to get hurt. As if it were an explanation my father said, "Boxers don't feel pain quite the way we do."

Pain, in the proper context, is something other than pain.

Consider: Gene Tunney's single defeat in a thirteen-year career of great distinction was to a notorious fighter named Harry Greb who seems to have been, judging from boxing lore, the dirtiest fighter in history. Greb was infamous for his fouls—low blows, butting, "holding and hitting," rubbing his laces against an opponent's eyes, routine thumbing—as well as for a fren-zied boxing style in which blows were thrown from all directions. (Hence, "The Human Windmill.") Greb, who died young, was a world middleweight champion for three years but a flamboyant presence in boxing circles for a long time. After the first of his several fights with Greb the twenty-two-year-old Tunney was so badly hurt he had to spend a week in bed; he'd lost an astonishing two quarts of blood during the fifteen-round fight. Yet, as Tunney said some years later:

> Greb gave me a terrible whipping. He broke my nose, maybe with a butt. He cut my eyes and ears, perhaps with his laces . . . My jaw was swollen

313

from the right temple down the cheek, along under the chin and partway up the other side. The referee, the ring itself, was full of blood . . . But it was in that first fight, in which I lost my American light-heavyweight title, that I knew I had found a way to beat Harry eventually. I was fortunate, really. If boxing in those days had been afflicted with the Commission doctors we have today—who are always poking their noses into the ring and examining superficial wounds—the first fight with Greb would have been stopped before I learned how to beat him. It's possible, even probable, that if this had happened I would never have been heard of again.

Tunney's career, in other words, was built upon pain. Without it he would never have moved up into Dempsey's class.

Tommy Loughran, light-heavyweight champion in the years 1927–29, 12 was a master boxer greatly admired by other boxers. He approached boxing literally as a science—as Tunney did—studying his opponents' styles and mapping out ring strategy for each fight, as boxers and their trainers commonly do today. Loughran rigged up mirrors in his basement so that he could watch himself as he worked out, for, as he said, no boxer ever sees himself quite as he appears to his opponent. He sees the opponent but not himself as an opponent. The secret of Loughran's career was that his right hand broke easily so that he was forced to use it only once each fight: for the knockout punch or nothing. "I'd get one shot then the agony of the thing would hurt me if the guy got up," Loughran said. "Anybody I ever hit with a left hook I knocked flat on his face, but I would never take a chance for fear if my [left hand] goes, I'm done for."

Both Tunney and Loughran, it is instructive to note, retired from boxing 13 well before they were forced to retire. Tunney became a highly successful businessman, and Loughran a highly successful sugar broker on the Wall Street commodities market. (Just to suggest that boxers are not invariably stupid, illiterate, or punch-drunk.)

Then there was Carmen Basilio!—much loved for his audacious ring 14 style, his hit-and-be-hit approach. Basilio was world middle- and welterweight champion 1953–57, stoic, determined, a slugger willing to get hit in order to deal powerful counter-punches of his own. Onlookers marveled at the punishment Basilio seemed to absorb though Basilio insisted that he didn't get hit the way people believed. And when he was hit, and hit hard—

> People don't realize how you're affected by a knockout punch when you're hit on the chin. It's nerves is all it is. There's no real concussion as far as the brain is concerned. I got hit on the point of the chin [in a match with Tony DeMarco in 1955]. It was a left hook that hit the right point of my chin. What happens is it pulls your jawbone out of your socket from the right side and jams it into the left side and the nerve there paralyzed the whole left side of my body, especially my legs. My left knee buckled and I almost went down, but when I got back to my corner the bottom of my foot felt like it

had needles about six inches high and I just kept stamping my foot on the floor, trying to bring it back. And by the time the bell rang it was all right.

Basilio belongs to the rough-and-tumble era of LaMotta, Graziano, Zale, Pep, Saddler; Gene Fullmer, Dick Tiger, Kid Gavilan. An era when, if two boxers wanted to fight dirty, the referee was likely to give them license, or at least not to interfere.

Of Muhammad Ali in his prime Norman Mailer observed, "He worked apparently on the premise that there was something obscene about being hit." But in fights in his later career, as with George Foreman in Zaire, even Muhammad Ali was willing to be hit, and to be hurt, in order to wear down an opponent. Brawling fighters—those with "heart" like Jake LaMotta, Rocky Graziano, Ray Mancini—have little choice but to absorb terrible punishment in exchange for some advantage (which does not in any case always come). And surely it is true that some boxers (see Jake LaMotta's autobiographical *Raging Bull*) invite injury as a means of assuaging guilt, in a Dostoyevskian exchange of physical well-being for peace of mind. Boxing is about being hit rather more than it is about hitting, just as it is about feeling pain, if not devastating psychological paralysis, more than it is about winning. One sees clearly from the "tragic" careers of any number of boxers that the boxer prefers physical pain in the ring to the absence of pain that is ideally the condition of ordinary life. If one cannot hit, one can yet be hit, and know that one is still alive.

It might be said that boxing is primarily about maintaining a body capable of entering combat against other well-conditioned bodies. Not the public spectacle, the fight itself, but the rigorous training period leading up to it demands the most discipline, and is believed to be the chief cause of the boxer's physical and mental infirmities. (As a boxer ages his sparring partners get younger, the game itself gets more desperate.)

The artist senses some kinship, however oblique and one-sided, with the professional boxer in this matter of training. This fanatic subordination of the self in terms of a wished-for destiny. One might compare the time-bound public spectacle of the boxing match (which could be as brief as an ignominious forty-five seconds—the record for a title fight!) with the publication of a writer's book. That which is "public" is but the final stage in a protracted, arduous, grueling, and frequently despairing period of preparation. Indeed, one of the reasons for the habitual attraction of serious writers to boxing (from Swift, Pope, Johnson to Hazlitt, Lord Byron, Hemingway, and our own Norman Mailer, George Plimpton, Ted Hoagland, Wilfrid Sheed, Daniel Halpern, et al.) is the sport's systematic cultivation of pain in the interests of a project, a life-goal: the willed transposing of the sensation we know as pain

315

(physical, psychological, emotional) into its polar opposite. If this is maso-chism—and I doubt that it is, or that it is simply—it is also intelligence, cunning, strategy. It is an act of consummate self-determination—the constant reestablishment of the parameters of one's being. To not only accept but to actively invite what most sane creatures avoid—pain, humiliation, loss, chaos—is to experience the present moment as already, in a sense, past. *Here* and *now* are but part of the design of *there* and *then:* pain now but control, and therefore triumph, later. And pain itself is miraculously transposed by dint of its context. Indeed, it might be said that "context" is all.

The novelist George Garrett, an amateur boxer of some decades ago, reminisces about his training period: 18

> I learned something . . . about the brotherhood of boxers. People went into this brutal and often self-destructive activity for a rich variety of motivations, most of them bitterly antisocial and verging on the psychotic. Most of the fighters I knew of were wounded people who felt a deep, powerful urge to wound others at real risk to themselves. In the beginning. What happened was that in almost every case, there was so much self-discipline required and craft involved, so much else besides one's original motivations to concentrate on, that these motivations became at least cloudy and vague and were often forgotten, lost completely. Many good and experienced fighters (as has often been noted) become gentle and kind people . . . They have the habit of leaving all their fight in the ring. And even there, in the ring, it is dangerous to invoke too much anger. It can be a stimulant, but is very expensive of energy. It is impractical to get mad most of the time.

Of all boxers it seems to have been Rocky Marciano (still our only undefeated heavyweight champion) who trained with the most monastic devotion; his training methods have become legendary. In contrast to reckless fighters like Harry "The Human Windmill" Greb, who kept in condition by boxing all the time, Marciano was willing to seclude himself from the world, including his wife and family, for as long as three months before a fight. Apart from the grueling physical ordeal of this period and the obsessive preoccupation with diet and weight and muscle tone, Marciano concentrated on one thing: the upcoming fight. Every minute of his life was defined in terms of the opening second of the fight. In his training camp the opponent's name was never mentioned in Marciano's hearing, nor was boxing as a subject discussed. In the final month Marciano would not write a letter since a letter related to the outside world. During the last ten days before a fight he would see no mail, take no telephone calls, meet no new acquaintances. During the week before the fight he would not shake hands. Or go for a ride in a car, however brief. No new foods! No dreaming of the morning after the fight! For all that was not *the fight* had to be excluded from consciousness. When Marciano worked out with a punching bag he saw his opponent before him, when he jogged he saw his opponent close beside him, no doubt when he slept he "saw" his opponent constantly—as the cloistered monk or nun chooses by an act of fanatical will to "see" only God.

Madness?—or merely discipline?—this absolute subordination of the self. In any case, for Marciano, it worked.   19

———— ■ ————

Tommy Hearns was a little cocky, and I had something for him.
(Marvin Hagler)

———— ■ ————

No sport is more physical, more direct, than boxing. No sport appears   20
more powerfully homoerotic: the confrontation in the ring—the disrobing—
the sweaty heated combat that is part dance, courtship, coupling—the frequent urgent pursuit by one boxer of the other in the fight's natural and
violent movement toward the "knockout": surely boxing derives much of its
appeal from this mimicry of a species of erotic love in which one man overcomes the other in an exhibition of superior strength and will. The heralded
celibacy of the fighter-in-training is very much a part of boxing lore: instead
of focusing his energies and fantasies upon a woman the boxer focuses them
upon an opponent. Where Woman has been, Opponent must be.

As Ali's Bundini Brown has said: "You got to get the hard-on, and then   21
you got to keep it. You want to be careful not to lose the hard-on, and cautious
not to come."

Most fights, however fought, end with an embrace between the boxers   22
after the final bell—a gesture of mutual respect and apparent affection that
appears to the onlooker to be more than perfunctory. Rocky Graziano sometimes kissed his opponents out of gratitude for the fight. One might wonder
if the boxing match leads irresistibly to this moment: the public embrace of
two men who otherwise, in public or in private, could never approach each
other with such passion. Though many men are loudly contemptuous of
weakness (as if eager to dissociate themselves from it: as during a boxing
match when one or both boxers are unwilling to fight) a woman is struck by
the admiration, amounting at times to awe, they will express for a man who
has exhibited superior courage while losing his fight. And they will express
tenderness for injured boxers, even if it is only by way of commentary on
photographs: the picture of Ray Mancini after his second defeat by Livingstone Bramble, for instance, when Mancini's face was hideously battered
(photographs in *Sports Illustrated* and elsewhere were gory, near-porno-
graphic); the much-reprinted photograph of the defeated Thomas Hearns
being carried to his corner in the arms of an enormous black man (a body-
guard, one assumes) in solemn formal attire—Hearns the "Hit Man" now
helpless, semiconscious, looking very like a black Christ taken from the cross.
These are powerful, haunting, unsettling images, cruelly beautiful, inextricably bound up with boxing's primordial appeal.

Yet to suggest that men might love and respect one another directly, [23] without the violent ritual of combat, is to misread man's greatest passion—for war, not peace. Love, if there is to be love, comes second. . . .

———■———

What time is it?—"Macho Time"!
(Hector "Macho Man" Camacho, WBC lightweight champion)

■

I don't want to knock my opponent out. I want to hit him, step away, and watch him hurt. I want his heart.
(Joe Frazier, former heavyweight champion of the world)

———■———

A fairy-tale proposition: the heavyweight champion is the most dangerous [24] man on earth: the most feared, the most manly. His proper mate is very likely the fairy-tale princess whom the mirrors declare the fairest woman on earth.

Boxing is a purely masculine activity and it inhabits a purely masculine [25] world. Which is not to suggest that most men are defined by it: clearly, most men are not. And though there are female boxers—a fact that seems to surprise, alarm, amuse—women's role in the sport has always been extremely marginal. (At the time of this writing the most famous American woman boxer is the black champion Lady Tyger Trimiar with her shaved head and theatrical tiger-striped attire.) At boxing matches women's role is limited to that of card girl and occasional National Anthem singer: stereotypical functions usually performed in stereotypically zestful feminine ways—for women have no natural place in the spectacle otherwise. The card girls in their bathing suits and spike heels, glamour girls of the 1950s, complement the boxers in their trunks and gym shoes but are not to be taken seriously: their public exhibition of themselves involves no risk and is purely decorative. Boxing is for men, and is about men, and *is* men. A celebration of the lost religion of masculinity all the more trenchant for its being lost.

In this world, strength of a certain kind—matched of course with intel- [26] ligence and tirelessly developed skills—determines masculinity. Just as a boxer is his body, a man's masculinity is his use of his body. But it is also his triumph over another's use of his body. The Opponent is always male, the Opponent is the rival for one's own masculinity, most fully and combatively realized. Sugar Ray Leonard speaks of coming out of retirement to fight one man, Marvin Hagler: "I want Hagler. I need that man." Thomas Hearns, decisively beaten by Hagler, speaks of having been obsessed with him: "I want the rematch badly . . . there hasn't been a minute or an hour in any day that I haven't thought about it." Hence women's characteristic repugnance for boxing per se coupled with an intense interest in and curiosity about men's fascination with it. Men fighting men to determine worth (i.e., masculinity) excludes women as completely as the female experience of childbirth excludes men. And is there, perhaps, some connection?

In any case, raw aggression is thought to be the peculiar province of men, as nurturing is the peculiar province of women. (The female boxer violates this stereotype and cannot be taken seriously—she is parody, she is cartoon, she is monstrous. Had she an ideology, she is likely to be a feminist.) The psychologist Erik Erikson discovered that, while little girls playing with blocks generally create pleasant interior spaces and attractive entrances, little boys are inclined to pile up the blocks as high as they can and then watch them fall down: "the contemplation of ruins," Erikson observes, "is a masculine specialty." No matter the mesmerizing grace and beauty of a great boxing match, it is the catastrophic finale for which everyone waits, and hopes: the blocks piled as high as they can possibly be piled, then brought spectacularly down. Women, watching a boxing match, are likely to identify with the losing, or hurt, boxer; men are likely to identify with the winning boxer. There is a point at which male spectators are able to identify with the fight itself as, it might be said, a Platonic experience abstracted from its particulars; if they have favored one boxer over the other, and that boxer is losing, they can shift their loyalty to the winner—or, rather, "loyalty" shifts, apart from conscious volition. In that way the ritual of fighting is always honored. The high worth of combat is always affirmed.

Boxing's very vocabulary suggests a patriarchal world taken over by adolescents. This world is young. Its focus is youth. Its focus is of course *macho*—*machismo* raised beyond parody. To enter the claustrophobic world of professional boxing even as a spectator is to enter what appears to be a distillation of the masculine world, empty now of women, its fantasies, hopes, and stratagems magnified as in a distorting mirror, or a dream.

Here, we find ourselves through the looking-glass. Values are reversed, evaginated: a boxer is valued not for his humanity but for being a "killer," a "mauler," a "hit-man," an "animal," for being "savage," "merciless," "devastating," "ferocious," "vicious," "murderous." Opponents are not merely defeated as in a game but are "decked," "stiffed," "starched," "iced," "destroyed," "annihilated." Even the veteran sportswriters of so respectable a publication as *The Ring* are likely to be pitiless toward a boxer who has been beaten. Much of the appeal of Roberto Durán for intellectual boxing *aficionados* no less than for those whom one might suppose his natural constituency was that he seemed truly to want to kill his opponents: in his prime he was the "baby-faced assassin" with the "dead eyes" and "deadpan" expression who once said, having knocked out an opponent named Ray Lampkin, that he hadn't trained for the fight—next time he would kill the man. (According to legend Durán once felled a horse with a single blow.) Sonny Liston was another champion lauded for his menace, so different in spirit from Floyd Patterson as to seem to belong to another subspecies; to watch Liston overcome Patterson in tapes of their fights in the early 1960s is to watch the defeat of "civilization" by

27

28

29

something so elemental and primitive it cannot be named. Masculinity in these terms is strictly hierarchical—two men cannot occupy the same space at the same time.

At the present time twenty-year-old Mike Tyson, Cus D'Amato's much-vaunted protégé, is being groomed as the most dangerous man in the heavyweight division. He is spoken of with awe as a "young bull"; his strength is prodigious, at least as demonstrated against fairly hapless, stationary opponents; he enters the arena robeless—"I feel more like a warrior"—and gleaming with sweat. He does not even wear socks. His boxing model is not Muhammad Ali, the most brilliant heavyweight of modern times, but Rocky Marciano, graceless, heavy-footed, indomitable, the man with the massive right-hand punch who was willing to absorb five blows in the hope of landing one. It was after having broken Jesse Ferguson's nose in a recent match that Tyson told reporters that it was his strategy to try to drive the bone back into the brain . . .

The names of boxers! *Machismo* as sheer poetry.

Though we had, in another era, "Gentleman Jim" Corbett (world heavyweight champion, 1892–97); and the first black heavyweight champion, Jack Johnson (1908–15) called himself "Li'l Arthur" as a way of commenting playfully on his powerful physique and savage ring style. (Johnson was a white man's nightmare: the black man who mocked his white opponents as he humiliated them with his fists.) In more recent times we had "Sugar Ray" Robinson and his younger namesake "Sugar Ray" Leonard. And Tyrone Crawley, a thinking man's boxer, calls himself "The Butterfly." But for the most part a boxer's ring name is chosen to suggest something more ferocious: Jack Dempsey of Manassa, Colorado, was "The Manassa Mauler"; the formidable Harry Greb was "The Human Windmill"; Joe Louis was, of course, "The Brown Bomber"; Rocky Marciano, "The Brockton Blockbuster"; Jake LaMotta, "The Bronx Bull"; Tommy Jackson, "Hurricane" Jackson; Roberto Durán, "Hands of Stone" and "The Little Killer" variously. More recent are Ray "Boom-Boom" Mancini, Thomas "Hit-Man" Hearns, James "Hard Rock" Green, Al "Earthquake" Carter, Frank "The Animal" Fletcher, Donald "The Cobra" Curry, Aaron "The Hawk" Pryor, "Terrible" Tim Witherspoon, "Bonecrusher" Smith, Johnny "Bump City" Bumphus, Lonnie "Lightning" Smith, Barry "The Clones Cyclone" McGuigan, Gene "Mad Dog" Hatcher, Livingstone "Pit Bull" Bramble, Hector "Macho Man" Camacho. "Marvelous" Marvin Hagler changed his name legally to Marvelous Marvin Hagler before his fight with Thomas Hearns brought him to national prominence.

It was once said by José Torres that the *machismo* of boxing is a condition of poverty. But it is not, surely, a condition uniquely of poverty? Or even of adolescence? I think of it as the obverse of the feminine, the denial of the feminine-in-man that has its ambiguous attractions for all men, however "civilized." It is a remnant of another, earlier era when the physical being was primary and the warrior's masculinity its highest expression. . . .

THE MYTH OF THE SEXUAL ATHLETE

DON SABO

Don Sabo's discussion of sports and sexuality made up
one of the viewpoints in a powerful collection of writ-
ings by men titled *Men and Intimacy: Personal Accounts
Exploring the Dilemmas of Modern Male Sexuality* (1990).
Sabo, an Associate Professor of Sociology at D'Youville
College in Buffalo, New York, is author of the book
Jock: Sports and Male Identity (1980), a study of the
psychological aspects of athletics. He has also co-ed-
ited a recent collection of essays with our next author,
Mike Messner, titled *Sport, Men, and the Gender Order:
Critical Feminist Perspectives* (1990).

The phrase "sexual athlete" commonly refers to male heterosexual virtuosity   1
in the bedroom. Images of potency, agility, technical expertise and an ability
to attract and satisfy women come to mind. In contrast, the few former
athletes like Dave Meggyesy and Jim Bouton who have seriously written on
the subject, and films such as *Raging Bull* and *North Dallas Forty*, depict the
male athlete as sexually uptight, fixated on early adolescent sexual antics and
exploitative of women. The former image of athletic virility, however, remains
fixed within the popular imagination and, partly for this reason, there has
been very little said about the *real* connections between sport and male
sexuality.

Locker Room Sex Talk

I played organized sports for 15 years and they were as much a part of my   2
"growing up" as Cheerios, television, and homework. My sexuality unfolded
within this all-male social world of sport where sex was always a major focus.
I remember, for example, when we as prepubertal boys used the old "buying
baseball cards" routine as a cover to sneak peeks at *Playboy* and *Swank* magazines at the newsstand. We would talk endlessly after practices about "boobs"
and what it must feel like to kiss and neck. Later, in junior high, we teased
one another in the locker room about "jerking off" or being virgins, and
there were endless interrogations about "how far" everybody was getting with
their girlfriends.

    Eventually, boyish anticipation spilled into *real* sexual relationships with   3
girls which, to my delight and confusion, turned out to be a lot more complex

than I ever imagined. While sex (kissing, necking, and petting) got more exciting, it also got more difficult to figure out and talk about. Inside, most of the boys, like myself, needed to love and be loved. We were awkwardly reaching out for intimacy. Yet publicly, the message that got imparted was to "catch feels," be cool, connect with girls but don't allow yourself to depend on them. Once when I was a high school junior, the gang in the weight room accused me of being wrapped around my girlfriend's finger. Nothing could be further from the truth, I assured them, and in order to prove it, I broke up with her. I felt miserable about this at the time and I still feel bad about it.

Within the college jock subculture, men's public protests against intimacy 4 sometimes became exaggerated and ugly. I remember two teammates, drunk and rowdy, ripping girls' blouses off at a mixer and crawling on their bellies across the dance floor to look up skirts. Then there were the Sunday morning late breakfasts in the dorm. We jocks would usually all sit at one table and be forced to listen to one braggart or another describe his sexual exploits of the night before. Though a lot of us were turned off by such kiss-and-tell, ego-boosting tactics, we never openly criticized them. Real or fabricated, displays of raunchy sex were also assumed to "win points." A junior fullback claimed to have defecated on a girl's chest after she passed out during intercourse. There were also some laughing reports of "gang-bangs."

When sexual relationships *were* "serious," that is, tempered by love and 5 commitment, the unspoken rule was silence. It was rare when we young men shared our feelings about women, misgivings about sexual performance or disdain for the crudeness and insensitivity of some of our teammates. I now see the tragic irony in this: we could talk about superficial sex and anything that used, trivialized or debased women, but frank discussions about sexuality that unfolded within a loving relationship were taboo. Within the locker room subculture, sex and love were seldom allowed to mix. There was a terrible split between inner needs and outer appearances, between our desire for the love of women and our feigned indifference toward them.

Sex as Sport

Sport is a social setting in which gender learning melds with sexual learning. 6 Our sense of "femaleness" or "maleness" influences the ways we see ourselves as sexual beings. Indeed, as we develop, *sexual* identity emerges as an extension of an already-formed *gender* identity, and sexual behavior becomes "scripted" by cultural meanings. The prevailing script for manhood in sport is basically traditional; it emphasizes competition, success (winning), domination, aggression, emotional stoicism, goal-directedness and physical strength. Many athletes buy into this hypermasculine image and it affects their relationships with women. Dating becomes a "sport" in itself and "scoring," or seeking sex with little or no regard for emotions, is regarded as a mark of masculine achievement. Sexual relationships get defined as "games" in which women are seen as "opponents," and "winners" and "losers" vie for dominance. Too often, women get used as pawns in men's quests for acceptance among peers and status within the male pecking order. I believe that for many of us jocks, these lessons somehow got translated into a "man-as-hunter/woman-as-prey" approach to sexual relationships.

How did this happen? What transformed us from boys who needed and depended on women to men who misunderstood, felt separated from, and sometimes mistreated women? One part of the problem is the expectation that we are supposed to act as though we want to be alone, like the cowboy who always rides off into the sunset alone. In sport, there is only one "most valuable player" on the team.

Too often this prevents male athletes from understanding women and their life experiences. Though women's voices may reach men's ears from the sidelines and grandstands, they remain distant and garbled by the clamor of male competition. In sport, communication gaps between the sexes are due in part to women's historical exclusion from sport, the failure to create coed athletic programs, and coaching practices which quarantine boys from the "feminizing" taint of female influence. One result of this isolation is that sexual myths flourish. Boys end up learning about girls and female sexuality *from other males*, and the information that gets transmitted within the male network is often inaccurate and downright sexist. I can see in retrospect that as boys we lacked a vocabulary of intimacy which would have enabled us to better share sexual experiences with others. The locker room language that filled our adolescent heads did not exactly foster insights into the true nature of women's sexuality—or our own, for that matter.

Performance and Patriarchy

Traditional gender learning and locker room sexual myths can also shape men's lovemaking behavior. Taught to be "achievement machines," many athletes organize their energies and perceptions around a performance ethic which influences sexual relations. The goal-directedness and preoccupation with performance and technique enters into male scripts of lovemaking. In the movie *Joe*, a sexually liberated woman tells her hardhat lover that "making love isn't like running a 50 yard dash."

When intercourse becomes the chief goal of sex, it bolsters men's performance inclinations and limits their ability to enjoy other aspects of sexual experiences. It can also create problems for both men and their partners. Since coitus requires an erection, men are under pressure to get and maintain erections. If erections do not occur, or men ejaculate "too quickly," their self-esteem as lovers and men can be impaired. In fact, sex therapists tell us that men's preoccupation and anxieties about erectile potency and performance can cause the very sexual dysfunctions they fear.

It is important to emphasize that it is not only jocks who swallow this 11 limiting model of male sexuality. Sport is not the only social setting which promotes an androcentric, eroticism-without-intimacy value system. Consider how male sexuality gets socially constructed in fraternities, motorcycle gangs, the armed forces, urban gangs, pornography, corporate advertising, MTV, magazines like *Playboy* or *Penthouse*, and the movies—to name but a few examples. These are not random and unrelated sources of traditional masculine values. They all originate in patriarchy.

Sexual relations between men and women in western societies have been 12 conducted under the panoply of patriarchal power. The sexual values which derive from patriarchy emphasize male dominance and the purely erotic dimensions of the sex act while reducing women to delectable but expendable objects. An alternative conception of human sexuality, however, is also gaining ascendancy within the culture. Flowing out of women's experiences and based on egalitarian values, it seeks to integrate eroticism with love and commitment. It is deeply critical of the social forces which reduce women (and men) to sex objects, depersonalize relationships and turn human sexuality into an advertising gimmick or commodity to be purchased. This is the sexual ethos proffered by the women's movement.

Today's young athletes don't seem as hooked on the hypermasculine 13 image that traditional sport has proffered. Perhaps it is because alternative forms of masculinity and sexuality have begun to enter the locker room subculture. Sex segregation in sport is not as pronounced as it was when I was a young man in the mid-sixties. More girls are playing sports than ever before, and coed athletic experiences are more common. As more women enter the traditionally male environments of sport, business, factories or government, men are finding it more difficult to perceive women in one-dimensional terms. Perhaps we are becoming better able to see them for what they really are and, in the process, we are beginning to search for alternative modes of being men.

What Do Men Really Want . . . Need?

Most of us do not really know what it is we want from our sexual lives. Men 14 seem torn between yearning for excitement and longing for love and intimacy. On one side, we feel titillated by the glitter of contemporary cosmetics and corporate advertising. Eroticism jolts our minds and bodies. We're sporadically turned on by the simple hedonism of the so-called sexual revolution and the sometimes-sleek-sometimes-sleazy veil of soft- and hard-pornography. Many of us fantasize about pursuing eroticism without commitment; some actually live the fantasy. On the other side, more men are recently becoming aware of genuine needs for intimate relationships. We are beginning to recognize that being independent, always on the make and emotionally controlled, are not meeting our needs. Furthermore, the traditional masculine script is certainly not meeting women's expectations or satisfying their emotional needs. More and more men are starting to wonder if sexuality can be a vehicle for expressing and experiencing love.

In our culture many men are suffering from "sexual schizophrenia." Their minds lead them toward eroticism while their heads pull them toward emotional intimacy. What they want rarely coincides with what they need. Perhaps the uneasiness and the ambivalence which permeates male sexuality is due to this root fact: the traditional certainties which men used to define their manhood and sexuality no longer fit the realities of their lives, and until equality between the sexes becomes more of a social reality, no new model of a more humane sexuality will take hold. 15

As for me, I am still exploring and redefining my sexuality. While I don't have all the answers yet, I do have direction. I am listening more closely to women's voices, turning my head away from the sexist legacy of the locker room and pursuing a pro-feminist vision of sexuality. It feels good to stop pretending that I enjoy being alone. I never did like feeling alone. 16

SPORTS AND THE POLITICS
OF INEQUALITY

◑

MIKE MESSNER

Mike Messner is a leading voice for men's rights, and many of his writings and commentaries deal with the phenomenon of sports in society. He is an editor of the men's studies collection *Men's Lives* (1989) and co-editor with Don Sabo of the collection *Sport, Men, and the Gender Order: Critical Feminist Perspectives* (1990). The following essay was first printed in 1986 in *Changing Men*.

Our town had two high schools. Ours was mostly the poor and blue collar workers, and the rich kids all went to Northside. They always beat us in sports, but my senior year we had a good basketball team, we all really hoped we could beat Northside. Well, by the middle of the first half our team was just totally *dominating* them—it was amazing—and the crowd on our side did this cheer: IN YOUR *FACE* NORTHSIDE! After a couple of minutes, the Northside crowd yelled back: THAT'S ALL RIGHT, THAT'S OK, YOU'LL BE WORKING FOR *US* SOMEDAY!

This story, told by a young man about his own high school experience in a small midwest town, illuminates some of the complex and contradictory aspects of sports in a society which is stratified along ethnic and class lines. It appears on the surface that the sporting contest exists *outside* the realm of everyday social experience in that it can bring together people of diverse cultural and economic backgrounds. Here every person (theoretically) has the same opportunity to excel, is judged by the same standards, must conform to the same set of rules under the watchful eye of a neutral authority (referees) and the community. The game thus reinforces the myth of fairness, equal opportunity, meritocracy and democracy.

But simmering just below the surface of this seemingly egalitarian contest are the hatreds, prejudices and antagonisms that result from social inequality. In a stratified society, when participation in sport is opened up to all, the sporting arena often becomes a "contested terrain" where intergroup antagonisms are played out. For the "blue collar" kids (and for their fans and families in the stands) the game becomes a place to prove that "we're just as good as they are—indeed, perhaps *better* than they are." For a fleeting moment in this arena, they can achieve this victory and shove it in the faces of their superiors. But this victory is immediately shoved back into their faces as meaningless and hollow in terms of life *outside* the sporting arena: inequality still exists after the final buzzer sounds, and the privileged classes have the luxury of pooh-poohing the importance of a mere game when compared to real life where you'll be working for *us* someday!

From the point of view of many who are concerned with dealing with the problems of the poor, the under-privileged, the oppressed in this society, the experience of athletes is often seen as meaningless. Sports are regarded by some as an "opiate" which keeps vital attentions and energies diverted away from the real political and economic tasks at hand. But there is another point of view which is not so immediately obvious. What goes on in the sporting arena is meaningful in understanding the making and re-making of social reality. When poor people, working class people, black or brown people participate with the dominant classes and achieve some success in sports, this does not automatically eliminate poverty and inequality, but it does change the context in which class and race relations take place.

Reinforcing Racism

Organized sports were originally set up in Britain and in the U.S. by white upper class males to measure themselves against each other and to "build character" in an expanding entrepreneurial environment. As long as a system of "sports apartheid" existed, the athletic accomplishments of white males from the upper classes could be used as an ideological justification for the existence of inequality. Blacks, women and other oppressed groups, it was argued, could not compete with white males in sports or in the economy because they would surely lose, given their "obvious" inherent inferiority.

But as some color bars began to fall in professional and amateur sports— Satchel Paige striking out top white professional baseball players in an exhibition, Jesse Owens capturing the Olympic Gold in Munich in 1936, Jackie Robinson excelling in the previously all-white professional baseball leagues— the old myths of white superiority were challenged. Today, athletes still symbolically embody the hopes, dreams—and prejudices—of different communities. For example, many whites hope that Gerry Cooney will be the "Great White Hope" who finally wins the heavyweight boxing championship. And a black friend tells me that Boston Celtics' star Larry Bird is the second most hated man in the black community (after Ronald Reagan) for daring to be among the best in a "black sport."

Behind the symbolic meaning of the mythological giants of professional sports are millions of people who compete in high schools, recreation leagues, and on playgrounds. Sociologist Harry Edwards argues that hundreds of thousands of black youth are "channeled" into sports by role models in the media, by peer group and family encouragement, and by the denial of access to white-dominated schools and professions. Thus, far from being an indicator of "black progress," the predominance of blacks in many sports is an indicator of the persistence of racism in society. And, as Edwards and others have pointed out, the "carnage" that results can be staggering due to the incredibly small number of people who actually ever make a living through sports. In Edwards' words,

> Despite the fact then that American basketball, boxing, football, and baseball competitions have come more and more to look like Ghana playing Nigeria, sport nonetheless looms like a fog-shrouded minefield for the overwhelming majority of black athletes. It has been a treadmill to oblivion rather than the escalator to wealth and glory it was believed to be. There is today disturbingly consistent evidence that the black athlete who blindly sets out to fill the shoes of Dr. J., Reggie J., Magic J., Kareem Abdul-J., or O.J. is destined to end up with "No J."—no job whatsoever that he is qualified to do in our modern, technologically sophisticated society. At the end of his career, he is not running through airports like O.J. He is much more likely to be sweeping up airports—if he has the good fortune to land even that job.[1]

Is the institution of sport simply a social mechanism through which existing social inequalities are reproduced and justified? Are there perhaps moments in sports—especially for the majority of participants who never come close to making it "big"—which might lead to the opposite tendencies? Specifically, does the day-to-day interaction of males "playing together" on the nation's playgrounds lead to a breakdown of racism and to a discovery of our common humanity with which we can challenge the inequities of the larger society?

In Your Face!

I drove the lane and put up what I thought was a pretty good-looking jump-hook in heavy traffic when, seemingly from nowhere, a large black hand swatted the ball away. "Try to come in here again with that weak shit and I'll kick your white ass!" Such was my introduction to Ron, who appeared to me the epitome of the black playground player: with his gangly 6′ 4″ frame, his shaved head, his quickness and style, his aggressive intensity, and his frequent verbal intimidation, he would usually dominate play at this mostly-white playground which I came to frequent.

After playing in pickup games with Ron for three years (yet rarely speaking with him), I decided he would be an interesting person to interview for my research on athletes. He quickly agreed ("You gonna make me *famous*?"). Although my goal was to learn about "The Black Athlete," my interview with this good-humored and thoughtful thirty-year-old "professional gym-rat" ultimately taught me more about my own deeply-ingrained attitudes and assumptions concerning black males. I admitted to Ron that his verbal and physical aggressiveness had certainly intimidated me. When playing against him I found myself playing a much more "passive" game, simply out of fear that if I "took the ball to the hoop," he would embarrass me—or even hurt me. Ron laughed and told me that much of his style is a persona which he has consciously constructed to intimidate "white boys" like me and get the edge.

> I'm tall, I'm thin, I'm a black person with a shaved head, and I'm fearful. You have to intimidate mentally, because that's the advantage you have. But you're not really out to hurt that individual—it's competitiveness—the whole realization is that you've *gotta* talk shit in this game, you *have* to say, you know, "If you come close to me, I'm gonna *hurt* you!"

I asked Ron if he had ever had to back up that bluster with his fists, and his answer was a real revelation to me: "No, never. Are you kidding? Never. (laughs)—I would run. I would *run*. I'd be scared to fight." Now, I've played basketball since I was old enough to count to two, and it had never occurred to me that the black players might be a bit scared too. It's fascinating to me to realize that I have always been a little more tentative—even passive—when playing against black guys, and underlying this tentativeness was my fear of what I assumed to be a potential for violence simmering just below the surface of that black skin. Where did this assumption come from? Certainly not from personal experience—I never have had overt violence committed against me by a black player in a game! But the fear was there nonetheless. And on some (semiconscious) level, I always felt that winning a particular game just wasn't so important if it meant that I had to get my face smashed in for it. If it's so important to him that he has to threaten me, then by God he can *have* the damned game! (Am I mistaken, or is there a faint echo of "You'll be working for *us* someday," here?) 10

Interestingly, even though my talk with Ron was disturbing to me in that it made me aware of how deeply-ingrained my own racist attitudes are, it also raised my hopes that sports can be an activity in which racism is undermined. Ron spent a good deal of time talking to me about how he met his best friend—a white man—on a basketball court, and when they play on the same team together, he told me, "We know each other's moves so well it's like magic sometimes." 11

Sports and the Politics of Inequality

If this discussion of sports and inequality seems to make contradictory points, it is because sports plays a contradictory role in the larger politics of inequality. On an ideological level, sports strengthens and legitimates class and ethnic 12 inequalities in society while simultaneously providing cultural space where ideologies supporting inequalities can be challenged and debunked. And for participants, sports offers a place where class and ethnic antagonisms and prejudices can be destructively played out *and* it can offer a space where participants can experience transcendent moments of play which are relatively free from the larger social inequities. In this space, it is possible to discover ourselves and each other as human beings. What all this means is that the role sports will play in the politics of inequality will be determined by "how we play the game," both individually and collectively.

Reference

1. Harry Edwards, "The Collegiate Athletic Arms Race," *J. of Sport and Social Issues*, 8(1) Winter/ Spring 1984.

MAKING CONNECTIONS

1. Discuss the tone of Dave Barry's piece. Is he making fun of men? Women? Both? Would you consider his humor "sexist"? Why or why not?

2. Try your own hand at comic writing, using Barry's techniques of description, overstatement, and understatement as a guide. Write a humorous description of the latest sports event you watched or participated in, in such a way as to answer Barry's theme: "why sports is a drag."

3. Are any of the elements of masculinity discussed in Chapter 3 illustrated in the arena of sports? Do you perceive any changes over the last few decades in the way sports are taught, played, or publicized that would challenge or support Bruce Kidd's view of sport as a "masculinizing" activity? How would a newly popular sport like All Star Wrestling fit into Kidd's argument? What influence might sports have on the homophobia discussed in Gary Kinsman's essay (Chapter 3)?

4. Conduct your own research on the history of women in professional sports. What advances have been made, and where might inequities still exist? Do you detect any differences in the ways men's and women's sports are funded or publicized? Do you believe women should be able to compete against men in professional sports, or play with men on professional teams? Explain and defend your position.

5. What do you make of Kidd's theory of an all-male sport like rugby constituting a type of "backlash" against feminism and the threat posed by women's independence? Explain in your own words the connection Kidd draws between Nancy Chodorow's theories of motherhood and boys' attraction to the world of sports. As men and women, what were your own childhood experiences of sports and games as a way to bond with your same-sex peers and/or exclude members of the opposite sex? Write a personal narrative about your own relationship to sports, either while growing up or today, which responds to Kidd's statements about gender and sports.

6. Discuss the tone of Joyce Carol Oates's essay. Is she in favor of boxing, opposed to it, or neutral in her observations? Look at individual sentences or passages that you feel best represent her point of view, and discuss her use of language to convey her perspective. How does she, as a woman and writer, attempt to identify with and understand the sport of boxing?

7. At one point in her essay, Oates describes the publicity surrounding boxing competition as "a fairy-tale proposition." To what extent can you compare the fantasy surrounding sports with that of fairy tales? Compare

and contrast messages about men and women found in Chapters 7 and 8. Are the separate "lessons" taught by fairy tales and by sports compatible? What expectations might they create in men's and women's sense of each other and themselves?

8. Throughout this chapter, various authors suggest that aggressive sports condition men to repress their emotions and feelings—both interpersonal emotions like intimacy and openness, as well as individual feelings like pain, weakness, or even enjoyment of the game without a concern for winning. Argue for or against this view—or find a middle ground—using examples from your own experience or research.

9. Sports can be seen as a metaphor that permeates society. Don Sabo shows how its imagery can shape men's view of sexuality, but themes of athletic aggressiveness, competition, and performance also crop up in other areas of life. List as many instances as you can of the athletic myth in war, business, love, education, or any other area of endeavor. Compare your list to those of your classmates. Are these valuable metaphors, or do they carry a double-edged and/or gendered message?

10. Compare Mike Messner's essay with Kidd's on the relationship between sports, class, and race. What, if any, relationship among them can you see today, whether in professional sports, college athletic scholarships, or on neighborhood playing fields? How about behind the scenes of the sports industry, in the hierarchy of coaches, managers, or owners? Write your own response to Messner's claim that organized sports reinforce class and race divisions in society.

11. List the positive attributes of sports as individual development, group activity, and cultural expression. In what instances do sports move away from those positive values and qualities, whether in children's sports, college athletics, or professional games? What suggestions could you make in those instances to remedy the situation? Write an essay that defends, attacks, or calls for change in one sport of your choice.

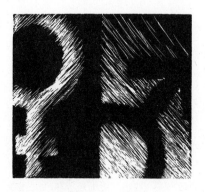

Gendered Images as Commodity

9
PRESS, FILM, TV

C O N T E X T S

We live in a society powerfully influenced by media. The newspapers we read, the films we watch, the television shows we tune in all shape our sense of the world and of ourselves. Opinions and attitudes we absorb help form our judgment about important issues; images and role models we see offer us a blueprint for our own identities and convey strong messages about family life, social roles, values, and ideals. Indeed, our very concept of reality is structured by the images and information we receive—and today much of that data is conveyed through the media.

Author Stephen Minot once demonstrated the conditioning power of the media by working out a simple calculation. He wanted to show students of creative writing why coming up with fresh ideas seemed so hard. Minot calculated that if an individual watched just five television shows a week for four years, he or she would have taken in around 1,040 separate story lines, been introduced to at least 3,120 different characters, seen over 4,160 separate dramatic scenes, and absorbed the equivalent of 20,800 pages of written dialogue. With such an overwhelming input of data, it's small wonder that having original ideas seems difficult at times! And, given that television's content, however mundane, is loaded with messages about the structures and values of our lives, imagine how powerfully even a conservative amount of television viewing can influence the ways we see ourselves and our society.

The question, of course, is not just how much data we absorb from the media, but what that information consists of. What are the assumptions and values that underlie the media's picture of the world? How fairly does it represent us as men and women? What stereotypes does it perpetuate and what prejudices might it uphold? And, in the case of sources we turn to for accurate, objective information—the newspapers, radio, and television news— how reliably are we being served?

In our first essay, media analysts Martin A. Lee and Norman Solomon address the issue of "Press and Prejudice," focusing on the news media's representation of gender. Their investigation looks both at examples of sexism in reporting and at what might be seen as more subtle indicators of bias. Does the press as an industry exercise equal opportunity in hiring and promotion? Who holds the positions of power, both behind the scenes as top executives as well as on-screen in the form of expert commentators, that "select group that constructs our national reality"? How are women's issues and issues of gay rights discussed in the media, and to what extent does the press accurately represent and inform all members of its audience? Lee and Solomon offer one perspective on the news and its role in shaping social attitudes.

The issue of discrimination also concerns our next author, journalist Ben Fong-Torres, who asks "Why Are There No Asian Anchor*men* on TV?" Fong-Torres shows how gender and race can intersect to initiate a double prejudice—in this case, calling up old stereotypes and myths about the Asian man from World War II and Vietnam. Whereas we frequently assume gender discrimination to be "a woman's problem," Fong-Torres illustrates how both sexes can be subject to injustice, particularly in an industry devoted to marketing image as much as information.

Our next three essays shift the focus onto film, providing three very distinct views on gender in motion pictures. Actress Meryl Streep's discussion of "When Women Were in the Movies" brings together her personal experience, industry statistics, and some thought-provoking predictions about women's future in motion pictures, a field that she shows to be shrinking in opportunity as it expands toward global markets. Next, film critic Kathi Maio takes a look at the image of the single woman in film, in her review of two movies of the 1980s, *Fatal Attraction* and *Someone to Watch Over Me*. With wit and insight, Maio argues that the independent woman depicted in these films might reveal much about society's fear of the changing status of women.

Images of men and masculinity have also been frequent subjects for the movies—indeed, critics claim that the "masculine myth" has its history in Westerns and action-adventure films. Anthony Easthope, in his essay from *What a Man's Gotta Do: The Masculine Myth in Popular Culture* (1990), takes a psychological approach to Hollywood's image of masculinity. He uses the theories of Sigmund Freud to explain the tensions and intensities of masculine love between fathers and sons and among men in general as portrayed on the silver screen.

We close this chapter with a look at television via Cynthia Hanson's evaluation of the popular TV series "China Beach." Although the series was advertised as the "female perspective" on the Vietnam War, Hanson argues that it contains numerous stereotypes and conveys disturbing messages about the nature and role of women. Among other topics, Hanson discusses the implications of how television assumes the viewer to be male, a theory that our next chapter takes up in its look at art and advertising.

Indeed, many of the themes introduced in Chapter 9—image and identity, how gender is represented in popular culture, and the media's power to shape reality—will surface again in the following chapters. We hope these essays stimulate you to think about your own relationship to media images and messages. By gaining perspective on how mass media reflects and shapes social attitudes, individuals can stay active participants in deciding how to see the world, each other, and themselves.

PRESS AND PREJUDICE

◑

MARTIN A. LEE AND NORMAN SOLOMON

> Martin A. Lee is an investigative journalist and media
> critic whose articles have appeared in such publications
> as *Rolling Stone*, *The Nation*, and *Newsday*. He is co-
> author with Bruce Shlain of *Acid Dreams: The CIA,
> LSD and the Sixties Rebellion* (1987) and is the publisher
> of *Extra!*, the journal of the organization FAIR (Fair-
> ness and Accuracy in Reporting). Journalist Norman
> Solomon's writings include the book *Killing Our Own:
> The Disaster of America's Experience with Atomic Radia-
> tion* (1982) and numerous commentaries published in
> newspapers and magazines across the country, from
> the *Boston Globe* and the *New Statesman* to the *Los An-
> geles Times*. This excerpt from their book *Unreliable
> Sources: A Guide to Detecting Bias in the News Media*
> (1990) examines some of the prejudices at work behind
> the news.

The printed pages we read, and the broadcasts we tune in, are said to mirror 1
society. But mass media also continue to *shape* our society—reinforcing certain
attitudes and actions while discouraging others. If television, for instance,
were not capable of fundamentally affecting people's behavior, then corporations would not be spending billions of dollars every month for commercials. If what appears in print had little impact on day-to-day lives, advertisers
would not be so heavily invested in newspaper and magazine ads.

For many women, media messages reflect the kind of attitudes that rudely 2
confront them on a daily basis. For people who are black, Latino, Native
American or of Asian ancestry, the largely white world of U.S. mass media
resonates with many of the prejudices that they repeatedly encounter in a
white-dominated country. And for those whose sexual orientation draws them
to people of the same gender, the main news media commonly leave them
out or put them down.

Media that habitually stereotype, debase and overlook the humanity of 3
some of us are not doing a good job of serving any of us. Rather than isolating
and pigeonholing the wide diversity of people in the United States, shouldn't
the mass media illuminate commonalities and differences, aiming to increase
genuine understanding? Instead of recycling the dregs of past prejudicial
views, media could help us all to take fresh looks at antiquated preconceptions.

All this may sound like nothing more than common sense. But despite   4
all the progress that's been made in recent decades, common nonsense still
finds its way into American mass media portrayals of issues surrounding
gender and race.

Women's Rights and Media Wrongs

Picture this scene at the 1987 Pan Am games: U.S. basketball player Jennifer   5
Gillom dribbles the ball up the court as millions of people across the United
States watch on TV. Then they hear CBS commentator Billy Packer say,
"Doesn't Gillom remind you of a lady who someday is going to have a nice
large family and is going to be a great cook? Doesn't she look like that? She's
got just a real pleasant face."

Or consider what happened on NBC Television at the 1984 Democratic   6
National Convention, as Geraldine Ferraro—the first woman nominated for
national office by a major party—looked out from the podium while the
convention hall erupted with cheers from the delegates. On the air, Tom
Brokaw provided this narration: "Geraldine Ferraro . . . The first woman to
be nominated for Vice President . . . Size six!"

When the *Washington Post*'s venerated columnist David Broder wrote that   7
the National Organization for Women was "strident and showboating," *USA
Today* founder Al Neuharth liked the comment so much that he quoted it in
his own column. Only ten days earlier, another Neuharth commentary had
called for the return of the "sky girls" he preferred to look at. "Many of the
young, attractive, enthusiastic female flight attendants—then called steward-
esses—have been replaced by aging women who are tired of their jobs or by
flighty young men who have trouble balancing a cup of coffee," Neuharth
complained. He yearned for the days when a flight attendant was "a nurse;
unmarried; under age 25; not over 5 feet 4 inches tall; weight less than 115
pounds." This conveyed something of the mentality of the man who invented
and ran *USA Today* for its first half-dozen years. His unabashed sexism so
appalled many staffers at the newspaper that 175 (out of 426 in the newsroom)
quickly signed a letter declaring they were "offended, outraged and embarrassed" by the founding father's column.

Male Media Dominance

Between the lines and between the transmitters is an invisible shrug about   8
the status of women in America. We are told that it's improving—but usually
without reference to how bad the situation remains. The mass media, ill-
equipped to play a constructive role, are key contributors to the problems
facing women. That's not surprising, since news media companies are bastions
of male supremacy themselves.

In 1989 men held 94 percent of the top management positions in the 9
U.S. news media. As for reporters, men had the highest profiles. A study of
the front pages of ten major newspapers found that only about one-quarter—
27 percent—of the bylines were women's. (*USA Today* ranked best at 41
percent; in contrast 16 percent of the *New York Times'* front-page bylines
belonged to women.) On network television the picture was similar; researchers found that on the nightly news, 22.2 percent of the stories on CBS were
reported by women, 14.4 percent on NBC, and 10.5 percent on ABC.

"I think women are going to continue to be a presence in broadcasting, 10
but we've had a slowdown [at the networks] in the last eight years," Marlene
Sanders said in 1989, after a long career as a reporter and producer at ABC
and CBS Television. "The move for affirmative action has been played down.
The pressure is off the people who hire. The women are there, but at a
quarter of staff." At commercial TV stations around the country, figures for
1988 showed that 18 percent of the news directors were women.

"There are fewer women on air at the networks now than there were in 11
1975 when I went to work at the networks," Linda Ellerbee said in 1989. The
situation farther up the hierarchy was even worse. "The reason you see us on
TV is so you don't notice our absence in that room marked 'executive producer' or 'CEO' or 'network president' . . . You get to a certain place where
you would reasonably expect that the next executive producer job will be
yours, for example. Then you see younger, less qualified men promoted over
you. It's much harder for the women on the management side than it is on
the air." Ellerbee added that with "younger women coming into this business
. . . I hear them saying that they'd better not make waves or they won't get
anywhere because that's the way corporations work."

Media commentators are overwhelmingly male. "For all their activity 12
now outside the home," said Fairleigh Dickinson University's dean of graduate
studies, Barbara Kellerman, "women are by and large still excluded from the
select group that constructs our national reality." While women are becoming
more visible as news reporters, "for a female to play the role of commentator,
expert, or analyst—that is, to be the resident sage—is still disturbingly rare."
During presidential campaigns, for instance, "television's stock experts" are
"almost invariably men." Studies of the nation's op-ed pages show a heavy
preponderance of males.

Women's voices are also scarce in news coverage. Surveys of ten leading 13
newspapers found that 11 percent of people quoted on the front page were
female. (For the *New York Times* the figure was five percent.) Betty Friedan
called the absence of women on front pages "a symbolic annihilation of
women. I don't think it's a systematic attempt to do that by editors, but I do
think it is clearly related to the style and content decisions of what makes
news, and those are still being defined by men." Said Junior Bridge, a
researcher for the surveys: "Is the news that appears on the front page really
the news we want? We raise men in this country to believe that things in our
daily lives are irrelevant, and things women do are irrelevant."

Abortion Lingo and the Floating Fetus

One of the experiences that can only be second-hand for the men dominating   14
the press is abortion. In 1989, the Supreme Court gave state legislatures more
latitude to interfere with abortions. Like the highest court itself, those legislatures were dominated by men who could rest assured they would never
get pregnant. And like the legislators, the pundits too were of a singularly
uninvolved gender as they uttered assorted wisdom on the topic. "The talk
shows are becoming just incredible," exclaimed Eleanor Smeal, president of
the Fund for the Feminist Majority. "The major national talk shows are white
male conservatives . . . The Washington gangs that you see on Sunday morning are all men essentially. Oh, they have a woman here and there, but it's
nowhere near balanced. And on a subject like abortion, don't tell me a 55-
year-old man feels like a 35-year-old woman, I mean it's just not possible."

Labeling has been central to media coverage of abortion. In the courts   15
and in politics, disputes center around whether abortion should be legal.
Activists and others who support that option are pro-choice. But some media
have insisted on calling them "pro-abortion." For instance, in an introductory
segment on ABC's *Nightline*, Jeff Greenfield repeatedly used "pro-abortion."
Throughout 1989, *Chicago Tribune* news articles frequently referred to "abortion supporters" and "pro-abortion" forces. And in an ironic twist the newspaper ran the headline "Abortion rights gain for fathers," over a report on
backing in the Illinois legislature for a bill to "give a father the right to seek
a court injunction to prevent a woman from terminating her pregnancy."

Use of the "pro-abortion" term implied that supporters of abortion rights   16
were trying to maximize the frequency of abortions. The term also masked
the realities of abortion as a last resort. "As a woman who was forced to
confront this decision, I can assure you that it is a rare woman, indeed, who
'wants' to have an abortion," said Kate Michelman, executive director of the
National Abortion Rights Action League. She added: "Our position, and the
position of the vast majority of Americans, is pro-choice, not pro-abortion."

Sometimes bias has been stark, as when *U.S. News & World Report* made   17
a sweeping reference to "abortion, pornography and other threats to families"—a favorite theme of many groups opposed to abortion rights. Broadcast
journalism has felt their sting, as when an ABC Radio special on the subject,
hosted by Barbara Walters, aired without commercials in summer 1989. "This
topic is one advertisers seem to be very cautious about," a network official
explained. And before NBC broadcast a two-hour TV movie, *Roe v. Wade*,
starring Holly Hunter, several advertisers pulled out as sponsors. They did
so at the request of a leading gendarme of social propriety, the American
Family Association based in Tupelo, Mississippi.

Abortion-rights activists have tried to buy commercial air time. But TV   18
networks refused to run paid spots for an upcoming Washington march for
legal abortion in spring 1989. The ads were blocked from the airwaves as too

"controversial"—an objection that, for instance, has not impeded pro-nuclear commercials which appear regularly on television.

Eleanor Smeal charged that while "the media has been very willing to show the opposition's films, such as *Silent Scream*, it worries about showing a real abortion. The rationale is that somehow it might be viewed as not good taste . . . One of the things we would love them to show is what comes out of an abortion at the typical abortion. It's only two tablespoons of tissue and blood. Well, they show the grotesque pictures of the opposition, and those pictures—we don't believe are real. The pictures are always of what they *purport* to be a typical abortion, but have to be either last trimester or still-births, or perhaps not even an abortion, and they're grotesque. Ninety-one percent of all abortions occur in the first trimester. Less than one one-hundredth of one percent of abortions are in the last trimester. Yet to show what is the truth is somehow more controversial than the distortion." 19

On TV, when an anchor reports the latest abortion news, a common background graphic is a well-developed fetus. While presented as a neutral symbol of the abortion issue, the fetal logo strongly tilts the debate—perhaps as much as a drawing of a coathanger (signifying harm caused by illegal abortions) would tilt in the opposite direction. The logo is in sync with tendencies to push women almost out of the mental pictures we have of the abortion issue. "The rise of the fetus as an independent figure in our national consciousness has transformed the debate—upstaging, and sometimes eclipsing, women and their stake in the legality of abortion," Barbara Ehrenreich has observed. Media framing of the issue brought us to a point where, in her words, "the fetus is viewed almost as a freestanding individual, while women have all but disappeared." 20

But if concerned women were to be pushed from the abortion picture, so were women journalists—at least according to some of the most powerful newspapers in the country. The *Washington Post* reprimanded staff reporters who, on their own time, marched for abortion rights with hundreds of thousands of other Americans one Sunday in April 1989. At the *Post*—as at the *Philadelphia Inquirer* and *Chicago Tribune*—the First Amendment seemed in disrepute. The *Post* handed down a memo ordering every "newsroom professional" not to take part in any abortion-related demonstration, no matter what subject areas they reported on for the newspaper. The preference seemed to be for training journalists not to have any convictions strong enough to impel public protest on a matter of principle. 21

An ironic *Post*script came a few weeks after issuance of the thou-shalt-not-demonstrate memo, when the *Washington Post* published a very favorable news article headlined "Chinese Journalists Demand Freedom," about more than 1,000 reporters and editors who were publicly petitioning in China. The featured photo was of a Chinese editor speaking through a bullhorn to demonstrators against press censorship. The specter of journalists on the march was laudable in Beijing, but unprofessional in Washington. 22

341

For all the uproar about abortion, there has been little media promotion 23
of contraception. Suggestive sexuality is unabashed in movies, TV shows,
newspapers and magazines. But the rudiments of contraception—and the
failures to come up with more reliable and less hazardous forms of birth
control—are not on the media agenda. Bloody violence and flip allusions to
sex are media staples, yet somehow a straightforward and continuing flow of
information about preventing unwanted pregnancies is deemed too "sensitive"
for the mass media to implement. That the need for abortions might be
appreciably lessened by such information is apparently too logical for the
media powers to acknowledge.

Domestic Violence and Rape

In 1974, Ann Simonton was the model who appeared on the cover of the 24
Sports Illustrated annual swimsuit issue. But, she now says, that type of media
emphasis dehumanizes women, encouraging violence against them. In an
interview, Simonton described the process this way: "The media indoctrinates
the masses to view women as consumable products. Women, now viewed
as 'things,' are much easier to violate and harm because they aren't seen as
human beings." She offered the following equation: *Woman = product =
consumption = what one purchases has no will of its own.*

Perhaps the situation in the USA is not much different than in France, 25
where the government Women's Rights Minister, Michele Andre, said: "If a
man beats a dog on the street, someone will complain to the animal protection
society. But if a man beats his wife in the street, no one moves." In the United
States, a country which has no high governmental post for women's rights,
the city of Chicago had three times as many shelters for animals as for battered
women in 1989; the animal shelters had a total budget several times higher
too.

The *Time* magazine cover story "Women Face the '90s" included poll 26
results showing that 88 percent of American women rated rape as an issue
"very important" to them. Yet nowhere else in the six-page spread did *Time*
so much as mention rape—or any other form of violence against women.
While the women of America are justifiably concerned, the media of America
paper over the issue.

A brutal assault is apt to be written off as the product of a sick mind, 27
unconnected to the cultural attitudes that go unchallenged and routinely
fueled by the dominant media of the country. But, as former Brooklyn district
attorney Elizabeth Holtzman says, "Rape is only superficially a sexual act. It
is foremost an act of violence, degradation and control . . . Sexual violence
against women exists because attitudes dehumanizing women exist." And, she
adds, "Society should stop identifying sex with violence and with denigration
of women, and that includes the images on television and in the other media."

According to the FBI's national statistics, a forcible rape gets reported to 28
police once every six minutes, and one woman in ten will be raped during

her lifetime—an extreme underestimate. Studies calculate that up to one-third of females in the United States will be raped during their lifetimes. Whatever the data, media usually report the figures fatalistically—as if rape were a natural occurrence.

News reporting of rape is selective. "Think of all the women" suggests 29 poet and essayist Katha Pollitt, "who have not entered the folklore of crime because their beatings and/or rapes and/or murders lacked the appropriate ingredients for full-dress media treatment—which include, alas, being white, young, middle-class and, as the tabloids love to say, 'attractive.'" These kinds of imbalances in coverage are magnified when sensationalized stories stress rape as a black-on-white crime. In fact, most rape is *intra*racial.

Also obscured is the reality that—whatever the race of the assailant— 30 rape is almost entirely a male-on-female crime. After the highly-publicized and extremely brutal gang rape of a woman jogging in New York's Central Park in 1989, such points were rarely discussed in mass media. That was certainly the case when six men and no women appeared on ABC's *This Week With David Brinkley* to discuss the Central Park rape—just another instance of how male voices dominate the media, defining what the "issues" are, and are not.

When a woman publicly charged that Senator Brock Adams—a longtime 31 friend of her family—had sexually assaulted her, *U.S. News & World Report* began its account this way: "The senator is not the first politician accused of hanky-panky." A press that uses "hanky-panky" as a synonym for sexual assault is part of the nation's milieu that tacitly accepts rape.

More than half of the rapes in the United States are perpetrated by men 32 who are not strangers to the women they attack—but you wouldn't know that from our mass media. When rape happens between people who know each other, news coverage is usually skimpy or nonexistent, says Robin Warshaw, author of the landmark book *I Never Called It Rape*. When people don't see "acquaintance rapes" or "date rapes" reported in the media, the implication is that such rapes don't happen, or that there's nothing much wrong with them when they do. And the reporting "still really focuses on what women should do, what limits they should do in order to be safe. There is very little examination of men and why they do it. The focus is on making the woman responsible for being raped."

Until the news media start reporting rape for what it is—a viciously 33 violent crime—society will fail to treat it that way. And until the media start defining the prevalence of rape in the U.S. as a crisis, the dominant public messages about rape will imply acceptance.

Our Homophobic Press

Along with portrayals of women, media outlooks toward gay people have 34 been slow to change. Some media continue to identify open homosexuality as a symbol of modern ills, as when a 1987 *Parade* magazine article fondly reminisced: "The '50s, viewed through the rosy prism of nostalgia, were the good old days . . . We had never heard of AIDS. Homosexuals stayed in the closet, not on the front pages."

While progress has been evident during the past two decades, prejudices continue to deeply influence the publicized images of lesbians and gay males in America. Clearly, journalism can provide excellent coverage about the nation's wide spectrum of gay people. Some articles and news broadcasts have shown sensitivity and insight—but such instances are much more the exception than the rule.   35

National Public Radio aired a superb retrospective report 20 years after gay resistance to a police raid at a bar in Greenwich Village set in motion the country's gay liberation movement. "Remembering Stonewall," a half-hour segment produced by Pacifica Radio and aired on *All Things Considered* one evening in the summer of 1989, was rich with oral history rendered vivid and alive. Those who produced "Remembering Stonewall" for a national radio audience of several million people showed that the boundaries of news media potential are far wider and more meaningful than the usual limits of American journalism.   36

In a city considered a mecca for homosexuals, San Francisco's morning *Chronicle* and afternoon *Examiner* have had plenty of incentive to improve news treatment of gay people. When the *Examiner* put together a 16-day "Gay in America" series—drawing on 50,000 hours of staff time—the result was 64 pages illuminating the lives and concerns of gays in the Bay area and elsewhere. The 1989 project was unprecedented for a U.S. daily paper. "I'd go to other cities and describe it to journalists and get blank looks," recalled a reporter and editor who worked on the series, Raul Ramirez. The series was notable for its broad scope and a tone affirming homosexuality as a sexual orientation as valid as any other.   37

The greatest success of the project, wrote a columnist for the city's alternative weekly *Bay Guardian*, "was that it dared to make visible gay men and lesbians who were real people, with all the differences and contradictions that entails." That set the *Examiner* series apart from mass media's usual cubbyhole approach. David Israels added: "For the most part, gays rarely see themselves in the newspaper or on the nightly TV news unless the story is about death (AIDS) or politics (usually the repeal of gay or AIDS rights statutes). As for the supreme arbiters of cultural acceptance—film and television—gay life is virtually nonexistent."   38

Attacks on Lesbians and Gay Males

Outside of San Francisco, U.S. media coverage is frequently equivocal or worse about gays. While generally avoiding overt put-downs of people because of their gender or the color of their skin, many journalists imply that   39 gay people may have already gained more than their fair share of human rights. "There is a myth that our community isn't oppressed any more," said *Village Voice* writer Donna Minkowitz. "On the TV news, we are a powerful minority beginning to flex its perversely huge muscles. But that image ignores much of our experience."

Underneath a thin layer of tolerance, media are routinely indifferent to 40 day-to-day realities. Attacks unleashed on lesbians and gay men get little censure in the mainstream press. Newspapers publicized a report by the National Gay and Lesbian Task Force documenting 7,248 acts of violence that targeted homosexuals in 1988—but mass media neither dwelled on the pattern nor defined it as a serious human rights problem. The links with other types of bigotry were clear to researchers, even though the press seemed disinclined to give the connections a second glance. "There has been an increase in homophobic behavior and it is not just within the general population," warned Janet Caldwell of the Center for Democratic Renewal. "It is also an outgrowth of the activities of organized hate groups, including the Klan and the neo-Nazis."

Anti-homosexual venom often is overlooked when the mass media criti- 41 cize other forms of bigotry. Some news outlets, however, have become more sensitive. In a 1989 broadcast that challenged the racist lyrics in a song by the rock group Guns N' Roses, *Entertainment Tonight* did not mention the song's reference to "faggots" or the album cover's urging that people be on guard against attacks by gays. But the TV show followed up with excellent coverage that raised issues about gay-bashing in mass-market music.

Selling the Straight Life

Sometimes media aversion to gays takes the form of a not-so-soft sell for the 42 superiority of the straight life. A *Christian Science Monitor* front-page article, headlined "Finding pathways out of homosexuality," chronicled the efforts of "ex-gays" to give others "an opportunity to change." The story, which was slanted toward a view of homosexuality as an affliction, did not mention that the newspaper itself refused to knowingly employ any homosexuals.

"The *Christian Science Monitor* is an activity of The First Church of Christ, 43 Scientist," the paper's circulation manager explained in a letter to an angry subscriber who had learned of the policy. "Consequently, the standards of the newspaper cannot be different from those of the church. Our moral standards are based on the Bible, which for us has very clear statements on sexual conduct." After firing employee Chris Madsen because she was a lesbian, the newspaper engaged in seven years of lethal battles rather than reinstate her.

While most newspapers are more accepting of employee diversity, homo- 44 phobic attitudes have a way of surfacing to the printed page. The *New York Times* published a news article which cited unnamed sources and baseless innuendos suggesting that lesbian parenting could damage children: "Some clinicians speculate that in the long term, girls might have difficulty in intimate relationships with men, and boys might be uncomfortable with their roles as males. If lesbian parents are openly hostile toward men, these difficulties could be worsened." After gay activists complained, the *Times* published an editor's note admitting that the comments in question "were added to the article during editing" after reporter Gina Kolata had submitted it. "In the absence of evidence that hostility toward men is common among lesbian parents," the *Times* conceded, "the reference to such hostility was unwarranted. The article should have given lesbian parents a chance to respond."

Contributing to American homophobia are nationally televised news accounts like a 1989 story by Fox TV's *The Reporters* about a male pedophile. The show linked homosexuality with sexual abuse of boys. In response, the Gay & Lesbian Alliance Against Defamation (GLAAD) asked: "Would a segment on Ted Bundy or Charles Manson describe them as killers, rapists and heterosexuals?" As GLAAD pointed out, "Statistically the vast majority of child sexual abuse cases involve heterosexual men who abuse girls (usually family members or friends), although the media's coverage has disproportionately focused on men who abuse boys." That imbalance of coverage "serves to perpetuate the popular myth that all molesters are gay, and all gays are molesters." 45

On Capitol Hill, the media periodically go wild over "scandals" involving sexual conduct, gay and straight. The matter of whether sex was between consenting adults sometimes seems to count less than whether the activities were heterosexual or homosexual. Thus, in 1989, when an Ohio jury convicted U.S. Representative Donald Lukens of having sex with a 16-year-old female, the media uproar was far less sustained than the tumult that greeted Lukens' colleague Barney Frank for his relationship with a man who worked as a prostitute. 46

For many millions of gay Americans a recurring message is that there is something wrong with their sexual orientation. Every time a news account speaks of an "accusation" of homosexuality, or refers to someone as an "admitted" homosexual, the harmful prejudices get reinforced. When the Republican National Committee issued a news release implying that House Speaker Tom Foley was a homosexual, few of the press commentators who vocally deplored the "smear" raised the question of why homosexuality—real or invented—should amount to a smear at all. 47

While homosexuals often face media negativity, prejudice also manifests in omissions; gays are frequently excluded from consideration as a legitimate minority group. After a New York City redistricting hearing in 1989, for example, the *New York Times* reported calls for fair representation of the black, Hispanic, and Asian-American communities without mentioning that gay and lesbian community activists had testified with similar concerns. Protests of the exclusion seemed to have little effect on the *Times*. In a follow-up article on redistricting, written by the same reporter, the *Times* again failed to give any ink to the views of gay and lesbian groups. 48

While instances of sensitive reporting about lesbians and gay males have been on the rise, serious defects persist. The media's discussions of gay rights in the abstract ignore the personal dimensions of daily life impinged upon by anti-gay bigotry. If American journalism were doing a better job, it would discover reasons to pay attention to voices like that of writer Jacqi Tully: "When I don't hold hands with my lover in the grocery store, the issue isn't how much I can display affection publicly. It's freedom. My freedom. I don't have as much of it as heterosexuals do." . . .

WHY ARE THERE NO ASIAN ANCHOR*MEN* ON TV?

◐

BEN FONG-TORRES

Journalist Ben Fong-Torres's previous writings include *The Rolling Stone Rock 'n' Roll Reader* (1974), a history of rock musicians and their music. The following piece, reprinted from the collection *Men's Lives* (1989), offers an insider's view of the television news. Here, Fong-Torres examines gender and race discrimination in media images—in particular the revealing case of "the missing Asian anchorman."

Connie Chung, the best-known Asian TV newswoman in the country, is a co-anchor of *1986*, a primetime show on NBC. Ken Kashiwahara, the best-known Asian TV newsman, has been chief of ABC's San Francisco bureau for seven years; his reports pop up here and there on ABC's newscasts and other news-related programs. 1

Wendy Tokuda, the best-known Asian TV newswoman in the Bay Area, is a co-anchor of KPIX's evening news. David Louie, the most established Asian TV newsman, is a field reporter, covering the Peninsula for KGO. 2

And that's the way it is: among Asian American broadcasters, the glamor positions—the anchor chairs, whose occupants earn more than $500,000 a year in the major markets—go to the women; the men are left outside, in the field, getting by on reporters' wages that top out at about $80,000. 3

The four Bay Area television stations that present regular newscasts (Channels 2, 4, 5, and 7) employ more than 40 anchors. Only two are Asian Americans: Tokuda and Emerald Yeh, a KRON co-anchor on weekends. There is no Asian male in an anchor position, and there has never been one. (Other Asian women who have anchored locally are Linda Yu [KGO] and Kaity Tong [KPIX], now prime-time anchors in Chicago and New York.) 4

None of the two dozen broadcasters this reporter spoke to could name a male Asian news anchor working anywhere in the United States. 5

Don Fitzpatrick, a TV talent headhunter whose job it has been for four years to help television stations find anchors and reporters, maintains a video library in his San Francisco office of 9,000 people on the air in the top 150 markets. 6

There are, in fact, several reasons proposed by broadcasters, station executives, talent agents and others. 7

- Asian men have been connected for generations with negative stereotypes. Asian women have also been saddled with false images, but, according to Tokuda, "In this profession, they work for women and against men."
- Asian women are perceived as attractive partners for the typical news anchor: a white male. "TV stations," says Henry Der, director of Chinese for Affirmative Action, "have discovered that having an Asian female with a white male is an attractive combination." And, adds Sam Chu Lin, a former reporter for both KRON and KPIX, "they like the winning formula. If an Asian woman works in one market, then another market duplicates it. So why test for an Asian male?"
- Asian women allow television stations to fulfill two equal-opportunity slots with one hiring. As Mario Machado, a Los Angeles-based reporter and producer puts it, "They get two minorities in one play of the cards. *They* hit the jackpot."
- Asian males are typically encouraged by parents toward careers in the sciences and away from communications.
- Because there are few Asian men on the air, younger Asian males have no racial peers as role models. With few men getting into the profession, news directors have a minuscule talent pool from which to hire.

And, according to Sumi Haru, a producer at KTLA in Los Angeles, the situation is worsening as stations are being purchased and taken over by large corporations. At KTTV, the ABC affiliate, "The affirmative action department was the first to go." At her own station, the public affairs department is being trimmed. "We're concerned with what little Asian representation we have on the air," said Haru, an officer of the Association of Asian-Pacific American Artists. 8

Honors Thesis

Helen Chang, a communications major at UC Berkeley now working in Washington, DC, made the missing Asian anchorman the subject of her honors thesis. Chang spoke with Asian anchorwomen in Los Angeles, Chicago and New York as well as locally. "To capsulize the thesis," she says, "it is an executive decision based on a perception of an Asian image. On an executive decision level, the image of the Asian woman is acceptable." 9

"It's such a white bread medium; it's the survival of the blandest," says a male Asian reporter who asked to remain anonymous. A native San Franciscan, this reporter once had ambitions to be an anchor, but after several static years at his station, "I've decided to face reality. I have a white man's credentials but it doesn't mean a thing. I'm not white. How can it not be racism?" 10

"Racism is a strong word that scares people," says Tokuda. 11

"But whatever's going on here is some ugly animal. It's not like segrega- 12
tion in the south. What it is is very subtle . . . bias."

To Mario Machado, it's not that subtle. Machado, who is half Chinese 13
and half Portuguese, is a former daytime news anchor in Los Angeles who's
had the most national television exposure after Kashiwahara. Being half-
Chinese, he says, has given him no advantage in getting work. "It's had no
bearing at all. There's a move on against Asians, period, whether part-Asian
or full-Asian."

TV executives, he charges, "don't really want minority males to be totally 14
successful. They don't want minority men perceived as strong, bright, and
articulate. We can be cute second bananas, like Robert Ito on *Quincy*. But
having an Asian woman—that's always been the feeling from World War II,
I guess. You bring back an Asian bride, and she's cute and delicate. But a
strong minority man with authority and conviction—I don't think people are
ready for that."

War Image

Bruno Cohen, news director at KPIX, agrees that "for a lot of people, the 15
World War II image of Japanese, unfortunately, is the operative image about
what Asian males are all about."

That image, says Serena Chen, producer and host of *Asians Now!* on 16
KTVU, was one of danger. "They may be small, but they're strong. So watch
out, white women!"

The Vietnam war and recent movies like *Rambo*, Machado says, add to 17
the historic negativity. "You never went to war against Asian women," he says.
"You always went to war against Asian men."

Today, says Tokuda, Asian men are saddled with a twin set of stereotypes. 18
"They're either wimpy—they have real thick glasses and they're small and
they have an accent and they're carrying a lot of cameras—or they're a
murderous gangster." "Or," says Les Kumagai, a former KPIX intern now
working for a Reno TV station, "they're businessmen who are going to steal
your jobs."

"The Asian woman is viewed as property, and the Asian male has been 19
denied sexuality," says Chen. "Eldridge Cleaver created a theory of the black
male being superglorified in the physical and superdecreased in the mental.
It's very difficult for people to see a successful black male unless he's an athlete
or a performer. If he's in a corporate situation, everyone says, 'Wow, he's the
product of affirmative action.' That theory holds that in this society, people
who have potential to have power have to be male, and have both mental and
physical [strength] to be the superior male. In this society, they took away
the black male's mental and gave him his physical. The Asian male has been
denied the physical and given the mental."

Veteran KRON reporter Vic Lee listens to a tally of stereotypes and   20
images associated with Asian men. "All those reasons limit where an Asian
American can work. I've always said to my wife, if I'm fired here, there're
only a couple of cities I can go to and get a job based on how well I do my
work, not how I look or what color my skin is. There are cities with Asian
American populations, and you can count them on one hand: Seattle, Los
Angeles, New York, Boston, and possibly Washington.

"The rest of the country? You might as well forget Detroit. They *killed*   21
a [Chinese] guy just 'cause he looked Japanese." Lee is referring to Vincent
Chin, who was beaten to death by two white auto workers who mistook him
for a Japanese and blamed him for their unemployment.

'Exotic' Females

In contrast to the threatening Asian male, says Les Kumagai, "Females are   22
'exotic.' They're not threatening to non-Asian females and they're attractive
to non-Asian males. You're looking to draw the 18-to-45-year-old female
demographic for advertising. You just won't get that draw from an Asian
male."

To Tokuda, the Asian woman's persisting stereotype is more insidious   23
than exotic. "It's the Singapore girl: not only deferential but submissive. It's
right next to the geisha girl."

At KGO, says one newsroom employee, "somebody in management was   24
talking about [recently hired reporter] Janet Yee and blurted out, 'Oh, she's
so cute.' They don't care about her journalistic credentials. . . . That type of
thinking still persists."

Aggressive

Janet Yee says she can take the comment as a compliment, but agrees that it   25
is "a little dehumanizing." Yee, who is half Chinese and half Irish-Swedish,
says she doesn't get the feeling, at KGO, that she was hired for her looks.
Stereotypes "are the things I've fought all my life," she says, adding that she
isn't at all submissive and deferential. "I'm assertive and outgoing, and I think
that's what got me the job."

Emerald Yeh, who worked in Portland and at CNN (Cable News Net-   26
work) in Atlanta before joining KRON, says she's asked constantly about the
part being an Asian woman played in her landing a job. "The truth is that it's
a factor, but at the same time, there is absolutely no way I can keep my job
virtually by being Asian."

Despite the tough competition for jobs in television, Yeh, like Tokuda   27
and several peers in Los Angeles, is vocal about the need to open doors to

Asian men. "People think Asians have done so well," she says, "but how can you say that if one entire gender group is hardly visible?"

George Lum, a director at KTVU who got into television work some 30 years ago at Channel 5, has a theory of his own. "The Asian male is not as aggressive as the Asian female. In this business you have to be more of an extrovert. Men are a little more passive." 28

Headhunter Don Fitzpatrick agrees. "Watching my tapes, women in general are much more aggressive than men. . . . My theory on that is that— say a boy and girl both want to get into television, and they have identical SATs and grade point averages. Speakers tell them, you'll go to Chico or Medford and start out making $17,000 to $18,000 a year. A guy will say, 'This is bull. If I stay in school and get into accounting or law . . .' And they have a career change. A woman will go to Chico or Medford and will get into LA or New York." 29

"In Helen Chang's paper," recalls Tokuda, "she mentions the way Asian parents have channeled boys with a narrow kind of guidance." 30

"With Japanese kids," says Tokuda, "right after the war, there was a lot of pressure on kids to get into society, on being quiet and working our way back in." In Seattle, she says, "I grew up with a whole group of Asian American men who from the time they were in junior high knew they were going to be doctors—or at least that they were gonna be successful. There was research that showed that they were very good in math and sciences and not good in verbal skills. With girls there's much less pressure to go into the hard sciences." 31

Most of the men who do make it in broadcasting describe serendipitous routes into the field, and all of them express contentment with being reporters. "Maybe I'm covering my butt by denying that I want to anchor," says Kumagai, "but I do get a bigger charge being out in the field." 32

Still, most Asian male reporters do think about the fame and fortune of an anchor slot. Those thoughts quickly meet up against reality. 33

David Louie realizes he has little chance of becoming the 6 o'clock anchor. "I don't have the matinee idol look that would be the most ideal image on TV. Being on the portly side and not having a full head of hair, I would be the antithesis of what an anchorman is supposed to look like." 34

Kind of like KPIX's Dave McElhatton? Louie laughs. "But he's white," he says, quickly adding that McElhatton also has 25 years of experience broadcasting in the Bay Area. 35

At least Louie is on the air. In Sacramento, Lonnie Wong was a reporter at KTXL (Channel 40), and Jan Minagawa reported and did part-time anchoring at KXTV (Channel 10). Both have been promoted into newsroom editing and production jobs. And neither is thrilled to be off the air. 36

Wong, who says he was made an assignment editor because, among reporters, he had "the most contacts in the community," says his new job is "good management experience. But I did have a reservation. I was the only minority on the air at the station; and I know that's valuable for a station." 37

Minagawa's station, KXTV, does have an Asian on the air: a Vietnamese   38
woman reporter named Mai Pham. "That made the decision easier," says
Minagawa, who had been a reporter and fill-in anchor for seven years. A new
news director, he says, "had a different idea of what should be on the air" and
asked him to become a producer. "I didn't like it, but there was nothing I
could do."

Mitch Farris rejects any notion of a conspiracy by news directors against   39
Asian American men. In fact, he says, they are "desperate" for Asian male
applicants. "Just about any news director would strive to get an Asian on the
air and wouldn't mind a man."

To which Machado shouts, "We're here! We're here! We're looking for   40
work."

WHEN WOMEN WERE IN THE MOVIES

◐

MERYL STREEP

Actress Meryl Streep has starred in numerous motion
pictures such as *Sophie's Choice* (1982), *Out of Africa*
(1985), and *Postcards from the Edge* (1990) and has been
active in addressing the role of women in film. The
following speech was delivered in Los Angeles as the
keynote address at the first national women's conference of the Screen Actors Guild (SAG) on August 1,
1990.

I won't slog through all the tragic statistics contained in the SAG report 1
"The Female in Focus: In Whose Image?," but some of the numbers are so
stunning that I really must share them with you.

Three years ago, women were down to performing only one-third of all
the roles in feature films. In 1989, that number slipped to 29 percent. Of
course, that was before the figures for this year were tabulated. Just wait till
they factor in our contributions to *Total Recall, Robocop II, Days of Thunder,
Die Hard 2, The Hunt for Red October, The Abyss, Young Guns II, Miami Blues,
Last Exit to Brooklyn, Dick Tracy* and *The Adventures of Ford Fairlane.* We
snagged a good six or seven major roles in those movies. If the trend continues,
by the year 2000 women will represent 13 percent of all roles. And in 20
years, we will have been eliminated from movies entirely.

But that's not going to happen, is it, ladies?! 2

There is some good news in these statistics. The average earnings by age 3
and sex show that "after the age of 10, men earn consistently higher average
annual earnings under SAG contracts than women do." That doesn't immediately sound like good news. However, it does mean that from birth through
age nine, a girl can make a pretty fair living. In fact, we may have located one
of the few areas in American enterprise where there *is* equal pay for equal
work. My advice is: little girls, hold out for the big money, invest wisely and
investigate other careers, because after fourth grade, it's all down hill.

By the way, as the mother of a 10-year-old boy, I would like to know 4
precisely *when* they begin to demonstrate their superior earning potential.
I'm always looking for the light at the end of the Nintendo tunnel.

What is the problem? We all know what the problem is. One, there's very 5
little work for women. And two, when we do work we get paid much

less than our male counterparts—about 40 cents to 60 cents on the male dollar.

And what work there is lately is odd. Somebody at *The New Yorker* said 6 recently that if the Martians landed and did nothing but go to movies this year, they'd come to the fair conclusion that the chief occupation of women on Earth is hooking. And I don't mean rugs.

"What has happened to women in the movies?" asked Janet Maslin, a 7 critic for the *New York Times*. Peter Rainer of the *Los Angeles Times* recently wrote, "an entire generation of female performers is being squelched by an industry that finds no percentage in accommodating their talents."

Why is this happening? The three monkeys volunteer their answers: 8

"I don't see any good scripts being written for women," say the producers, 9 covering their eyes.

"I can't continue to write screenplays that won't sell," say the writers, 10 covering their mouths.

"We'd *love* to make that picture, but nobody would go to see it—nobody 11 wants to hear from women," say the studios, covering their ears and their bases, their wallets and their faces all at the same time.

Bottom line: the real reason for the disappearance of women from films 12 has a lot to do with the way movies are financed today. Many films are currently financed by foreign pre-sales. Production costs are significantly offset by fees paid to secure a certain film for foreign markets. So the big scramble is now on for international money.

Revenues from overseas can represent half or more of a picture's total 13 haul. Action-adventure films traditionally presell best. You don't have to un-derstand what little English is contained in a film to know that something is exploding and enjoy the spectacle. This also means that sometimes the movies *we* get to see at home are pre-determined by what deal makers believe will eventually go big in the Far East or Southeast Asia.

The trouble is, when the bottom line drives the dream machine, some 14 things get paved over and flattened (they don't call it the bottom line for nothing). Anyone wondering nostalgically where the crackling wit and stylish verbal surprise of classic films has gone can look under the wheels of the blockbuster. They do make money—sometimes. And sometimes they just *cost* money.

For whatever reason, the targeted worldwide audience—the audience that 15 studios *most* want to reach—seems to be 16- to 25-year-old males. In a recent article in *Los Angeles* magazine, 20th Century-Fox production executive Me-lissa Bachrach stated, "Most moviegoers are men. You can't make movies just for the women's audience anymore. There has to be broad appeal. Men have the power, and women respond to that power."

In that same article, screenwriter Michael Mahern says, "Women got 16 pushed aside. Movies today must appeal to both men and women. Relatively few women go to the movies alone. It's easier for men to be appealing to both men and women."

So people will tell you it's all about sex appeal. "Women's careers don't last as long as men's," says Interscope production exec David Madden. "There's a romanticism about the older male, not the female." [17]

Well, certainly in a season where most of the female leads are prostitutes there's not going to be a lot of work for women over 40. Like hookers, actresses seem to lose their market appeal around that age. At the age of 40, however, most male actors are just approaching their peak earning potential. This boon continues into their 50s and 60s. According to the 1989 SAG statistics, men aged 60 to 69 years of age earned on average almost twice the annual salary of women 30 to 39 years old. Does this really reflect what the market demands? [18]

It's interesting that everybody knows who goes to the movies now, but there's not a lot of data on who is deliberately staying home. If I were in the business end of this business, I would certainly be looking worldwide for markets, especially as the known one shrinks, for whatever reason. [19]

There is, for instance, a generation (or two) of people out there who represent a huge (and with the greying of America, growing) market. These people grew up going to the movies not twice a month, but two and three times a week. They had the *habit* of going out to the movies. They have the money to go, and they don't need a sitter because the kids are grown. They have a VCR but they don't know how to program it, and they can't be bothered to sit down for an hour to plod through the Satellite/Cable Guide (which is now as big as a phone book) in order to find the two or three things they'd like to tape. And the novelty of cassette rentals has worn off as the overwhelming supermarket effect of video stores sends them slouching back to the car empty-handed. [20]

These people are grouchy, but with reason. They are being ignored by the movie industry. We should find market strategies that court this audience which has forcibly weaned itself from its moviegoing habit. They have the time, the money *and* the inclination to go out to the movies—and not just on weekends. [21]

Who else is staying home? [22]

I always wonder about the people who came out to see the story of a little known (in this country) Danish woman writer who tried to make a go of coffee farming in East Africa. I have little doubt that if Sydney Pollack went seeking financing for *Out of Africa* in the current marketplace he'd be told "nobody wants to see that—it's a woman's story." [23]

Janet Maslin, in her recent *New York Times* article "Bimbos Embody Retro Rage" (great title), tells of an agent who informed her client, a writer, that if he wanted to get his script financed he'd better change the female protagonist to a male. Centering a story on a woman makes it harder to sell. [24]

Anne Thompson, in her *LA Weekly* article entitled "Battling the Big Boys: The Decline of the Woman Star," says, "Actresses are as unclear about their [25] screen roles as American men and women seem to be about their roles in real life."

I'm not sure that's true. I do know what roles are around, and I'm not confused about which ones realistically I'm able to portray. But the *range* of roles simply doesn't exist. All through my career, I've been barely able to contain a guffaw when an interviewer asked, "What drew you to this specific character? Why, out of everything available, did you choose *this* role?" As if there always existed a veritable rainbow of well-written roles for women! "The blue, the orange, the red, the green, the yellow, the puce, the vermilion—and you chose the olive green. Why this odd Australian film? Are you drawn to accents?" They happily pounce upon the obvious. 26

No. It's because I'm drawn to good writing and ideas and controversy and drama and feeling and emotion all packed into the character of the protagonist—the *person* who drives the action, not his girlfriend. Now in the prime of my life, I want to play the lead. Why? Because I grew up and was nourished on the legacy of the great female stars: the grand and glorious work of Bette Davis and Barbara Stanwyck, Carole Lombard and Lucille Ball, Katharine Hepburn and Greta Garbo, and on stage, Geraldine Page, Irene Worth, Maggie Smith, Colleen Dewhurst, Ethel Merman, Kim Stanley, Jessica Tandy and many, many others. 27

These women inspired me. The derivation of that word is from the Latin *in-spirare:* to breathe life into, to fill with life, to breathe in—and I did. I gasped when I saw these women. It made me want to be something, to achieve something, to express my humanity, my aliveness, my connection to that radiant, important creation which was woman. 28

I was inspired by actors, too. In fact, the first time I was aware that there was such a thing as the craft of acting was when in high school I saw Marlon Brando in the film of *Julius Caesar*. What he was doing was so in essence different from everyone else that it pulled me out of the theatrical reality and made me aware of his choices as an actor. Elements of his technique, his timing (which was odd), his movements, his use of an unlovely voice which became nevertheless unforgettable, excited and intrigued me and inspired me as an actor. 29

But when I saw those actresses, I was inspired *as a woman*. When I saw them on the 4:30 movie or on screen or on stage, what sent me out of the theater buzzing like a hovercraft was the idea that if *she* counted, if that woman was significant in the shimmering landscape that was a movie, then *I* counted, *girls* counted, we *mattered*. Evidence to that effect is not always manifest in this culture. If we don't have these images of women we feel for, admire, recognize and esteem, then we stifle the dreams of our daughters; we put our hands over the mouth of their inspiration. If we erase our dreams, we disappear. 30

If most of the women we've seen in films this year are slapped, kicked, raped, murdered, bruised, begging for help or duplicitous and just asking for 31 it, this is *not* an indication that *actresses* are confused about their roles. It is rather an indication of the kinds of images the industry has confidence in, green lights and feels will sell.

One thing is clear: the two questions, "Why are there so few roles for women?," and "Why are we paid, relatively, so little?," are linked. My dad said it to me, "Supply and demand, Meryl, supply and demand." As long as there are a lot of us to fill only a few parts, the economics are very pleasant for the people who pay us. Why *should* the studios create more jobs for us so that we no longer undercut each other's salary demands? (If we can't get her cheap, we'll get her, or her, or her.) Imagine what these stupendously-budgeted movies would cost if we were working in equal numbers and paid commensurately with our brothers, the male actors. 32

If it's not in the financial interest of the studios to change the status quo, then I don't have much hope it will change. But the market *will* dictate what is on the screen. That's up to you and me and millions of moviegoers to demonstrate. This summer's disappointing performance of some of the expensive self-styled blockbusters may be evidence that our voices are being heard. 33

Michael Brenson, who is a fine arts critic in New York, recently wrote an article entitled, "Is Quality an Idea Whose Time Has Gone?" In it, he talks about that feeling that overtakes you in confronting certain masterful works of art. I've extrapolated a bit of it to refer to an experience that you and I and anyone who works in the movies has had once or twice in a darkened theater, in the face of a certain performance or some such cinematic wonder. He calls that feeling "aesthetic emotion," and it's part of what I would hope is the legacy of our generation of filmmakers to our children, because we really are at a turning point now. 34

"Aesthetic emotion," he says, "is an experience at once personal and impersonal, specific and general. It is rooted in the object, but it also suggests something beyond the object. It suggests the depth of feeling and knowledge of which human beings are capable. It brings an intensified awareness of life and death. It is related to the experience of revelation and love, and is ultimately just as resistant to theory and language. Indeed, it suggests that what is most profound can never be analyzed or held in words." 35

This past weekend we celebrated my mother's 75th birthday (she'll be thrilled I told everyone which birthday). As I agonized to her about what in hell I was going to say in this speech, she said, "Why don't you just tell them that when there were more women in the movies, the movies were better?" 36

SEX AND THE SINGLE TERRORIST
Fatal Attraction and *Someone to Watch Over Me*

KATHI MAIO

Feminist film critic Kathi Maio's reviews have been
called "intelligent, incisive, and reliably feminist without sacrificing either wit or complexity." Here, she
takes a penetrating look at two box-office hits of the
1980s: *Fatal Attraction* and *Someone to Watch Over Me.*
Her reviews have been collected in the books *Feminist
in the Dark: Reviewing the Movies* (1988), from which
our selection is taken, and *Popcorn and Sexual Politics*
(1991).

The current obsession with the "new" monogamy would be hilarious if it 1
weren't so depressing—and so based in gut-wrenching fear. The fear of AIDS
is the most obvious source of the current sexual paranoia. But it's not the only
reason our popular culture is once again embracing the simple, cracked logic
that love and marriage go together like a horse and carriage. When Carly
Simon (former troubadour of the exciting, cynical world of sexual freedom
in the 70s) admonishes her girlfriend to stay in her dull long-term relationship
because it's "The Stuff That Dreams Are Made Of," she isn't playing on her
(or our) fear of AIDS. Her message is rather that a good, or at least bearable,
man is exceedingly hard to find. Once you latch onto one, you'd better stick
like a leech.

This warning against the single lifestyle and toward a "Stand By Your 2
Man" monogamy reflects the agonized frenzy the media has tried to stir in
the hearts of single female baby boomers during the last few years. Our
biological clocks are at two minutes to midnight, they keep telling us. And,
as *Newsweek* gleefully warned in their infamous article of June 1986, women
in their thirties have probably already missed the boats when it comes to
finding a husband. Once you hit forty, it's all over. In their immortal words:
"Forty-year-olds are more likely to be killed by a terrorist" than to marry.
The message is: You tarried too long with your freedom, girls, and now you've
got to pay. You're used goods. No one would want you for a life partner. You
used to scoff at the nuclear family. Now you realize that you'd kill to have a
hubby and bambinos in your own golden little house.

Of course, when *Newsweek* preaches a sermon on the desperate plight of 3
single women, can Hollywood be far behind? Enter two tales of the horrors

of spinsterhood masquerading as thrillers, *Fatal Attraction* and *Someone to Watch Over Me.*

Fatal Attraction is one of the cleverest examples of woman-hating to ever roll off a movie reel. Adrian Lyne, creator of such slick trash as *Flashdance* and *9 1/2 Weeks,* has done it again with a movie which continues to gross a million dollars *a day* weeks after its release. The premise of the movie is a simple extension of *Newsweek's* statistics. When the alarm on a woman's biological clock goes off, she becomes a demon that will not be denied. If she's more likely to be killed by a terrorist than find a husband, she's likely to *become* a terrorist to get what every woman is in heat for—a "suitable" father for her children.

Alex Forrest (Glenn Close) is just such a terrorist. And the nastiest thing about Lyne's portrayal of this woman is that she doesn't start off looking or acting like a terrorist. When we first see Alex, she is at a crowded cocktail party to launch a new book on Samurai self-help. She is a particularly cool, beautiful, and completely self-assured blonde in a room full of sleek and attractive New York yuppies. When she cuts dead the rather crude flirtation of a not-very-sleek schlump, we may (as Lyne hopes we will) think her a bit of a ball-breaker, but her reaction seems reasonable enough. Later, she is perfectly gracious (and mildly flirtatious) with the schlump's colleague, Dan Gallagher (Michael Douglas). And when Alex and Dan meet again at a legal huddle where she, as editor, is called in to discuss a suit against one of her author's books with Gallagher, the publishing house's attorney, she is calm, intelligent, and professional. She is also clearly interested in Dan.

As Lyne carefully builds the attraction between his two leads, it is hard to mistake the power balance. Although Dan is portrayed as the handsome and bright rising star of his law firm, in social-sexual matters he is seen as a klutz and an innocent. Here is a guy who gets cream cheese on his nose eating a bagel, who can't open his cheap umbrella in the middle of a downpour, and can't seem to catch the attention of cabdrivers or waiters. He is bedazzled by Alex's come-hither looks and her cool sophistication. When the two discuss, playfully, whether or not to end their friendly dinner in bed, Dan acknowledges that the choice is hers. Decision-making power belongs to Alex because she is the stronger personality of the two and Dan doesn't know his own mind. Of course, according to the filmmakers, any sexual situation where the woman is empowered is a situation ripe for disaster—a feminist violation of the natural order.

When the decision is made, by Alex, to defile this married man, Lyne and Close (in a brilliant, haunting performance) start to build their image of imbalance and iniquity. Alex brings Dan back to her stark white loft in the middle of the meat-packing industry: a she-devil leading her prey past smudge pot fires and hanging animal carcasses to her own little hell. She makes love to him in a pointed debasement of domesticity, among the dirty pots and pans in her kitchen sink.

While the sex, expressed in all the exaggerated panting and moaning of 8 cheap porn, is good for Dan, it (and Alex) are clearly too much for this simple, domestic fellow. When Dan tries to toddle home, Alex turns petulant and possessive and eventually self-destructive. Dan is puzzled and dismayed. How could a simple roll in the hay suddenly get so complicated? It is a philandering husband's worst nightmare when Alex refuses to play by "the rules" that say that a woman who sleeps with a married man has no rights, no power. Such women do not deserve loyalty, tender consideration, or respect in the morning, say those rules. The fact that Alex does want, indeed *demands*, these things is proof of her insanity, which becomes more and more pronounced from this point on.

Meanwhile, Dan's lovely and sweet wife, Beth (Anne Archer), knows 9 nothing of her husband's betrayal. She tends to their adorable daughter Ellen (Ellen Hamilton Latzen), and plots to buy an even cozier nest for her family in the country. Dan confesses his infidelity only after little Ellen's bunny rabbit is found dead and boiled in the Gallagher kitchen. The sides are then drawn in this life-and-death struggle for suitable husband material; the good/chaste/suburban/wife/homemaker must fend off the attack of the evil/sexy/urban/slut/career woman. When the Mother and the Whore do battle, can the victor be in question?

To reinforce the message that single women are the enemy of married 10 women, and that married women must reject, if necesssary destroy, their unnatural and envious sisters, Lyne makes use of another popular anti-feminist stereotype: that of the emasculated modern American man. Dan is seen as a passive victim, a tethered goat to Alex's predatory female. At home he is un-macho, too. His approach to his wife is less sexual (i.e., dominant) than worshipful. And unlike his own father, he is nurturing and approving toward his daughter. Sounds good, except that Lyne's point seems to be that tenderness makes a man a total wimp. When Dan has both the opportunity and provocation, on two separate occasions, to protect his family by killing Alex, he is unable (despite the loud encouragement of the movie audience) to be effectively violent. Destruction of the temptress is therefore left to the enraged lioness protecting her den and cub. Beth doesn't hesitate: She blows away her rival with a single shot to the heart.

The fact that such a story is doing such boffo box office is due in part to 11 Lyne's clever direction, James Dearden's tight scripting, and excellent performances by all the lead players. But this is by no means the best movie of the year, nor does it boast any superstars in its cast. *Fatal Attraction* is a mega-hit for other, more disturbing, reasons. It feeds into the general public's deepest fears about single, successful (read: feminist) career women and the danger they represent to the nuclear family. When Alex challenges Dan's professed happiness in marriage with "So what are you doing here?" or when she later informs him, "I won't let you treat me like some slut you can bang a couple of times and then throw away like a piece of garbage," she is being strong and assertive and justly angry at "the rules" of a male-dominated society. Yet by making Alex a self-destructive madwoman, Dearden and Lyne are encouraging us to equate a woman's independence and anger with madness. They are also trying to convince us that the single woman's confidence and success are merely a mask for her deep-seated self-hatred at her failure as a real woman. She is a monster without the Day-Glo eyes or the bloody fangs or other accoutrements of the fantastical fiend. Alex is no fantasy. Lyne and Dearden want us to believe that she is real.

And the unmarried, career woman monster is one Americans, even women, need little encouragement to believe in and hate. At the show I attended, a young woman sitting in front of me joined the throng in egging Dan on to murder and in clapping and cheering when Beth finally shot Alex. This woman, as the filmmakers hoped, identified strongly with Beth. As the shot rang out, she yelled out, "Take that, Bitch, I'm sick of your shit!" 12

Someone to Watch Over Me would probably evoke a less dramatic reaction from my young friend. It is a very similar film, made with just as much visual style by Ridley Scott. But *Someone* doesn't ask us to hate the single woman, only to pity her. Claire Gregory (Mimi Rogers) is the single woman in question, a wealthy member of New York's beautiful people. At a fashionable club, Claire is the only witness to the murder of a friend by a mafia-connected psychotic named Venza (Andreas Katsulas). While she has a rich, anal-retentive lover (played to perfection by John Rubenstein), he's another of those emasculated American males. He doesn't even make a pretense of protecting her. He leaves town soon after the murderer threatens to kill Claire. 13

Now, even if her boyfriend were no help, a rich woman would still have plenty of resources to call on for protection. This is a woman who could easily afford to hire an army of Sly Stallones (or Brigitte Nielsens) to protect her day and night. But what kind of story would that make? Claire is instead portrayed as a frightened, isolated (evidently she has no family or real friends) woman who must rely on the kindness of strangers: namely the New York Police. One of her guardians is a good-looking, happily married joe who just made detective. Mike Keegan (Tom Berenger) is your basic, boring, lower-middle-class cop. Like Dan Gallagher, Mike Keegan is a bit of a klutz. Unlike him, he is still a man's man capable of protecting a woman. 14

In fact, when Mike strays from monogamy, it is not because of the lure of Claire's she-devil sexuality, but because Claire shows herself to be a weak, womanly woman. She collapses, weeping out of her terror, and Mike offers her sex as a pledge of his comfort and protection. Unlike the monstrous Alex, Claire admits that she has no claim on Keegan. She is pathetically grateful for any attention or help she can get from a manly, good-looking husband type like Mike. 15

Meanwhile, Keegan also has a nice wife at home, an ex-cop named Ellie (Lorraine Bracco) who is not appeased when he tries to soften the blow of his infidelity by sobbing out, "I respect you so much!" Ellie knows how much 16 such proclamations are worth, and she doesn't try to soften the blow at all when she decks her husband in a restaurant parking lot, screaming "Don't talk to *me* about *respect!*"

Let me say here and now that the little spirit and warmth found in *Someone* all belong to Lorraine Bracco in her first major screen role. Bracco is able to perfectly blend a genuine toughness and strength with all the expected attributes of the idealized Hollywood homemaker. Ellie, unlike Beth in *Fatal Attraction*, is allowed her sexuality and her full measure of anger toward her husband. When Keegan is expelled from his cozy home, Ellie becomes the household protector. In a short, hilarious scene, she takes her son to the practice range to watch as she polishes her shooting skills. She is still quite a markswoman, but instead of aiming for the heart, Ellie shoots out the groin area on her paper target with much grim satisfaction. 17

The dynamics of the triangle in *Someone* are much different from those in *Fatal Attraction*, since the real enemy is the male murderer and not the female interloper. Claire is never a villainess, just a lonely woman in need of help. Neither woman sees the other as the enemy. In fact, Claire freely offers to put herself at risk when the bad guy threatens Keegan's family. But, as in *Fatal Attraction*, it is the lioness who saves the day, blowing away the villain to protect her son and husband. 18

Even without the rigid Mother-Whore roles, there is no question who will win and who will lose in this movie. After the shooting is over, the Keegan family unites in (I kid you not) a group fetal hug. The nuclear family is re-solidified, and poor Claire is left out in the cold, in the dark. 19

And *that* is what both of these films are really about. The most poignant, pointed, and exploitive scene in *Fatal Attraction* is not, to my mind, the murder of Alex and her unborn child by Beth. It is a much earlier scene when Alex stalks Dan home to his new suburban home. It is winter, and Alex is shivering in the dark and cold. She peers into the window of the Gallagher living room like a child at a toy store. Inside, Beth and Ellen snuggle in the golden glow of their fireplace. Dad comes home after a rough day to this peace and joy. The three form an enchanting tableau of the perfect beatific family unit. Alex stumbles away from the window and vomits. 20

While *Fatal Attraction* expresses a much more virulent form of misogyny than *Someone to Watch Over Me*, both of these flashy thrillers argue that the nuclear unit of mommy-and-daddy-and-baby-makes-three must not be put asunder. And since the heterosexual nuclear family unit is *the* natural order, single women are the ultimate losers in life. *Fatal Attraction* tells us to hate the unmarried woman as an unnatural and evil creature. *Someone to Watch Over Me* tells us to pity her for her sterile and exposed life. Both tell us that an unmarried woman deserves what she gets—as long as it's bad. 21

As I thought about these movies, another pop song came to mind, Maggie Roche's "Married Men," in which she lists her various conquests among the attached male population. The song ends: "All o' that time in Hell to spend, 22 for kissin' the married men." The Roches are being ironic when they make that statement, but the same cannot be said for the boys in Hollywood. Adrian Lyne, and many of the thousands of people flocking to see *Fatal Attraction*, really see the single woman as a social evil deserving of fire and brimstone.

Scary? Definitely. But, call me an optimist, maybe the unmarried uppity women of the world should be cheered by the woman-hating of these films. After all, the single woman's blissful independence must be viewed as a serious threat to the patriarchy to warrant such open attacks in the popular culture. 23

WHAT A MAN'S GOTTA DO

ANTHONY EASTHOPE

This discussion of the masculine image in film is taken
from Anthony Easthope's recent study, *What a Man's
Gotta Do: The Masculine Myth in Popular Culture* (1990),
in which he applies social and psychological theories
to the ways men are portrayed in today's world. Easthope teaches English and Cultural Studies at Man-
chester Polytechnic in England and is also the author
of three books on literary criticism and theory, *Poetry
as Discourse* (1983), *British Post-Structuralism* (1988) and
Poetry and Phantasy (1989).

Masculine Style: Banter

> *Yet each man kills the thing he loves,*
> *By each let this be heard,*
> *Some do it with a bitter look,*
> *Some with a flattering word*
> (Oscar Wilde, *The Ballad of Reading Gaol*)

Banter or repartee is not an exclusively masculine style. It is used between 1
friends and between lovers. But it is used so much and so often as a form of
male exchange, it is so widespread and powerful, both in life and its fictional
representation, that it must be considered an example of masculine style. As
such it can be analysed into three features: one governs its mode of operation,
the other two its content. As humour or comedy, banter makes use of every
kind of irony, sarcasm, pun, clichéd reply, and so is an example of the
joke. . . . The content of banter has a double function. Outwardly banter is
aggressive, a form in which the masculine ego asserts itself. Inwardly, however,
banter depends on a close, intimate and personal understanding of the person
who is the butt of the attack. It thus works as a way of affirming the bond of
love between men while appearing to deny it. The analysis is straightforward,
but repartee figures so largely in masculine style it needs to be looked at in
detail. There are two examples here: one of the elder/younger brother relationship, another of father and son.

When *Butch Cassidy and the Sundance Kid* came out in 1969 the free- 2
floating life style it celebrated could not but signal the values of the counter-

culture, just as the frequently expressed unwillingness of its heroes to join the army made them sound like college kids escaping the Vietnam war. Drawing on Truffaut's *Jules et Jim* (1962) and borrowing its ending from *Viva Zapata!* (1951), the movie has a sketchy plot which is really not more than an occasion to dramatise a classic buddy relationship. Women in it are treated as marginal, objects in exchange between the two men.

Following a confessional scene in the brothel during which the two men tell each their real names, a prostitute puts her arms round Cassidy. A trifle disconsolately his partner says he's going off to find a woman who is beautiful, gentle, refined. He goes to Etta, the 'teacher-lady'. When they wake up in bed they hear Butch cycling round the house saying in a melodramatic voice, 'You're mine'. He takes Etta off on his bike.

> SUNDANCE: What're you doing?
> CASSIDY: Stealing your woman.
> SUNDANCE: Take her.
> CASSIDY: You're a romantic bastard, I'll give you that.

Their banter covers the aggression towards Etta who, of course, threatens their own love for each other. After a surly invitation for her to come with them to Bolivia, Sundance warns 'if you whine or make a nuisance, I'm dumping you flat' to which Cassidy responds, 'Don't sugar-coat it like that, Kid, tell her straight.'

Unlike the situation in *Jules et Jim*, Etta doesn't make love with Cassidy as well as Sundance, but she matters only a little more to them than the bar-girls they meet. Once when they are hiding in a brothel, Cassidy is making love with a woman on the bed while his buddy watches out for the posse. Cassidy objects that it puts him off for the other to be 'staring out the window like that', and Sundance says, with only slight conviction, 'Don't ask me to stay.'

In their characters the two men form a pair of opposites. Cassidy is reason, ideas, quick talk, sociability, the pleasure principle; Sundance is body, action, not given to words, isolated, the reality principle. Unfailingly optimistic, Cassidy has a touch of cowardice in his scheming; Sundance, though he hides it well, is stupid. While Cassidy represents the older brother, in terms of the dominant myth he is less Butch than his name supposes—when he complains at length 'I don't like jungles, I don't like snakes', Sundance cuts him short with 'Bitch, bitch, bitch.' Yet they are willing to die for each other, as in the end they do. Challenged to a fight by Harvey, Cassidy whispers 'If when it's done, I'm dead—kill him', and Sundance replies 'Love to.' Their sublimated love for each other comes out not only in their lingering exchange of looks but in continual banter which reveals close sympathy for each other's weaknesses. Mainly in the film this is a matter of dialogue exposing Cassidy's brave pretensions:

> SUNDANCE: What's your idea this time?
> CASSIDY: Bolivia.

SUNDANCE:	What's Bolivia?
CASSIDY:	That's a country, stupid—Central or South America, one or the other.

During the second raid on 'The Flyer' Cassidy lays the dynamite with the words 'That oughter do it'; after a large explosion, with dollar bills drifting through the air, Sundance asks with a smile, 'Think you used enough dynamite then, Butch?' Pursued, Cassidy explains 'They can't track us over rock'—Sundance snipes back, 'Tell *them* that.' Sundance always expects the worst because he cannot think through the consequences of his actions. As Cassidy sneers, 'For a gunman, you're one hell of a pessimist.' When the Kid won't jump into the torrent because he can't swim it's left to his partner to point out: 'Are you crazy? The fall will probably kill you!'   7

Both are doomed: partly by the changing West in which banks get harder to rob, mainly by their refusal to grow up, submit to the symbolic father and accede to adult heterosexuality. This is why most of the movie consists of them being chased by an indistinct figure, the lawman Lefors. In Bolivia, Cassidy's fantasy kingdom, the law of the father catches up with them. Holed up in the cantina, Cassidy says, 'Bet it's just one guy'; when the hat he throws out the door is immediately shot to pieces in a fusillade of bullets, Sundance's rejoinder is 'Don't you get sick of being right all the time?' Their ammunition is across the square on a mule. Sundance says he'll go; Cassidy replies, 'This is no time for bravery, I'll let you.' But after a long exchange of looks he points out the logic of the situation: 'Hell, I'm the one that has to go . . . I could never give you cover, you can cover me.' He runs for the bandoleer and could escape, but comes back to his friend; both are wounded: 8

CASSIDY:	Is that what you call giving cover?
SUNDANCE:	Is that what you call running? If I knew you were going to stroll . . .
CASSIDY:	You never could shoot, not from the very beginning.
SUNDANCE:	And you were all mouth.

To the end they cannot admit their love for each other except through attack. In banter explicit antagonism between two masculine egos covers the implicit male bond. Personal criticism like this would never be allowed to an outsider for it depends on a disavowed but fond awareness of 'how like you that is.' And much of the viewer's pleasure arises from appreciating this.   9

Banter between Father and Son

Indiana Jones and the Last Crusade, directed by Steven Spielberg (1989), is the third of the 'Indiana Jones' series and follows its hero from the United States to Venice, Salzburg, Berlin and the Middle East in search of the Holy Grail, which is able to confer immortality on its bearer. In the narrative Sean Connery and Harrison Ford are father and son, but they are also father and son   10 in the genre because this movie marks Indiana Jones's claim to take over the role of prime popular hero from James Bond.

As British posters for the movie claimed, 'The Man with the Hat is [11] Back—and This Time He's Bringing his Dad': for psychoanalysis the hat may symbolise the phallus. If so, the assonance which links 'hat' and 'dad' is no accident, because what is at issue between father and son is the phallus, as can be seen in the poster for the film, epitomising the look of the father. There is the son in the foreground confidently engaging the look of the

"Indiana Jones and the Last Crusade" (Courtesy of Lucasfilm Ltd. TM & © Lucasfilm, Ltd. (LFL) 1989. All Rights Reserved.

viewer ('Yes, I *know* I've got it'), while the father seeks to dominate him from behind. The father's beady sidelong stare perfectly mingles self-regarding pride ('my son, chip off the old block') and suspicion ('if he thinks he's got it, he may use it against me').

In *Indiana Jones and the Last Crusade* the feminine side of masculinity is 12 associated with books and scholarship, the masculine side, as so often, with physical aggression. Jones Junior partakes of both since he is the scholarly gent with glasses and no hat who turns into the violently active hero with fedora hat and bullwhip. Relatively, in terms of behaviour, Jones Senior is feminized, an eccentric academic, an archaeologist over-concerned with books, fragile with age, wearing granny glasses, whose voice occasionally breaks up an octave. Yet he is still capable of masculinized action in his own way; at one point he raises his umbrella to frighten a flock of seagulls into the path of an attacking Messerschmitt.

The love between them cannot speak its name. When a brief lull in the 13 action leaves them drinking together in a bar, Indiana tells his father 'You never talked to me'; Jones replies, 'OK, let's talk'—but they can't find anything to say. Their love is expressed through the action; father sometimes saves son, but mostly the son saves his father. In fact, Indiana firmly risks life and limb to get hold of the Grail so he can heal the old man's wound. It is also negotiated by their banter, especially in the way Jones Senior keeps calling his son 'Junior'. He therefore refuses to accord him a name and place of his own (Indiana) by insisting he is only a qualified repetition of himself.

The intensity of their relationship leaves little room for Indiana's heter- 14 osexual desires. After he has proved his masculinity with 'the girl' (Alison Doody, androgynously named in the film as 'Dr. Schneider'), she turns out to be a Nazi, and falls to her death trying to get hold of the Grail for herself. She is not much more than an object in exchange and joke between the two men. When the father warns the son against 'the girl' because she's a Nazi, Indiana asks 'How do you know?' and is told 'She talks in her sleep.'

Banter or repartee as a masculine style is effective by operating a double 15 bluff. Because it is comic and relies on the joke form it seems to be genial, permissive and open. It is not in fact genial because it actully supports the aggression of the masculine ego. And it is not open because it sets out to protect the male bond—sublimated homosexual desire—and exclude women.

THE WOMEN OF *CHINA BEACH*

◑

CYNTHIA A. HANSON

In 1988, the television series "China Beach" made its
debut as a revolutionary drama presenting the "female
perspective" on the Vietnam war. This essay by Cynthia Hanson, written while she was a doctoral student
in speech communications at the University of Minnesota and first published in the *Journal of Popular Film
and Television* in 1990, analyzes the show's portrayal of
both gender and war.

Clad in a poppy-red bathing suit, the woman stretches out on the beach. A
closeup reveals her toes digging lazily into the sand. The camera pans slowly
up her smooth, toned calves and thighs to her face, which is shielded by
sunglasses. The sound of an approaching helicopter disturbs her reading, and
she lowers her head. The next shot tracks her marching resolutely from the
beach, oblivious to the wolf whistles from the men around her. She enters
her hut, removes her sunglasses, and slips into her gown. As she steps to the
doorway, her face is flooded with light and her hair is blown back by the wind
from the landing chopper. The camera assumes her point of view and zooms
in on the broken, twisted bodies that soldiers are rushing frantically to unload.

Such is the viewer's introduction to Nurse Colleen McMurphy in the
telefilm *China Beach*. The film served as the pilot for the current ABC series
that—according to a network press release—depicts the "drama about the
unsung heroism of American women in Vietnam."[1] Film and television portrayals of U.S. involvement in the Vietnam war have virtually excluded mention of women who served their country. Programming that gives voice to
the experiences shared by the approximately 50,000 nurses, entertainers, Red
Cross volunteers, and other women who were there is welcome and long
overdue.[2] From a feminist perspective, however, the portrayal of the women
of *China Beach* is highly problematic, as the telefilm's opening scene might
suggest. . . .*

China Beach was created by writer John Sacret Young and William
Broyles, Jr., former editor-in-chief for *Newsweek* magazine. Young's concept

---

* This essay is an edited version of the original. Footnotes after this point in the text have been
renumbered. [Editor's note]

of the program, which was referenced frequently in the publicity surrounding the show, was that of "a women's steam bath in the middle of a men's locker room."[3] Broyles, a veteran, illustrated his belief in the importance of the women's effort with a description of his encounter with a Red Cross volunteer while he was serving in Vietnam with the Marine Corps: "I couldn't say a word when I saw that 'doughnut dolly.' I was in awe of them. Just to see an American woman was a powerful sort of symbol. After the life I'd been living out in the jungle, and all that she represented, you felt at least somebody cares."[4] Although seven women who served in Vietnam act as advisors to the show, its concept is the product of men. Young's description of the show as an essentially female equivalent of the male Vietnam experience (women's steam bath=men's locker room) and Broyles's idealized vision of the woman as "a powerful sort of symbol" suggest that rather than a depiction of women's experiences, *China Beach* might be two men's approximation of the female presence in Vietnam.

Because of its unique concept, *China Beach* received a great deal of advance press, the majority of it favorable.[5] The publicity, which allowed Broyles and Young to articulate their rationale for the series, clearly attempted to establish *China Beach* as emanating from a female perspective. The marketing of the show as a women's series is succinctly summed up by an advertisement in *TV Guide*: 4

---■---

50,000 American women
volunteered to serve in
Vietnam.
This is the war.
The way they saw it.[6]

---■---

The photographs accompanying the copy, however, hint at a different perspective. Full-page advertisements in *TV Guide* feature the women of *China Beach* clad only in bathing suits. One photograph features Nurse McMurphy standing next to a bare-chested man; they both are smiling invitingly as McMurphy makes the sign of "thumbs up." Another photograph depicts McMurphy and USO singer Laurette Barber reclining on the sand beneath a lifeguard tower. Both women smile and direct their gaze toward the lifeguard, who is not visible (he is represented by a rifle and a life preserver bearing the name "China Beach," both hanging from the tower). Meanwhile, a man in shorts and a woman in a bathing suit frug happily in the background. In both cases, the women are depicted as nonprofessional, physical, inviting, and protected by men. The most egregious example of a publicity photograph that undercuts the show's ostensible message appeared in *Rolling Stone* magazine: an article about the show is accompanied by an overhead shot of 5

McMurphy seductively reclining on a gurney, one hand wrapped around an IV stand, the other caressing the exposed section of midriff where her olive-drab t-shirt has separated from her fatigue pants.[7] The publicity alone would indicate that the viewer ought to expect mixed messages about the role of women in the Vietnam war.

The telefilm pilot of *China Beach* focuses on the experiences of four women. McMurphy is introduced first. A short-timer, she has seven days remaining in her tour of duty. While clearly competent (several scenes show her at work, assisting in surgery, performing triage, and so on), she has "gone robot" and is numb to both the horrors of war and the supportive friends around her. Similar to characters revealed in nonfictional, woman-authored accounts of the war (see, for example, Lynda Van Devanter's *Home Before Morning*), she also epitomizes the television character type identified by Kalisch et al. as the "professional nurse."[8] The next character shown is Red Cross volunteer Cherry White, whose name is an apt descriptor. The viewer first sees her on the plane en route to Vietnam, where she is the target of a pickup attempt by an ambassador's aide. A "doughnut dolly" from Iowa, she is naive, incompetent, and victimized in the course of the show. Her portrayal is consistent with television's penchant for portraying "nursing students, candy-stripers, and recently graduated nurses . . . as very naive and clumsy rookies who need constant supervision. . . ."[9] She also has an ulterior motive for going to Vietnam: to find her brother.

The second newcomer to China Beach is Laurette Barber, a backup singer in a "girl group." Her essential loneliness and low self-image is heightened by the references of others to the lead singer as the "looker" of the group. She eagerly anticipates her tour of Vietnam as a "men-o-rama." An orphan from Paoli, Pennsylvania, her brash manner, wacky clothes, and reference to experiences with "a long list of Pennsylvania bar juiceheads" suggest that she is the Sally Bowles type: apolitical, good natured, soiled but vulnerable.

The final character is K.C., the entrepreneurial "good-time bad girl" who "graduated" from her status as doughnut dolly and now provides "a *real* service" to the fighting men. As a result of her efforts, China Beach—a combination R & R station and medical unit—can offer comforts to soldiers that go beyond the Koolaid, doughnuts, and board game available in the rec center.

All four women represent instantly recognizable character types, which is not surprising, given television's fundamental (and economically motivated) conservatism. In Meehan's catalog of women characters on television, McMurphy, Cherry White, Laurette Barber, and K.C. would inhabit the categories of harpy, victim, imp, and courtesan, respectively.[10] The fit between the characters of *China Beach* and easily identified stereotypes of women is an indicator of their essentially traditional conception. The roles also represent various degrees of the most fundamental and oppressive polarization in the depiction of women: the virgin-whore dichotomy. The dichotomy exists in its traditional form and is replicated in the relative positions of newcomer and veteran. . . . Cherry and K.C. represent the newcomer-virgin and the veteran-whore, respectively. McMurphy, who is "soiled" by her experience in the war, spurns male advances in the manner of a "virgin." Barber, who makes no secret of her desire for men, is a "virgin" to Vietnam.

The virgin-whore opposition has been described by Ellen Seiter as the [10] "conventional melodramatic treatment of women" in which "the positive characterization of a female character was achieved through comparison to another female character who was morally condemned, thus emphasizing normative definitions of women's roles."[11] Characterization consistent with traditional portrayals of women would highlight and isolate female characters in the *virgin* and *whore* categories, most likely through comparison of opposites. However, subversion of that "normativeness" could occur in the narrative as events and interaction between characters can increase the potential for character development beyond the conventional types. Noting the patterns of this interaction makes possible the identification of the underlying messages of *China Beach*.

Even the *amount* and *direction* of the interaction between female charac- [11] ters—apart from the content—would suggest that the telefilm is perpetuating traditional characterizations of women by the juxtaposition of the most extreme representatives of virgins and whores . . . Sixty-seven percent (or 15:17) of the interaction between the four female characters takes place between the newcomer-virgin Cherry and the veteran-whore K.C. Twenty-five percent (5:40) occurs between the veteran-virgin McMurphy and the newcomer-whore Laurette. There is little interaction *within* the virgin and whore categories: newcomers, veterans, and whores do not interact at all with one another. Significantly, the only intra-category interaction—between virgins Cherry and McMurphy—involves a blatant reference to their object status (this will be discussed later).

The amount, direction, and content of interaction among the four main [12] female characters support three generalizations about the women of *China Beach*.

1. Veterans take on the characteristics of newcomers. A round, developing char- [13] acter is bound to change as a result of her exposure to and interaction with others. In the K.C.-Cherry dyad, the change in K.C.'s character becomes clear in her behavior at a reception at the U.S. embassy. She arrives at the party with Cherry, who hopes to receive information about her brother from the ambassador's aide. K.C.'s protective questioning of Cherry shows her concern: Are you sure you want to do this? Are you sure you know what you're doing?" When they enter the embassy, Cherry finds the aide, and K.C. spots the China Beach lifeguard. K.C.'s conversation with the lifeguard indicates that their relationship has a history that went beyond physical intimacy. He asks her when she plans to retire and makes disparaging references to the monetary aspect of their relationship. Her response is bitter: "I'm just a one-stop full-service center. I went from a bad pimp to a good one—the U.S. Armed Forces, war in Vietnam." "Keep telling yourself that," he responds. "I'm never gonna buy it." Whether the last statement refers to his inability to accept her description of herself as a "service center" or his refusal to "buy" her love is unclear. Nevertheless, K.C.'s feelings for the lifeguard, the occurrence of the exchange at a party where she initially acts as Cherry's chaperone, and the change in her behavior toward Cherry suggest that she is taking on some of the vulnerability that is one of Cherry's most prominent traits.

The transformation of McMurphy, facilitated by Laurette, is far more 14 blatant and disconcerting. In the McMurphy-Laurette narrative thread, McMurphy initially rejects Laurette's friendly overtures, but they establish a bond through their knowledge of lyrics to popular songs. Eventually, they open up to each other about their lives in the States and make a bargain that sets up the climax of the show. The bargain results in the metamorphosis of McMurphy from professional nurse to love object. The groundwork for this change is laid during a surprise farewell party thrown by the medical staff. The convivial atmosphere is destroyed by Austin, a chopper pilot whose romantic overtures McMurphy has repeatedly rebuffed. He tells her that although he'd like to get to know her—even the "hot and sexy" part of her— it is clearly time for her to go home because she's "gone robot." He leaves, and the room is silent. The next two shots show the chopper rising into the sky and McMurphy's face, eyes skyward, as she watches Austin's departure. Her closeup is gauzy and diffused, and a melancholy piano and harmonica accompany the scene.

The "feminization" of McMurphy continues in the following scene 15 where, inexplicably, she sits alone in her hooch wearing a tight off-the-shoulder mini-dress and black stiletto heels. McMurphy's contemplative mood leads her to the beach, where she encounters Laurette. They talk about their lives in the States. Laurette attempts to persuade her to sing backup in the show that evening (the "looker," felled by dysentery, has long since departed the camp, leaving Laurette to sing lead). "You'll love it," she wheedles. "Men *everywhere*. You wouldn't *believe* what a huge dose of unadulterated male lust can do for your outlook on life." McMurphy reluctantly consents but tells Laurette that she must promise to help in the hospital on the last night.

The metamorphosis of McMurphy is depicted in detail. Laurette gives 16 her a silver lamé mini-dress, a push-up bra, tights, go-go boots, and a brunette fall. She shows her how to hike her skirt for maximum exposure. The performance itself is depicted in a series of shots alternating between an audience view of the stage and closeups of the male audience members. When McMurphy is recognized, the men begin shouting her name, cheering, and applauding. Laurette pushes her to center stage. The melancholy piano theme overtakes the song of the performance, the camera slowly moves from a medium shot to a closeup, and McMurphy begins to cry; certainly not the response of a robot. The dominance of the melancholy theme and the un-interrupted singing and cheering barely audible in the background indicate that the viewer has entered McMurphy's subjective reality. The operation of narcissistic voyeurism is apparent; as the viewer identifies with McMurphy, she is objectified and fetishized through the performance setting and the closeup. The music of the performance is foregrounded again for only a few seconds before a bomb shakes the building and cuts the electricity. Never-theless, McMurhy's transformation is complete: By appearing on stage in the costume of a go-go girl and receiving "a huge dose of unadulterated male lust," she has restored her ability to cry and disproved the horny pilot's accusation of "going robot."

Although the bombing ends the performance and forces McMurphy to return to the horrors of the hospital, her decision to remain at China Beach at the end of her tour is no surprise. The next morning, she sits reflectively in the wreckage of her bombed-out hooch and announces her decision to stay: "I have an even bigger family here . . . I *am* home." Her on-stage experience of the previous evening is clearly instrumental in her decision. Her perception of the audience-performer relationship as "family" suggests that the family supports woman-as-spectacle. It also echoes television's crea-tion of the family to foster unity between viewer and viewed and mask the voyeurism encouraged by the images.[12]

2. Newcomers do not take on the characteristics of veterans. Although one might expect the newcomers to change with their experiences in the war, they do not. Cherry remains the naive victim. The ambassador's aide claims to have information about her brother, but this is a ploy to get her alone in his jeep. He lunges for her. She bites his hand and escapes, running hysterically through the jungle in her pink party dress and heels. Finally, she is rescued by a beefy, filthy, taciturn soldier who had stared at her at the rec center and remarked upon her "round eyes." The only time that Cherry appears in the program after her rescue is at the USO show, where she arrives arm in arm with her beefy soldier. The only change apparent for the Cherry character is her acquisition of a protector.

Nor does Laurette Barber appear to be markedly changed by her expe-rience. To uphold her end of the "bargain," she assists McMurphy in the hospital during the bombing. McMurphy commends her the next morning for "being there" for the men, but her compassion appears to be the result of her encounter with one badly burned soldier. They joke about a USO singer with a nice voice and a great "set of knockers" of whom he has a photograph. With his last breath, the dying man begs Laurette to fish the snapshot out of his pocket. It is a picture of her. She holds his hand and begins to cry, choking in her attempt to sing "I Believe" for him. While her tears certainly are the product of compassion, at least part of her sorrow comes from the realization that the one man who adores her sufficiently to carry her photo (he adores her image, not her person; he does not even know her) in his wallet is about to die. Her compassion, ultimately, is expressed in song; the hospital becomes the site of another "performance." The next morning, there is no suggestion that she will continue to minister to the wounded, and she is incredulous at McMurphy's decision to remain at China Beach. (In fact, Laurette's involvement in the war effort in the six episodes of the series in which her character appears consists entirely of her attempts to become a "star" and leave China Beach.) For Laurette, the war still seems to be the "men-o-rama" that she eagerly anticipated at the beginning.

3. Whores call attention to the object status of virgins. When Cherry inter- 20 rupts K.C. at her "work" and expresses disgust (a scene that titillates viewers while allowing them to participate in Cherry's disapproval), K.C. calls Cherry a tease in her short little Red Cross uniform and says "we both do the same thing" for the soldiers. Laurette identifies McMurphy as "Competition Number One" in the "men-o-rama": "Body like Monroe, hair like silk, heart as big probably as all America." McMurphy protests that she is "just one of the guys." The camera's exploration of the bathing-suit-clad McMurphy on the beach has already proved otherwise, and her participation in the musical performance cements her position as object of the male gaze within the narrative as well as of the (male) camera. Curiously, the tendency of the women to point out to one another their status as objects sanctions the television viewer's voyeurism. The viewer can sympathize—indeed, *identify*— with the virgin's status as an object while receiving pleasure from regarding her. . . .

Of course, objectification is not unique to the virgins, nor are the whores 21 the only figures to call attention to this status. The welcoming speech given to the newcomers by the special services officer addresses the need for women to keep "their hair short and their skirts long." The women's status as objects is reflected in the male responses to them, ranging from harassment (the ambassador's lecherous aide, the doctor who pinches McMurphy at the operating table and the USO singers at the bar) to adoration (Cherry's protector, Laurette's dying soldier, the male audience at the USO performance).

In many cases, the camera's gaze replicates that of the male character. 22 The introduction of each female character depicts her as an object of fascination. The camera's slow examination of McMurphy on the beach fetishizes her physical image. Cherry's first appearance is as the object of the gaze of the ambassador's aide, a position established by a reverse-shot setup of the ambassador preparing to take his seat on the plane and a cut to Cherry seated and looking out the window. (Furthermore, he initially mistakes her for an entertainer.) The USO singers are introduced shortly afterwards with a shot that begins at their knees and slowly moves to their faces. The effect is similar to that of the introduction of McMurphy.

The fascination with women's legs continues in the first shot of K.C. Her [23] presence during the special services officer's speech is first signaled by the click of her high heels. The shot shifts from the faces of the USO singers to K.C.'s feet, shod in slides with embroidered vamps that read "Viet Nam." (The two parts of the name are placed so that the viewer can read the name correctly only when K.C.'s legs are crossed.) The camera pans her scantily clad body, reaching her face just in time to catch her exhaling a puff of cigarette smoke. She leans seductively against the doorframe until the officer makes a disparaging remark about her morals.

This scene is characteristic of the contradictory message that *China Beach* [24] conveys: The camera continually presents the woman as pleasurable object, yet the viewer is expected to condemn her status as such. This expectation is most apparent in the unsympathetic portrayal of the harassing men and the women's willingness to defend themselves. Cherry bites her attacker, and McMurphy mouths off to the surgeon. When the surgeon (appropriately named Dick Richard) gooses Laurette in the bar, she responds by thanking him and squeezing his crotch until he doubles over. The effect of these scenes is to allow the viewer to participate in the voyeurism as the on-screen voyeurs are chastised.

The scene that epitomizes this paradox occurs on the plane, where a [25] soldier attempts to coerce a stewardess into helping him with his seatbelt. She whips out a switchblade and warns him, "If I find anything else hanging around down here, I'm gonna cut it off and take it with me." This scene seems to serve no narrative point except to add humor and to establish that women are equipped to deal with male harassment. However, the latter purpose of the scene is largely undercut by the camera's fixation on the rump of the stewardess throughout the exchange.

The objectification of the women of *China Beach* occurs on two levels. [26] The women are addressed as objects within the *narrative*. The sole exception to this is K.C., perhaps because she is already aware of and willing to manipulate her fascination for men for profit. This is both threatening to the male spectator and uncomfortably similar to the television apparatus, which itself manipulates images for economic gain. Instead, the potential of K.C. to relinquish the rewards of her status is presented at the embassy reception. All four women, however, are addressed as objects by the *camera*.

Although detailed analysis of subsequent episodes of *China Beach* is be- [27] yond the scope of this work, tentative exploration suggests that their portrayal of women has been consistent with the patterns established in the pilot tele-film, the introduction of new characters and the departure of old ones notwithstanding. The arrival of Airman Wayloo Marie Holmes is a near substitution for the departed Laurette Barber. Like Laurette, Holmes is sexually aggressive and an ambitious performer; with microphone in hand and cameraman in tow, she perpetually searches for material for a story that will be her ticket to a job with the Armed Forces Network. Her interaction with

McMurphy is marked by hostility; McMurphy fears Holmes will abuse the affections of Dr. Richard. Holmes assumes the position of newcomer-whore vacated by Laurette and serves as a reminder of McMurphy's "virgin" status (at least, where Dr. Richard is concerned).

Because the pilot telefilm depicted McMurphy's emotional "thaw," her romantic activity during the 1988–89 season is not surprising. She becomes involved to varying degrees with Austin, the figher pilot; Hyams, a young medic; Dodger, a soldier; and Dr. Richard. (As the 1989–90 season begins, she is contemplating a liaison with a French doctor.) All of these entanglements provide a rationale for McMurphy to don beachwear or evening clothes, allowing the camera and the viewer to continue the exploration of McMurphy's body begun in the pilot. Although McMurphy seems to have relinquished her "virgin" status by the end of the season, her "purity" finds an outlet in expressions of disgust concerning K.C.'s heroin addiction, paralleling Cherry's earlier shock at K.C.'s sexual conduct. 28

The episodes that explore K.C.'s addiction are also the last to feature Cherry. Cherry's death follows a scene where she offered comfort to a panicked fellow doughnut dolly and admitted that she was no longer frightened by the war. Her display of courage and maturity reveals her transcendence of her newcomer-virgin status; she is subsequently blasted at the entrance to a foxhole. 29

Cherry's death is compensated not by the introduction of a similar character but by fundamental changes in the character of K.C., her polar opposite in the virgin-whore dichotomy. In the pilot, the character of Cherry serves to both condemn and soften K.C. In Cherry's absence, the character of K.C. continues to soften and does little worthy of condemnation. Although her work as a prostitute is foregrounded in the pilot, this aspect of her character all but disappears in later episodes as she becomes an all-purpose "entrepreneur," dabbling in the black market and opening up a beauty salon. She becomes a junkie, but several episodes later she goes straight, kicking the habit back in the States while escorting Cherry's body home. (Cherry's goodness apparently is sufficiently potent to transcend the grave.) The character of K.C., potentially radical in its representation of a woman in the sex industry, becomes merely a "bad girl" who does shady business. 30

China Beach has introduced additional female regulars (Mai, a Vietnamese who falls in love with the hospital mortician; Frankie Bunsen, a black disc jockey) and has expanded the role of others (Lila Garreau, a career Army officer). Each woman has been objectified to varying degrees. Mai, an unspoiled native woman, is a stereotype. Frankie, in "All About E.E.V.," is coerced into performing on stage in gold lamé. In the same episode, Lila's anxiety about menopause is salved by her successful competition with Wayloo and K.C. for the amorous attentions of a visiting officer. 31

Perhaps the clearest evidence of the lack of change in the portrayal of the women of *China Beach* is the episode "Vets." This show juxtaposes snap- 32 shots and interviews of women who had served in Vietnam with clips from previous episodes in an attempt to authenticate the series. The majority of the clips included in this episode are from the pilot, and the longest clips are those of McMurphy on stage in go-go gear and Laurette singing in the hospital; *performances*, where objectification of women is most troubling. The narration accompanying these clips features veterans discussing the importance of women's efforts to boost soldier morale. The effect of the juxtaposition of narration and image transcends authentication of the series; indeed, the commentary elevates viewer participation in objectification to the status of a patriotic act.

That *China Beach* perpetuates ways of looking at women that are deeply disturbing to feminists is clear. The underlying message of the pilot telefilm is this: The woman in war can lose her sense of self. She can be rehabilitated by becoming desirable and desired sexually. Each of the four women of *China Beach* represents a character type familiar to television viewers and assumes the role of "virgin" or "whore" with respect to men or to the war. Such roles inaccurately represent the women involved in the war and women in general. Voyeuristic viewers of *China Beach* get the best of both worlds: They can enjoy women as spectacle while participating in their on-screen attempts to escape that position by combating their harassers. The viewers identify with the characters in their efforts to escape objectification—by individual men or by war in general, which separates men and women and encourages the former to view the latter as that for which they fight. The unity of the television "I" and the viewer "You" against the objectifying "They" conceals the fact that the viewer, too, receives pleasure from the women's object status.[13]

"I have an even bigger family here," says McMurphy. "This is my home." Her decision to remain at China Beach enables the series to continue and explicitly acknowledges the importance of the narrative "family." The "family" of viewers is encouraged to reach a parallel decision. However, the viewer who does so believing that the show gives voice to feminist perspectives on the experiences of women in Vietnam has bought into a fiction as illusory as the peaceful white sands of China Beach.

Notes

1. John J. O'Connor, "'China Beach,' Women at War," *New York Times*, 26 April 1988, Sec. C, p. 18.

2. Mark Morrison, "'China Beach' Salutes the Women of Vietnam," *Rolling Stone*, 19 May 1988, p. 76.

3. See, for example, Morrison, 19 May 1988; Matt Rush, "Vietnam's Prime-Time Hour of Duty," *USA Today*, 26 April 1988, Sec. D, p. 3.

4. Rush, 26 April, 1988, Sec. D, p. 3.

5. See, for example, Monica Collins, "Women and War Hit the 'Beach,'" *USA Today*, 26 April 1988, Sec. D, p. 1; *Daily Variety*, 26 April 1988, p. 10; O'Connor, 26 April 1988, Sec. C, p. 18;

People, 23 April 1988, p. 11; Howard Rosenberg, "Women in War," *Los Angeles Times*, 26 April 1988, Sec. 6, p. 1; *TV Guide*, 23–29 April 1988, p. A81.

6. *TV Guide*, 23–29 April 1988, p. A108.

7. Morrison, p. 75.

8. Lynda Van Devanter, *Home Before Morning: The Story of an Army Nurse in Vietnam* (New York: Beaufort, 1983); Philip A. Kalisch, Beatrice J. Kalisch, and Margaret Scobey, *Images of Nurses on Television* (New York: Springer, 1983), pp. 195–200.

9. Kalisch et al., p. 177.

10. Meehan.

11. Ellen Seiter, "The Political Is Personal: Margarethe von Trotta's *Marianne and Julianne*," *Journal of Film and Video*, 37, No. 2 (Spring 1985), p. 15.

12. Ellis, p. 135.

13. Ellis noted television's tendency to adopt the direct address "I" in speaking to the viewer "You" about "They" groups such as blacks and housewives. The result of this opposition is the unity of "I/You" and the inability of the consensus to recognize that it may rightfully belong to "They." Ellis, pp. 139–140. The "I/You" unity seems to have a similar masking effect in *China Beach*; they may not recognize their participation in the objectification of women.

MAKING CONNECTIONS

1. Analyze the instances of sexism and homophobia discussed by Lee and Solomon. Try reversing the allusions to refer to men or heterosexuals—for instance, imagine Billy Packer commenting on a male basketball player's pleasant face and future home life, or Tom Brokaw announcing George Bush's inseam length. What happens?

2. Study one news station, financial network, newspaper, or news magazine and take notes on who seems to have which jobs—reporters, anchors, editors, "experts" (analysts, columnists, commentators). How do these jobs divide up according to gender and race? Do you find any conspicuous omissions (like Fong-Torres' example of the invisible Asian male) or special groupings (like pairing minority anchors with white anchors or men with women) or predictable assignments (men reporting on sports or politics, women reporting "lifestyle" or soft news)? Which positions seem to have the most power in "constructing national reality" and who fills those jobs? In the form of a letter to the editor or station manager, write an evaluation of the network or newspaper you've chosen.

3. Lee and Solomon analyze the ways in which abortion is reported and discussed on the news. They conclude that the press seems to lack a balanced view and sufficient coverage of important, related issues such as sex education and birth control. Do you agree or disagree with their assessment? How would you evaluate the press's coverage of other topics, such as homelessness, crime, illness, or drugs? Does the news focus merely on the sensational aspects of social debates, as Lee and Solomon suggest? Or do you feel the press does try to present underlying problems or solutions? In your own experience, how well do you feel the media provides you with informed, objective coverage? Write an essay that expresses and gives evidence for your point of view.

4. Compare and contrast Gloria Steinem's essay "The Politics of Talking in Groups" (Chapter 4) with Lee and Solomon's point about male voices dominating the media and deciding what the issues are. Are there any points of connection between interpersonal conversation and the nationwide "conversation" of media coverage? How feasible is an analogy between the two?

5. Streep lists a number of reasons for the "disappearance" of women from the movies. How might film and literature be similar in this respect? Imagine a dialogue between Streep and Dale Spender (Chapter 5) on the representation of women in culture. Where might they agree or disagree?

6. What are your own feelings about the motion picture industry—does it speak to and reflect your own interests and realities, or are there things

you would like to see represented in the movies that are not currently covered? Write a review of a recent film you felt "spoke to you" or represented an issue well and one that did not. Discuss your choices in class—are there any areas of disagreement among your classmates?

7. Using Deborah Tannen's study in Chapter 4 ("Sex, Lies and Conversation"), expand and develop Anthony Easthope's analysis of masculine communication styles like banter. What insights can Tannen's study bring to the evaluation of film images? Do the images of male communication, conflict, and bonding in the movies simply reflect established ways of being, or do you think they help shape how men learn to relate to each other?

8. Compare Maio's essay with the messages conveyed in fairy tales (Chapter 7). What lessons seem to be the same? Can you think of other movies that illustrate Maio's point about the sanctity of the family and the dangers of independent women? Are there any films that challenge Maio's point?

9. Compare the images of mothers and daughters with the images of fathers and sons in popular culture—what is the difference, say, between Sara Maitland's analysis of mothers and daughters (Chapter 7) and Easthope's view of the father-son bond? What do these relationships have in common with each other, and where do they diverge? To what extent are parent-child relationships (or our expectations for them) created by mass media images? Do you think they might profit by being changed? Why or why not?

10. Write an essay that analyzes the roles of women in "masculine" films like Westerns, police dramas, or action-adventure movies. How does Easthope's analysis compare with your own? Are there any parallels with the roles of men in productions meant primarily for a female audience, such as soap opera or romance? Use examples to explain and support your points.

11. Using Hanson's evaluation of "China Beach" as a model, analyze other dramas about professional women, either on television or in film. Are the women depicted as true professionals, or are they stereotypes? Compare your findings to television or print advertisements that use images of professional women. What products are being sold? What do these images convey? Write a descriptive essay on the media's image of professional women that presents your findings.

12. How is homosexuality depicted in television and film? As a class, you might view and analyze a movie like *Longtime Companion*, *Desert Hearts*, *Maurice*, or *My Beautiful Laundrette* and discuss the representation of homosexuality in film. How might you recast Jane Rule's essay (Chapter 5) to apply to the way movies make "the real visible"?

10
ART AND
ADVERTISING

C O N T E X T S

One of the earliest and most detailed studies of gender images in popular culture was conducted by social scientist Erving Goffman. In 1976, his book *Gender Advertisements* gave readers a model and a vocabulary with which to examine the social and psychological nature of advertising images, particularly those representing men and women. Goffman posited that advertisements present more than just a static image or depiction of a product. Rather, they display an entire "scene" made up of the most minute elements—gesture, expression, posture, mood, placement—constituting a vivid script of social arrangements and behaviors. The reason advertising is so magnetic to viewers is that as social beings we are constantly engaged in the project of defining ourselves and our relation to others—a lifelong process of learning, so to speak, who we are. Advertising attracts us, not because we have an intense fascination for toothpaste or floor wax, but because it sends out clear and vivid messages about how to act, feel, and be in any situation.

Goffman gives the example of a family on vacation, taking its cues for what "having a good time" is about from idealized ads depicting happy families on vacation. Long after the product (soft drinks, rental cars, or suntan lotion) has been forgotten, these messages about how ideal people act are remembered. The "product" sold wasn't really Coca-Cola or Avis, but "having fun"—specifically, how people who *are* having fun look and act. The use of gender in advertising can be described in much the same way. What is most lastingly

383

"sold" to viewers is not perfume, but femininity, not a sportscar, but an image of manliness. Of course, the advertiser's interest is in making money, hoping the ad will link the product closely enough to the mood or message to convince us to buy the item. But what remains most powerfully, whether or not we purchase the Ferrari or Chanel No. 5, is the lesson that "this is how men and women *are,* or want to be, or should be."

Goffman's study looks specifically at how femininity is depicted in advertisements through the use of women's gestures, body postures, expressions, and their physical placement in relation to men. In photograph after photograph, he shows women posed to convey messages of powerlessness, subordination, dreaminess, and especially childishness, displaying all of the physical gestures and postures we usually associate with children. We see adult women with babyish pouts, the head wistfully cocked to the side or tucked down, eyes looking up in a "seductive-gamin" style, displaying clownish gestures and facial expressions of mischief or childish glee. Above all, Goffman comments on the sensation of women being perpetually on display, conscious of and available to the unseen viewer.

This concept of women as objects for display is not new to twentieth-century advertising. The first essay in our chapter reflects on the history of art and the female nude in painting to show the objectification of women under the power of the male gaze. What is the difference between a man's social "presence" and that of a woman as depicted in art? John Berger's famous television series *Ways of Seeing,* from which this excerpt is taken, was groundbreaking in demonstrating how visual representation can be used to understand culture.

In our next essay, "A Gentleman and a Consumer," Diane Barthel examines images of men in advertisements and definitions of masculinity conveyed by the advertising industry. Barthel argues that ads geared toward a male audience speak to men's discriminating judgment as consumers, their sense of competitiveness and power, and the "masculine" privilege of ownership. She also looks at the ways some of these images might be changing to include men in the more "feminized" market of grooming and beauty items. In the end, however, Barthel concludes that the masculine imperatives of independence, adventure, competition, and "cool" remain intact in the advertising world.

Another area of gender representation that has received a great deal of attention is the "body-beautiful" industry for women. Incessant information about diets, cosmetics, body-structuring exercises, even surgery, make up the foundation of a booming advice industry for women in our society, creating a near-obsessive focus on achieving the "perfect" female body. Rosalind Coward looks at the social fears and perceptions about women that underlie this relentless drive toward "The Body Beautiful."

What impact might culture's emphasis on youth and physical perfection have on the fragile, complex experience of love? In our next selection, poet Robert Hass offers an allegory of human contact through his prose poem, "A Story About the Body." With delicacy and grace, Hass touches on the impact of image and how it sometimes conflicts with real emotion.

Finally, in our closing essay, Wendy Chapkis expands the horizons of the beauty industry to cover its impact on Third World and non-Western countries. "Skin Deep" looks at how advertisers market the "white, Western and wealthy" image of The Good Life throughout the world, raising important issues about race, class, and gender in the advertising industry. Taken together, this chapter's essays offer the beginnings of a deeper look at the image industry—how it works, who it affects, what it conveys.

WAYS OF SEEING

◐

JOHN BERGER

John Berger's landmark public television series and its companion book *Ways of Seeing* (1973) began a revolution in the ways we analyze art, advertising, and popular images throughout our culture. In this excerpted famous chapter, Berger looks at representations of the female figure as the eternal object of the male gaze. Berger's writings include many other books on art, photography, and culture, such as *The Look of Things* (1975), *Another Way of Telling* (1982), and *The Sense of Sight* (1985).

Reclining Bacchante by Felix Trutat, 1824–48 (*Musée des Beaux Arts, Dijon*)

According to usage and conventions which are at last being questioned but have by no means been overcome, the social presence of a woman is different in kind from that of a man. A man's presence is dependent upon the promise of power which he embodies. If the promise is large and credible his presence is striking. If it is small or incredible, he is found to have little presence. The promised power may be moral, physical, temperamental, economic, social, sexual—but its object is always exterior to the man. A man's presence suggests what he is capable of doing to you or for you. His presence may be fabricated, in the sense that he pretends to be capable of what he is not. But the pretence is always towards a power which he exercises on others.

By contrast, a woman's presence expresses her own attitude to herself, and defines what can and cannot be done to her. Her presence is manifest in her gestures, voice, opinions, expressions, clothes, chosen surroundings, taste—indeed there is nothing she can do which does not contribute to her presence. Presence for a woman is so intrinsic to her person that men tend to think of it as an almost physical emanation, a kind of heat or smell or aura. 2

To be born a woman has been to be born, within an allotted and confined space, into the keeping of men. The social presence of women has developed as a result of their ingenuity in living under such tutelage within such a limited space. But this has been at the cost of a woman's self being split into two. A woman must continually watch herself. She is almost continually accompanied by her own image of herself. Whilst she is walking across a room or whilst she is weeping at the death of her father, she can scarcely avoid envisaging herself walking or weeping. From earliest childhood she has been taught and persuaded to survey herself continually. 3

And so she comes to consider the *surveyor* and the *surveyed* within her as the two constituent yet always distinct elements of her identity as a woman. 4

She has to survey everything she is and everything she does because how she appears to others, and ultimately how she appears to men, is of crucial importance for what is normally thought of as the success of her life. Her own sense of being in herself is supplanted by a sense of being appreciated as herself by another. 5

Men survey women before treating them. Consequently how a woman appears to a man can determine how she will be treated. To acquire some control over this process, women must contain it and interiorize it. That part of a woman's self which is the surveyor treats the part which is the surveyed so as to demonstrate to others how her whole self would like to be treated. And this exemplary treatment of herself by herself constitutes her presence. Every woman's presence regulates what is and is not 'permissible' within her presence. Every one of her actions—whatever its direct purpose or motivation—is also read as an indication of how she would like to be treated. If a woman throws a glass on the floor, this is an example of how she treats her own emotion of anger and so of how she would wish it to be treated by others. If a man does the same, his action is only read as an expression of his anger. If a woman makes a good joke this is an example of how she treats the joker in herself and accordingly of how she as a joker-woman would like to be treated by others. Only a man can make a good joke for its own sake. 6

One might simplify this by saying: *men act* and *women appear*. Men look
at women. Women watch themselves being looked at. This determines not
only most relations between men and women but also the relation of women
to themselves. The surveyor of woman in herself is male: the surveyed female.
Thus she turns herself into an object—and most particularly an object of
vision: a sight.

In one category of European oil painting women were the principal, ever-
recurring subject. That category is the nude. In the nudes of European painting we can discover some of the criteria and conventions by which women
have been seen and judged as sights.

The first nudes in the tradition depicted Adam and Eve. It is worth
referring to the story as told in Genesis:

> And when the woman saw that the tree was good for food, and that it was a
> delight to the eyes, and that the tree was to be desired to make one wise,
> she took of the fruit thereof and did eat; and she gave also unto her husband
> with her, and he did eat.
>
> And the eyes of them both were opened, and they knew that they were
> naked; and they sewed fig-leaves together and made themselves aprons. . . .
> And the Lord God called unto the man and said unto him, 'Where are thou?'
> And he said, 'I heard thy voice in the garden, and I was afraid, because I was
> naked; and I hid myself. . . .'
>
> Unto the woman God said, 'I will greatly multiply thy sorrow and thy
> conception; in sorrow thou shalt bring forth children; and thy desire shall
> be to thy husband and he shall rule over thee'.

What is striking about this story? They became aware of being naked
because, as a result of eating the apple, each saw the other differently. Nakedness was created in the mind of the beholder.

The second striking fact is that the woman is blamed and is punished by
being made subservient to the man. In relation to the woman, the man
becomes the agent of God.

In the medieval tradition the story was often illustrated, scene following
scene, as in a strip cartoon. . . .

During the Renaissance the narrative sequence disappeared, and the single moment depicted became the moment of shame. The couple wear fig-
leaves or make a modest gesture with their hands. But now their shame is not
so much in relation to one another as to the spectator.

Adam and Eve by Jan Gossart called Mabuse, Early
16th Century, (*Copyright Reserved To Her Majesty
Queen Elizabeth II*)

. . . .

When the tradition of painting became more secular, other themes also 14
offered the opportunity of painting nudes. But in them all there remains the
implication that the subject (a woman) is aware of being seen by a spectator.

She is not naked as she is. 15

She is naked as the spectator sees her. 16

Often—as with the favourite subject of Susannah and the Elders—this is 17
the actual theme of the picture. We join the Elders to spy on Susannah taking
her bath. She looks back at us looking at her.

Susannah and the Elders by Jacopo Tintoretto, 1518–94, (*Louvre, Paris*)

In another version of the subject by Tintoretto, Susannah is looking at   18
herself in a mirror. Thus she joins the spectators of herself.

Susannah and the Elders by Jacopo Tintoretto, 1518–94, (*Kunsthistorisches Museum, Vienna*)

The mirror was often used as a symbol of the vanity of woman. The   19
moralizing, however, was mostly hypocritical.

Vanity by Hans Memling, 1435–94, (*Strasbourg Museum*)

The Judgement of Paris by Lucas Cranach the Elder, 1472–1553, (*Landesmuseum, Gotha*)

You painted a naked woman because you enjoyed looking at her, you put a mirror in her hand and you called the painting *Vanity*, thus morally condemning the woman whose nakedness you had depicted for your own pleasure.

20   The real function of the mirror was otherwise. It was to make the woman connive in treating herself as, first and foremost, a sight.

21   The Judgement of Paris was another theme with the same inwritten idea of a man or men looking at naked women.

22   But a further element is now added. The element of judgement. Paris awards the apple to the woman he finds most beautiful. Thus Beauty becomes competitive. (Today The Judgement of Paris has become the Beauty Contest.) Those who are not judged beautiful are *not beautiful*. Those who are, are given the prize. . . .

23   The prize is to be owned by a judge—that is to say to be available for him. Charles the Second commissioned a secret painting from Lely. It is a highly typical image of the tradition. Nominally it might be a *Venus and Cupid*. In fact it is a portrait of one of the King's mistresses, Nell Gwynne. It shows her passively looking at the spectator staring at her naked.

Nell Gwynne and the infant Duke of St. Albans by Sir Peter Lely, 1618–1680, (*Denys Eyre Bower Bequest, Chiddingstone Castle, Kent, England*)

This nakedness is not, however, an expression of her own feelings; it is a sign of her submission to the owner's feelings or demands. (The owner of both woman and painting.) The painting, when the King showed it to others, demonstrated this submission and his guests envied him. . . .   24

We can now begin to see the difference between nakedness and nudity in the European tradition. In his book on *The Nude* Kenneth Clark maintains that to be naked is simply to be without clothes, whereas the nude is a form of art. According to him, a nude is not the starting point of a painting, but a way of seeing which the painting achieves. To some degree, this is true— although the way of seeing 'a nude' is not necessarily confined to art: there are also nude photographs, nude poses, nude gestures. What is true is that the nude is always conventionalized—and the authority for its conventions derives from a certain tradition of art. . . .   25

What do these conventions mean? What does a nude signify? It is not sufficient to answer these questions merely in terms of the art-form, for it is quite clear that the nude also relates to lived sexuality.   26

To be naked is to be oneself. 27

To be nude is to be seen naked by others and yet not recognized for 28 oneself. A naked body has to be seen as an object in order to become a nude. (The sight of it as an object stimulates the use of it as an object.) Nakedness reveals itself. Nudity is placed on display.

To be naked is to be without disguise. 29

To be on display is to have the surface of one's own skin, the hairs of 30 one's own body, turned into a disguise which, in that situation, can never be discarded. The nude is condemned to never being naked. Nudity is a form of dress.

In the average European oil painting of the nude the principal protagonist 31 is never painted. He is the spectator in front of the picture and he is presumed to be a man. Everything is addressed to him. Everything must appear to be the result of his being there. It is for him that the figures have assumed their nudity. But he, by definition, is a stranger—with his clothes still on.

Consider the *Allegory of Time and Love* by Bronzino. The complicated 32 symbolism which lies behind this painting need not concern us now because

Venus, Cupid, Time and Love by Agnolo Bronzino, 1503–1572, (*National Gallery, London*)

it does not affect its sexual appeal—at the first degree. Before it is anything else, this is a painting of sexual provocation.

The painting was sent as a present from the Grand Duke of Florence to the King of France. The boy kneeling on the cushion and kissing the woman is Cupid. She is Venus. But the way her body is arranged has nothing to do with their kissing. Her body is arranged in the way it is, to display it to the man looking at the picture. This picture is made to appeal to *his* sexuality. It has nothing to do with her sexuality. (Here and in the European tradition generally, the convention of not painting the hair on a woman's body helps towards the same end. Hair is associated with sexual power, with passion. The woman's sexual passion needs to be minimized so that the spectator may feel that he has the monopoly of such passion.) Women are there to feed an appetite, not to have any of their own. . . . 33

It is true that sometimes a painting includes a male lover. 34

Bacchus, Ceres and Cupid by Hans von Aachen, 1552–1615, (*Kunsthistorisches Museum, Vienna*)

But the woman's attention is very rarely directed towards him. Often she looks away from him or she looks out of the picture towards the one who considers himself her true lover—the spectator-owner.

There was a special category of private pornographic paintings (especially in the eighteenth century) in which couples making love make an appearance. But even in front of these it is clear that the spectator-owner will in fantasy oust the other man, or else identify with him. By contrast the image of the couple in non-European traditions provokes the notion of many couples making love. 'We all have a thousand hands, a thousand feet and will never go alone.'

Almost all post-Renaissance European sexual imagery is frontal—either literally or metaphorically—because the sexual protagonist is the spectator-owner looking at it.

The absurdity of this male flattery reached its peak in the public academic art of the nineteenth century. Men of state, of business, discussed under

Les Oréades by William Bouguereau, 1825–1905, (*Paris, Private Collection. Scala/Art Resource, New York*)

paintings like this. When one of them felt he had been outwitted, he looked up for consolation. What he saw reminded him that he was a man.

There are a few exceptional nudes in the European tradition of oil paint- 39 ing to which very little of what has been said above applies. Indeed they are no longer nudes—they break the norms of the art-form; they are paintings of loved women, more or less naked. Among the hundreds of thousands of nudes which make up the tradition there are perhaps a hundred of these exceptions. In each case the painter's personal vision of the particular women he is painting is so strong that it makes no allowance for the spectator. The painter's vision binds the woman to him so that they become as inseparable as couples in stone. The spectator can witness their relationship—but he can do no more: he is forced to recognize himself as the outsider he is. He cannot deceive himself into believing that she is naked for him. He cannot turn her into a nude. The way the painter has painted her includes her will and her intentions in the very structure of the image, in the very expression of her body and her face.

Danäe by Rembrandt van Ryn, 1606–1669, (*Hermitage Museum, Leningrad* [*detail*]. *Scala/Art Resource, New York*)

The typical and the exceptional in the tradition can be defined by the 40
simple naked/nude antinomy, but the problem of painting nakedness is not
as simple as it might at first appear.

What is the sexual function of nakedness in reality? Clothes encumber 41
contact and movement. But it would seem that nakedness has a positive visual
value in its own right: we want to *see* the other naked: the other delivers to
us the sight of themselves and we seize upon it—sometimes quite regardless
of whether it is for the first time or the hundredth. What does this sight of
the other mean to us, how does it, at that instant of total disclosure, affect
our desire?

Their nakedness acts as a confirmation and provokes a very strong sense 42
of relief. She is a woman like any other: or he is a man like any other: we are
overwhelmed by the marvellous simplicity of the familiar sexual mechanism.

We did not, of course, consciously expect this to be otherwise: uncon- 43
scious homosexual desires (or unconscious heterosexual desires if the couple
concerned are homosexual) may have led each to half expect something different. But the 'relief' can be explained without recourse to the unconscious.

We did not expect them to be otherwise, but the urgency and complexity 44
of our feelings bred a sense of uniqueness which the sight of the other, as she
is or as he is, now dispels. They are more like the rest of their sex than they
are different. In this revelation lies the warm and friendly—as opposed to
cold and impersonal—anonymity of nakedness.

One could express this differently: at the moment of nakedness first 45
perceived, an element of banality enters: an element that exists only because
we need it.

Up to that instant the other was more or less mysterious. Etiquettes of 46
modesty are not merely puritan or sentimental: it is reasonable to recognize
a loss of mystery. And the explanation of this loss of mystery may be largely
visual. The focus of perception shifts from eyes, mouth, shoulders, hands—
all of which are capable of such subtleties of expression that the personality
expressed by them is manifold—it shifts from these to the sexual parts, whose
formation suggests an utterly compelling but single process. The other is
reduced or elevated—whichever you prefer—to their primary sexual category:
male or female. Our relief is the relief of finding an unquestionable reality to
whose direct demands our earlier highly complex awareness must now yield.

We need the banality which we find in the first instant of disclosure 47
because it grounds us in reality. But it does more than that. This reality, by
promising the familiar, proverbial mechanism of sex, offers, at the same time,
the possibility of the shared subjectivity of sex.

The loss of mystery occurs simultaneously with the offering of the means 48
for creating a shared mystery. The sequence is: subjective—objective—subjective to the power of two.

We can now understand the difficulty of creating a static image of sexual   49
nakedness. In lived sexual experience nakedness is a process rather than a
state. If one moment of that process is isolated, its image will seem banal and
its banality, instead of serving as a bridge between two intense imaginative
states, will be chilling. This is one reason why expressive photographs of the
naked are even rarer than paintings. The easy solution for the photographer
is to turn the figure into a nude which, by generalizing both sight and viewer
and making sexuality unspecific, turns desire into fantasy.

Let us examine an exceptional painted image of nakedness. It is a painting   50
by Rubens of his young second wife whom he married when he himself was
relatively old.

Hélène Fourment in a Fur Coat by
Peter Paul Rubens, 1577–1640,
(*Kunsthistorisches Museum, Vienna*)

We see her in the act of turning, her fur about to slip off her shoulders.   51
Clearly she will not remain as she is for more than a second. In a superficial
sense her image is as instantaneous as a photograph's. But, in a more profound

sense, the painting 'contains' time and its experience. It is easy to imagine that a moment ago before she pulled the fur round her shoulders, she was entirely naked. The consecutive stages up to and away from the moment of total disclosure have been transcended. She can belong to any or all of them simultaneously.

Her body confronts us, not as an immediate sight, but as experience— 52 the painter's experience. Why? There are superficial anecdotal reasons: her dishevelled hair, the expression of her eyes directed towards him, the tenderness with which the exaggerated susceptibility of her skin has been painted. But the profound reason is a formal one. Her appearance has been literally re-cast by the painter's subjectivity. Beneath the fur that she holds across herself, the upper part of her body and her legs can never meet. There is a displacement sideways of about nine inches: her thighs, in order to join on to her hips, are at least nine inches too far to the left.

Rubens probably did not plan this: the spectator may not consciously 53 notice it. In itself it is unimportant. What matters is what it permits. It permits the body to become impossibly dynamic. Its coherence is no longer within itself but within the experience of the painter. More precisely, it permits the upper and lower halves of the body to rotate separately, and in opposite directions, round the sexual centre which is hidden: the torso turning to the right, the legs to the left. At the same time this hidden sexual centre is connected by means of the dark fur coat to all the surrounding darkness in the picture, so that she is turning both around and within the dark which has been made a metaphor for her sex.

Apart from the necessity of transcending the single instant and of admit- 54 ting subjectivity, there is, as we have seen, one further element which is essential for any great sexual image of the naked. This is the element of banality which must be undisguised but not chilling. It is this which distinguishes between voyeur and lover. Here such banality is to be found in Ruben's compulsive painting of the fat softness of Hélène Fourment's flesh which continually breaks every ideal convention of form and (to him) continually offers the promise of her extraordinary particularity.

The nude in European oil painting is usually presented as an admirable 55 expression of the European humanist spirit. This spirit was inseparable from individualism. And without the development of a highly conscious individualism the exceptions to the tradition (extremely personal images of the naked), would never have been painted. Yet the tradition contained a contradiction which it could not itself resolve. A few individual artists intuitively recognized this and resolved the contradiction in their own terms, but their solutions could never enter the tradition's *cultural* terms.

The contradiction can be stated simply. On the one hand the individu- 56 alism of the artist, the thinker, the patron, the owner: on the other hand, the person who is the object of their activities—the woman—treated as a thing or an abstraction. . . .

Dürer believed that the ideal nude ought to be constructed by taking the   57
face of one body, the breasts of another, the legs of a third, the shoulders of
a fourth, the hands of a fifth—and so on. . . .

The result would glorify Man. But the exercise presumed a remarkable   58
indifference to who any one person really was.

In the art-form of the European nude the painters and spectator-owners   59
were usually men and the persons treated as objects, usually women. This
unequal relationship is so deeply embedded in our culture that it still structures the consciousness of many women. They do to themselves what men
do to them. They survey, like men, their own femininity.

In modern art the category of the nude has become less important. Artists   60
themselves began to question it. In this, as in many other respects, Manet
represented a turning point. If one compares his *Olympia* with Titian's original, one sees a woman, cast in the traditional role, beginning to question that
role, somewhat defiantly.

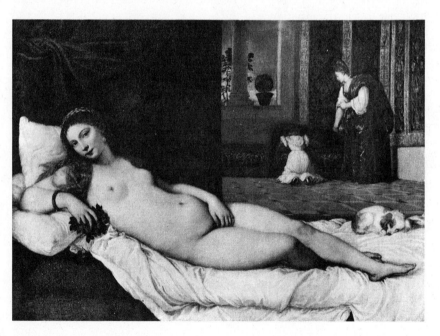

The Venus of Urbino by Titian, 1487/90–1576, (*Uffizi, Florence Alinari/Art Resource, New York*)

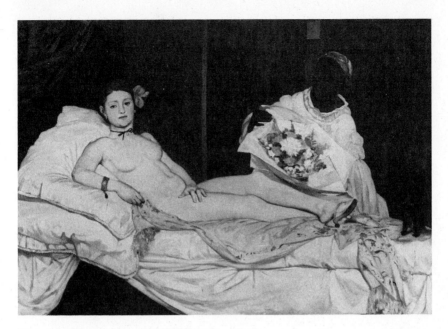

Olympia by Edouard Manet, 1832–1883, (*Louvre, Paris*)

The ideal was broken. But there was little to replace it except the 'realism'   61
of the prostitute—who became the quintessential woman of early avant-garde
twentieth-century painting. (Toulouse-Lautrec, Picasso, Rouault, German
Expressionism, etc.) In academic painting the tradition continued.

Today the attitudes and values which informed that tradition are ex-   62
pressed through other more widely diffused media—advertising, journalism,
television.

But the essential way of seeing women, the essential use to which their   63
images are put, has not changed. Women are depicted in a quite different
way from men—not because the feminine is different from the masculine—
but because the 'ideal' spectator is always assumed to be male and the image
of the woman is designed to flatter him. If you have any doubt that this is so,
make the following experiment. Choose from this book an image of a traditional nude. Transform the woman into a man. Either in your mind's eye or
by drawing on the reproduction. Then notice the violence which that transformation does. Not to the image, but to the assumptions of a likely viewer.

A GENTLEMAN AND A CONSUMER

DIANE BARTHEL

Diane Barthel's essay is taken from her study of 1988, *Putting On Appearances: Gender and Advertising*, a book that looks at the many ways men and women are defined by the advertising industry. Barthel's studies of American culture span a wide range. She is also author of a book on the Amana Society, a midwestern religious sect, titled *Amana: From Pietist Sect to American Community* (1984).

There are no men's beauty and glamour magazines with circulations even approaching those of the women's magazines. . . . The very idea of men's beauty magazines may strike one as odd. In our society men traditionally were supposed to make the right appearance, to be well groomed and neatly tailored. What they were *not* supposed to do was to be overly concerned with their appearance, much less vain about their beauty. That was to be effeminate, and not a "real man." Male beauty was associated with homosexuals, and "real men" had to show how red-blooded they were by maintaining a certain distance from fashion.

Perhaps the best-known male fashion magazine is *GQ* founded in 1957 and with a circulation of 446,000 in 1986. More recently, we have seen the launching of *YMF* and *Young Black Male*, which in 1987 still have few advertising pages. *M* magazine, founded in 1983, attracts an audience "a cut above" that of *GQ*.[1]

Esquire magazine, more venerable (founded in 1933), is classified as a general interest magazine. Although it does attract many women readers, many of the columns and features and much of the advertising are definitely directed toward attracting the attention of the male readers, who still make up the overwhelming majority of the readership.

The highest circulations for men's magazines are for magazines specializing either in sex (*Playboy*, circulation 4.1 million; *Penthouse*, circulation nearly 3.8 million; and *Hustler*, circulation 1.5 million) or sports (*Sports Illustrated*, circulation 2.7 million).[2] That these magazines share an emphasis on power—either power over women or over other men on the playing field—should not surprise. In fact, sociologist John Gagnon would argue that sex and sports now represent the major fields in which the male role, as defined by power, is played out, with physical power in work, and even in warfare, being less important than it was before industrialization and technological advance.[3]

If we are looking for comparative evidence as to how advertisements define gender roles for men and women, we should not then see the male role as defined primarily through beauty and fashion. This seems an obvious point, but it is important to emphasize how different cultural attitudes toward both the social person and the physical body shape the gender roles of men and women. These cultural attitudes are changing, and advertisements are helping to legitimate the use of beauty products and an interest in fashion for men, as we shall see. As advertisements directed toward women are beginning to use male imagery, so too advertisements for men occasionally use imagery resembling that found in advertisements directed toward women. We are speaking of two *modes*, then. As Baudrillard writes, these modes "do not result from the differentiated nature of the two sexes, but from the differential logic of the system. The relationship of the Masculine and the Feminine to real men and women is relatively arbitrary."[4] Increasingly today, men and women use both modes. The two great terms of opposition (Masculine and Feminine) still, however, structure the forms that consumption takes; they provide identities for products and consumers.

Baudrillard agrees that the feminine model encourages a woman to please herself, to encourage a certain complacency and even narcissistic solicitude. But by pleasing herself, it is understood that she will also please others, and that she will be chosen. "She never enters into direct competition. . . . If she is beautiful, that is to say, if this woman is a woman, she will be chosen. If the man is a man, he will choose his woman as he would other objects/signs (HIS car, HIS woman, HIS eau de toilette)."[5]

Whereas the feminine model is based on passivity, complacency, and narcissism, the masculine model is based on exactingness and choice.

> All of masculine advertising insists on rule, on choice, in terms of rigor and inflexible minutiae. He does not neglect a detail . . . It is not a question of just letting things go, or of taking pleasure in something, but rather of distinguishing himself. To know how to choose, and not to fail at it, is here the equivalent of the military and puritanical virtues: intransigence, decision, "virtus."[6]

This masculine model, these masculine virtues, are best reflected in the many car advertisements. There, the keywords are masculine terms: *power, performance, precision*. Sometimes the car is a woman, responding to the touch and will of her male driver, after attracting him with her sexy body. "Pure shape, pure power, pure Z. It turns you on." But, as the juxtaposition of shape and power in this advertisement suggest, the car is not simply other; it is also an extension of the owner. As he turns it on, he turns himself on. Its power is his power; through it, he will be able to overpower other men and impress and seduce women.

> How well does it perform?
> How well can you drive? (Merkur XR4Ti)

The 1987 Celica GT-S has the sweeping lines and aggressive stance that promise performance. And Celica keeps its word.

Renault GTA:
Zero to sixty to zero in 13.9 sec.
It's the result of a performance philosophy where acceleration and braking are equally important.
There's a new Renault sports sedan called GTA. Under its slick monochromatic skin is a road car with a total performance attitude. . . . It's our hot new pocket rocket.

In this last example, the car, like the driver, has a total performance attitude. That is what works. The slick monochromatic skin, like the Bond Street suit, makes a good first impression. But car, like owner, must have what it takes, must be able to go the distance faster and better than the competition. This point is explicitly made in advertisements in which the car becomes a means through which this masculine competition at work is extended in leisure. Some refer directly to the manly sport of auto-racing: "The Mitsubishi Starion ESI-R. Patiently crafted to ignite your imagination. Leaving little else to say except . . . gentlemen, start your engines." Others refer to competition in the business world: "To move ahead fast in this world, you've got to have connections. The totally new Corolla FX 16 GT-S has the right ones." Or in life in general. "It doesn't take any [Japanese characters] from anyone. It won't stand for any guff from 300ZX. Or RX-7. Introducing Conquest Tsi, the new turbo sport coupe designed and built by Mitsubishi in Japan." Or Ferrari, which says simply, "We are the competition." In this competition between products, the owners become almost superfluous. But the advertisements, of course, suggest that the qualities of the car will reflect the qualities of the owner, as opposed to the purely abstract, apersonal quality of money needed for purchase. Thus, like the would-be owner, the BMW also demonstrates a "relentless refusal to compromise." It is for "those who thrive on a maximum daily requirement of high performance." While the BMW has the business attitude of the old school ("aggression has never been expressed with such dignity"), a Beretta suggests what it takes to survive today in the shark-infested waters of Wall Street. In a glossy three-page cover foldout, a photograph of a shark's fin cutting through indigo waters is accompanied by the legend "Discover a new species from today's Chevrolet." The following two pages show a sleek black Beretta similarly cutting through water and, presumably, through the competition: "Not just a new car, but a new species . . . with a natural instinct for the road . . . Aggressive stance. And a bold tail lamp. See it on the road and you won't soon forget. Drive it, and you never will."

And as with men, so with cars. "Power corrupts. Absolute power corrupts absolutely" (Maserati). Not having the money to pay for a Maserati, to corrupt and be corrupted, is a source of embarrassment. Advertisements reassure the consumer that he need not lose face in this manly battle. Hyundai promises, "It's affordable. (But you'd never know it.)"

> On first impression, the new Hyundai Excel GLS Sedan might seem a trifle beyond most people's means. But that's entirely by design. Sleek European design, to be exact.

Many advertisements suggest sexual pleasure and escape, as in "Pure shape, pure power, pure Z. It turns you on." Or "The all-new Chrysler Le Baron. Beauty . . . with a passion for driving." The Le Baron may initially suggest a beautiful female, with its "image of arresting beauty" and its passion "to drive. And drive it does!" But it *is* "Le Baron," not "La Baronness." And the advertisement continues to emphasize how it *attacks* [emphasis mine] the road with a high torque, 2.5 fuel-injected engine. And its turbo option can blur the surface of any passing lane." Thus the object of the pleasure hardly has to be female if it is beautiful or sleek. The car is an extension of the male that conquers and tames the (female) road: "Positive-response suspension will calm the most demanding roads." The car becomes the ultimate lover when, like the Honda Prelude, it promises to combine power, "muscle," with finesse. Automobile advertisements thus play with androgyny and sexuality; the pleasure is in the union and confusion of form and movement, sex and speed. As in any sexual union, there is ultimately a merging of identities, rather than rigid maintenance of their separation. Polymorphous perverse? Perhaps. But it sells.

Though power, performance, precision as a complex of traits find their strongest emphasis in automobile advertisements, they also appear as selling points for products as diverse as shoes, stereos, and sunglasses. The car performs on the road, the driver performs for women, even in the parking lot, as Michelin suggests in its two-page spread showing a male from the waist down resting on his car and chatting up a curvaceous female: "It performs great. And looks great. So, it not only stands out on the road. But in the parking lot. Which is one more place you're likely to discover how beautifully it can handle the curves" (!).

As media analyst Todd Gitlin points out, most of the drivers shown in advertisements are young white males, loners who become empowered by the car that makes possible their escape from the everyday. Gitlin stresses the advertisements' "emphasis on surface, the blankness of the protagonist; his striving toward self-sufficiency, to the point of displacement from the recognizable world."[7] Even the Chrysler advertisements that coopt Bruce Springsteen's "Born in the USA" for their "Born in America" campaign lose in the process the original political message, "ripping off Springsteen's angry anthem, smoothing it into a Chamber of Commerce ditty as shots of just plain productive-looking folks, black and white . . . whiz by in a montage-made community." As Gitlin comments, "None of Springsteen's losers need apply—or rather, if only they would roll up their sleeves and see what good company they're in, they wouldn't feel like losers any longer."[8]

This is a world of patriarchal order in which the individual male can and must challenge the father. He achieves identity by breaking loose of the structure and breaking free of the pack. In the process he recreates the order and reaffirms the myth of masculine independence. Above all, he demonstrates that he knows what he wants; he is critical, demanding, and free from the constraints of others. What he definitely does not want, and goes to some measure to avoid, is to appear less than masculine, in any way weak, frilly, feminine.   13

Avoiding the Feminine

Advertisers trying to develop male markets for products previously associated primarily with women must overcome the taboo that only women wear moisturizer, face cream, hair spray, or perfume. They do this by overt reference to masculine symbols, language, and imagery, and sometimes by confronting the problem head-on.   14

There is not so much of a problem in selling products to counteract balding—that traditionally has been recognized as a male problem (a bald woman is a sexual joke that is not particularly amusing to the elderly). But other hair products are another story, as the March 1987 *GQ* cover asks, "Are you man enough for mousse?" So the advertisements must make their products seem manly, as with S-Curl's "wave and curl kit" offering "The Manly Look" on its manly model dressed in business suit and carrying a hard hat (a nifty social class compromise), and as in college basketball sportscaster Al McGuire's testimonial for Consort hair spray: 15

> "Years ago, if someone had said to me, 'Hey Al, do you use hair spray?' I would have said, 'No way, baby!'"
> "That was before I tried Consort Pump."
> "Consort adds extra control to my hair without looking stiff or phony. Control that lasts clean into overtime and post-game interviews . . ."
> Grooming Gear for Real Guys. *Consort.*

Besides such "grooming gear" as perms and hair sprays, Real Guys use "skin supplies" and "shaving resources." They adopt a "survival strategy" to fight balding, and the "Fila philosophy"—"products with a singular purpose: performance"—for effective "bodycare." If they wear scent, it smells of anything *but* flowers: musk, woods, spices, citrus, and surf are all acceptable. And the names must be manly, whether symbolizing physical power ("Brut") or financial power ("Giorgio VIP Special Reserve," "The Baron. A distinctive fragrance for men," "Halston—For the privileged few").   16

As power/precision/performance runs as a theme throughout advertising to men, so too do references to the business world. Cars, as we have seen, promise to share their owner's professional attitude and aggressive drive to beat out the competition. Other products similarly reflect the centrality of business competition to the male gender role. And at the center of this competition itself, the business suit.

> At the onset of your business day, you choose the suit or sportcoat that will position you front and center . . .
> The Right Suit can't guarantee he'll see it your way. The wrong suit could mean not seeing him at all.

Along with the Right Suit, the right shirt. "You want it every time you reach across the conference table, or trade on the floor, or just move about. You want a shirt that truly fits, that is long enough to stay put through the most active day, even for the taller gentleman." The businessman chooses the right cologne—Grey Flannel, or perhaps Quorum. He wears a Gucci "timepiece" as he conducts business on a cordless telephone from his poolside—or prefers the "dignity in styling" promised by Raymond Weil watches, "a beautiful way to dress for success."

Men's products connect status and success; the right products show that you have the right stuff, that you're one of them. In the 1950s C. Wright Mills described what it took to get ahead, to become part of the "power elite":

> The fit survive, and fitness means, not formal competence . . . but conformity with the criteria of those who have already succeeded. To be compatible with the top men is to act like them, to look like them, to think like them: to be of and for them—or at least to display oneself to them in such a way as to create that impression. This, in fact, is what is meant by "creating"—a well-chosen word—"a good impression." This is what is meant—and nothing else—by being a "sound man," as sound as a dollar.[9]

Today, having what it takes includes knowing "the difference between dressed, and well dressed" (Bally shoes). It is knowing that "what you carry says as much about you as what you put inside it" (Hartmann luggage). It is knowing enough to imitate Doug Fout, "member of one of the foremost equestrian families in the country."

> Because of our adherence to quality and the natural shoulder tradition, Southwick clothing was adopted by the Fout family years ago. Clearly, they have as much appreciation for good lines in a jacket as they do in a thoroughbred.

There it is, old money. There is no substitute for it, really, in business or in advertising, where appeals to tradition form one of the mainstays guaranteeing men that their choices are not overly fashionable or feminine, not working class or cheap, but, rather, correct, in good form, above criticism. If, when, they achieve this status of gentlemanly perfection, then, the advertisement suggests, they may be invited to join the club.

When only the best of associations will do

> Recognizing style as the requisite for membership, discerning men prefer the natural shoulder styling of Racquet Club. Meticulously tailored in pure wool, each suit and sportcoat is the ultimate expression of the clubman's classic good taste.

Ralph Lauren has his Polo University Club, and Rolex picks up on the polo theme by sponsoring the Rolex Gold Cup held at the Palm Beach Polo and Country Club, where sixteen teams and sixty-four players competed for "the pure honor of winning, the true glory of victory":

> It has added new lustre to a game so ancient, its history is lost in legend. Tamerlane is said to have been its patriarch. Darius's Persian cavalry, we're told, played it. It was the national sport of 16th-century India, Egypt, China, and Japan. The British rediscovered and named it in 1857.
> The linking of polo and Rolex is uniquely appropriate. Both sponsor and sport personify rugged grace. Each is an arbiter of the art of timing.

In the spring of 1987, there was another interesting club event—or non-event. The prestigious New York University Club was ordered to open its doors to women. This brought the expected protests about freedom of association—and of sanctuary. For that has been one of the points of the men's club. It wasn't open to women. Members knew women had their place, and everyone knew it was not there. In the advertisements, as in the world of reality, there is a place for women in men's lives, one that revolves around: [20]

Sex and Seduction

As suggested earlier, the growing fascination with appearances, encouraged by advertising, has led to a "feminization" of culture. We are all put in the classic role of the female: manipulable, submissive, seeing ourselves as objects. This "feminization of sexuality" is clearly seen in men's advertisements, where many of the promises made to women are now made to men. If women's advertisements cry, "Buy (this product) and he will notice you," men's advertisements similarly promise that female attention will follow immediately upon purchase, or shortly thereafter. "They can't stay away from Mr. J." "Master the Art of Attracting Attention." She says, "He's wearing my favorite Corbin again." Much as in the advertisements directed at women, the advertisements of men's products promise that they will do the talking for you. "For the look that says come closer." "All the French you'll ever need to know." [21]

Although many advertisements show an admiring and/or dependent female, others depict women in a more active role. "I love him—but life in the fast lane starts at 6 A.M.," says the attractive blonde tying on her jogging shoes, with the "him" in question very handsome and very asleep on the bed in the background. (Does this mean he's in the slow lane?) In another, the man slouches silhouetted against a wall; the woman leans aggressively toward him. He: "Do you always serve Tia Maria . . . or am I special?" She: "Darling, if you weren't special . . . you wouldn't be here." 22

The masculine role of always being in charge is a tough one. The blunt new honesty about sexually transmitted diseases such as AIDS appears in men's magazines as in women's, in the same "I enjoy sex, but I'm not ready to die for it" condom advertisement. But this new fear is accompanied by old fears of sexual embarrassment and/or rejection. The cartoon shows a man cringing with embarrassment in a pharmacy as the pharmacist yells out, "Hey, there's a guy here wants some information on Trojans." ("Most men would like to know more about Trojan brand condoms. But they're seriously afraid of suffering a spectacular and terminal attack of embarrassment right in the middle of a well-lighted drugstore.") Compared with such agony and responsibility, advertisements promising that women will *want* whatever is on offer, and will even meet the male halfway, must come as blessed relief. Men can finally relax, leaving the courting to the product and seduction to the beguiled woman, which, surely, must seem nice for a change. 23

Masculine Homilies

A homily is a short sermon, discourse, or informal lecture, often on a moral topic and suggesting a course of conduct. Some of the most intriguing advertisements offer just that, short statements and bits of advice on what masculinity is and on how real men should conduct themselves. As with many short sermons, many of the advertising homilies have a self-congratulatory air about them; after all, you do not want the consumer to feel bad about himself. 24

What is it, then, to be a man? It is to be *independent*. "There are some things a man will not relinquish." Among them, says the advertisement, his Tretorn tennis shoes. 25

It is to *savor freedom*. "Dress easy, get away from it all and let Tom Sawyer paint the fence," advises Alexander Julian, the men's designer. "Because man was meant to fly, we gave him wings" (even if only on his sunglasses). 26

It is to live a life of *adventure*. KL Homme cologne is "for the man who lives on the edge." Prudential Life Insurance preaches, "If you can dream it, you can do it." New Man sportswear tells the reader, "Life is more adventurous when you feel like a New Man." 27

It is to *keep one's cool.* "J. B. Scotch. A few individuals know how to keep   28
their heads, even when their necks are on the line."

And it is to stay one step *ahead of the competition.* "Altec Lansing. Hear   29
what others only imagine." Alexander Julian again: "Dress up a bit when you
dress down. They'll think you know something they don't."

What is it, then, to be a woman? It is to be *dependent.* "A woman needs   30
a man," reads the copy in the Rigolletto advertisement showing a young man
changing a tire for a grateful young woman.

The American cowboy as cultural model was not supposed to care for or   31
about appearances. He was what he was, hard-working, straightforward, and
honest. He was authentic. Men who cared "too much" about how they looked
did not fit this model; the dandy was effete, a European invention, insufficient
in masculinity and not red-blooded enough to be a real American. The other
cultural model, imported from England, was the gentleman. A gentleman did
care about his appearance, in the proper measure and manifestation, attention
to tailoring and to quality, understatement rather than exaggeration.[10]

From the gray flannel suit of the 1950s to the "power look" of the 1980s,   32
clothes made the man fit in with his company's image. Sex appeal and corporate correctness merged in a look that spelled success, that exuded confidence.

Whether or not a man presumed to care about his appearance, he did   33
care about having "the right stuff," as Tom Wolfe and *Esquire* call it, or "men's
toys," as in a recent special issue of *M* magazine. Cars, motorcycles, stereos,
sports equipment: these are part of the masculine appearance. They allow the
man to demonstrate his taste, his special knowledge, his affluence: to extend
his control. He can be and is demanding, for only the best will do.

He also wants to be loved, but he does not want to appear needy. Adver-   34
tisements suggest the magic ability of products ranging from cars to hair
creams to attract female attention. With the right products a man can have
it all, with no strings attached: no boring marital ties, hefty mortgages, corporate compromises.

According to sociologist Barbara Ehrenreich, *Playboy* magazine did much   35
to legitimate this image of male freedom. The old male ethos, up to the
postwar period, required exchanging bachelor irresponsibility for married
responsibility, which also symbolized entrance into social adulthood.[11] The
perennial bachelor, with his flashy cars and interchangeable women, was the
object of both envy and derision; he had fun, but and because he was not
fully grown up. There was something frivolous in his lack of purpose and
application.

This old ethos has lost much of its legitimacy. Today's male can, as   36
Baudrillard suggests, operate in both modes: the feminine mode of indulging
oneself and being indulged and the masculine mode of exigency and competition. With the right look and the right stuff, he can feel confident and
manly in boardroom or suburban backyard. Consumer society thus invites

both men and women to live in a world of appearances and to devote ever more attention to them.

Notes

1. Katz and Katz, *Magazines*, pp. 703–5.

2. Ibid.

3. John Gagnon, "Physical Strength: Once of Significance," in Joseph H. Pleck and Jack Sawyer, eds., *Men and Masculinity* (Englewood Cliffs, N.J.: Prentice-Hall, 1974), pp. 139–49.

4. Baudrillard, *La société de consommation*, pp. 144–47.

5. Ibid.

6. Ibid.

7. Todd Gitlin, "We Build Excitement," in Todd Gitlin, ed., *Watching Television* (New York: Pantheon, 1986), pp. 139–40.

8. Ibid.

9. C. Wright Mills, *The Power Elite* (New York: Oxford University Press, 1956), p. 141.

10. See Diane Barthel, "A Gentleman and a Consumer: A Sociological Look at Man at His Best," paper presented at the annual meeting of the Eastern Sociological Society, March 1983, Baltimore.

11. Barbara Ehrenreich, *The Hearts of Men: American Dreams and the Flight from Commitment* (New York: Anchor Books, 1983).

THE BODY BEAUTIFUL

◑

ROSALIND COWARD

Cultural critic Rosalind Coward is author of the revealing book *Female Desires: How They Are Sought,
Bought, and Packaged* (1985), from which this selection
is taken. Here, she discusses society's negative obsession with the "perfect" female body. Her other books
include an investigation of alternative medicine titled
The Whole Truth: The Myth of Alternative Health (1989)
and a study of *Patriarchal Precedents: Sexuality and Social
Relations* (1983).

The essence of fashion is that it represents an almost annual—but usually   1
subconsciously perceived shift in what is deemed to look good. Colour, length
and shape of clothing have all changed drastically from year to year over the
last few decades. What is more, there have been considerable changes in the
type of woman whose beauty is taken as exemplary—the difference, for example, between Twiggy or Julie Christie in the sixties, Maria Schneider in
the seventies and Nastassia Kinsky in the eighties. But this diversity of col-
ouring, hairstyles, and dress styles disguises what has been a consistent trend
in fashion for the last thirty years. The images which have bombarded us
over these years leave little doubt that there is one very definite ideal, the
ideal of the perfect body.

This is the one fundamental point of agreement in fashion, advertising   2
and glamour photography; the rules are rigid and the contours agreed. There
is a definite female outline which is considered the cultural ideal. This 'perfect'
female body would be between five foot five and five foot eight, long-legged,
tanned and vigorous looking, but above all, without a spare inch of flesh.
'Brown, slim, lively and lovely . . . that's how we would all like to see ourselves
on holiday. Here are a few tips on achieving this and maintaining it' (*Ideal
Home*).

Ever since the sixties, with its key image of Twiggy, there has been a   3
tendency with fashion- and beauty-writing and imagery towards the idealization of a female body with no fat on it at all. Concern with achieving this
'fashionable slimness' has become a routine part of many women's lives;
dieting, watching what you eat, feeling guilty about food, and exercising affect
most women to a greater or lesser degree.

The ideal outline is the silhouette which is left behind after the abolition   4
of those areas of the body which fashion-writing designates 'problem areas.'
First, bottoms:

> Female behinds—whether sexy and shapely or absolutely enormous—have
> long been the subject of saucy seaside postcards. But this important structure
> can make or mar flimsy summer clothes . . . to say nothing of beachwear. If
> what goes on below your back is no joke to you, join Norma Knox as she
> looks at ways to smooth down, gently reshape and generally improve the
> area between your waist and your knees.   (*Woman's Own*, 24 July 1982)

We are encouraged to 'beat saddle-bag hips' because pear-shaped buttocks
tend to wear badly in middle age if they have lacked exercise or have been
constantly flattened in over-tight trousers' (ibid.). Next we learn of the disadvantages of flabby thighs. We are told to 'ride a bike and firm up *slack* calves
and *floppy* thighs.' Elsewhere we learn of the horrors of loose stomach muscles
and their dire consequence, 'the pot belly.' Bosoms are a little more recalci-
trant but even these can be 'toned up' which means 'your bust's firmness can
be improved if the circulation is encouraged' (*Annabel*, December 1980).
Finally we should 'Take a Long Look at Legs' (*Woman's Own*, 1 May 1982).
The 'best' are 'smooth, flawless, unflabby, and golden.' But there is good
news, because 'legs are leaner . . . thanks to dieting and exercise' (ibid.).

And if all or any of these problem parts continue to cause you trouble,   5
you can always resort to the knife—cosmetic surgery. Women's magazines,
beauty books and beauty advice regularly give out information about this or
make it the subject of light-hearted asides: 'The only known way to remove
surplus body fat (short of an operation!) is to consume fewer calories' (John
Yudkin). Cosmetic surgery is offered not just for altering the shape of your
nose but for cutting away bits of flesh that cling stubbornly to those problem
areas.

These exhortations leave us in little doubt that the West has as constrict-   6
ing an ideal of female beauty and behaviour as exists in some non-European
societies where clitoridectomy is practised. In the West, the ideal of sexual
attractiveness is said to be upheld voluntarily, rather than inflicted by a compulsory operation to change the shape of women's anatomy. But the obsession
with one particular shape, everywhere promoted by the media, is no less of a
definite statement about expectations for women and their sexuality.

Confronted with the strictness of this cultural ideal, we need to under-   7
stand the meanings and values attached to this shape. We also need to understand the mechanisms which engage women in a discourse so problematic
for us; and we need to know how women actually perceive themselves in
relation to this idealized image.

What are the values which Western society attributes to this body shape?   8

The shape is slim, lacking in 'excess fat' which is defined as any flesh   9
which appears not to be muscled and firm, any flesh where you can 'pinch an
inch,' as a current slimming dictum suggests. The only area where flesh is
tolerated is around the breasts. The totally androgynous style of the sixties
has relaxed somewhat—perhaps men couldn't stand the maternal deprivation,
when it came to it. But even with breasts, the emphasis is on the 'well-
rounded' and 'firm' in keeping with the bulgeless body.

The most striking aspect of this body is that it is reminiscent of adoles-   10
cence; the shape is a version of an immature body. This is not because with
the increase in the earnings of young people, the fashion industry now has
them in mind (though there may be an element of truth in this), because the
ideal is not exactly a young girl. Rather it is an older woman who keeps an
adolescent figure. Witness the eulogies over Jane Fonda's body; a woman of
nearly fifty with the 'fantastic body' of a teenager.

This valuation of immaturity is confirmed by other practices concerned   11
with rendering the female body sexually attractive. The practice of shaving
under the arms and shaving the legs removes the very evidence that a girl has
reached puberty. It is considered attractive that these 'unsightly' hairs are
removed. Body hair is considered ugly and beauty advice strongly recom-
mends shaving the body to restore pre-pubescent smoothness. A recent hair-
removal advertisement spelled out the ideology: 'Go as Bare as You Dare.
With Bikini Bare you can wear the briefest bikini, the shortest shorts or the
new "thigh-high" cut swim suits with confidence.' Strange paradox here.
Pubic hair appearing in its proper place is unsightly. Yet fashion is designed
precisely to reveal this part.

The aim is constantly to produce smoothness, 'no razor stubble.' The   12
aim of shaving legs is to produce these firm, lean, smooth objects which,
naturally, have a far higher incidence on a rangy, sexually immature body than
on an older woman.

It is no coincidence that this sexual ideal is an image which connotes   13
powerlessness. Admittedly, the ideal is not of a demure, classically 'feminine'
girl, but a vigorous and immature adolescent. Nevertheless, it is not a shape
which suggests power or force. It has already been fairly widely documented
how women often choose (albeit unconsciously) to remain 'fat' because of the
power which somehow accrues to them.[1] And it is certainly true that big
women can be extremely imposing. A large woman who is not apologizing
for her size is certainly not a figure to invite the dominant meanings which
our culture attaches to femininity. She is impressive in ways that our culture's
notion of the feminine cannot tolerate. Women, in other words, must always
be seen as women and not as impressive Persons with definite presence.

1. See S. Orbach, *Fat Is a Feminist Issue* (Hamlyn, 1979).

The cultural ideal amounts to a taboo on the sexually mature woman. 14
This taboo is closely related to other ideologies of sexually appropriate behaviour for men and women. Historically, for instance, the law has had difficulty in recognizing women as sexually responsible individuals. In the statutes of the law, in fact, it is only men who are deemed capable of committing
sexual crimes, and this is not just because it is indeed men who tend to attack
women. These legal ideologies are constructed on the belief that only men
have an active sexuality, therefore only men can actively seek out and commit
a sexual crime. Women in these discourses are defined as the sexually responsive or passive victims of men's advances. Actually (as much recent feminist
writing on the law has made us realize) the *workings* of the law do embrace
very definite beliefs about female sexuality.[2] In rape cases, there are frequent
attempts to establish women's culpability, to establish that women 'asked for
it' in some way, and gave out messages which invited a male sexual attack.
Thus even though the *statutes* of the law appear to protect women against
men's active sexuality, in fact the *workings* of the law often put women on trial
and interrogate them about their degree of responsibility for the attack.

The ideology in the legal treatment of rape corresponds closely with 15
general ideologies about masculine and feminine behaviour. It is acknowledged that women have a sexuality, but it is a sexuality which pervades their
bodies almost as if *in spite of themselves*. It is up to women to protect themselves
by only allowing this sexual message to be transmitted in contexts where it
will be received responsibly, that is, in heterosexual, potentially permanent
situations. This is why the defence of a rapist is often conducted in terms of
attempting to cast doubt on a woman's sexual 'morality.' If she can be proved
to have used her sexuality 'irresponsibly,' then she can be suspected of having
invited the active attack of the man. It is only women who have expressed
their sexuality within the safety of the heterosexual couple who can be guaranteed the protection of the law.

The sexually immature body of the current ideal fits very closely into 16
these ideologies. For it presents a body which is sexual—it 'exudes' sexuality
in its vigorous and vibrant and firm good health—but it is not the body of a
woman who has an adult and powerful control over that sexuality. The image
is of a highly sexualized female whose sexuality is still one of response *to* the
active sexuality of a man. The ideology about adolescent sexuality is exactly
the same; young girls are often seen as expressing a sexual need even if the
girl herself does not know it. It is an image which feeds off the idea of a fresh,
spontaneous, but essentially *responsive* sexuality.

But if this image is somewhat at variance with how the majority of women, 17
especially the older ones, experience their sexual needs, their choices and their

2. See S. Edwards, *Female Sexuality and the Law* (Martin Robertson, 1982).

active wants, then how is it that this body image continues to prevail? How does that image continue to exist in women's lives, making them unhappy by upholding impossible ideals? How is it that these images have a hold when most women would also express extreme cynicism about advertising stereotypes and manipulation, not to mention knowledge of the techniques by which these body forms are sometimes achieved? (It is not just the real body that is subjected to the knife. Far more common is the cutting off of excess flesh on the photographic image.)

Perhaps the mechanism most important in maintaining women's concern with this ideal is that it is built on a *disgust* of fat and flesh. It is not just a simple case of an ideal to which some of us are close and others not, which we can take or leave. The ideal says as much about its opposite, because the war with fat and excess flesh is a war conducted in highly emotive language. And this language constructs the meanings and therefore the emotions which surround body image. The most basic point about this is that it is difficult to find a non-pejorative word to describe what after all is the average female shape in a rather sedentary culture. When it comes down to it, 'plump,' 'well-rounded,' 'full,' and so on all sound like euphemisms for fat and therefore carry negative connotations. No one wants to be plump when they could be firm; it would be like choosing to be daft when you could be bright. But perhaps more important is that language pertaining to the female body has constructed a whole regime of representations which can only result in women having a punishing and self-hating relationship with their bodies. First, there is the fragmentation of the body—the body is talked about in terms of different parts, 'problem areas,' which are referred to in the third person: 'flabby thighs . . . they.' If the ideal shape has been pared down to a lean outline, bits are bound to stick out or hang down and these become problem areas. The result is that it becomes possible, indeed, likely, for women to think about their bodies in terms of parts, separate areas, as if these parts had some separate life of their own. It means that women are presented with a fragmented sense of the body. This fragmented sense of self is likely to be the foundation for an entirely masochistic or punitive relationship with one's own body. It becomes possible to think about one's body as if it were this thing which followed one about and attached itself unevenly to the ideal outline which lingers beneath. And the dislike of the body has become pathological. The language used expresses absolute disgust with the idea of fat. Fat is like a disease: 'if you *suffer* from cellulite . . .' The cures for the disease are even worse. The body has to be hurt, made to suffer for its excess. *Company* magazine reports on 'Pinching the Fat Away.' Pummelling is regularly recommended, as is wringing out and squeezing: 'Use an oil or cream lubricant and using both hands, wring and twist the flesh as though you were squeezing out water, then use fists to iron skin upwards, kneading deeper at the fleshier thigh area' (*A–Z of Your Body*). And under the title of 'Working Hard at Looking Good' we are told about actress Kate O'Mara's 'beauty philosophy':

18

'I'm determined to do all I can to help myself. If I cheat on my regime, I write myself abusive notes. Anyway, all this masochistic stuff gives me a purpose in life' (*Cosmopolitan*).

It is almost as if women had to punish themselves for existing at all, as if any manifestation of this too, too-solid flesh had to be subjected to arcane tortures and expressions of self-loathing. [19]

I have already suggested that one of the reasons behind this self-disgust may be the conflict surrounding the cultural valuation of the sexually imma-ture image. It seems as though women have to punish themselves for growing up, for becoming adults and flaunting their adulthood visibly about their bodies. It is as if women feel that they are too big, occupying too much space, have overgrown their apportioned limits. And a punishment is devised which internalizes the negative values which this society has for such women. It is of course sensual indulgence which is seen as the root cause for women overspilling their proper space. Women who feel themselves to be overweight also invariably have the feeling that their fatness demonstrates weakness and greed. Being fat is tantamount to walking around with a sandwich board saying, 'I can't control my appetite.' [20]

This belief is fostered by the slimming industry and by the literature on fatness. Yudkin, for instance, in the *A–Z for Slimmers*, writes: 'It's not very nice having to admit you are fat. It's much more attractive to suppose that the extra weight isn't due to overeating but is caused by fluid retention . . .' And *Slimmer* magazine ran a spread asking whether children were helpful when their mothers were dieting. They gave a sample of the answers: 'An eight-year-old concerned about his mother's figure is Daniel Hanson of Ash-ford, Middlesex. "I'm not going to let my mum have any more sweets," he declared firmly. "I want her to be thin like other mums." And nine-year-old Kerry Wheeler says of her mother, "She's looking thinner now, but we can't stop her eating sweets. I have to take them away from her."' [21]

At the heart of these caring offspring's anxieties about their mother's body shape, and at the heart of the discourses on the ideal body, lies a paradox. The *sexual* ideal of the slim, lithe, firm body is also a statement of self-denial, the absence of any other form of sensuality. This adds a further dimension to the cultural connotations of immaturity. The ideal body is also evidence of pure devotion to an aesthetic ideal of sexuality, a very limited aesthetic ideal. Ideal sexuality is limited sensuality; the ideal excludes any form of sensual pleasure which contradicts the aspiration for the perfect body. Again it is a statement about a form of sexuality over which women are assumed to have no control, since it is a statement about not having grown up and pursued other pleasures. [22]

The ideal promoted by our culture is pretty scarce in nature; there aren't all that many mature women who can achieve this shape without extreme effort. Only the mass of advertising images, glamour photographs and so on makes us believe that just about all women have this figure. Yet the ideal is [23] constructed artificially. There are only a very limited number of models who make it to the billboards, and the techniques of photography are all geared towards creating the illusion of this perfect body.

Somewhere along the line, most women know that the image is impossible, and corresponds to the wishes of our culture rather than being actually attainable. We remain trapped by the image, though, because our culture generates such a violent dislike of fat, fragmenting our bodies into separate areas, each of them in their own way too big. Paradoxically, though, this fragmentation also saves us from despair. Most women actually maintain an ambiguous relation to the ideal image; it is rarely rejected totally—it pervades fantasies of transforming the self. But at the same time, there's far more narcissistic self-affirmation among women than is sometimes assumed. Because of the fragmentation of the body into separate areas, most women value certain aspects of their bodies: eyes, hair, teeth, smile. This positive self-image has to be maintained against the grain for the dice are loaded against women liking themselves in this society. But such feelings do lurk there, waiting for their day, forming the basis of the escape route away from the destructive and limiting ideals which are placed on women's bodies.

24

A STORY ABOUT THE BODY

◑

ROBERT HASS

Robert Hass's delicate, insightful poems have delighted readers since his first collection, *Field Guide*, was published in 1973. Hass has been the recipient of the prestigious MacArthur Fellowship and was awarded the 1984 National Book Critics Circle Award in criticism for his collection of essays, *Twentieth Century Pleasures*. The following piece is taken from his latest volume of poetry, *Human Wishes* (1989), and is an example of a "prose poem"—a creation with the evocative intensity of a poem, yet without the traditional line breaks of verse.

The young composer, working that summer at an artist's colony, had watched her for a week. She was Japanese, a painter, almost sixty, and he thought he was in love with her. He loved her work, and her work was like the way she moved her body, used her hands, looked at him directly when she made amused and considered answers to his questions. One night, walking back from a concert, they came to her door and she turned to him and said, "I think you would like to have me. I would like that too, but I must tell you that I have had a double mastectomy," and when he didn't understand, "I've lost both my breasts." The radiance that he had carried around in his belly and chest cavity—like music—withered very quickly, and he made himself look at her when he said, "I'm sorry. I don't think I could." He walked back to his own cabin through the pines, and in the morning he found a small blue bowl on the porch outside his door. It looked to be full of rose petals, but he found when he picked it up that the rose petals were on top; the rest of the bowl—she must have swept them from the corners of her studio—was full of dead bees.

SKIN DEEP

WENDY CHAPKIS

In this excerpted chapter of her book *Beauty Secrets: Women and the Politics of Appearance* (1986), Wendy Chapkis focuses on the impact of Western advertising on developing or non-Western countries. Much of her other work has involved an awareness of the situation of women around the world as well. She has also written a study on sex discrimination in international employment titled *Of Common Cloth: Women in the Global Textile Industry* (1983).

"Mirror, mirror on the wall, who is the fairest of them all?" As children we 1
accept that "the fairest" is the same sort of measure as the fastest, the tallest or the richest. Later, in the growing sophistication of adulthood, we determine that the most beautiful is more like the bravest, the most popular or the most powerful. It becomes a judgement about which one might have an *opinion* but remains a quality that ultimately can be established by an independent and attentive authority. "Ladies and Gentlemen, the judges have reached a decision. The new Miss World is. . . ."

Adults thus continue to pose the question "who is the fairest" as though 2
it were meaningful, even when the category of "them all" includes women of diverse races and nationalities. Indeed female beauty is becoming an increasingly standardized quality throughout the world. A standard so strikingly white, Western and wealthy it is tempting to conclude there must be a conscious conspiracy afoot.

But in fact no hidden plot is needed to explain the pervasiveness of this 3
image. The fantasy of the Good Life populated by Beautiful People wearing The Look has seized the imagination of much of the world. This Western model of beauty represents a mandate for a way of life for women throughout the world regardless of how unrelated to each of our ethnic or economic possibilities it is. We invest a great deal in the fantasy, perhaps all the more, the further we are from being able to attain it. This international fantasy becomes the basis of our myths of eroticism, success and adventure.

It is "Charlie's Angels" (women on a 1970s U.S. TV show) who appear 4
to have a good time in the world, not women who are fat or small or darkskinned. As the center of a world economic system, the U.S. owns the biggest share of the global culture machine. By entering that world in imagination,

each woman aims to be whiter, more Western, more upper class. This goes beyond simple manipulation.

While the Hearst Corporation is trying to maximize profits on a global scale, that does not fully explain *Cosmopolitan*'s popularity in seventeen languages around the world. The Cosmo package seems to offer everything: sexuality, success, independence and beauty. It is powerful and compelling. A woman working all day making microchips who buys lipstick or cigarettes is buying some tiny sense of dignity and self-esteem along with the glamour.

In large part, the content of the global image is determined by the mechanics of the sell: who creates the images for what products to be marketed through which media controlled by whom? The beauty trade (cosmetics, toiletries, fragrance and fashion) is expanding its market worldwide. And a world market means global marketing. For instance, during the Christmas season of 1982, the same commercials for Antaeus and Chanel No. 5 perfumes were being used throughout Europe, the U.S. and Latin America.[1] And in 1985, *Business Week* reported that Playtex had kicked off:

> . . . a one ad fits all campaign . . . betting that a single marketing effort can sell a new bra around the world . . . At one point several years ago, Playtex had 43 versions of ads running throughout the world with local managers in charge . . . This year Playtex gave all its world wide business to New York's Grey Advertising.[2]

Tony Bodinetz, vice-chair of KMP in London (a division of the huge international advertising corporation Saatchi and Saatchi) believes this kind of advertising campaign arises in part from cultural chauvinism:

> The use of the same ad in various countries is in part based on a calculation of cost effectiveness, but partly it is simply a reflection of an attitude of mind. Some company executive in Pittsburg or Los Angeles or somewhere thinks "if it works in Pittsburg it'll work in London . . . why the hell would they be any different?" One of the things we fight against here is the fact that American solutions are often imposed on us.[3]

Bodinetz appears to be a minority voice in a company committed to just such a global advertising strategy: "They are committed to it because they need to be. They are looking to get those huge world clients and the way to get the clients is to sell this concept, so they have to believe it," says Bodinetz. The competition among the advertising giants for the large corporate accounts is intense. And the world of multinational product and image is very small indeed.

About a dozen advertising agencies worldwide represent the majority of major multinational corporations and themselves operate across national boundaries.[4] The number three advertising agency in the U.S., J. Walter Thompson, for example, is also the most important agency in Argentina, Chile and Venezuela, number two in Brazil and number four in Mexico. The majority (35 of the top 50) of these global image makers are American advertising agencies. The products they hype are also overwhelmingly American. U.S. companies alone account for nearly half of global expenditures on advertising, outspending the closest rival, Japan, by five to one. Small wonder then that advertising images tend to be recognizably North American.[5]

These global advertising campaigns increasingly ignore national differences in determining the products to be marketed and the images used to sell them. The ads contribute to the belief that success and beauty are brand names with a distinctly white American look to them. Trade journals *Advertising Age* and *Business Abroad* note the trend: "Rubinstein Ads Not Altered for Señoras"; "World Wide Beauty Hints: How Clairol Markets Glamour in Any Language." 10

The advertising agency Saatchi and Saatchi is enthusiastic about "world branding" and global culture: 11

> Market research will be conducted to look for similarities not seek out differences. Similarities will be exploited positively and efficiently . . . developing advertising for an entire region of the world, and not simply for one market to find a real advertising idea so deep in its appeal that it can transcend national borders previously thought inviolate.[6]

Western corporations are not alone in pursuing this transcendent advertising ideal. Shiseido, the Japanese giant in cosmetics, has recently revamped its advertising to present a "determinedly international thrust."[7] "It is easy to create an ordinary, nice picture with a nice model and a nice presentation for the product," explains a company executive, "but we wanted to be memorable without being too realistic. Realism would have too closely defined our market." Shiseido hints at its Asian origin—"intrigue from the Orient"—but its models are white and its targeted market is "the international affluent elite."[8] Saatchi and Saatchi agrees that this is the strategy of the future: 12

> Are social developments making outmoded the idea that the differences between nations with regard to this or that durable, cosmetic or coffee were crucial for marketing strategy? Consumer convergence in demography, habits and culture are increasingly leading manufacturers to a consumer-driven rather than a geography-driven view of their marketing territory . . . Marketers will be less likely to tailor product positioning to the differing needs of the country next door and more likely to operate on the basis of the common needs for their products.[9]

A "consumer-driven" view of marketing means focusing on that segment of any society likely to purchase a given product. For many products, in particular luxury items, the potential market in large parts of the world remains extremely limited. It is certainly true that members of these national elites often more closely resemble their counterparts in other countries than they do their own less affluent compatriots. 13

In turn, the upper class serves as the model of success and glamour for the rest of the nation. All the pieces of the picture begin to fit neatly together, confirming that there is but one vision of beauty. The woman on the imported American television program resembles the woman in the Clairol ad resembles the wife of the Prime Minister or industrial magnate who dresses in the latest French fashion as faithfully reported in the local version of *Cosmopolitan*. 14

Corporate advertising is not, then, uniquely responsible for the homogenization of culture around the world. But it is an important team player. Tony Bodinetz explains: 15

> I don't think you can just point the finger and blame advertising, because advertising never leads. But admittedly it is very quick to sense what is happening on the streets or around the world and to jump on a bandwagon. Of course while it is true that advertising never sets the pace, it cannot escape its share of the responsibility for confirming the view that to "join the club" you've got to look like this, smell like this, speak like this and dress like this.[10]

This vision of beauty and success has been made familiar around the world not only through ads but via the American media of magazines, television and motion pictures. In much of the world, a large portion of television programming is composed of American imports. Foreign programs make up well over half of television fare in such countries as Ecuador, Chile and Malaysia.[11] In Western Europe, the Middle East and parts of Asia more than 20 percent of all television programs are made in the U.S. One popular American program, "Bonanza," was once seen in 60 countries with an estimated audience of 350 million. The contemporary equivalent, "Dallas," is watched by millions from Malaysia to South Africa.[12] 16

The Americanization of the world media has had useful spinoffs for marketing. Saatchi and Saatchi again: 17

> . . . television and motion pictures are creating elements of shared culture. And this cultural convergence is facilitating the establishment of multinational brand characters. The world wide proliferation of the Marlboro brand would not have been possible without TV and motion picture education about the virile rugged character of the American West and the American cowboy, helped by increasing colour TV penetration.[13]

That American television should be so omnipresent is not entirely due to chance or to the excellence of the U.S. "sitcom." In the 1950s, ABC—the American Broadcasting Corporation, a private television company, received U.S. government AID funding to create the first television stations in Ecuador, Colombia and Peru. They also provided technical assistance for the development of many others. By the early 1970s, ninety countries throughout the world were buying ABC programs and business agreements between ABC and its Latin American affiliates allow the corporation to choose both 18 programs and sponsors for peak viewing hours.[14] Even without such direct control, foreign imports are often the programming of choice because small local networks find it much cheaper to buy American programs than to produce their own.

Television, and the related Hollywood film industry, are not the only media plying their wares around the world. Many of the top twenty American magazine corporations also produce for a world market. Hearst Corporation, the third largest magazine corporation in the U.S., produces a Latin American version of *Good Housekeeping—Buenhogar—*and *Vanidades* (the women's magazine with the largest circulation in Latin America). Hearst also publishes the internationally popular *Cosmopolitan.* Condé Nast, number six on the U.S. list, publishes and distributes adapted versions of *Vogue* magazine in many countries.[15]

Researchers in Latin America studied the content of these transnational women's magazines and found striking similarities from country to country. The majority of articles focused on beauty, fashion or products for use in the home. Perhaps even more telling, almost a third of the total space was devoted to advertising and 60 percent of all advertisements were for the products of transnational corporations.[16]

Of course, the media have always relied heavily on advertising. Now, though, the relationship is so intimate that one corporation may own both the magazine advertising a product and the company producing it. Media authority Ben Bagdikian puts it bluntly: "The major media and giant corporations have always been allies; they are now a single entity."[17]

Four of the fifty largest U.S. media corporations are among the fifty largest advertisers. All three of the major American television networks and three of the four leading movie studios are part of companies so large that they appear on the list of the 500 largest corporations in the United States.[18] Thus, not only does one country determine the jingle much of the world will hum, but a very few, large corporations own the piper.

While it would be wrong to suggest that this is the result of a conscious conspiracy among the various parts of the global culture machine (U.S.-based multinational corporations, U.S.-dominated international advertising and the U.S. entertainment and media industries) it is safe to say that they all benefit from a collective global fantasy of success and beauty defined by white skin, Western culture and imported products.

> Elaborate make-up is part of the electronics image in Malaysia, and the factories even provide classes in how to apply it. This allows the workers to feel they are part of a global culture which includes the choice between Avon and Mary Quant products.[19]

> There just seems to be a great desire to aspire to Western values and Western culture . . . Often an ad will be written in English because that is one way of flattering the audience: "You are smart, sophisticated and educated." I suppose that is also why the models tend to be white . . .[20]

. . . Dr. Fu Nong Yu [a plastic surgeon in Peking] performs "eye jobs" to create folded or "double" eyelids, considered a mark of wide-eyed beauty . . . Most northern Chinese are born without double eyelids and Fu takes a few stitches to remove the epicanthal fold in the upper eyelid that is typical of Asians . . .[21]

Japanese television commercials are a paean to the American way of life, full of glamorous movie stars and famous sports heroes . . . Despite a growing pride in things Japanese, the United States remains a cultural pacesetter for Japan . . . If a Japanese company cannot find an American celebrity to endorse its product, it may opt for displaying the product in a recognizably U.S. setting or placing a blue-eyed, blond model alongside it.[22]

Naturally, this trend toward global cultural homogenization has not gone unchallenged. Indigenous culture remains a powerful alternative to the white Western model of success and beauty. In some countries, traditional images are officially promoted as a response to the flood of imported Western culture. In other countries, local culture acts subversively as the bearer of otherwise illegal messages of political, economic and cultural resistance.

Following the Sandinista victory over the Somoza dictatorship in Nicaragua, sexist advertising was banned. If a woman now appears in an advertisement, there must be a reason other than providing a sexual come-on to the potential buyer. While *Vanidades* and *Cosmopolitan*, with their transnational advertising, can still be purchased in Managua, the local billboards do not offer images of the wealthy white glamour girl.

Another, although very different reaction to Western sexualized imagery of women, is evidenced in the Islamic countries of North Africa and the Middle East. A dramatic symbol of religious, national and patriarchal culture, the veil, is increasingly being adopted by women in these countries. The use of the veil to reclaim (and in some cases to re-invent) indigenous culture is clearly problematic but hardly inexplicable. Shortly before the overthrow of the Shah in Iran, the most popular women's magazine in that country was *Zan-e Ruz* (*Woman of Today*) with a circulation of over 100,000. The periodical was filled with love stories starring blonde, blue-eyed heroines lifted directly from Western magazines. Of the 35 percent of the periodical taken up with ads, much focused on beauty and cosmetic products again often featuring blonde models. One researcher observed "the great stress on physical appearance in a situation of acute sexual repression is . . . somehow ironic."[23] More than ironic, the resulting tensions may have helped encourage both the Islamic revival and the subsequent return to the veil.

Significantly, while the veil may be an important and visible symbol of resistance to Western culture and values, it is worn by women only. Women throughout the world tend to be designated as culture bearers and given the burdensome responsibility of preserving traditional values and aesthetics. In recent studies in several African countries, researchers discovered that women were seen both as repositories of traditional culture and those most likely to succumb to Western influences. Women in Uganda, for example, were seen as:

> . . . scapegoats not only for male confusion and conflict over what the contemporary roles of women should be, but for the dilemmas produced by adjusting to rapid social change. Where men have given up traditional customs and restraints on dress, but feel traitors to their own culture, they yearn for the security and compensation of at least knowing that women are loyal to it.[24]

In much the same way, women in Zambia have been held responsible "when the state of morality was chaotic . . ." and when cultural traditions became "contaminated by Western influence."[25] Unfortunately, women of the Third World singlehandedly can no more turn back Western cultural domination than they can be held responsible for its powerful and enduring influence. And while women certainly *are* at the forefront of many forms of resistance including the cultural, "tradition" may not be the only element women will choose to draw on in creating a culture that speaks of and to their lives.

At the international festival of women's culture, Black women fill the stage night after night with their presence. To watch them is not simply to admire but to feel pride. They allow for no less. Their self-respect is utterly contagious and offers a vision of power beyond the borders of white commercial culture.

These women using music, language and movement different from my own, still speak directly to me. "This is a heart beat. This is all of our heart beats. And it is beating for you. And for you. And for you." (Edwina Lee Tyler playing her African drum.)

The destructive effect of racism on the self-image of people of color[26] is well-documented and much bemoaned—especially among anti-racist whites. Isn't it terrible that Blacks have felt a need to "relax" their curly hair to appear more attractive? Isn't it shocking that eye jobs creating a Western eyelid were popular among certain Vietnamese women during the war? Isn't it distressing that the model for female beauty sold to developing nations is the same White Woman sold to the West?

Yes. But at some level it is also profoundly reassuring to white women; we are, after all, the model. We do embody at least one element of the beauty formula. Our white Western lives are the stuff of global fantasy and demonstrably enviable.

This international commercial trend can easily be misrepresented as evidence of a unanimous esthetic judgement. But people of color are not alone in buying fantasies packaged in a distant ethnic reality. For the Western white, paradise is tropical, and passion, rhythmic movement and sensuality all wear dark skin. Just as the white Western world serves as the repository for certain elements of a global myth of success and beauty, so too does the world of color represent related myths of sensuality, adventure and exoticism.

The fantasy of the Western Good Life is grounded in the reality of the economic privilege of the industrialized West. Perhaps the fantasy of sensuality and passion ascribed to the Third World reflects something similar about the realities of privilege and oppression. It is certainly true that to maintain a position of privilege in a world of tremendous poverty requires some measure of emotional shutting down, a distancing of the self from the unentitled other. Puerto Rican poet Aurora Levins Morales suggests that this has consequences for white culture:

> There is a kind of aliveness that has been obtained in oppressed cultures that gets shut down in dominant culture. There is a lot of fear that comes with privilege. Fear that others want to take your stuff away from you. It means an incredible locking down. Also you have to be in control all the time. Being always in control is not conducive to sensuality.[27]

Power is the arbiter determining which characteristics will be ascribed to the self and which will be projected onto the other. These complimentary images are the basis of myths of white and black, male and female, the self and Other. . . .

. . . the world of advertising is a rich source of imagery of women of color, often combining racist and sexist stereotypes in one picture. Advertisements using Asian women, for example, are evocative not only of the sexual mystery but also the docility and subservience supposedly "natural to the oriental female." This is true whether the product is the woman herself (as an assembly line worker or a "hospitality girl" in a holiday "sex tour") or another good or service enhanced by the female touch. A Malaysian electronics firm advertising brochure reads:

> The manual dexterity of the oriental female is famous the world over. Her hands are small and she works fast with extreme care. Who, therefore, could be better qualified by nature and inheritance to contribute to the efficiency of the bench assembly line than the oriental girl?

And this from Thai International Airlines:

> Gentle people . . . caring for you comes naturally to the girls of Thai. The gentle art of service and courtesy is one they learn from childhood . . . Beautiful Thai.

As the advertising technique of "world branding" helps spread white Western culture to developing nations, Third World women increasingly appear in advertisements in the West promising entry to that vanishing world of the exotic. These women thus become metaphors for adventure, cultural difference and sexual subservience; items apparently increasingly hard to come by in the industrialized West.

Especially interesting are those ads selling travel and tourism. Their invitation is to escape to paradise on earth—in itself fascinating given the way Third World countries are represented in the other media. The split images are quite remarkable: the exotic is marketed as a holiday fantasyland while "the underdeveloped world" is used in the West as shorthand for poverty, hunger, political corruption and religious fanaticism. 39

Of course, airlines and other branches of the tourist industry are in the business of selling fantasy not theories of underdevelopment. "A taste of Paradise to Sri Lanka . . . Discover the infinite beaches with the people of Paradise" whispers the Air Lanka ad. The text is set against a picture of a deserted white sandy beach with a small inserted photo of a smiling Asian flight hostess. 40

The use of foreign locales and peoples to enhance the magic properties of a product is an effective marketing technique. It is easier to suspend judgement and accept the promise of the fantastic if it is set far from familiar soil. Just as we doubt that the truly romantic can happen to people who look too ordinary, it is harder to believe that the truly fantastic can happen too close to home. 41

In the past, travel belonged to a small, very privileged elite. We saw pictures of Brigitte Bardot in St. Tropez and knew both were the stuff of dreams. Now we can choose to visit the Côte d'Azur on a holiday, taking advantage of bargain flights or package tours. But when we walk the streets of our collective dreams, we don't look like Bardot. And the romantic adventures that befell her seem to pass us by. Perhaps we are not beautiful enough, or rich enough, to bring out the true magic of St. Tropez? 42

Rather than concluding that the fantasy was never a full and true reflection of reality, we simply set our sights on ever more distant shores. The more inaccessible the better. Travel brochures almost always suggest that this spot is still "unspoiled"; perhaps the compulsive clicking of cameras is an attempt to recapture the quiet, frozen images of the dream we thought we bought. Back home, looking through the carefully composed shots, the exotic again resembles the airline ads that fed our fantasies. 43

Ironically, travel to exotic lands actually robs us of their exoticism; the exotic must remain unfamiliar in order to retain its mystery. Experience creates familiarity, something our culture teaches us is the antithesis of romance. So while travel ads promise access to the exotic, they must also emphasize its unknowable Otherness. A Singapore Airlines ad reads: "Across four continents of the earth . . . you are an unsolved mystery in a *sarong kebaya*. Who are you Singapore Girl?" 44

A serenely beautiful Asian woman stares directly into the camera, an intimate look, steady and deep: "The airline with the most modern fleet in the world still believes in the romance of travel." And, as Singapore Airlines 45 reminds us, there is nothing more romantic than the mysterious Asian woman. Nothing else appears in their ads. Exotic cloth is wrapped around undemanding oriental gentleness: "Enjoy the kind of inflight service even other airlines talk about, with gentle hostesses in sarong kebayas caring for you as only they know how." Yes, their girls have a reputation, but they don't mind.

Hilton International promotes their hotels in Hong Kong, Jakarta, Kuala 46 Lumpur, Manila, Singapore, Taipei and Tokyo with the picture of five Asian women (some dressed in traditional outfits, others in Western service uniforms): "Life Oriental style . . . A carefully melded crossroads of East and West. You've focused on Hilton International. A unique blend of Oriental hospitality and international service."

The ad speaks to the fantasy and the *fear* of travel in exotic lands. Hilton 47 will help smooth out the cultural confusions by carefully melding East and West. A safe way to enjoy exoticism. You can "enter a world where a myriad of surrounding sights and sensations tantalize your imagination, and let the Hilton International world of thoughtful services *put your mind at ease*." The hotel is no simple place to sleep, no more than an airline is simply a means of transportation. It is a fantasy, indeed A Way of Life, or at least the safe imitation of one. "Specializing in the unexpected—a lobby in exact replica of a sultan's palace. Our own cruising replica of a pirate chasing brigantine . . ."

Perfumes, cosmetics and certain fashion lines promise the look of the 48 exotic for those unable or unwilling to actually travel to distant countries. The Ultima II cosmetic line by Revlon is marketed as a way for East to meet West. "The collection is Ultima's lyrical translation of the loveliest colors the Orient has to offer." Note the use of the word orient in so many of these ads. Orient is a realm of fantasy; Asia is a real life place. Orient brings to mind the mystery of the exotic region of the East; Asia says Vietnam, Red China, Toyota car competition. The most striking thing about the Ultima II "East Meets West" advertisement is the photograph accompanying it. Lauren Hutton sits on a cushion wearing something reminiscent of a kimono (but showing too much flesh). She looks down with a slightly amused smile at her hands folded in her lap. Across from her, an Asian woman dressed in a real kimono bows to this symbol of daring Western womanhood. This is apparently the proper attitude for East when meeting West.

Perfume ads are particularly fond of the exotic motif. And here again the 49 racial stereotypes and the promise of exotic fantasy reign: "Island Gardenia by Jovan: Delicate. Exotic. Above all . . . Sensuous. Only in the islands do the most delicate flowers grow a little wilder." "Fidji by Guy Laroche: Fidji, le parfum des paradis retrouvés." "Mitsouko by Guerlain: Serenely mysterious . . ."

Even such a mundane product as panty hose can be sold with a touch of 50 the exotic: "The look . . . the feel . . . of the Orient. Now yours in a pantyhose. Sheer Elegance. Silky smooth, radiant . . ." This ad points out one of the stereotypes that may help make the Asian woman the model of acceptable

Ultima II "East Meets West" (*Copyright 1982 Charles Revson Inc.*)

exotic sexuality. Like an idealized child, she is described as small, docile, available and never demanding. Her body is as "smooth and silky," as the hairless body of a sexually innocent child.

High fashion, too, often makes use of exotica. *Vogue* magazine is especially fond of setting its white models, dressed in "native inspired" fashions, against such backdrops as the Tunesian Oasis of Nefta. Magazines for working class women, on the other hand, only rarely show such exotic fashions or locales. In part this may reflect the fact that the Hilton International Way of Life is a much more familiar fantasy to *Vogue* readers. And while *Vogue* suggests that, for the wealthy, fashion is artful play, the *Cosmopolitan* reader knows that in the realm of Dress for Success, clothing is serious business.

For working women, the exotic is, at best, an *after hours* image created through cosmetics, perfumes and daring sexual practices—all important elements of the "Sex and the Single Girl" success package. Apparently only those who are beyond any doubt white, Western and wealthy can afford to look Third World.

Notes

1. *Advertising Age*, "Toiletries and Beauty Aids Supplement," February 28, 1983.
2. *Business Week*, December 16, 1985, p. 64.

3. Bodinetz, Tony, interview 23 November 1984, London.

4. Saatchi and Saatchi Annual Report, 1982, p. 19.

5. Cavanagh, John and Selvaggio, Kathy, "Who's Behind the Media Blitz?" *Multinational Monitor*, August 1983, p. 20–21. And Clairmonte, Frederick and Cavanagh, John, "Transnational Corporations and Services: The Final Frontier," Trade and Development: an *UNCTAD Review*, no. 5, 1985, p. 262.

6. *op. cit.*, Saatchi and Saatchi, p. 15.

7. *op. cit.*, *Advertising Age*.

8. *Ibid.*

9. *op. cit.*, Saatchi and Saatchi, p. 10.

10. *op. cit.*, Bodinetz.

11. Gay, Jill, "Sweet Darlings in the Media," *Multinational Monitor*, August 1983, p. 20.

12. Gallagher, Margaret, *Unequal Opportunities, the case of women and the media*, UNESCO, 1981. And *op. cit.*, Gay.

13. *op. cit.*, Saatchi and Saatchi, p. 12.

14. *op. cit.*, Cavanagh and Selvaggio, p. 21.

15. Bagdikian, Ben, *The Media Monopoly*, Beacon Press, Boston, 1983, p. 12. And *op. cit.*, Gay.

16. Santa Cruz, Adriana and Erazo, Viviana, *Compropolitan: el orden transnacional y su modelo feminino*, Edition Nueva Imagen, Mexico, 1980, cited in Gallagher, p. 46. The U.S. is a relative newcomer to the Third World and is not the only Western voice selling its products and values. The colonial relationship remains important. In her UNESCO study, *Unequal Opportunities* (1981, p. 25), Margaret Gallagher notes that the magazine *Amina*, edited and produced in France, is distributed throughout francophone Africa. Its advertising, almost exclusively for beauty and fashion, directs readers to French mail order firms.

17. *op. cit.*, Bagdikian, p. 233.

18. *Ibid.*, p. 123 and p. 21.

19. Grossman, Rachel, *Southeast Asia Chronicle*, no. 66, p. 6.

20. *op. cit.*, Bodinetz.

21. "Cosmetic Surgery Gains in Popularity in China," *Los Angeles Times*, December 16, 1982.

22. "U.S. Sets the Pace," *International Herald Tribune*, October 1, 1984, p. 12.

23. Sreberny-Mohammadi, Annabelle, "At the Periphery," unpublished paper, Sweden, 1978, cited in Gallagher, p. 58.

24. Obbo, Christine, *African Women: their struggle for economic independence*, Zed Press, London 1980.

25. Glazer Shuste, Ilse, *New Women of Lusaka*, Mayfield, Palo Alto, California, 1979, cited in Gallagher, p. 59.

26. Choice of the appropriate words to refer to so-called "non-white" women is problematic as political preferences differ from country to country. The expression "women of color," or, alternatively, "Third World women," is commonly used in the United States, while elsewhere (Britain and the Netherlands, for example), "Black" is the inclusive political description. I have chosen to use these expressions interchangeably throughout the text.

27. Levins Morales, Aurora, interview, February 21, 1983, Oakland, California.

MAKING CONNECTIONS

1. Visit your local art museum, or an art gallery, bookstore, or magazine stand and take a close look at the representations of women in art and advertising. Are women still depicted in the same ways that Berger suggests? Try the experiment at the end of Berger's article, substituting a male for a female figure in any given picture. What happens to both the figure and the position of the viewer? Write a description of your experiment and its results.

2. Compare Cynthia Hanson's article on "China Beach" (Chapter 9) with Berger's discussion of the male gaze and the function of the viewer. How do the two correspond? Try applying the points made about oppression in Marilyn Frye's essay "Oppression" (Chapter 2) to these analyses of art and television images. Could such representations of women be seen as "oppressive"? Why or why not?

3. Discuss Berger's distinction between the "naked" and the "nude." What does he mean by the phrase, "the nude is condemned to never being naked"? Can you identify the difference in your own analysis of art and advertising images? How would you compare Berger's essay with Barthel's statement about advertising's impact on everyone: "We are all put in the classic role of the female: manipulable, submissive, seeing ourselves as objects." Do you agree or disagree with this statement?

4. One area of growing interest for analysts of popular culture is the sexual imagery in music videos and MTV. How do music videos conform to or break the mold of previously commodified sexuality? Is exposure a form of vulnerability or a form of power for artists like Madonna? Write an essay that looks at sex and gender imagery in a representative sample of music videos.

5. In the style of Barthel's piece, write your own essay comparing and contrasting advertisements aimed at a male audience with those that target a female audience. Try to organize them according to the types of products or lifestyles they seem to be selling. What differences do you find in the images used, the feelings conveyed, and the messages implicit in each?

6. Using Coward's essay as a starting point, research the growing instance of eating disorders among young adults today. Use your findings to write a paper that examines this phenomenon both as a medical problem and as a product of cultural attitudes about the body.

7. Select one of the themes that recur in this chapter, such as the focus on aging vs. youth, infantilization, or the fragmenting of body parts, and

discuss its use in a cross-section of essays, such as Berger, Barthel, Coward, and/or Hass.

8. Spend a few minutes writing your response to Hass's prose poem. What is the "meaning" of the tale? What do you think the bowl of rose petals and bees was meant to say to the young composer? Compare your responses and thoughts to those of your classmates. Do you find any difference in responses? Do men respond to the story differently than women? If so, can you use essays like Elizabeth Flynn's or Robert Crosman's in Chapter 6 to explore those differences?

9. What is your own experience with the way advertising packages sex, beauty, wealth, a desirable lifestyle? How much does it affect your own choices? Try listing the last five items you bought—or make an imaginary "wish list" of items you would like to obtain. To what extent is your list influenced by the promises of The Good Life or The Look that these specific products hold out? Do these products carry any links to gender or messages about men's and women's lifestyles? Discuss your findings.

10. What are the negative aspects of commercializing the white, Western standard of beauty, here and abroad? In what ways is it reassuring to those of us who belong to the dominant culture, and what false images of ourselves might it reinforce? What might it mean for those of us who don't belong to that group, either in this country or in other countries? Does such advertising affect men and women differently?

11. Compare and contrast the image of the Asian woman in Chapkis's essay with the image of Asian men and women in Ben Fong-Torres's piece (Chapter 9) and with the woman in Hass's poem. Do you agree that there are stereotypes that affect this ethnic group? Write an essay that describes images of Asian men and women in American society. You might also include facets of public image that these authors haven't addressed, such as competition in the auto industry, electronics, or education. Can you draw any conclusions about how stereotypes are formed?

12. Chapkis demonstrates how some stereotypes of marginal cultures can contain desirable elements, like her example of "the Orient," which is constructed to represent the exotic and the sensual. What are some "positive" stereotypes about other groups, such as African Americans, Native Americans, or others? Are there differences in the ways we see men and women belonging to these groups? What might the desirable traits projected onto others reflect about the desires or lacks in the dominant culture? Do such stereotypes limit members of these groups or present them in a positive light?

11
PORNOGRAPHY

C O N T E X T S

> We define pornography as the graphic sexually
> explicit subordination of women through pictures or
> words that also includes women dehumanized as sexual
> objects, things, or commodities; enjoying pain or hu-
> miliation or rape; being tied up, cut up, mutilated,
> bruised, or physically hurt; in postures of sexual sub-
> mission or servility or display; reduced to body parts,
> penetrated by objects or animals, or presented in sce-
> narios of degradation, injury, torture; shown as filthy
> or inferior; bleeding, bruised, or hurt in a context that
> makes these conditions sexual. (MacKinnon, *Feminism
> Unmodified: Discourses on Life and Law* [Cambridge:
> Harvard University Press, 1987], p. 176)

With this definition, launched in 1983 as an amendment to the Minneapolis
City Council Code of Ordinances Relating to Civil Rights, lawyer Catharine
MacKinnon and author-activist Andrea Dworkin opened a new phase in the
public debate over pornography. Their proposal presented guidelines that
defined pornography as discrimination on the basis of sex and therefore a
violation of civil rights. In the past, the case against obscenity had been argued
on highly subjective moral grounds, using vague terms and fuzzy definitions.
This definition, however, allowed MacKinnon and Dworkin to present a
different argument against pornography—not for portraying explicit sex, but

for portraying sex in such a way as to subordinate, demean, or denigrate women. Their distinction was a crucial one: it is not what pornography *is* but what it *does* which violates individual rights and serves to reinforce social injustice and sexual violence. Yet despite the new focus offered by this interpretation, the problem of censorship in a free society continues to be a pressing issue in the debate about pornography, with many voices (including feminists) arguing strongly against censorship in any form.

What is the difference between material that is merely sexually explicit and pornography? Our first author in this chapter, Gloria Steinem, establishes a classic distinction between "Erotica vs. Pornography." Steinem examines the difference between mutual pleasure and the unequal exercise of power to dominate another. Much of the current confusion over obscenity comes, Steinem argues, from confusing sex and violence, a dangerous intertwining of elements that lies at the heart of a society in which men dominate women. Yet untangling sex from aggression, a necessary process to return dignity and affection to the concept of sexuality, meets with numerous obstacles in society. Steinem's essay traces how moralism, antifeminism, misguided liberalism, and the economics of the billion-dollar pornography industry frequently stand in the way of objectively analyzing the meaning and impact of pornography.

The links between pornographic fantasies and behavior are explored in our next two essays. Philip Weiss's "Forbidden Pleasures" offers the point of view of a consumer of pornography, a man who enjoys pornographic fantasies even while he recognizes that they are not "right" and represent a sexual double standard. Nonetheless, he asserts that pornography remains a "successfully private" activity for men—something to be indulged in secretly but not actually acted out in life. In his reponse to Weiss, "One Man's Pleasures," Douglas Campbell states what he believes are the limitations of such a view. Focusing on pornography's more subtle ideological messages, Campbell shows how the "social fantasy" marketed by pornography—the idea of male power and female victimization—is far from private, but does in fact directly shape many social and sexual practices.

Fred Small's essay, "Pornography and Censorship," offers another important perspective on the antipornography debate, as he outlines the dangers of censorship in society. Addressing specifically the Minneapolis ordinance of 1983 put forth by MacKinnon and Dworkin, Small demonstrates how such legislation may not always be used "in the spirit of its creation," and in fact may come to harm the very groups whose rights it was meant to protect.

In our final essay, "Pornography and Freedom," John Stoltenberg looks at society's concept of sexual freedom, particularly the complex relationship between sexual freedom and sexual justice. Drawing on his years of activism for men's rights, Stoltenberg demonstrates how pornography creates a false sense of freedom for men by equating sexuality with male dominance, aggression, and anger. According to Stoltenberg, it is the responsibility of men themselves to recognize this cultural "setup," resist its influence, and advocate for change.

The issues about gender and society raised by pornography are multiple and complex. To what extent is pornography protected under the First Amendment? Would restrictions on the portrayal of graphic sexual images gradually lead to further and further censorship, possibly encroaching onto artistic, medical or educational materials? What is the link between pornography and crime, in a culture in which it is estimated that one out of every three women will be the victim of sexual assault? What about exploitation and criminality within the industry itself? Is the existence of pornography a symptom or a cause of societal attitudes towards men and women? Does it offer sexual freedom or does it desensitize and dehumanize? These questions and more are part of the cultural debate about pornography, a debate whose consequences are far-reaching in terms of personal rights, freedom of expression, and social justice.

EROTICA VS. PORNOGRAPHY

GLORIA STEINEM

In this famous essay, written in 1977, Gloria Steinem
discusses the distinctions between "erotica" and "pornography"—sex as mutual sensual pleasure or as the
unequal power of one group over another. Steinem, a
noted speaker, writer, and activist for the cause of
women's rights, is also author of *Marilyn* (1987), a
biography of "sex symbol" Marilyn Monroe.

Look at or imagine images of people making love; really making love. Those
images may be very diverse, but there is likely to be a mutual pleasure and
touch and warmth, an empathy for each other's bodies and nerve endings, a
shared sensuality and a spontaneous sense of two people who are there because
they *want* to be.

Now look at or imagine images of sex in which there is force, violence,
or symbols of unequal power. They may be very blatant: whips and chains of
bondage, even torture and murder presented as sexually titillating, the clear
evidence of wounds and bruises, or an adult's power being used sexually over
a child. They may be more subtle: the use of class, race, authority, or just
body poses to convey conqueror and victim; unequal nudity, with one person's
body exposed and vulnerable while the other is armored with clothes; or even
a woman by herself, exposed for an unseen but powerful viewer whom she
clearly is trying to please. (It's interesting that, even when only the woman is
seen, we often know whether she is there for her own pleasure or being
displayed for someone else's.) But blatant or subtle, there is no equal power
or mutuality. In fact, much of the tension and drama comes from the clear
idea that one person is dominating another.

These two sorts of images are as different as love is from rape, as dignity
is from humiliation, as partnership is from slavery, as pleasure is from pain.
Yet they are confused and lumped together as "pornography" or "obscenity,"
"erotica" or "explicit sex," because sex and violence are so dangerously intertwined and confused. After all, it takes violence or the threat of it to maintain
the unearned dominance of any group of human beings over another. Moreover, the threat must be the most persuasive wherever men and women come
together intimately and are most in danger of recognizing each other's
humanity.

The confusion of sex with violence is most obvious in any form of sado-
masochism. The gender-based barrier to empathy has become so great that

a torturer or even murderer may actually believe pain or loss of life to be the natural fate of the victim; and the victim may have been so deprived of self-respect or of empathetic human contact that she expects pain or loss of freedom as the price of any intimacy or attention at all. It's unlikely that even a masochist expects death. Nonetheless, "snuff" movies and much current pornographic literature insist that a slow death from sexual torture is the final orgasm and ultimate pleasure. It's a form of "suicide" reserved for women. Though men in fact are far more likely to kill themselves, male suicide is almost never presented as sexually pleasurable. But sex is also confused with violence and aggression in all forms of popular culture, and in respectable theories of psychology and sexual behavior as well. The idea that aggression is a "normal" part of male sexuality, and that passivity or even the need for male aggression is a "normal" part of female sexuality, are part of the male-dominant culture we live in, the books we learn from, and the air we breathe.

Even the words we are given to express our feelings are suffused with the same assumptions. Sexual phrases are the most common synonyms for conquering and humiliation (*being had, being screwed, getting fucked*); the sexually aggressive woman is a *slut* or a *nymphomaniac*, but the sexually aggressive man is just *normal*; and real or scientific descriptions of sex may perpetuate the same roles, for instance, a woman is always *penetrated* by a man though she might also be said to have *enveloped* him. 5

Obviously, untangling sex from aggression and violence or the threat of it is going to take a very long time. And the process is going to be greatly resisted as a challenge to the very heart of male dominance and male centrality. 6

But we do have the common sense of our bodies to guide us. Pain is a warning of damage and danger. If that sensation is not mixed with all the intimacy we know as children, we are unlikely to confuse pain with pleasure and love. As we discover our free will and strength, we are also more likely to discover our own initiative and pleasure in sex. As men no longer can dominate and have to find an identity that doesn't depend on superiority, they also discover that cooperation is more interesting than submission, that empathy with their sex partner increases their own pleasure, and that anxieties about their own ability to "perform" tend to disappear along with stereotyped ideas about masculinity. 7

But women will be the main fighters of this new sexual revolution. It is our freedom, our safety, our lives, and our pleasure that are mostly at stake. 8

We began by trying to separate sex and violence in those areas where the physical danger was and is the most immediate: challenging rape as the one crime that was considered biologically irresistible for the criminal and perhaps invited by the victim; refusing to allow male-female beatings to be classified as "domestic violence" and ignored by the law; exposing forced prostitution and sexual slavery as national and international crimes. With the exception of wife beating, those challenges were made somewhat easier by men who wanted to punish other men for taking their female property. Women still rarely have the power to protect each other. 9

Such instances of real antiwoman warfare led us directly to the propa- 10
ganda that teaches and legitimizes them—pornography. Just as we had begun
to separate rape from sex, we realized that we must find some way of separating pornographic depictions of sex as an antiwoman weapon from those
images of freely chosen, mutual sexuality.

Fortunately, there is truth in the origin of words. *Pornography* comes from 11
the Greek root *porné* (harlot, prostitute, or female captive) and *graphos* (writing
about or description of). Thus, it means a description of either the purchase
of sex, which implies an imbalance of power in itself, or sexual slavery.

This definition includes, and should include, all such degradation, re- 12
gardless of whether it is females who are the slaves and males who are the
captors or vice versa. There is certainly homosexual pornography, for instance,
with a man in the "feminine" role of victim. There is also role-reversal
pornography, with a woman whipping or punishing a man, though it's significant that this genre is created by men for their own pleasure, not by or for
women, and allows men to *pretend* to be victims—but without real danger.
There could also be lesbian pornography, with a woman assuming the "masculine" role of victimizing another woman. That women rarely choose this
role of victimizing is due to no biological superiority, but a culture that doesn't
addict women to violence. But whatever the gender of the participants, all
pornography is an imitation of the male-female, conqueror-victim paradigm,
and almost all of it actually portrays or implies enslaved woman and master.

Even the 1970 Presidential Commission on Obscenity and Pornography, 13
whose report is often accused of suppressing or ignoring evidence of the
causal link between pornography and violence against women, defined the
subject of their study as pictorial or verbal descriptions of sexual behavior
characterized by "the degrading and demeaning portrayal of the role and
status of the human female."

In short, pornography is not about sex. It's about an imbalance of male- 14
female power that allows and even requires sex to be used as a form of
aggression.

Erotica may be the word that can differentiate sex from violence and 15
rescue sexual pleasure. It comes from the Greek root *eros* (sexual desire or
passionate love, named for Eros, the son of Aphrodite), and so contains the
idea of love, positive choice, and the yearning for a particular person. Unlike
pornography's reference to a harlot or prostitute, *erotica* leaves entirely open
the question of gender. (In fact, we may owe its sense of shared power to the
Greek idea that a man's love for another man was more worthy than love for
a woman, but at least that bias isn't present in the word.) Though both erotica
and pornography refer to verbal or pictorial representations of sexual behavior, they are as different as a room with doors open and one with doors locked.
The first might be a home, but the second could only be a prison.

The problem is that there is so little erotica. Women have rarely been 16
free enough to pursue erotic pleasure in our own lives, much less to create it
in the worlds of film, magazines, art, books, television, and popular culture—

all the areas of communication we rarely control. Very few male authors and filmmakers have been able to escape society's message of what a man should do, much less to imagine their way into the identity of a woman. Some women and men are trying to portray equal and erotic sex, but it is still not a part of popular culture.

And the problem is there is so much pornography. This underground 17 stream of antiwoman propaganda that exists in all male-dominant societies has now become a flood in our streets and theaters and even our homes. Perhaps that's better in the long run. Women can no longer pretend pornography does not exist. We must either face our own humiliation and torture every day on magazine covers and television screens or fight back. There is hardly a newsstand without women's bodies in chains and bondage, in full labial display for the conquering male viewer, bruised or on our knees, screaming in real or pretended pain, pretending to enjoy what we don't enjoy. The same images are in mainstream movie theaters and respectable hotel rooms via closed-circuit TV for the traveling businessman. They are brought into our homes not only in magazines, but in the new form of video cassettes. Even video games offer such features as a smiling, rope-bound woman and a male figure with an erection, the game's object being to rape the woman as many times as possible. (Like much of pornography, that game is fascist on racial grounds as well as sexual ones. The smiling woman is an Indian maiden, the rapist is General Custer, and the game is called "Custer's Revenge.") Though "snuff" movies in which real women were eviscerated and finally killed have been driven underground (in part because the graves of many murdered women were discovered around the shack of just one filmmaker in California), movies that simulate the torture murders of women are still going strong. (*Snuff* is the porn term for killing a woman for sexual pleasure. There is not even the seriousness of a word like *murder*.) So are the "kiddie porn" or "chicken porn" movies and magazines that show adult men undressing, fondling, and sexually using children; often with the titillating theme that "fathers" are raping "daughters." Some "chicken porn" magazines offer explicit tips on how to use a child sexually without leaving physical evidence of rape, the premise being that children's testimony is even less likely to be believed than that of an adult woman.

Add this pornography industry up, from magazines like *Playboy* and *Hus-* 18 *tler*, to movies like *Love Gestapo Style, Deep Throat*, or *Angels in Pain*, and the total sales come to a staggering eight billion dollars a year—more than all the sales of the conventional film and record industry combined. And that doesn't count the fact that many "conventional" film and music images are also pornographic, from gynocidal record jackets like the famous *I'm "Black and Blue" from the Rolling Stones—and I Love It!* (which showed a seminude black woman bound to a chair) to the hundreds of teenage sex-and-horror movies in which young women die sadistic deaths and rape is presented not as a crime but as sexual excitement. Nor do those industries include the sales of the supposedly "literary" forms of pornography, from *The Story of O* to the works of the Marquis de Sade.

If Nazi propaganda that justified the torture and killing of Jews were the theme of half of our most popular movies and magazines, would we not be outraged? If Ku Klux Klan propaganda that preached and even glamorized the enslavement of blacks were the subject of much-praised "classic" novels, would we not protest? We know that such racist propaganda precedes and justifies the racist acts of pogroms and lynchings. We know that watching a violent film causes test subjects to both condone more violence afterward and to be willing to perpetuate it themselves. Why is the propaganda of sexual aggression against women of all races the one form in which the "conventional wisdom" sees no danger? Why is pornography the only media violence that is supposed to be a "safety valve" to satisfy men's "natural" aggressiveness somewhere short of acting it out? 19

The first reason is the confusion of *all* nonprocreative sex with pornography. Any description of sexual behavior, or even nudity, may be called pornographic or obscene (a word whose Latin derivative means *dirty* or *containing filth*) by those who insist that the only moral purpose of sex is procreative, or even that any portrayal of sexuality or nudity is against the will of God. 20

In fact, human beings seem to be the only animals that experience the same sex drive and pleasure at times when we can and cannot conceive. Other animals experience periods of heat or estrus. Humans do not. 21

Just as we developed uniquely human capacities for language, planning, memory, and invention along our evolutionary path, we also developed sexuality as a form of expression, a way of communicating that is separable from our reproductive need. For human beings, sexuality can be and often is a way of bonding, of giving and receiving pleasure, bridging differentness, discovering sameness, and communicating emotion. 22

We developed this and other human gifts through our ability to change our environment, adapt to it physically, and so in the very long run to affect our own evolution. But as an emotional result of this spiraling path away from other animals, we seem to alternate between periods of exploring our unique abilities and feelings of loneliness in the unknown that we ourselves have created, a fear that sometimes sends us back to the comfort of the animal world by encouraging us to look for a sameness that is not there. 23

For instance, the separation of "play" from "work" is a feature of the human world. So is the difference between art and nature, or an intellectual accomplishment and a physical one. As a result, we celebrate play, art, and invention as pleasurable and important leaps into the unknown; yet any temporary trouble can send us back to a nostalgia for our primate past and a conviction that the basics of survival, nature, and physical labor are somehow more worthwhile or even more moral. 24

441

In the same way, we have explored our sexuality as separable from con-   25
ception: a pleasurable, empathetic, important bridge to others of our species.
We have even invented contraception, a skill that has probably existed in
some form since our ancestors figured out the process of conception and
birth, in order to extend and protect this uniquely human gift. Yet we also
have times of atavistic suspicion that sex is not complete, or even legal or
intended by God, if it does not or could not end in conception.

No wonder the very different concepts of "erotica" and "pornography"   26
can be so confused. Both assume that sex can be separated from conception;
that human sexuality has additional uses and goals. This is the major reason
why, even in our current culture, both may still be condemned as equally
obscene and immoral. Such gross condemnation of all sexuality that isn't
harnessed to childbirth (and to patriarchal marriage so that children are
properly "owned" by men) has been increased by the current backlash against
women's independence. Out of fear that the whole patriarchal structure will
be eventually upset if we as women really have the autonomous power to
decide our sexual and reproductive futures (that is, if we can control our own
bodies, and thus the means of reproduction), anti-equality groups are not
only denouncing sex education and family planning as "pornographic," but
are trying to use obscenity laws to stop the sending of all contraceptive
information through the mails. Any sex or nudity outside the context of
patriarchal marriage and forced childbirth is their target. In fact, Phyllis
Schlafly has denounced the entire women's movement as "obscene."

Not surprisingly, this religious, visceral backlash has a secular, intellectual   27
counterpart that relies heavily on applying the "natural" behavior of some
selected part of the animal world to humans. This is questionable in itself,
but such Lionel Tiger-ish studies make their political purpose even more
clear by the animals they choose and the habits they emphasize. For example,
some male primates carry and generally "mother" their infants, male lions
care for their young, female elephants often lead the clan, and male penguins
literally do everything except give birth, from hatching the eggs to sacrificing
their own membranes to feed the new arrivals. Perhaps that's why many male
supremacists prefer to discuss chimps and baboons (many of whom are studied
in atypical conditions of captivity) whose behavior is suitably male-dominant.
The message is that human females should accept their animal "destiny" of
being sexually dependent and devote themselves to bearing and rearing their
young.

Defending against such repression and reaction leads to the temptation   28
to merely reverse the terms and declare that *all* nonprocreative sex is good.
In fact, however, this human activity can be as constructive or destructive,
moral or immoral, as any other. Sex as communication can send messages as
different as mutual pleasure and dominance, life and death, "erotica" and
"pornography."

The second kind of problem comes not from those who oppose women's   29
equality in nonsexual areas, whether on grounds of God or nature, but from

men (and some women, too) who present themselves as friends of civil liberties and progress. Their opposition may take the form of a concern about privacy, on the grounds that a challenge to pornography invades private sexual behavior and the philosophy of "whatever turns you on." It may be a concern about class bias, on the premise that pornography is just "workingmen's erotica." Sometimes, it's the simple argument that they themselves like pornography and therefore it must be okay. Most often, however, this resistance attaches itself to or hides behind an expressed concern about censorship, freedom of the press, and the First Amendment.

In each case, such liberal objections are more easily countered than the   30
anti-equality ones because they are less based on fact. It's true, for instance, that women's independence and autonomy would upset the whole patriarchal apple cart: the conservatives are right to be worried. It's not true, however, that pornography is a private concern. If it were just a matter of men making male-supremacist literature in their own basements to assuage their own sexual hang-ups, there would be sorrow and avoidance among women, but not the anger, outrage, and fear produced by being confronted with the preaching of sexual fascism on our newsstands, movie screens, television sets, and public streets. It is a multi-billion-dollar industry, which involves the making of public policy, if only to decide whether, as is now the case, crimes committed in the manufacture and sale of pornography will continue to go largely unprosecuted. Zoning regulations on the public display of pornography are not enforced, the sexual slavery and exploitation of children goes unpunished, the forcible use of teenage runaways is ignored by police, and even the torture and murder of prostitutes for men's sexual titillation is obscured by some mitigating notion that the women asked for it.

In all other areas of privacy, the limitation is infringement on the rights   31
and lives and safety of others. That must become true for pornography. Right now, it is exempt: almost "below the law."

As for class bias, it's simply not accurate to say that pornography is erotica   32
with less education. From the origins of the words, as well as the careful way that feminists working against pornography are trying to use them, it's clear there is a substantive difference, not an artistic or economic one. Pornography is about dominance. Erotica is about mutuality. (Any man able to empathize with women can easily tell the difference by looking at a photograph or film and putting himself in the woman's skin. There is some evidence that poor or discriminated-against men are better able to do this than rich ones.) Perhaps the most revealing thing is that this argument is generally made *on behalf* of the working class by pro-pornography liberals, but not *by* working-class spokespeople themselves.

Of course, the idea that enjoying pornography makes it okay is an over-   33
whelmingly male one. From Kinsey forward, research has confirmed that men are the purchasers of pornography, and that the majority of men are turned on by it, while the majority of women find it angering, humiliating, and not a turn-on at all. This was true even though women were shown

sexually explicit material that may have included erotica, since Kinsey and others did not make that distinction. If such rare examples of equal sex were entirely deleted, pornography itself could probably serve as sex aversion-therapy for most women; yet many men and some psychologists continue to call women prudish, frigid, or generally unhealthy if they are not turned on by their own domination. The same men might be less likely to argue that anti-Semitic and racist literature was equally okay because it gave them pleasure, or that they wanted their children to grow up with the same feelings about people of other races, other classes, that had been inflicted on them. The problem is that the degradation of women of all races is still thought to be normal.

Nonetheless, there are a few well-meaning women who are both turned on by pornography and angered that other women are not. Some of their anger is misunderstanding: objections to pornography are not condemnations of women who have been raised to believe sex and domination are synonymous, but objections to the idea that such domination is the only form that normal sexuality can take. Sometimes, this anger results from an underestimation of themselves: being turned on by a rape fantasy is not the same thing as wanting to be raped. As Robin Morgan has pointed out, the distinguishing feature of a fantasy is that the fantasizer herself is in control. Both men and women have "ravishment" fantasies in which we are passive while others act out our unspoken wishes—but they are still *our* wishes. And some anger, especially when it comes from women who consider themselves feminists, is a refusal to differentiate between what may be true for them now and what might be improved for all women in the future. To use a small but related example, a woman may now be attracted only to men who are taller, heavier, and older than she, but still understand that such superficial restrictions on the men she loves and enjoys going to bed with won't exist in a more free and less-stereotyped future. Similarly, some lesbians may find themselves following the masculine-feminine patterns that were our only model for intimate relationships, heterosexual or not, but still see these old patterns clearly and try to equalize them. It isn't that women attracted to pornography cannot also be feminists, but that pornography itself must be recognized as an adversary of women's safety and equality, and therefore, in the long run, of feminism.

Finally, there is the First Amendment argument against feminist anti-pornography campaigns: the most respectable and public opposition, but also the one with the least basis in fact.

Feminist groups are not arguing for censorship of pornography, or for censorship of Nazi literature or racist propaganda of the Ku Klux Klan. For one thing, any societal definition of pornography in a male-dominant society (or of racist literature in a racist society) probably would punish the wrong people. Freely chosen homosexual expression might be considered more "pornographic" than snuff movies, or contraceptive courses for teenagers more "obscene" than bondage. Furthermore, censorship in itself, even with the

34

35

36

444

proper definitions, would only drive pornography into more underground activity and, were it to follow the pattern of drug traffic, into even more profitability. Most important, the First Amendment is part of a statement of individual rights against government intervention that feminism seeks to expand, not contract: for instance, a woman's right to decide whether and when to have children. When we protest against pornography and educate others about it, as I am doing now, we are strengthening the First Amendment by exercising it.

The only legal steps suggested by feminists thus far have been the prosecution of those pornography makers who are accused of murder or assault and battery, prosecution of those who use children under the age of consent, enforcement of existing zoning and other codes that are breached because of payoffs to law-enforcement officials and enormous rents paid to pornography's landlords, and use of public-nuisance statutes to require that pornography not be displayed in public places where its sight cannot reasonably be avoided. All of those measures involve enforcement of existing law, and none has been interpreted as a danger to the First Amendment. 37

Perhaps the reason for this controversy is less substance than smokescreen. Just as earlier feminist campaigns to combat rape were condemned by some civil libertarians as efforts that would end by putting only men of color or poor men in jail, or in perpetuating the death penalty, anti-pornography campaigns are now similarly opposed. In fact, the greater publicity given to rape exposed the fact that white psychiatrists, educators, and other professionals were just as likely to be rapists, and changes in the law reduced penalties to ones that were more appropriate and thus more likely to be administered. Feminist efforts also changed the definition to sexual assault so that men were protected, too. 38

Though there are no statistics on the purchasers of pornography, clerks, movie-house owners, video-cassette dealers, mail-order houses, and others who serve this clientele usually remark on their respectability, their professional standing, suits, briefcases, white skins, and middle-class zip codes. For instance, the last screening of a snuff movie showing a real murder was traced to the monthly pornographic film showings of a senior partner in a respected law firm; an event regularly held by him for a group of friends including other lawyers and judges. One who was present reported that many were "embarrassed" and "didn't know what to say." But not one man was willing to object, much less offer this evidence of murder to the police. Though some concern about censorship is sincere—the result of false reports that feminist anti-pornography campaigns were really calling for censorship, or of confusion with right-wing groups who both misdefine pornography and want to censor it—much of it seems to be a cover for the preservation of the pornographic status quo. 39

In fact, the obstacles to taking on pornography seem suspiciously like the virgin-whore divisions that have been women's only choices in the past. The 40 right wing says all that is not virginal or motherly is pornographic, and thus they campaign against sexuality and nudity in general. The left wing says all sex is good as long as it's male-defined, and thus pornography must be protected. Women who feel endangered by being the victim, and men who feel demeaned by being the victimizer, have a long struggle ahead. In fact, pornography will continue as long as boys are raised to believe they must control or conquer women as a measure of manhood, as long as society rewards men who believe that success or even functioning—in sex as in other areas of life—depends on women's subservience.

But we now have words to describe our outrage and separate sex from   41
violence. We now have the courage to demonstrate publicly against pornography, to keep its magazines and films out of our houses, to boycott its purveyors, to treat even friends and family members who support it as seriously as we would treat someone who supported and enjoyed Nazi literature or the teachings of the Klan.

But until we finally untangle sexuality and aggression, there will be more   42
pornography and less erotica. There will be little murders in our beds—and very little love.

FORBIDDEN PLEASURES

PHILIP WEISS

Speaking as a consumer of pornography, Weiss presents another viewpoint on the antipornography debate, in this article first published in *Harper's Magazine* in 1986. His position is that antipornography activists are asking men to deny their masculinity. Far from being the dangerous social influence that feminists make it out to be, Weiss sees pornography instead as a harmless male indulgence that may be enjoyed in private but never actually acted on in life.

The first unsettling thing about being a man in Minneapolis during the city's yearlong debate over antipornography legislation was the sense of having been preempted.[1] The women were all so articulate. It wasn't that they were persuasive or even logical, but they had the words. They'd been thinking about these issues and talking about them for some time, and as soon as they struck they changed the language. Certain terms were used, and certain ideas. Other ideas had already been cashiered or were the subject of caricature. I felt that I was starting out at such a deficit, I had to keep my mouth shut. To say, I am a man who feels aroused by looking at and reading some of this stuff was no argument. It was like saying, I am a lizard.

I've always consumed pornography, in more or less passive ways, often guiltily. *Playboy*s were a staple of my teenage years—I can still smell the dust of the barn loft to which my confederate, a giant friend with a straw thatch of hair, brought the magazines. Into adulthood I consumed porn on the sly, seldom buying "the slicks," as the mainstream publications are known, but finding ways to see them, at men friends' homes. There is always porn around.

Among most of my friends, the porn issue rarely came up. But then it never had to. Everyone knew porn wasn't right. Its double standard was too obvious; women didn't traffic in sexually explicit pictures of men.

In Minneapolis the antiporners brought these issues to the surface, and in the process disrupted my own pattern of covert consumption. To look at

---

1. Weiss refers to the amendment to the Minneapolis City Council Code of Ordinances Relating to Civil Rights, by Catharine MacKinnon and Andrea Dworkin, which proposed that pornography is a violation of civil rights.

the proposed pornography law was to see elements of my lust pulled out like so many glistening fish guts, to have my unexamined guilt about the matter yanked from its shell. The ordinance defined as a violation of a woman's civil rights the "graphic sexually explicit subordination of women, whether in pictures or in words." Any woman might claim that she had been discriminated against by material depicting women "as sexual objects for domination, conquest, violation, exploitation, possession or use, through postures or positions of submission or servility or display." Harsh, yes, but there, in part— once you have crowbarred off the manhole covers—I am.

Those words were point iv in the ordinance that the mayor ultimately   5 vetoed. Point vi had to do with women shown bleeding, bruised, or hurt in a sexual context. I couldn't argue in favor of the male excesses, the stuff that seemed reptilian; I was happy to draw the line somewhere, probably through the use of obscenity laws. But I kept waiting for other men to stand up and defend at least the postures-of-display portion of point iv. No one did. There was the power of the feminist language—its newness, its passion about issues men did not generally discuss.

Often it seemed that the feminists were not really interested in what men   6 had to say.

The city council had hired Catharine A. MacKinnon and Andrea Dwor-   7 kin to draft the antiporn legislation at the same time the pair were teaching a course on pornography at the University of Minnesota Law School to sixty students, fifty-six of them women. The course analyzed, among other things, "the significance of penetration," and became a locus of the antiporn movement. Meanwhile, someone reported that MacKinnon had dismissed persistent questions about what material was and wasn't covered by the amendment as "a man's questions." MacKinnon, a respected constitutional scholar, argued convincingly that the report was a slur. But the gender issue was always there, and the feeling lingered that, in order to take part in the discussion, I had somehow to step out of my maleness, leave it like a husk, repudiate it.

No one induced this feeling as much as Andrea Dworkin. The author,   8 visiting from New York, could be seen everywhere, armored in girthy overalls, roofed by tumultuous dark curls. She gave amazing performances. One night she read from her work in the basement of a church. I came late, held my ear to a half-inch crack in the door, and heard the husky Dworkin oratory. In a voice that seemed less a means of expression than an internal organ, something bloody, personal, and injured that she tore out of herself regularly in public, she invoked her hoarse vocabulary of cunts, assholes, blood, violation.

I shifted my head to peep at the audience. Attentive, calm, nearly   9 churchly, they sat with shoulders squared.

Their faith in Dworkin, and the city's faith, amazed me. She was the one   10 who had written eight years before that sexual relations between a man and a woman were politically acceptable only when the man had a "limp penis." It was a line I found myself repeating to women friends, each time studying the friend's face to capture even a flicker of agreement. How was it that this quotation had not been hung about Dworkin's neck like a bell when she came to town? How was it that the law the city had hired her to write was being discussed as though it involved snow emergencies or other quotidian civil processes, and not treated as an attempt to govern sexual politics, "the significance of penetration"?

Then something happened that pushed me toward Dworkin's side and made   11
me wonder about my own role. It was a debate between Dworkin and Matthew Stark, the head of the Minnesota Civil Liberties Union. Stark stood up first. He spoke with a bullish eloquence about the difference between word and act, and about the First Amendment. He didn't talk about pornography really. Pornography, he seemed to agree in passing, was disgusting, but that was not the point. Then Dworkin got up and plunged headfirst into pornography. The audience was behind her. Her heavy left arm shook in the air, tears stained the spaces around her eyes into violet saucers. Unless the law were passed, Dworkin said, reducing matters to an attractively simple proposition, women would be regarded only as cunts. "We are to provide total access to every orifice and allow forced sex as if there is nothing that can fill that aching void."

Two seats away from me in the front row, a middle-aged man in cowboy   12
boots kept shaking his head. He had an unruly mustache and a somewhat gone-to-seed look. He turned to me—another man, a presumed ally—in disbelief. Then he began exclaiming aloud. At last he interrupted the speech with an obscene comment about Dworkin's thighs.

I hissed as loudly as anyone. Dworkin put him down, and he stood and   13
walked out. One could sense a rush of satisfaction among the antiporners at having living proof. For he had provided, in corpus, Exhibit A: the scumball, the lizard, the consumer of pornography, the man for whom women were not human beings.

If you were a man who opposed the amendment, this was the choice you   14
were left with: be like him and regard women as cunts, or be as aloof and granitey as the First Amendment, like Matt Stark, and say that porn was disgusting but that Nazis, too, must be able to express themselves. The qualities the women had brought to the table—sincerity, an emotional intensity about sexual issues—were somehow not available to men. You could be either a scumball or a constitutionalist, though in between there was a large and uncharted territory whose existence it would be easy to deny as long as no one opened his mouth.

But who would speak up? The public discourse had been narrowed; there   15
was a sort of licensing of acceptable opinion at work. For a year the antiporn movement seemed to be the strongest voice in the city, and I now see that shame, the manipulation of traditional pruderies, was an important factor in its success. It specialized in demonstrations at which male "secrets" were

unveiled and linked with criminal behaviors. I especially remember the "porn drive," when antiporn groups, including the Pornography Resource Center (or PRC, a think tank and mobilization committee), issued a call for donations of pornography. Antiporners littered the marble floor of City Hall with the stuff, asserting that women had smuggled it out of their homes at great risk.

The rhetoric hardly mattered; the antiporners' triumph was in confronting City Hall with men's closet items. Reporters—mostly men, among them myself—buzzed around, uncertain where to focus the Minicams. Crouched over a tangle of oro-genitally fastened bodies just a few feet from the Father of Waters statue (naked himself, but judiciously draped), I fought my prurience by taking indecipherable notes against my knee. 16

And then, in a posture the public mind associates with a group of law enforcement officials brandishing confiscated goods, three of the organizers came to the microphone, one of them holding under her chin a magazine opened to a randy bedroom scene. A woman in dishabille straddled a man who appeared to be whacking her with a brush. Both of them leered at the camera. I wanted to look at the pictures—in fact, the PRC seemed to be daring us to—but I kept my face on the granite faces of the antiporners, only occasionally stealing glances at what they'd seized. Their point was that if you liked that stuff you liked to batter women, and I walked out of City Hall a few minutes later trilling vaguely with shame. 17

In responding to such assaults, I tended to be oblique. One thing I did was telephone the PRC and, as a reporter, ask a series of what might have been characterized as a man's questions. 18

"Five million people bought the Vanessa Williams issue of *Penthouse*. Who are they?" I asked. "Wife batterers? Why did they want to see her?" 19

I might as well have been asking about the behavior of vermin. "I don't know or care," said the PRC lady on the line. 20

Another time I called and asked her if she could give me the name of one man who had reformed himself because of the antiporn movement, one man who was formerly aroused by pornography and now sees that he was wrong. She told me such men exist, that she would try and find one for me. But she never called back. 21

Sometimes I wondered if I ought to reform myself. Partly this was the effect of my girlfriend's house, which she shared with three other women and where, upstairs by the bathroom door, someone had tacked a poem about men not being able to dance. Sitting on the old couch downstairs and listening to one of the roommates talk about patriarchal structure, I would glance across the room into the pier glass, see myself nodding to what was being said, and think, Who is that nodding? Someone who was under construction, someone unmanned, lifted out of his male husk. Often I felt as if I'd wandered into a city of women. 22

The PRC's women were stone-faced, square-shouldered, in that city of women, they were the caryatids. I saw two of them at one of the cooperative 23 restaurants where I ate; they were clearly gay, and my sense was heightened of living in a place where a culture that had little to do with my own appetites was establishing itself. The *Star and Tribune* raised the gay question as an aside in a news story but never addressed it head-on. There were things people didn't talk about. When a male writer in a gay newspaper wrote an article characterizing the porn amendment as a sort of radical-feminist-lesbian Trojan horse wheeled into City Hall by women in flannel shirts (male gays tended to oppose the bill), I quoted the line in a story and later opened the paper to find it had been cut. Time to keep your head down, I thought.

The other side had the floor. When anything happened, everyone waited 24 to hear what the PRC had to say about it. After a disturbed, previously institutionalized woman set herself afire in a protest against porn inside a news shop that summer, all the media called the PRC. A spokeswoman likened the burn victim to Norman Morrison, a Quaker who had killed himself outside the Pentagon in 1965 after U.S. bombing raids had killed scores of Vietnamese civilians. Then a group of PRC women gathered on the sidewalk outside a porn theater on Lake Street to make an official statement. While lamenting the woman's decision, it acknowledged that burning "as an act of political protest" and noted that women live "under conditions of political and sexual terrorism." They dispersed without answering questions (though they did regroup and reread the statement for a late-arriving TV crew).

The conference had the urgency of a meeting with guerrillas in the 25 mountains. I respected their power, and wanted to know what their agenda meant for me.

"A socially constructed sexuality": that was what one feminist had termed the 26 goal of the antiporn amendment. This was what I'd wanted to see when I asked the PRC lady to show me one reformed man, it was the concept I was always struggling with.

A night last winter. My girlfriend and I have gone to see the film *Blade* 27 *Runner*, about which the paper I work for had printed a listing written in the winking language of men. "Watch for the snake lady," it said. I understood from that, correctly, that the snake lady would be nude.

And now, on the way back, my girlfriend says she agrees with a friend's 28 statement that the movie was violent toward women.

Irritated, I pause to calculate. "There were five people killed in that 29 movie," I say. "Three of them were men."

"Yes, but the *way* the women were killed." 30

"The way they were killed?" I whacked the steering wheel. "Those 31 schmucks were killed horribly. They crushed that guy's skull on camera."

She's quiet. I've been yelling. I refocus on the road. 32

She says, "It was sexual, the way they were killed. The snake woman was 33 naked through that clear raincoat. And Daryl Hannah looked like she was having an orgasm when she died."

"What do you mean?" I say.   34

"The leotard she had on. She might as well have been naked."   35

"That's ridiculous," I say. In fact, I am disappointed in Hannah; I had   36
thought the movie was made early enough in her career that there would be
a nude scene, but there hadn't been.

"You could practically see her nipples," my girlfriend says.   37

"You couldn't."   38

"You could."   39

"You couldn't," I say.   40

My voice, swelling with anger, fills the car. "I know," I say. "I was looking 41
for them."

The sound reverberates. I haven't lost my temper like this in years, and   42
there's a stunned silence. She and I pad into her house separately.

It's another hour before we speak to each other. I apologize. "You're   43
right," I say. "I see now that the deaths of the women were sexualized in a
way that the men's were not."

I hear myself speaking in an alien language. The words pile up, lodge in   44
my throat like something friable and dry that others have formed with their
hands.

Reconstruction started and stalled. Sexualized violence was abhorrent, yes.   45
But mere objectification? I faltered.

The antiporners were emphatic. The very act of looking at a naked model   46
was an artifact of male supremacy, the reduction of women to chattel. The
women in the pictures had had no choice when they posed. In fact, the
ordinance would have allowed participants in pornography to sue for its
suppression on the grounds that they had been coerced. The ordinance defined coercion very broadly; it could include consensual agreements that the
models later simply regretted.

The ordinance was saying that pornography is the inevitable condition   47
of women in our society. Often I saw right-thinking men express similar
views. Thus, *Washington Post* columnist Richard Cohen, who suggested that
Vanessa Williams was a social victim; she had learned to value herself for the
wrong things, both as beauty queen and porn subject.

What both Cohen and the antiporn legislation said was, in essence, just: 48
people should be able to make of themselves what they want. And yet a
universe of feeling was being flattened in the ethical rush. Vanessa Williams
had a beautiful body. More, its display was plainly something she too had
taken pleasure in. Sexual display is a way in which people feel valued, connect
themselves without really connecting.

But there was still the sexism. Women were almost universally the subjects   49
of porn (that endless line of $10-an-hour models), and though they might
enjoy it, they were passive. It seemed always to be a man's eyes at work.

Of course, I could reply to myself, the roles were changing. Women also 50
could be producers, like the women who were putting out porn focusing on
male subjects for a women's home video market. I was like the urban liberal
who hopes that a criminal suspect will turn out to be white—I wanted the
blame spread equally. I got encouragement from *Elbowing the Seducer*, a fine
and sexually explicit novel by T. Gertler, a woman, in which it was suggested
that the protagonist, a writer, had taken the genderless byline D. Lietman so
that she might appropriate a male privilege: the creation of prose with a
pornographic component. Progress, I thought.

In the end, though, women's porn wasn't going to resolve my Minneapolis 51
problem. As long as men's and women's roles in society were different, the
porn would be, too. There would always be objections. This was the cul-de-
sac the year kept driving me toward: men and women would always be at
odds. I could never forget a scene at one of Matthew Stark's appearances
when a woman friend of his, crouched and crying, her hands tensed like claws,
renounced their friendship. My own women friends would always disagree
with me. And there'd always be the women's reverence for their own fantasies,
which they felt were inherently purer than the stuff of iv, v, vi, etc. Pornography "*is* violence" against women, Sheila Kitzinger, a respected anthropologist, baldly stated on one page of *Woman's Experience of Sex*, while elsewhere
in the book, amid photographs of a woman pleasuring herself, women were
told that "fantasy can be the poetry of sex."

Of course, we men didn't have Kitzingers. We had Gucciones, ethical 52
Richard Cohens, and so on. But there was no corresponding male language
of sexuality, no poets, intellectuals, advocates.

In retrospect, I see that we did have Tim Campbell. But Tim Campbell 53
had been easy to ignore, and I didn't read him till months after the furor died
down. Campbell was gay and ran the *GLC Voice*, a newspaper largely serving
gays ("poofters," he called them). I'd avoided him for a bunch of reasons. He
was given to ad hominem attacks (Dworkin suffered, he said, from a "lack of
prettiness"). Also, he'd become a participant in the conflict. "I believe that
the objectification of the sensual model is a healthy part of sexual experience,"
he'd said, and his home had been spray-painted, perhaps by the same people
who decorated the sex shop a few blocks away with the slogan "Castrate Porn
Users."

When I read Campbell's back issues in the library, I saw that he'd had 54
my number. "I believe that men are going to have to do more than avoid the
issues of content of pornography to satisfactorily deal with the 'radical
feminists,'" he wrote. "Men are going to have to stand up and own their use
of pornography. They are going to have to explain what goes on with them
as they view pornography. And they are going to have to communicate a little
better with straight women over their use of *Playboy*-like material . . . the
Brownmillers of the world have got a lot of women convinced that dirty,

rotten, awful things pass through straight men's minds when they look at pornography. There will be no peace over this issue until that lie is squashed. If it is not a lie, then maybe the 'radical feminists' should win."

His challenge still hangs there. I picture him: big and gourd-shaped, a redheaded satyrish figure in a tight brown suit at the back of the room during City Hall press conferences, "asking" his 50-second questions about porn. He wants an answer from me.

What I'd say is that porn's reductions, even its degradations, seem to go on in a feverish, removed zone. Because these thoughts are unspoken, because they violate norms, they've always seemed grotesque to me; they breed the conviction that I'm different and outrageous. Yet what relation do they bear to my actions? A study by two female researchers of women who read romance novels—a form of "mild pornography" generally entailing the rape of a young woman by an older man with whom she later falls in love—found that, despite savoring such Neanderthal fantasies, the readers expressed "liberal views" of a woman's place in society. Their porn is private, and I'm with them there. Porn, and the fantasies porn fosters, is like so many of the other dreams and movies that go on in one's head, that make life interesting. But I don't visualize emirs and pashas, nothing B.C. It's American, rock and roll era. What makes it male? Maybe that it's so gritty in detail, so aggressively superficial, nothing gossamer, nothing violent either. It's kaleidoscopic, with the frantic pacing and sudden absorption of an MTV video, and featuring the weird synecdoche of photographs, the reduction of a person to a close-up detail. As I say, often it seems grotesque. But I observe myself—living in Minneapolis has made me do that much—and I'm convinced that world is successfully private. It's about connecting without real connection: the flaring wants one has and does not act on, but which are still desires, that one turns in one's mind and does not seek to make into facts of life.

ONE MAN'S PLEASURES: A RESPONSE TO WEISS

◑

DOUGLAS CAMPBELL

This response to Philip Weiss's article soon followed in the pages of *Harper's Magazine* (1986), with writer Douglas Campbell analyzing the problems inherent in Weiss's assumptions about pornography. Campbell argues that the "social fantasy" portrayed by pornography—the image of men dominating women—is not merely a "private" indulgence, but does in fact directly influence many of the ways people behave in society.

In his attempt to come to terms personally with what one feminist he quotes calls a "socially constructed sexuality," Philip Weiss does manage to speak to a conspicuous gap in the ongoing debate over pornography. But his perspective as a "passive," "often guilty" consumer of pornography reveals a limited appreciation of some of the key issues of that debate. Specifically, his assumptions about the nature of pornography and its social role are problematic.

Weiss claims that pornography is appealing, in general, because it is "gritty," "aggressively superficial," and "male." This characterization enables him to find entertainment in "the reduction of a person to a closeup detail," and to conclude that men relate to pornography in much the same way they relate to rock and roll. He suggests that there is a qualitative difference between the pornography that arouses him and that which seems "reptilian," the stuff of "male excesses." And he is content to allow traditional standards of obscenity to define that distinction.

Weiss's confidence that sexually explicit imagery can be judged solely on the basis of its subject matter reflects a shallow view of pornography. This is a relatively accessible approach, since if we focus only on visual content, pornography becomes easy to recognize and, in theory, easy to regulate. The depiction of certain activities—pedophilia or extreme sexual violence, for example—is so unambiguously objectionable that few among even the most vigilant guardians of free speech will openly justify it. Hence the task of establishing the lowest common denominator of acceptable morality is fairly uncomplicated. And pornography thus ceases to pose much of a problem.

The "problem" of pornography, however, has to do not only with what the specific images are and how they represent sex, but also with what they

1

2

3

4

say, implicitly, about the nature of social-sexual relations between men and women. The ideological message in a given porn spread may not have been consciously engineered.

But the scenarios, postures, and facial expressions commonly represented in pornographic images speak for themselves. What they tell us is that the exercise of power, by men, within (and, by implication, beyond) the realm of sex is virtuous, desired, and fun. Therein lies the essence of pornographic fantasy. 5

Weiss argues reasonably that the fantasies *inspired* by pornography are harmless because they are private, contained, and have no bearing on actions: "Porn's reductions, even its degradations, seem to go on in a feverish, removed zone." While this may be true to some extent, it does not follow that sexual fantasies—and more general fantasies about male power—have no bearing on our attitudes toward social-sexual conduct. 6

Through its sheer prevalence and endurance, pornography has acquired a degree of social acceptance. We are, as noted, generally content to regulate the grossly obscene; the vast majority of porn is dismissed as little more than a curious aspect of contemporary culture. As a result, the social fantasy manifest through its images is quietly legitimized. Is it unreasonable to suggest that this fantasy of the pleasure of male power exerts a passive but nonetheless real influence on perceptions of social reality? The fine line of reason or instinct that separates fantasy and reality may well become obscured. In this context, pornography is properly understood not simply as a product, but as part of a social process. 7

The victims of this process are many. They include women who are compelled to participate in the business of pornography and who come to judge themselves as they are judged by men. They include all men who have been conditioned to objectify sex—to view it and value it in isolation from its essential personal or social context. (It is the absence of social context and the tendency to cater to a fixation on sexual anatomy which distinguishes traditional pornography from that which Weiss suggests is consumed by women in the form of romance novels and other pseudo-erotica.) Among the victims too are all men and women who find themselves falsely characterized as, respectively, sexual aggressors and sexual targets. 8

We must be actively concerned with more than the surface appearance of pornography. And we must not confine our critical analyses to the realm of traditional morality, where porn is judged according to a sense of "right and wrong." Rather, our attention should be directed to the social dimension of pornography. As such, porn should be judged in the context of social ethics: according to a reasoned assessment of the extent to which the interests of one group of individuals are being pursued at the expense of another's. 9

The challenge to men is not, as Weiss presents it, to venture into the fray of anti-pornographers, there to slay the myth that "dirty rotten, awful 10 things pass through straight men's minds when they look at pornography." The real challenge is to recognize pornography's role as a pernicious socializing agent. Only then can we begin to appreciate its potential to inhibit the development of social-sexual relations between men and women that are not based on the exploitation of power. Only then can we understand the extent to which it inhibits the realization of a socially constructed sexuality.

PORNOGRAPHY AND CENSORSHIP

◑

FRED SMALL

This essay by Fred Small, first printed in the journal *Changing Men* (1985), questions whether the "blunt and dangerous instrument" of censorship is really the best strategy against sexism in society, or whether it might remove more rights than it restores. If antipornography legislation can ban pornography because it encourages violence against women, then what is to stop censorship from spreading to other areas of culture, including the suppression of materials some see as educational or artistic?

Writing about pornography[1] I shoulder two burdens: guilt and fear. Each clouds reason and impedes communication. I feel guilty about patriarchy, about the injuries women have for centuries suffered at the hands of men and the oppression against which they struggle today. While I have actively supported their struggle, I have also unwittingly participated in their oppression. This knowledge is painful. I worry about making more mistakes, causing more hurt.

And I am afraid of controversy, afraid of criticism and denunciation by sisters and brothers who share my critique of patriarchy and my commitment to equality. I fear their anger. When Andrea Dworkin says that "any defense of pornography is war" against women,[2] I am discouraged from contemplative and free-ranging discussion. Pornography is so complicated and so vast a subject. My thinking on it has changed more than once and will change again. Dare I cast my thoughts in unchangeable print?

The pain of pornography is not equally shared. As a man, I am not hurt and enraged by pornography in the same way as women. Some will feel I have nothing to contribute, no moral ground to stand on. But I am concerned enough about the dangers of censorship and about my priorities for activism that I offer my thoughts.

I oppose censorship because I believe it threatens our freedom to express unpopular ideas, to create subversive images, to make radical culture. I think that the legislative restrictions proposed for pornography are so vague that they could and would be used against feminist publications. Even if worded more precisely, these restrictions would set a precedent for governmental repression dangerous to us all.

My views on pornography itself are less strongly held. They are tentative, admitting of error, colored by personal experience and inexperience. As an artist I strive to create a new culture that fully respects all women and men as human beings. Pornography has no place in such a culture. I denounce pornography as I denounce all sexist propaganda. But I suspect that pornography is not the central problem of patriarchy, that it is more symptom than disease. I suspect it may account for less direct harm than is sometimes attributed to it. I suspect that strategies other than antiporn activism may be more effective against sexism and violence. Pornography may not be the best target for our rage.

Censorship: Too Blunt and Dangerous an Instrument

Misogynist violence in this country has imposed a state of siege against women. Responding to these intolerable conditions, women and men in Minneapolis proposed an ordinance in 1983 that would permit individuals to sue to prevent the production or sale of pornography as a civil rights violation. Slightly modified, the Minneapolis ordinance has been offered as model legislation against pornography. Initially appealing, this legislation threatens grave dangers.

While proponents of the ordinance argue that its meaning is plain, many people—including widely respected feminist leaders—find its language vague and confusing. It defines pornography as "the graphic sexually explicit subordination of women through pictures and/or words" that satisfies *any one* of nine criteria. These include the presentation of women "dehumanized as sexual objects" or "in postures of sexual submission" or "as whores by nature" or "being penetrated by objects" or "in scenarios of degradation," or the exhibition of "women's body parts . . . such that women are reduced to those parts."

These terms do not mean what you or I or Catharine MacKinnon or Andrea Dworkin thinks they should mean. *They mean whatever a commissioner or judge or jury or the Supreme Court of the United States thinks they should mean in the political and social climate of the moment.*

Is fellatio "subordination"? Is genital exposure? Is wearing high heels? Is a short story about lesbians making love a "scenario of degradation"? Is the missionary position a "posture of sexual submission"? Does the word "objects" include a speculum demonstrated in a woman's self-help health manual or a dildo described in a lesbian sex guide? Does a documentary on prostitution depict women as "whores by nature"? Does an illustration teaching women how to examine their breasts "reduce" women to their "parts"? Don't ask me. Ask a juror in Attapulgus, Georgia, or Brigham City, Utah, or New York, New York. Ask William Rehnquist.

459

Advocates of this legislation may believe that they command its destiny,   10
that it will be used forever in the spirit of its creation. Historically, however,
censorship is invoked not against the powerful and ideologically dominant,
but against the weak, the outlaw, the radical. Ordinance coauthor Dworkin
concedes—indeed, she asserts proudly—that this ordinance will be applied
against materials produced by and for the gay and lesbian community.[3] She
even concedes that it could be used against her own writing on pornography.[4]
She is willing to take that chance. I am not. A time when *Our Bodies, Our
Selves* is being removed from library shelves under pressure from the Right
is no time to devise a new rationale for censorship.

Writers, photographers, artists, models, producers, directors, actors, pub-   11
lishers, clerical workers, magazine distributors, news dealers, and art exhibi-
tors are all potential defendants under this legislation. They can't be sure how
its language will be interpreted, either—and they can't afford to find out.
Many will refrain from producing, selling, or exhibiting legally protected
materials because of the possibility of a ruinous adverse ruling or because the
costs of defending a lawsuit would be prohibitive.

Proponents of the ordinance emphasize that its enforcement provisions   12
are civil, not criminal. But civil law can have the same impact as criminal law.
When individuals sue for damages or to enjoin publication, the power of the
state is invoked. A judge or jury looks at the material and decides if it is
"pornography." If the judge issues an injunction, and the defendant refuses
to comply, he or she can be sent to jail. The result is censorship: the materials
are forbidden, banned by state decree.

Censorship advocates argue that if pornography contributes to violence   13
against women, then censorship is *ipso facto* justified. Research in this area is
very new. The studies some find conclusive others find ambiguous or flawed.
But even if we assume for the sake of argument that pornography does
influence violence against women, censorship is still not the answer. It is too
dangerous, and it will not work.

The lethal effects of alcohol on the victims of crimes (including rape and   14
drunk driving) committed under its influence, on alcoholics, and on people
close to them are unarguable. But when prohibition was tried it failed utterly,
and succeeded only in romanticizing liquor further, feeding organized crime,
and breeding public cynicism. Likewise, prostitution is an abhorrent way for
human beings to relate to one another. It systematically exploits and brutalizes
women and girls forced by economic oppression to engage in it. But its
illegality in forty-nine states has done nothing to protect women or to improve
sexual relations. Banning porn will not make it unavailable, just illegal—
thereby enhancing its allure.

If the state can ban pornography because it "causes" violence against   15
women, it can also ban *The Wretched of the Earth* because it causes revolution,
Gay Community News because it causes homosexuality, *Steal This Book* because
it causes thievery, and *The Feminine Mystique* because it causes divorce. When

speech is abridged in order to prevent crime, the precedent is set for censoring any book, magazine, or film documentary that encourages civil disobedience or draft resistance, suggests herbal remedies unapproved by the F.D.A., explains home birth techniques, or approves gay or lesbian sex. Despite its shortcomings, failures, and misapplications, the First Amendment does protect ideas worth protecting. Carving out special exceptions to it will return to haunt us.

Pornography is a concrete, stationary target for our rage against misogynist violence, a horrifying and seemingly intractable problem. It is an issue on which feminists and our old foes, the religious Right, can at last agree, and thus united, win. It is just a start, goes the argument, but at least it's winnable. 16

But a start to what? After the porn shop is closed down, the Moral Majority's next target will not be the businessmen's club that excludes women or the sweatshop that exploits them; it will be the gay bookstore, another purveyor of "perversion." I am in favor of building coalitions with those who disagree with us on other issues, but people who rail against pornography, abortion, sex education, and gay rights in the same breath are too dangerous to dignify with alliance or embolden with victory. We in the men's movement are all sexual outlaws: sissies, gays, bisexuals, egalitarians, nudists, abortionists, sodomists, pacifists. Let us not arm those who would destroy us. 17

Pornography: A Picture of the Pain

Revolting as pornography can be, it does not exist in a cultural vacuum. I perceive it as just one band in a continuous spectrum of sexist media. Other media, it seems to me, are equally destructive and more pervasive. 18

The critics of pornography are right. Pornography is relentlessly sexist, displaying women as objects for men's sexual gratification. It wrenches sex from any human context of affection, understanding, or commitment. It depicts intercourse without reference to either contraception or conception. It generally presents a viciously narrow and rigid physical stereotype of women: young, slim-waisted, large-busted, with virtually no body hair. Often it associates sex with violence. It is patriarchal, produced by a multimillion-dollar, male-dominated industry in which women are exploited and frequently mistreated. 19

In each of these particulars pornography seems indistinguishable from American mass media as a whole. Advertising (including TV, radio, print, billboard, and shop window display), movies, television, music videos, recorded music (including album cover art), magazines, and written fiction inculcate the same values and perpetuate the same stereotypes. Sexism and violence are epidemic in our society. Sexism and violence run in a seamless continuum from *The New Yorker* to *Esquire* to *Playboy* to *Hustler*. The sole 20 unique feature of pornography is that its sexism and violence involve women, and frequently men, with their genitalia graphically displayed.

Personally, I am no more offended by sexism and violence unclothed than 21
clothed. I am no more offended by *Playboy* than by *Bride's* magazine, nor more by *Gallery* than by the mercenary magazine *Soldier of Fortune*, no more by *Behind the Green Door* than by *Porky's*, no more by an s/m video than by *The Texas Chainsaw Massacre*. One of the top-grossing films of all time was also one of the most sexist and violent: *Indiana Jones and the Temple of Doom*, targeted at and enthusiastically promoted to a juvenile audience. The "classic" *Gone with the Wind* panders vicious racist and sexist stereotypes while it celebrates rape.

Among so many media abuses, why does pornography strike us as pat- 22
ently, uniquely offensive? Nearly all of us, women and men, are survivors of deep hurt and humiliation around sexuality and nudity. As children we were reprimanded if we touched our genitals, punished if we engaged in sex play, yelled at if we wandered outside naked. Our questions about sex provoked adult discomfort, hostility, and sometimes violence. Many of us were victims of sexual abuse. Nudity is still taboo in public and in most households. Sex remains largely forbidden, mysterious, charged with cloudy memories of pain and powerlessness. No wonder the depiction of women and men in a sexual context brings intense response, whether revulsion or stimulation. Both may be a distorted measure of reality.

My own observations of pornography do not rise to the level of scientific 23
research. Feminism has taught us, however, that personal experience may be at least as true as what passes for science. My observations suggest that most pornography is not inherently violent, and that explicitly violent pornography is not as ubiquitous as some have alleged.

Playboy: Violence in Disguise?

Playboy, Penthouse, and their imitators are commonplace in the United States. 24
They are generally available at newsstands and convenience stores and are advertised in mass-circulation newspapers. These magazines are slightly slicker and subtler than the "hardcore" magazines found in porn shops. They use more sophisticated photography, more "discreet" poses, and more articles on nonsexual subject matter to project a "classier" image than their raunchy brethren. With few exceptions (which are apparently increasing), they avoid explicitly violent imagery in their photographs of women. Antiporn activists argue, however, that the images in these magazines are inherently violent because they depict women as powerless, subservient, and subjugated.

I think the images in these magazines operate differently. Economic and 25
political realities notwithstanding, most men do not perceive women as pow-

erless, in part because women hold the power of rejection. I suspect that a man who whistles at women on the street actually perceives women as having more sexual power than he. We are trained from childhood to believe that real men get sex from women, that if we do not get sex from women we are not men, we are nothing. Women can deny sex to men, thereby denying our manhood, our existence. Men do not want to hurt women. Men hurt women only when they have been fooled into believing with all the force of hallucination that they must hurt women in order to save their own lives. It is a brutal order that robs the humanity of both women and men.

Playboy offers men a dream vacation from this system. In its pages, women   26
are not aloof and rejecting, but welcoming and sexually accessible. *Playboy* delights in showing "nice girls"—The Girls of the Ivy League, The Girls of the Big Ten—wanting sex, wanting us. In these purposefully constructed images, women greet us with flattery and invitation, with airbrushed smiles that speak eager, delighted consent; they are not powerless; they freely surrender their power of rejection; they are not coerced or hurt; they are on our side. They seem to say to us: "I want sex with you. Therefore, you are a man." If the fantasy sounds pathetic or preposterous, it is a measure of male terror and desperation.

The fabricated letters to these magazines, sold separately in compilations   27
like *Forum*, complete this picture. These letters, which offer the wildest, most nonsensical of male reveries, do not celebrate rape, violence, or coercion. Rather, they are tales of male passivity and female assertiveness, stories of an ordinary guy minding his own business when a beautiful woman offers or, more typically, demands to have sex with him. The male burden of initiative and performance is lifted by these voracious, undiscriminating, approving women. The image that typifies pornography is not men raping women, but women seducing men.

Of course, all this ignores the *context* of women's social and economic   28
powerlessness. Real life "seduction" is frequently rape or harassment. It is possible that these nonviolent images operate within men's psyches to contribute to actual violence. But the heart of the antiporn argument is that the violence lies *in the pornography itself*. If porn is violent only because society is violent, then every depiction of relations between women and men is violent.[5] If the roots of violence lie outside pornography, pruning its branches with censorship is a diversion from more vital work.

Violent Pornography: Core or Fringe?

Violent pornography is repellent. In the context of the real-world sexual   29
violence that threatens every woman, pornographic melding of sex and violence is especially obscene. Antiporn activists suggest that nearly all porn is

violent, that porn is everywhere, and therefore violent porn is everywhere, relentless, inescapable.

My own investigations, deliberate if inexhaustive, indicate that violent porn is not ubiquitous. I looked first at the corner grocery. They carried no porn at all. (I thanked the owner for that policy.) I went to the nearest 7-Eleven. They carried *Playboy*, *Penthouse*, *Cheri*, and the like behind the counter with only the titles showing. To study these and other porn magazines, I went to the biggest news dealer in town, where men linger furtively at the porn racks. Combining the scores of porn magazines on display— *Swank*, *Stag*, *Pub*, *Oui*, *Velvet*, *Partner*—I could find not one photograph depicting physical violence, bondage, or coercion.[6] 30

So I took the subway into the city, to Boston's Combat Zone. My roommate warned me to be careful. You don't go there unless you work there, you want something sexual, or you're lost. Cops stand around in clusters on the street, waiting for trouble. 31

My search ended at the Liberty Book Shop. They carried bondage and s/m magazines, maybe five to ten percent of their stock. The back cover of *Slave Auction* pictured a naked black woman bound and gagged. My stomach turned. Then I saw the cover of *Enslave*, which showed a leather-clad black woman yanking a bound and gagged white man on a chain leash. As I looked further, I discovered that the majority of these magazines showed women as "dominatrixes" (Aggressive Women . . . Who Demand to Meet You!) over captive, humiliated men. Whoever was in charge, the scenes looked less realistic than professional wrestling. I saw no pictures of cutting, bleeding, mutilation, or death. I know these images exist, but I spent the better part of a day looking for them in a major urban center and could not find them.[7] 32

My modest research suggests, first, that explicitly violent pornography is not pervasive or predominant. It seems apparent that these magazines account for a small fraction of the porn market.[8] The Liberty Book Shop is not a place you'll walk into by mistake. With rare exception, the only way you'll encounter violent pornography is by seeking it out—or by living with someone who does. 33

Second, the frequency of male-submissive imagery in sadomasochistic magazines raises questions in my mind about assumptions that pornographic images translate directly into behavior. I don't pretend to know how these images operate in the lives of men and women, but the answer is not self-evident. 34

Finally, I was struck by the ferocity of images of male violence in magazines more readily available than pornographic magazines. Magazines glorifying guns and mercenary warfare are common at newsstands. Boxing and wrestling magazines carried at the corner grocery are filled with photographs of men brutally beating men, faces sometimes covered with blood, and men being subjected to severe pain and humiliation. Clearly, these images are 35 propaganda for male violence against men. Horrible as is violence against women, male violence against men is more frequent. Men are three times more likely to be murdered than women and twice as likely to be assaulted.[9] Of course, we are trained from childhood to believe that men are appropriate victims of male violence while women are inappropriate (albeit frequent) victims. But the men's movement should know better. If we are outraged at images of male violence against women, where is our outrage at images of male violence against men?

The Road to a Just Society: No Shortcuts

If censorship is too blunt and dangerous an instrument to use against pornography, and if the role of pornography in real world violence is not clear cut, how do we fight sexual exploitation and violence? 36

The remedy to bad speech is not less speech, but more. The messages of pornography are insidious in part because they are virtually the only messages most men get about sex. In the absence of free and open discussion of sexuality, porn speaks to men without rebuttal. It is frequently the only sex "education" boys receive. It flourishes in the darkness. It thrives on taboo. In a society that encouraged inquisitive, guilt-free discussion of sex from childhood on, pornography would be an absurd irrelevancy. In the long term, the only effective strategy against porn and the values it represents is to build that society. 37

We need to bring sex out in the open, into the light. We need universal, relaxed, nonreproachful, nonhomophobic sex education. We need stories, drawings, photographs, poems, songs, street theater, movies, advertisements, and TV shows about the ways real sex with real people can be. We need to see each other naked, casually and nonsexually, at the beach and in our backyards, to know what real people look like, to preempt prurience. We need to think about and heal the hurts in our lives that have left us with sexual compulsions, addictions, and obsessions. 38

We need to continue the long struggle against sexism and violence. There are no shortcuts. We need more shelters for battered women and effective police response to domestic violence. We need to counsel men to stop abusing women and women not to tolerate it. We need a massive education campaign against rape—in schools, at workplaces, on the airwaves. We need boycotts of products advertised with sexist imagery. We need nonsexist textbooks and sports programs. We need to encourage children to feel proud and powerful. We need to elect feminist women and antisexist men to public office. We need to organize working women. We need gay rights. We need to involve men fully in raising and loving our children. 39

We must crack down on crime in the porn industry. Assault, battery, rape, and coercion occur in that industry like any other and should be prosecuted. The production of child pornography is virtually always child abuse and should be prosecuted. Publication and distribution of pornography that is made possible by unlawful coercion or violence against a "model" should be enjoined as a violation of her or his privacy rights. We can regulate the time, place, and manner of pornography sale and display so as not to offend the unwary. We can use picket lines to challenge the consumers of pornography to reexamine the way they think about women and about themselves. 40

A century ago, many feminists turned their energies away from women's rights toward moral purity. Alcohol became a scapegoat for innumerable social ills. It was widely believed that booze, by loosening men's inhibitions, brought out their inherently degraded nature. The result of this historic shift was the temperance movement, short-lived prohibition, and slowed gains for women. Let us not repeat this mistake with pornography out of frustration with the pace of our progress against the injustice that surrounds us. 41

Our society is misogynist and violent. Pornography is a sign of the times. Killing the messenger, however tempting, will not change the bad news. Sex and sexuality are complicated and poorly understood. The history of sexual legislation is frightening. It is the wrong course. We need more speech about sex, not less. Let us continue to talk in a way that cherishes the humanity in all of us. 42

Notes and References

1. I confine my discussion to pornography aimed at heterosexual males because I am most familiar with it and most qualified to assess it.

2. Andrea Dworkin, address delivered at Boston University, April 3, 1985.

3. Dworkin, *op. cit.*

4. *Ibid.*

5. See Ellen Willis, "Feminism, Moralism, and Pornography," in Snitow *et al.*, eds., *Powers of Desire: The Politics of Sexuality* (New York: Monthly Review Press, 1983), p. 464; Carole S. Vance and Ann Bar Snitow, "Toward a Conversation About Sex in Feminism: A Modest Proposal," *Signs*, Vol. 10, No. 1 (Autumn 1984), pp. 128–129.

6. *Hustler* editor Larry Flynt's vicious and deliberately provocative stances on sex and politics lead to hideous images. The May 1985 issue contained the most disturbing image I saw in my survey of pornography: a staged photograph of a black "family" cannibalizing an infant, with this text: "FOOD FOR THOUGHT. Millions of poor Africans are starving to death every day while lunch and dinner may be staring them right in the face. We're not saying that cannibalism is the only solution to the continent's massive hunger problem—it's just an idea the natives may find easy to digest," p. 27. Because this image does not concern sex, it would not be covered by a Minneapolis-type ordinance.

7. See Gayle Rubin, "Censored: Antiporn Laws and Women's Liberation," *Gay Community News*, Dec. 22, 1984, p. 8, for a similar impression of porn inventory. I assume one can obtain violent materials through the mails or by a more thorough search.

8. The Pornography Resource Center cites a study indicating that "depictions of bondage, domination, and spanking" constitute 17.2 percent of *hardcore* pornographic magazine covers surveyed in New York City's Times Square. *Women Against Pornography Newsreport* (no date, no page), citing *American Journal of Psychiatry*, Vol. 139, No. 11, Nov. 1982, pp. 1493–1495.

9. See U.S. Bureau of the Census, *Statistical Abstract of the United States: 1985* (Washington, D.C.: 1984), p. 170; Edward J. Brown, Timothy J. Flanagan, and Maureen McLead, eds., *Sourcebook of Criminal Justice Statistics—1983* (Washington, D.C.: U.S. Department of Justice, Bureau of Justice Statistics, 1984), pp. 341–42.

PORNOGRAPHY AND FREEDOM

☽

JOHN STOLTENBERG

A leading voice in men's studies, John Stoltenberg addresses the paradox of sexual freedom in society. Why, he asks, has "sexual freedom" gradually come to look so much like injustice and domination? This essay asks us to consider the debate about pornography in light of the difficult balance between freedom and justice in a democratic society. Stoltenberg is editor of the book *Refusing To Be a Man: Essays on Sex and Justice* (1989), from which this selection is taken.

There is a widespread belief that sexual freedom is an idea whose time has come. Many people believe that in the last few decades we have gotten more and more of it—that sexual freedom is something you can carve out against the forces of sexual repressiveness, and that significant gains have been won, gains we dare not give up lest we backslide into the sexual dark ages, when there wasn't sexual freedom, there was only repression.

Indeed many things seem to have changed. But if you look closely at what is supposed to be sexual freedom, you can become very confused. Let's say, for instance, you understand that a basic principle of sexual freedom is that people should be free to be sexual and that one way to guarantee that freedom is to make sure that sex be free from imposed restraint. That's not a bad idea, but if you happen to look at a magazine photograph in which a woman is bound and gagged and lashed down on a plank with her genital area open to the camera, you might well wonder: Where is the freedom from restraint? where's the sexual freedom?

Let's say you understand that people should be free to be sexual and that one way to guarantee that freedom is to make sure people can feel good about themselves and each other sexually. That's not a bad idea. But if you happen to read random passages from books such as the following, you could be quite perplexed:

> "Baby, you're gonna get fucked tonight like you ain't never been fucked before," he hissed evily down at her as she struggled fruitlessly against her bonds. The man wanted only to abuse and ravish her till she was totally broken and subservient to him. He knelt between her wide-spread legs and gloated over the cringing little pussy he was about to ram his cock into.[1]

And here's another: 4

> He pulled his prick out of her cunt and then grabbed his belt from his pants.
> He seemed to be in a wild frenzy at that moment. He slapped the belt in
> the air and then the leather ripped through the girl's tender flesh. "Sir, just
> tell me what it is you want and I'll do it." "Fuck you, you little two-bit whore!
> I don't need nothin' from a whore!" The belt sliced across her flesh again
> and then she screamed, "I'm willing!" "That's just it! You're willing! You're
> a whore and you are an abomination . . ."[2]

Passages such as this might well make you wonder: Where are the good   5
feelings about each other's body? where's the sexual freedom?

Let's say you understand that people should be free to be sexual and that   6
one way to guarantee that freedom is to make sure people are free from
sexualized hate and degradation. But let's say you come upon a passage such
as this:

> Reaching into his pocket for the knife again, Ike stepped just inches away
> from Burl's outstretched body. He slid the knife under Burl's cock and balls,
> letting the sharp edge of the blade lightly scrape the underside of Burl's
> nutsack. As if to reassert his power over Burl, Ike grabbed one of the bound
> man's tautly stretched pecs, clamping down harder over Burl's tit and muscle,
> latching on as tight as he could. He pushed on the knife, pressing the blade
> into Burl's skin as hard as possible without cutting him. "Now, you just let
> us inside that tight black asshole of yours, boy, or else we're gonna cut this
> off and feed it to the cattle!"[3]

After reading that, you might well ask: Where's the freedom from hatred?   7
where's the freedom from degradation? where's the sexual freedom?

Let's say you understand people should be free to be sexual and that one   8
way to guarantee that freedom is to make sure people are not punished for
the individuality of their sexuality. And then you find a magazine showing
page after page of bodies with their genitals garroted in baling wire and leather
thongs, with their genitals tied up and tortured, with heavy weights suspended
from rings that pierce their genitals, and the surrounding text makes clear
that this mutilation and punishment are experienced as sex acts. And you
might wonder in your mind: Why must this person suffer punishment in
order to experience sexual feelings? why must this person be humiliated and
disciplined and whipped and beaten until he bleeds in order to have access to
his homoerotic passion? why have the Grand Inquisitor's most repressive and
sadistic torture techniques become what people do to each other and call sex?
where's the sexual freedom?

If you look back at the books and magazines and movies that have been   9
produced in this country in the name of sexual freedom over the past decade,
you've got to wonder: *Why has sexual freedom come to look so much like sexual
repression? why has sexual freedom come to look so much like unfreedom?* The
answer, I believe, has to do with the relationship between freedom and justice,

and specifically the relationship between *sexual* freedom and *sexual* justice. When we think of freedom in any other sense, we think of freedom as *the result* of justice. We know that there can't truly *be* any freedom until justice has happened, until justice exists. For any people in history who have struggled for freedom, those people have understood that their freedom exists on the future side of justice. The notion of freedom *prior* to justice is understood to be meaningless. Whenever people do not have freedom, they have understood freedom to be that which you arrive at by achieving justice. If you told them they should try to have their freedom without there being justice, they would laugh in your face. Freedom *always* exists on the far side of justice. That's perfectly understood—except when it comes to sex.

The popular concept of sexual freedom in this country has never meant 10 sexual justice. Sexual-freedom advocates have cast the issue only in terms of having sex that is free from suppression and restraint. Practically speaking, that has meant advocacy of sex that is free from institutional interference; sex that is free from being constrained by legal, religious, and medical ideologies; sex that is free from any outside intervention. Sexual freedom on a more personal level has meant sex that is free from fear, guilt, and shame—which in practical terms has meant advocacy of sex that is free from value judgments, sex that is free from responsibility, sex that is free from consequences, sex that is free from ethical distinctions, sex that is essentially free from any obligation to take into account in one's consciousness that the other person is a *person*. In order to free sex from fear, guilt, and shame, it was thought that institutional restrictions on sex needed to be overthrown, but in fact what needed to be overthrown was any vestige of an interpersonal ethic in which people would be real to one another; for once people are real to one another, the consequences of one's acts matter deeply and personally; and particularly in the case of sex, one risks perceiving the consequences of one's acts in ways that feel *bad* because they do not feel *right*. This entire moral-feeling level of sexuality, therefore, needed to be undone. And it was undone, in the guise of an assault on institutional suppression.

Sexual freedom has never really meant that individuals should have sexual 11 self-determination, that individuals should be free to experience the integrity of their own bodies and be free to act out of that integrity in a way that is totally within their own right to choose. Sexual freedom has never really meant that people should have absolute sovereignty over their own erotic being. And the reason for this is simple: Sexual freedom has never really been about *sexual justice between men and women*. It has been about maintaining men's superior status, men's power over women; and it has been about sexualizing women's inferior status, men's subordination of women. Essentially, sexual freedom has been about preserving a sexuality that preserves male supremacy.

What makes male supremacy so insidious, so pervasive, such a seemingly 12 permanent component of all our precious lives, is the fact that erection can be conditioned to it. And orgasm can be habituated to it. There's a cartoon; it's from *Penthouse*. A man and woman are in bed. He's on top, fucking her. The caption reads: "I can't come unless you pretend to be unconscious." The joke could as well have taken any number of variations: "I can't get hard unless—I can't fuck unless—I can't get turned on unless—I can't feel anything sexual unless— . . ." Then fill in the blanks: "Unless I am possessing you. Unless I am superior to you. Unless I am in control of you. Unless I am humiliating you. Unless I am hurting you. Unless I have broken your will."

Once sexuality is stuck in male supremacy, all the forms of unjust power [13] at the heart of it become almost physically addictive. All the stuff of our primitive fight-or-flight reflexes—a pounding heart, a hard sweat, heaving lungs—these are all things the body does when it is in terror, when it is lashing out in rage, and these are all things it is perfectly capable of doing during sex acts that are terrifying and sex acts that are vengeful. Domination and subordination—the very essence of injustice and unfreedom—have become culturally eroticized, and we are supposed to believe that giving eroticized domination and subordination free expression is the fullest flowering of sexual freedom.

Prepubescent boys get erections in all kinds of apparently nonsexual [14] situations—being terrified, being in physical danger, being punished, moving perilously fast, simply being called on to recite in class. A boy's body's dilemma, as he grows older, as he learns more about the cultural power signified by the penis and how it is supposed to function in male-supremacist sex, is how to produce erections reliably in explicitly heterosexual contexts. His body gets a great deal of help. All around him is a culture in which rage and dread and hazard and aggression are made aphrodisiacs. And women's bodies are made the butt of whatever works to get it up.*

The sexuality of male supremacy is viscerally committed to domination [15] and subordination, because those are the terms on which it learned to feel, to feel anything sexual at all. Its heart pounds and its blood rushes and its autonomic nervous system surges at the thought and/or the action of forced sex, bullying sex, violent sex, injurious sex, humiliating sex, hostile sex, murderous sex. The kind of sex that puts the other person in their place. The kind of sex that keeps the other person *other*. The kind of sex that makes you know you're in the presence of someone who is palpably a man.

Some of us know how male-supremacist sexuality feels better than do [16] others. Some of us know how that sexuality feels inside because we do it, or we have done it, or we would like to do it, or we would like to do it more than we get a chance to. It's the sexuality that makes us feel powerful, virile, in control. Some of us have known how that sexuality feels when someone

* See "Sexual Objectification and Male Supremacy," pp. 51–53.

else is doing it to us, someone who is having sex with us, someone whose body is inhabited by it, someone who is experiencing its particular imperative and having male-supremacist sex against our flesh. And some of us don't really know this sexuality directly; in fact our bodies haven't adapted to male supremacy very successfully at all—it is not the sexuality that moves us, that touches us, that comes anywhere near feeling as good as we imagine we want our sexual feelings to feel. We don't recognize a longing for anything like it in our own bodies, and we've been lucky so far—very lucky—not to have experienced it *against* our bodies. Nonetheless, we know that it exists; and the more we know about pornography, the more we know what it looks like.

Pornography and Male Supremacy

Male-supremacist sexuality is important to pornography, and pornography is important to male supremacy. Pornography *institutionalizes* the sexuality that both embodies and enacts male supremacy. Pornography says about that sexuality, "Here's how": Here's how to act out male supremacy in sex. Here's how the action should go. Here are the acts that impose power over and against another body. And pornography says about that sexuality, "Here's who": Here's who you should do it to and here's who she is: your whore, your piece of ass, yours. Your penis is a weapon, her body is your target. And pornography says about that sexuality, "Here's why": Because men are masters, women are slaves; men are superior, women are subordinate; men are real, women are objects; men are sex machines, women are sluts. 17

Pornography institutionalizes male supremacy the way segregation institutionalizes white supremacy. It is a practice embodying an ideology of biological superiority; it is an institution that both expresses that ideology and enacts that ideology—makes it the reality that people believe is true, keeps it that way, keeps people from knowing any other possibility, keeps certain people powerful by keeping certain people *down*. 18

Pornography also *eroticizes* male supremacy. It makes dominance and subordination feel like sex; it makes hierarchy feel like sex; it makes force and violence feel like sex; it makes hate and terrorism feel like sex; it makes inequality feel like sex. Pornography keeps sexism sexy. It keeps sexism *necessary* for some people to have sexual feelings. It makes reciprocity make you go limp. It makes mutuality leave you cold. It makes tenderness and intimacy and caring make you feel like you're going to disappear into a void. It makes justice the opposite of erotic; it makes injustice a sexual thrill. 19

Pornography exploits every experience in people's lives that *imprisons* sexual feelings—pain, terrorism, punishment, dread, shame, powerlessness, self-hate—and would have you believe that it *frees* sexual feelings. In fact the sexual freedom represented by pornography is the freedom of men to act sexually in ways that keep sex a basis for inequality. 20

You can't have authentic sexual freedom without sexual justice. It is only   21
freedom for those in power; the powerless cannot be free. Their experience
of sexual freedom becomes but a delusion borne of complying with the demands of the powerful. Increased sexual freedom under male supremacy has
had to mean an increased tolerance for sexual practices that are predicated
on eroticized injustice between men and women; treating women's bodies or
body parts as merely sexual objects or things; treating women as utterly
submissive masochists who enjoy pain and humiliation and who, if they are
raped, enjoy it; treating women's bodies to sexualized beating, mutilation,
bondage, dismemberment. . . . Once you have sexualized inequality, once it
is a learned and internalized prerequisite for sexual arousal and sexual gratification, then anything goes. And that's what sexual freedom means on this
side of sexual justice.

Pornography and Homophobia

Homophobia is absolutely integral to the system of sexualized male suprem-   22
acy. Cultural homophobia expresses a whole range of antifemale revulsion: It
expresses contempt for men who are sexual with men because they are believed to be "treated like a woman" in sex. It expresses contempt for women
who are sexual with women just *because* they are women and also because they
are perceived to be a rebuke to the primacy of the penis.

But cultural homophobia is not merely an expression of woman hating;   23
it also works to protect men from the sexual aggression of other men. Homophobia keeps men doing to women what they would not want done to themselves. There's not the same sexual harassment of men that there is of women
on the street or in the workplace or in the university; there's not nearly the
same extent of rape; there's not the same demeaned social caste that is sexualized, as it is for women. And that's thanks to homophobia: Cultural homophobia keeps men's sexual aggression directed toward women. Homophobia
keeps men acting in concert as male supremacists so that they won't be
perceived as an appropriate target for male-supremacist sexual treatment.
Male supremacy *requires* homophobia in order to keep men safe from the
sexual aggression of men. Imagine this country *without* homophobia: A
woman raped every three minutes *and a man* raped every three minutes.
Homophobia that keeps that statistic at a "manageable" level. The system is
not foolproof, of course. There are boys who have been sexually molested by
men. There are men who have been brutalized in sexual relationships with
their male lovers, and they too have a memory of men's sexual violence. And
there are many men in prison who are subject to the same sexual terrorism
that women live with almost all the time. But for the most part—happily—
homophobia serves male supremacy by protecting "real men" from sexual
assault by other real men.

Pornography is one of the major enforcers of cultural homophobia. Por- 24
nography is rife with gay-baiting and effemiphobia. Portrayals of allegedly
lesbian "scenes" are a staple of heterosexual pornography: The women with
each other are there for the male viewer, the male voyeur; there is not the
scantest evidence that they are there for each other. Through so-called men's-
sophisticate magazines—the "skin" magazines—pornographers outdo one another in their attacks against feminists, who are typically derided as lesbians—
"sapphic" at best, "bulldykes" at worst. The innuendo that a man is a "fairy"
or a "faggot" is, in pornography, a kind of dare or a challenge to prove his
cocksmanship. And throughout pornography, the male who is perceived to
be the passive orifice in sex is tainted with the disdain that "normally" belongs
to women.

Meanwhile gay male pornography, which often appears to present an 25
idealized, all-male, superbutch world, also contains frequent derogatory references to women, or to feminized males. In order to give vent to male sexual
aggression and sadism in homosexual pornography and also to circumvent
the cultural stigma that ordinarily attaches to men who are "treated like a
woman" in sex, gay male pornography has developed several specific "codes."
One such code is that a man who is "capable" of withstanding "discipline"—
extremely punishing bondage, humiliation, and fistfucking, for instance—is
deemed to have achieved a kind of supermasculinity, almost as if the sexual
violence his body ingests from another man enhances his own sexual identity
as a man. (This is quite the reverse in heterosexual pornography, where sexual
sadism against a woman simply confirms her in her subordinate status.) Another code common in gay male pornography, one found frequently in films,
is that if a man is shown being assfucked, he will generally be shown assfucking
someone else in turn—this to avoid the connotation that he is at all feminized
by being fucked. Still another code in gay male pornography is that depictions
of mutuality are not sustained for very long without an intimation or explicit
scene of force or coercion—so you don't go limp out of boredom or anxiety
that you've been suckered into a scene where there's no raw male power
present.

There is, not surprisingly, an intimate connection between the male 26
supremacy in both heterosexual and homosexual pornography and the woman
hating and femiphobia in them both as well. That connection is male-supremacist sex—the social power of men over women acted out as eroticized domination and subordination. The difference is that gay male pornography in-
vents a way for men to be the *objects* of male-supremacist sex without seeming
to be its *victims*. In its own special fashion, gay male pornography keeps men
safe from male-supremacist sex—by holding out the promise that you'll come
away from it more a man.

Needless to say, for heterosexual men who don't buy this, it's repellent 27
and a crock. Needless to say, for homosexual men who *do* buy into this, it can
become a really important part of one's sexual identity as a gay man. Because

if you think the problem facing you is that your masculinity is in doubt because you're queer, then the promise of gay male pornography looks like forgiveness and redemption. Not to mention what it feels like: communion with true virility.

Pornography and Men

Now this is the situation of men within male supremacy: Whether we are straight or gay, we have been looking for a sexual freedom that is utterly specious, and we have been looking for it through pornography, which perpetuates the very domination and subordination that stand in the way of sexual justice. Whether we are straight or gay, we have been looking for a notion of freedom that leaves out women; we have been looking for a sexuality that preserves men's power over women. So long as that is what we strive for, we cannot possibly feel freely, and no one can be free. Whatever sexual freedom might be, it must be after justice.

28

I want to speak directly to those of us who live in male supremacy as men, and I want to speak specifically to those of us who have come to understand that pornography does make sexism sexy; that pornography does make male supremacy sexy; and that pornography does define what is sexy in terms of domination and subordination, in terms that serve *us as men*— whether we buy it or not, whether we buy into it or not—because it serves male supremacy, which is exactly what it is for.

29

I want to speak to those of us who live in this setup as men and who recognize—in the world and in our very own selves—the power pornography can have over our lives: It can make men believe that anything sexy is good. It can make men believe that our penises are like weapons. It can make men believe—for some moments of orgasm—that we are just like the men in pornography: virile, strong, tough, maybe cruel. It can make men believe that if you take it away from us, we won't have sexual feelings.

30

But I want to speak also to those of us who live in this setup as men and who recognize the power that pornography has over the lives of women: because it can make us believe that women by nature are whores; because it can make us believe that women's body parts belong to us—separately, part by part—instead of to a whole real other person; because it can make us believe that women want to be raped, enjoy being damaged by us, deserve to be punished; because it can make us believe that women are an alien species, completely different from us so that we can be completely different from them, not as human as us so that we can be human, not as real as us so that we can be men. I want to talk to those of us who know in our guts that pornography can make us believe all of that. We know because we've watched it happen to men around us. We know because it has happened in us.

31

And what I want to say is simply this: We've got to be about making   32
some serious changes, and we've got to get busy and *act*. If we sit around and
don't do anything, then we become the ones who are keeping things the way
they are. If we sit around and all we do is intellectual and emotional dithering,
then we stay in the ranks of those who are the passive enforcers of male
supremacy. If we don't take seriously the fact that pornography is a radical
political issue and an issue about *us* and if we don't make serious progress in
the direction of *what we're going to do about it*, then we've just gone over to
the wrong side of the fight—the morally wrong, historically wrong side of a
struggle that is a ground swell, a grass-roots *people's* movement against sexual
injustice.

We've got to be telling our sons that if a man gets off by putting women   33
down, *it's not okay.*

We've got to be telling merchants that if they peddle women's bodies and   34
lives for men's consumption and entertainment, *it's not okay.*

We've got to be telling other men that if you let the pornographers lead   35
you by the nose (or any other body part) into believing that women exist to
be tied up and hung up and beaten and raped, *it's not okay.*

We've got to be telling the pornographers—Larry Flynt and Bob Guc-   36
cione and Hugh Hefner and Al Goldstein and all the rest—that whatever
they think they're doing in our names as men, as entertainment for men, for
the sake of some delusion of so-called manhood . . . well, it's not okay. It's
not okay with *us.*

Freedom and Equality

Historically, when people have not had justice and when people have not had   37
freedom, they have had only the material reality of injustice and unfreedom.
When freedom and justice don't exist, they're but a dream and a vision, an
abstract idea longed for. You can't really know what justice would be like or
what freedom would feel like. You can only know how it feels *not* to have
them, and what it feels like to hope, to imagine, to desire them with a passion.
Sexual freedom is an idea whose time has *not* come. It can't possibly be truly
experienced until there is sexual justice. And sexual justice is incompatible
with a definition of freedom that is based on the subordination of women.

Equality is still a radical idea. It makes some people very angry. It also   38
gives some people hope.

When equality is an idea whose time has come, we will perhaps know sex   39
with justice, we will perhaps know passion with compassion, we will perhaps
know ardor and affection with honor. In that time, when the integrity within
everyone's body and the whole personhood of each person is celebrated whenever two people touch, we will perhaps truly know the freedom to be sexual
in a world of real equality.

According to pornography, you can't get there from here. According to [40] male supremacy, you should not even want to try.

Some of us want to go there. Some of us want to be there. And we know [41] that the struggle will be difficult and long. But we know that the passion for justice cannot be denied. And someday—*someday*—there will be both justice and freedom for each person—and thereby for us all.

Notes

1. Edward Baker, *Tricked Into White Slavery* (South Laguna, CA: Publisher's Consultants, 1978), p. 132.
2. *The Shamed Beauty* (New York: Star Distributors, Ltd.), p. 60.
3. Eli Robeson, "Knife Point," *Folsom Magazine*, No. 2 (1981?), p. 27.

MAKING CONNECTIONS

1. Explain Steinem's use of important words like "erotica," "pornography," and "obscenity." What distinguishes these terms from each other in Steinem's definitions? Look up other definitions of these terms, either in the dictionary or as used by other essayists, and compare them to Steinem's. What is your own definition of these terms? How would you, for instance, label a story like Angela Carter's "The Company of Wolves" (Chapter 7), particularly its depiction of sex? Would you call this story pornographic? Would Steinem? Why or why not?

2. Compare and contrast Steinem's essay with John Berger's discussion of the female nude (Chapter 10). What connections can you draw between Berger's analysis of the depiction of "loved women" and Steinem's views on erotica? How might Berger's points about the female figure and the male gaze apply to pornography in general?

3. List the obstacles to disentangling sex and violence that Steinem discusses in her essay. Does Steinem believe obscenity to be immoral? Is she for or against censorship? Compare her views on censorship to those of Small. What are your own opinions on the points she raises?

4. Select any previous chapter that deals with gender and image—either Chapter 7, 8, 9, or 10. How might social messages about gender discussed in these chapters contribute to or resist an acceptance of pornography?

5. Outline the arguments of Weiss and Campbell. How well does Campbell answer Weiss? Are there any other points in Weiss that remain to be addressed? What is the significance of Weiss's interchange with his girlfriend after the movie? How valid is Weiss's point that feminists ask men to throw off their masculinity? Do other essays in this chapter seem to demand that? If not, how do they avoid it?

6. Campbell talks about the dangerous "social fantasy" of men's domination and women's subordination that pornography disseminates. Does this "social fantasy" really exist in other areas of culture, as Campbell seems to suggest? If so, where should one draw the line in prohibiting such messages? Do the paintings discussed in Berger's essay (Chapter 10) illustrate this same fantasy? If so, should they be censored? How might paintings differ from pornography, and how might they be similar?

7. Explain Small's statement that "pornography may not be the best target for our rage." What are his objections to the Minneapolis ordinance of 1983? How do they differ from Weiss's objections? What in general are the problems of censorship that Small addresses? Do you agree or dis-

agree that censorship might work against the very people it was designed to protect? Write an imaginary dialogue between Small and the proponents of the Minneapolis ordinance, Catharine MacKinnon and Andrea Dworkin, that presents both points of view.

8. Analyze Small's writing style, particularly in his opening paragraphs, where he introduces a difficult stand on a difficult subject. How does he use devices like parallelism, sentence length and structure, word choice and questions to present his topic and ease the reader into the essay? Where is his main thesis stated? How does he qualify his position and suggest concerns that will be discussed more fully in the rest of his essay? Find examples throughout the essay where Small uses short, forceful sentences to make his point and where he uses more complex sentences to elaborate, qualify, or explain his stand. Try writing an essay—or revising a previous essay you've written—in which you attempt to use some of Small's strategies of writing style to present and develop your points.

9. Do you agree or disagree with Stoltenberg's concepts of freedom and justice? Construct your own argument about how freedom and justice are to be balanced, particularly as regards sexuality and expression.

10. Stoltenberg argues that pornography conditions people by eroticizing male supremacy and making sexual equality leave the viewer "cold." Does culture have this powerful conditioning effect on people? Can you think of any examples in your own experience that would prove or disprove the impact of socialization on people's concept of what is erotic and what is not? How do individuals learn about sex, and can they unlearn lessons that are embedded in culture?

11. The question of censorship is ongoing and complex. As a class, choose sides on the issue of pornography, examining and representing three positions:

    1) defending freedom of speech, as guaranteed by the First Amendment of the Constitution,

    2) defending censorship,

    3) defending the view of pornography as a violation of civil rights, and explaining how this view is distinct from the first two.

    Your library should have a number of resources to get you started in exploring the many facets of this debate.

12. Research the phenomenon of sexual violence in our culture by collecting some statistics on rape, domestic violence, sexual harassment, and assault. Look in particular at studies that explore the connections between pornography and aggression. You may find some conclusive, others inconclusive. Discuss and analyze your findings with your class.

5
PART

GENDER AND WORK,
VALUE, POWER

12
WOMEN
WORKING

C O N T E X T S

Women have always worked, but the visibility and the value of their work has changed over time. Prior to the Industrial Revolution the activities of work and family took place together, and women and men worked alongside one another. As the industrial economy developed in the early 1800s, however, production of goods that women had always made for their families was gradually removed from the home to the factory. The growth of the textile industry in New England is a good example of how the concept of "work" was progressively redefined, as the manufacture of cloth and clothing moved from a "cottage industry" in the home to factories outside the home.

By the middle of the nineteenth century there were clear gender and class divisions in employment in America. While new immigrants filled the factory jobs, the "middle class" was emerging as growing numbers of men earned incomes from industry and commerce. Business was conducted away from home and men, not women, were involved in the transactions. Separated from the "public" world of commerce, women's labor in the private sphere of the home was no longer considered real work. Motherhood became the middle class woman's calling. She devoted her life to making her home a safe haven for her children and a place of respite for her husband from the competitiveness of the marketplace. Because the family depended on his income, the man's labor gradually came to carry a high level of power and prestige. No matter what his status in the workplace, to the extent that the family relied on his income, a man was "king in his castle."

Since the 1950s, society has become increasingly aware of the problems that financial dependence poses for women. New phrases have entered our vocabulary to describe the predicament of women who are not economically self-sufficient. The term "displaced homemaker," for example, refers to a woman who, due to divorce or widowhood, finds it necessary to enter the paid work force after years of working at home. Without a history of paid employment, her skills seldom translate into a well-paid position. Likewise, the "feminization of poverty," a frequent issue in economic discussions today, describes the increasing numbers of female-headed households in America whose incomes fall below the poverty line.

Today more than ever we are faced with the question of what we value as real work and how we compensate it. Paid work provides for one's needs. It is also a concrete measure of one's worth and can be a vehicle for personal fulfillment and creative expression. In our first selection, Marge Piercy looks at one meaning of work in her poem "To Be of Use." In it, she celebrates the world of physical labor and shows the satisfaction of work with a purpose, the real work that has to be done to keep the rhythms of life flowing. A different vision of work is presented by our second author, Ruth Sidel, who takes a revealing look at today's "New American Dreamers." Sidel's interviews with young women of the 1990s show the pervasive mystique of glamorous careers that color the dreams of many women today. Without exception, these future workers from all walks of life imagine that what awaits them are interesting jobs, rapid promotion, wealth, and a life unencumbered by family responsibilities or blocked opportunities.

In sharp contrast, Hilary Lips looks at the realities of "Women and Power in the Workplace." Lips explores the definitions of power in today's corporate world and looks at the obstacles facing women in gaining access to real influence, decision-making opportunities, and recognition in the workplace. Next, Marilyn Waring returns us to the concept of work's value in her essay "A Woman's Reckoning: An Introduction to the International Economic System." Asking the question, "who works and who doesn't?," Waring examines how current economic theories devalue and make invisible women's work around the world. Patricia J. Williams closes the chapter by further broadening our understanding of the work women do. Her essay "On Being the Object of Property" draws attention both to the history of black women's slavery and to the contemporary issue of women's reproductive labor. Examining the legal and personal complexities of Mary Beth Whitehead's agreement to be a surrogate mother in the famous case of "Baby M," Williams considers how reproduction, too, can become a center for the exercise of power and bias in society.

The essays in this chapter raise questions that are a long way from being answered in society. What are the differences between wage labor and a "labor of love," and what do those differences mean in concrete terms for women and men? When is work valued, and who performs society's most "valuable" work? When society begins to value more equally the contributions of women's labor, will the "rules of the game" for success and achievement change? How can we ensure that every human being, regardless of race, sex, or class, has the opportunities to achieve the satisfaction, respect, and rewards that working provides?

TO BE OF USE

MARGE PIERCY

Marge Piercy is the most widely anthologized feminist poet of her generation. Her poems and essays have appeared in such periodicals as *The Nation*, *The Trans-atlantic Review*, and *Women: A Journal of Liberation*. Her novels include *Small Changes* (1973) and *Woman on the Edge of Time* (1976). An ardent activist, Piercy writes about women's issues, social justice, and war. "To Be of Use" is the title poem of her 1973 volume of poetry.

The people I love the best
jump into work head first
without dallying in the shallows
and swim off with sure strokes almost out of sight.
They seem to become natives of that element,
the black sleek heads of seals
bouncing like half-submerged balls.

I love people who harness themselves, an ox to a heavy cart,
who pull like water buffalo, with massive patience,
who strain in the mud and the muck to move things forward,
who do what has to be done, again and again.

I want to be with people who submerge
in the task, who go into the fields to harvest
and work in a row and pass the bags along,
who stand in the line and haul in their places,
who are not parlor generals and field deserters
but move in a common rhythm
when the food must come in or the fire be put out.

The work of the world is common as mud.
Botched, it smears the hands, crumbles to dust.
But the thing worth doing well done

has a shape that satisfies, clean and evident.
Greek amphoras for wine or oil,
Hopi vases that held corn, are put in museums
but you know they were made to be used.
The pitcher cries for water to carry
and a person for work that is real.

THE NEW AMERICAN DREAMERS

RUTH SIDEL

A professor of sociology at Hunter College of the City
University of New York, Ruth Sidel has conducted
research on the well-being of families and the social
position of women. She places gender issues in context
by focusing on the ways that such issues are embedded
in social class, race, and culture. Among her books are
Women and Child Care in China: A Firsthand Report
(1972), *Women and Children Last: The Plight of Poor
Women in Affluent America* (1987), and *On Her Own:
Growing Up in the Shade of the American Dream* (1990),
from which this selection is taken.

> *It's your life. You have to live it yourself . . . If you work
> hard enough, you will get there. You must be in control of
> your life, and then somehow it will all work out.*
>
> (Angela Dawson
> high-school junior, Southern California)

She is the prototype of today's young woman—confident, outgoing, knowl- 1
edgeable, involved. She is active in her school, church, or community. She
may have a wide circle of friends or simply a few close ones, but she is
committed to them and to their friendship. She is sophisticated about the
central issues facing young people today—planning for the future, intimacy,
sex, drugs, and alcohol—and discusses them seriously, thoughtfully, and forth-
rightly. She wants to take control of her life and is trying to figure out how
to get from where she is to where she wants to go. Above all, she is convinced
that if she plans carefully, works hard, and makes the right decisions, she will
be a success in her chosen field; have the material goods she desires; in time,
marry if she wishes; and, in all probability, have children. She plans, as the
expression goes, to "have it all."

She lives in and around the major cities of the United States, in the towns 2
of New England, in the smaller cities of the South and Midwest, and along
the West Coast. She comes from an upper-middle-class family, from the
middle class, from the working class, and even sometimes from the poor.

What is clear is that she has heard the message that women today should be the heroines of their own lives. She looks toward the future, seeing herself as the central character, planning her career, her apartment, her own success story. These young women do not see themselves as playing supporting roles in someone else's life script; it is their own journeys they are planning. They see their lives in terms of *their* aspirations, *their* hopes, *their* dreams.

Beth Conant is a sixteen-year-old high-school junior who lives with her mother and stepfather in an affluent New England college town. She has five brothers, four older and one several years younger. Her mother is a librarian, and her stepfather is a stockbroker. A junior at a top-notch public high school, she hopes to study drama in college, possibly at Yale, "like Meryl Streep." She would like to live and act in England for a time, possibly doing Shakespeare. She hopes to be living in New York by the age of twenty-five, in her own apartment or condo, starting on her acting career while working at another job by which she supports herself. She wants to have "a great life," be "really independent," and have "everything that's mine—crazy furniture, everything my own style."

By the time she's thirty ("that's so boring"), she feels, she will need to be sensible, because soon she will be "tied down." She hopes that by then her career will be "starting to go forth" and that she will be getting good roles. By thirty-five she'll have a child ("probably be married beforehand"), be working in New York and have a house in the country. How will she manage all this? Her husband will share responsibilities. She's not going to be a "supermom." They'll both do child care. He won't do it as a favor; it will be their joint responsibility. Moreover, if she doesn't have the time to give to a child, she won't have one. If necessary, she'll work for a while, then have children, and after that "make one movie a year."

Amy Morrison is a petite, black, fifteen-year-old high-school sophomore who lives in Ohio. Her mother works part-time, and her father works for a local art museum. She plans to go to medical school and hopes to become a surgeon. She doesn't want to marry until she has a good, secure job but indicates that she might be living with someone. She's not sure about having children but says emphatically that she wants to be successful, to make money, to have cars. In fact, originally she wanted to become a doctor "primarily for the money," but now she claims other factors are drawing her to medicine.

Jacqueline Gonzalez is a quiet, self-possessed, nineteen-year-old Mexican-American woman who is a sophomore at a community college in southern California. She describes her father as a "self-employed contractor" and her mother as a "housewife." Jacqueline, the second-youngest of six children, is the first in her family to go to college. Among her four brothers and one sister, only her sister has finished high school. Jacqueline's goal is to go to law school and then to go into private practice. While she sees herself as eventually married with "one or two children," work, professional achievement, and an upper-middle-class life-style are central to her plans for her future.

If in the past, and to a considerable extent still today, women have hoped to find their identity through marriage, have sought to find "validation of . . . [their] uniqueness and importance by being singled out among all other women by a man," the New American Dreamers are setting out on a very different quest for self-realization. They are, in their plans for the future, separating identity from intimacy, saying that they must first figure out who they are and that then and only then will they form a partnership with a man. Among the young women I interviewed, the New American Dreamers stand apart in their intention to make their own way in the world and determine their own destiny prior to forming a significant and lasting intimate relationship.

Young women today do not need to come from upper-middle-class homes such as Beth's or middle-class homes such as Amy's or working-class homes such as Jacqueline's to dream of "the good life." Even young women with several strikes against them see material success as a key prize at the end of the rainbow. Some seem to feel that success is out there for the taking. Generally, the most prestigious, best-paying careers are mentioned; few women of any class mention traditional women's professions such as teaching or nursing. A sixteen-year-old unmarried Arizona mother of a four-and-a-half-month-old baby looks forward to a "professional career either in a bank or with a computer company," a "house that belongs to me," a "nice car," and the ability to buy her son "good clothes." She sees herself in the future as dating but not married. "There is not so much stress on marriage these days," she says.

Yet another young woman, a seventeen-year-old black unmarried mother of an infant, hopes to be a "professional model," have "lots of cash," be "rich," maybe have another child. When asked if a man will be part of the picture, she responds, "I don't know."

An eighteen-year-old Hispanic unmarried mother hopes to "be my own boss" in a large company, have a "beautiful home," send her daughter to "the best schools." She wants, in her words, to "do it, make it, have money."

These young women are bright, thoughtful, personable. And they are quintessentially American: they believe that with enough hard work they will "make it" in American society. No matter what class they come from, their fantasies are of upward mobility, a comfortable life filled with personal choice and material possessions. The upper-middle-class women fantasize a life even more upper-middle-class; middle-class and working-class women look toward a life of high status in which they have virtually everything they want; and some young women who come from families with significant financial deprivation and numerous other problems dream of a life straight out of "Dallas," "Dynasty," or "L.A. Law." According to one young woman, some of her friends are so determined to be successful that they are "fearful that there will be a nuclear war and that they will die before they have a chance to live their lives. If there is a nuclear war," she explained, "they won't live long enough to be successful."

Young women are our latest true believers. They have bought into the 12 image of a bright future. Many of them see themselves as professional women, dressed in handsome clothes, carrying a briefcase to work, and coming home to a comfortable house or condo, possibly to a loving, caring husband and a couple of well-behaved children. How widespread is the dream? How realistic is it? What is the function of this latest American dream? What about those young women who cling to a more traditional dream? What about those who feel their dreams must be deferred? What about those with no dream at all? And what about those who "share the fantasy," as the Chanel No. 5 perfume advertisement used to say, but have little or no chance of achieving it.

Perhaps the most poignant example of the impossible dream is Simone 13 Baker, a dynamic, bright, eighteen-year-old black woman from Louisiana. Simone's mother is a seamstress who has been off and on welfare over the years, and her father is a drug addict. Simone herself has been addicted to drugs of one kind or another since she was five. She has been in and out of drug-abuse facilities, and although she attended school for many years and was passed from grade to grade, she can barely read and write. When I met her in a drug rehabilitation center, she was struggling to become drug free so that she could join the Job Corps, finish high school, and obtain some vocational training. Her dream of the future is so extraordinary, given her background, that she seems to epitomize the Horatio Alger myth of another era. When asked what she would like her life to be like in the future, Simone replies instantly, her eyes shining: "I want to be a model. I want to have a Jacuzzi. I want to have a *big*, BIG house and a BIG family—three girls and two boys."

"And what about the man?" I ask her. 14

"He'll be a lawyer. He'll be responsible, hardworking, and sensitive to 15 my feelings. Everything will be fifty-fifty. And he'll take the little boys out to play football and I'll have the girls inside cooking. That would be a dream come true!"

Simone's dream is an incredible mixture of the old and the new—a Dick- 16 and-Jane reader updated. And she's even mouthing the supreme hope of so many women in this age of the therapeutic solution to personal problems— that she'll find a man who is "sensitive" to her "feelings." She has lived a life far from the traditional middle class and yet has the quintessential image of the good life as it has been formulated in the last quarter of the twentieth century. But for Simone, it is virtually an impossible dream. One wishes that that were not so; listening to her, watching her excitement and hope at the mere thought of such a life, one gets caught up and wants desperately for it all to happen. The image is clear: the white house in the suburbs with the brass knocker on the front door, the leaves on the lawn in the fall, the boys playing football with this incredibly wonderful husband/father, and Simone sometimes the successful model, other times at home, cooking with her daughters. But we know how very unlikely it is that this particular dream will come true. And yet, maybe . . .

How have young women come to take on the American Dream as their own? That this is a relatively new dream for women is clear. Until recent years women, for the most part, did not perceive themselves as separate, independent entities with their own needs and agendas. Women fit themselves into other people's lives, molded their needs to fit the needs of others. For the full-time homemaker the day began early enough to enable husband and children to get to work and school on time. Chores had to be done between breakfast and lunch or between lunch and the end of school. Dinnertime was when the man of the house returned from work. When a woman worked outside of the home, her work hours were often those that fit into the schedules of other family members. Her needs were determined by the needs of others, as often her identity rested on her affiliation with them.

What some women seem to be saying now is that they will form their own identities, develop their own styles, and meet their own needs. They will be the central characters in their stories. They will work at jobs men work at, earn the money men earn; but many of them also plan at the same time to play all the roles women have traditionally played.

What has become clear in talking with young women throughout the country is that many of them are planning for their future in terms of their "public" roles as well as their "domestic" roles, that they are "laying claim to significant and satisfying work . . . as a normal part of their lives and laying claim also to the authority, prestige, power, and salary that . . . [that] work commands." Historically, women have been confined primarily to the "domestic" sphere of life, particularly to child rearing and homemaking, and men, for the most part, have participated in the "public" sphere—that is, in social, economic, and political institutions and forms of association in the broader social structure. This dichotomy between "public" and "domestic" has led to "an asymmetry in the cultural evaluation of male and female that appears to be universal." Margaret Mead noted this asymmetry when she observed that "whatever the arrangements in regard to descent or ownership of property, and even if these formal outward arrangements are reflected in the temperamental relations between the sexes, the prestige values always attach to the activities of men."

In New Guinea, women grow sweet potatoes and men grow yams; yams are the prestige food. In societies where women grow rice, the staple food, and men hunt for meat, meat is the most valued food. Traditionally, the more exclusively male the activity, the more cultural value is attached to it. Because male activities have been valued over female activities and women have become "absorbed primarily in domestic activities because of their role as mothers," women's work of caring has traditionally been devalued. However, as political scientist Joan Tronto has pointed out, it is not simply the dichotomy between the public and the private that results in the devaluation of the female but the immense difference in power between the two spheres. So long as men have a monopoly on the public sphere and it in turn wields great power within society, women, identified with the private sphere, which is seen as relatively powerless, will be devalued.

Since the emergence of the women's movement in the 1960s, women in the U.S. as well as in many other parts of the world have been questioning the traditional asymmetry between men and women, seeking to understand its roots, its causes, and its consequences, and attempting to modify the male monopoly of power. Many strategies have developed toward this end: laws have been passed in an attempt to eliminate discrimination; groups have formed to elect more women to positions of power, those already in power have been urged to appoint more women to administrative roles; dominant, high-status, high-income professions have been pressured to admit more women to their hallowed ranks; and strategies to bring greater equity to male and female salaries have been developed.

Great stress has been placed on raising the consciousness of both women and men concerning this imbalance of power, but particular attention has been devoted to raising the consciousness of women. Discussion about the relative powerlessness of the non-wage-earning "housewife" has been widespread. Books and articles about the impoverishment of the divorced woman, the problems of the displaced homemaker, and the often desperate plight of the single, female head of household have been directed at women. During the 1970s and 1980s, the message suddenly became clear to many women: perhaps they are entitled to play roles formerly reserved for men; perhaps they would enjoy these challenges; perhaps they have something special to offer and can make a difference in the practice of medicine or law or in running the country. Moreover, it became clear that if women want power, prestige, and paychecks similar to those men receive, if they want to lessen the asymmetry between male and female, then perhaps they must enter those spheres traditionally reserved for men. If men grow yams, must women grow yams? If men hunt and women gather, must women purchase a bow and arrow? If men are in the public sphere while women are at home caring for children and doing the laundry, the consensus seems to say that women must enter the public sphere. If men are doctors and lawyers and earn great rewards while women are nurses and teachers and earn meager rewards, then women see what they obviously must do. If men have focused on doing while women have focused on caring, then clearly women must become doers.

It is not sufficient, however, to become a doer in a traditionally female occupation, for, as we know, these occupations are notoriously underpaid and underesteemed. Women must become *real* doers in the arena that counts: they must learn to play hardball, or, as Mary Lou Retton says in her breakfast-cereal advertisements, "eat what the big boys eat." For real power, status, money, and "success," it's law, medicine, and finance—also, possibly, acting, modeling, or working in the media, if one is very lucky.

An illustration of the current emphasis on male-dominated careers as the   24
road to success for young women are the career goals of *Glamour* magazine's
"Top Ten College Women '88." One woman hopes to become an astronaut;
a second plans to work in the area of public policy, another to be a biologist,
another to obtain a degree in business administration, yet another to obtain
a degree in acting; and one young woman is currently working in journalism.
One college senior is undecided between journalism and law, and the last
three are planning to go to law school. These young women, according to
Glamour, "possess the talents and ambition necessary to shape tomorrow's
society." It is noteworthy that none of the women *Glamour* chose to honor
are entering any traditionally female occupation or any "helping" profession—not even medicine. Don't nurses, teachers, and social workers "possess
the talents and ambition necessary to shape tomorrow's society"? The word
has gone out and continues to go out that the way to "make it" in American
society and the way to "shape tomorrow's society" is the traditional male
route.

Once singled out, these young women play their part in spreading the   25
ideology of the American Dream. Three of the ten honorees appeared on
NBC's "Today" show. When asked about the significance of their being
chosen, one woman replied without hesitation that if you work hard, you can
do whatever you want to do. This statement was greeted by smiles and nods;
she had clearly given the right message.

In addition to wanting to break out of the mold of a secondary worker   26
receiving inferior wages and benefits and having little authority or opportunity
for advancement, women have been motivated to make real money and to
acquire valued skills and some semblance of security because of their relatively
recent realization that women, even women with children, may well be forced
to care for themselves or, at the very least, to participate in providing for the
family unit. Women have come to realize that whether because of divorce
(which leaves women on the average 73 percent poorer and men on the
average 42 percent richer), childbearing outside of marriage, the inability of
many men to earn an adequate "family wage," or their remaining single—
either through design or through circumstance—they must be prepared to
support themselves and anyone else for whom they feel responsible.

But what of all that caring women used to do—for children, for elderly   27
parents, for sick family members, for the home? What about Sunday dinner,
baking chocolate-chip cookies with the kids eating up half the batter, serving
Kool-Aid in the backyard on a hot summer day? What about sitting with a
child with a painful ear infection until the antibiotic takes effect, going with
a four-year-old to nursery school the first week until the child feels comfortable letting you leave, being available when there's an accident at school and
your second grader must be rushed to the emergency room? Who's going to
do the caring? Who is going to do the caring in a society in which few
institutions have been developed to take up the slack, a society in which men

have been far more reluctant to become carers than women have been to become doers. Members of the subordinate group may gain significantly in status, in self-image, and in material rewards when they take on the activities and characteristics of the dominant group, but there is little incentive for members of the dominant group to do the reverse.

Above all, how do young women today deal with these questions? How do they feel about doing and caring, about power, prestige, and parenting? What messages is society giving them about the roles they should play, and how are they sorting out these messages? 28

A key message the New American Dreamers are both receiving and sending is one of optimism—the sense that they can do whatever they want with their lives. Many Americans, of course—not just young people or young women—have a fundamentally optimistic attitude toward the future. Historically, Americans have believed that progress is likely, even inevitable, and that they have the ability to control their own destinies. A poll taken early in 1988 indicates that while the American public was concerned about the nation's future and indeed more pessimistic about "the way things [were] going in the United States" than they had been at any other time since the Carter presidency in the late 1970s, they nonetheless believed that they could "plan and regulate their own lives, even while the national economy and popular culture appear[ed] to be spinning out of control." As one would expect, those with higher incomes and more education are more optimistic than those with less; Republicans are more optimistic than Democrats or Independents; and, significantly, men are more hopeful than women. In looking toward the future, young men clearly dream of "the good life," of upward mobility and their share of material possessions. While young women historically have had far less control over their lives than men, for the past twenty-five years they have been urged to take greater control, both in the workplace and in their private lives, and they have clearly taken the message very much to heart. 29

Angela Dawson, a sixteen-year-old high-school junior from southern California, sums up the views of the New American Dreamers: "It's your life. You have to live it yourself. You must decide what you want in high school, plan your college education, and from there you can basically get what you want. If you work hard enough, you will get there. You must be in control of your life, and then somehow it will all work out." . . . 30

This increased commitment on the part of women to enter the "public" sphere and, in many cases, to aim for the most prestigious jobs, to reach for the top, to "go for it," is reflected in other aspects of their lives. One of these is young women's increased participation in athletic activities. A recent survey indicates that among a random sample of girls aged seven to eighteen, 82 percent said that they currently participate in sports. Eighty-seven percent of the parents polled believe that sports are as important for girls as for boys. 31

Young women clearly have a great deal to gain from intense athletic involvement: the confidence that comes with the development of skills, an understanding of the importance of teamwork, improved body image, and, of 32 course, the friendships that can develop from continuous commitment to and participation in activities one cares about deeply. But perhaps the most important benefit was spelled out by the mother of a teenage female athlete: The "message of sports," she writes, is to "be aggressive . . . Go for the ball. Be intense." It must be noted that in this case it was the athlete's father who continuously counseled her to really "go for it," not to be content to "sit on the bench." The writer notes how girls have been trained for generations to "Be quiet, Be good, Be still . . . not to get dirty" and that being intense is "neither quiet nor good. And it's definitely not pretty." What participation in athletics can teach a young woman, and what she must learn if she is really to be a force in this society, is to not be "afraid to do her best." This is part of what Angela and some of the other young women seem to be saying—they are going to go out there and not be afraid to do their best.

These women have a commitment to career, to material well-being, to success, and to independence. To many of them, an affluent life-style is central to their dreams; they often describe their goals in terms of cars, homes, travel to Europe. In short, they want their piece of the American Dream. Many of them plan eventually to weave marriage and children into the superstructure; some of them are not so sure. But for now their priorities are to figure out who they are, get on with their education, and become successful in their chosen field.   33

What is new about the dreams of many young women today is not only that they are the central characters in their plans for the future but that they believe they must prepare themselves to go it alone. Young women of all classes talk about the need to be independent. Some quote their mothers and other female relatives who are urging them to organize their lives so that they can take care of themselves. A seventeen-year-old midwestern daughter of divorced parents reports, "My mom tells me I have to be self-secure. I don't want to have to depend on anyone." Another says, "My mother wants me to be happy and she wants me to be able to take care of myself." Yet another: "My grandmother says 'Have your own nest egg.'" Several young women in the Southwest agree. A seventeen-year-old whose parents are divorced: "I want to be independent—financially and emotionally. I want to be stable and independent. I do not want to rely on anyone else," she says emphatically. A twelve-year-old agrees and says her friends talk about the need for women to be able to support themselves and their families. She was five months old when her parents divorced and freely admits she still wishes they would get back together. A sixteen-year-old whose mother is a "housewife" and whose father does "sales-type jobs" but is currently unemployed isn't sure what she wants to do but knows she wants a "decent job" and doesn't want "to end up dependent."   34

This perception on the part of young women that success is there for the taking, that affluence is a necessary ingredient in any life plan, and that they need to be able to stand on their own can be seen as a coming together of several strands of American thought: the American Dream promises upward   35 mobility to those who plan and work sufficiently hard; the women's movement has taught at least two generations of women that they are entitled to play virtually any roles in society that they are capable of and that they are entitled to reap the appropriate rewards; and the ideology of the Reagan years has both stressed individualism and undermined Americans' belief in the necessity of creating a more humane and equitable environment in which all people can thrive. During the 1980s we have witnessed, I believe, the merging of these three lines of thought against a backdrop of ever-increasing disparities in wealth and well-being between rich and poor, black and white, and ever-increasing emphasis on materialism, often at any cost—what one social critic has called the "empty ostentation and narcissistic culture of the 1980s." Is it any wonder that young women feel they are on their own? The message that they must go it alone is being given to many Americans: the homeless; the hungry; the elderly nursing-home residents; the children who are essentially lost in the foster-care system; the millions who are uninsured for health care and those who do not have access to care because of inadequate or nonexistent services; the numbers of young people receiving inferior education that cannot possibly prepare them for living and working in the next century. Moreover, young women see on a personal level that individuals must be able to care for themselves. They see their divorced parents floundering; they hear the cautionary tales about relying too much on men; they are all too aware of the status and respect given in American society to those who embody the traditional male characteristics of autonomy and power, and know that to protect themselves they must have no less.

The feminist movement did not, of course, set out to bolster and extend   36
to yet another group the ideology of individualism and the American Dream. With its appeal to "sisterhood" and its use of consciousness-raising groups, it set out, rather, on a far more collective course, encouraging women to see themselves not simply as individuals but as part of a long, international struggle for equality. But movements do not exist in a vacuum. The women's movement originated within a class system that drew largely middle- and upper-middle-class adherents and then was in part shaped by their concerns and their needs. It exists today within an individualistic, hierarchical system committed for the most part to private enterprise and profit making. Once it became clear that the movement was not going to disappear, elements of that structure began admitting "the best and the brightest" to their hallowed halls. Leaders of the movement might call for widely available day care, paid parental leave, larger welfare grants, and more money for prenatal care, but what was picked up by the media were the upper-middle-class women in the courtrooms, the board rooms, and the emergency rooms, often putting off marriage and children in order to go for the brass ring of success.

This ideology of independence and individualism can be seen to some   37
degree in all three groups, but it is far more prevalent among the New American Dreamers, and adds significantly to the pressure these young

women already feel. They feel pressure to succeed not only for the status and material rewards success bestows but because they recognize the likelihood that they may be the sole support of themselves and their children.

This sense of responsibility, of aloneness, brings a new intensity to the need to be "successful." Many young women see the choices as "making it" or "not making it," being "independent" versus being "dependent." Understood in those terms, the pressure is to work out a way for oneself to live the good life. . . .

Stacy Steinberg, a soft-spoken yet articulate seventeen-year-old high-school junior, whose mother is a school nurse and whose father is an auditor, analyzes the pressures young women feel: "It's so hard to be an adolescent today, and it's only going to get harder. Kids today have to worry about liquor, drugs, sex, *and* their academic work. And your parents want you to do better than they did, but it's harder to do better today than when they were growing up."

She goes on: "Guys have different pressures; they're more into sexual experiences. But it's harder to be a girl. You see models in ads and say, 'I don't look like that; how can I fit into that?' Parents say, 'When you lose a few more pounds, you can get a new outfit.' And the pressure about grades—the girls who cry if they don't do perfectly on a quiz!

"You want to be feminine but independent. What's an independent woman? Someone who if left on her own could fend for herself.

"The world is changing and it's hard to figure out where you belong. I have an anorexic friend; she just wants control over her life. What with competition, SATs, parents pressuring kids, and divorce, kids need their parents more than ever but they just can't communicate with them."

While the emphasis among the New American Dreamers is on doing, on career, on material rewards, these young women almost always include commitment to family as one of their central concerns. Although they have taken on the goals of high achievement, success, and independence, they have for the most part kept the values of caring for others. They now see a dual responsibility, at work and at home, both public and private. The New American Dreamers may at this time in their lives place their career goals first, but as they look ahead it becomes clear that many fully expect to care for family and children as well.

Alexandra Morgan, a black seventeen-year-old from the Midwest, whose mother is a high-school teacher and whose father is a chemist, hopes to be an oceanographer. She plans to "settle down" after she completes a B.S. and an M.S. in science and oceanography, but only when she finds the right person, one with whom she wants to "share the future." He must be "what I want in a guy"; what is important is "how he carries himself and if he knows what he wants out of life." She plans to have "no more than two children" and worries about "juggling work and coming home to the children—they need to know they are loved." She recalls that her mother always worked but was always there. But her mother had a work life based on the school calendar—Christmas and spring vacations, summers off. How will Alexandra manage to do both? In her plans for the future the doing is clear and concrete; the caring is hazier, harder to imagine.

Wendy Jackson has the dream, too. A twenty-year-old junior from one of the campuses of the University of North Carolina, Wendy is the youngest of three children and comes from a working-class family. Her father, now retired, was a supervisor in a local textile plant, and her mother still works as a winder in another textile plant. Wendy's dream seems in many ways to be at odds with the life she is leading. An undergraduate major in social work, she plans to work with handicapped people, probably as a school social worker. She is also engaged; her fiancé is studying, in her words, "ag ed"—agricultural education—and they plan to live in Raleigh. But Wendy does not see herself marrying until she is at least twenty-six. "The most important thing is independence," she says. "You have to be secure within yourself before making a connection with someone else. If something ever happens, you must be able to stand alone.

"I want to expand, to see things and meet people. I don't want to stay in one place. I don't want to hold back. I want to be released into a new world. I know social work might put me back because of the money; it might not allow me to do the things I want to do. I plan to go on and get an MSW so that I can make more money."

Wendy isn't sure whether she wants children. She does know that she wants to travel and that she wants a different kind of marriage than her mother had. "My father came home and lay on the couch." What kind of relationship does she want? "I'm selfish—call me greedy. I'm not going to come home and wash his clothes. I'd rather not get married than be someone's maid!"

Wendy is on course for a very different life than the one she says she wants. She's studying for a bachelor's degree in social work; as she comments, she is likely to be paid a meager salary and have few opportunities for promotion. Her professional options will improve somewhat with an MSW, but will these opportunities get her where she wants to go? She's engaged at the age of twenty and yet has an image of independence and adventure that seems at odds with the life of a married social worker living in a small city in North Carolina. Wendy's relatively unconventional ideas and dreams seem directly in conflict with her far more conventional life choices. It is almost as though Wendy's hopes for the future were taken from *Ms.* magazine while her real options were rooted in *Good Housekeeping*.

Other young women have this inner drive, this vision of what they want to become that impels them onward when others from similar backgrounds might choose more modest goals. Sandra Curran grew up in New York City, the youngest of four children. Her parents came to this country from Trinidad when Sandra was ten; they have both worked in a hospital for many years— her father as a security guard, her mother as a unit secretary. From the time she was a junior in college, Sandra has had a vision of her future life: she planned to get her master's degree in social work, work a couple of years, and then go on to law school. And she has done exactly that. Along the way she married a young man who is working in computers and also getting his master's degree; she is currently holding down a full-time, extremely demanding job in foster care while attending law school at night. Why is she doing all this? Where does the drive, the impetus come from? Sandra tries to explain:

"I have a picture of a certain life-style that I want. By the time I'm forty 50 I want to be able to enjoy my family, live in the suburbs. I want to work by choice rather than out of necessity.

"Law will enable me to speak out—to advocate for individuals and fam- 51 ilies. I plan to practice either family or criminal law, and with my MSW and my law degree I can deal with counseling, advocating, and legal issues in a holistic way.

"I just have an image of how I see myself in the future, how I will be 52 comfortable emotionally. I have always had high expectations."

Like many other New American Dreamers, Sandra is clear about how to 53 develop her career but far less clear about how she will manage family and career. As with so many women who are firmly set on their quest, she sees what she must do to get where she wants to be professionally, but while she is also committed to children, to family, and to caring, that aspect of life is less mapped out, more sketchily drawn. One of the characteristics of the New American Dreamers is their focus on what they need to accomplish *before* they become emotionally involved. Their focus is on their professional lives, on doing; caring is part of the picture but less clearly visualized. Nonetheless it is always there, in the background, for though young women understand that they must be active participants in society, they also understand that new arrangements have yet to be worked out to provide the caring that women once provided. The New American Dreamers know that they want to be prepared to take on new roles and responsibilities even as they suspect they will still be expected to perform the old ones as well. . . .

WOMEN AND POWER IN THE WORKPLACE

HILARY M. LIPS

A psychologist who has conducted extensive research on gender, Hilary Lips has written *Women, Men and the Psychology of Power* (1981), *Sex and Gender: An Introduction* (1988), and *The Psychology of Sex Differences* (1978) with Nina Colwill. Lips's research on gender has covered topics as diverse as attitudes toward childbearing and careers, the use of computers, stereotyping, sex discrimination, and stress in the workplace. In this essay, she discusses women's exclusion from and marginalization in the workplace.

During most of our recent history, the major thrust of women's struggle for power has been toward increased access to the major institutions in society. The struggle simply not to be excluded—from voting rights, jobs, organisations, full legal status as persons—has taken up much of women's collective energy for decades. A strong emphasis in the struggle has been on access to and equality in the world of paid employment, for women have intuited rightly that the income, status, knowledge and social networks that come with employment are crucial resources on which power, both individual and collective, can be based.

Power, it should be noted at the outset, is the capacity to have an impact on one's environment, to be able to make a difference through one's actions. It is the opposite of helplessness. There is no use in debating whether or not women should really want power, or whether it is appropriately feminist to strive for power. Such debates are based on a long outdated, narrow notion of power as a static quality possessed only by tyrants. In talking about women increasing their power, I am referring to an increase in effectiveness of influence, in strength.

More power for women means two things: increasing women's access to resources and to the positions from which these resources are controlled; and increasing women's impact on the formation of policy about how our institutions function. Because women have a long history of exclusion, the initial focus in the struggle to increase women's power has been to gain access for women to a variety of institutions.

The universities are a good case in point. For years, women were excluded from higher education on the grounds that we were unsuited for it and might even be damaged by it. Some "experts" even went so far as to argue that too much use of a woman's brain would damage her reproductive organs and thus endanger her vital child-bearing function (see Shields, 1975). Universities in many countries accept female students as a matter of course now. In Canada, we have come a long way from the time when the principal of a Laval University-affiliated college for women had to placate critics of her institution by interspersing piano recitals and afternoon teas with normal academic pursuits. Such activities were supposedly necessary to keep her delicate female students from breaking under the strain of uninterrupted intellectual work (Danylewycz, 1981). However, arguments about damaging the reproductive system are still being used in some quarters to exclude women from various arenas of professional and amateur sports.

We rejoice in the knowledge that women now have access to the universities as students, and that there is even a growing minority of women in faculty and administrative positions. Having increased their access to this one important institution, have women, in fact, begun to make any impact on it? And has women's access to university education increased their power to gain entry to other previously restricted arenas: employment, government, business? 5

The answer is yes to both questions. The universities have changed since women were admitted. The curriculum shows their influence: courses dealing with the female half of the human race are growing in number and respectability. Many Canadian universities have formal programmes in Women's Studies, and the federal government has recently moved to endow five "Chairs" in Women's Studies at universities across the country. University structure and policy reflect women's presence too. Such issues as parental leave and day care are being taken a little more seriously. Real effort is made to meet the needs of part-time students. Great transformations have not taken place, but neither has the institution absorbed women without a trace. Most interesting of all, perhaps, is the change that has been wrought in the dreams and ambitions of female students. A survey done in the U.S. in the mid-1970s revealed that no fewer than one in six female college students were planning careers in the traditionally male-dominated fields of business, engineering, law or medicine (Astin, King, and Richardson, 1975). Clearly, these women are getting the messages about the increased possibilities for access into these fields, and are exercising their newfound power to choose these professions. However, the sense of power that comes with women's perception of an increased range of career choices may be short-lived. Statistics on women's employment indicate that they may often get in the door, but no further. Females in almost every professional field, for example, are underemployed and underpaid relative to their male counterparts (Abella, 1984) and women in trade occupations still have a great deal of difficulty finding employment (Braid, 1982). Moreover, the research bleakly suggests that, as women grow more numerous in a particular profession or occupation, its status declines (Touhey, 1974). 6

Thus, although women's problems with access to the workplace are far 7
from over, there is an increasing recognition that simply being allowed in—
to a profession, a business organisation, a trade union—is only half the battle.
How can women avoid being marginal members of the workplace community—tokens whose presence supposedly illustrates that "women can make
it," but who are not at the centre of decision making and who are powerless
to rise to the top of, or change the shape of, the institutions in which they
work?

Much advice has been aimed at women in an effort to answer this ques- 8
tion. Most of it boils down to a prescription that women carefully observe
and follow the models provided by successful men. Successful businesswomen
profiled in the media are (like their male counterparts) often heard to comment that, in the service of success, they have given up their social life,
hobbies, and recreation, and find it difficult to make time for family and
friendship.

Such an ideal, based on the model of a small number of high-achieving, 9
powerful, visible men in high-status jobs, creates discomfort among many
women. For some, the discomfort may stem from a fear of being labelled
tough, competitive or ambitious—qualities that are incongruent with our
culture's definition of femininity. For others, the idea of subordinating all
other priorities to one's paid work seems unrealistic and unpleasant. The first
objection is easily dealt with, at least in theory. The attention paid to the
concept of androgyny in recent years has, if nothing else, shown that the
qualities associated with strength are not necessarily antithetical to the traditional "feminine" virtues of nurturance, sensitivity and care for others (Colwill and Lips, 1978). It is possible to be tough without losing sight of what is
fair, to be ambitious without trampling on everyone else on one's way to the
top—and if women are going to make an impact in the workplace or anywhere
else they are simply going to have to figure out how to blend these qualities.

The second objection, however, is one to be taken more seriously. How 10
realistic, how desirable is it for women to adopt wholesale the myth that
gaining success and power requires the subordination of all other activities,
values, and interests to one's career? This model, which is held out to men as
an ideal, is unworkable and destructive even for most of *them*, even though
they have been socialised toward it and are provided by society with many
more supports for this life style than are women (Harrison, 1978).

In order to devote all of her energy to a career, a woman needs someone 11
taking care of the other aspects of her life: feeding her, cleaning up after her,
making sure she has clean clothes, making dental appointments for her, keeping her social life organised, looking after her children, and so on. She needs,
in essence, a wife. Employed women do not have wives, and it is simply
impractical to try to follow the male model for career success without one.
Now that fewer career men have wives who fill the traditional role, perhaps
the male career model itself will begin to change. At any rate, business and
professional women will have to develop their own model for career success.

The male model, presented in such glowing terms, is largely a myth. It is an ideal that is used to keep men in line, and there is no reason why women should fall in line behind them. While popular writers are exhorting women to map out career strategy years in advance the way men supposedly do, research suggests that, despite the ideal, most men do not plan their careers any more carefully than women do (Harlan and Weiss, 1980). While the advice-mongers are saying knowingly that women have not got what it takes to wheel and deal in the business world because they have never learned not to take conflict personally, many business and professional women have found to their chagrin that their male counterparts grow silent, withdraw, or become bitter and vindictive in their relationships to colleagues after being opposed on some policy or economic issue. While popular writers are fond of saying that women lack the training necessary to be good "team players" because they never passed through the proving ground of football, basketball and hockey, many a male ex-athlete will admit that his main legacy from high school football was a recurring knee injury and a sense of failure. 12

The writers who say these things have taken our society's definition of the male role and life pattern and elevated it unquestioningly to an ideal. If the shoe were on the other foot, if women were in the majority in business and the professions, these same writers would be telling aspiring career men that they were at a disadvantage in knowing how to be part of a co-operative business partnership because they had never gone through the "proving ground" of rearing children. Instead of advising women to bone up on football and hockey so that they would not feel left out of casual conversations with the men in the office, the experts (presuming traditional gender roles in this mythical situation) would be advising men to read romance novels, keep up with the latest recipes, talk about their children, and follow the careers of the great women runners and tennis players. Since men hold the majority of powerful business and professional positions, it is assumed that there must be something right about men's upbringing and life style—something that leads them into powerful positions—and if women would only emulate that pattern they too could make it to "the top" in large numbers. Not only does this analysis overlook the fact that our society is arranged in a way that makes it horribly impractical for the majority of women to follow the male model (i.e., not only do most women *not* have partners who fulfill the role of the traditional wife, but also they *do* have children for whom they usually have primary responsibility), but also the whole approach is rooted in our all-too-human need to rationalise the status quo. 13

Psychologists have been finding for years that people in general like to believe that the world is a reasonably fair and just place, that there is an order to things, and that people basically get what they deserve (e.g., Lerner, 1974). Thus, people are very good at thinking up reasons why things are the way they are—at justifying and rationalising our social arrangements rather than questioning them. It is easier, for example, to think of women as "unassertive" or poorly trained for leadership in order to explain how few women reach 14 visible leadership positions than to think that there may be something askew with a system or an organisation in which this is the case. Since men are on top and women are the bottom, such thinking goes, what women are doing must be wrong . . . and men are the ones doing it right. Teach the women how to act like men, and their problems will be solved.

Perhaps the clearest way to see how this type of rationalisation works is to imagine the changes in explanation for the status quo that would be required if the positions of the two groups were reversed. Gloria Steinem provides an amusing example of this process in her article "If Men Could Menstruate" (Steinem, 1983). She fantasises that if men and not women had menstrual cycles, menstruation would be regarded as a sign of superiority. The fact that men were "in tune" with nature and the cycles of the moon would be thought to give them an advantage in making important decisions, and women's non-cyclic nature would be used as a reason for excluding them from high positions. In fact, women's menstrual cycle has been cited repeatedly (on very flimsy evidence) as a handicap that makes them unfit for certain possible positions. Here too, though, the only logic in the argument is that relating it to the status quo. Nowhere is it argued that, since women supposedly become so unreliable and irrational at certain times of the month, they should be relieved of the delicate job of caring for small, helpless children during such times. Similar logic asserts that women's allegedly superior manual dexterity makes them uniquely fit to be typists, while ignoring the possibility that it might make them uniquely fit to be surgeons or television repairpersons. 15

It is reasonable to be suspicious of any approach that purports to explain women's failure to advance, or their lack of impact, solely on the basis of flaws in their own behaviour. Of course there are things most women can learn to make themselves more effective, but that is also true for most men. What *may* be more true for women than for men in many organisations, however, is that support and security from the organisation is lacking. Women, while inside an organisation, often find that they are still outsiders. As Rosabeth Kanter's (1977) work shows, the issue is not whether or not women know how to play on teams, but whether a token woman can play on a team that does not want her on it. 16

It is becoming clear, then, that having broken down many initial access barriers, women taking up their newly-won positions in mainstream organisations often find that they are still far from the centres of power. Having dealt with many of the formal barriers to career participation, they find themselves blocked by less tangible but equally frustrating obstacles. They feel invisible. They feel (and they are often right) that no one takes them seriously. Such feelings are not limited to women in business, engineering, or other male-dominated professions, or to women in "white-collar" jobs. Women in teaching, nursing, secretarial work, carpentry and other trades, and factory work all report similar frustrations in their struggles to make an impact in their work environment. Understanding of the dilemmas faced by 17 women trying to be effective in the workplace can be enhanced by examining their problems within the framework provided by psychological research on power.

Psychologists argue that power—the ability to make an impact or to get others to do what one wants them to do—is based on a person's access to certain resources that can be used to "back up" her influence attempts (French and Raven, 1959). In other words, in order for a person (or a group) to exert power, there have to be reasons—fear, respect, admiration, greed, loyalty— for others in the environment to co-operate or comply. The resources that provide the reasons for compliance include control over rewards (for example, the capacity to reward a person who complies with one's wishes by promoting her, giving her a raise, giving her the day off, giving her a gift) and control over punishments (such as the capacity to discipline someone, fire her, take something away from her). The resources on which power is based also include legitimacy, expertise, personal attractiveness or likableness, and the sheer amount of knowledge or information one can muster to support one's arguments. The amount of power or influence a person can wield depends at least partly on how much access she has, and is seen to have, to these kinds of resources. 18

A person's ability to influence others depends not only on her actual access to resources, but also on the amount of control over these resources that others see her as having. If a woman is an expert in a given field, for instance, that expertise will not provide her with a source of power with respect to others who do not recognise her as an expert. While women are often blocked from control over certain kinds of resources in their work settings, it is just as often true that the resources they do have go unrecognised. In the case of expertise, the stereotype of feminine incompetence often works against the perception of women as experts, particularly in traditionally male fields. In the case of legitimacy, not only do women rarely find themselves in positions of authority, but, even when they do, their automatic low status as women acts to contradict and undermine their authority in the eyes of others. 19

A consequence of these difficulties is that women sometimes find them-selves relying more than they should or would like to on the resources of personal attractiveness or likableness to exert influence in the workplace. They smile a lot, try to win the friendship and good will of the people they must influence, and may sometimes use their sexuality in overt or covert ways as a basis of power. This is a strategy that often does work, but it tends to be a trap if relied on exclusively. A person using it does not enhance anyone's view of her competence and must be rather too careful about staying on everyone's good side. 20

It must be remembered also that attempts to exert influence do not usually involve an active influencer and a totally passive target person. The power interaction is often a complex one, involving conflict, with both parties using several bases of power at once in the effort to win the struggle. Thus, for instance, a woman who has enormous resources in terms of information, 21 control over rewards, and personal attractiveness may find herself in a struggle with a supervisor who is not averse to using the coercive power of sexual harassment. A group of women workers that has done enough extensive research on an issue to earn the label of "experts" and has a large base of informational power may confront an employer who knows much less than they do, but who uses the power of position and status to try to delegitimise the group and their statements. Any attempt to exert influence involves making an accurate assessment of the amount and type of resistance likely to be encountered and the strategies most likely to overcome the resistance.

Not the least of the problems a person can face in trying to wield power is a negative bias in her own view of the resources she controls. If a person who is an expert lacks confidence in her own expertise, she will have difficulty exerting influence based on that expertise. Since women are continually being given the message that they are not expected to be experts, that people are pleasantly surprised when they know anything about important issues, lack of confidence is a dangerously seductive trap for them. Men too feel inadequate when they compare themselves to their colleagues. Our culture's specialised, competitive workplaces tend to foster this feeling. Men, however, have developed more strategies than women have for hiding this feeling of inadequacy. What must be kept in mind is that the exercise of power depends not only on what kinds of resources one controls, but also on the way one thinks one's own resources compare to everyone else's. In other words, how powerful a person or group feels can make a difference in how powerful they are. 22

A person's exercise of power is also affected by what she and others see as appropriate behaviour. Since "feminine" behaviour is, almost by definition, powerless behaviour, the woman trying to act in a powerful way is placed in a double bind. There may be times when she has the resources and knows she has the resources to wield power, but holds back out of a fear of being labelled pushy, aggressive, tough, or just plain not nice. 23

The three factors just described (what resources a person controls, how powerful she feels, and what she and others see as appropriate behaviour) affect not only the amount of impact she can have in a particular situation, but also the style or strategy of influence she employs. Her style of influence may be more or less direct, for example (Johnson, 1976). Someone who uses a direct style of influence asks for or demands openly what she wants, making it clear that she is the one who wants it. Someone using a very indirect style of influence, on the other hand, tries to get what she wants to happen without acknowledging that she is the source of the influence. A common example of the latter is the strategy of talking to someone behind the scenes rather than personally bringing up an issue at a meeting. 24

Both styles carry some risks, especially at the extremes. The person using the direct approach to influence may be viewed as abrasive, may be disliked, and may often find herself involved in conflict. The payoff is that, when she gets something positive to happen, she gets credit for it—credit that adds to 25 her competence and expertise in the eyes of others and thus adds to the store of resources she can draw on in future situations.

The person using the indirect approach to influence, on the other hand, avoids the risk of being openly associated with an idea that turns out to be unpopular or unworkable, while keeping the opportunity for private satisfaction when she is the source of an initiative that works. However, sometimes this satisfaction can be a little too private. No matter how many good ideas she generates, a person can never build up her credibility if she is never seen as the originator of these ideas, if her influence is always indirect. 26

Clearly, to increase one's competence in the eyes of others, it is necessary to use influence directly and openly, at least some of the time. However, this is not to say that women should always avoid using indirect strategies. There are times when it is simply more important to get something done than to make an issue of it or get credit for it. In some organizations, for instance, people have managed to advance the cause of women considerably without ever being so obvious about it that they generated a fight. 27

Since it seems to be important to use influence directly and openly at least some of the time, it would seem to be a simple matter for women to get the message and start using more direct power styles in order to enhance their personal effectiveness and increase their acceptance within institutions. This, in essence, is what assertiveness training is supposed to be about: teaching people, especially women, to exert influence directly. Men rarely sign up for assertiveness training. Does this mean men have no trouble exerting influence openly? Perhaps, but it could also mean that men are more reluctant than women to accept for themselves the label of "unassertive." Also, many of the programmes are geared to women, on the unproven assumption that women need the training more. In fact, some Canadian research suggests that women are actually more appropriately assertive than men in many situations (Wine, Smye and Moses, 1980). 28

But while basic skills in assertiveness can only be helpful, they provide no magic cure for the power problems that women face in their working lives. How direct a woman is able to be in her attempts to exert influence depends only in a limited way on these skills. More importantly, it depends on the degree of actual control over resources that she brings to an interaction, how powerful she feels, and what kinds of behaviour she and those around her see as appropriate. 29

Women are often accused of relying on indirect or hidden power styles— of being manipulative and sneaky rather than open when trying to exert influence. In cases where this accusation is true, there are probably a number of factors operating that favour an indirect strategy. For example, the more resources one can command to back up one's requests or demands, the easier it is to be direct. This is particularly true of such resources as legitimacy, status and support. The more authority a person has in her position, the higher her status, and the more backing she feels from her co-workers, the easier it is for her to make strong, clear demands on people. For this reason, 30 a teacher may have no hesitation about making certain clear demands on her students, but may be wary about adopting the same strong, direct style with school administrators. When dealing with students, she is operating from a position of recognised authority and of higher status within the institution. Moreover, she usually knows she is working within guidelines that are accepted by and will be supported by her colleagues. If she had no recognised authority over the people she was trying to influence, if she were operating from a position of lower status, if she felt isolated from her colleagues on a particular issue (all of which are more likely to be the case when she is trying to exert influence over an administrator instead of a student), it would be more difficult for her to be direct and assertive.

For women (or men, for that matter) who find themselves at the bottom 31
of the ladder in a workplace that operates on a very hierarchical basis, it is unrealistic to expect a lot of direct, open use of power. This is doubly true if a woman has no network of support among her co-workers—a problem that plagues women who are breaking ground in a traditionally male job. Finally, it must be noted that women tend to start with a strike against them when it comes to status. The status ascribed to females in many jobs is automatically lower than that ascribed to men in the same job. Simply trying to teach or convince women to be more assertive and direct under these conditions is not the answer. Most women know how to be assertive under the right circumstances, but they avoid behaviour that is going to get them into more trouble than they want to handle.

Intervention to increase women's capacity to exert power in a direct way 32
should not focus mainly on the behaviour of individual women. Rather, a more useful focus is on finding ways to increase women's access to resources, and to change the culture's image of femininity so that it is no longer synonymous with weakness or incompetence.

How can such changes be accomplished? They have already begun to 33
happen. A crucial aspect of increasing women's access to resources in the workplace is the formation of support groups. Such groups not only provide much needed support (a resource in itself) for women who are isolated or ignored in male-dominated workplaces, they also enable women to share information and expertise—thus potentially increasing the competence (another resource) of all members. In some situations, these groups can also provide the political clout to help attain certain kinds of change beneficial to women (yet another resource). Also, the existence of network groups may provide a significant source of encouragement for more women to enter certain fields, an eventuality that will make it less common for women to find themselves isolated as tokens in their jobs.

It does not take a psychologist to tell most women that another extremely 34
important aspect of increasing women's access to the resources on which power is based involves eliminating women's "double shift". Time and energy are themselves precious resources on which all attempts to have influence or make an impact on the world are based. For years, women's time and energy

have been stolen from them by economic and cultural systems that have allocated to women virtually all of the responsibility for child care and the daily maintenance functions of cooking, cleaning, shopping and errand-running. Even in countries where serious attempts have been made to "socialise" child care functions, women are the ones faced with the housework when they return from work each day. And in Sweden, where new fathers and mothers are equally entitled to parental leave at 90 per cent of salary, few fathers avail themselves of the opportunity to stay home with their infants. No modern economic system has yet solved this problem of women's double day.

On an individual level, a woman is seriously handicapped in her attempts   35
to have an impact outside of her own family by this double burden of labour. On a group level, the double shift weakens and dilutes women's impact on the values that shape the political process, the educational process, the arts, our own culture, and the future of the world. In the power terms discussed in this chapter, the cultural requirement that women perform a disproportionately large share of home-related work interferes with their access to almost every type of resource on which power can be based. Household responsibilities may make a woman less available for the extra meetings or social events where information is exchanged and contacts that lead to promotions and better jobs are made. They slow down her education, keeping her at a lower level in the job market. Thus, her access to information and expertise is curtailed, as is her access to the reward and punishment power that accompanies control over economic resources, and to the legitimacy that comes with holding a position of recognised authority. The only power base that is not guaranteed to be adversely affected by this situation is that of personal attractiveness or likability—and there is many a bleary-eyed, irritable woman with no time for exercise or sleep who will say that even that traditional source of female power is compromised by the double shift. Clearly, for women as individuals or for women as a group to have a greater impact on our cultural institutions, the relegation to women of most child care and household responsibilities would have to be changed.

The "powerless/incompetent" image of femininity would also have to be   36
changed. While that change is beginning to happen as strong, competent women become more visible, efforts in some specific areas are called for. Ripe for revision, for instance, is the notion that women are incompetent to handle all things mathematical and technical. The pernicious stereotype of women as beings who cannot deal with numbers and who are too muddleheaded to balance a chequebook is not only wrong, it is dangerous in an age that is increasingly dominated by the computer. It will be helpful to remember that when the typewriter was first invented, it was thought to be too complicated a machine for women to handle!

It would also be useful to work against the idea that women must be   37
physically weak. Not only is this view of women an obstacle to their employment in a variety of jobs requiring strength and stamina, but it may also be

509

related to the general perception of women's effectiveness and their sense of power. Being weak fosters a need for protection from men—and this generates an attitude of protectiveness on men's part that generalises far beyond the physical realm into other aspects of women's lives.

A third aspect of the femininity stereotype that would-be powerful women need to challenge is that women are quiet, soft-spoken and polite. A growing body of research in psychology shows that, in the first place, people who talk more in groups tend to be accorded more status in those groups; and, in the second place, men tend to discourage women from speaking up in group situations by interrupting them and by ignoring their input. These tactics used by men tend to subdue women's efforts at participation in the discussion, allowing the men conversational control. Then, in a vicious circle, women are discounted more and more as they become increasingly silent, and they try less and less often to enter the conversation as they feel increasingly ignored. One approach to this problem is for women to try to train their male colleagues to stop interrupting them, but such training may not come easily. It is a rare and lucky woman who, after bringing the problem to the attention of the men she works with, finds she is never interrupted again! More probably, she will have to work actively to invalidate the feminine stereotype of politeness by refusing to defer to male speakers who try to interrupt her and by protesting such interruptions again and again. Since old habits die hard, and since change is more in women's interest than men's, it is unrealistic to rely too heavily on men to relinquish their conversational control tactics without continuous pressure from women.

As women gain more access to the resources on which power is based, they will find it easier to challenge the "powerless" image of femininity. And, concurrently, as the powerless image fades, women will find it easier to be recognised as strong, as competent, as experts. Thus, in a reversal of a "vicious circle", the two processes will feed into each other, ultimately making it easier for women to use such resources as expertise, information and legitimacy. These resources become springboards for acquiring access to other resources—tangible ones such as money and control over decision making—and for opening the doors to these resources to other women. This is an optimistic perspective to be sure, but one that is consistent with the way many advances for women have been achieved over the years. For women, as for any relatively powerless group, the key to starting the "nonvicious circle" rolling is to use their most available resource: their numbers, their collectivity, pooled energy and shared support. The payoff may well be not only more access to and impact in the workplace for women, but a more humane workplace for everyone.

References

Abella, R. S. *Equality in Employment: A Royal Commission Report*. Ottawa: Canadian Government Publishing Centre, 1984.

Astin, A. W., King, M. R., and Richardson, G. T. *The American Freshman: National Norms for Fall 1975*. Los Angeles: University of California Laboratory for Research in Higher Education, 1975.

Braid, K. "Women in Trades in British Columbia". In M. Fitzgerald, C. Guberman, and M. Wolfe (eds.), *Still Ain't Satisfied! Canadian Feminism Today*. Toronto: The Woman's Press, 1982.

Colwill, N. L., and Lips, H. M. "Masculinity, Femininity and Androgyny: What Have You Done for Us Lately?" Chapter in H. M. Lips and N. L. Colwill, *The Psychology of Sex Differences*. Englewood Cliffs, N.J.: Prentice-Hall, 1978.

Danylewycz, M. "Changing Relationships: Nuns and Feminists in Montréal, 1890–1925". *Histoire Sociale—Social History*, 14: 28 (1981), 413–434.

French, J. P. R., and Raven, B. "The Bases of Social Power". In D. Cartwright (ed.), *Studies in Social Power*. Ann Arbor: Institute for Social Research, University of Michigan, 1959.

Harlan, A., and Weiss, C. L. "Moving Up: Women in Managerial Careers". Third progress report. Wellesley, Mass.: Wellesley College Centre for Research on Women, 1980.

Harrison, J. "Warning: The Male Sex Role May Be Dangerous to Your Health". *Journal of Social Issues*, 34: 1 (1978), 65–86.

Johnson, P. "Women and Power: Toward a Theory of Effectiveness". *Journal of Social Issues*, 32: 3 (1976), 99–110.

Kanter, R. M. *Men and Women of the Corporation*. New York: Basic Books, 1977.

Lerner, M. J. "Social Psychology of Justice and Interpersonal Attraction". In T. L. Huston (ed.), *Foundations of Interpersonal Attraction*. New York: Academic Press, 1974.

Shields, S. A. "Functionalism, Darwinism and the Psychology of Women: A Study in Social Myth". *American Psychologist*, 30: 7 (1975), 739–754.

Steinem, G. *Outrageous Acts and Everyday Rebellions*. New York: Holt, Rinehart and Winston, 1983.

Touhey, J. C. "Effects of Additional Women Professionals on Rating of Occupational Prestige and Desirability". *Journal of Personality and Social Psychology*, 29: (1974), 86–89.

Wine, J. D., Smye, M. D., and Moses, B. "Assertiveness: Sex Differences in Relationships between Self-report and Behavioural Measures". In C. Stark-Adamec (ed.), *Sex Roles: Origins, Influences, and Implications for Women*. Montreal: Eden Press, 1980.

A WOMAN'S RECKONING

An Introduction to the International Economic System

◖

MARILYN WARING

Marilyn Waring is a political economist and former member of the New Zealand Parliament. She is the author of *Women, Politics, and Power* (1985) and *If Women Counted: A New Feminist Economics* (1989), from which this selection is taken. Waring, who holds a doctorate in economics, has been called an iconoclast for encouraging readers to question the traditional economic definitions of value and work.

I am awake in a glistening morning ready to write. From the window, the lush green grass, thick with autumn dew, leads to the empty beach. The sea and sky beyond—both blue and unpolluted—are washed clear and clean by the sun. The only sounds are the early dawn chorus and the roaring of the waves. I sit, as writers and artists have sat for centuries, laboring unpaid. Yet I am sure this is work. I am sure it is productive, and I hope it will be of value. But as far as the International Labor Organization (ILO) is concerned, on this late summer day in 1986, it is none of the above.

I consider the hills rising directly from the sea. They were once covered in thick native bush, which must have been nonproductive, for it was burned or cleared off. Now thousands of pine trees inch their way to a harvest at twenty years. That will make them "productive." If the mineral prospecting licenses on the hills reveal minerals in quantity, the hills, too, will be productive. As they are—untouched, unscathed—they have no value. That's what the international economic system says.

My tenancy of this house is unproductive. While its owner will have a market rental value of the house imputed for the sake of the national accounts, I contribute nothing, as I am a guest here. I consume a little water and electricity. Now that has value! If modern plumbing conveniences were not providing water and I walked with my bucket to the foothills four hundred meters away to collect it from the streams there, it would be worthless. That's what the international economic system says.

If I were to take commercially prepared, prepackaged food from the refrigerator, I would be economically consumptive. But I choose to eat the feijoas, tamarillos, and apples from the domestic garden, items of no value.

512

All in all, I seem to be having a very worthless sort of day—like the beach, the birds, and the clear and unpolluted skies.

Tell Me a Riddle: Who Works and Who Doesn't

Consider Tendai, a young girl in the Lowveld, in Zimbabwe. Her day starts   5
at 4 a.m., when, to fetch water, she carries a thirty-litre tin to a borehole about eleven kilometers from her home. She walks barefoot and is home by 9 a.m. She eats a little and proceeds to fetch firewood until midday. She cleans the utensils from the family's morning meal and sits preparing a lunch of sadza for the family. After lunch and the cleaning of the dishes, she wanders in the hot sun until early evening, fetching wild vegetables for supper before making the evening trip for water. Her day ends at 9 p.m., after she has prepared supper and put her younger brothers and sisters to sleep. Tendai is considered unproductive, unoccupied, and economically inactive. According to the international economic system, Tendai does not work and is not part of the labor force.

Cathy, a young, middle-class North American housewife, spends her days   6
preparing food, setting the table, serving meals, clearing food and dishes from the table, washing dishes, dressing and diapering her children, disciplining children, taking the children to day-care or to school, disposing of garbage, dusting, gathering clothes for washing, doing the laundry, going to the gas station and the supermarket, repairing household items, ironing, keeping an eye on or playing with the children, making beds, paying bills, caring for pets and plants, putting away toys, books, and clothes, sewing or mending or knitting, talking with door-to-door salespeople, answering the telephone, vacuuming, sweeping, and washing floors, cutting the grass, weeding, and shoveling snow, cleaning the bathroom and the kitchen, and putting her children to bed. Cathy has to face the fact that she fills her time in a *totally* unproductive manner. She, too, is economically inactive, and economists record her as unoccupied.

Ben is a highly trained member of the U.S. military. His regular duty is   7
to descend to an underground facility where he waits with a colleague, for hours at a time, for an order to fire a nuclear missile. So skilled and effective is Ben that if his colleague were to attempt to subvert an order to fire, Ben would, if all else failed, be expected to kill him to ensure a successful missile launch. Ben is in paid work; he is economically active. His work has value and contributes, as part of the nuclear machine, to his nation's growth, wealth, and productivity. That's what the international economic system says.

Mario is a pimp and a heroin addict in Rome. He regularly pays graft.   8
While Mario's services and his consumption and production are illegal, they are, nonetheless, marketed. Money changes hands. Mario's activities are part

of Italy's hidden economy. But in a nation's bookkeeping, not all transactions are accounted for. A government treasury or a reserve bank measures the money supply and sees that more money is in circulation than has been reported in legitimate business activities. Thus some nations, including Italy, regularly impute a minimal value for the hidden economy in their national accounts. So part of Mario's illegal services and production and consumption activities will be recognized and recorded. That's what the international economic system says.

Ben and Mario work. Cathy and Tendai do not. Those are the rules. I believe that women all over the world, with lives as diverse as those of Cathy and Tendai, are economically productive. You, too, may believe that these women work full days. But according to the theory, science, profession, practice, and institutionalization of economics, we are wrong.

Blind Man's Bluff: How Economic Theory Constructs Reality

The major twentieth century British economist, John Maynard Keynes, called economics "a method rather than a doctrine, an apparatus of the mind, a technique of thinking which helps its possessor to draw correct conclusions."[1] My "technique of thinking" has me conclude that Cathy and Tendai work, that they are productive, and that their economic activity is of value. My technique of thinking leads me to conclude that Ben and Mario work, that they are destructive, and that their economic activity is a major cost and threat to the planet. But that is not how the established economic theory views their activities.

Theory is used, first of all, in order to decide what facts are relevant to an analysis. As the lives of Tendai, Cathy, Ben, and Mario illustrate, only some everyday experiences are stated, recognized, and recorded by economic theory. Overwhelmingly, those experiences that are economically visible can be summarized as *what men do*.

Most propositions in economics are explained and illustrated by using words and mathematics. These are seen to be alternative languages that are translatable into each other. Mathematical formulas assist the illusion that economics is a value-free science: propaganda is less easily discerned from figures than it is from words. The process of theorizing takes place when economists reason about simplified models of an actual economy or some part of an economy. From this model, "factual predictions" are made. Clearly, if you do not perceive parts of the community as economically active, they will not be in your model, and your "correct conclusions" based on the model will not include them.

The belief that value results only when (predominantly) men interact 13
with the marketplace means that few attempts are made to disguise this
myopic approach.

For example, Baron Lionel Robbins, an economist who was a member 14
of the British House of Lords, wrote:

> The propositions of economic theory . . . are all *assumptions* involving in
> some ways *simple* and *indisputable* facts of *experience.* . . . We do not need
> controlled experiments to establish their *validity:* they are so much *the stuff
> of our everyday experience* that they have only to be stated to be recognized as
> *obvious* (my emphasis).[2]

Whatever else Baron Robbins's "everyday experience" might involve, it 15
will not account for the everyday experience of Cathy and Tendai. We are
taught to read through or over such rhetoric, never to question it. It is the
language of economic texts, and their assumptions that the male experience
encompasses female experience have enslaved women in the male economic
system.

Feminist theorist Sheila Rowbotham reminds us: 16

> Language conveys a certain power. It is one of the instruments of domina-
> tion. . . . The language of theory—censored language—only expresses a
> reality experienced by the oppressors. It speaks only for their world, for their
> point of view.[3]

And something else happens to language in its colonizing by male theo- 17
rists.

Xenophon coined the word *oikonomikos* to describe the management or 18
rule of a house or household. In general usage, the word *economy* still retains
some links with its Greek origins. *Roget's Thesaurus* lists as synonyms management, order, careful administration, frugality, austerity, prudence, thrift,
providence, care, and retrenchment.[4] These synonyms are unlikely candidates
for what is called the "science" of economics. The meanings of words, our
words, change inside a "discipline."

When I look at the index of any major journal of economics, it is difficult 19
to think of subjects that have remained unscathed in terms of invasion by this
discipline. Nobel Prize winner Paul Samuelson, Professor of Economics at
Massachusetts Institute of Technology, writes:

> In recent years, economists have begun to infiltrate the field of demography.
> This is part of the imperialist movement in which we economists try to apply
> our methodologies to everything—to the law, to the sociology of the family,
> courtship, marriage, divorce, and cohabitation.[5]

But women are generally presumed to know little about economics, or 20
the world's or a nation's economy. Yet a "simple and indisputable fact of
everyday experience" is that most women know how to be economical, to use

things sparingly, to cut down on expenses. For some this knowledge and skill sustains the lives of themselves and their children from one hour or one day to the next. But what "everyday experience" would British Baron Lionel Robbins call on to give the "obvious" answers to some simple questions?

- Case studies in Gambia show that women's working time in agriculture rose from nineteen to twenty hours when improved methods were introduced, but men's working time fell from eleven to nine hours.[6] How does that happen?
- Why do nutritional deficiencies result, when family food availability declines as subsistence (nonmonetary) farmland is taken for cash crops and men get paid an income?
- Why, when men take over responsibility for women's tasks as soon as they are mechanized, or when they are transformed from subsistence into market production, are the tasks suddenly "productive"?
- Housework is implicitly taxed by not being valued. Shouldn't it then be recognized in the distribution of benefits?
- A chemical spillage creates increased value in the labor and expenditure required to clean it up; it contributes to a nation's growth. Why is that so?
- As I write, NASA has announced a "successful" Star Wars experiment. Two missiles were launched and chased each other about the sky before one deliberately blew up the other and then self-destructed. This success follows a failed Challenger shuttle mission, failed Titan and Cruise missile tests, and failed satellite launches. But for the purpose of recording production, both the success and failures contributed billions of dollars in growth to the U.S. economy.

This is not a sane state of affairs. What is the origin of such madness? [21]

According to Baron Robbins the authoritative definition of economics is [22] "the study of human behaviour in disposing of scarce means which have alternative uses to satisfy ends of varying importance."[7]* Then shouldn't the basic questions of economics involve those who are seen to be "economically inactive"? What particular mix of goods and services best meets the needs and wants of a community—how they are to be produced, from whom they are to be provided, and how they are to be distributed—are questions that should include the community and the environments in which we live. But the system says that forests, rainfall, water resources, fossil fuels, seafood, soil, grasslands, and the quality of the air that we breathe are worthless when preserved for future generations. It is their use, exploitation, and payment for

---

* This is an edited version of Waring's chapter. All footnotes that follow have been renumbered. [Editor's Note]

them in the market that, in Robbins's terms, "establishes their validity." It is in their destruction that they become "simple and indisputable facts of experience."

Defining Economic Terms

Disciples of economics are likely to see it as a science that treats things from the standpoint of price. Words that we think we all understand (such as *value*, *work*, *labor*, *production*, *reproduction*, and *economic activity*) have been hijacked into the service of this science. As a result, such words come to have two very different definitions: an economic definition and a noneconomic one.

Work, Labor, and Economic Activity

When I was a child, one of my grandmothers would bring her work into the sitting room. She would sit sewing buttons and darning socks while we sat reading at leisure, listening to the radio in front of the fire. My grandmother never stopped. When I got up in the morning she would already be in the kitchen working the dough for the day's baking. My other grandmother was a member of the church and a number of charity organizations. She did what our village called good works. Arriving home from school, I might see the clothesline flagged with washing or piles of weeds in the pathways or bottles full of freshly preserved fruit on the kitchen bench, and I would know my mother had been working hard. I, in turn, would have to do my schoolwork.

Every time I see a mother with an infant, I know I am seeing a woman at work. I know that work is not leisure and it is not sleep and it may well be enjoyable. I know that money payment is not necessary for work to be done. But, again, I seem to be at odds with economics as a discipline, because when work becomes a concept in institutionalized economics, payment enters the picture. *Work* and *labor* and *economic activity* are used interchangeably (though different schools of economics will argue that this is not the case). So my grandmother did not work, and those mothers I see with their infants are not working. No housewives, according to this economic definition, are workers.

The criterion for "productive" work proposed over fifty years ago by home economist Margaret Reid was that any activity culminating in a service or product, which one can buy or hire someone else to do, is an "economic activity" even if pay is not involved.[8] Yet in major texts used in college economics courses in North America, it is not unusual to find sentences such as "Most of us prefer no work to work with no pay."[9] Who is "us," I wonder. Adam Smith defined work as an activity requiring the worker to give up "his [*sic*] tranquility, his freedom and his happiness."[10] Charlotte Perkins Gilman, a leading intellectual of the women's movement in the United States in the early twentieth century, called this a particularly masculine view:

Following that pitiful conception of labour as a curse, comes the very old and androcentric (i.e., male-centered) habit of despising it as belonging to women and then to slaves . . . for long ages men performed no productive industry at all, being merely hunters and fighters.

Our current teachings in the infant science of political economy are naively masculine. They assume as unquestionable that "the economic man" will never do anything unless he has to; will only do it to escape pain or attain pleasure; and will, inevitably, take all he can get and do all he can to outwit, overcome, and if necessary destroy his antagonist.[11]

But the view of the world that Gilman despised has been institutionalized, so that work, according to Katherine Newland, "is still the primary means by which people establish a claim to a share of production. To be without work is to place that claim in jeopardy."[12] Housewives clearly do not "work." Mothers taking care of children are not working. No money changes hands.   27

Those who are in the grey area of informal work—between the recognized labor market and the housewife—may not claim to be workers either, in this economic sense. Invisible, informal work includes bartering, the trading of goods in informal settings (for example, in flea markets), and "off the books" or "under the table" employment. Workers who do not report work or pay income taxes on earnings and workers who are paid in cash at below minimum wages fall into this category. In addition, volunteer work can be considered informal work.[13] (And note that volunteer *work* is generally done by women while *financial contributions* to voluntary organizations—which take place in the market, are tax-deductible, and have special rules within the economic system—are generally made by men.)   28

"Home-based work activities"—including housekeeping, home repair and maintenance, do-it-yourself building, and child care—are informal work. So are "deviant work activities"—which include anything from organized crime to petty fraud. The social exchange of services, which is the giving and receiving of services within social networks of relatives, friends, neighbors, and acquaintances, is also regarded as economically unimportant and remains unacknowledged.   29

The *labor force*, then, is defined in economics as all members of the working age population who are either employed formally or are seeking or awaiting formal employment. The labor force consists of the employed and unemployed but not the underemployed, the marginally employed, the would-be employed, and certainly not those who work in the informal sector or who work as housewives.   30

Production and Reproduction

The skewed definitions of work and labor that are used by economists result in an equally skewed concept of *production*. As we have seen, economists usually use *labor* to mean only those activities that produce surplus value (that   31 is, profit in the marketplace). Consequently, labor (work) that does not produce profits is not considered production.

So, for example, the labor of childbirth may be work for a paid surrogate 32 mother or for the paid midwife nurse, doctor, and anaesthetist. Despite the *Oxford English Dictionary's* description of labor as "the pains and effort of childbirth: travail," the woman in labor—the reproducer, sustainer, and nurturer of human life—does not "produce" anything. Similarly, all the other reproductive work that women do is widely viewed as unproductive. Growing and processing food, nurturing, educating, and running a household—all part of the complex process of *reproduction*—are unacknowledged as part of the production system. A woman who supplies such labor is not seen by economists as performing work of value. Yet the satisfaction of basic needs to sustain human society is fundamental to any economic system. By this failure to acknowledge the primacy of reproduction, the male face of economics is fatally flawed.

We frequently hear from politicians, theologians, and military leaders 33 that the wealth of a nation is its children. But, apparently, the creators of that wealth deserve no economic visibility for their work.

But what value is a unit of production which cannot guarantee its own 34 continuous and regular reproduction? As a means of reproduction, woman is irreplaceable wealth. Reproducing the system depends on her. Gold, cloth, ivory, and cattle may be desirable, but they are only able to produce and reproduce wealth in the hands of progeny. Control derives ultimately not from the possession of wealth, but the control of reproduction. In terms of value, reproduction of the human species is either the whore, debased, or no worth, or the virgin on the pedestal, valued beyond wealth.

In support of this point of view, Gerda Lerner, Professor of History at 35 the University of Wisconsin, argues that women's reproductive power was the first private property amassed by men, and that domination over women provided the model for men's enslavement of other men.[14]

The basic definitions and concepts in the male analyses of production 36 and reproduction also reflect an unquestioned acceptance of biological determinism. Women's household and child care work are seen as an extension of their physiology. All the labor that goes into the production of life, including the labor of giving birth to a child, is seen as an activity *of* nature, rather than as interaction of a woman *with* nature. "Nature" apparently produces plants, animals, and Homo sapiens unconsciously, and women play no active or conscious part in the process.

Pivotal to this analysis is the fixation on paid labor alone as productive. 37 Even Frederick Engels's brief insight on reproduction is now forgotten. Engels was the long-time friend of Karl Marx and Marx's collaborator on *The Origin of the Family, Private Property and the State*. In it, Engels wrote:

> According to the materialist concept . . . the determining factor of history
> is, in the final instance, the production and reproduction of the immediate

essentials of life. This, again, is of a two-fold character. On the one side, the production of the means of existence of articles of food and clothing, dwellings and of the tools necessary for that production; on the other side, the production of human beings themselves, the propagation of the species.[15]

Yet today the liberal-conservative spectrum of economists speak of reproduction (in some of its forms) as privatized and domestic (and thus only of its microeconomic significance). The Marxist economists speak of it (in some of its forms) as having only "use value." Reproduction in all its forms is not fully addressed within any discipline. While recent feminist writers are an exception (see, for example, Gena Corea's *The Mother Machine* or Mary O'Brien's *The Politics of Reproduction*), reproduction is generally seen as part of nature and, thus, not within the scope of analysis or change.   39

Counting Women Out of the Labor Force

In the rain forest of southern Cameroon, the Beti people practice a form of agriculture that involves clearing two new half-acre fields each year and cultivating them for two or three years. Thus, the food farmer, always a woman, has four to six fields under cultivation at any one time. The major crops are groundnuts, cassava, cocoyams, plantain, and a variety of vegetables. Men's agricultural labor consists primarily of the cultivation of cocoa, one of Cameroon's major exports.   40

Beti men labor for a total of seven and a half hours a day. They spend less than an hour a day on food-related tasks, about two hours a day on their cocoa plots, and four hours on work such as beer or palm-wine production, house building and repair, production of baskets, production of housing materials or other simple commodities intended for the market, and part-time wage work.   41

Beti women, on the other hand, labor for eleven hours a day. They spend about five hours a day on food production—four hours to provide for family needs and one hour to produce surplus for the urban market. In addition, they spend three to four hours a day for food processing and cooking and two or more hours for water and firewood collection, washing, child care, and care of the sick.[16]   42

The International Labor Organization (ILO), a UN agency, counts the Beti man as an "active laborer." But since none of the Beti woman's working day is spent "helping the head of the family in his [*sic*] occupation"[17]—and since housework done by members of a family in their own homes is also specifically excluded—the ILO concludes that she is not an active laborer.*   43

---

* The I.L.O. will also exclude Tendai and Cathy, and much of the world's invisible child labor

Thus the international economic system constructs reality in a way that   44
excludes the great bulk of women's work—reproduction (in all its forms),
raising children, domestic work, and subsistence production. Cooking, according to economists, is "active labor" when cooked food is sold and "economically inactive labor" when it is not. Housework is "productive" when
performed by a paid domestic servant and "nonproductive" when no payment
is involved. Those who care for children in an orphanage are "occupied";
mothers who care for their children at home are "unoccupied."

The American contributor to the *International Encyclopedia of Social Science*,   45
A. J. Jaffe, further demonstrates the peculiar reasoning inherent in the international economic system. In the section "The Labour Force—Definitions
and Measurement," he writes that "housewives are excluded from what is
measured as the working force because such work is outside the characteristic
system of work organization or production. Moreover their inclusion in the
working force would not help policy makers to solve the significant economic
problems of American society."[18]

I would have thought that domestic work was about the oldest "system   46
of work organization or production." And as for "significant economic problems of American society," what about the problems of the more than 30
million Americans—77.7 percent of them women and children—who lived
below the poverty line in 1980? What about the fact that 36 percent of all
female-headed households in America and 56.2 percent of black female-
headed households were at or below the poverty level in 1982? And how
about the 20 percent of all American children and 50 percent of all American
black children who lived in poverty in 1983?[19] Doesn't such poverty represent
a significant enough problem for policymakers to address? Evidently not,
since most women and children do not count in the reckoning of the international economic system. . . .

Notes

1. J. M. Keynes, *The General Theory of Employment, Interest and Money* (London: Macmillan, 1965; New York: Harcourt Brace Jovanovich, 1936).

2. Lionel Robbins, as quoted in Tjalling C. Koopmans, *Three Essays on the State of Economic Science* (New York: McGraw-Hill, 1957), 140–42.

3. Sheila Rowbotham, *Woman's Consciousness, Man's World* (Baltimore: Penguin Books, 1973), 32–34.

---

force. International guidelines set the age of eligibility for the economically active population at 15 years, although countries may set lower limits. In 25 of 40 countries for which comparisons are possible by age, females form a significantly higher proportion of child labor than of adult labor. In 14 countries the sex ratios are similar for both age groups, and in only one is the child labor force disproportionately male.

4. Norman Lewis (editor), *The New Roget's Thesaurus of the English Language in Dictionary Form* (New York: G. P. Putnam's Sons, 16th Imp, 1964), 165.

5. Paul A. Samuelson, "Modes of Thought in Economics and Biology." *American Economic Review* 75 (May 1985): 167.

6. Ulrike Von Buchwald and Ingrid Palmer, *Monitoring Changes in the Conditions of Women—A Critical Review of Possible Approaches.* UNR15D/78/C.18, Geneva, 19.

7. L. C. R. Robbins, *An Essay on the Nature and Significance of Economic Science.* (London: Macmillan, 1969).

8. "If an activity is of such a character that it might be delegated to a paid worker then that activity shall be deemed productive." Margaret G. Reid, *Economics of Household Production* (New York: Wiley, 1934).

9. Ralph T. Byrns and Gerald W. Stone, *Economics*, 2d ed. (Glenview, IL: Scott, Foresman, 1984), 5.

10. Smith, *The Wealth of Nations.*

11. Charlotte Perkins Gilman, *The Man-Made World or Our Androcentric Culture* (New York: Johnson Reprint Corp., 1971), 232–36.

12. Katherine Newland, *Global Employment and Economic Justice: The Policy Challenge* (Washington: *Worldwatch Paper*, 28).

13. Louise A. Ferman, "The Work Ethic in the World of Informal Work," Industrial Relations Research Association Series: *The Work Ethic—A Critical Analysis* (Madison, WI: Industrial Relations Research Association, 1983), 211.

14. *New York Times Book Review*, April 20, 1986, p. 12.

15. Frederick Engels, *The Origin of the Family, Private Property and the State* (London: Lawrence and Wishart, 1940 [1884]), 1–2.

16. "Female Farmers—the doubly ignored," *Development Forum* (September 1986), 7.

17. D. J. Casley and D. A. Lury, *Data Collection in Developing Countries* (New York: Clarendon Press), 440.

18. *International Encyclopedia of Social Sciences*, s.v. "labor force."

19. Robin Morgan (ed.), *Sisterhood is Global* (Garden City, NY: Doubleday, 1984), 700.

ON BEING THE OBJECT OF PROPERTY

◑

PATRICIA J. WILLIAMS

An attorney and professor in the law school at the
University of Wisconsin-Madison, Patricia Williams
teaches commercial and consumer law and jurispru-
dence. Currently she is at work on a book that examines the intersection of constitutional rights and commercial interests. In this essay, which first appeared in
a 1988 issue of *Signs: Journal of Women in Culture and
Society*, Williams draws on her experience as an African
American woman and professional, raising troubling
questions about how the value of human life is determined by legal contract and the rules of the marketplace.

On Being Invisible

Reflections

For some time I have been writing about my great-great-grandmother. I have   1
considered the significance of her history and that of slavery from a variety
of viewpoints on a variety of occasions: in every speech, in every conversation,
even in my commercial transactions class. I have talked so much about her
that I finally had to ask myself what it was I was looking for in this dogged
pursuit of family history. Was I being merely indulgent, looking for roots in
the pursuit of some genetic heraldry, seeking the inheritance of being special,
different, unique in all that primogeniture hath wrought?

I decided that my search was based in the utility of such a quest, not   2
mere indulgence, but a recapturing of that which had escaped historical scrutiny, which had been overlooked and underseen. I, like so many blacks, have
been trying to pin myself down in history, place myself in the stream of time
as significant, evolved, present in the past, continuing into the future. To be
without documentation is too unsustaining, too spontaneously ahistorical, too
dangerously malleable in the hands of those who would rewrite not merely
the past but my future as well. So I have been picking through the ruins for
my roots.

What I know of my mother's side of the family begins with my great-   3
great-grandmother. Her name was Sophie and she lived in Tennessee. In

1850, she was about twelve years old. I know that she was purchased when she was eleven by a white lawyer named Austin Miller and was immediately impregnated by him. She gave birth to my great-grandmother Mary, who was taken away from her to be raised as a house servant.[1] I know nothing more of Sophie (she was, after all, a black single mother—in today's terms—suffering the anonymity of yet another statistical teenage pregnancy). While I don't remember what I was told about Austin Miller before I decided to go to law school, I do remember that just before my first day of class, my mother said, in a voice full of secretive reassurance, "The Millers were lawyers, so you have it in your blood."[2]

When my mother told me that I had nothing to fear in law school, the law was "in my blood," she meant it in a very complex sense. First and foremost, she meant it defiantly; she meant that no one should make me feel inferior because someone else's father was a judge. She wanted me to reclaim that part of my heritage from which I had been disinherited, and she wanted me to use it as a source of strength and self-confidence. At the same time, she was asking me to claim a part of myself that was the dispossessor of another part of myself; she was asking me to deny that disenfranchised little black girl of myself that felt powerless, vulnerable and, moreover, rightly felt so.

In somewhat the same vein, Mother was asking me not to look to her as a role model. She was devaluing that part of herself that was not Harvard and refocusing my vision to that part of herself that was hard-edged, proficient, and Western. She hid the lonely, black, defiled-female part of herself and pushed me forward as the projection of a competent self, a cool rather than despairing self, a masculine rather than a feminine self.

I took this secret of my blood into the Harvard milieu with both the pride and the shame with which my mother had passed it along to me. I found myself in the situation described by Marguerite Duras, in her novel *The Lover:* "We're united in a fundamental shame at having to live. It's here we are at the heart of our common fate, the fact that [we] are our mother's children, the children of a candid creature murdered by society. We're on the side of society which has reduced her to despair. Because of what's been done to our mother, so amiable, so trusting, we hate life, we hate ourselves."[3]

Reclaiming that from which one has been disinherited is a good thing. Self-possession in the full sense of that expression is the companion to self-

4

5

6

7

1. For a more detailed account of the family history to this point, see Patricia Williams, "Grandmother Sophie," *Harvard Blackletter* 3 (1986): 79.

2. Patricia Williams, "Alchemical Notes: Reconstructing Ideals from Deconstructed Rights," *Harvard Civil Rights—Civil Liberties Law Review* 22 (1987): 418.

3. Marguerite Duras, *The Lover* (New York: Harper & Row, 1985), 55.

knowledge. Yet claiming for myself a heritage the weft of whose genesis is my own disinheritance is a profoundly troubling paradox. . . .*

On Ardor

The Child

One Saturday afternoon not long ago, I sat among a litter of family photo-graphs telling a South African friend about Marjorie, my godmother and my mother's cousin. She was given away by her light-skinned mother when she was only six. She was given to my grandmother and my great-aunts to be raised among her darker-skinned cousins, for Marjorie was very dark indeed. Her mother left the family to "pass," to marry a white man—Uncle Frederick, we called him with trepidatious presumption yet without his ever knowing of our existence—an heir to a meat-packing fortune. When Uncle Frederick died thirty years later and the fortune was lost, Marjorie's mother rejoined the race, as the royalty of resentful fascination—Lady Bountiful, my sister called her—to regale us with tales of gracious upper-class living. 8

My friend said that my story reminded him of a case in which a swarthy, crisp-haired child was born, in Durban, to white parents. The Afrikaner government quickly intervened, removed the child from its birth home, and placed it to be raised with a "more suitable," browner family. 9

When my friend and I had shared these stories, we grew embarrassed somehow, and our conversation trickled away into a discussion of laissez-faire economics and governmental interventionism. Our words became a clear line, a railroad upon which all other ideas and events were tied down and sacrificed. 10

The Market

As a teacher of commercial transactions, one of the things that has always impressed me most about the law of contract is a certain deadening power it exercises by reducing the parties to the passive. It constrains the lively in-volvement of its signatories by positioning enforcement in such a way that parties find themselves in a passive relationship to a document: it is the contract that governs, that "does" everything, that absorbs all responsibility and deflects all other recourse. 11

Contract law reduces life to fairy tale. The four corners of the agreement become parent. Performance is the equivalent of obedience to the parent. 12

---

* This essay is an edited version of the original. Footnotes after this point in the text have been renumbered. [Editor's Note]

Obedience is dutifully passive. Passivity is valued as good contract-socialized behavior; activity is caged in retrospective hypotheses about states of mind at the magic moment of contracting. Individuals are judged by the contract unfolding rather than by the actors acting autonomously. Nonperformance is disobedience; disobedience is active; activity becomes evil in contrast to the childlike passivity of contract conformity.

One of the most powerful examples of all this is the case of Mary Beth   13
Whitehead, mother of Sara—of so-called Baby M. Ms. Whitehead became a vividly original actor *after* the creation of her contract with William Stern; unfortunately for her, there can be no greater civil sin. It was in this upside-down context, in the picaresque unboundedness of breachor, that her energetic grief became hysteria and her passionate creativity was funneled, whorled, and reconstructed as highly impermissible. Mary Beth Whitehead thus emerged as the evil stepsister who deserved nothing.

Some time ago, Charles Reich visited a class of mine.[4] He discussed with   14
my students a proposal for a new form of bargain by which emotional "items"—such as praise, flattery, acting happy or sad—might be contracted for explicitly. One student, not alone in her sentiment, said, "Oh, but then you'll just feel obligated." Only the week before, however (when we were discussing the contract which posited that Ms. Whitehead "will not form or attempt to form a parent-child relationship with any child or children"), this same student had insisted that Ms. Whitehead must give up her child, because she had *said* she would: "She was obligated!" I was confounded by the degree to which what the student took to be self-evident, inalienable gut reactions could be governed by illusions of passive conventionality and form.

It was that incident, moreover, that gave me insight into how Judge   15
Harvey Sorkow, of New Jersey Superior Court, could conclude that the contract that purported to terminate Ms. Whitehead's parental rights was "not illusory."[5]

(As background, I should say that I think that, within the framework of   16
contract law itself, the agreement between Ms. Whitehead and Mr. Stern was clearly illusory.[6] On the one hand, Judge Sorkow's opinion said that Ms.

---

4. Charles Reich is author of *The Greening of America* (New York: Random House, 1970) and professor of law at the University of San Francisco Law School.

5. See, generally, In the Matter of Baby "M," A Pseudonym for an Actual Person, Superior Court of New Jersey, Chancery Division, Docket no. FM-25314-86E, March 31, 1987. This decision was appealed, and on February 3, 1988, the New Jersey Supreme Court ruled that surrogate contracts were illegal and against public policy. In addition to the contract issue, however, the appellate court decided the custody issue in favor of the Sterns but granted visitation rights to Mary Beth Whitehead.

6. "An illusory promise is an expression cloaked in promissory terms, but which, upon closer examination, reveals that the promisor has committed himself not at all" (J. Calamari and J. Perillo, *Contracts*, 3d ed. [St. Paul: West Publishing, 1987], 228).

Whitehead was seeking to avoid her *obligations.* In other words, giving up her child became an actual obligation. On the other hand, according to the logic of the judge, this was a service contract, not really a sale of a child; therefore delivering the child to the Sterns was an "obligation" for which there was no consideration, for which Mr. Stern was not paying her.)

Judge Sorkow's finding the contract "not illusory" is suggestive not just   17
of the doctrine by that name, but of illusion in general, and delusion, and the righteousness with which social constructions are conceived, acted on, and delivered up into the realm of the real as "right," while all else is devoured from memory as "wrong." From this perspective, the rhetorical tricks by which Sara Whitehead became Melissa Stern seem very like the heavy-worded legalities by which my great-great-grandmother was pacified and parted from her child. In both situations, the real mother had no say, no power; her powerlessness was imposed by state law that made her and her child helpless in relation to the father. My great-great-grandmother's powerlessness came about as the result of a contract to which she was not a party; Mary Beth Whitehead's powerlessness came about as a result of a contract that she signed at a discrete point of time—yet which, over time, enslaved her. The contract-reality in both instances was no less than magic: it was illusion transformed into not-illusion. Furthermore, it masterfully disguised the brutality of enforced arrangements in which these women's autonomy, their flesh and their blood, were locked away in word vaults, without room to reconsider—*ever.*

In the months since Judge Sorkow's opinion, I have reflected on the   18
similarities of fortune between my own social positioning and that of Sara Melissa Stern Whitehead. I have come to realize that an important part of the complex magic that Judge Sorkow wrote into his opinion was a supposition that it is "natural" for people to want children "like" themselves. What this reasoning raised for me was an issue of what, exactly, constituted this "likeness"? (What would have happened, for example, if Ms. Whitehead had turned out to have been the "passed" descendant of my "failed" godmother Marjorie's mother? What if the child she bore had turned out to be recessively and visibly black? Would the sperm of Mr. Stern have been so powerful as to make this child "his" with the exclusivity that Judge Sorkow originally assigned?) What constitutes, moreover, the collective understanding of "un-likeness"?

These questions turn, perhaps, on not-so-subtle images of which mothers   19
should be bearing which children. Is there not something unseemly, in our society, about the spectacle of a white woman mothering a black child? A white woman giving totally to a black child; a black child totally and demandingly dependent for everything, for sustenance itself, from a white woman. The image of a white woman suckling a black child; the image of a black child sucking for its life from the bosom of a white woman. The utter interdependence of such an image; the selflessness, the merging it implies; the giving up of boundary; the encompassing of other within self; the un-

bounded generosity, the interconnectedness of such an image. Such a picture says that there is no difference; it places the hope of continuous generation, of immortality of the white self in a little black face.

When Judge Sorkow declared that it was only to be expected that parents would want to breed children "like" themselves, he simultaneously created a legal right to the same. With the creation of such a "right," he encased the children conforming to "likeliness" in protective custody, far from whole ranges of taboo. Taboo about touch and smell and intimacy and boundary. Taboo about ardor, possession, license, equivocation, equanimity, indifference, intolerance, rancor, dispossession, innocence, exile, and candor. Taboo about death. Taboos that amount to death. Death and sacredness, the valuing of body, of self, of other, of remains. The handling lovingly in life, as in life; the question of the intimacy versus the dispassion of death. [20]

In effect, these taboos describe boundaries of valuation. Whether something is inside or outside the marketplace of rights has always been a way of valuing it. When a valued object is located outside the market, it is generally understood to be too "priceless" to be accommodated by ordinary exchange relationships; when, in contrast, the prize is located within the marketplace, all objects outside become "valueless." Traditionally, the Mona Lisa and human life have been the sorts of subjects removed from the fungibility of commodification, as "priceless." Thus when black people were bought and sold as slaves, they were placed beyond the bounds of humanity. And thus, in the twistedness of our brave new world, when blacks have been thrust out of the market and it is white children who are bought and sold, black babies have become "worthless" currency to adoption agents—"surplus" in the salvage heaps of Harlem hospitals. . . . [21]

MAKING CONNECTIONS

1. In "To Be of Use" Piercy contrasts the "parlor generals and field desert-ers" with those who "stand in line and haul" or "move in a common rhythm/when the food must come in." What images come to mind with these two descriptions? What kinds of work is Piercy contrasting? Is she suggesting that nonphysical work is valueless? What are some of the words Piercy selects to convey the "feel" of heavy labor? Are these words generally considered positive or negative terms? Does her portrait of solid, satisfying labor make a distinction between women's work and men's work?

2. Write an essay contrasting the phrase "to be of use" with the phrase "being used" with regard to work. You might refer to your own experi-ences of working and the sense of control, of purpose, of power or powerlessness that you have experienced at work. Has the work you've done been "a thing worth doing well," or has it been less than satisfying? Would you consider your education a form of "work"? Why or why not?

3. On average, a woman today still earns approximately 65 cents for every dollar earned by a man. What factors might contribute to this phenom-enon? Are women's jobs less valuable than men's? Discuss your own position on the concept of comparable worth (equal pay for jobs of equal value) by integrating the information from essays in this chapter with the stance taken by Katherine Kersten in Chapter 2.

4. Sidel comments that all women, no matter what their economic back-grounds are, expect to be upwardly mobile. How realistic is this "Amer-ican dream" for women or men today? Is upward mobility more realistic for some than for others? Why? Why do you think the young women whom Sidel interviewed have these ideas about work? How do your own dreams of future work compare to the respondents in Sidel's essay?

5. Sidel understands that women today are aware of the need to support themselves and have therefore incorporated achievement and success into their dreams of the future. She wonders, however, who is going to do the work of caring—for children, for elderly or sick parents—that women used to do. What are the personal advantages and the costs of caregiving? Write an essay discussing your ideas of who will nurture children or the elderly. Consider how flexible jobs, role sharing, community care arrange-ments, or other innovations might be employed to handle these problems.

6. As a class project, collect newspapers from several different communities and compare their classified ads. Does the language of these ads reveal anything about the gendered nature of work in our culture? Now read

the personals column and list the characteristics that single men and women are looking for in a mate. How often and when do such traits as caring, nurturing, independence, or achievement occur? If children are mentioned, by whom are they mentioned and in what context? Do you find any points of connection between the gendered nature of jobs and the gendered qualities of personal relationships?

7. Discuss Lips's definition of power as it contrasts to qualities we tradition-ally associate with femininity. Referring back to the essays by Susan Brownmiller and Marilyn Frye in Chapter 2, do you think it is true that a woman risks "losing her femininity" by gaining access to power? What aspects of the feminine stereotype do Lips, Brownmiller, and Frye cri-tique, and what are the perceived risks and benefits of challenging those aspects? In a brief descriptive paper, try constructing your vision of what the "new feminine ideal" would have to look like to incorporate women's move toward professional achievement and power.

8. Lips contends that the male model of success in the corporation (being a team player, planning career strategies) is largely a myth. Discuss spe-cific ways in which this myth might make work in the corporation alien-ating for *both* women and men. Refer to the selections on sports in Chapter 8. In what ways is the male model of success in the corporation similar to the model of masculinity in sports? What would a more "fem-inine" or "androgynous" model of success look like?

9. In light of Lips's view that women use indirect strategies to exert power in the workplace, discuss the essays on women and language in Chapter 4. Do you see any similar strategies at work in women's styles of discus-sion? In what ways might the insecurities revealed in women's use of language be accommodations that they develop in order to be heard at all? What can you conclude about social structure and power relations in private and public settings?

10. Waring has a different definition of "work" than the one used in tradi-tional economic theories. Compare Waring's definition of work with the images of work in Piercy's poem "To Be of Use." If work is not highly valued, does it (and those who do it) become invisible? Is it important to know that other individuals and society see a purpose in what we are doing with our time? What types of satisfaction and value are emphasized in Piercy's poem, and which are emphasized in Waring's essay?

11. Williams introduces her essay with a discussion of her need as an African American to recapture that part of her heritage that had "escaped histor-ical scrutiny." Compare Williams's essay to Alice Walker's in Chapter 5. What part does history—the recording of experience for posterity—play in our perceptions of what is valuable in society? What does Williams mean when she says that being without a history leaves one vulnerable

to "those who would rewrite not merely the past but [the] future as well"? How might Walker respond to Williams's statement that "Reclaiming that from which one has been disinherited" can be both a source of strength as well as a "profoundly troubling paradox"? How do both these authors attempt to "reclaim" and "rewrite" their personal and collective pasts?

12. How does the title of Williams's essay reframe the concept of human beings and the work they do? What are the various ways that she presents the concept of "property" in her essay? Is reproduction a useful example by which to explore the many meanings of ownership, legal agreement, racial boundaries, and human labor? What aspects of reproduction make it a particularly complex form of labor to discuss?

13

MEN WORKING

Work is a search for daily meaning as well as daily bread, for recognition as well as cash. . . . in short, for a life rather than a Monday through Friday sort of dying.
(Studs Terkel, *Working*)

The provider role has long been a standard for measuring a man's status in the family and the community. The neighborhood in which a man's family resides, the car he drives, the caliber of his son's or daughter's college—all of these are public statements about the breadwinner's success. The very clothes a man wears on the job ("white collar" or "blue collar") tell us something about his standing in society. His success is measured not merely in income but in the independence, the amount of decision-making, and the power he exercises in his job. Although women also earn incomes that support families, the breadwinner role is still largely seen as a man's way of validating his masculinity. If he fails in any form as a provider, he may be criticized for being lazy, shiftless, irresponsible, "not much of a man"—accusations that cut to the core of his character. Yet even if he is successful in the role, the pressure to earn money and recognition in the outside world can exert a strain on other areas of a man's life. Currently, a growing number of men are questioning whether the costs and tensions of the breadwinner role outweigh its potential rewards.

The first essay in this chapter deals with the conflicts inherent in the myth of "The Breadwinner." Mark Gerzon reflects on how a man's roles as provider, husband, and father are pitted against one another in modern life. According to Gerzon, men face a perplexing double bind. If a man spends time with his family, he runs the risk of losing a competitive edge in today's fast-paced marketplace. However, if he slaves for the company, he risks becoming a stranger at home, turning into one of the many fathers chained to the breadwinner role whose children grow up "without knowing him." As with the other essays in his book *A Choice of Heroes: The Changing Face of American Manhood*, from which this excerpt is taken, Gerzon challenges narrow definitions of manhood that limit men's opportunities for personal development. For Gerzon, women's emergence as partners to men in the role of provider signals a healthy, liberating change for both sexes.

Not all men, however, share this positive outlook on women in the workforce. Our next author, Anthony Astrachan, explores the tensions and dilemmas that face "Men and the New Economy" and the ways in which men perceive women workers as a threat to their role in society. Astrachan looks at the changes in the nature and meaning of men's work in today's economy, including jobs that involve repetitive, unskilled, and unsatisfying tasks and the displacement of many men from jobs they once saw as secure. For Astrachan, the prospect of women "taking over men's jobs" presents just one more target for the insecurities of men in an unstable economic climate.

In our next selection, John Lippert provides a personal account of his work in an automobile assembly plant. His essay, "Sexuality as Consumption," provides an incisive commentary on the ways sex and sexuality are used in the workplace, and how the feeling of being "used" in a repetitive, dehumanizing job can be reproduced in personal relationships. Lippert offers insights on male competition and identity, on the causes of sexual harassment on the job, and on the feelings of alienation and boredom that can result in the modern workplace.

Edward Hirsch ends this chapter with his poem "Commuters," which captures the feeling of everyone who has learned that work is not always filled with excitement and challenge. Trapped among a sea of commuters, "buckled into a steel box," wondering who he is and what his life is really about, Hirsch's narrator presents yet another facet of the world of work.

The sense of men losing control—of the work process, of the provider role—is a strong theme of the selections in this chapter. As you read these essays, think about the effects that a changing economy may be having on your generation. What impact does the changing character of work have on society, the family, and personal relationships? Are men still trapped by the image of the breadwinner role, or is it a relic from past eras, ripe for change? Are there ways to make work a more meaningful endeavor for men and women? How might other variables like race or class affect the opportunities and experiences of people in the workplace?

THE BREADWINNER
Images of Family

MARK GERZON

Mark Gerzon's works have dealt with topics such as the generation gap, the social responsibility of parents, and, most recently, the changing ideals of masculinity and men's social roles in America. His books include *A Childhood for Every Child: The Politics of Parenthood* (1973), *The Whole World is Watching: A Young Man Looks at Youth's Dissent* (1969), and *A Choice of Heroes: The Changing Face of American Manhood* (1984), from which this selection is taken.

Only if we perpetuate the habit of speaking about "the position of women" in a vacuum will we fail to recognize that where one sex suffers, the other sex suffers also.
(Margaret Mead, Male and Female, 1949)

In Mary Lavin's short story "Lilacs," an old man, Phelim Malloy, provides   1
for his wife and two daughters by selling manure. The dunghill, located in the corner of their small yard, produces such a foul odor that his wife and his daughters complain constantly.

"But if it could be put somewhere else," suggests his wife, Ros, "and not   2
right under the window of the room where we eat our bit of food."

"What I don't see," interjects his daughter Kate, "is the need for us   3
dealing in dung at all."

His daughter Stacy says nothing; she is in bed with a headache, which   4
afflicts her every Wednesday, when a fresh load of manure is dumped. She wants to have lilacs in the yard and get rid of the smelly muck altogether.

But when Malloy suddenly dies, Ros takes over the manure trade. To her   5
daughters' amazement, she argues that they must keep the dunghill where it is. It is their only livelihood.

Soon afterward, unaccustomed to the heavy work, Ros passes away. It is   6
then that Kate, who is concerned about her dowry, leaps to the dung's defense. Then Kate marries, and Stacy becomes the sole mistress of the house. The

first thing she plans to do, she tells the family lawyer enthusiastically, is to plant a few lilac trees and get rid of the dunghill.

"But what will you live on, Miss Stacy?" asks the lawyer. And there the story ends. 7

Poor Phelim Malloy! For decades he made a living that permitted his wife to live comfortably and his daughters to go to boarding school. And he worked knee-deep in manure for most of his adult life. 8

Neither I nor my friends have such malodorous occupations. Our wives and children live with lilacs, not dung. What we have in common with Phelim Malloy, however, is that our families are becoming aware of how our occupations detract from their lives. They want us to work, of course, but they want us to be husbands and fathers too. 9

Perhaps if I had lived a generation earlier, I could have seen the commuter train that I rode every weekday for more than three years as a symbol of my worldly success. But times have changed. My wife expected to see her husband and expected me to see my children. And I expected it too. Therein was the dilemma. No matter how I stretched myself, I could not be a father *and* a breadwinner. 10

So the commuter train became, instead, a symbol of my dilemma. In the morning, I would catch the 7:44 or the 8:12. The first would bring me to the office before most of my colleagues; the second, only after everyone else was hard at work. Whenever I could, I took the 8:12. That way I could at least say good-morning to my children. 11

I would leave the office between five and six, while many of my colleagues were still at work. An hour would pass before I was home. My sons, then both under five, would already have eaten dinner by the time I arrived. 12

I wanted to be with them, and they wanted to be with me. But it was the end of their day and time for bed. "They're tired," my wife would say to me. "Better let them sleep." Of course, she was right. And yet my day with them, and theirs with me, was just beginning. 13

I was also tired, quick to lose my temper, and hungry. After several years of this shuttlecock schedule, I was confused too. I was making a living, my wife was taking care of the kids (and teaching part-time), and the children were growing up. We were all doing what we were supposed to do, but it was not working—not for me, not for my wife, and not for our children. 14

We are among the lucky ones. My income is higher and my schedule more flexible than most. I miss fewer events in my children's lives than, for example, my friend George, a foreman at a nearby factory. George wants to see his son play football after school "more than anything else in the world," he tells me. His son plays quarterback on his junior high school team, but George has yet to see a game. When the traffic is good, he catches part of the last quarter (by which time the coach has put in the second-string quarterback). When the traffic is bad, his son is already showering in the locker room. 15

"Paul set a school passing record, but I never saw him complete a single pass," says George. "Again and again I apologized: 'Gee, Paul, sorry I missed the game.' He used to say, 'That's okay, Dad,' but now he just grunts." 16

George has stopped trying. Paul has stopped caring. 17

The problem is not limited to clock-punchers. Richard earns twice as much as George but sees his son even less. A sought-after lawyer, Richard reached the top, and stays at the top, by "doing what needs to be done." This means that he may be in Europe or Japan for several weeks or preparing briefs under intense pressure. His job is flexible (at least in theory), so he squeezes out time now and then to watch a baseball game or to reserve a weekend for skiing. But in a competitive world, any time "lost" to family puts his firm at a disadvantage. He may forfeit a client, miss an opportunity, lose the "inside track." 18

Several years my senior, Richard met me over lunch one day shortly after I had been promoted. I told him how much I regretted missing out on my children's lives. "Welcome to the club!" he replied heartily. Was he sardonically commiserating with me? Or was he genuinely welcoming me to that relatively exclusive professional club whose members' time has such a high market value that they cannot refuse to sell it? I now think he was doing both: congratulating me on my success and forewarning me about its ultimate price. (He is now divorced. His wife has custody of their children.) 19

I used to think that Carl, a professor of history, had this problem solved. When my wife and I both worked, he and his wife once advised us on how to organize a two-career family. Their method was to take turns. When he was under pressure, she would cut back, and when she had to switch into high gear, he would slow down. It all sounded so simple. Most afternoons, Carl could be seen picking up his daughter at school. 20

What I did not realize was that this freedom from external encumbrances did not resolve his masculine dilemma. When I talked with him a few months later, he was fuming. He resented other faculty members' subtle but unmistakable jokes. "They have no right to question my allocation of time," he argued. "They prefer leisurely lunches or gossiping in the faculty club to spending time with their own children. But why do they try to impose their priorities on me?" 21

Beneath his irritation, Carl had his own doubts. Although he had tenure, he still felt the spur of academic competition in his flank. "I'm working at a competitive disadvantage," he said. "How can I convince myself, much less them, that my work is to be taken seriously—that I am producing? Maybe I *am* drifting. If I really cared about this book, if I really thought that it was any good, I wouldn't be leading my life like this." 22

George, Richard, Carl, myself—we were all struggling with a predicament we could not even name. Once we have families, we cannot afford to take our shoulders from the wheel without being inundated with unpaid bills. There is no time left in our lives to think about it. And even if we thought 23 about it, what good would it do? We have to make a living. We have to support our families. Our only way out, it often seems, is to become so successful that at last we can stop. But then it is too late.

Late one night, holding high a blazing torch, Daniel Boone went hunting for deer. After waiting for the gleaming light to reflect in the eyes of his prey, he saw a pair of firelit eyes through the underbrush. He raised his rifle but did not fire. Something about the eyes seemed odd. Moving toward them slowly, he finally realized that they were a woman's. She ran away, but according to legend, Daniel soon came courting and made her his wife. 24

In reality, she was much more than Boone's wife. Nearly as tall as her husband, Rebecca Bryan Boone was a remarkable woman. Single-handedly, and often under harsh frontier conditions, she cared and provided for their children while Daniel was gone for months on various expeditions. When Daniel was kidnapped by the Shawnee, she moved her children hundreds of miles on horseback through hostile Indian territory. When her aging husband was racked by rheumatism, she went hunting and brought back enough game to feed them all. Yet she is depicted in the popular nineteenth-century biographies of the legendary "Col. Daniel Boone" as merely an "amiable Spouse" without any personality of her own. Why, in the legend of Daniel Boone, was the courage and competence of Rebecca Bryan Boone omitted? One suspects that his early biographers, if given the opportunity, would have erased her from the legend altogether. 25

After all, this is precisely what the writers of frontier fiction did. Their heroes avoided all intimate relationships with women. James Fenimore Cooper's Natty Bumppo, whose life was chronicled in a series of five novels published between 1823 and 1841, *The Leatherstocking Tales*, was perhaps the first American literary figure to become famous abroad as well as at home. He became the symbol of the frontier man for more than one generation of readers. Yet he never once loved a woman. Wedded to the wilderness, accompanied by his loyal friend, Chingachgook, he speaks of heterosexual love as if it were alien to him. When he refers to marriage, it is clear that he considers it a form of captivity. It symbolized "a kind of *emasculation*," suggested Leslie Fiedler in *Love and Death in the American Novel*, "since the virility of Natty is not genital but heroic and cannot survive in the marriage bed any more than beside the hearth." 26

To be a hero, then, a man either should avoid becoming entangled with women altogether or should marry a woman who remains obediently in the background. It is as if man becomes heroic by virtue of the distance he places between himself and the feminine. 27

Whether on the frontier of yesteryear or in the inflationary, urban economy of today, a competent and enterprising woman would be an extraordinary asset. Just as Rebecca's hunting abilities made the Boone family more secure, so today do wives' professional skills enable a family to derive greater rewards 28 from the marketplace and to live more comfortably than would be possible with only a single wage earner.

Yet such a woman has not been highly prized by American men. A woman able to earn enough to support herself and her family did not appeal to us, she threatened us. In a poll conducted in 1946 by *Fortune* magazine, men were asked whether they would prefer to marry a girl who had never worked, one who had been moderately successful in her work, or one who had been very successful. By a wide margin, men preferred the woman of *moderate* success.

Men do not mind a woman who "helps out" or who may "supplement" the family's income. But the notion that one's wife can function just as capably in the marketplace as oneself breeds anxiety. It deprives us of another dimension of heroism—the heroism of The Breadwinner.

The Breadwinner's virtue is equal to his productivity. To his wife and children, he is a hero because he provides for them. To his country, he is a hero because he makes the economy work and grow. The Breadwinner prides himself on his family's material well-being: the more they have, the better a man he is. Even if the Breadwinner's wife works as long and hard as he does, he is nevertheless the provider. If she is employed, he earns more money. If she works as a homemaker, the economy puts money in his pockets and nothing in hers. He can make money; she can only spend it.

In an economy that assumes men are the providers and sets wages accordingly, many women need the Breadwinner. Without him, their lives are strained. Consider the plight of women whose husbands are laid off, or who turn to drink, or who are incapacitated by illness or injury, or who abandon their families and evade child support. The wives of such men consider the Breadwinner to be a model of masculinity without equal. They revere the Breadwinner, the man who brings home a paycheck every week and who works year after year without complaint.

This ideal image of the Breadwinner, however, has been politicized. Instead of inspiring reverence, it triggers debate. Narrow-minded advocates of women's rights declare that the Breadwinner oppresses his wife. According to them, he does not serve his family; he rules over them. He does not take care of his wife; he exploits her. He does not work to provide for his loved ones; he works to achieve success for himself. He is driven by ambition, not love.

Equally narrow-minded men's rights advocates avow precisely the opposite. The Breadwinner is not the oppressor; he is the victim. "My first wife was completely dependent on me," complained one man. "I was always playing a role of some sort. She wanted me to take on three jobs so she could have the kinds of things she wanted."

By placing both arguments side by side, it is clear that they are rationales for rage at the other sex. Fortunately for all of us, the truth is both more complex and more human. As Studs Terkel's *Working* poignantly revealed, most men today do not see themselves as powerful, dominating figures. On the contrary, they portray themselves as struggling to find ways to survive and, if possible, to grow, despite the mounting pressures of making enough money to support themselves and their families.

Our bodies often speak more eloquently than our words. When the twentieth century began, men could expect to live nearly as long as women. A woman's life expectancy was 48 years, a man's 46. But by the mid-1970s, according to the U.S. Department of Health, Education and Welfare, the average woman could expect to live 76.5 years, while the life expectancy of the average man was only 68.7 years. According to some estimates, by the year 2000, men may die a full decade sooner than women. 36

"It is time that men . . . comprehended," advised James Harrison of the Albert Einstein College of Medicine, "that the price paid for belief in the male role is shorter life expectancy. The male sex role will become less hazardous to our health only insofar as it ceases to be defined as opposite to the female role . . ." 37

Of the many lethal aspects of masculinity, none is more so than the pressure of work. What is debilitating is not work itself (the chronically unemployed die earlier than other men), but the anxiety and helplessness of bureaucratic employment. Those who are self-employed or who can run their own shop outlive those who are trapped between superior and subordinate. "Longevity depends less upon fitness or genetic inheritance," observed John Stickney in *Self-Made*, a study of entrepreneurship, "than upon work satisfaction, a quality linked to autonomy." 38

Some men reject the role altogether. Others defend it as the wisdom of tradition. Both responses are oversimplified. All human societies and all human families face the question of how work is to be divided among its members. Every society and every family must find its own answer. In America, our response has varied enormously over our two-hundred-year history. 39

In colonial America, women had relatively greater occupational freedom than in some later periods. Colonial women were butchers and gunsmiths. They ran mills and shipyards. They worked as midwives and sextons, journalists and printers. They learned a trade, as did men, through apprenticeship. But in the 1800s, a woman's role narrowed. By midcentury, fewer female shopkeepers and business women were at work than before the Revolutionary War. They might be allowed to indulge in such careers before marriage, but once appropriated by a man in marriage, they were, as Alexis de Tocqueville pointed out, "subjected to stricter obligations" than were women in Europe. 40

Between these two periods came industrialization, a process in which the "home become *divorced* from the workplace," with femininity identified with the former, masculinity with the latter. Before the Industrial Revolution, both sexes usually worked at home. Indeed, home *meant* work. Although women's tasks were different, they were interdependent with men's. They focused on household care: spinning wool and flax, cooking, preserving and curing, animal care, gardening, and countless other productive tasks. But after the 41

Industrial Revolution, concludes historian Amaury de Riencourt, "the wife as the husband's productive partner and fellow worker disappeared."

Before industrialization, men frequently took responsibility for training   42
boys as young as six years of age. If a boy did not work with his father, he was apprenticed to another man to learn a trade. Accordingly, most child-rearing manuals in colonial America were written for mothers *and* fathers. Because fathers were nearby, working in a family farm or shop, they played a large role in the rearing of their children, particularly their sons. After industrialization, when men went away to a job, their sons could not follow, and child-rearing advice more often was directed to women only. Boys were still expected to be men, of course, but they spent the first decade of their lives in a world in which they rarely saw grown men at work.

This transition to an industrial society was neither immediate nor simple.   43
Not all men left the farms and family-run shops; not all women lost their productive functions. But the shift was nevertheless profound. The home came to be seen, in Christopher Lasch's phrase, as a "haven in a heartless world."

In marriage, the role of the Breadwinner became paramount. The hus-   44
band-wife relationship was a union of opposites.

She was:	*He was:*
family oriented	success oriented
pure	worldly
gentle	aggressive
moral	pragmatic
emotional	rational
delicate	tough
weak	strong

By splitting the national character in half, one feminine and the other masculine, the nineteenth-century family engaged in a holding action against the tumult of history. Women would embody tradition; men would embody change.

Feminist historians have every reason to question this unwritten patriar-   45
chal contract that governed the American family. One does not need a lawyer to realize that some of its clauses make it a dangerous document for women to sign. Dare a woman renounce a career so her husband will provide for her? Once a career is foregone, what will assure the quality of his care? Who will guarantee that the contract will be honored? What will happen should the marriage end? Do women want to spend their lives being taken care of by the Breadwinner?

These questions were first raised by early feminists, such as Angelina   46
Grimké, Amelia Bloomer, and Charlotte Perkins Gilman. They are now being

posed again by today's feminist historians, economists, and sociologists. But one issue rarely raised is: If women were being discriminated against, what was happening to men? Were they ruthlessly forcing the second sex out of the professions and back into the home? Were they reducing women to economic dependence and domestic isolation in order to ensure their own supremacy? Or were they themselves oppressed, struggling workers caught in the grinding gear of industrialization? Were they merely downtrodden and disillusioned men who sought in women a nurturant refuge from a heartless world?

Some contemporary feminists who have blamed the Breadwinner for relegating women to domesticity do not feel obliged to try to understand men's experience. "What is a man, anyway?" asks the narrator of *The Women's Room.* "Everything I see around me in life tells me a man is he who makes money." She dismisses the question of why men act as they do with ignorance and arrogance: "I don't claim to know, and I don't even care much. I figure that's their problem." Of course, women are entitled to be as indifferent and bitter as they want to be; after all, they have much about which to be angry. But it will not serve their cause. To pretend that men's pain is irrelevant to women is understandable, but unwise. It will not result in equality, much less in intimacy. 47

Consider, in contrast, the portrait a male historian draws of nineteenth-century American men. "How was a man to be manly?" asked contemporary historian Peter Gabriel Filene, summarizing the insecurity and confusion of men in the closing decades of the century. "Feminism aroused such furious debate less because of what men thought about women than because of *what men were thinking about themselves.* They dreaded a change in sex roles because . . . they were finding it acutely difficult to be a man. The concept of manliness was suffering strain in all its dimensions—in work and success, in family patriarchy, and in . . . sexuality. The masculine role was uncertain." 48

Unaccustomed to such expressions of concern for men, some feminists have criticized Filene. In a review of his work, Cynthia Russet wrote, "Many men were antagonized by the very first stirrings of women's rights around 1848, and many of them continued to be hostile thereafter. Are we to assume an uncertainty in the masculine role that extended over half a century? Might the reason be less subtle? Might Victorian males, early and late, perceiving the advantages that accrued to them as 'Lords of Creation,' have simply opposed rocking the boat?" 49

It is odd that a woman historian would find prolonged masculine uncertainty so hard to accept. After all, for both women *and* men, the economic world was being transformed. To provide for a family, then considered to be a masculine responsibility, was a far different task at the end of the century than at the beginning. 50

As historian Mary P. Ryan observed, men now labored in "a world gone mad with change, acquisitiveness, and individualism." From countryside to city, from farm to factory, from self-employment to company employee, work- 51 ers were entering an unfamiliar and often threatening world. The foundations of the marketplace were shifting. While promoting the cult of the true woman, men were becoming enmeshed in its masculine counterpart: the cult of the self-made man. As early as the 1830s, men began to feel the pressure of a new, frustrating, and contradictory definition of success. While fantasizing about the heroic exploits of Daniel Boone or the mythical world of Natty Bumppo, the Breadwinner found himself faced with jobs that were anything but heroic. He was not a solitary figure on the landscape. He was part of an organization that was becoming increasingly complex and bureaucratic. He was not his own boss, but an employee whose livelihood depended on pleasing the man who was.

How, then, was a man to become a success? The hero of Horatio Alger's novels emphasized the importance of dressing neatly and modestly, of being punctual and reliable, of eliminating slang and colloquialism from one's speech. In short, he symbolized "the qualities of character and intellect which make the hero a good employee." 52

Hero and employee: the words themselves jar when juxtaposed. They seem antithetical, and in Horatio Alger's own life they were. Although we associate his name with virile success, Horatio Alger never married, and he spent his life in boarding houses. The only woman he ever lived with was his sister. He attended Harvard Divinity School and briefly served as minister to a small congregation in Brewster, Massachusetts. He left the ministry for reasons that were, until recently, obscure. In fact, he was accused by a parish committee of "unnatural familiarity with boys." Alger did not deny the charge; he acknowledged that he had been "imprudent" and left. 53

No wonder men felt insecure. They were caught between the too-good-to-be-true heroes of Horatio Alger and an increasingly bureaucratic reality where only aggressive, often ruthless men could become Carnegies and Rockefellers. "The inner conflict in young Americans between the will for righteousness and the will for success," observed historian Bernard Wishy, "must have been extraordinary." The conflict had a direct impact on masculinity, for it was men who were supposed to climb the ladder of success. They placed on women the burden of being righteous because the burden of success was heavy enough. 54

As Daniel Boone and Davy Crockett etched their virile exploits in the national consciousness, the workingman in Boston, New York, and Philadelphia was caught in the web of industrial civilization. Coping with rent, work, children, and urban life, he had little reason to feel secure, much less heroic. To have a wife at home who took care of him, and who was grateful for his hard-earned wages, was the least he could expect. Regardless of what his work might be, he could feel manly because only men performed his particular function. 55

The most reliable method of ensuring the manliness of the Breadwinner's role was to construct an economy in which only men could be providers, which is precisely what we did. From the Civil War to World War II, women 56 were excluded from the work force to a greater degree than either before or since. "The isolation of women from work was a significant phenomenon," concluded the economist Eli Ginzburg, "for only about eighty years"— roughly from 1860 to 1940.

Although Rosie the Riveter led postwar women back into the economy, women are still unable to be the Breadwinner. Even if they are allowed and sometimes even encouraged to bring a second income into the family's bank account, the economy is structured to ensure their continued dependency on the *real* provider. Compared to men, women earn less money today than they did a quarter-century ago. In 1955, they earned 64 percent of what men earned. Today they earn less than 59 percent. Two thirds of full-time working women earn less than $10,000 a year, and less than 7 percent of all working women are managers. In other words, whether working or not, all but a few women still depend on the Breadwinner.*

This sexual division of labor, however, takes its toll on both men and women. The syndromes are so common that they now have names: women suffer from the "Cinderella complex," men from the "Breadwinner complex." "Women are brought up to depend on a man and to feel naked and frightened without one," wrote Colette Dowling. "We have been taught to believe that as females we cannot stand alone, that we are too fragile, too delicate, too needful of protection." To avoid being responsible for themselves (and their offspring) and to avoid the hardships and indignities of working for a living, such women cling to men. Even if the relationship is not emotionally fulfilling, at least these wives have a security blanket to protect them from economic woes.

Except for their unhappiness, men who suffer from the Breadwinner complex have precisely the opposite symptoms. They are addicted to their work. Although it causes physical and emotional strain, they climb the ladder of success as quickly as they can. They feel completely responsible for their families' economic well-being. They are determined to stand alone and to admit to no feelings of weakness or vulnerability. They expect themselves to stand up under the strain. Unable to spend much time or energy on their children, they numb themselves to their fathering role and focus increasingly on their career.

The Cinderella/Breadwinner marriage obviously does not work very well anymore. The husband sees his wife as free from the stress of a job, and envies her; she sees him as having a paying job and social recognition, and envies him. Both of them, observed Margaret Mead in *Male and Female*, are "dissatisfied and inclined to be impatient with the other's discontent."

---

* In 1979, 5.5 million wives earned more than their husbands. This is twice the figure in 1970. All indications are that the number of "Mrs. Breadwinners" will continue to increase.

Even though men are still considered to be the Breadwinner, the two-career family is now common. Old expectations clash with new realities. The Breadwinner still expects to be greeted by the housewife; the working woman expects her husband to share her domestic duties. The Breadwinner expects his wife to be an old-fashioned mother who bakes bread, while she expects him to be a modern father who shares household chores. With work and home no longer divided neatly between the sexes, problems proliferate. When workers in the late sixties were asked about job-related problems, only 1 percent of the conflicts cited related to the family. By the late seventies, the percentage had risen to 25 percent, and it is still rising. 61

A typical conflict is that if the Breadwinner is to compete successfully, his wife and children must move when the company wants to relocate him. His wife's career (if any) and friends must be forfeited. The children's school life must be disrupted. The family, like excess baggage, must be crated and shipped to accompany the Breadwinner on his quest for success. 62

In addition to practical matters are the interpersonal ones. Unrivaled by any nation on earth, America extols competitiveness. The Breadwinner is willing to compete for success against other men, but not against women. For women, competition has been deemed unfeminine. Nineteenth-century child-rearing manuals enjoined parents to have their daughters avoid the "ruder and more daring gymnastics of boys." Never was she to try to swing higher than her friends, to outdo, to excel. Her virtues rested in solidarity, unity, attachment. 63

As the sexes split, so do the philosophies of work and family. The capitalist marketplace must be competitive, or waste and corruption ensue. The loving family must be cooperative, or animosity and envy take root. 64

It is a bizarre division of life. Unwieldy and unworkable, the arrangement is bound to produce tension. Competition cannot be worshiped outside the home and banished within it. A world in which men compete and women cooperate is nothing more than a prescription for inequality. 65

As long as men cast themselves (or are cast by their wives) as Breadwinners, the pressure on them to achieve will be intense. If a man expects to spend the prime of his life single-handedly supporting his wife, his children, and his home, he has locked himself into a role that cannot help but produce physical and psychological stress. In addition to this stress, he may now bear the resentment of his wife, who is trapped in the home, and the alienation of his children, who complain that he is distant. In such a family, the Breadwinner will neither live long nor live happily. Indeed, the family itself may come apart. 66

Instead of resenting feminists for attempting to rewrite the masculine-feminine contract, we should be grateful. They are challenging a contract that serves us no better than it does them. 67

MEN AND THE NEW ECONOMY

ANTHONY ASTRACHAN

Anthony Astrachan is author of *How Men Feel: Their Response to Women's Demands for Equality and Power* (1988). Based on interviews with 400 people, 350 of whom were men, the book "tries to show how men feel about women's quests for independence, equality, and power." In this essay he examines issues raised by the "new economy": job loss, financial insecurity, and the changing character of men's work.

Pete used to be proud of the work he did as a machinist in an auto parts factory. Now he's just tired—and scared. Half the workers in his plant have been laid off because carmakers have been buying parts from Japan. On top of that, his company is automating in order to compete. "That means they only need a quarter of the workers they used to," Pete says, "and if they move the plant or write new job descriptions that get around the union and seniority, they can hire women. With the computer running the operation they don't need my muscle. And they don't need my skill with the lathe and the drill presses anymore. Work gets simple enough and they turn it over to the girls." 1

Pete is one of the many men in the United States who see themselves as casualties of the changes occurring in the workplace over the past 30 years. Some, like Pete, string together complaints about imports, automation, and women as though they were all part of the same great shift. 2

In fact, men are facing very different kinds of change. One thing these changes have in common, however: They alter the nature of work itself. In the United States more than in other countries, and for men more than for women, what you do defines who you are. A man's work is an important part of his identity as a man. 3

Economics vs. Man the Provider

Historically, men grew up expecting to provide for themselves and for their family. Providing was a man's job—whether he did it as doctor or lawyer, merchant or corporate executive, cop or soldier, auto worker or miner. 4

Today the role of man as provider is being transformed, and economic change is the main force responsible. Note the measure of the shift: In 1960, 5

83.3 percent of all men over the age of 16 were in the labor force; in 1985, it was 76.2 percent. By contrast, 37.7 percent of women 16 and over were in the labor force in 1960, but the figure had risen to 54.4 percent by 1985.

Men are no longer the sole providers for their families. The traditional family—a husband who goes out to work while his wife stays home and raises children—now accounts for only 10.7 percent of U.S. households. Now, more than 32 percent of all households are two-earner families in which the wife shares the role of provider. 6

There are two reasons for these changes. First, the cycle of inflation and recession and the shift from manufacturing to services have produced an economy in which the family needs more than one income to live decently or even survive. Second, rising competition from imports, dwindling jobs in manufacturing, the high Reagan budget, and growing trade deficits occurring over the past five years have helped to destroy thousands of the jobs that enabled men to provide. 7

Imports and Jobs

The boom in imports has had so much impact in everyday life and in the media recently that we may forget it's part of a broader decline in manufacturing and connected with the switch from smokestack to high-tech industry over the past 20 years. Economists estimate that we have lost about 2 million jobs, 30,000 of them in the textile industry alone, since the U.S. dollar and U.S. imports started to climb in 1981. The rise in imports and the fall in manufacturing seem like statistical abstractions, but the abstract soon becomes concrete: Brown Shoe Company of St. Louis closed eight of its 30 domestic shoe plants and bought a company that imports Italian shoes; Caterpillar Tractor cut its total work force by a third; Dixie Yarns in Chattanooga spun 45 percent less yarn in 1985 than the year before. 8

Then the statistics hit home: Theodore McBryar, a 43-year-old Dixie Yarns dye-machine operator, made only half as much in 1985 as he did the year before and couldn't afford to replace his 1973 Chevrolet, which had 213,000 miles on it when *U.S. News* reported his plight. Kevin Englert, 30, a roving tender at the same mill, couldn't buy his three children new clothes for last school year. That kind of hardship undermines a man's faith in himself. A man unable to "do his job" as provider has lost more than just money. 9

Ironically, the economic policies that have hurt traditional men (and traditional corporations) by bringing on the import crisis came from the conservative administration of Ronald Reagan, whose supporters labor so hard—and most fruitlessly—in behalf of traditional values in both personal and economic life. 10

Technology vs. a "Man's Job"

Automation, like economics, brings losses beyond jobs or money. "A man's job" once required skill, strength, and the ability to work long hours—all admirable qualities that used to be thought of as exclusively male. Thanks to technological advances, many such jobs now require less and less skill in the use of a worker's hands, eyes, and judgment. Pride and craftsmanship become irrelevant.

This seems brand new, something very modern. In fact, it's the latest stage in a long historical process that began with the Industrial Revolution and the development of factories 200 years ago and gathered force with the invention of the assembly line in the early years of this century.

Today's jobs require more and more obedience to company rules and the tyranny of electronic monitoring. Management often translates these new conditions to mean that the work has become suitable for women, whom they see as reliable, punctual workers who like repetitious work and believe that they profit when the company does. Male managers, in fact, do not try to hide this. Most technological changes in one factory "were of a type that would tend to increase the percentage of women. For example, we have broken down the alignment of components and simplified [the] job, and as the jobs called for less skill, they became women's work." That was one New Jersey executive quoted in Georgina Smith's study of the job market, which cited many more.

Women in Men's Jobs

The arrival of women in the workplace, particularly in what were once labeled masculine occupations, is a social and psychological shift that is more significant and far reaching than the economic changes caused by the five-year boom in imports or by automation, though these may have higher and more visible immediate costs.

A woman employed in what was once called a man's job is a more radical departure from tradition because she violates a division of labor that goes back millennia. She is also more universal. Imports hurt some industries, automation primarily affects factory workers, but we all meet this working woman, whether or not we are employed. She is in every kind of work and from every racial and ethnic group.

The idea that a woman can and should do "a man's job" is the product of social and psychological forces that are reshaping both the male role as provider and the male monopoly on certain occupations.

These powerful traditions deprived women of independence and equality, confining them to low-paid work that brought few of the satisfactions of mastery and achievement that many of us find so necessary for happiness. For the past 20 years women have been fighting to do away with these restrictions on equality and power. Their struggle has produced changes in U.S. politics, culture, and psychology. They have shown that the old strengths and skills and the ability to work long hours that were needed for what used to be seen as a man's job are not exclusively male—or even often required now. The number of women has increased in many occupations, from factory worker to police officer to corporate manager to physician—18 percent of blue-collar workers and 16 percent of doctors and lawyers, for example, are now women.

Frequently overlooked, however, is the part economic forces have played 18 in these changes. Women have been pushed in this direction by the same shifts that have done so much to change the role of work in men's lives.

This affects both men's acceptance of change and their resistance to it. 19 Most men recognize the injustice of the old division of labor and have learned to live with some of the ways women are changing that division. Our acceptance reflects recognition of many realities—a family needs two incomes to survive; women perform as well as men in many jobs; women have the right to equal opportunity in any occupation they choose.

But for most men, I believe, resistance is still stronger than acceptance. 20 The very economic necessities that bring women into "a man's job" underline the erosion of the male role as provider and thus produce conflict. Polls that show acceptance must be seen in this context. It appears that many men give pollsters views that they think are socially acceptable, but behave differently. A recent survey by the *Harvard Business Review*, for instance, shows that only 5 percent of male executives have an unfavorable view of female executives, compared to 41 percent in 1965. But more than half the men surveyed made $100,000 or more a year, while only 10 percent of the women did. However low the expressed bias, many women attribute such measurable discrimination to male resistance.

Most men can't accept that a woman no longer devotes herself primarily 21 to housekeeping and childcare, even though they know it's true and still value her as a partner. It is hard to welcome change when the myths and emotions of the traditional system remain strong. It's especially hard when men are confronted at the same time with such economic and technological changes, just described, that damage or destroy many of the satisfactions of work that might otherwise survive the introduction of women into the workplace. Generally, men find it more difficult to feel support for the women they work with than a wife or daughter going out to face a similar situation.

My own research indicates that most men also feel some combination of 22 anger, fear, and anxiety toward women in traditionally masculine jobs, often treating women co-workers in any or all of three ways. They show *hostility;* *deny* their competence, sometimes their very presence; or *transform* them in fantasy—into nuns, whores, lovers, mothers, wives, daughters, sisters—any role that allows them to treat women as traditional females rather than peers.

These behaviors take different forms in different occupations. Hostility 23 is often expressed sexually. Some factory workers, for instance, put porn pictures in their tool chests and display them when women workers walk by.

Suggestive propositions and other forms of sexual harassment directed at women are common occurrences in offices. Recruiters from the investment banking firm Goldman, Sachs asked women at Stanford University if they would have an abortion rather than jeopardize their careers, thus attacking both their right and their ability to combine motherhood and career.

Denial is what's being expressed by the committee of men who direct all   24
their comments to the man from the ad agency, though the woman on the team, sitting next to him at the table, is his boss and the designer of the campaign. It's denial also when men insist that most women are not as career-oriented as men, despite statistics showing that in many industries women in technical, professional, supervisory, and managerial positions have the same rate of turnover as men.

Transformation can take forms as nasty as a sexual assault on a woman   25
coal miner or as "innocent" as a request by a male executive that his female colleague sew on an errant button for him, thus transforming her into a mother.

The Bright Side

The fearsome changes discussed here are changes in work that alter the shape   26
of society and of individual lives, that change the very way we see ourselves as men. The answer to these threats isn't to block imports, stop automation, or deny women the right to work. It's to find ways that government, corporations, and individuals can cushion the effects of change.

One way is to remember that in every change there's a bright side as well   27
as a dark side. In every case, the promise can alter our lives as much as the threat does.

On the economic front, for instance, the threat of imports has been   28
accompanied by the arrival of foreign firms to build factories here that may make up for some of the jobs lost, like Komatsu, the Japanese manufacturer of earth-moving machines, in Chattanooga.

Technology has improved living standards for everyone and working   29
conditions for the people who master new tools. It can lead to increased responsibility and demand higher skills in operators, as Paul Adler points out in his book *Dollars and Sense*. Responsibility increases because machines cost more and produce more. Operators need higher skills because they must understand the control program logic well enough to correct errors on the line or help write new programs. When the Communications Workers of America polled members in 1979, about 78 percent said technological change had increased the skill requirements of their jobs.

A woman in "a man's job" constitutes a more personal challenge to a man   30
than economic or technological change. It's a challenge he meets at home as well as at work, in his gut, often in his crotch, as well as in his head. Despite

or because of the challenge she represents, a man can probably enrich his life more by learning to work with women in his kind of job than by switching jobs to escape the threat of imports or mastering automation.

Men can start by seeking the positive emotions that are generated by the arrival of women in the workplace, and by their assertion of equality. These emotions are admiration, identification, and pleasure. Such feelings produce positive behavior—acceptance, support, and association. 31

I also believe a man can work with a woman in "her kind" of job. A small but increasing number of men are now sharing the work of raising their children. They find it enriches both their own and their children's lives. 32

Few men, however, even those who welcome women as peers, do literally half the household work. There will always be economic crises and technological changes that alter our work patterns, but society will truly be transformed only when men do half the work of childcare and take half the responsibility for it from the moment of birth. Unhappily, we can't take more than a small step toward this day until individuals and trade unions, government and corporations, change the way work is organized. 33

SEXUALITY AS CONSUMPTION

JOHN LIPPERT

John Lippert's research focuses on the automobile industry and the implications of contemporary change for that industry's employees. Lippert has written about job security and salary and pension issues in the collective bargaining process, and about contract negotiations between auto workers' unions and industry management. In this essay, which first appeared in *Brother: A Forum for Men Against Sexism* in 1976, he describes his own experience on the assembly line, relating how alienation and dehumanization at work carry over into personal life.

I work at a Fisher Body plant over in Elyria, Ohio. And so I spend about sixty hours each week stacking bucket seats onto carts. I used to spend all my time here in Oberlin as a student. But I had to give up that life of comfort as it became financially impossible and as it became psychologically and politically a less and less satisfactory alternative. I still try to remain rigorous about my intellectual growth, though, and so I still take a few courses here at the College. Such a schizophrenic role is at times hard to bear psychologically, and the work load is often staggering. But such a dual life-style also gives me something of a unique perspective on both Oberlin and Fisher Body. I feel this perspective is a useful contribution to this conference on men's sexuality.

One of the things that really surprised me when I went to work for Fisher Body is that it really is hard to go to work every day. I don't know why that surprised me. At first I thought that everyone around me was pretty well adjusted and that I was still an irresponsible hippie at heart. But then I found that just about everyone I know at the plant has to literally struggle to go back to work every day. Again I was surprised, but this time also encouraged, because I made the very casual assumption that I could look to the people around me for help in facing the strain of that factory. But I soon found that there is nothing "casual" about this kind of support: it is incredibly difficult to find. I have lots of friends now, from all over Northern Ohio and from all different kinds of cultural backgrounds. But most of these relationships seem based on a certain distance, on an assumption that we really do face that factory alone. At first I had to look to see if it was my fault, to see if there was something in me that made it hard to have nurturing relationships with the people I work with. I soon found out that it is my fault, but that it is part of more general phenomena. I began to explore these "phenomena" as completely as I could: this exploration became an essential part of my struggle to go to work every day.

In trying to look at these barriers between me and the people around me, I was struck immediately with the kind of role sexuality plays in mediating the relationships of people in the factory. I spend much time working with men in almost complete isolation from women. I soon found that instead of getting or giving nurture to these men that I was under intense pressure to compete with them. We don't seem to have any specific goal in this competition (such as promotions or status, etc.). Each member of the group seems concerned mainly with exhibiting sexual experience and competency through the competition. Past sexual history is described and compared in some detail: as a newcomer, I was asked to defend my sexual "know-how" within a week of joining the group. Also, we try to degrade each other's sexual competency verbally, through comments like, "Well, why don't you introduce your wife to a *real* man," or "Well, I was at your house last night and taught your wife a few things she didn't know." But it is important to note that none of what happens between men in the plant is considered "sexuality." That remains as what we do with (or to) our women when we get home. And so even though homosexuality is generally considered to be some kind of disease, most men are free to engage in what seems to be a pretty basic need for physical intimacy or reassurance. This can be expressed very simply, through putting arms around shoulders or squeezing knees, but it can also become much more intense and explicit, through stabbing between ass cheeks or pulling at nipples. But all of this physical interaction occurs within this atmosphere of competition. It takes the form of banter, horseplay, thrust and parry seemingly intended to make the need for such physical interaction seem as absurd as possible. But even through this competition, it is easy to see that many, many men enjoy this physical interaction and that they receive a kind of physical satisfaction from it that they just don't get when they go home. 3

My relationships with women seem somehow equally distorted. Entry of women into the factory is still a relatively recent event, at least recent enough so that contact between men and women is still unique and very noticeable. Much occurs before words are even spoken. Like every other man there, I discuss and evaluate the physical appearance of the women around men. This analysis is at times lengthy and involved, as in "She's pretty nice but her legs are too long in proportion to the rest of her body." Of course this evaluation goes on in places other than the factory, but here it seems particularly universal and intense. Perhaps a reason for this intensity is that the factory is an ugly place to spend eight or ten hours a day, and attractive people are much nicer to look at. 4

I guess I really do get some sort of satisfaction from engaging in this analysis. But there is an incredible gap between the kind of pleasure I get 5 when I sleep with someone and the kind of pleasure I get when I see someone attractive in the shop. And yet I behave as if there is some connection. Many men are completely unabashed about letting the women know they are being watched and discussed, and some men are quite open about the results of their analysis. Really attractive women have to put up with incredible harassment, from constant propositions to mindless and obscene grunts as they walk by. Men who call out these obscenities can't actually be trying to sleep with the women they are yelling at; they are simply making the women suffer for their beauty.

In this attack they are joined by some older men who just don't like the thought of working with women. Many women have been told they ought to leave the factory and get a husband, and then they are told in some detail what they have to do to get a husband! It is really difficult for women to work in that factory. In many cases women have merely added eight hours a day of boredom and frustration in the factory to eight or more hours a day of housework and childcare at home. And they have to contend with this harassment on top of all that.

But women are getting more secure in the factory. More and more now, men who are particularly offensive in this harassment are responded to in kind, with a flippant, "Up your ass, buddy!" In any case, by the time I get close enough to a woman to actually talk to her, I feel like a real entrepreneur. By that time I've already completed my analysis of the woman's physical appearance, and in the beginning of the conversation we are both trying to find out the results of the analysis. And to reinforce this feeling of entrepreneurship, when I get back to the men I'm working with, I get all kinds of comments like "Did you tap it?" or "Are you going to?"

But one thing that really amazes me about my sexuality at the factory is that it has a large effect on my sexuality at home. I first began to notice this when, in the first week, I began to feel an incredible amount of amorphous and ill-defined sexual energy at the moment I left the plant. This energy makes the drive home pretty exciting and it influences my behavior the rest of the day. I often think something like, "Well, I have two hours before I go back to work, and it would really be nice if I could get my rocks off before then." I found that dissipating this sexual energy really does make it easier to go back. Also, I began to notice that my sexuality was becoming less physically oriented (as in just being close to someone for a while) and more genitally oriented (as in making love and going to sleep). Also, as household chores were becoming more formidable while working, I began to ask people who came to my house—and for some reason, especially my sexual partners—to take more responsibility in keeping the place fixed up.

In trying to understand how my sexuality was being influenced by the factory, this relationship between sexuality at home and at work became an important clue. Working is much more than an eight-hour-a-day diversion; it influences everything I do. If I'm not actually working I'm either recuperating or getting ready to go back. Because I confront this fact every day, it's not hard for me to imagine the changes in my sexuality as essentially in response to the fact that I have to go to work every day.

Now there is an important contradiction in this "I go to work." When I'm at work, I'm not really "me" any more, at least in some very large ways. I don't work *when* I want to; I don't work *because* I want to; I don't work *at* something I'd like to be doing. I don't enjoy my job; I feel no sense of commitment to it; and I feel no satisfaction when it's completed. I'm a producer; my only significant role is that I make money for Fisher Body. Now Fisher Body values me highly for this, and at the end of each week they reward me with a paycheck which is mine to consume as I like. But notice: I have to spend a large part of that check and much of my time off in preparation for my return to my role as producer. To a large extent, I don't consume so that I can feel some satisfaction or something like that. Now I consume so that I can go back to work and produce. And that part of my consumption which I actually do enjoy is influenced by my work in that what I enjoy has to be as completely removed from my work as possible. I build elaborate and often expensive systems (such as families, stereos, or hot rods) into which I can escape from my work each day. And this is as true of my sexuality as it is true of the music I consume for escape each day, the car I consume to get back and forth, or the soap I consume to wash the factory's dirt off me when I get home. 10

There is an important adjunct to this: the specifically asexual or even antisexual nature of the work I do. For the last three months my role as producer has consisted of stacking bucket seats on carts. That's it; nothing more and nothing less. Many parts of me are stifled by this type of work; we've all read about the monotony and so on. What is relevant here is that whatever dynamic and creative sexual energy I have is ignored for eight hours each day and at the end, is lost. 11

I hope that by now a picture is beginning to emerge which explains much of what is happening to me sexually as a function of this split between my role as producer and my role as consumer. What is the nature of this picture? The essential conflict is that in my role as producer, much of what is organic and natural about my sexuality is ignored for eight hours each day and at the end lost. I have to spend much of the rest of the day looking for it. 12

But notice: already I have lost much of what seems such a basic part of me. My sexuality is something which is no longer mine simply because I am alive. It is something which I have to look for and, tragically, something which someone else must give to me. And because my need to be sexually revitalized each day is so great, it becomes the first and most basic part of a contract I need to make in order to ensure it. The goal of this contract is stability, and it includes whatever I need to consume: sex, food, clothes, a house, perhaps children. My partner in this contract is in most cases a woman; by now she is as much a slave to my need to consume as I am a slave to Fisher Body's 13 need to consume me. What does she produce? Again: sex, food, clothes, a house, babies. What does she consume for all this effort?—all the material wealth I can offer plus a life outside of a brutal and uncompromising labor market. Within this picture, it's easy to see why many women get bored with sex. They get bored for the same reason I get bored with stacking bucket seats on carts.

But where did this production/consumption split originate and how does   14
it exert such a powerful influence over our lives? The essential conflict is that we really do have to go to work and we really do have to let our employers tell us what to do. There's nothing mysterious about this. People who will not or can not make a bargain similar to the one that I have made with Fisher Body are left to starve. If we are unable to convince ourselves of this by looking around this room or this College, we need only expand our observation slightly. Furthermore, Fisher Body and other employers have spent decades accumulating bureaucracies and technologies which are marvelous at producing wealth but which leave us with some awfully absurd jobs to perform. We have no say in deciding the nature of these jobs; they are designed only from the point of view of profit maximization.

But to question the economic power of Fisher Body is to question most   15
of what is to our lives essential and leads us to an intellectual tradition which most of us find repugnant. But if we are to have an adequate look at our sexuality we must begin with these observations: that our society is largely influenced by two relationships which are universal in our society: *that as producers we are forced into roles which we cannot design and which ignore our sexuality precisely because it is an unprofitable consideration, and that as consumers our sexuality becomes a pawn in our need to escape from the work we do and our need to return to work each day refreshed and ready to begin anew.*

Now what is the power of the conclusion we have just made? It is a   16
conclusion which was reached through the exploration of day-to-day experience, but at this point it is an intellectual abstraction which leaves much out. For instance, it doesn't consider important influences of family and school on sexuality. At this point, the conclusion is general enough to apply equally well to blue and white collar workers (the main conflict is that we really do have to go to work). The conclusion doesn't attempt to explain every detail of the life of every worker. It does, however, attempt to describe a certain dynamic to which those lives respond and certain boundaries within which those lives occur. This conclusion is necessary for us in this conference if only from the point of view of intellectual clarity; we can hardly proceed unless we are aware that we as men and the College as an institution play a particular kind of economic role in society. Enough self-awareness to include the discussion of sexuality is a form of consumption that is simply not available to the mass of the people in our society. And it is to their time spent as producers that we owe our own extravagant consumption.

But what is the political significance of the conclusions we have reached?   17
That is, can our discussion of sexuality affect the evolution of Fisher Body's

power over us? For today, the answer seems no, that for today Fisher Body is incredibly strong because, like myself, the majority of people who work for it are basically committed to their jobs. But we need only consider individual survival for a moment to see that it can only be sought in the long run in a collective consciousness which is capable of challenging the power Fisher Body has over our lives. And this is why we need to confront our sexuality; because our sexuality is based on competition among men and at best distorted communication between men and women, it will make building that collective consciousness an incredibly difficult task.

In a short time we in the United States will feel the need for that collective [18] consciousness much more sorely than we feel it today. The Third World is in revolt and the U.S. economy is in the midst of an economic collapse which rivals the collapse of the Thirties in proportions. As a result, we face massive unemployment in this country and the awesome prospect of battles between different groups of people fighting for the "privilege" of working for Fisher Body. If people see that it is only Fisher Body that can gain from such a battle, they may decide not to fight it. And if people see that a victory for Fisher Body means inevitably a return to a lifetime of alienation and oppression inside offices and factories, they may decide to fight instead for the right to control their own lives.

COMMUTERS

EDWARD HIRSCH

Edward Hirsch is a poet who teaches creative writing at the University of Houston. His many honors include awards from the Academy of American Poets and the National Endowment for the Arts. In this poem, from Hirsch's second book, *Wild Gratitude*, published in 1986, the narrator recognizes himself among the commuters, repeating again and again the mundane trek to work. Hirsch's other books of poetry are *For the Sleepwalkers* (1981) and *The Night Parade* (1989).

It's that vague feeling of panic
That sweeps over you
Stepping out of the #7 train
At dusk, thinking, *This isn't me*
Crossing a platform with the other
Commuters in the worried half-light
Of evening, *that must be*

Someone else with a newspaper
Rolled tightly under his arm
Crossing the stiff, iron tracks
Behind the train, thinking, *This*
Can't be me stepping over the tracks
With the other commuters, slowly crossing
The parking lot at the deepest
Moment of the day, wishing

That I were someone else, wishing
I were anyone else but a man
Looking out at himself as if
From a great distance,
Turning the key in his car, starting
His car and swinging it out of the lot,

Watching himself grinding uphill
In a slow fog, climbing past the other

Cars parked on the side of the road,
The cars which seem ominously empty
And strange,
           and suddenly thinking
With a new wave of nausea
This isn't me sitting in this car
Feeling as if I were about to drown

In the blue air, *that must be*
Someone else driving home to his
Wife and children on an ordinary day
Which ends, like other days,
With a man buckled into a steel box,
Steering himself home and trying
Not to panic

In the last moments of nightfall
When the trees and the red-brick houses
Seem to float under green water
And the streets fill up with sea lights.

MAKING CONNECTIONS

1. Gerzon argues that men in modern times no longer have the traditional "frontier" outlets to prove their masculinity. As a result, he claims, the breadwinner role is all that they have left to validate themselves as men. Do you agree or disagree with this assessment? List the heroic feelings that might accompany success in the breadwinner role. How do these compare with the heroism of the frontier? Write your own essay about avenues for heroism and male validation today. How might Gerzon's points correspond to those of a writer like Robert Bly (Chapter 3)?

2. Psychologist David Gutmann coined the phrase "the parental imperative" to describe the tendency of couples, even those committed to equality and role-sharing in their marriages, to become more stereotyped in their roles after the birth of their first child. He contends that women become more domestic and nurturant and men begin to worry about being adequate providers for their families. Using Gerzon's essay and anecdotes from your friends' or family members' experiences, write an essay that supports or discounts the "parental imperative."

3. Astrachan outlines several threats that the "new economy" poses for working class men. How have changes in the U.S. economy affected the kinds of jobs men and women do? Consider the work that your grandparents and parents have done and compare it to the kind of work you are (or will be) doing. What are some of the differences in the conditions of work, the income from work, and the relationship of personal life to work life between your experience and that of past generations? Write an essay that summarizes your findings.

4. Both Gerzon and Astrachan discuss the issue that women's paid employment can threaten a man's sense of competence in the provider role. Do you agree or disagree? What other factors might contribute to the undermining of the male provider role? In your opinion, what risks do men face in giving up the role of provider, and what benefits might they gain? Are women opening themselves to the same pressures and anxieties that men have long faced by assuming the role of breadwinner? What do women win or lose by competing for the right to participate equally in the world of paid labor?

5. All of the writers in this chapter allude at some point to a loss of identity in their discussion of the working world. These experiences of work seem to be in direct contrast to the "quintessentially American" images of glamor and fulfillment that Ruth Sidel (Chapter 12) relates from her interviews of young women. How can you explain the gap between these

two views of work? Do men and women have different images of work and its rewards? Compare your own thoughts about work with those of your classmates. What promises does society hold out to its future workers, and how possible is it to avoid "losing one's identity" in the work one does?

6. Compare and contrast Marge Piercy's poem (Chapter 12) with Hirsch's. What images about work, value, and identity come across in each poem? How do the tone, rhythm, line breaks, and word choice of each poem work to convey its message? Do the views of labor in these two poems contradict one another, or do the poems share an implicit agreement about the nature of work? Try writing your own poem that expresses your ideas about work—it could be a recollection of one moment in the life of a worker, like Hirsch's poem, or a catalogue of labors, like Piercy's. Use as many vivid images and concrete words as you can to bring your subject to life.

7. Sociologist Melvin Kohn has studied the relationship between the conditions of a workplace and an individual's personality. His findings showed that workers who are allowed more opportunities for self-direction and independent decision-making on the job respond by exhibiting a greater degree of personal autonomy and responsibility than workers who are constantly supervised. In fact, Kohn found that those who are continually supervised tended to exhibit more conformity and less initiative even outside the workplace in their personal lives. What other aspects of jobs might shape features of personality? Are there differences in traditionally male and female jobs in terms of the personality traits they encourage? As a class project, make a list of a number of professions, including some traditionally filled only by men or women. Have each member of the group brainstorm on the personality traits that might be encouraged by one of those professions. Compare and discuss your findings, concentrating particularly on what insights you can draw about gender and work.

8. At the beginning of his essay, Lippert contrasts his college experiences with his work at the Fisher Body plant. Explain Lippert's use of the term "schizophrenic role." What does he learn about the conditions of work in the factory? Are these experiences similar to or different from your experiences in college? Compare Lippert's use of personal experience with the more objective tone of Astrachan's essay. What would happen to their subjects if the styles of these essays were switched?

9. List the many uses and meanings of sexuality brought up in Lippert's essay. How convincing are the parallels he draws between conditions at the plant, the change in his personal relationships, and the general ways in which men sometimes treat women? Is Lippert erroneously "blaming the system" for attitudes and behaviors that are an individual's

responsibility to avoid? Or do you agree with his claim that the structures of the workplace can have an effect on people's actions and values outside of work, even in such "private" areas as sexuality? Write an essay that argues for one or the other position or that attempts to mediate between the two.

10. In *The Peter Pan Syndrome*, Dan De Kiley contends that some men in contemporary society are choosing the lifestyle of Peter Pan, the boy who "refused to grow up." Likewise, in her book titled *The Hearts of Men: American Dreams and the Flight from Commitment*, Barbara Ehrenreich argues that the image of "the playboy"—the man free of commitments—has replaced that of the dull, responsible breadwinner. Do you agree that we are witnessing a flight from commitment among American men? Based on your own observations, is there any truth to the idea that young men today are delaying "growing up"? Can the same be said for young women today? Write an essay that expresses your views on "The New Man" or "The New Woman" of today.

11. Write an essay that attempts to pull together the social factors that contribute to masculine anxiety, as discussed in this chapter and in previous chapters. You might select a representative sample of writers from Chapter 3 on masculinity, Chapter 8 on sports, Chapter 10 on advertising or Chapter 11 on pornography, and this chapter on men and work. Compare these writers' views on the pressures facing men in society today. Do any of the demands and rules of the masculine role overlap? Are there any contradictions, paradoxes, or double binds that characterize what it means to be a man today?

14
THE WORKPLACE INSIDE THE HOME

C O N T E X T S

National surveys of high school seniors show that today most young women and men expect to have both a career and a family as adults. The difference in their expectations is reflected in the amount of time and commitment women and men plan to allocate to these respective roles. Even by the time they reach high school many women are wondering how they will balance the competing demands of work and family. Some will resolve the issue by lowering their career aspirations. Others will maintain high career goals but will pay the price by sacrificing a family life. Still others, as the saying goes, will try to "have it all." While young men have the same goals of work and family, their plans for the future focus almost exclusively on building their careers. The idea that they might quit their jobs one day to raise a family, or that they would perhaps choose a less prestigious career because it offered them more time to bring up their children are infrequent themes in men's plans for the future.

Why *do* many of us still assume that the woman will manage the home and family, even if she works full-time? What rewards and opportunities for growth do men miss out on when they take a secondary role in raising children? How do society's assumptions about who is best suited to nurture or to provide reveal preconceptions about gender and sex roles? Do these role assignments reflect natural differences between men and women, or are these arrangements socially constructed? The essays in this chapter examine the work of being a parent and homemaker, and ask us to reflect on the ways in which private life is influenced by the politics and values of the culture at large.

In our first essay, "Why Men Don't Rear Children: A Power Analysis," Margaret Rivka Polatnick contends that automatically allocating child rearing responsibilities to women both reflects and maintains male dominance in society. Men don't rear children, Polatnick argues, because childrearing is a job that offers few benefits and demands many sacrifices. The job of raising children, which usually falls to women, carries a high price in terms of lost wages, reduced independence, lowered social status, and arrested career advancement. In very practical terms, women ultimately give up power both in the home and in society when convention places the burden of parenting exclusively on their shoulders.

Our next two selections offer views on housework, from a female and a male perspective. In her classic essay, Pat Mainardi explores "The Politics of Housework," a politics that has nothing to do with campaign slogans or party platforms. Instead, Mainardi is referring to power relationships within the home, the personal negotiations between men and women about "sharing" housework and the subtle assumptions about privilege and power that such negotiations reveal. Another view is offered by Joel Roache in "Confessions of a Househusband." Roache's personal essay recounts how, after switching roles with his wife, he began to suffer from the alienation, frustration, and resentment brought on by a life of full-time housework. We see his initial enthusiasm at the experiment give way to feelings of exhaustion, lethargy, and depression when the realities of housework set in. Roache's reflections on his diminishing sense of self-worth and personal control during these weeks reveal much about the occupational hazards of the workplace inside the home.

In "Listening," our final essay, Sey Chassler reflects on the privileges that being a married, white, middle-class man have granted him. After a series of personal and public revelations about the situation of women, he begins to acquire an understanding of the extraordinary demands that others—and often he himself—have placed on women. Through his thoughtful and imaginative style of writing, Chassler offers us a glimpse into the struggles of a man trying to become aware of his own role in perpetuating society's expectations for women.

The statement "the personal is political" has been a prominent theme of the women's movement. It states that the issues we deal with in our private lives—who cares for the children, how we negotiate housework, who should make career sacrifices, and who should miss out on the experience of parenting—may not at first look like subjects for public discussion. But these issues are not unique to individual relationships; instead, they reflect inadequacies in social organization and larger cultural assumptions about gender and work, value, power. These issues, moreover, are becoming more pronounced as growing numbers of women pursue full-time careers, yet find that they are expected to fulfill around-the-clock roles as mothers and housekeepers as well. We invite you to add your own opinions to this important discussion of the "hidden industry," the workplace inside the home.

WHY MEN DON'T REAR CHILDREN
A Power Analysis

M. RIVKA POLATNICK

Margaret Rivka Polatnick is a sociologist who has re-
searched the connections between gender and power
and gender and privilege. This essay is a shorter version of an article that first appeared in 1973 in the
Berkeley Journal of Sociology. In it Polatnick argues that
power differences between men and women are maintained by the allocation of child-rearing responsibilities to women. These responsibilities exact a cost in
women's careers in terms of training, salary, and promotion.

The starting point for this essay is a simple fact of contemporary social life: 1
in our society (as in most societies familiar to us), women rather than men
have the primary responsibility for rearing children. Of course, fathers are
not devoid of obligations vis-à-vis their offspring, but the father who accepts
the routine day-to-day responsibility for supervising his children and servicing
their needs, at the expense of outside employment and activity,* is a rare bird
indeed.

In examining why this is so, I plan to steer clear of two potential pitfalls.   2
First, I will make no attempt to unravel historical causes in pursuit of a
primeval "first cause." Anthropological evidence about the origin of male and
female behaviors is inconclusive and sheds little light on the contemporary
situation, where the conditions of life are substantially different. This essay
will deal only with current reasons why men don't rear children. Second, I
have no intention of discussing individuals and their personal motivations. I
treat men as a gender and women as a gender, and my conclusions will be
generalizations about groups and group relations.

The choice of who rears a society's children and the implications of that   3
choice for the whole social structure seem to me extremely fruitful subjects

---

* Let this suffice as my definition of childrearing responsibility, with the qualification that outside
employment and activity are possible if children spend part of the day with babysitters, at day-
care centers, in school, or alone.

for sociological examination. Yet social scientists have shown little inclination to consider the allocation of childrearing responsibility as a matter of social choice. Instead they have been surprisingly willing to lay things at nature's door and ask no more: men don't rear children because women are the natural rearers of children.

For social scientists to rest so content with biological determinist expla- 4 nations is at best intellectually unproductive, and at worst politically suspect. Elsewhere I have discussed in detail how the use (primarily misuse) of "nature" arguments has obscured the sociological understanding of childrearing as a social job.[1] My own explanation for why men don't rear children rests upon a basic premise about male/female relations: in our society (as in most societies familiar to us), men as a gender enjoy a superior power position in relation to women as a gender. That is, they are in control of the major sources of societal power (political, economic, social, physical),[2] and their superordinate position and the subordinate position of women are buttressed by an ideology of male supremacy and female inferiority.* It is not my purpose here to "prove" the existence of an overall power inequality between the sexes; by now there is a sufficient corpus of Women's Liberation literature that documents painstakingly the subordinate status of women in the various spheres of societal life.[3] I am interested instead in demonstrating how the assignment of childrearing responsibility to women articulates with a general pattern of male domination of our society. My analysis will illuminate and illustrate certain aspects of the gender power dynamic, but those unhappy with the basic premise will simply have to suspend misgivings and come along for the ride.

If, as I will argue, the current allocation of childrearing responsibility to 5 women must be understood in the context of their subordinate position in society, then two different causal relationships suggest themselves:

1. Because women are the rearers of children, they are a powerless group vis-à-vis men.
2. Because women are a powerless group vis-à-vis men, they are the rearers of children.

The first proposal is of course wholly compatible with a biological determinist position. If those who regard females as the biologically designated rearers of children had at least examined the implications of this "fact" for the overall societal status of women, I would already have an important ingredient of my

---

* Modern democratic ideology requires that groups be defined as "different" rather than unequal, but the essence of a power relationship shines clearly through most of the basic decrees about male and female natures: women are soft, weak, passive, helpless, compliant, in need of care and protection; men are strong, active, assertive, commanding, suited for leadership and managerial roles.

"power analysis." Unfortunately, biological determinists have been largely associated with the "different but equal," "complementary," "separate spheres" school of thought about male/female relations, in which power is a foreign concept.

Women's responsibility for childrearing certainly contributes to their societal powerlessness, but this is only one component of the total "power picture." It will be my contention in the rest of this paper that the second causal relationship is operative as well. Thus, the causal model that will inform my discussion can be represented best by a feedback arrangement: 6

Women are a powerless group vis-à-vis men.

Women are the rearers of children.

My task will be to explain, elaborate, and justify this "power analysis."

Two final cautionary comments are in order. First, the subordinate position of women is rooted in multiple causes and is reinforced by many different institutions and practices. The causal model above is by no means intended as a complete statement about women's powerlessness; many other variables besides childrearing responsibility would have to be included in the picture. Freeing women from childrearing duties would not in and of itself eliminate the power differential between the sexes. For example, if domestic responsibilities didn't bar women from most influential jobs, discrimination in education, training, hiring, and promotion would. When I isolate the effects of any one variable upon the position of women, keep in mind that many other variables are left behind. 7

Second, I will be unable to do justice here to the complexities of social class. The gender dynamic of male superordination/female subordination operates across the entire range of socioeconomic status, but different realities and norms in each socioeconomic group produce variations in the basic pattern. Some of my specific statements, and some of the quotations I use, will be slanted toward middle-class realities; nevertheless, the essentials of my argument apply equally well to all social classes. 8

Social Advantage: The Power Analysis

Having elsewhere addressed and dispensed with the argument that men don't rear children because of "biology," I can now present and defend the central thesis of this essay: men (as a group) don't rear children because they don't *want* to rear children. (This implies, of course, that they are in a position to enforce their preferences.) It is to men's advantage that women are assigned childrearing responsibility, and it is in men's interest to keep things that way. 9

I should emphasize at once that I have no intention of measuring the $\quad$ 10 "inherent worth" of childrearing as compared to other pursuits. On some "absolute" scale of values, childrearing would probably rank higher than many a work-world job. But my topic is not "the good life," it is power advantages. Thus my view of childrearing must be unabashedly pragmatic: will it get you ahead in the world? Does it even get you power in the family?

I will discuss the undesirability of the childrearing job under two general $\quad$ 11 categories: (a) the advantages of avoiding childrearing responsibility (which are, primarily, the advantages of breadwinning responsibility), and (b) the disadvantages attached to childrearing responsibility.

Breadwinning Beats Childrearing

Full-time childrearing responsibility limits one's capacity to engage in most $\quad$ 12 other activities. However, the most important thing, in power terms that childrearers can't do is to be the family breadwinner.[4] This is the job that men prefer as their primary family responsibility. It offers important power advantages over the home-based childrearing job.

Money, Status, Power

First, and of signal importance, breadwinners earn money. "Money is a source $\quad$ 13 of power that supports male dominance in the family. . . . Money belongs to him who earns it, not to her who spends it, since he who earns it may withhold it."[5]

Second, occupational achievement is probably the major source of social $\quad$ 14 status in American society.

> In a certain sense the fundamental basis of the family's status is the occupa-
> tional status of the husband and father. [The wife/mother] is excluded from
> the struggle for power and prestige in the occupational sphere [while the
> man's breadwinner role] carries with it . . . the primary prestige of achieve-
> ment, responsibility, and authority.[6]

Even if one's occupation ranks very low in prestige and power, other $\quad$ 15 tangible and intangible benefits accrue to wage earners, such as organizational experience, social contacts, "knowledge of the world," and feelings of independence and competence. Moreover, the resources that breadwinners garner in the outside world do not remain on the front porch; breadwinning power translates significantly into power within the family. This is in direct contradiction to the notion of "separate spheres": the man reigning supreme in extrafamilial affairs, the woman running the home-front show. (I'll return to this theme later.)

The correlation between earning power and family power has been sub-   16
stantiated concretely in a number of studies of family decision-making.[7] These·
studies show that the more a man earns, the more family power he wields;
and the greater the discrepancy between the status of the husband's and wife's
work, the greater the husband's power. When the wife works too, there is a ·
shift toward a more egalitarian balance of power and more sharing of household burdens.*

Lois Hoffman has proposed four explanations for the increased family   17
power of working wives, which convey again some of the power resources
connected with breadwinning:

1. [Women who work have more control over money] and this control can
    be used, implicitly or explicitly, to wield power in the family.
2. Society attaches greater value to the role of wage earner than to that of
    housewife and thus legitimizes for both parents the notion that the former
    should have more power.
3. An independent supply of money enables the working woman to exert
    her influence to a greater extent because she is less dependent on her
    husband and could, if necessary, support herself in the event of the dis-
    solution of the marriage.
4. Working outside the home provides more social interaction than being a
    housewife. This interaction has been seen as leading to an increase in the
    wife's power because of: (a) the development of social skills which are
    useful in influencing her husband; (b) the development of self-confidence;
    (c) the greater knowledge of alternative situations that exist in other
    families; and (d) the more frequent interaction with men, which may
    result in the feeling that remarriage is feasible.[8]

Not only does the woman's working modify the power relation between   18
husband and wife, it also affects the gender power distribution in the whole
family: when the mother works, daughters are likely to become more independent, and sons more dependent and obedient.[9]

Power Structure of the "Normal" Family

It is worth noting, in this connection, how sociological definitions of the   19
"normal" family situation and "normal" personality development for sons and
daughters sanction the status quo of male power and female powerlessness.
Healthy families are those that produce strong, independent *sons*, ready to
take on strong, independent "masculine roles." (Strong, independent daugh-

---

* This should not imply, however, that women who earn more than their husbands necessarily
have superior power, since the subordinate position of women stems from multiple causes.

ters are not a goal; they're a symptom of deviance.) For the proper "masculine" upbringing, boys must have "male role models." What little importance academics have attached to fathers' playing a greater role in childrearing has been largely motivated by this concern. Lest they develop "nurturant" personalities, boys, brought up by "nurturant" mothers, should have strong male role models close at hand, but not too actively involved in childrearing, for "a child whose father performs the mothering functions both tangibly and emotionally while the mother is preoccupied with her career can easily gain a distorted image of masculinity and femininity."[10]

Precisely.

20

Men Want to be the Breadwinners

Men have good reason, then, to try to monopolize the job of principal family breadwinner (much as they may appreciate a second income). Husbands' objections to wives working "stem from feelings that their dominance is undermined when they are not the sole or primary breadwinners."[11] There is also

21

> the feeling of being threatened by women in industry, who are seen as limiting opportunities for men, diminishing the prestige of jobs formerly held only by men, and casting a cold eye on masculine pretentions to vocational superiority.[12]

These feelings are quite justified; as Benson so neatly understates it, "The male fear of competition from women is not based solely on myth."[13]

Where outright forbidding of the wife to work is no longer effective, the continued allocation of childrearing responsibility to women accomplishes the same end: assuring male domination of the occupational world. Should all other barriers to economic power for women suddenly vanish, childrearing responsibility would still handicap them hopelessly in economic competition with men.

22

Of course, children are not just a handy excuse to keep women out of the job market. Most people—male and female—want to have them, and somebody has to rear them. Men naturally prefer that women do it, so that having children need not interfere with their own occupational pursuits.

23

> Since housewife and mother roles are preferred for women, it is considered distasteful and perhaps dangerous to upgrade their occupational status. Apparently there is a fear of mass defections from maternal responsibility. Perhaps there is also a hidden suspicion that the woman's employment is symptomatic of a subversive attitude toward motherhood.[14]

Both these motives, therefore—the desire to limit females' occupational activities, and the desire to have children without limiting their own occu-

24

pational activities—contribute to a male interest in defining childrearing as exclusively woman's domain. Thus,

> there has been consistent social effort as a norm with the woman whose vocational proclivities are completely and "naturally" satisfied by childbearing and childrearing, with the related domestic activities.[15]

One of the controls operating to restrict women's breadwinning activities [25] is the social pressure against mothers who "neglect their children." Where financial need compels mothers with young children to work, their absence from the home is accepted as a "necessary evil." (Welfare departments, however, will generally support mothers of young children without pressuring them to seek work.) In the middle classes, sentiments about male/female responsibility are less obscured by immediate economic considerations:

> Some public disapproval is still directed toward the working mother of young children and the mother who devotes her primary attention to a career; the feeling persists that a mother who creates a full life for herself outside the home may be cheating her children, if not her husband.[16]

Fathers, on the other hand, have public license (in fact, a veritable public [26] duty) to devote primary attention to job or career. Sandra and Daryl Bem have illustrated the existent "double standard" of parental responsibility with the example of a middle-class father who loses his wife:

> No matter how much he loved his children, no one would expect him to sacrifice his career in order to stay home with them on a full-time basis—even if he had an independent source of income. No one would charge him with selfishness or lack of parental feeling if he sought professional care for his children during the day.[17]

Men Want Women to be the Childrearers

By propagating the belief that women are the ones who really desire children, [27] men can then invoke a "principle of least interest": that is, because women are "most interested" in children, they must make most of the accommodations and sacrifices required to rear them. Benson says that "fatherhood . . . is less important to men than motherhood is to women, in spite of the fact that maternity causes severe limitations on women's activities."[18] My own version would be that fatherhood is less important to men than motherhood is to women *because* childrearing causes severe limitations on the childrearer's activities.

In a discussion of barriers to careers for women, Alice Rossi cites some [28] very revealing findings about which sex advocates a more rigid standard of "mothering responsibility."

On an item reading "Even if a woman has the ability and interest, she should not choose a career field that will be difficult to combine with childrearing," half of the women but two-thirds of the men agreed. Again, although half the women thought it appropriate for a woman to take a part-time job if a child was a preschooler, only one-third of the men approved. A quarter of the men, but only 14% of the women, thought a full-time job should not be taken until the children were "all grown up."[19]

Women too imbibe the ideology of motherhood, but men seem to be its strongest supporters. By insuring that the weight of childrearing responsibility falls on women's shoulders, they win for themselves the right of "paternal neglect." As Benson observes, "The man can throw himself into his work and still fulfill male obligations at home, mainly because the latter are minimal. [Men have] the luxury of more familial disengagement than women."[20]

Of course, men as family breadwinners must shoulder the *financial* burden involved in raising children: they may have to work harder, longer hours, and at jobs they dislike. But even factory workers enjoy set hours, scheduled breaks, vacation days, sick leave, and other union benefits. To the extent that men *can* select work suited to their interests, abilities, and ambitions, they are in a better position than women arbitrarily assigned to childrearing. And to the extent that breadwinning gains one the resources discussed earlier (money, status, family power, etc.), financial responsibility is clearly preferable, in power terms, to "mothering" responsibility.

Childrearing Responsibility Handicaps Women

From the perspective of women—the more affluent women faced with "mother/career conflict," the poorer women faced with "mother/any job at all conflict"—men possess the enviable option to "have their cake and eat it too," that is, to have children without sacrificing their activities outside the home. A woman knows that becoming a parent will adversely affect her occupational prospects. "For a period, at least, parenthood means that . . . whatever vocational or professional skills she may possess may become atrophied.[21] During this period of retirement the woman

> becomes isolated and almost totally socially, economically, and emotionally dependent upon her husband. . . . She loses her position, cannot keep up with developments in her field, does not build up seniority. . . . If she returns to work, and most women do, she must begin again at a low-status job and she stays there—underemployed and underpaid.[22]

Not only during the period of childrearing do women become economically or professionally disadvantaged vis-à-vis men; most women's lives have already been constructed in anticipation of that period. "Helpful advice" from family, friends, and guidance counselors, and discriminatory practices in the schools and in the job market steer women toward jobs and interests compatible with a future in childrearing.

With the assistance of relatives, babysitters, or the few day-care centers that exist, women can hold certain kinds of jobs while they're raising children (often part-time, generally low-status). Women without husbands, women with pressing financial needs, women who can afford hired help, may work fulltime despite the demands of "mothering."[23] But to an important extent, occupational achievement and childrearing responsibility are mutually exclusive. A 40-hour work-week permits more family involvement than did a 72-hour work-week, but it's still difficult to combine with primary responsibility for children (given the lack of institutional assistance). Furthermore, the higher-status professional jobs frequently demand a work week commitment closer to the 72-hour figure. Men can hold these jobs and also father families only because they can count on a "helpmeet" to take care of children and home. Thus it is said that the wages of a man buy the labor of two people. Without this back-up team of wife/mothers, something would have to give.

Alice Rossi has suggested that the period of women's lives spent at home rearing children is potentially the peak period for professional accomplishment:

> If we judge from the dozens of researches Harvey Lehman has conducted on the relationship between age and achievement, . . . the most creative work women and men have done in science was completed during the very years contemporary women are urged to remain at home rearing their families. . . . Older women who return to the labor force are an important reservoir for assistants and technicians and the less demanding professions, but only rarely for creative and original contributors to the more demanding professional fields.[24]

The woman who tries to work at home while raising children finds that this is not too practicable a solution. Writer/critic Marya Mannes noted with regard to her own profession: "The creative woman has no wife to protect her from intrusion. A man at his desk in a room with closed door is a man at work. A woman at a desk in any room is available."[25]

Maintaining the Status Quo

If working hours and career patterns were more flexible, if childcare centers were more widely available, and if "retired mothers" reentering the workforce received special preference rather than unfavorable treatment,* childrearing

---

* Consider how the reentry of veterans into the workforce is eased by special benefits and preferential treatment.

would exact a less heavy toll on women's occupational achievement. Because men benefit from the status quo, they ignore, discourage, or actively resist such reform proposals. Alternative arrangements for rearing children, for balancing work commitment with family commitment, are not pressing concerns for men; the structural relegation of women to domestic service suits their interests very well.

Women's responsibility for children in the context of the nuclear family is an important buttress for a male-dominated society. It helps keep women out of the running for economic and political power. As Talcott Parsons states:

37

> It is, of course, possible for the adult woman to follow the masculine pattern and seek a career in fields of occupational achievement in direct competition with men of her own class. It is, however, notable that in spite of the very great progress of the emancipation of women from the traditional domestic pattern only a very small fraction have gone very far in this direction.* It is also clear that its generalization would only be possible with profound alterations in the structure of the family.[26]

I have chosen to focus upon breadwinning (economic activity) as the most important thing, from a power perspective, that childrearers can't do. Moreover, other activities—educational, political, cultural, social, recreational—suffer when one's life becomes centered around children and home.** The "on call" nature of "mothering" responsibility militates against any kind of sustained, serious commitment to other endeavors. A full-time mother loses

38

> the growth of competence and resources in the outside world, the community positions which contribute to power in the marriage. The boundaries of her world contract, the possibilities of growth diminish.[27]

While women are occupied with domestic duties, men consolidate their resources in the outside world and their position of command in the family. By the time most women complete their childrearing tenure, they can no longer recoup their power losses.

39

Childrearing: Not an Equal Sphere

By my explicit and implicit comparisons of breadwinning with childrearing, I have already asserted that the former is the more desirable "sphere" of action. Now I will discuss more directly the disadvantages of the childrearing job.

40

---

* One might well inquire what this "very great progress" is, if "only a small fraction" of women are actually involved.

** Here again, there's been little effort, for the sake of *female* childrearers, to develop more flexible programs of higher education and professional training.

Money, Status, Power

Once again, let's begin with the simple but significant matter of money. Money is a prime source of power in American society, and tending one's own children on a full-time basis is not a salaried activity.

> In sheer quantity, household labor, including child care, constitutes a huge amount of socially necessary production. Nevertheless, in a society based on commodity production, it is not usually considered "real work" since it is outside of trade and the market place. . . . In a society in which money determines value, women are a group who work outside the money economy. Their work is not worth money, is therefore valueless, is therefore not even real work. And women themselves, who do this valueless work, can hardly be expected to be worth as much as men, who work for money.[28]

Performing well at the job of childrearer may be a source of feminine credentials, but it is not a source of social power or status. Of all the possible adult roles for females, "the pattern of domesticity must be ranked lowest in terms of prestige," although "it offers perhaps the highest level of a certain kind of security."[29] When a woman bears and raises children, therefore, she is fulfilling social expectations and avoiding negative sanctions, but she "is not esteemed, in the culture or in the small society of her family, in proportion to her exercise of her 'glory,' childbearing."[30]

The rewards for rearing children are not as tangible as a raise or a promotion, and ready censure awaits any evidence of failure: "if the child goes wrong, mother is usually blamed."[31] Thus the male preference for the breadwinner role may reflect (among other things) an awareness that "it's easier to make money than it is to be a good father. . . . The family is a risky proposition in terms of rewards and self-enhancement."[32]

Family Power

If childrearers don't accumulate power resources in the outside world, do they at least win some advantage in the family balance of power? I have already cited the evidence that family power is directly related to earning power. It is not surprising that researchers have also found that the wife's power declines with the arrival of children; an inverse relationship exists between number of children and the wife's power vis-à-vis her husband.[33]

Two major theories of conjugal power suggest explanations for this effect. Blood and Wolfe's "resource theory" posits that "power will accrue to the spouse who has the more imposing or relevant resources, and thus has the greater contribution to make to the family."[34] If one considers occupational status and income as the most imposing of resources, then this explanation is little different from the "earning power equals family power" thesis. Yet Blood and Wolfe don't illuminate why breadwinning should be a "greater contribution" to the family than childbearing.

David Heer's "exchange value theory" postulates that "the spouse who could most likely marry another person who would be as desirable as or much more desirable than his (her) present spouse"[35] enjoys the superior power position. When a woman has children and becomes a full-time childrearer, she grows more dependent on her husband, her opportunities to meet men decrease, and her prospects for remarriage decline. The husband thus possesses the more promising alternatives outside the marriage, and his power increases.

The woman's power is at its lowest point during the preschool period, when childrearing responsibilities are most consuming.

> When her children start school, the mother can be more autonomous and exercise more power because she is better able to handle outside employment; the children can now take care of themselves in many ways and are supervised to a greater extent by the school and other community agencies.[36]

Childrearing: Not a Separate Sphere

Despite the empirical evidence that women lose family power when they become mothers, one is still tempted to believe that by leaving childrearing to women, men have surrendered a significant area of control. This belief is based on the erroneous notion that women preside over childrearing as a separate sovereign domain. On the contrary, men's authority as family provider/family "head" carries right over into childrearing matters. Men may have surrendered the regular responsibility and routine decision-making, but they retain power where important decisions are concerned (including what the routine will be).

> In a sample of adolescents studied by Charles Bowerman and Glen Elder (1964), the father was reported to be the dominant parent in childrearing matters as often as the mother, in spite of the fact that mother does most of the actual work; apparently she often finds herself responsible for doing the menial chores without having the stronger voice in "childrearing policy."[37]

Constantina Safilios-Rothschild found that American men delegate to their wives many of the minor decisions related to rearing children and running a home—"those decisions, the enactment of which involves time-consuming tasks." This suggests to her that

> American husbands do not wish to take on "bothersome" decisions which are not crucial . . . and take too much of the time and energy that they prefer to dedicate to their work or leisure-time activities.[38]

Fathers may default from the daily childrearing routines but, much like male principals supervising female teachers, they still tend to wield the ultimate force and the ultimate decision-making power. Consider these statements of Benson's on the nature of paternal authority:

> The father as threatener is superimposed upon the mother's more basic pattern and is therefore more likely to appear as a terrorizing intruder, but one who speaks as authority and therefore ought to be obeyed. [page 14] . . . Family members can forsee his judgments and are constrained to act correctly according to their conception of his wishes. [page 18] . . . Even the social pattern that mother establishes is typically legitimized by the larger, more insistent parent lurking in the background. . . . Father is the embodiment of a basic form of social control: coercive power. . . . Father is an agent of both internal and external control, and the child responds to him in terms of both his respect for the man and his respect for the man's power. [pages 50–52] . . . But when order breaks down or is openly challenged the need for a new approach assumes an immediate, deliberative significance, and father is customarily expected to help meet the crisis. In fact, it is common for him to take charge. [page 59][39]

Taking care of children, therefore, does not provide women with any real power base. Men can afford to leave childrearing *responsibility* to women because, given their superior power resources, they are still assured of substantial childrearing *authority*. 51

The Nature of the Job

Childrearing, I have argued, is not a source of money, status, power in the society, or power in the family. The childrearing job is disadvantageous in terms of these major assets, but there are also drawbacks inherent in the nature of the work itself. The rearing of children "involves long years of exacting labor and self-sacrifice," but 52

> the drudgery, the monotonous labor, and other disagreeable features of childrearing are minimized by "the social guardians." On the other hand, the joys and compensations of motherhood are magnified and presented to consciousness on every hand. Thus the tendency is to create an illusion whereby motherhood will appear to consist of compensations only, and thus come to be desired by those for whom the illusion is intended.[40]

The responsibilities of a childrearer/homemaker are not confined to a 40-hour work-week. Margaret Benston estimates that for a married woman with small children (excluding the very rich), "the irreducible minimum of work . . . is probably 70 or 80 hours a week."[41] In addition to the actual hours of work, there is the constant strain of being "on call." Thus, another consideration in why the husband's power is greatest when the children are young "may be the well-described chronic fatigue which affects young mothers with preschoolers."[42] 53

Furthermore, women are adults (assertions that they have "childlike" natures notwithstanding), and they need adequate adult company to stimulate their mental faculties.

> A lot of women become disheartened because babies and children are not only not interesting to talk to (not everyone thrills at the wonders of da-da-ma-ma- talk) but they are generally not empathic, considerate people.[43]

Although interaction with young children is certainly rewarding in many ways, childrearers can lose touch with the world outside their domestic circle. In addition, American society segregates the worlds of childhood and adulthood; adults who keep close company with children are *déclassé*.

Since the "less-than-idyllic childrearing part of motherhood remains 'in small print,'"[44] new mothers are often in for some rude shocks. Betty Rollin quotes some mothers interviewed in an Ann Arbor, Michigan, study:

> Suddenly I had to devote myself to the child totally. I was under the illusion that the baby was going to fit into my life, and I found that I had to switch my life and my schedule to fit *him*.
>
> You never get away from the responsibility. Even when you leave the child with a sitter, you are not out from under the pressure of the responsibility.
>
> I hate ironing their pants and doing their underwear, and they never put their clothes in the laundry basket. . . . Best moment of the day is when all the children are in bed. . . . The worst time of day is 4 p.m., when you have to get dinner started, and the kids are tired, hungry, and crabby—everybody wants to talk to you about *their* day. . . . Your day is only half over.
>
> Once a mother, the responsibility and concern for my children became so encompassing. . . . It took a great deal of will to keep up other parts of my personality.
>
> I had anticipated that the baby would sleep and eat, sleep and eat. Instead, the experience was overwhelming. I really had not thought particularly about what motherhood would mean in a realistic sense. I want to do *other* things, like to become involved in things that are worthwhile—I don't mean women's clubs—but I don't have the physical energy to go out in the evenings. I feel like I'm missing something. . . . the experience of being somewhere with people and having them talking about something—something that's going on in the world.[45]

Avoiding the Job

When women are wealthy enough to afford it, they often hire nurses and governesses to relieve them of the more burdensome aspects of childcare. They can then enjoy the children's company when they want to, be active mothers when it suits them, but avoid the constant responsibility and the more unpleasant parts of the job (diapers, tantrums, etc.). The relationship between rich mother and governess resembles in significant respects the relationship between average father and average mother. The father "hires" the mother (by providing her with support), in the expectation that she will relieve him of the major burdens of childrearing. (However, even a rich mother is expected to pay a lot more personal attention to her children than any father is.)

From the perspective of an ambitious person, taking full-time care of your own children is rather like baking your own bread: it might be nice if one had the time, but there are more important things to be done. Thus you pay for the service of having someone else do it, increasing your financial burden but freeing yourself of a time-consuming task. 57

Fathers, with full social support, can buy a significant degree of freedom from direct family responsibility. They have a category of people at hand—women—constrained by social forces to accept that responsibility. Women have no such convenient group to whom they can pass the childrearing buck. For mothers, the price of escape from childrearing—financial, social, psychological—is usually too high. 58

"Motherly Selflessness"

A final relevant feature of the childrearing job itself is that mothers are obliged to subordinate their personal objectives and practice "selflessness"—putting the needs of others first, devoting themselves to the day-to-day well-being of other family members, loving and giving "unconditionally."* Such domestic service may be deemed virtuous, but it isn't a path to power and success. Males primed for competitive achievement show no eagerness to suppress their personal ambitions and sacrifice their own interests to attend to others' immediate wants. 59

Furthermore, men desire from women the same services and support, the same ministration to everyday needs, that mothers are supposed to provide for children. ("I want a wife to keep track of the children's doctor and dentist appointments. And to keep track of mine too. . . . a wife who will pick up after my children, a wife who will pick up after me.")[46] "Mothering" behavior is not very different from "feminine" behavior. By grooming females for "nurturance," men provide a selfless rearer for their children and an accommodating marriage partner for themselves. 60

Several movies and television serials have been constructed around the situation of a father/widower with a son or two, all in need of a "nurturant" woman to take care of them. The fact that children and fathers "compete" 61

---

* Erich Fromm, in *The Art of Loving*, waxes eloquent about mothers' "unconditional" love.

for similar services from the mother may explain why the Oedipus Complex is more pronounced than the Electra Complex (if these concepts still have any credibility).[47]

Margaret Adams has discussed the negative effects of this obligatory "selflessness" upon women. 62

> Both family and professional commitments incorporate the insidious notion that the needs of others should be woman's major, if not exclusive, concern. Implicit in the role that derives from this notion is the supposed virtue of subordinating individual needs to the welfare of others and the personal value and supposed reward of vicarious satisfaction from this exercise. . . . Women must abandon the role of the compassionate sibyl who is at everyone's beck and call, because being permanently available to help others keeps women from pursuing their own chosen avocations with the concentration that is essential for their successful completion.[48]

Men have a stake in ensuring that women remain unable to "abandon the role of the compassionate sibyl." They derive double benefit—as husbands wanting wifely services, as fathers wanting childrearing services—from the "emotional indenture" of women.[49] 63

More Evidence That Men Don't Want the Job

Despite all the disadvantages of childrearing responsibility, men often protest that they'd love to be able to stay home with the kids. Nonetheless, two additional sources of evidence indicate that men don't really find the job desirable. 64

The first relates to the widely noted phenomenon that boys who behave like girls draw stronger negative reactions than girls who behave like boys. A "sissy" playing with dolls elicits unmixed scorn, while an adventurous "tomboy" (as long as she's not too old) gets a certain amount of approval. In overall social estimation, female activities and traits are not as worthy or desirable as those of males. "The fact that . . . both sexes tend to value men and male characteristics, values, and activities more highly than those of women has been noted by many authorities.[50] 65

All this suggests the essential hypocrisy of men who laud female achievements as "different but equal," or who claim they'd gladly switch. Studies have consistently shown that far fewer men than women wish they had been born the opposite sex. The work of women, including most prominently the "nurturing" of children, is socially devalued, and a minuscule number of men have actually taken it on. 66

The second source of evidence relevant here is the attitude of men toward working with children as a salaried job. The overwhelming majority of people in occupations involving close interaction with children (elementary school 67 teachers, day-care and nursery school personnel, child welfare workers, etc.) are women.* Judging by the statistics, men have not chosen working with children as suitable employment for their sex.

However, men are willing to enter such "female" fields as children's education at the upper echelons. In 1968, 78 percent of elementary school *principals* were men.[51] Men dominate the top of the profession of child study[52] and dispense highly professional advice on childrearing to the actual rearers of children (for example, Dr. Spock). 68

Thus, working with children might not be such an unattractive prospect for males if the rewards (money, status, power) could be made commensurate with their expectations. In fact, there seems to be a current trend toward increased male participation in elementary education. This development is probably the result of several causes: a tight job market; a new concern that men be present in schools as "male role models";[53] and a general societal shift toward evaluating early childhood as a crucial learning period, and early education as a more important business. If the last factor is the predominant one, it's possible that the occupation of elementary school teacher could undergo a sex change, with the improvements in salary, benefits, job conditions, etc., that result when males move into female occupations. But even with a radical change in the status of salaried work with children, it is doubtful that unsalaried rearing of children will ever attract many males. 69

Conclusion

The allocation of childrearing responsibility to women, I have argued, is no sacred fiat of nature, but a social policy which supports male domination in the society and in the family. 70

Whatever the "intrinsic desirability" of rearing children, the conditions of the job as it's now constituted—no salary, low status, long hours, domestic isolation—mark it as a job for women only. Men, as the superordinate group, don't want childrearing responsibility, so they assign it to women. Women's functioning as childrearers reinforces, in turn, their subordinate position. Thus we come back again to the causal model of my Introduction— 71

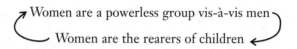

Women are a powerless group vis-à-vis men
Women are the rearers of children

—a vicious circle that keeps male power intact.

---

* The closer children approach to adulthood, the higher the percentage of males teaching them.

Notes

Much appreciation for the bloodcurdling critiques of Judie "Tenspeed" Gaffin, "Diesel" Dair Gillespie, Carol "Boss" Hatch, Ann "The Man" Leffler, Elinor "Bulldog" Lerner, Maria "Muscle" Mendes, and "Stompin" Stacey Oliker; much indebtedness to the Women's Movement in general.

1. See the original, longer version of this essay in *Berkeley Journal of Sociology* 18 (1973–74): 45–86.

2. "The general definition of 'power' is 'a capacity to get things done.' Either resources (rights in things) or authority (rights in persons) increases the ability of a person to do what he decides to do." (Arthur Stinchcombe, *Constructing Social Theories* [New York: Harcourt, Brace, & World, 1968], p. 157).

3. See, for example, Caroline Bird, *Born Female: The High Cost of Keeping Women Down* (New York: David McKay, 1968); Cynthia Fuchs Epstein, *Women's Place: Options and Limits in Professional Careers* (Berkeley: University of California Press, 1971); Kirsten Amundsen, *The Silenced Majority* (Englewood Cliffs, N.J.: Prentice-Hall, 1977); and Simone de Beauvoir, *The Second Sex* (New York: Alfred A. Knopf, 1952).

4. Many women work during some of the childrearing years, but if they have husbands, they are very rarely the principal breadwinner. In 1978, working wives contributed about 26% to family income (U.S. Dept. of Labor, *Monthly Labor Review*, April 1980, p. 48).

5. Reuben Hill and Howard Becker, eds., *Family, Marriage, and Parenthood* (Boston: D.C. Heath, 1955), p. 790.

6. Talcott Parsons, "Age and Sex in the Social Structure" in *The Family: Its Structure and Functions*, edited by Rose Laub Coser (New York: St. Martin's Press, 1964), pp. 258, 261–62.

7. For a full report, see Leonard Benson, *Fatherhood: A Sociological Perspective* (New York: Random House, 1968).

8. Lois Wladis Hoffman, "Effects of the Employment of Mothers on Parental Power Relations and the Division of Household Tasks," *Marriage and Family Living* 22 (February 1960): 33.

9. Benson, *Fatherhood*, pp. 302–3.

10. Norman W. Bell and Ezra F. Vogel, eds., *A Modern Introduction to the Family*, rev. ed. (New York: The Free Press, 1968).

11. Phyllis Hallenbeck, "An Analysis of Power Dynamics in Marriage," *Journal of Marriage and the Family* 28 (May 1966): 201.

12. Helen Mayer Hacker, "The New Burdens of Masculinity," *Marriage and Family Living* 19 (August 1957): 232.

13. Benson, *Fatherhood*, p. 293.

14. Ibid.

15. Leta S. Hollingworth, "Social Devices for Impelling Women to Bear and Rear Children," *The American Journal of Sociology* 22 (July 1916): 20.

16. Benson, *Fatherhood*, p. 292.

17. Sandra L. Bem and Daryl J. Bem, "Training the Woman to Know Her Place" in *Roles Women Play*, edited by Michele Hoffnung Garskof (Belmont, Calif.: Wadsworth, 1971), p. 94.

18. Benson, *Fatherhood*, p. 292.

19. Alice S. Rossi, "Barriers to the Career Choice of Engineering, Medicine, or Science Among American Women" in *Women and the Scientific Professions*, edited by Jacquelyn A. Mattfeld and Carol G. Van Aken (Westport, Conn.: Greenwood Press, 1965), p. 87.

20. Benson, *Fatherhood*, pp. 132, 134.

21. Robert F. Winch, *The Modern Family*, rev. ed. (New York: Holt, Rinehart and Winston, 1964), p. 434.

22. Dair L. Gillespie, "Who Has the Power? The Marital Struggle," *Journal of Marriage and the Family* 33 (August 1971): 456.

23. In 1960, 18.6 percent of mothers with children under the age of six were in the labor force in some capacity; 11.4 percent were working 35 hours or more per week. By 1970, the proportion of these mothers in the paid labor force at least part time or looking for paid jobs reached 32 percent, and in March 1979, 45 percent. The percentage actually working full time, year-round, remains low, however (U.S. Department of Labor, *Monthly Labor Review*, April 1980, p. 49). The increase in those working at least part time can probably be explained by the economy's need for more service and clerical workers, families' needs for more income because of recession and inflation, the increase in the percentage of mothers who are single, and the effects of the Women's Liberation Movement. Ongoing research will reveal to what extent men have taken on more childrearing work (U.S. Bureau of the Census, *Statistical Abstract of the U.S.: 1971* [Washington, D.C.: U.S.G.P.O., 1971], Table 332; and *A U.S. Census of Population: 1960, Subject Reports: Families* [Washington, D.C.: U.S.G.P.O., 1963], Final Report PC(2)–44, Table 11).

24. Rossi, "Barriers to the Career Choice," pp. 102–3, 107.

25. Quoted in Betty Rollin, "Motherhood: Who Needs It?" in *Family in Transition*, edited by Arlene S. Skolnick and Jerome H. Skolnick (Boston: Little, Brown, 1971), p. 352.

26. Parsons, "Age and Sex in the Social Structure," pp. 258–59.

27. Gillespie, "Who Has the Power?" p. 456.

28. Margaret Benston, "The Political Economy of Women's Liberation" in Garskof, *Roles Women Play*, p. 196.

29. Parsons, "Age and Sex in the Social Structure," p. 261.

30. Judith Long Laws, "A Feminist Review of Marital Adjustment Literature," *Journal of Marriage and the Family* 33 (August 1971): 493.

31. Benson, *Fatherhood*, p. 12.

32. Myron Brenton, *The American Male* (New York: Coward-McCann, 1966), p. 133.

33. David M. Heer, "The Measurement and Bases of Family Power: An Overview" in *Marriage and Family Living* 25; Robert O. Blood and Donald M. Wolfe, *Husbands and Wives: The Dynamics of Married Living* (New York: The Free Press, 1960); Lois Wladis Hoffman and R. Lippitt, "The Measurement of Family Life Variables" in P. H. Mussen, ed., *Handbook of Research Methods in Child Development* (New York: Wiley and Sons, 1960); and Frederick L. Campbell, "Demographic Factors in Family Organizations" (Ph.D. dissertation, University of Michigan, 1967).

34. Benson, *Fatherhood*, p. 149.

35. Constantina Safilios-Rothschild, "The Study of Family Power Structure: A Review 1960–1969," *Journal of Marriage and the Family* 32 (November 1970): 548.

36. Herr, "The Measurement and Bases of Family Power," quoted in Benson, *Fatherhood*, p. 152.

37. Benson, ibid., p. 157.

38. Constantina Safilios-Rothschild, "Family Sociology or Wives' Family Sociology?" in *Journal of Marriage and the Family* 31 (May 1969): 297.

39. Benson, *Fatherhood*.

40. Holingsworth, "Social Devices," pp. 20–21, 27.

41. Benston, "Political Economy," p. 199.

42. Hallenbeck, "An Analysis of Power Dynamics in Marriage," p. 201.

43. Rollin, "Motherhood," p. 353.

44. Ibid., p. 349.

45. Ibid.

46. Judy Syfers, "Why I Want a Wife," in *Notes From the Third Year* (New York, 1971), p. 13.

47. See Shulamith Firestone, *The Dialectic of Sex* (New York: Bantam, 1970) for an excellent analysis of these complexes in power terms.

48. Margaret Adams, "The Compassion Trap," *Psychology Today* 5 (November 1971): 72, 101. Reprinted in *Women in Sexist Society*, edited by Vivian Gornick and Barbara K. Moran (New York: Basic Books, 1971).

49. Ibid., p. 100.

50. Jo Freeman, "The Social Construction of the Second Sex" in Garskof, *Roles Women Play*, p. 126 (references included).

51. Epstein, *Women's Place*, p. 10.

52. Bird, *Born Female*, p. 102.

53. See Patricia Sexton, *The Feminized Male* (New York: Random House, 1969).

THE POLITICS OF HOUSEWORK

PAT MAINARDI

When Pat Mainardi first wrote this piece for the collection *Sisterhood is Powerful* (1970), she noted that she
owed her insights into masculine culture to her
mother, grandmother, and four aunts. Together, she
maintained, those six women and she put in over 200
years of housework! Their reflections on the job, like
those of other women, are captured in Mainardi's humorous account of a man and a woman negotiating
housework.

Though women do not complain of the power of husbands,
each complains of her own husband, or of the husbands of
her friends. It is the same in all other cases of servitude; at
least in the commencement of the emancipatory movement.
The serfs did not at first complain of the power of the lords,
but only of their tyranny.
(John Stuart Mill, On the Subjection of Women*)*

Liberated women—very different from women's liberation! The first signals   1
all kinds of goodies, to warm the hearts (not to mention other parts) of the
most radical men. The other signals—*housework*. The first brings sex without
marriage, sex before marriage, cozy housekeeping arrangements ("You see,
I'm living with this chick") and the self-content of knowing that you're not
the kind of man who wants a doormat instead of a woman. That will come
later. After all, who wants that old commodity anymore, the Standard American Housewife, all husband, home and kids. The New Commodity, the
Liberated Woman, has sex a lot and has a Career, preferably something that
can be fitted in with the household chores—like dancing, pottery, or painting.

On the other hand is women's liberation—and housework. What? You   2
say this is all trivial? Wonderful! That's what I thought. It seemed perfectly
reasonable. We both had careers, both had to work a couple of days a week
to earn enough to live on, so why shouldn't we share the housework? So I
suggested it to my mate and he agreed—most men are too hip to turn you
down flat. "You're right," he said, "It's only fair."

Then an interesting thing happened. I can only explain it by stating that   3
we women have been brainwashed more than even we can imagine. Probably

too many years of seeing television women in ecstasy over their shiny waxed floors or breaking down over their dirty shirt collars. Men have no such conditioning. They recognize the essential fact of housework right from the very beginning. Which is that it stinks. Here's my list of dirty chores: buying groceries, carting them home and putting them away; cooking meals and washing dishes and pots; doing the laundry, digging out the place when things get out of control; washing floors. The list could go on but the sheer necessities are bad enough. All of us have to do these things, or get some one else to do them for us. The longer my husband contemplated these chores, the more repulsed he became, and so proceeded the change from the normally sweet considerate Dr. Jekyll into the crafty Mr. Hyde who would stop at nothing to avoid the horrors of—*housework*. As he felt himself backed into a corner laden with dirty dishes, brooms, mops, and reeking garbage, his front teeth grew longer and pointier, his fingernails haggled and his eyes grew wild. Housework trivial? Not on your life! Just try to share the burden.

So ensued a dialogue that's been going on for several years. Here are   4
some of the high points:

"I don't mind sharing the housework, but I don't do it very well. We should   5
each do the things we're best at."
Meaning: Unfortunately I'm no good at things like washing dishes or cooking. What I do best is a little light carpentry, changing light bulbs, moving furniture (*how often do you move furniture?*).
Also Meaning: Historically the lower classes (black men and us) have had hundreds of years experience doing menial jobs. It would be a waste of manpower to train someone else to do them now.
Also Meaning: I don't like the dull stupid boring jobs, so you should do them.

"I don't mind sharing the work, but you'll have to show me how to do it."   6
Meaning: I ask a lot of questions and you'll have to show me everything everytime I do it because I don't remember so good. Also don't try to sit down and read while I'm doing my jobs because I'm going to annoy hell out of you until it's easier to do them yourself.

"We used to be so happy!" (Said whenever it was his turn to do something.)   7
Meaning: I used to be so happy.
Meaning: Life without housework is bliss. (*No quarrel here. Perfect agreement.*)

"We have different standards, and why should I have to work to your standards. That's unfair."   8
Meaning: If I begin to get bugged by the dirt and crap I will say "This place sure is a sty" or "How can anyone live like this?" and wait for your reaction. I know that all women have a sore called "Guilt over a messy house" or "Household work is ultimately my responsibility." I know that men have caused that sore—if anyone visits and the place *is* a sty, they're not going to

leave and say, "He sure is a lousy housekeeper." You'll take the rap in any case. I can outwait you.

Also Meaning: I can provoke innumerable scenes over the housework issue. Eventually doing all the housework yourself will be less painful to you than trying to get me to do half. Or I'll suggest we get a maid. She will do my share of the work. You will do yours. It's women's work.

"I've got nothing against sharing the housework, but you can't make me do   9
it on your schedule."

Meaning: Passive resistance. I'll do it when I damned well please, if at all. If my job is doing dishes, it's easier to do them once a week. If taking out laundry, once a month. If washing the floors, once a year. If you don't like it, do it yourself oftener, and then I won't do it at all.

"I *hate* it more than you. You don't mind it so much."   10

Meaning: Housework is garbage work. It's the worst crap I've ever done. It's degrading and humiliating for someone of *my* intelligence to do it. But for someone of *your* intelligence . . .

"Housework is too trivial to even talk about."   11

Meaning: It's even more trivial to do. Housework is beneath my status. My purpose in life is to deal with matters of significance. Yours is to deal with matters of insignificance. You should do the housework.

"This problem of housework is not a man-woman problem! In any relation-   12
ship between two people one is going to have a stronger personality and dominate."

Meaning: That stronger personality had better be *me*.

"In animal societies, wolves, for example, the top animal is usually a male   13
even where he is not chosen for brute strength but on the basis of cunning and intelligence. Isn't that interesting?"

Meaning: I have historical, psychological, anthropological, and biological justification for keeping you down. How can you ask the top wolf to be equal?

"Women's liberation isn't really a political movement."   14

Meaning: The Revolution is coming too close to home.

Also Meaning: I am only interested in how *I* am oppressed, not how I oppress others. Therefore the war, the draft, and the university are political. Women's liberation is not.

"Man's accomplishments have always depended on getting help from other   15
people, mostly women. What great man would have accomplished what he did if he had to do his own housework?

Meaning: Oppression is built into the System and I, as the white American male receive the benefits of this System. I don't want to give them up.

Postscript

Participatory democracy begins at home. If you are planning to implement your politics, there are certain things to remember.

1. He *is* feeling it more than you. He's losing some leisure and you're gaining it. The measure of your oppression is his resistance.

2. A great many American men are not accustomed to doing monotonous repetitive work which never ushers in any lasting let alone important achievement. This is why they would rather repair a cabinet than wash dishes. If human endeavors are like a pyramid with man's highest achievements at the top, then keeping oneself alive is at the bottom. Men have always had servants (us) to take care of this bottom strata of life while they have confined their efforts to the rarefied upper regions. It is thus ironic when they ask of women—where are your great painters, statesmen, etc? Mme. Matisse ran a millinery shop so he could paint. Mrs. Martin Luther King kept his house and raised his babies.

3. It is a traumatizing experience for someone who has always thought of himself as being against any oppression or exploitation of one human being by another to realize that in his daily life he has been accepting and implementing (and benefiting from) this exploitation; that his rationalization is little different from that of the racist who says "Black people don't feel pain" (women don't mind doing the shitwork); and that the oldest form of oppression in history has been the oppression of 50 percent of the population by the other 50 percent.

4. Arm yourself with some knowledge of the psychology of oppressed peoples everywhere, and a few facts about the animal kingdom. I admit playing top wolf or who runs the gorillas is silly but as a last resort men bring it up all the time. Talk about bees. If you feel really hostile bring up the sex life of spiders. They have sex. She bites off his head.

    The psychology of oppressed people is not silly. Jews, immigrants, black men, and all women have employed the same psychological mechanisms to survive: admiring the oppressor, glorifying the oppressor, wanting to be like the oppressor, wanting the oppressor to like them, mostly because the oppressor held all the power.

5. In a sense, all men everywhere are slightly schizoid—divorced from the reality of maintaining life. This makes it easier for them to play games with it. It is almost a cliché that women feel greater grief at sending a son off to war or losing him to that war because they bore him, suckled him, and raised him. The men who foment those wars did none of those

things and have a more superficial estimate of the worth of human life. One hour a day is a low estimate of the amount of time one has to spend "keeping" oneself. By foisting this off on others, man gains seven hours a week—one working day more to play with his mind and not his human needs. Over the course of generations it is easy to see whence evolved the horrifying abstractions of modern life.

6. With the death of each form of oppression, life changes and new forms evolve. English aristocrats at the turn of the century were horrified at the idea of enfranchising working men—were sure that it signaled the death of civilization and a return to barbarism. Some working men were even deceived by this line. Similarly with the minimum wage, abolition of slavery, and female suffrage. Life changes but it goes on. Don't fall for any line about the death of everything if men take a turn at the dishes. They will imply that you are holding back the Revolution (their Revolution). But you are advancing it (your Revolution).

7. Keep checking up. Periodically consider who's actually *doing* the jobs. These things have a way of backsliding so that a year later once again the woman is doing everything. After a year make a list of jobs the man has rarely if ever done. You will find cleaning pots, toilets, refrigerators and ovens high on the list. Use time sheets if necessary. He will accuse you of being petty. He is above that sort of thing—(housework). Bear in mind what the worst jobs are, namely the ones that have to be done every day or several times a day. Also the ones that are dirty—it's more pleasant to pick up books, newspapers, etc. than to wash dishes. Alternate the bad jobs. It's the daily grind that gets you down. Also make sure that you don't have the responsibility for the housework with occasional help from him. "I'll cook dinner for you tonight" implies it's really your job and isn't he a nice guy to do some of it for you.

8. Most men had a rich and rewarding bachelor life during which they did not starve or become encrusted with crud or buried under the litter. There is a taboo that says that women mustn't strain themselves in the presence of men: we haul around 50 pounds of groceries if we have to but aren't allowed to open a jar if there is someone around to do it for us. The reverse side of the coin is that men aren't supposed to be able to take care of themselves without a woman. Both are excuses for making women do the housework.

9. Beware of the double whammy. He won't do the little things he always did because you're now a "Liberated Woman," right? Of course he won't do anything else either . . .

I was just finishing this when my husband came in and asked what I was doing. Writing a paper on housework. Housework? he said, *Housework?* Oh my god how trivial can you get. A paper on housework. . . . 17

CONFESSIONS OF A HOUSEHUSBAND

◑

JOEL ROACHE

Joel Roache is a writer whose book, *Richard Eberhart: The Progress of an American Poet,* was published in 1971. This essay, originally published in *Ms.* magazine in 1972, traces Roache's transformation into a househusband after he and his wife switched work roles. Roache describes his initial decision to stay home, care for the children, and do the housework. His enthusiasm wanes, however, as he learns that the conditions of housework, the interruptions and the constant undoing of work that's been done, can defeat even the best-laid plans.

Many men are coming to realize that sex-role privilege inflicts enormous damage on them, turning half of humanity into their subordinates and the other half into their rivals, isolating them and making fear and loneliness the norm of their existence. That ponderous abstraction became real for me in what many men consider a trivial realm: housework.

Every movement produces its truisms, assumptions that very soon are scarcely open to argument. The Women's Movement is no exception, and one of its truisms is that the home is a prison for women, trapping them in housework and child care, frustrating and distorting their need for fulfillment as whole persons. Whatever reality lies behind many situation comedy stereotypes—the nag, the clinging wife, the telephone gossip—is rooted in this distortion. Only after I had assumed the role of househusband, and was myself caught in the "trap of domesticity," did I realize that the reality behind those stereotypes is a function of the role, not the person.

Two years ago, my wife Jan and I tried to change (at least within our own lives) society's imposed pattern of dependent servant and responsible master by deciding to share equally the responsibility of housework. We made no specific arrangement (a mistake from which I was to learn a great deal); it was simply understood that I was going to take on roughly half of the domestic chores so that she could do the other work she needed to do.

There was something of a shock for me in discovering the sheer quantity of the housework, and my standards of acceptable cleanliness fell rapidly. It became much easier to see my insistence on neatness as an inherited middle-class hang-up now that I had to do so much of the work myself. One of the long-standing sources of tension between Jan and me was almost immediately understood and resolved. What's more, I enjoyed it, at first. When not interrupted by the children I could, on a good day, do the kitchen and a bedroom, a load of laundry, and a meal in a little over two hours. Then I'd clean up after the meal and relax for a while with considerable satisfaction. So I approached the work with some enthusiasm, looking forward to seeing it all put right by my own hand, and for a while I wondered what all the fuss was about.

But within a few weeks that satisfaction and that enthusiasm began to 5 erode a little more each time I woke up or walked into the house, only to find it all needed to be done again. Finally, the image of the finished job, the image that encouraged me to start, was crowded out of my head by the image of the job to do all over again. I became lethargic, with the result that I worked less efficiently, so that even when I did "finish," it took longer and was done less well, rendering still less satisfaction. At first I had intellectual energy to spare, thinking about my teaching while washing dishes; pausing in the middle of a load of laundry to jot down a note. But those pauses soon became passive daydreams, fantasies from which I would have to snap myself back to the grind, until finally it was all I could do to keep going at all. I became more and more irritable and resentful.

Something similar happened even sooner and more dramatically to my 6 relationship with our three children. I soon found myself angry with them most of the time, and I almost never enjoyed them. Then I watched myself for a couple of days and realized what was going on. They were constantly interrupting. I had tried simply to be available to them in case they needed me while I went on reading, writing, cleaning, or watching television. But of course with a six-year-old, a four-year-old, and a one-year-old, someone would need me every five to 15 minutes. Just enough time to get into something, and up Jay would come with a toy to be fixed, or Matthew would spill his juice, or Eric would get stuck between the playpen bars and scream. In everything I tried to do, I was frustrated by their constant demands and soon came, quite simply, to hate them; and to hate myself for hating them; and at some level, I suspect, to hate Jan for getting me into this mess. My home life became a study in frustration and resentment.

I soon reached the conclusion that if I was going to keep house and take 7 care of the children, I might as well give up doing anything else at the same time if I hoped to maintain any equilibrium at all. So I deliberately went through my housekeeping paces in a daze, keeping alert for the children but otherwise concentrating on whatever was before me, closing down all circuits not relevant to the work at hand. I maintained my sanity, I think, and I ceased to scream at the children so much, but neither they nor anyone else got the benefit of any creative energy; there just wasn't any. In half a day I could feel my mind turning into oatmeal, cold oatmeal, and it took the other half to get it bubbling again, and by then it was bedtime, and out of physical exhaustion I would have to go to sleep on whatever coherent ideas I might have got together in my few hours of free time.

Things went on this way for quite some time, partly because I couldn't [8] think of an acceptable alternative, and partly because I was on a kind of guilt trip, possessed by the suicidal notion that somehow I had to pay for all those years Jan was oppressed. After a while I began to "adjust"; even cold oatmeal has a certain resilience. I began to perceive my condition as normal, and I didn't notice that my professional work was at a standstill. Then Jan became involved in community organizing, which took up more and more of her time and began to eat into mine, until finally I found myself doing housekeeping and child care from eight to 16 hours a day, and this went on for about eight weeks. The astonishing thing now is that I let this masochistic work load go on so long. I suppose my guilt trip had become almost equivalent to a woman's normal conditioning, in reducing my ability to resist effectively the demands of Jan's organizing. And the excitement of her newly discovered self-sufficiency and independence (after eight years of her struggle to make me recognize what I was doing to her) functioned in the same way as the normal assumption of the superior importance of a male's work as provider.

I can pinpoint the place in time when we saw the necessity for a more [9] careful adjustment of responsibilities, defining duties and scheduling hours more precisely and adhering to them more faithfully. It was at a moment when it became clear that Jan's work was beginning to pay off and her group scored a definite and apparently unqualified success. I went around the house for a full day feeling very self-satisfied, proud of her achievement, *as if it were my own*, which was fine until I realized, somewhere near the end of the day, that much of that sense of achievement resulted from the fact that I had no achievement of my own. I was getting my sense of fulfillment, of self-esteem, *through her*, while she was getting it *through her work*. It had happened: I was a full-fledged househusband.

A similar moment of illumination occurred at about the same time. Jan [10] had spent the afternoon with a friend while I took care of the children and typed a revision of the bibliography for the book I was trying to finish at the time, the kind of drudgery more prosperous authors underpay some woman to do. By the time Jan got home I was in a state of benumbed introversion, and when she began to talk about the substance of her afternoon's conversation, I was at first bored and finally irritated. Before long I was snapping at her viciously. She sat there looking first puzzled, then bewildered, and finally withdrawn. In a kind of reflexive self-defense she cut me off emotionally and went on thinking about whatever was on her mind. As I began to run down, I realized that what she had been trying to talk about would normally be interesting and important to me, yet I had driven her away. Then I looked at her and suddenly had the really weird sensation of seeing myself, my own isolation and frustration when I used to come home and try to talk to her. I realized that I was in her traditional position and felt a much fuller understanding of what that was. In that moment, on the verge of anger, an important part of what we had been doing to each other for all those years became clearer than it had ever been to either of us.

Another problem was suddenly clear to me also. The loneliness and 11
helplessness I had felt before we traded responsibilities had been a function
of my own privilege. My socially defined and reinforced role as *the* responsible
party to the marriage had cut me off from Jan's experience; had made inevitably futile our attempts to communicate with each other from two very
different worlds. Since she has a strong sense of herself as a responsible adult,
Jan was bound to resist the limits of her role as dependent and (though we
would never have said it) subordinate. When I found myself muttering and
bitching, refusing to listen, refusing to provide any positive feedback on her
experience in the outside world, I realized that her preoccupation, her nagging
and complaining, her virtual absence from my psychic world, had not been
neurotic symptoms but expressions of resistance to my privilege and to the
power over her life that it conferred.

Jan's failure to force a real change in our life together for so long is a 12
grim tribute to the power of socialization, and to my ability to exploit that
power in order to protect myself from reality. When Jan realized how really
minimal were the satisfactions of housework, there was also a voice within
her (as well as mine without) suggesting that perhaps she was just lazy. If she
began to hate the children, she knew that it was because they were helping
to prevent her meeting real and legitimate personal needs, but the voices were
always there hinting that the real trouble was that she was basically a hateful
person and thus a poor mother. If her mind became sluggish, she knew at
some level that she was making an adaptive adjustment to her situation, but
those voices whispered in a thousand ways that she might be going crazy, or
perhaps she was just stupid. And when she became sullen and resentful toward
me, the voices were always there to obscure her perception that I had it
coming. They even encouraged her to feel guilty, finally, when she did not
feel my success as her reward, the payoff for all her drudgery. They kept her
from realizing that such a payoff cost her a sense of her independent selfhood;
that it was at best the pittance of exploitation: shit wages for shit work.

Those voices, within and without, kept reminding us both that Jan's real 13
destiny was to keep me comfortable and productive and to raise "our" children. The feelings I'd come to experience in a few months had for years made
Jan feel lazy, selfish, and egotistic; unable to empathize with the needs of the
family (read: my need for success). Just as importantly, her knowledge that
the sources of her troubles were not all within herself could not have received
any reinforcement in the social world. I was her only link with that world;
my affection and "respect" were her only source of assurance that she was
real. To the extent that identity depends on recognition by others, she depended on me for that as surely as she depended on me for grocery money.
The result was that she was afraid to share with me huge areas of her life,
any areas which might threaten my regard for her. She could not afford,
psychologically or economically, to challenge me overtly. And when she managed to make any suggestion that her discontent was a function of what was

being done to her, it was battered down, by my recriminations, into a quagmire of guilt.

I had had some inkling of all this before I ever committed myself to 14 cooking a meal or washing a single pair of socks (as my responsibility, rather than a favor to her). But at every stage of our experiment in role reversal (or rather our attempt to escape roles) my understanding of her position became more real. I had got a lot of domestic services but I had been denied real contact with a whole human being, and hard upon my guilt came anger, rage at what had been done to us both.

I don't have space here to go on and extend our experience into the world 15 outside the family. It is enough to say that when someone has concrete power over your life, you are going to keep a part of yourself hidden and therefore undeveloped, or developed only in fantasy. Your identity becomes bound up in other people's expectations of you—and that is the definition of alienation. It did not take long for me to make connections between the alienating ways in which Jan had to deal with me in the early years of our marriage and the way that I was dealing with my "senior colleagues," the men and women who had power to fire me and did.

Our experience also helped me to understand the distortions of percep- 16 tion and personality that result from being the "superior" in a hierarchical structure. The nuclear family as we know it is one such structure, perhaps the crucial one. But the alienation which results from privilege pervades all our experience in a society which values human beings on the basis of sex, race, and class and which structures those standards into all its institutions. Housework is only a tip of that iceberg, but for Jan and me it has helped to make the need to fundamentally transform those institutions a gut reality.

LISTENING

◐

SEY CHASSLER

Writer, editor, and editorial consultant Sey Chassler is
a former Editor-in-Chief of *Redbook* magazine. Chassler is currently a consulting editor of *Parade* magazine
and Vice-President of the Childcare Action Campaign.
In 1987 he was the recipient of the National Women's
Political Caucus's Good Guy award.

One morning, about 20 years ago, my wife and I were arguing about whether   1
or not I ever listened to her. It was one of those arguments that grow into
passion and pain and, often, for me at least, into a kind of hysteria. This one
became one of those that do not go away with the years. Suddenly, she threw
something at me, and said: "From now on you do the shopping, plan the
meals, take care of the house, everything. I'm through!"

I was standing in the kitchen looking at the shelves of food, at the oven,   2
at the sink, at the refrigerator, at the cleaning utensils. At my wife.

My reaction was orgasmic. Somewhere inside of me there was screaming,   3
hurting, a volcanic gush of tears flooded my head and broke down over me.
I shook and sobbed. I was terrified. No matter what, I knew I could not
handle the burden. I could not do my job and be responsible for the entire
household. How could I get through a day dealing with personnel, budgets,
manuscripts, art departments, circulation statistics, phone calls, people,
agents, management, writers, and *at the same time* plan dinner for tonight and
tomorrow night and breakfast and a dinner party Thursday night and shopping for it all and making sure the house is in good shape and the woman
who cleans for us is there and on time and the laundry done and the children
taken to the doctor, and the children taken care of? How could *any* one
person do all that and stay sane? No one could do that properly. No one.
Natalie simply watched me for awhile. Finally she said: "Okay. Don't worry.
I'll keep on doing it." She put on her coat and went to her office.

Despite her simple statement that she would go on doing it, I stood   4
awhile telling myself that *no one* could do all of that. No one. There was a
click in my head—and it dawned on me that *she* was doing it.

How invisible my wife's life was to me. How invisible to men women are.   5

Shortly afterward, in 1963 or 1964, not long after *The Feminine Mystique*   6
was published, Betty Friedan and I were invited to speak to the nation's largest

organization of home economists. As executive editor of *Redbook* magazine, I was asked to talk about the magazine's view of women. Betty was talking about the thesis of her book—that all American women were trapped in their homebound positions and that women's magazines, among others, put out propaganda to keep them trapped.

I had read *The Feminine Mystique*, of course, and felt I was fully prepared to answer it and, thereby, to defend not only *Redbook* from Friedan's attack but to defend American women, as well. 7

In mid-speech I proclaimed that, despite what Friedan had written, women, in this day and in this country, were free to be whatever they wished to be, that they were not children to be told what they might and might not do, that they could work at whatever profession they chose or whatever job, that they were free to be wives if they wished, and truck drivers if they wished, and mothers if they wished or homemakers if they wished. The list was growing longer and the speech was getting more and more impassioned in its proclamation of freedoms. I paused and waited for the applause. I had, after all, just proclaimed freedom throughout the land! I looked out at the audience. The hall was silent. 8

My pause became a dark empty cavern, and I could feel myself groping for a way out, wondering what had gone awry. I felt naked, stripped bare before 800 women. I could not understand what I had said that was wrong. Looking for comfort, I thought of my wife, and—*click!* I suddenly realized that my wife was a woman who was free to choose a career and *had*—but who also had delayed that career until her children—*her* children!—were in school. She was not as free as I thought, nor was any married woman. 9

While my enthusiasm had diminished, I went on with my speech. But whatever it was that had clicked in my head first in the kitchen and then in Kansas City, stayed there. And for a long time afterward, there were things going on in my head that I couldn't quite get hold of. 10

Whatever they were, I found myself listening for clicks in my head while thinking about, talking to, or dealing with women. And since I worked with more than 60 women every day and came home to my wife every night, I had a good deal of listening to do. 11

At home one night after dinner, I sat down to read the paper, as usual, while my wife went into the kitchen to do the dishes. I could see her in the kitchen. She looked happy, or at least not unhappy, there in the pretty kitchen she had designed—and she was probably appreciating the change of pace after a hard day as chief of service in a mental hospital dealing with a staff of three or four dozen employees and a hundred or more patients, some of whom threatened her from time to time. Yes, she was using the time well, since she had no hobbies to break the tension. I was feeling comfortably and happily married, when—*click!*—the view changed, and I saw a hardworking woman doing something she'd rather not be doing just now. 12

When my wife finished and sat down near me, I kissed her with a special 13
tenderness, I thought. She didn't. As a matter of fact, she turned the other
cheek. Something was going on in both our heads.

The next night *I* decided to do the dishes and she read the paper. At the 14
sink, I began to think about male arrogance. Why did I have the choice of
doing or not doing the dishes, while my wife did not? By the same token,
why had she had to wait until our children were in school to exercise her
"free" choice of working at her career? Our jobs were equally pressured and
difficult (hers more harrowing than mine) and yet, if I chose to sit and read
after dinner, I could. She could not, unless I decided she could by *offering* to
do the dishes. My definition of freedom was based on a white male conception:
the notion that because I am free, because I can make choices, anyone can
make choices. I was defining "anyone" in my terms, in masculine terms. I am
anyone, unqualified. She is anyone, gender female. So you can take your
tender kisses and shove them.

I felt I had caught the edge of an insight about the condition of women 15
and while I wanted to, I found I couldn't discuss it with men; it made them
uneasy and defensive. They'd fight off the conversation. They'd say things
like "But that's the way it is supposed to be, Sey. Forget it!" After awhile, I
began to feel like one of those people who carry signs in the street announcing
the end of the world. Pretty soon I got defensive, too—and my questions
produced terrific dinner-table fights with other male guests. The women
almost always remained silent, seeming to enjoy watching the men wrestle.
The men were convinced that I was a nut. And several, including my father,
accused me of "coming out for women," because in my job as editor of a
women's magazine that would be "smart" and "profitable."

I certainly couldn't talk to any woman directly, because I was embarrassed. 16
I didn't believe women would tell me the truth—and, more important, I was
not going to let them know I was worried or thinking about the matter or
afraid to find the answer.

If you are one of those men who feel trapped by women, who think they 17
are fine for sex but interfere with living, all of the above may not be very
clear to you. Maybe the following will set some clicks off for you.

The other day I was reading *The Intimate Male*, by Linda Levine, ACSW, 18
and Lonnie Barbach, Ph.D. It is one of those books in which men reveal all
their sexual secrets, fantasies, and so on. It is supposed to help us understand
each other, I guess. All I ever get out of such books is the discovery that other
guys and I share the same fantasies. Well, in this one, I read about a guy who
likes his wife to walk around the house without any underwear under her
skirt. Innocent enough, you guess? But what he *really* likes is to "lay on the
floor while my wife does the dishes, and look up her dress"!

I told this story to a couple of men I know, and they thought it beat all 19
hell how he got his wife to walk around without her pants on. They loved it.
Hey, what a crazy guy!

But wait. Let's try it from the wife's point of view: here is this nice woman who has spent her day working somewhere, either out on a job of some kind or taking care of this romantic fellow's house. She is about as beat as he is by the end of the day and maybe she'll be ready for sex later, but not right now. Right now her hands are full of dirty dishes and wet garbage, so what can she be thinking of? *He* doesn't have to do anything but work his eyeballs.

Everyone to her or his own kink, of course. But it isn't kink that is going on here. What is going on here is a neat exercise in power. The man on the floor is proving to his wife and to himself that he is the boss. He can take his pleasure while she works. Of course, she can tell him to knock it off and keep her pants on, but that is going to make him very unhappy. Unhappy enough maybe to go out for a few beers until she comes to her senses. "This freaking wife of mine," he'll say to the guys in the bar, "every time I want it, she's doing the dishes or too tired or something."

So the chances are she doesn't tell him to knock it off, because the implied threat of walking out for a while gains the husband the privilege of turning his wife into a dancing girl while she's doing the dishes. In other words, here is a neat form of blackmail—"Do as I say, or you'll get my mad side and everyone will know I married a cold little bitch." This is known as dominance—and you should have heard a click in your head.

The episode on the kitchen floor is, admittedly, a bit unusual. That sort of thing doesn't go on with most people. Here's one that is more familiar. As reported in *The Wall Street Journal* in a story on sex discrimination in law firms, King & Spalding of Atlanta had a company picnic last summer. Initially proposed for the festivities was a "wet T-shirt" contest, but, in the end, the firm merely decided to hold a bathing-suit competition. It was open only to the company's women summer associates. A third-year law student from Harvard University won. While awarding her the prize, a partner of the firm said, "She has the body we'd like to see more of." King & Spalding is no small company. Among its clients are Coca-Cola Company, Cox Broadcasting Corporation, and General Motors.

The question here is: why would a Harvard law student parade around in a bathing suit for a bunch of rowdy male lawyers? It's easy to say she was looking for a job with a good firm. Since the bathing-suit competition incident, King & Spalding has promised it will not practice sex discrimination, and the student who won the contest has agreed to join the firm. But the question remains: why would she enter such a contest?

I refer you to the woman in the kitchen, above. Why did she take her pants off?

Dominance. Male dominance. Someone calls the shots, someone else does as she is told.

What would you say to your boss if he announced that he was thinking of having a wet jockstrap contest at the company picnic? Or if your best girl asked you to take your pants off, while you crawled under the car to have a

•

look at the manifold? What would you say? If your wife asked you to stay home with the baby or to meet the plumber or to do the shopping or to clean the toilet bowl some day, what would you say?

Click? 28

My wife and I have been married 41 years. We think of ourselves as being 29 happily married—and we are. But the dominance is there. It means that in my relationship with my wife, I am almost totally the boss. When we have a discussion (that's marital-ese for argument), more often than not it is I who declare when the end of it arrives. If we make a plan together and she does most of the work on the plan, it is given to me for *approval.* If I do most of the work on the plan, I submit it to her for her *information.* If she agrees to the plan, she'll say "Good, should we do it?" If *I* agree to the plan, I'll say, "Good, let's go." That doesn't mean that I make all the decisions, control all the funds, make all the choices, talk louder than she does. I don't have to. It simply means that I do not have to ask my wife for permission to do anything. Whether she does or says anything about it or not, everything my wife does is to a large extent qualified by what I think or will think. In effect, she must ask my permission. What's more, as husband, I seem—no matter how I try to avoid it—to assign all the jobs in our family. In effect, I win all the arguments—even the ones we don't have. That's emotional dominance—and it means that everything that occurs between us, everything we do together, is monitored by me.

Once during a lecture tour I was talking to undergraduates at the Uni- 30 versity of Indiana about the Women's Movement and how important it is. One of the women, a senior, asked a question and then she said: "I don't want to get married when I graduate. I want to be someone." *Click.*

That statement haunts me. I never had to say anything like that. I had 31 always thought I would get married *and* be somebody. What's more, I took it for granted that my wife would be responsible for the family in addition to her job. I would love and care for my children, but I wouldn't have to deal with their phone calls at the office. They'd call my wife at the office. That's what mommies are for, aren't they? No one had to tell the children that. No one had to tell me that. No one had to tell my wife that. We all *knew* it. And everyone knew that men not only had freedom of choice but freedom to grant permission to women to make choices.

I had freedom, yes, but as my children were growing up, as I looked at 32 my family, I began to struggle with a barely conscious knowledge that the happy group of people with whom I lived—my two sons, my daughter, my wife—were feeling uneasy when I was around. They shifted stiffly, muffled their voices, stifled their laughter when I arrived in their midst. They could feel the dominant grown male arrive. I didn't want that. It was simply there— where I was.

As the years went by and my consciousness grew, I began to recall for 33 examination not only those uneasy days, but really angry ones. What was I angry about? I was angry that I was not always my wife's center of attention.

I had been brought up thinking I would be. That made our early days very rough, indeed. I was angry when our first son was born. Those were the days when women had babies and men simply were proud, frightened, and prepared to pay the bills.

The birth of my first child was traumatic, as it was with each of the others. 34 Beyond admiring the growing child in my wife's body, I played virtually no part in any of their births. As each child was about to be born, I got to drive my wife to the hospital. I was kept in the waiting room for expectant fathers. I could read and smoke and bite my nails. No one came to tell me anything. The movies had told me childbirth is painful, dangerous, life-threatening for a woman. I stood in the corner of the waiting room—all three times—fearful, out of touch with whatever dark things were happening in an operating room somewhere above me, sick with wanting to be near my wife.

In the evening before my second son was born, it was extremely hot, and 35 the nurses sent me home to await his arrival. Nervous and feeling abandoned, I took a shower with an electric fan whirring in the bathroom. As I reached for the towel, I stuck my fingers into the metal blades of the fan. I screamed for my wife and cursed that she was not there. I raced around looking for bandages, found a handkerchief, wrapped it around my fingers, shoved a months-old condom on them to stem the flow of blood, dressed, ran to a doctor down the street, was stitched up, and finally rushed off to the hospital—to wait. And he was born. But I didn't get to see him right away.

It was always the same: when my first son was born, they didn't let me 36 see him for a while. A nurse simply came and told me to be proud. "It's a boy!" she said. I had to ask if my wife was all right. I had to ask when I would see our baby. After a half hour or so, they took me up to a nursery window and pointed to a bundle in a tiny basket. They took me to see my wife and let me kiss her. They sent me away. They did the same with our second son. They did the same with my daughter. Only, they didn't say, "Be proud," they said, "You have a beautiful little girl this time!" I was proud. But they did not let me use my love, touch my world.

I was angry. I felt left out, put off, unable to feel entirely that I, too, had 37 had a baby, had given (*given*) birth to a child—just as my wife had. I think sometimes that the anger of those days has carried into all of our lives. I, in some kind of crazy partnership with my past, my traditions, put it there—in the lives of my wife, and of our children.

Now, as I look back at the time of the births, when I was kept out, given 38 no choice over urgent and vital matters affecting my life, I understand how it feels to be a woman and have no choices—how it feels not to be heard. I have finally discovered what it is to be like the undergraduate who wanted to be someone. She, too, I realize now was in a waiting room waiting to be proud—and knowing her pride would be controlled by others.

Last year, after a board meeting of one of the nation's best-known wom- 39 en's organizations, I was sitting with a group of women who are legislators, corporate executives, lawyers, broadcasters—big shots. One of them said:

"We've been at it for about twenty years now, and we've made real progress—why then does the pain still linger?" Another answered simply: "Because the men still keep the lid on."

Click. 40

The Women's Movement has made some remarkable changes in our lives, 41
but it hasn't changed the position of the male much at all. Men still make the moves. They are the ones who, in their own good time, move in. And in their own good time, move out. Someone makes the rules, someone else does as she is told.

About eight years ago, my wife suggested—finally—that I must be hard 42
of hearing because I never seemed to hear what she said, even though I answered all questions and conducted real conversations with her. She made me promise to see an ear doctor. I did. He found nothing wrong. When I told him that this whole idea was my wife's, he sent me home. "Most of my male patients," he said, "are here on the advice of their wives." I laughed. But . . . *click!*

We don't have to listen. As men we simply are in charge. It comes with 43
the territory. Popeye sings "I am what I am." God said the same thing to Moses in the wilderness. Male images. They're built into us. Images of dominance.

I got to be the editor of *Redbook* because I was the second in line. There 44
was at least one woman on the staff who could have done the job as well or better than I, but the president of the company had, in his time, passed over many women—and this time there was no exception. While I knew about editing and writing and pictures, I didn't know beans about fiction or recipes and fashion and cosmetics and all of those things; still, having the responsibility and the authority, I had to act as if I did. I was forced, therefore, to listen very carefully to the women who worked with me and whose help I needed. And, listening, I learned to talk with them and talking with them I began to hear them.

Most of the editors in the company were women, most of the sales and 45
business people were men. The men could never figure out how to talk to the women. They seemed to think that I had learned some secrets about women, and they'd stop me in the halls and say things like "How can I tell Anne such and such about this advertising account?" And I'd say, "Just tell her." And they'd say, "But can you say that to a woman? Will she understand?"

Click. 46

In the beginning, I found myself using my position as a male. I *talked* to 47
the men; I gave orders to the women.

By the same token, the men and women dealt with me differently. In an 48
argument, a man would feel comfortable telling me I was wrong and, if necessary, call me a damn fool. Two hours later we'd be working together without grudge. But most women would give silent assent and do as they were told. They obeyed. The stronger ones *would* call me stupid or whatever

they needed to, but they (and I) would hurt for days. They had breached the rules. Some would come up to apologize, and we both would wind up with tears in our eyes. Dominance. When we learned to work with each other as equals, we learned to be angry as equals—and to respect each other, to love each other as equals.

And yet, while I began to feel some measure of equality with the women, I could not, for a very long time, figure out how to achieve the kind of camaraderie, the palship, the mutual attachment to team, the soldierly equality of action, that men feel for each other. I could never feel comfortable putting my arm around a woman as we walked down a corridor talking business or conspiring against some agent or corporate plan—as I would with a man. Out of sheer good feeling and admiration for a job well done and a fight well fought, there were days when I wanted to throw my arms around women I worked with—as I would with a man—but I never really felt fully free to.

While it was hard to achieve camaraderie, as we worked hand-in-hand, eye-to-eye, shoulder-to-shoulder, mind-to-mind warm, erotic, sexy—yet not sexy—feelings would begin to flow. While they were mutual, they were not feelings to be turned into acts of sex. They were feelings that came out of— and went into—the intensity of the work at hand.

What were they like, these erotic feelings? They were like the feelings of a locker room after a game played hard and won. They felt like sweat. They felt like heroism. They felt like bodies helping bodies. They felt like those urges that make it all right to smack a guy on the ass in congratulation and gratitude, to throw your arms around him and hug him for making the winning point. And they felt like the secret admiration of his body—because he was a hero—as he stood in the shower. How marvelous to feel that way about a woman—and not want to go to bed with her! Just to admire and love her for being with you—and for helping you to play the game. I recommend the feeling. And I think, perhaps, in prehistory when female and male hunted and gathered side-by-side in the frightening wilderness—sharing their fears, their losses, their gains and their triumphs equally—it must have been this way. In the time before the gods. In the time before I-am-what-I-am.

I was telling a woman friend about all of this. She asked: "Do you deal with your women colleagues and friends differently from the way you deal with your wife?"

Click.

I was sitting with a man friend, when, in relation to nothing in particular, he said: "Guys get to be heroes. Girls get to be cheerleaders. Guys get to be dashing womanizers, great studs. Women get to be sluts."

Click.

A lot of us men think of these things and we hurt when we do. And a lot of us—most of us—simply don't think of these things. Or we think of them as something that will go away—the complaints from women will go away, as they always seem to.

Still, as men, we recognize Freud's question: "Good God, what do women 57
want?"

To be heard. 58

My 89-year-old mother, married 65 years to my 89-year-old father, says 59
to him, "Someday you'll let me talk when I want to."

On the grimy wall of the 23rd Street Station of the New York subway a 60
woman's hand has written: "Women Lib gonna get your girl!"

In H. G. Wells's book, *The Passionate Friends*, Mary writes to Stephen: 61
"Womankind isn't human, it's reduced human."

Margaret Mead, in a conversation, remarks that in American households, 62
the man decides whether the toilet paper leads from the top of the roll or the
bottom of the roll.

Will men ever appreciate fully what women are saying? 63

I don't think I will ever, fully. No matter what clicks in my head. 64

The world belongs to men. It is completely dominated by us—and by 65
our images.

What men see when they look out and about are creatures very like 66
themselves—in charge of everything. What women see when they look out
and about is that the creatures in charge of everything are *unlike* themselves.

If you are a man, think of a world, your world, in which for everything 67
you own or do or think you are accountable to women. Women are presidents,
bankers, governors, door holders, traffic cops, airline pilots, bosses, supervi-
sors, landlords, Shakespeare. The whole structure is completely dominated
by women. Your doctor, your lawyer, your priest, minister, rabbi are women.
The figure on the cross is a woman. God is a woman. Every authoritative
voice and every authoritative image is the image and voice of women: Buddha,
Mohammed, Moses, Matthew, Luke, Paul, the guy who does the voice-over
on the commercial and Ben Franklin—all are women. So are Goliath and
David. So are the Supreme Court, the tax collector, the head of the CIA, the
mechanic who fixes your transmission, the editor of your daily newspaper,
the doctor who handed you to your mother. Jack the Giant Killer. Walter
Mondale. St. Patrick. Ronald Reagan is a woman. Walter Cronkite is a
woman. George Steinbrenner is a woman. Think of such a world. The Pope
is a woman. JR is a woman. Casper Weinberger. Think of yourself in such a
world. Think of your father in it. Think of *him* as a woman. Think about it.

Don't just brush it off, for Mary's sake—think about it. 68

MAKING CONNECTIONS

1. Do women and men face different problems in balancing career and family? Discuss the ways in which male and female socialization prepares them for the roles of breadwinner and parent. If a husband and wife decide that they both will have careers and will share the responsibilities of parenting, what problems might they encounter in terms of balancing time, energy, social status, and careers? Pair up with a classmate and negotiate these issues, with one person taking the position of the husband and one person playing the wife. Be imaginative in selecting the details of your couples' lives—the schedules and demands of two teachers in a small town will pose different problems than those of a broker and a flight attendant. Try to formalize your agreement by writing out an imaginary contract, then share your efforts with the rest of the class, discussing the problems that arose and your strategies for compromise.

2. Changes in gender roles (like men sharing more of the work of parenting) can sometimes be difficult to initiate since there are few role models. What is the function of role models in learning about or changing gender norms? Research shows that in traditional families, fathers play with infants and preschoolers, while mothers tend to all other aspects of child rearing. In nontraditional families, fathers do more of the feeding, diapering, cleaning, and putting the baby to bed. Using Holly Devor's (Chapter 1) discussion of how gender schemata develop in infants and young children, what do you think the differences would be in the development of gender schemata in children whose parents follow traditional vs. nontraditional roles?

3. In what ways do laws dealing with divorce and child custody reveal assumptions about gender and the task of parenting? Research the child custody and support laws in your state, including any movements to change them. What indicators, if any, do you find that point to gender role images underlying these laws? Write an essay that documents your findings.

4. Taking Polatnick's "power analysis" of child-rearing as a starting point, analyze the economic and social situation of a mother of two preschoolers after a divorce. Using Polatnick's discussion of "exchange value theory," write an essay that compares this woman's options to those of her ex-husband. What if society paid parents to care for their children? Are there any societies that provide such support? How might Katherine Kersten (Chapter 2) respond to Polatnick's analysis of the social organization of child-rearing in the United States?

5. Few of the "New American Dreamers" that Ruth Sidel interviewed (Chapter 12) talked about child-rearing. Discuss the absence of children in their dreams of success. Are young women today no longer as interested in motherhood? Do children somehow conflict with the particular types of futures Sidel's respondents envisioned? Or are these young women's dreams simply looking more like many young men's dreams, in which family plays a part, but it is assumed that someone else will take care of the children and manage the home? What are the practical options, such as daycare and housecleaning services, that might make this freedom possible? What considerations might make such services problematic or less available than expected?

6. Discuss the different implications of Polatnick's and Mark Gerzon's (Chapter 13) positions on the roles of breadwinning and child-rearing for men and women. Write an essay that compares the views of these two authors and Roache on the subject of women working and the dilemmas it presents for men. How do you think each author would solve these dilemmas? What are your own opinions on women and men working inside and outside the home?

7. National surveys indicate that, despite the dramatic increase of women in the paid workforce over the past two decades, the increase in men's housework and child care is small. How do you account for these discrepancies? Develop your own research paper on changes in men's and women's family roles over the past two decades.

8. Compare the images of working in the selections by John Lippert and Edward Hirsch (Chapter 13) with the images of housework in the essays by Roache and Mainardi. What similarities and differences do you perceive between "paid" and "unpaid" jobs? If many jobs outside the home seem repetitive and dehumanizing, why would women want to leave the home to pursue paid work? What advantages might a dull job have over housework? What disadvantages might it pose? What if a housewife received a salary for her work inside the home? In monetary terms, how much is housework worth, and how would you go about establishing a fair wage?

9. Mark Gerzon (Chapter 13) contends that the lack of autonomy experienced in most workplaces is one of the "lethal aspects of masculinity." Using the selections by Polatnick, Mainardi, and Roache, list the characteristics of housework and parenting and evaluate the amount of autonomy that one might experience in these tasks. Are there any "lethal aspects" of these work roles? Write a brief essay on the "occupational hazards"—both physical and mental—of the workplace inside the home.

10. Think back to the readings in Chapters 2 and 3, on femininity and masculinity, and discuss how male and female socialization emphasize

"doing" vs. "being," respectively. Trace Roache's transformation from "doing" in the first weeks of his househusband role to "being" later on. What happens to his sense of personal control as the realities of house-work set in? Imagine yourself in Roache's situation and write a short fictional account of "a day in my life."

11. Roache and Chassler come to similar realizations about the power and privilege they have enjoyed as husbands, yet each author frames the issue in a different way. Compare the use of such devices as humor, pathos, and descriptive anecdotes in their respective essays. Do you agree or disagree with these authors' assessments of male privilege? Do women have special privileges as wives? If so, how do these privileges differ from men's? How might social class play a part in determining the privileges of husbands and wives?

12. Using Chassler's device of a "click," write a personal essay drawing on incidents in your life—or even in your responses to selections in this book—that caused you to reflect on or examine your preconceptions about gender, value, and power. Alternately, you might write an essay using "click" to talk about moments when you resisted or felt uncom-fortable with such reflections. Like Chassler, use the essay as a place to explore your feelings and discover connections.

GENDER AND CULTURE

A CASE STUDY

15
REFLECTIONS
ON WAR

C O N T E X T S

The previous chapters in this book have looked at many facets of gender in society. In this final section we open the doors to a debate that integrates all these aspects—language and image, media and popular culture, social roles and responsibilities, and the many definitions of what it means to be a man or a woman. This section, "Gender and Culture: A Case Study," looks at the complex cultural phenomenon of war and presents the voices of thinkers, activists, and participants in America's most recent and controversial military engagements: Vietnam and the Persian Gulf.

In the words of our opening author, poet Margaret Atwood, war is a topic that presents many sides: "courage and atrocities," "glamour" and "horror," "banality" and "bravery." It can be argued that soldiering and warfare have been glorified in Western culture since the beginning of recorded history. Some of our earliest literature sings the praises of warriors and soldiers: Odysseus, Hector, and Achilles. Much of the glory of ancient civilizations such as Rome was due to a history of warfare and conquest. Atwood's poem, "The Loneliness of the Military Historian," offers a different, more snail's-eye view of war and those who write its history. Walking a difficult line between her feelings as a woman and her role as impartial researcher, Atwood's narrator contemplates the many interpretations of war, from the splendid to the tragic.

Even today, warfare continues to be the focus of much cultural attention, and in many contemporary societies the soldier remains the archetype of the consummate man, embodying all the elements of "true" masculinity. He is physically disciplined, mentally tough, courageous enough to put his life on the line, aggressive enough to kill and to survive. Our second author, Sam Keen, takes a look at "The Rite of War and the Warrior Psyche" in American culture today. According to Keen, all men are deeply marked by society's expectation that they "must be prepared to suffer, die, and kill" in battle. He examines the ways society has constructed a "warfare system" and how that system victimizes men, as well as those elements within the male psyche that respond to fierceness as a source of primal power and a way to masculine wholeness.

The image of the ideal warrior, of course, is not one that is found ready-made. Soldiers are not born; they are molded in boot camp and tested on the battlefield, perhaps the ultimate proving ground of "masculinity." Our next selection listens to the voices of men in the military, collected in Helen Michalowski's piece "The Army Will Make a 'Man' Out of You." These excerpts from interviews, recollections of basic training, and stories about life in the military raise troubling questions about the equation of masculinity with violence and its consequences for men's subsequent personal lives.

Journalist Walter J. Gottlieb highlights another aspect of gender and war in "The Sexual Connection," an examination of the rhetoric and imagery surrounding the Persian Gulf war. The association between sex and war made graphic in the language of military action may not be a literal one, Gottlieb argues, but may point to a dangerous juxtaposition between war and male sexual power. For Gottlieb, it is imperative that individuals learn to read the subtle (and not-so-subtle) images used by politicians and military leaders that help generate public excitement for war and conquest.

If war is equated with power and domination, what happens when that power fails? Our next two essays examine the aftermath of the Vietnam war on the American man's sense of self-confidence and masculinity. In "Do We Get to Win This Time?" Susan Jeffords analyzes images of manhood presented by the press and popular media after Vietnam. She contends that in the context of that war the public perceived the American male as a victim. As a result, she argues, the media began to reconstruct the image of the Vietnam veteran in such a way as to reclaim his lost masculinity. For Jeffords, Rambo stands as the symbol of this new man, who lives by his own laws, abolishes all ties to women, and rescues the manhood of all American men lost in Vietnam. In contrast, psychotherapist Edward Tick, in "Apocalypse Continued," offers a more personal side of the erosion of self-confidence brought about by Vietnam. While presenting the disabling experiences of his patient Ron, a veteran of the war now suffering from post-traumatic stress disorder, Tick also explores his own guilt at having escaped the draft and his subsequent shame about his own "incomplete" masculinity.

Men, of course, are not the only group affected by war. The Gulf War in particular brought the topic of women and the military into public discourse. For the first time, American women were present in large numbers in the military and reserve units sent to the Middle East. After the war, the policies that had kept these women soliders out of active combat in the army, navy, and air force elicited sharp debate as discriminatory practices. But what are the implications of "equal opportunity" for women in the military? In "Requiem for a Soldier," a meditation on the death of Major Marie T. Rossi whose helicopter was downed in Saudi Arabia during the Gulf War, Linda Bird Francke asks us to contemplate the very real costs of equality in the "new military."

We end with companion pieces on the memorials of war. In the photograph by Seny Norasingh from the collection *The Wall: Images and Offerings from the Vietnam Veterans Memorial,* a young boy leans from the shoulders of a veteran to kiss the name of a soldier etched in the memorial's famous black marble. Similarly, Yusef Komunyakaa's poem "Facing It" leans toward the wall's more ghostly reflections to find meaning in the human history of the war that it memorializes.

THE LONELINESS OF THE MILITARY HISTORIAN

MARGARET ATWOOD

Margaret Atwood is a Canadian writer whose many novels include *The Edible Woman* (1969), *Surfacing* (1972), *Life Before Man* (1979), *Bodily Harm* (1982), *The Handmaid's Tale* (1986), and *Cat's Eye* (1989). Her poetry has appeared in numerous magazines, including the following poem, which was published in *Harpers* in 1990. Here, she takes a close look at the many ways one can understand war and its aftermath.

Confess: it's my profession
that alarms you.
This is why few people ask me to dinner,
though Lord knows I don't go out of my way to be scary.
I wear dresses of sensible cut
and unalarming shades of beige,
I smell of lavender and go to the hairdresser's:
no prophetess mane of mine
complete with snakes, will frighten the youngsters.
If my eyes roll and I mutter,
if my arms are gloved in blood right up to the elbow,
if I clutch at my heart and scream in horror
like a third-rate actress chewing up a mad scene,
I do it in private and nobody sees
but the bathroom mirror.

In general I might agree with you:
women should not contemplate war,
should not weigh tactics impartially,
or evade the word *enemy*,
or view both sides and denounce nothing.
Women should march for peace,
or hand out white feathers to inspire bravery,
spit themselves on bayonets
to protect their babies,
whose skulls will be split anyway,

or, having been raped repeatedly,
hang themselves with their own hair.
These are the functions that inspire general comfort.
That, and the knitting of socks for the troops
and a sort of moral cheerleading.
Also: mourning the dead.
Sons, lovers, and so forth.
All the killed children.

Instead of this, I tell
what I hope will pass as truth.
A blunt thing, not lovely.
The truth is seldom welcome,
especially at dinner,
though I am good at what I do.
My trade is in courage and atrocities.
I look at them and do not condemn.
I write things down the way they happened,
as near as can be remembered.
I don't ask *why* because it is mostly the same.
Wars happen because the ones who start them
think they can win.

In my dreams there is glamour.
The Vikings leave their fields
each year for a few months of killing and plunder,
much as the boys go hunting.
In real life they were farmers.
They come back loaded with splendor.
The Arabs ride against Crusaders
with scimitars that could sever
silk in the air.
A swift cut to the horse's neck
and a hunk of armor crashes down
like a tower. Fire against metal.
A poet might say: romance against banality.
When awake, I know better.

Despite the propaganda, there are no monsters,
or none that can be finally buried.
Finish one off and circumstances
and the radio create another.
Believe me: whole armies have prayed fervently
to God all night and meant it,

and been slaughtered anyway.
Brutality wins frequently,
and large outcomes have turned on the invention
of a mechanical device, viz. radar.

True, sometimes valor counts for something,
as at Thermopylae. Sometimes being right,
though ultimate virtue by agreed tradition
is decided by the winner.
Sometimes men throw themselves on grenades
and burst like paper bags of guts
to save their comrades.
I can admire that.
But rats and cholera have won many wars.
Those, and potatoes
or the absence of them.
It's no use pinning all those medals
across the chests of the dead.
Impressive, but I know too much.
Grand exploits merely depress me.

In the interests of research
I have walked on many battlefields
that once were liquid with pulped
men's bodies and spangled with burst
shells and splayed bone.
All of them have been green again
by the time I got there.
Each has inspired a few good quotes in its day.
Sad marble angels brood like hens
over the grassy nests where nothing hatches.
(The angels could just as well be described as *vulgar*,
or *pitiless*, depending on camera angle.)
The word *glory* figures a lot on gateways.
Of course I pick a flower or two
from each, and press it in the hotel
Bible, for a souvenir.
I'm just as human as you.

But it's no use asking me for a final statement.
As I say, I deal in tactics.
Also statistics:
for every year of peace there have been four hundred
years of war.

THE RITE OF WAR AND
THE WARRIOR PSYCHE

SAM KEEN

Philosopher and writer Sam Keen was a consulting
editor for *Psychology Today* for many years and has written extensively on topics ranging from human development to the psychology of war. His acclaimed PBS
documentary, *Faces of the Enemy: Reflections of the Hostile
Imagination* was nominated for an Emmy Award and
appeared in book form in 1986. The essay below is
taken from his most recent book, *Fire in the Belly: On
Being a Man* (1991).

If men were Homo sapiens there would be no war.

I was fourteen when I had my last real fight, with fists and feet and anything   1
handy. I don't remember anymore what it was about, maybe a girl, or a casual
insult on the school bus, or maybe it was just because "the enemy" lived across
the imaginary line on Bellefonte Street and went to another school. By my
reckoning, Charley was a bit of a sissy. Chest caved in, shoulders slumping,
he walked with a monkey lope. At any rate, war was declared and we agreed
to meet in the vacant lot next to Nancy Ritter's house. At the appointed time,
we appeared on the battleground, each accompanied by selected members of
our respective tribes. For a while we circled round each other, each waiting
for the other to throw the first punch. "You want to start something, you
chicken-shit bastard?" "You touch me and I'll bust your ass." We moved closer.
Push came to shove, fists flew, and the first one hit me in the nose. "Hell with
this," I said. I was better at wrestling than boxing, I strategized. So I ducked,
grabbed his legs, and took him to the ground. After much rolling, arm bend-
ing, and cursing I ended up on the bottom, unable to move. "Give up," he
said. "Or I'll break your arm." He ratcheted my arm up a notch or two and
pushed my face into the gravel. "Do you surrender?" "Fuck off." My face
hurt, but not as much as my pride. We both knew I was defeated even though
I wouldn't surrender, so he released my arm and after a few rounds of mandatory cursing and name-calling we went home.

That night, true to the scenario in the comic books, I vowed I would   2
never again be beaten up by some goddamn sissy. For $3.95 I sent away for

a Charles Atlas course and began to transform a ninety-eight-pound weakling into a lean and mean fighting machine. In the secrecy of my room I practiced "dynamic tension," lifted weights, did push-ups and leg lifts. Later I graduated to wrestling. For years, well into my midthirties, I worked out at the YMCA. I perfected my take-downs and pinning combinations and occasionally entered competitions as a light-heavyweight. I was never a champion but I learned to love fighting. And no one rubbed my face in the dirt.

Meanwhile I was studying philosophy and honing the weapons of dialectic, debate, and argumentation. By the time I was a practicing Ph.D. my mind was even more skilled than my body in the art of self-defense. As a professor I engaged in daily combat with colleagues and students. I was good at the academic game, enjoyed it, and played to win. I hardly noticed that, over the years, I had gradually adopted a combative stance toward others—the mind and posture of a warrior. I was much better at fighting than at wondering or loving. 3

Agents of Violence

Why has the gender that gave us the Sistine Chapel brought us to the edge of cosmocide? Why have the best and brightest exercised their intelligence, imagination, and energy and managed only to create a world where starvation and warfare are more common than they were in neolithic times? Why has the history of what we dare to call "progress" been marked by an increase in the quantity of human suffering? 4

Could it be that men are determined to be greedy, aggressive, and brutish? Does some selfish gene, some territorial imperative, drive us blindly into hostile action? Is the story of Cain and Abel etched on our DNA? Does excess testosterone condemn us to violence and early heart attacks? 5

Because men have historically been the major agents of violence, it is tempting to place the blame on our biology and to conclude that the problem lies in nature's faulty design rather than in our willfulness. But all deterministic explanations ignore the obvious: men are systematically conditioned to endure pain, to kill, and to die in the service of the tribe, nation, or state. The male psyche is, first and foremost, the warrior psyche. Nothing shapes, informs, and molds us so much as society's demand that we become specialists in the use of power and violence, or as we euphemistically say, "defense." Historically, the major difference between men and women is that men have always been expected to be able to resort to violence when necessary. The capacity and willingness for violence has been central to our self-definition. The male psyche has not been built upon the rational "I think; therefore I am" but upon the irrational "I conquer; therefore I am." 6

In what has come to be the normal state of emergency of modern life, we grant the state the power to interrupt the lives of young men, to draft 7 them into the army, and to initiate them into the ritual of violence. Clichés that pass for wisdom tell us: "The army will make a man out of you," and "Every man must have his war."

Induction into the army or, if you are one of the lucky "few" into the marines, involves the same process of systematic destruction of individuality that accompanied initiation in primitive tribes. The shaved head, the uniform, the abusive drill instructors, the physical and emotional ordeal of boot camp, are meant to destroy the individual's will and teach the dogface that the primary virtue of a man is not to think for himself but to obey his superiors, not to listen to his conscience but to follow orders. Like the rites of all warrior societies it teaches men to value what is tough and to despise what is "feminine" and tenderhearted. Nowhere so clearly as in the military do we learn the primitive maxim that the individual must sacrifice himself to the will of the group as it is represented by the authorities.

In the mythic initiation, the neophyte identifies with the tribal heroes. Their story provides the pattern that will be superimposed on his autobiography. That this mythical-mystical mode of initiation is still in force in our so-called modern mind can be seen in the continual references to the great American hero, John Wayne, in the literature that is now coming out of the Vietnam experience. "The war was billed on the marquee as a John Wayne shoot-'em-up test of manhood . . . I had flashes of images of John Wayne films with me as the hero . . . You see the baddies and the goodies on television and at the movies . . . I wanted to kill the bad guy."[1] Early Christians learned that the authentic life was an "imitation of Christ"; initiates in the mystery cults became the god Dionysius; nice American boys going into battle became John Wayne, the mythic man who had been divinized and made immortal by the media.

For the last four thousand years the baptism by fire has been a great male initiation rite. To win the red badge of courage was the mark of a man. Phillip Caputo reporting on Vietnam states the tradition in classical form: "Before the firefight, those Marines fit both definitions of the word *infantry*, which means either 'a body of soldiers equipped for service on foot,' or 'infants, boys, youths collectively.' The difference was that the second definition could no longer be applied to them. Having received that primary sacrament of war, baptism of fire, their boyhoods were behind them. Neither they nor I thought of it in those terms at the time. We didn't say to ourselves, We've been under fire, we've shed blood, now we're men. We were simply aware, in a way we could not express, that something significant had happened to us."[2]

Although only a minority of men actually serve in the military and fewer still are initiated into the brotherhood of those who have killed, all men are marked by the warfare system and the military virtues. We all wonder: Am I a man? Could I kill? If tested would I prove myself brave? Does it matter whether I have actually killed or risked being killed? Would you think more or less of me if I had undergone the baptism of fire? Would I think more or less of myself? What special mystery surrounds the initiated, the veteran? What certification of manhood matches the Purple Heart or the Congressional Medal of Honor?

Men have all been culturally designed with conquest, killing, or dying in mind. Even sissies. Early in life a boy learns that he must be prepared to fight or be called a sissy, a girl. Many of the creative men I know were sissies. They were too sensitive, perhaps too compassionate to fight. And most of them grew up feeling they were somehow inferior and had flunked the manhood test. I suspect that many writers are still showing the bullies on the block that the pen is mightier than the sword. The test shaped us, whether we passed or flunked.

We are all war-wounded.

The Warrior Psyche

To understand men and the twisted relations that exist between men and women, we need to look at what happens to a man when his mind, body, and soul are socially informed by the expectation that he must be prepared to suffer, die, and kill to protect those he loves.

These are not the kinds of topics we usually consider when we think about men. Why not? Why do we so seldom wonder if the habit of war has made men what they are rather than vice versa? The warfare system has become such an accepted part of the social and psychological horizon within which we live, that its formative influence on everything we are and do has become largely invisible. Or to put the matter another way, the warfare system has formed the eyes through which we see war, which means we are encompassed within the myth of war. We assume war is "just the way things are." It is an inevitable outcome of the power dynamics that exist among tribes, groups, nations. And because we rarely examine our basic assumptions about war, generation after generation, we continue to beg the crucial question about the relationship between the warfare system and the male and female psyche.

Lately we have generated a new, and I believe, false hope that women can gain enough power to solve the problems men create. The recent feminist slogan "Peace is Matriotic" reveals in a single phrase the degree to which the warfare system has bewitched us all. It assumes the opposite, that "War is Patriotic," a problem caused by men. But as we will see, the warfare system unfortunately shapes both the male and female psyche equally (although in opposite ways). History offers us the chance to take responsibility and change what we previously considered our fate. What it does not offer is virgin births, pure heroes, guiltless saviors, or morally immaculate groups (the faithful, the bourgeoisie, the moral majority, the sons of God or the daughters of the goddess) whose innocence gives them the leverage to change the course of things in the twinkling of an eye or the length of a sermon.

Our best hope is to see how the war system has been constructed, and then to undertake the hundred-year task of taking it apart piece by piece.   17

Modern psychology has given us two great intellectual tools that can help us understand the warrior psyche: Freud's idea of "defense mechanisms" and Wilhelm Reich's notion of "character armor."   18

Freud assumed he was offering an objective, empirical, scientific, and universally valid account of the essential nature of the human psyche. But nowhere was he so much a product of his time as in his assumptions that his own theories were not conditioned by his time and social milieu. Like most nineteenth-century scientists, he assumed he could see reality as if from a god's-eye perspective—the way it really was. But Freud is interesting and useful to us precisely when we see his psychology not as a description of the inevitable structure of the human psyche, but as a psychogram of the way the minds and emotions of men and women have been shaped by the warfare system. His account of the self inadvertently lays bare the logic of the warrior psyche. The psychological landscape he describes, no less than the political landscape Matthew Arnold described in *Dover Beach*, is that of a battlefield where "ignorant armies clash by night."   19

The psyche, according to Freud, is like a miniaturized nation that is organized to guard against the threats real or imagined, from internal or external sources. It is the scene of a perpetual conflict in which the embattled ego is constantly fending off angelic legions and moralistic forces of the superego and the dark powers of the libidinal underworld. Even in the healthy individual there is a continual conflict between the instinctual drives that propel the organism toward gratification and the defenses and counterforces that oppose the expression and gratification.   20

The weapons used in this struggle, the defense mechanisms, are well honed but for the most part are used automatically, with little awareness. In fact, defense mechanisms, like the propaganda apparatus of a modern state, function best when they censor awareness of the actual (ambiguous) situation of the self. They foster comforting illusions and keep unpleasant realities out of consciousness.   21

Consider the obvious parallels between the modus operandi of the warfare state and some of the defense mechanisms Freud considered the armamentum of the ego.[3]   22

Repression, "the exclusion of a painful idea and its associated feeling from consciousness," is like the repression of our genocide against native Americans and the consequent sense of appropriate guilt.   23

Isolation, the splitting off of appropriate feelings from ideas, is obvious in our habit of thinking calmly about nuclear destruction.   24

Reaction formation, "replacing an unacceptable drive with its opposite," is at work in naming the MX missile "the peacekeeper."   25

Displacement, directing an unacceptable wish away from its original to a less threatening object, e.g., occurs when a man rapes a woman to give vent to the anger he feels toward his mother or toward the authorities who brutalized the "feminine" aspects of himself. 26

Projection, attributing an unacceptable impulse to somebody else, allows us to claim that the enemy is planning to destroy us. 27

Denial, remaining unaware of the painful reality, is evident in the pretense that we can use nuclear weapons against an enemy without destroying ourselves. 28

Rationalization, using reasons to disguise one's unconscious motives, is used when we announce to the world that "We sent arms to the Contras only because we wanted to help them remain free, not because we want to dominate Central America." 29

Wilhelm Reich added a crucial twist to the notion of defense mechanisms. Not only the mind, but the body is formed by living in the ambiance of threat and violence. When we perceive danger, the body immediately prepares itself for fight or flight, glands and muscles switch to emergency status. Adrenaline courses through our system, the heart rate increases, and we assume a "red alert" stance. In the natural course of things, a threat arises and recedes, the lion approaches and retreats or is killed. But a culture that is at war or constantly preparing for a possible war conspires to create the perception, especially among its male citizens, that the threat from the enemy is always present, and therefore we can never let down our guard. "Eternal vigilance is the price of liberty." So men, the designated warriors, gradually form "character armor," a pattern of muscular tension and rigidity that freezes them into the posture that is appropriate only for fighting—shoulders back, chest out, stomach pulled in, anal sphincter tight, balls drawn up into the body as far as possible, eyes narrowed, breathing foreshortened and anxious, heart rate accelerated, testosterone in full flow. The warrior's body is perpetually uptight and ready to fight. 30

Recently, on an ordinary afternoon, I watched an early stage of the education of a warrior in my side yard. Two boys, four and six years old, were swinging on a rope that hung from a tall limb of an old cottonwood tree. For a while they took turns in an orderly way, but then the bigger boy seized power and began to hog the swing. The little boy protested, "It's my turn," and went over and tried to take the rope. "Bug off!" shouted the big boy, and pushed the little boy roughly to the ground. The man-child struggled to his feet, jaw quivering, fighting to hold back his tears, and said defiantly, "That didn't hurt." 31

Condition a man (or a woman) to value aggression above all other virtues, and you will produce a character type whose most readily expressed emotion will be anger. 32

Condition a woman (or a man) to value submission above all other attitudes and you will produce a character type whose most readily expressed emotion will be sadness. 33

Depending on how you look at it, aggression may be man's greatest virtue   34
or his greatest vice. If our destiny is to conquer and control, it is the prime
mover. If our destiny is to live in harmony, it is the legacy of an animal past.
Or maybe it is only focused energy that may be as easily directed toward
making a hospital as making war.

Research has shown it is not simple aggression but aggression mixed with   35
hostility that predisposes Type A personalities to heart attacks. Unfortunately,
the majority of men, being novices at introspection, have a hard time separating aggression and anger. Thus, the social forces that encourage a man to
be an extrovert, hard-driving and iron-willed, prepare him equally for success
and a heart attack. (And why does the heart "attack" a man if not because he
has become an enemy to his own heart? And why does it most frequently
attack a man at 9 a.m. on Mondays?)[4] Arguably, the fact that men die seven
to nine years before women on an average is due to the emotions, behavior,
and character-armor that make up the warrior psyche. Statistically, in modern
times the traditional female stance of submission has proven to have greater
survival value than the traditional male stance of aggression. The meek do
inherit the earth for nearly a decade longer than the conquistadors. Men pay
dearly for the privilege of dominating. As women enter the arenas where
competition and conquest are honored above all other virtues, both their
character armor and their disease profiles are likely to begin to resemble
men's.

In the psyche no less than in a machine, "form follows function." Thus   36
a man's mind-body-spirit that has been informed by the warfare system will
necessarily be shaped by the actuality or anticipation of conflict, competition,
and combat. The following are some of the characteristics of the warrior
psyche:

- A dramatic, heroic stance. The warrior's world is structured on one of
  the oldest dramatic principles—the conflict between an antagonist and
  protagonist, a hero and a villain. It is filled with the stuff of which good
  stories are made: crucial battles, brave deeds, winning and losing. And
  violent emotions: hate and love, loyalty and betrayal, courage and cowardice. It is not accidental that we speak of the "theater" of war. The
  warrior finds the meaning of his life in playing a part in an overarching
  story of the cosmic struggle between good and evil.
- Willpower, decision and action. The warrior psyche has little time for
  contemplation, appreciation, and simple enjoyment. It is a mind disciplined to strategic thinking, to the setting of goals and the elaboration of
  means. It asks "how" rather than "why."
- A sense of adventure, danger, excitement, and heightened awareness that
  comes from living in the presence of death. Many men who have been
  to war confess that for all its horror it was the one time in their lives
  when they felt most alive. The warrior denies death, lives with the illusion

of his own invulnerability and his immortality in being a part of the corps, the brotherhood of Valhalla. By remaining in the excitement of the ambiance of violent death he escapes the anxiety (and courage) of having to live creatively with the prospect of normal death.

- The identification of action with force. When politics reaches a point of impotence the warrior's imagination turns immediately to the use of force. Thus the specter of impotence always shadows the warrior. He must constantly prove he is powerful by his willingness to do and endure violence.

- A paranoid worldview. The warrior is marked by a negative identity; his life is oriented against the enemy, the rival, the competition. He moves with others only when he conspires to make them allies in his struggle against a common enemy.

- Black-and-white thinking. The more intense a conflict becomes, the more we oversimplify issues, and screen information to exclude anything that is not relevant to winning the struggle. The warrior's eye and mind narrow to stereotypes that reduce the enemy to an entity that can be defeated or killed without remorse. In the heat of battle life it is: Kill or be killed; You are either for or against us.

- The repression of fear, compassion, and guilt. The warrior psyche automatically manufactures propaganda that allows it to feel morally self-righteous by transferring blame to the enemy.

- Obsession with rank and hierarchy. The military world is organized on the basis of a hierarchy of command and submission, a pecking order in which the private obeys the corporal, the corporal the sergeant, etc. In such a world rank limits responsibility. Because obedience is required there is always a rationale denying one's radical freedom—"I was only following orders, doing my duty."

- The degrading of the feminine. To the degree that a culture is governed by a warfare system, it will reduce women to second-class citizens whose function is essentially to service warriors.

Cannon Fodder, Gang Rape, and the War System

In the last generation, the women's movement has made us aware of the ways women have been victims of men's violence. Recent estimates[5] are that, in the U.S., three out of four women will be victims of at least one violent crime in their lifetime. Every eighteen seconds a woman is beaten, and the rate of rape is thirteen times higher than in Britain. Short of some theory that attributes violence to the innate sinfulness of men, the only way we can make sense of this propensity to brutalize women is by looking for the factors that

37

cause men to be violent. We must assume, as they say about computers, "Garbage in, garbage out." Violence in, violence out. Men are violent because of the systematic violence done to their bodies and spirits. Being hurt they become hurters. In the overall picture male violence toward women is far less than male violence against other males. For instance, the F.B.I. reports that of the estimated 21,500 murders in the United States in 1989 two-thirds of the victims were males. What we have refused to acknowledge is that these outrages are a structural part of a warfare system that victimizes both men and women.

The advent of total war and nuclear weapons has recently forced women   38
and children to live with the deadweight of the threat of annihilation that men have always felt in times of war or peace. In the old war code, warriors were expendable but women and children were to be protected behind the shield. Granted, the sanctity of innocence was violated as often as it was respected in warfare. The point is: no one even suggested that men's lives have a claim to the sanctity and protection afforded, in theory, to women and children. It is wrong to kill women and children but men are legitimate candidates for systematic slaughter—cannon fodder.

Every man is "the Manchurian candidate," a hypnotized agent of the state   39
waiting to be called into active service by the bugle call of "Duty," "Honor," "Patriotism." While the official stories all rehearse the glory of the crusade, men harbor the secret knowledge from the time we are young that war is more gory than glory. As a boy, I read the names on the Rolls of Honor on the bronze plaques in churches and memorial auditoriums and imagined what it was like for Harvey Jackson 1927–1945, still a boy at eighteen, to die in the mud on a remote island in the Pacific. And we all saw the crippled veterans who had nothing between their bitterness and despair except war stories and wondered if we would still want to live with such perpetual wounds.

The wounds that men endure, and the psychic scar tissue that results   40
from living with the expectation of being a battlefield sacrifice, is every bit as horrible as the suffering women bear from the fear and the reality of rape. Rise a hundred miles above this planet and look at history from an Olympian perspective and you must conclude that when human beings organize their political lives around a war system, men bear as much pain as women. Our bodies are violated, we are regularly slaughtered and mutilated, and if we survive battle we bear the burden of blood-guilt. When we accept the war system, men and women alike tacitly agree to sanction the violation of the flesh—the rape of women by men who have been conditioned to be "warriors," and the gang rape of men by the brutality of war. Until women are willing to weep for and accept equal responsibility for the systematic violence done to the male body and spirit by the war system, it is not likely that men will lose enough of their guilt and regain enough of their sensitivity to weep and accept responsibility for women who are raped and made to suffer the indignity of economic inequality.

If we are to honor as well as be critical of manhood we need to remember 41 that most men went to war, shed blood, and sacrificed their lives with the conviction that it was the only way to defend those whom they loved. For millennia men have been assigned the dirty work of killing and have therefore had their bodies and spirits forged into the shape of a weapon. It is all well and good to point out the folly of war and to lament the use of violence. But short of a utopian world from which greed, scarcity, madness, and ill will have vanished, someone must be prepared to take up arms and do battle with evil. We miss the mark if we do not see that manhood has traditionally required selfless generosity even to the point of sacrifice. "To support his family, the man has to be distant, away hunting or fighting wars; to be tender, he must be tough enough to fend off enemies. To be generous, he must be selfish enough to amass goods, often by defeating other men; to be gentle, he must first be strong, even ruthless in confronting enemies; to love he must be aggressive enough to court, seduce, and 'win' a wife."[6] It was historical necessity and not innate hardness of hearts or taste for cruelty that caused masculinity to evolve into a shell of muscle and will wrapped around a vacuum.

I think what I have said about the warfare system and the warrior psyche is 42 mostly true. But another voice rises up from some primitive depth within myself, the voice of a proud warrior, that I found first in a dream:

I go down into a dark, smoky basement where I am to be initiated into 43 one of the mysteries of manhood. As I enter the room I see that men are sitting around a ring in which two men are fighting. I watch as the fighters batter each other with their fists, but my fascination turns to horror when they pull knives and start slashing at each other. Blood flows. Then one of the fighters stabs and kills the other. I rush from the room in revulsion and moral indignation and report the incident to the police.

I woke from the dream in a sweat, filled with anxiety, unable to go back 44 to sleep. As I began to probe I realized that in the dream I was the "good," moral judgmental observer of the violence and that the fighters were "bad" men. As I lay tossing and turning, it occurred to me to experiment by changing roles in the dream and becoming one of the fighters. After all, it was my dream and all the characters in it were parts of myself. No sooner did I project myself inside the bodies of the fighters than my anxiety vanished and was replaced by a feeling of power and the elation. I was inside the ecstasy of hitting and being hit, lost in the excitement of the battle. I was no longer the moral observer but the warrior lost in the primal battle to survive. And it was not pain I felt but a fierce animal power, raw courage, and the strong knowledge that, if my life was threatened, I would fight with everything in me.

It has been twenty years since my blood-dream, but I remember it vividly 45 because it signaled some kind of change in the depth of my being. It put me in touch with the animal that, if threatened, would defend its life. It told me that although I was moral I was also capable of the primitive amoral violence necessary for survival. After the dream I lost a measure of my fear, paranoia, and feeling of vulnerability, because I knew I would instinctively defend myself if attacked.

This is the dilemma a sensitive man must face: So long as the world is 46 less than perfect the warrior can never wholly retire. It still takes gentleness and fierceness to make a whole man.

Notes

1. Mark Baker, *Nam: The Vietnam War in the Words of the Men and Women Who Fought There* (New York: Morrow, 1982), p. 22.

2. Phillip Caputo, *A Rumor of War* (New York: Ballantine, 1978), p. 120.

3. *American Handbook of Psychiatry*, Vol. 1 (New York: Basic Books, 1974), p. 750.

4. Larry Dossey, M.D., *Recovering the Soul* (New York: Bantam Books, 1989).

5. *Newsweek* (July 16, 1990), *New York Times* (August 6, 1990).

6. David Gilmore, *Manhood in the Making: Cultural Concepts of Masculinity* (New Haven, CT: Yale University Press, 1990), p. 230.

THE ARMY WILL MAKE A "MAN" OUT OF YOU

◑

HELEN MICHALOWSKI

An activist with the War Resisters League West, Helen Michalowski has been an ardent speaker against violence. She co-edited the book *Power of the People: Active Nonviolence in the U.S.* (1977), a photographic history of pacifism and nonviolent social movements in America. In the following essay, she presents the stories and thoughts of men who have experienced the often inhuman rigors of military basic training.

Male children are set up to be soldiers. The military takes the attitudes and behaviors already developed in young males and hones them to a fine edge. The attitudes include being emotionally closed, preferring power over pleasure, and feeling superior to women. The behaviors include domination, aggression, and physical violence to oneself and to others.

The military prefers to work on young men who are still unsure of their individual identity and place in the world. (Today the work force in the military is more than half under the age of 24. The median age for teamsters is 38.4, longshoremen and stevedores 44.8 years, policemen 36 years and firemen 38 years. From *Enlisted Times*, Oct. 79, p. 14). In basic training young men are isolated from everyone but people like themselves where they are totally under the control of drill sergeants who conduct a not so subtle form of brainwashing.

Steve Hassna, Army Drill Sergeant:

There's Joe Trainee doing what Joe does best—being dumb. And it's not the man's fault. But it is such a shock to his—to his whole being. You take that man, and you totally strip him, and then you make him like a big ball of clay, and you take and you make him a soldier. Whether he wants to be a soldier or not, you make him a soldier.

. . . They taught me in drill sergeant's [school], get the psychological advantage off the top. Remain on top; remain the aggressor. Keep the man in a state of confusion at all times, if you want to deal with him in that way, but do not let him get his thing together so he can retaliate in any way, you know what I mean? If in doubt, attack.

. . . I was gruff—I was gruff to the point where I was letting you know *I am in command.* You might as well strike anything in your mind, any feeling, that you are going to do anything but what I tell you. (*Smith*)

Victor DeMattei, Army Paratrooper:

Basic training encourages woman-hating (as does the whole military experience), but the way it does it is more complex than women sometimes suppose. The purpose of basic training is to dehumanize a male to the point where he will kill on command and obey his superiors automatically. To do that he has to be divorced from his natural instincts which are essentially nonviolent. I have never met anyone (unless he was poisoned by somebody's propaganda) who had a burning urge to go out and kill a total stranger.

So how does the army get you to do this? First you are harassed and brutalized to the point of utter exhaustion. Your individuality is taken away, i.e., same haircuts, same uniforms, only marching in formation. Everyone is punished for one man's "failure," etc. You never have enough sleep or enough to eat. All the time the drill instructors are hammering via songs and snide remarks that your girl is off with "Jody." Jody is the mythical male civilian or 4F who is absconding with "your" girl, who by implication is naturally just waiting to leave with Jody.

After three weeks of this, you're ready to kill anybody. Keep in mind there is no contact with the outside world. The only reality you see is what the drill instructors let you see. I used to lie on my bunk at night and say my name to myself to make sure I existed. (*Letter to Helen Michalowski, December 1978*)

In basic training, the man is made an object, dehumanized, subjugated. The system starts to break down when people are seen as people.

Robert McLain, Marine:

Talk to anybody who was going through Marine Corps boot camp . . . the dehumanizing process is just hard to describe. I wish somebody had a record of suicides that go on at these places . . . [and] the beatings that go on daily. Boys are turned not into men, but beasts—beasts that will fight and destroy at a moment's notice, without any regard to what they are fighting or why they are fighting, but just fight. I have seen men fight each other over a drink of water when there was plenty for both of them. (*Lifton*)

Steve Hassna:

. . . I hated that thing of embarrassing a man in front of 40 people. Basic training is such a dehumanizing process to begin with that when you stand there and dehumanize a person in front of his peers, that he's got to sleep with, and in the same building, that's hard. They lose respect for the man.

... But I don't like dying. And killing. It's very weird because I started   12
realizing again, thousands and thousands of men, 18, 19, 20, 22-years-old—
I'm thinking, Jesus Christ, man, they're gonna kill every swinging dick in the
country! You know, there won't be a male American over 25 left standing. I
can't—it just—it got to be bodies. I started to get personal with them. Instead
of looking at them as Joe Trainee and that was it, I was looking at them as
McNulty and Peterson and Nema and Hill and the other thousand that I
can't remember. Well, when you do that ... it don't set too well. Now it sets
even worse because it's taken me seven years to get to the point where I can
look back on that and realize—you know, I trained troops. I was a staff
sergeant, E-6, with the hat, who trained troops for a year. And probably half
of them are dead. And I'll never know. (*Smith*)

The military is a blatant hierarchy. Power and privilege correspond di-   13
rectly with one's rank, but feelings of superiority are encouraged throughout.
Especially those men in less desirable, more hazardous assignments are encouraged to feel superior. Inevitably, someone has to be on the bottom.
Somebody has to be the scapegoat, the enemy.

Ernie "Skip" Boitano, 9th Division Army:

... The military has this thing where if your platoon sergeant gets down   14
on you and you don't have any kind of karma, something going for you to
get him off your back, then all of a sudden the platoon leader's down on you,
and if the platoon leader and the platoon sergeant start making you the kicking
boy of the platoon, then all of a sudden the CO's [commanding officer] down
on you. All he hears about you is bad. And the next thing you know, you're
up for an article 15 and then you're up for a battalion article 15 because the
colonel's heard a lot of bad things about you. He sees you goofing off and he
catches you. You don't necessarily have to be doing anything anybody else
wouldn't be doing, but because everybody kind of knows who you are negatively, you're it. It keeps building on top of that. It just starts with one person
with a little bit of power to get down on you. He can bend someone else's
ear and say, "Hey, look at this clown." It may even be that the whole platoon
starts working on him. They want to get in tight with the sergeant or they
want to feather their cap. So they're all working on this one poor guy. Once
these people get down on you, it's downhill from there. There's no getting
out from under it ... Maybe that's something about people ... I know guys
who tried. They went to the field all the time. They did everything they could
and it never got any better. It was like somebody got picked out and they put
a sign around your neck and from then on everybody just let them have it.
Any time they had trouble, that person got it. (*Smith*)

During basic training, the man's insecurity about his own sexuality is   15
manipulated so as to link sexuality with aggression and violence.

Unnamed soldier:

. . . I [was] very stirred, patriotically [and thought] that I someday was 16
going to have to, might have to, do this . . . That I would get my chance . . .
I remember questioning myself . . . saying this may all be a pile of crap . . .
this stuff about patriotism and yet because of this indecision . . . the confusion
within myself, I said . . . I don't think I'll ever be able to live with myself
unless I confront this, unless I find out, because if I [do not] I'll always wonder
whether I was afraid to do it . . . I had the whole question of whether I was
a man or not . . . whether I was a coward. (*Lifton*)

Wayne Eisenhart, Marine:

One of the most destructive facets of bootcamp is the systematic attack 17
on the recruits' sexuality. While in basic training, one is continually addressed
as faggot or girl. These labels are usually screamed into the face from a
distance of two or three inches by the drill instructor, a most awesome,
intimidating figure. During such verbal assaults one is required, under threat
of physical violence, to remain utterly passive. A firm degree of psychological
control is achieved by compelling men to accept such labels. More importantly, this process is used as a means to threaten the individual's sexual
identity. The goals of training are always just out of reach. We would be
ordered to run five miles when no one was in shape for more than two or
were ordered to do 100 push-ups when they and we both knew we could only
do 50. In this manner, one can be made to appear weak or ineffective at any
time. At this point, the drill instructor usually screams something in your face
like "You can't hack it, you goddamned faggot."

. . . Once the sexual identity was threatened, psychological control 18
achieved, and sexuality linked with military function, it was made clear that
the military function was aggression. The primary lesson of boot camp, towards which all behavior was shaped, was to seek dominance. Our mission
was always "close with the enemy and destroy him." To fail in this, as in all
else, was non-masculine. Aggression and seeking dominance thus was equated
with masculinity. Recruits were brutalized, frustrated, and cajoled to a flash
point of high tension. Recruits were often stunned by the depths of violence
erupting from within. Only on these occasions of violent outbursts did the
drill instructor cease his endless litany of "You dirty faggot" and "Can't you
hack it, little girls." After a day of continuous harassment, I bit a man on the
face during hand-to-hand combat, gashing his eyebrow and cheek. I had lost
control. For the first time the drill instructor didn't physically strike me or
call me a faggot. He put his arm around me and said that I was a lot more
man than he had previously imagined. Similar events occurred during bayonet
drill. In several outbursts I utterly savaged men. In one instance, I knocked a
man off his feet and rammed a knee into his stomach. Growling and roaring
I went for his throat. I was kicked off the man just before I smashed his voice

box with my fist. In front of the assembled platoon the DI (drill instructor) gleefully reaffirmed my masculinity. The recruit is encouraged to be effective and to behave violently and aggressively. (*Eisenhart, J. of Humanist Psychology*)

Physical violence against troops is more central to basic training in the Marines than in other branches of the armed forces. All branches associate masculinity with insensitivity, invulnerability and violence—only more subtly. 19

Wayne Eisenhart, Marine and Counselor:

. . . In [Marine] boot camp, there was a Private Green who had a good deal of difficulty with the rigorous physical regime. He was slender and light complexioned. Private Green was a bright, well-intentioned young man who had volunteered and yet lacked the composite aggressive tendencies thought to comprise manhood. Although not effeminate by civilian standards, he was considered so in boot camp. He was continually harassed and called girl and faggot. We began to accept the stereotyping of him as effeminate, passive, and homosexual. 20

While in the midst of a particularly grueling run, Private Green began to drop out. The entire platoon was ordered to run circles around him each time he fell out. Two men ran from the formation to attempt to carry him along. His eyes were glazed and there was a white foam all around his mouth. He was beyond exhaustion. He fell again as the entire formation of 80 men continued to run circles around him. Four men ran from the formation and kicked and beat him in an attempt to make him run. He stumbled forward and fell. Again he was pummelled. Finally four men literally carried him on their shoulders as we ran to the base area where we expected to rest. We were then told that "No goddamned bunch of little girl faggots who can't run seven miles as a unit are going to rest." We were ordered to do strenuous calis-thenics. Private Green, the weak, effeminate individual who had caused the additional exercises, was made to lead us without participating. He counted cadence while we sweated. Tension crackled in the air, curses were hurled, and threats made. As we were made to exercise for a full hour, men became so exhausted their stomachs cramped and they vomited. Private Green was made to laugh at us as he counted cadence. The DI looked at Private Green and said, "You're a weak no-good-for-nothing queer." Then turning to the glowering platoon he said, "As long as there are faggots in this outfit who can't hack it, you're all going to suffer." As he turned to go into the duty hut he sneered, "Unless you women get with the program, straighten out the queers, and grow some balls of your own, you best give your soul to God 'cause your ass is mine and so is your mother's on visiting day." With a roar, 60 to 70 enraged men engulfed Private Green, knocking him to the ground, kicking and beating him. He was picked up and passed over the heads of the roaring, densely packed mob. His eyes were wide with terror, the mob beyond reason. Green was tossed and beaten in the air for about five minutes and 21 was then literally hurled onto a concrete wash rack. He sprawled there dazed and bleeding.

Private Green had almost been beaten to death in a carefully orchestrated ritual of exorcism. In him were invested those qualities most antithetical to the military ethos and most threatening to the sexual identity of the individual Marines. Masculinity is affirmed through aggression and completion of the military function. We had been ordered to run around Private Green in order to equate passivity and nonaggression with being a clear and present danger. (*Eisenhart, J. of Humanistic Psychology*) 22

Basic training not only links sexuality with dominance, aggression and violence, it also teaches that the man's very survival depends upon maintaining these attitudes and behaviors. By associating qualities that are stereotypically considered common to women and homosexual men with all that is undesirable and unacceptable in the male recruit, misogyny and homophobia are perpetuated in the military and in society at large. It is understandable that it would take a long time and a lot of work for men to undo the effects of military training as it pertains to their own male self-image and these images of women and gays. 23

To my knowledge, no studies have been done to establish or refute a connection between military training/experience and violence against women; however, it seems reasonable to suspect such a connection. The purpose of basic training is to prepare men for combat. That experience certainly affects men in their relationships with other people, especially women. 24

Robert McLain:

. . . When I came back home I was very much anti-war, and yet there was a hostility in me toward other people . . . If someone irritated me, my first impulse was to kill the fucker. . . . I'd catch myself and I'd think of another alternative to deal with whatever the problem was. . . . Today there is still a lot of hate in me—a hatred that makes it difficult to form . . . relationships with anyone. (*Lifton*) 25

Wayne Eisenhart:

. . . One young veteran I have worked with became completely impotent three years after discharge. Unable to maintain an erection during the last three attempts at intercourse, he was afraid to try again. At this time he purchased a weapon, a pistol, and began brandishing and discharging it. His sexuality was blocked by a frustrated idealized male role which could not tolerate intimacy. The means to affirm manhood was through face to face combat, aggressive behavior, and the seeking of dominance. 26

. . . [There] is a constant fear of being harmed by someone and a constant elimination of real or fantasized adversaries in order to maintain a feeling of adequacy and security. My personal experience directly validates this. Since I 27 was not exposed to much combat in Vietnam, I can only conclude that this process originated for me in basic training.

Perhaps this can best be articulated if I share some observations concern- 28 ing my own intrusive imagery. Generally these take the form òf daydreams. They consist of brief, very violent eye-gouging, throat-ripping fantasies revealing an underlying hypermasculine ideal. There is usually a woman involved and I am always dominant and inordinately violent in defeating some adversary. These brief images leave me with a feeling of power and supermasculinity. I usually find that my muscles tense during such imagery . . .

As a civilian, one generally attempts to create a more authentic masculine 29 self-image that cannot help but be influenced by the military experience. Constantly in social and sexual relationships I have found myself trying to be "heavy," feeling at times foolishly as if I were a caricature of myself. I have striven constantly to achieve dominance. In the past more so than now, I felt insecure sexually and had a very low tolerance for feeling threatened. Occasional outbursts of violence have shamed and frightened me. This all has cost me dearly in social relationships. (*Eisenhart, J. of Social Issues*)

Robert Lifton, Psychologist who worked with Vietnam veterans:

A number of veterans told how, when brushed by someone on the street— 30 or simply annoyed by something another person had done—they would have an impulse to "throttle" or kill him. And they would directly associate this impulse with patterns of behavior cultivated in Vietnam: with "wasting" whomever passed for the enemy, with the numbing and brutalization underlying that behavior, but also with the rage beneath the numbing. (*Lifton*)

Steve Hassna:

. . . A lot of times I'd wake up in the middle of the night and throw [my 31 wife] out of bed and throw her behind the bunker. And start screaming. She was scared of me. She finally left me. Because I would get to the point where I was so pissed off, I'd tell her, "Don't do it again; don't push me." I didn't want to hurt nobody, but I'd get to the point where I can't relate to people no more and so I just snapped. I was going like this until I realized what it was that sent me to Vietnam, indoctrinated from childbirth, the whole thing, I stopped having these bad dreams. Because I could see it wasn't me that was fucked up, it was my government and my whole society that got me this way. (*Smith*)

Robert Lifton, Psychologist:

Falling in love, or feeling oneself close to that state, could be especially 32 excruciating—an exciting glimpse of a world beyond withdrawal and numbing, but also a terrifying prospect. A typical feeling, when growing fond of a girl [sic] was, "You're getting close—watch out!" The most extreme emotion of this kind expressed was:

"If I'm fucking, and a girl says I love you, then I want to kill her . . . [because] if you get close . . . you get hurt." [33]

. . . It is possible that he and many others continue to associate the nakedness of sex with Vietnam images of grotesque bodily disintegration—as did Guy Sajer, with memories from the German Army experience of World War II: "As soon as I saw naked flesh [in a beginning sexual encounter] I braced myself for a torrent of entrails, remembering countless wartime scenes, with smoking, stinking corpses pouring out their vitals." (*Lifton*) [34]

When people are divided into distinct sex roles, the function of the female is to give birth and nurture, while the function of the male is to kill and die. Powerful cultural myths support the idea that the purpose of the son is to be a blood sacrifice—Jesus sacrificed to God the Father, Isaac to Abraham. [35]

There are some parallels between the oppression of women and men according to sex roles. The media/cultural hype is similar—women love being sex objects and men love getting their heads beaten, whether on a football field or a battlefield. The appeal to virtue is similar. Women sacrifice themselves to serving their family, while men sacrifice themselves to the Armed Service. The cover-up is similar. Until recently no one heard about rape or battered women, and no one ever talked about men who come back from war sound in body but emotionally disabled. And who ever talks about the physically disabled? [36]

One wonders if there is a statistical difference between the incidence of women coming to women's shelters who associate with men having had military or para-military (police) experience and those who associate with men not having had this background. Let's interview women—mothers, sisters, lovers—who have had before-and-after basic training relationships with men. What, if any, changes do they notice? Let's also interview women "dependents," particularly military wives. What is their place in the "pecking order"? What kinds of friendships get formed when the family gets transferred every one and a half to four years? Do these women feel isolated? What do they think about the "security" of military life? [37]

Because women have not been in the military in significant numbers until recently, there does not exist a great body of material relating their experience. Let's interview women in the military. Is the training comparable? How do men in the military view and treat women they work with? Women they command? How do women in the military view other military women? [38]

For the last several years women have been recruited to the military in unprecedented numbers; not because the military has any great interest in "equality" for women, but because the male population ages 17–21 has declined by 15%. There is a great and urgent need to deepen and broaden the popular understanding that while women certainly have the right and capability to be soldiers, for women to become like men have been would not be a step toward anyone's liberation. [39]

We have to redefine the word "service" so that it is neither forced nor [40] armed. Rather than women being trained to kill, let men learn to nurture life.

Sources

Wayne Eisenhart, "You Can't Hack It Little Girl: A Discussion of the Covert Psychological Agenda of Modern Combat Training," *Journal of Social Issues*, Vol. 31, No. 4, 1975.

Wayne Eisenhart, "Flower of the Dragon: An example of Applied Humanistic Psychology," *Journal of Humanistic Psychology*, Vol. 17, No. 1, Winter 1977.

Robert J. Lifton, *Home From the War: Vietnam Veterans, Neither Victims Nor Executioners* (New York: Simon & Schuster, 1973).

Clark Smith, editor, "The Short-timers: Soldiering in Vietnam," unpublished manuscript.

THE SEXUAL CONNECTION

◖

WALTER J. GOTTLIEB

In this essay, Walter Gottlieb examines the sexual imagery in the rhetoric surrounding the Persian Gulf war. What connections does military and political language make between sex and the violence of war? What effect do these metaphors have on our thinking? Gottlieb is a free-lance writer in Washington, D.C. This article first appeared in *The Progressive* magazine in April 1991.

When the war began, a male colleague and I were watching some videotape 1
of a B-52 bomber dropping its load over Iraq. My colleague, a former Army Ranger who might have been called into action at any time, said: "Look at that B-52. It's like a large flying dick with wings! Doesn't that give you a hard-on?"

I asked if he was serious. "Absolutely," he said. 2

It got me thinking. Was there a connection between sex and the Gulf 3
war?

Listening to reporters and military officers talk about the war, I was struck 4
by the sexual images and language they used. A U.S. attack on Iraqi tanks was a "hard" kill. The Iraqis "penetrated Saudi Arabia"—their first "thrust" into that country. There was much talk of the "big sixteen-inch guns" on the battleship *Missouri*.

I noticed that the Pentagon's "bomb's-eye-view" videotapes had an almost 5
sexual quality. A long, flying projectile climactically made contact with its target—a munitions depot with a huge set of barn doors down the middle— and exploded. Even those of us who were against the war felt a tinge of exhilaration and release.

"That excitement is really obscene," says Michael Rogin, a political- 6
science professor at the University of California, Berkeley. "It's the excitement that machines bring as an extension of the body." Releasing the videotapes to the media, Rogin says, is the military's way of "hooking people into the action."

Warfare and sex are not literally equivalent, of course. But the sexual 7
imagery of the Persian Gulf war does provide clues to the underlying mentality of warfare and to our fascination with its high-tech tools. The connection is not so much between warfare and sex as between warfare and male sexual *power*. For what is war but the ultimate form of male competition?

The military itself has been known to exploit this connection. In one 8
drill, male recruits are commanded to march around—sometimes in their
underwear—grabbing their crotches with one hand and their firearms with
the other, chanting: "This is my rifle/This is my gun/One is for fightin'/The
other's for fun."

Sometimes the metaphor is almost comically real. A British company won 9
a contract to ship 500,000 "camouflaged condoms" to the Gulf. The condoms
were not to be placed on the soldiers' sexual organs but on the barrels of their
guns as protection against the desert sand. "A condom can fit over a twenty-
millimeter cannon and, in action, a round can be shot straight through," the
Toronto Globe and Mail reported.

At other times, the sexual dimension of warfare can be downright scary. 10
In the Persian Gulf, Navy pilots on the *U.S.S. Kennedy* told an Associated
Press reporter they had been watching pornographic movies before flying
bombing runs. *The Washington Post* reported that the military censored the
story, claiming it would be "too embarrassing." Pilots' songbooks are known
to equate getting killed on a bombing mission with necrophilia—they call it
"fucking a dead whore."

Just as the Pentagon uses images of aggressive male sexuality to train its 11
soldiers, so Washington resorts to sexual imagery to justify its interventions.

Think of how often the word "rape" was evoked in the Persian Gulf 12
crisis. George Bush constantly referred to the "rape of Kuwait" as justification
for the war. But Kuwait is not a person; it cannot be raped. Then why this
imagery?

Rogin says America's white male leaders have historically used vengeance 13
for rape—especially the rape of white females by men of color—as a pretext
for military and political offensives. That explains, he says, why Bush not only
used rape as a justification for the war against Iraq, but also why he cited the
sexual assault of an American officer's wife by a Panamanian soldier as a reason
for invading that country, and why he used the rape of a white woman by
black convict Willie Horton to attack Michael Dukakis in 1988. According
to Rogin, Bush has turned the American military into "the defenders of some
kind of violated womanhood." In the process, Bush proves his manhood and
overcomes his "wimp" image.

The war's male-sexual overtones may help explain why fewer women than 14
men supported the war in the Gulf. That is not to say that women are immune
to the sexual imagery and exhilaration of high-tech warfare. "For God's sake!"
a female colleague told me. "Watching those videotapes gives *me* a hard-on!"

To some, it may seem perverse to talk about sexuality and warfare in the 15
same breath. But if policymakers and soldiers feel a quasi-sexual need to flex
male power, to go on conquests, to compete and dominate, and if we, caught
up in the vicarious excitement of war, cheer them on, then *that* is what's truly
perverse.

DO WE GET TO WIN THIS TIME?

◐

SUSAN JEFFORDS

In this excerpted chapter from her book *The Remasculinization of America: Gender and the Vietnam War*
(1989), Susan Jeffords analyzes the images of the Vietnam veteran in popular culture after the war. For Jeffords, the figure of Rambo reveals much about society's
need to restore what it felt to be the lost manhood of
the American man in Vietnam, but with some dangerous implications for women. Jeffords is Associate Professor of English at the University of Washington.

II

The Vietnam War provided the context in which American males could most   1
clearly be identified as victims of a wide range of factors, most of them
articulated in the personal narratives of veterans.* This list is long and diverse.

The clearest example of American soldiers as victims comes with the   2
depiction of the nearly six hundred American POWs held prisoner by the
North Vietnamese. Soldiers were seen to be subjected to mental and physical
torture, conditions of near starvation, harassment, isolation, and deprivation.
These soldiers' narrations of beatings, humiliation, and illness at the hands
of the North Vietnamese serve, for the American public at large, as distinctive
evidence of the victimization of a segment of the American population.[1] To
the extent that the war in Vietnam is seen to be the cause of a general
disillusionment with American government and ideals, POWs are taken to
be emblematic of the American public as a whole, victims of a war it never
understood. As *Newsweek's* lead story of its special issue "The Legacy of
Vietnam" states, "We're Still Prisoners of War."[2] Fears about the estimated
twenty-five hundred MIAs possibly still being kept in camps create anxieties
about the continuation of such victimization. In Wheeler's terms, the North
Vietnamese "created" "niggers" out of the American POW.

Yet another way in which Vietnam soldiers/veterans were seen as victims   3
was in treatment they received by the American public on their return from

---

* Because this essay is an excerpted chapter, footnotes have been renumbered throughout.
[Editor's Note]

war. Ron Kovic's *Born on the Fourth of July*, an account of Kovic's Vietnam service and paralysis from a gunshot wound, recalls his first exposure to the American public's reaction to Vietnam and its veterans: "I was in Vietnam when I first heard about the thousands of people protesting the war in the streets of America. I didn't want to believe it at first—people protesting against *us* when we were putting our lives on the line for our country. . . . How could they do this to us?"[3] Asked to be grand marshal for a Memorial Day parade after his return, Kovic experiences firsthand the response of the American public. Expecting the rousing cheers he had heard as a child at earlier parades, Kovic is stunned when he and another veteran receive only stares and dis-ease. He becomes convinced that the crowds do not know who they are, for if they did,

> they'd have been flooding into the streets, stomping their feet and screaming and cheering. . . . They'd have been swelling into the streets, trying to shake their hands just like in the movies, when the boys had come home from other wars. . . . If they really knew who they were, he thought, they'd be roaring and clapping and shouting. (pp. 103–104)

But instead, "he couldn't help but feel like he was some kind of animal in a zoo or that he and Eddie were on display in some trophy case" (p. 104). Rejected by the very people whom they were defending, Vietnam veterans feel they were deprived of the reintegrating homecoming given soldiers from earlier wars and made scapegoats of the country's discomfort with the war and its outcome.

Vietnam soldiers/veterans were also seen to be victims, not only of the people they were defending, but of the very government who sent them to war in the first place. In addition to criticizing what appeared to them an often confused and misguided government policy, veterans' accounts speak most forcefully to the government's failure to make an all-out commitment to winning the war once the decision had been made to engage in it. Two comments are representative, both from soldiers in the Army's Charlie Company serving in Vietnam during 1967–69. David Brown:

> They might have won anyway . . . if they hadn't been bound down like Gulliver in Lilliput by the rules and the tactical restraints of a limited war. *A nine-to-five-war* . . . ; they could have used all that power to blow the whole country to hell, but instead they kept bumping around on little nickle-and-dime, hit-and-run operations.[4]

And Frank Goins:

> It could have been over within six months. . . . Easy. We could have took the 57,000 troops that got killed and put them all in a line behind tanks and APCs instead and just started them at one end and walked across the country. (p. 102)

By refusing to use its technological superiority, these veterans reason, the U.S. Government willingly sacrificed its own soldiers' lives and bodies for limited warfare.

Vietnam soldiers are seen as well as victims of an inequitable draft. Early on it provided deferments for primarily college-educated and middle- and upper-class draftees, and later it enabled systematic preferences to be given those who were middle and upper class and white, leaving a disproportionate amount of combat fighting to blacks, southerners, Hispanics, and the urban lower class. As Ruben Treviso puts it, "The draft boards chose those individuals who were most vulnerable. . . . Unlike middle America, many of the poor and minorities did not have money for frivolous-type deferments."[5] Of blacks in the military during the Vietnam era, 55 percent served in Vietnam, as opposed to 47 percent of whites, primarily because more blacks entered the military through the draft than whites (28 percent versus 24 percent) and more draftees served in combat. In the state of New Mexico in 1970, Hispanics made up 27 percent of the population, but 69 percent of those drafted and 44 percent of combat deaths. When it came to serving in heavy combat, minorities were disproportionately represented. 48 percent of Hispanics and 34 percent of blacks as opposed to 29 percent of whites served in heavy combat. One of every two Hispanics who went to Vietnam served in a combat unit; one of every five was killed in action; one of every three was wounded in action. Educational level was an even more important factor. Of those serving in Vietnam with less than a high school education, 49 percent were in heavy combat, whereas of those with college educations, only 15 percent served in heavy combat.[6] Whereas at the end of World War II, blacks made up 12 percent of all combat troops, by the start of the Vietnam War blacks composed 21 percent of combat troops so that in 1965, 24 percent of all Army combat deaths were blacks.[7] As General S. L. A. Marshall commented: "In the average rifle company, the strength was 50% composed of Negroes, Southwestern Mexicans, Puerto Ricans, Guamanians, Nisei, and so on, but a real cross-section of American youth? Almost never" (p. 10).

Perhaps the most distressing form of victimization came for American soldiers in their sense that they were betrayed by the very people for whom they were fighting—the Vietnamese. As Sgt. Phillip L. Woodall wrote in a letter home:

> [My platoon leader died] fighting for a people who have no concern for the war, people he did not understand, [who] knew where the enemy were, where the booby traps were hidden, yet gave no support. People that he would give portions of his food to yet would try to sell him a coke for $1. . . . This country is no gain that I can see, Dad. We're fighting, dying, for a people who resent our being over here.[8]

Many veterans recount their realizations that the Vietnamese who seemed most to serve them—hootch maids, barbers, washerwomen, prostitutes—

turned out to be spies for the NLF. As Michael Herr wrote, "the VC got work inside all the camps as shoeshine boys and laundresses and honey-dippers, they'd starch your fatigues and burn your shit and then go home and mortar your area."[9] In John Wayne and Ray Kellog's *Green Berets* (1968), Sergeant Muldoon catches a member of the Strike Force, a special team of Vietnamese who work with the American military to "kill all stinking Commie," pacing off the grounds of their base camp for mortaring. Loren Baritz summarizes what many soldiers saw as "the open hostility of some South Vietnamese, the people they had come to defend," throwing grenades into troop trucks, turning American food over to guerillas, giving information on troop strength to the NLF, and so on.[10] In narrative after narrative, American soldiers speak of the people whom they were defending as, at best, indifferent to their survival and, at worst, a threat to it.

To compound matters, soldiers felt that they could not count on those they were fighting with, the Army of the Republic of Vietnam. Again and again these soldiers are spoken of as cowardly, disorganized, unmotivated, and poorly trained. The American television-viewing public saw firsthand what seemed to be incontrovertible evidence of the cowardice of ARVN when, after announcing his policy of "Vietnamization," President Nixon launched the secret invasion of Cambodia. Sent on a major operation with nothing but American air support, the ARVN troops were ambushed. Fleeing from North Vietnamese troops, American cameras captured ARVN soldiers clinging to American helicopter skids and apparently faking wounds in order to be evacuated (p. 202).

The widespread belief in South Vietnamese corruption added to the general sense that American soldiers had of being betrayed by their ally. An example is in one of the U.S.'s most favored plans for defeating the Viet Cong, the strategic hamlet program, in which entire villages were relocated in order to isolate the Viet Cong and deprive them of both food and recruits. In addition to being forcibly removed from their ancestral lands, peasants were often "forced to construct [the hamlets] by corrupt officials who had pocketed a percentage of the money allocated for the projects."[11] Edward Brady, Combat Operations and Intelligence Advisor for the United States Military Assistance Command in Vietnam in the late sixties, recalls that ARVN command positions were bought and sold, a practice laid principally at the door of the wives of the General Staff members. He recalls that mistresses of general officers often supported themselves through selling their influence to obtain military posts for male relatives.[12]

The final and apparently clearest evidence of a victimization of Vietnam soldiers/veterans is in the growing evidence for the physical destruction caused by the exposure of thousands of U.S. troops to Agent Orange. Yet officially unestablished by government studies, some link exists between exposure to Agent Orange and the numerous cases of cancer, skin disease, birth defects, and other disorders experienced by these soldiers and their families.

Innocent of the possible effects of such exposure, soldiers did not even become aware of their danger until years after the war was over, so that their bodies continue to be literal evidence of a victimization by U.S. government war policies. The 1986 television film, *Unnatural Causes* (dir. Lamont Johnson) presents this victimization in its clearest narrative form. William V. Taylor, a veteran whose body began producing tumors several years after his service in Vietnam, felt this victimization most clearly:

> For the first time in Taylor's experience, Vietnam veterans were being portrayed on television as something other than dupes or murderers; for the first time, they were being regarded with sympathy, instead of indifference or disdain. They were victims, entitled (as their opponents had been, ten years earlier) to all the dignity victimization seems to confer in the media. He saw the change in attitude—the interest, the concern, the *respect*—among his friends, and felt rather important as a result.[13]

As Taylor's response indicates, an alteration has occurred in recent years in American popular attitudes toward the Vietnam War and the people who fought in it, one that has solidified the image of the veteran as a victim of this and other factors, many part of the war itself, but many also products of American responses to that war and its warriors. Even during the years when the Vietnam War was still unpopular, in the late 1970s, many representations led toward a perception of the soldier as sympathetic victim. Films like *The Boys in Company C* (1978) urged us to sympathize with the young men who entered the war naively or unwillingly and who, in the later controversial metaphor of *The Deer Hunter*, lost all control over their own lives, thoughts, and futures in the confusing and indiscriminate Russian roulette game that was Vietnam.

In the years following the war, the plight of the veteran became more apparent—the increasing visibility of numbers of injured or disabled veterans returning from the wars to their homes (according to hearings before the Committee on Veterans' Affairs conducted in February, March, and May 1980, over half a million veterans were receiving disability compensation from the Vietnam War as of 1980[14]); the declaration by President Carter of Vietnam Veterans' Week, from May 28 to June 3, 1979; the popularization of knowledge about Post-Traumatic Stress Syndrome (estimated to afflict anywhere from 500,000 to 700,000 Vietnam veterans); and the publicization of the rise in deaths and child deformities linked to Agent Orange. Through all of these highly visible representations, American audiences were increasingly encouraged to see the Vietnam veteran as a victim.

Time magazine concluded in 1985 that "the most important change in American attitudes toward the war in the past few years has been the public acceptance of those who fought. The Viet Nam veteran, after a long struggle, has acquired a considerable respect . . . that he deserves."[15] And on Memorial Day, 1984, President Reagan presided over the burial of the Unknown Soldier from Vietnam at Arlington National Cemetery. Signaling his "pardon" of the Vietnam veteran, Reagan declared: "We may not know his name, but we know his courage. He is the heart, the spirit, and the soul of America."[16] Laying the "old man" of Vietnam officially to rest—the individual, named soldier who had been rejected, spat on, and denied—Reagan has authorized the entrance of the "new man," the emblematic soldier whose unknown identity lays him open to a renaming by those who signify him, a renaming that retrieves him from his marginalized position and places him at the "heart of America." A 1980 Veterans Administration study of American attitudes toward Vietnam-era veterans offers testimony to this changing perception. As its authors conclude, "one detects an increasing sense of sympathy for these veterans among the public as a whole. . . . Public sentiment that 'veterans of the Vietnam war were made suckers, having to risk their lives in the wrong war in the wrong place at the wrong time' has significantly increased between 1971 (49%) and today [1979] (64%)."[17] Similar responses were given to the statement, "Veterans who served in Vietnam are part of a war that went bad": in 1971, 62 percent agreed, and in 1979, the figure rose to 81 percent (p. 87). As the authors of the report conclude: "if anything, negative attitudes toward the war are associated with higher levels of sympathy toward these veterans" (p. 85).

Receiving greatest sympathy from the American public is the American POW. With responses on a scale from 1 to 10, a 1979 Lou Harris survey asked people to rate their feelings toward different groups of people. The category "veterans who were captured and held prisoner in Vietnam" received 10s across the board, and veterans who served in Vietnam during the war received an average of 9.8, somewhat above veterans of World War II or Korea (9.6). In contrast, "our military leaders" rated only a 6.3 (behind doctors, a 7.9), and "United States Congressmen and Senators" warranted a 5.2, only slightly higher than "people who demonstrated against the war in Vietnam," who were given an average of 5.0. (Lowest on the scale were "oil company executives," who scored a 2.9) (p. 88). Because Vietnam veterans, especially POWs, rate very high in their reception of public sympathy (significantly higher than government officials), it is efficient use of cultural perception for recent Vietnam narratives to have featured both rescues of POWs and rejections of indifferent and deceptive government representatives as their primary themes. 13

This shift in public opinion has been so severe that political scientist Jean Bethke Elshtain can conclude, "Vietnam is even now in the process of being reconstructed as a story of universal victimization—of Vietnamese by us; of our soldiers by the war—and by us when we didn't welcome them home; of our nation by the war at home and *the* war; of wives and girlfriends by disturbed veterans; of nurses by the war and later nonrecognition of *their* victims."[18] Although this sense of "universal victimization" is now operating in American culture, Vietnam representation in general speaks, not to the 14 situations of nurses or even of the Vietnamese (the numbers of narratives that actually include Vietnamese people as other than stereotypes is extremely small[19]), but to the men who fought there, in particular to white men. In spite of the fact that 9.3 percent of Vietnam-era soldiers were black and disproportionately higher numbers of blacks served in heavy combat, that approximately 5 percent were Hispanics and 3.2 percent were women,[20] most media and film attention has focused on the white male. The stars of recent films like *Missing in Action* (1984) and *Missing in Action 2* (1985) and *First Blood* (1982), *Rambo: First Blood, Part II* (1985),[21] and *Rambo III* (1988) are white males.[22] Even the black veteran in *Uncommon Valor* (1985), a decorated helicopter pilot, is an outsider, not a member of the original LRRP team that has been reassembled to rescue one of their members in a POW camp, and in *Missing in Action 2* the only POW to defect to the Vietnamese cause is black.

This must make us question the social function of this recent shift in cultural attitudes toward the Vietnam veteran as more than a simple cultural apologetic for mistreatment of American soldiers and guilt over an uncertain war experience. If, in spite of the facts of war service, only certain veterans are being chosen as emblems of this cultural shift, then the production of the Vietnam veteran as victim must be further interrogated. More important, we must examine the consequences of the production of victimization in these emblems, specifically, the images and constructions generated by the scenario of victimization. A look at two of Vietnam representations' most popular films, *First Blood* and *Rambo: First Blood, Part II*, shows that the proposition of victimization, once established in films like *First Blood*, is being used to bolster a call for the regeneration of these victims—particularly white men—for a restitution of their "rights" and a return of their identity. It is, as *Time* magazine declares, "a very literal and significant transaction . . . [that] suggests that in the American imagination, the Viet Nam veteran erstwhile psychotic, cripple and loser, has been given back his manhood."[23]

III

In *First Blood,* John Rambo returns from Vietnam where he served on a Special Forces team and escaped from a POW camp in which he was severely tortured (within the opening minutes of the film, we see the numerous scars on his back from this torture). Having lost all but one of the men in his unit, Rambo hitchhikes to the town of Hope, Oregon, where he has finally traced the one remaining member of his team, Delmar Berry, but is told by Berry's mother that he died the year before of Agent Orange. Alone, rejected, purposeless, Rambo goes into the town of Hope, only to be "escorted" out by Sheriff Teasle, who sees Rambo as an undesirable hippie who doesn't belong in his town. Not willing to be told what to do, Rambo returns to town, where he is arrested by Teasle. When the sheriff's men strip, hose down, and shave Rambo by force, he experiences flashbacks of the torture he suffered at the hands of the Vietnamese in the POW camp. Breaking out of the jail, Rambo begins a one-man war against the town, in which he succeeds in destroying much of the town's property and injuring (not killing) most of its police officers and national guard.

Finally, trapped inside a gun shop, surrounded by police cars and the burning flames of his rampage, Rambo is confronted by his former teacher and mentor, Colonel Trautman. Facing Trautman, the only man who can understand his plight, Rambo breaks down. Collapsing in Trautman's arms, Rambo cries tears of loss for his dead buddies and of frustration for his treatment on returning from the war. Once in charge of "million dollar equipment," Rambo is now unable to even hold down a job at a car wash. And the job that he has been trained to do and at which he excels—killing— is disallowed. But "You don't just turn it off," he cries. Winning medals and praise for the job he did in Vietnam, Rambo comes home to find only rejection, scorn, and prejudice from the country whose ideals he fought to defend. Trautman finally escorts the broken Rambo out of the gunshop under his own trenchcoat, his arm around Rambo's shoulders. As the police handcuff Rambo and take him off to prison, the camera freezes on his pacified image, now controlled, not only by the military (Trautman) and the government (the police), but by the camera as well, frozen in his confusion.

From the film's outset, Rambo is produced as a victim, first of his Vietnamese torturers, then of the war that took his buddies away, then of an autocratic sheriff who doesn't like Rambo's looks and thinks he's inappropriate for his town, and, finally of the very military apparatus he fought for when he is trailed by the National Guard. In addition, Rambo's friend, Delmar Berry, was a victim of Agent Orange contamination. And, as Rambo tells Trautman, he was himself a victim of his government's policy, for though he and his friends fought well and in his mind could have won the war, "Somebody wouldn't let us win." Rambo comes to stand as emblem of the multiple avenues of victimization available to Vietnam representation. The close of the film freezes Rambo's status as victim. For all of his expertise, desire to be reintegrated and pacifism (Rambo only fights when goaded and, importantly, he *kills no one* in this first film, though it is very clear he could have done so with ease), he does not step out of his role as victim. Instead, he steps only into the arms of Colonel Trautman and the waiting police.

But in 1985 the confused and lonely veteran of *First Blood* became the triumphant hero of *Rambo: First Blood, Part II* (dir. George P. Cosmatos). As Harry Haines puts it, "*Rambo* proclaims a regeneration of pride in the Vietnam veteran and . . . hails him as a warrior hero."[24] Rejected and persecuted by his government in *First Blood*, Rambo is finally taken into custody by the police to be punished for stepping outside of the law. But in *Rambo*, after

17

18

19

pinning down a government representative and threatening to "find" him if he doesn't expedite the rescue of American POWs, Rambo, now strong and self-reliant (bare-chested instead of hidden beneath Trautman's raincoat), strides into the sunset toward Thailand. Whereas in *First Blood* Rambo accepts the government's demands for order and reintegration by surrendering and going to prison, in *Rambo* he refuses assimilation (walking away from a presidential pardon), institutes his own law ("Find 'em [the POWs]. Or I'll find you"), and sets forth his own conditions for reintegration: "For our country to love us as much as we love it!" The fires that illuminated the end of *First Blood* have been washed into the pastel shades of a setting sun, and the divisive fighting going on "outside your front door" has given way to the unified closing song of the "Home of the brave," where "we'll never fall" because "the strength of our nation belongs to us all."

Rambo: First Blood, Part II begins with Rambo in a prison labor camp, where he is forced to break rocks in a hot sun that is reflected off the mirrored sunglasses of the prison guards. In the film's ethical balance, Rambo is completing his penance for destroying property in *First Blood* by "serving time" in the purposeless destruction of useless property. Colonel Trautman, who rescued Rambo from his first victimization, now arrives to retrieve him from his second—victimization by a state institution that is punishing Rambo for its own failures to deal properly either with him or the war in which he fought. Trautman offers Rambo a possible presidential pardon if he can complete an unnamed "mission," suggesting that Reagan, whose photograph appears in several key shots of the film, unlike the government he represents, understands the value of the veteran and wants to "pardon" his errors and mistreatments, in some ways himself stepping outside of the law, much as Rambo must do to rescue the POWs. (Reagan's repeated photographic appearance suggests as well that he would endorse the devictimization of the white male if Rambo succeeds.) Rambo pointedly asks Trautman, "Do we get to win this time?" Trautman's reply records the shift in the narration of victimization that has taken place between this film and its predecessor: "This time, it's up to you."

Rambo is released to attempt a Special Operations mission that will try to find American POWs left in Vietnam, to find prisoners being held and tortured by the government of Vietnam, just as Rambo, in similar though less severe terms, has been released from a prison where he was held by his own government. His task is not only to achieve his own "pardon," but that of his victimized buddies as well, showing that he is to be seen, not as an exception in his treatment but as the rule. And this time, unlike in *First Blood*, Rambo does win, defeating not only the Vietnamese who guard the POW camp from which he rescues five POWs, but the Russian soldiers who advise them as well. And, perhaps more to the point, he defeats his own government, retrieving the very men the government has denied for years.

Rambo's worst "enemy" in the film is not the Vietnamese or even the Russians, but Marshall Murdock, a Washington bureaucrat who was sent to supervise Rambo's mission and finally, when it appears that evidence of POWs does exist contrary to his own government's policy statements, tries to sabotage Rambo's mission. Murdock's pronouncement on the POWs makes the victimization of POWs and veterans clear; to him and the government he represents, they are worthless: "Do you think somebody's going to stand up on the floor of the United States Senate and ask for a couple billion dollars for a couple of forgotten ghosts?" Trautman's reply fixes the film's response: "Men, goddamn it! *Our* men!" When Trautman accuses Murdock of just "trying to cover his ass," Murdock makes his function clear, that it is not his ass, but "a nation's!" So the POWs and, by analogy, veterans as a whole, are being made to pay the price, again with their lives, for a misguided and misdirected government policy about the Vietnam war.

But Rambo and the film that displays him confront this victimization   23 directly, not only by insisting that there are still POWs, but also by showing their continued valor, heroism, and patriotism. Although their country has betrayed them, they have retained, to use Wheeler's terms, their "ability to make a commitment." Rambo's final speech instantiates the reversal that *Rambo* has inscribed. When Trautman asks what he wants, Rambo speaks not only for himself but for all veterans: "I want what they want, and what every other guy who came over here and spilt his guts and gave everything he had wants—For our country to love us as much as we love it!" In the economy of *Rambo*, veterans are not asking then for "special treatment," only for the fulfillment of a bargain, to be paid fairly for their work and sacrifice. And, as Rambo's brutally enunciated words to Murdock make clear, *Rambo* reiterates the government's debt in this agreement. Unlike the government's "mission" in Vietnam, Rambo can grittily declare for himself, "Mission accomplished!" The failure of Vietnam, to echo Richard Halloran's paean to the U.S. soldier, owed not to the individual soldier/veteran, but to the government that sent him to war in the first place. *Rambo* blares into thousands of movie theaters and homes the message that not only did the soldier/veteran perform his job well, but he can still accomplish his "mission," one for which he has never been adequately paid.

Thus, from *First Blood* to *Rambo* the character of the veteran has shifted   24 dramatically. No longer a confused and tearfully inarticulate misfit, he is now a determined and demanding leader; no longer destroying property in a blaze of revenge, he rescues other forgotten heroes, bringing them home as well; no longer under the protection of the military or subject to the law, he now strides independently out to a brilliant landscape that awaits the institution of his own law; no longer a victim, he is a hero, reviving for a disillusioned nation the very ideas of heroism itself; no longer feminized, he has "been given back his manhood."[25] *First Blood* and *Rambo: First Blood, Part II* set the poles for the alteration in the image of the veteran that has transpired in recent years, an alteration in which the image of the victimized soldier/veteran/American male has been regenerated into an image of strength and revived masculinity.

IV

While offering a message of victory in Rambo's extravagantly successful mis-   25
sion,[26] *Rambo* reinforces the theme of regeneration through a simple and
repetitive symbolic program: purification through fire and rebirth through
immersion in water. As a common feature not only of *Rambo* but of other
recent Vietnam films as well, the symbolic significance of this imagery is
crucial to understanding the power of these narratives to renew the image of
the American male, "reborn" from the waters that have purified him of his
tainted past images. Mircea Eliade's explanation indicates the force of this
imagery: "In whatever religious complex we find them, the waters invariably
retain their function: they disintegrate, abolish forms, 'wash away sins': they
are at once purifying and regenerating."[27]

The most explicit of these images appears in *Missing in Action* when   26
Colonel Braddock (Chuck Norris) appears to have been defeated by Vietnamese guards in his effort to free American POWs being transferred from one
camp to another.[28] Riding in a high-speed assault raft, Braddock is thrown
from the boat when it is hit by a Vietnamese bazooka and explodes in flames.
With the boat overturned and no sign of Braddock or his accomplice above
water, the Vietnamese soldiers begin laughing among themselves at the ease
with which they have defeated the Americans (again). But, as with Rambo,
this time there is a new soldier, a "new man," who is not so easily defeated
or humiliated. In a slow motion straight-on shot, Braddock is shown rising
out of the river, droplets of water creating an aura around him, firing his
M-16. As the triumphant music reaches its climax, Braddock kills the laughing
Vietnamese soldiers and rescues the POWs. The slow-motion camera (only
one of two uses of this technique in an otherwise mundane cinematography)
draws our attention to this as mythic action and underscores its significance
for the audience.

Rambo endorses this imagery by rising from the waters no fewer than   27
four times in *Rambo*. In the first of two important scenes, Rambo is immersed
in the waters of a river as he leaps from an exploding boat. Both his guide,
Co Bao, and a rescued POW watch the waters tensely, believing that Rambo
was killed, but he bursts from the river to their cheers and the rising strains
of an exultant background score. And later, in a still more miraculous resur-
rection, Rambo dives into a pool at the bottom of a waterfall, escaping from
a napalm bomb dropped by a Russian helicopter. The waters explode into
flames, and the door-gunner shatters the water's surface with multiple,
seemingly unsurvivable rounds. But as the helicopter lowers to the water's
surface to find the body, Rambo leaps from the water, throws the door-gunner
overboard, and lands on the helicopter.

These scenes, like the one in *Missing in Action*, link the regeneration   28
through water to the defeated veteran—to the victim. Braddock is being
laughed at by the confidently conquering Vietnamese; Rambo has been be-

trayed by Vietnamese pirates who have sold knowledge of his whereabouts to a Vietnamese patrol boat, and later, after excruciating torture, he is brutally bombarded by the overwhelming technological superiority of the Russians. In each case, the veteran was submerged long enough to be believed dead; in each case, the presumed "victors" look arrogantly pleased by this confirmation of the weakness of their American opponent; and in each case, the "old man" gives way to the "new man," the revived American male.

Klaus Theweleit's complex reading of Fascist literature establishes the 29 link between this kind of purification and the constructions of masculinity. Thus, we can read in these films not simply the rebirth of a victimized character, but the simultaneous regeneration of masculinity itself in contemporary American cultural productions. Theweleit locates the regenerative imagery of water in the ascendent bourgeois self-image of the eighteenth century as a signifier of "the bourgeoisie's 'moral superiority' over the absolutist nobility."[29] As a result of this moral fixation, water's purifying powers came to be associated closely with sexual purity, an image vital to the self-perception of what Theweleit calls the "soldier male" in Fascist Germany.

> Water was precisely the substance that possessed adequate redemptive qualities. No other substance could make people feel "reborn" after such a brief immersion. Water acquired the function of providing healthy competition for true "rebirths," those that involved real orgasms. (p. 422)

Theweleit traces the release of waters prominent in Fascist literature— 30 floods, streams, rivers, burst dams—to its function as sublimated "release" of sexual energies. In an uncontrolled state, it is a release to be feared, possibly overrunning the soldier male and drowning him. What is preferred are controlled streams of water in which the soldier male can immerse himself to be reborn. As Theweleit shows again and again, intimately connected to these fears are women, especially women of the lower class, for women are reminders of that sexuality from which purifying water has rescued the soldier male.

> In the guise of the promised ocean, the "infinite vagina," water not only hides the reality of women, but flows forth against the ("dirty") sexuality of the women of oppressed classes and strata: that is, "proletarian" women. At the same time, splashing out of the sink and on to the bodies of bourgeois men, water became the new religion of Asexuality. . . . Water guarantees that the desires of these men are clean, that their unconsciouses are pure. (p. 421)

In these terms, the taint of impure sexuality is identified with "dirty" women, women who must be rejected in order for the soldier male to maintain his purity and energy.

Both Braddock and Rambo are radically disassociated from women in 31 *Missing in Action* and *Rambo: First Blood, Part II*. Ms. Fitzgerald, an assistant to the State Department accompanying Senator Powers on his fact-finding mission to Vietnam, thinks Braddock initially rude and uncivil, trying more to disrupt than to further negotiations about POWs. She confesses that her job is to "keep an eye" on him while they are in Ho Chi Minh City. Believing that he is coming to her room for a nightcap and suggesting that he is being forward when he starts immediately to undress, Fitzgerald is dumbfounded to find Braddock redressing in nightgear and sneaking out of her hotel room. Anxiously awaiting his return, Fitzgerald, now dressed in low-cut black negligee, sees Braddock sneaking back into the hotel moments before a military patrol that pursues him for killing Vietnamese general Trang. Braddock enters Fitzgerald's room, grabs her, strips off her negligee and throws her on the bed. As Braddock jumps under the covers with her and soldiers burst down the door to her room, she swears that Braddock has been with her all night. The next morning, with a decided change in attitude toward Braddock, even displaying some jealousy about whom he is traveling to Bangkok to see, Fitzgerald wishes him a wistful good-bye at the airport, telling him, "I'm sorry you have to leave." Fitzgerald appears again in the film only at the end, when, seated with the government negotiators who have just accepted the Vietnamese statement that "there are no American POWs in the Republic of Vietnam," she is witness to Braddock bursting into the negotiating room with one POW under his arm and several behind him.

Rambo's contact for his POW rescue mission is, to his surprise, a Vietnamese woman, Co Bao, daughter of an ARVN intelligence officer killed during the war. She is tough, resourceful, and a capable fighter, though she cautions Rambo to "follow orders" when he goes into the POW camp (he is only supposed to take pictures as evidence of POWs, not rescue them, an intertextual reference to Rambo's own victimization as frozen by the cameras at the end of *First Blood*, an act *Rambo* will not repeat). And although Rambo must first rescue her when she is caught by a Vietnamese guard, she later rescues him from his Russian torturers, showing no inequality in terms of their abilities to work together. But Co's rescue is somewhat different than Rambo's. Whereas he saves her by coming up on her captor from behind and overpowering him, she uses a decidedly feminine deception to rescue him. After sneaking into the camp dressed as a prostitute, she kills the captain she has gone in to have sex with and then goes to Rambo's aid. When they escape from the camp chased by dozens of Vietnamese and Russian soldiers, Co is killed by an unexpected bullet, only moments after Rambo has agreed to take her to Thailand with him after the mission is over. After burying her body, Rambo places her necklace around his own neck.

Fitzgerald and Co, for all of their differences of character and role in these films, share a number of features important to the accomplishment of masculine regeneration. First, both initially side with "order," with their respective governments' rules (Co's are clearly the U.S.'s not the Vietnamese government's) against the veterans. Fitzgerald chastises Braddock for being rude and Co urges Rambo to do only what he has been assigned. But both also shift their allegiances to the veterans' cause—the rescue of the POWs.

Fitzgerald helps Braddock with his alibi and Co assists Rambo in his first rescue attempt of a POW. Second, both women are quickly attracted to the veterans: Fitzgerald says she will miss Braddock while he is gone and Co pleads with Rambo to take her with him to Thailand. And while Braddock (questionably) and Rambo (clearly) are attracted in turn, neither initiates a bonding; this must come from the women. As if negating Rambo's interest, the more powerful ethics of the narration kill Co immediately after Rambo agrees to take her with him. Third, neither woman has anything to do with the actual rescue of the POWs. Fitzgerald seems to side still with the government negotiating teams that believe there are no camps, and Co is killed before Rambo's final rescue attempt that actually achieves the release of the POWs.

But a more important shared feature, one that returns to Theweleit's tie 34 between purifying waters and sexuality, is that both women are eliminated from the plots almost immediately after sexual encounters. (Although Fitzgerald is still alive, she does not speak again in the film after her good-bye to Braddock.) No evidence exists for an actual sexual liaison between Braddock and Fitzgerald, but her milder, fonder, and more sensual attitude the morning following Braddock's leap into her bed (she is dressed now in a frilled dress and not a suit) suggests that they have had sex. More austere in its reinforcement of the purity of the soldier male, *Rambo* rejects Co, not after she slept with Rambo, but with the Vietnamese captain whom she killed in order to rescue Rambo. The behavior of these women is distinct from that of their male counterparts, neither of whom expresses sexual desire or appears interested in establishing bonds with women. Braddock is nothing less than brutal in his treatment of Fitzgerald, stripping her and throwing her to her bed before leaping in after her. And although Rambo is clearly interested in Co in some way, he expresses no sexual desire for her.

After signs of their sexuality have been displayed, both women are force- 35 fully eliminated from the narrative, both now somehow tainted and unfit to accompany these men any longer. It is as if Braddock and Rambo can accomplish their "missions" only by severing themselves from women and the sexuality they represent. In order to be regenerated and to reestablish both the POWs and their masculinity in the face of a disbelieving and hostile audience, Braddock and Rambo must be sexually pure, their masculinity unsullied by any suggestions of femininity, domesticity, order, or the body.[30]

In keeping with Theweleit's linkage of purification and masculinity, both 36 Braddock and Rambo are regenerated after their dissociation from now "dirty" women. In order for these men to achieve their goals—the rescue of POWs/the rescue of American masculinity—they must sever their ties to women and sexuality. They must depend instead only on the male bonds (apparently desexualized) that precede and succeed the appearance of the women (Braddock knew Tuck, the man who provides boats and equipment for him and accompanies him on the mission, during the war; Rambo, although he did not know these POWs personally, is linked to them, as is

Braddock, by having been himself in a prison camp). Women are, as has been seen in so many cases, excluded from these bonds. But what makes this distinction unique is its causal link to the mythology of regeneration of a victimized manhood. In order for the POWs to "come home," the bonds of masculinity must be reaffirmed and severed from women, sexuality, and the body. More to the point, these regenerative bonds are confirmed, not simply by the exclusion of women but at their expense as well. Women are forced in these representations (Fitzgerald literally) to bear the burden of masculine victimization through their "dirty" sexuality, becoming the repositories of discarded traits that do not fit the character of the "new man" being reborn in Vietnam. . . .

Notes

1. The most complete narratives of POWs are contained in Zalin Grant's *Survivors: American POWs in Vietnam* (New York: Berkley Books, 1975). The 1987 film *Hanoi Hilton* depicts some of the scenes narrated in *Survivors*. In addition to providing evidence of victimization, the narratives of POWs support racism as well by reinforcing an American identity in contradistinction to a third-world people.

2. Tom Morganthau, "We're Still Prisoners of War," *Newsweek*, April 15, 1985, p. 34.

3. Ron Kovic, *Born on the Fourth of July* (New York: Pocket Books, 1976), p. 134.

4. Quoted in *Charlie Company: What Vietnam Did to Us*, ed. Peter Goldman and Tony Fuller (New York: Ballantine, 1983), p. 88.

5. Ruben Treviso, "Hispanics and the Vietnam War," in *Vietnam Reconsidered*, ed. Salisbury, p. 185.

6. These figures were compiled from *Myths and Realities: A Study of Attitudes toward Vietnam Era Vets*, U.S. Senate Committee on Veterans' Affairs, *Hearings*, 92nd Congress, 2d sess. (Washington: Government Printing Office, 1980) and Treviso, "Hispanics and the Vietnam War."

7. Figures quoted in Horne, ed., *Wounded Generation*, p. 10.

8. Quoted in Morrow, "Bloody Rite of Passage," p. 59.

9. Michael Herr, *Dispatches* (New York: Avon, 1978), pp. 13–14.

10. Loren Baritz, *Backfire: Vietnam—A History of How American Culture Led Us into Vietnam, and Made Us Fight the Way We Did* (New York: Ballantine, 1985), pp. 285–86.

11. Stanley Karnow, *Vietnam: A History* (New York: Viking, 1983), p. 323.

12. Quoted in Al Santoli, *To Bear Any Burden: The Vietnam War and Its Aftermath in the Words of Americans and Southeast Asians* (New York: Ballantine, 1985), pp. 118–24. For a summary discussion of the extent to which American interests were invested in Vietnamese government corruption, see Barbara W. Tuchman's "America Betrays Herself in Vietnam," in her *The March of Folly: From Troy to Vietnam* (New York: Knopf, 1984, chap. 5). We must keep in mind that these constructions of connection, service, and duty were interpreted in quite other ways by the Vietnamese themselves and that the term "corruption" applies principally to the identification of American interests.

13. Joe Klein, *Payback* (New York: Ballantine, 1984), p. 272.

14. U.S. Congress, Senate, Committee on Veterans' Affairs, *Hearings*, 96th Congress, 2d sess. (Washington: Government Printing Office, 1980).

15. Morrow, "Bloody Rite of Passage," pp. 23–24.

16. *New York Times*, May 26, 1984.

17. *Myths and Realities*, p. 85.

18. Jean Bethke Elshtain, *Women and War* (New York: Basic Books, 1987), p. 218.

19. The most prominent exception to this is Vietnamese director Ho Quang Minh's film, *Karma* (1986), which records the impact of the war on a South Vietnamese family. Ho Quang Minh plans two other films to complete his trilogy, one a view of the war for a North Vietnamese family and the other for an American family.

20. These figures are compiled from various government documents (*Myths and Realities*, and U.S. Veterans' Administration, *Annual Report* [Washington: Government Printing Office, 1983]). There is some disagreement about the number of women serving in the Vietnam-era military. Early figures of 2 percent (*Myths and Realities*) were rejected in favor of the more recent 3.2 percent (*Annual Report*).

21. Rambo's representativeness as a white male would seem to be contradicted by his early and brief assertion in *Rambo: First Blood, Part II* that he is part Indian. But Sylvester Stallone's widely proclaimed Italian heritage outweighs "Rambo's statement as a cultural signifier and draws him back into the circle of a white American male who can effectively capitalize on his absorbed "heritage," appropriating it within his image rather than being challenged by it. Secondarily, Rambo's image from *First Blood*, in which no such statement was made, was already fully established as a cultural artifact. His subsequent acknowledgment of Native American ancestry thus stands, not as a detractor from his image as a white male, but as reinforcement, both of his "natural" abilities as a soldier and, more importantly, of his genuine "Americanness." As Harry Haines explains, "[Rambo's] Indian origins enable him to move deftly through the jungle, using the natural environment as a weapon; his German origins explain his superior command of technology and strategy" (The Pride Is Back: *Rambo, Magnum, P.I.*, and the Return Trip to Vietnam," in *The Cultural Legacy of Vietnam: Uses of the Past in the Present*, ed. Peter Ehrenhaus and Richard Morris [Ablex Press, forthcoming]).

22. The television program "Tour of Duty" includes black and Hispanic soldiers, though the officers are white.

23. Morrow, "Bloody Rite of Passage," p. 24.

24. Haines, *The Pride is Back* (forthcoming).

25. Morrow, "Bloody Rite of Passage," p. 24.

26. David H. Van Biema, "With a $100 Million Gross(out), Sly Stallone Fends Off *Rambo's* Army of Adversaries," *People*, July 8, 1985, p. 37.

27. Mircea Eliade, *The Sacred and the Profane* (New York: Harcourt, 1959), p. 131.

28. The power of Norris's role here to regenerate masculinity within and without *Missing in Action* becomes doubled when it is known that his own brother died in a POW camp (Peter Travers, "Picks and Pans," *People*, June 24, 1985, pp. 9–10).

29. Klaus Theweleit, *Male Fantasies*, vol. 1, trans. Stephen Conway (Minneapolis: University of Minnesota Press, 1987), p. 420.

30. These themes are in sharp contrast to an earlier film like Hal Ashby's *Coming Home*, in which the veteran-as-victim is celebrated, with Luke rejecting the war and its masculine values in favor of the feminism and femininity of Sally Hyde (a feminism that, problematically, he is instrumental in bringing about). He accepts not only a more passive and negotiating posture, but is firmly established in a domesticity as well. Finally, his disability marks his rejection of the masculine body, and his love scenes with Sally Hyde reinforce his association with her sexuality. *Coming Home*, like *First Blood*, is the representation of veterans to which *Rambo: First Blood, Part II* and *Missing in Action* are responding.

APOCALYPSE CONTINUED

EDWARD TICK

Edward Tick is a writer and psychotherapist who has worked with Vietnam veterans since 1979. He is author of Sacred Mountain: Encounters with the Vietnam Beast *(1989) and editor of* Voices, *the Journal of the American Academy of Psychotherapists. In the following essay, which first appeared in the* New York Times Magazine *in 1990, Tick describes his therapeutic work with Vietnam veterans.*

Like seventeen million other men who came of age during Vietnam, I did not serve in the armed forces. It was a blessing, then, to have escaped; it is a burden now. I find there is something missing in me. I have unwanted feelings that nag me in unexpected ways and at unexpected times.

Although a number of other nonveterans years ago began expressing similar problems in print and on television, I did not know that the problems applied to me. Perhaps I blocked out my feelings. In any case, I first became aware of these feelings when a man named Fred sought my psychotherapeutic services. Exactly my age, Fred wanted help for anxiety attacks and recurring nightmares. In his dreams, he was pursued by a galloping horseman determined to cut out his heart.

Through psychotherapy, we searched his past for reasons for his present suffering. Nothing proved promising until, because he could bear it no longer, Fred confessed: he had fulfilled his military obligation by spending two years stateside unloading and processing body bags from Vietnam.

We had found the horseman. Fred had handled the bodies of other men like so much supermarket ware, listing names and numbers and arranging transportation. He had never been in danger himself until much later, when the deaths he processed and his profound guilt returned to haunt him.

But I, also, changed with Fred's admission. I felt uneasy, incomplete. If Fred was one step removed from the war, I was too. If he was haunted, what was I?

I searched for clues to my discomfort. The work of the psychiatrist Robert J. Lifton and others on combat veterans suffering post-traumatic stress told me what I had not experienced. Another small body of writing, on an elusive subject known as "Vietnam guilt," told me that I was not the only man who had been happy to escape service in my teens only to feel angry, confused and incomplete years later.

In high school, during the mid-1960s, I had considered enlisting as a 7
medic, not because I believed in the war, but because many of my neighbors
and classmates were fighting it. Later, my objections to the war overrode my
desire to be counted among those serving. I was prepared, during my junior
year in college, to apply for conscientious-objector status. If it were not
granted, I would then decide whether I would go to jail, flee the country or
take some other course. I was unsure what I would do.

In the end, Lottery No. 244 rescued me from that dilemma. But it 8
plunged me into a state of permanent moral ambiguity, because part of our
heritage insists that, if there is a war to be fought, young men are expected
to fight it. War, if it exists, is a required course, and a course with a final
examination. I was, I came to feel, among those men of my generation who
had never been tested.

After learning of Fred's horseman, I began to seek out psychotherapeutic 9
work with Vietnam veterans. They had a need to tell their stories, and I could
join them in the jungle in this way.

Ron was the first veteran of jungle combat with whom I worked. "*Apoc-* 10
alypse Now," he chuckled during one session. "A picnic compared to the real
thing." Ron was emotionally disabled by his combat experiences and his
reception when he came back to America. He had been spat on, jailed and
hospitalized. In the hospital, he had been drugged into a stupor. "Why get
better?" he asked. "The government pays me more for being disabled than I
could ever make working."

Ron wanted my help to find meaning in a life whose usefulness had 11
officially ended at age twenty-two. But, sitting across from him, I felt weak,
inadequate, physically smaller, although we were the same size. I had to fight
the urge to look at the floor instead of directly into the eyes that were avoiding
mine.

This was because I felt Ron had something over me. He had survived a 12
long tour in the demilitarized zone and the decimation of his battalion. The
closest I had come to physical danger was being chased down a deserted
Washington street on the night of the first Moratorium Against the War. The
guardsman who had chased me was my age, spoke my language and, though
he prodded me with his bayonet, ordered me to move with a "please."

It is not because I protested the war that I felt guilty before Ron. In fact, 13
I am even more convinced now that the war was a mistake. I think it hurt all
of us in ways that linger long into adulthood. The warriors, honorable men
like Ron who served in Vietnam, suffer, unlike veterans of other wars, because
the correctness of what our nation did will forever be in question. Those like
me who, for one reason or another, did not serve, suffer because we chose
not to perform a primary and expected rite of passage. We were never in-
ducted, not merely into the Army, but into manhood. Recently, I was con-
tacted by Sam, a former draft resister who fled to Canada to avoid prison. He
told me: "I think about Vietnam every day. I can't join in with others. Can a
resister also suffer post-traumatic stress?"

I have had some of the usual rites—marriage, educational and professional 14
recognition. But no matter how many passages or accomplishments I garner,
I never quite feel complete. Nor do I think that, had I served in Vietnam, I
would now be enjoying the contentment I seek. A nonveteran I know says,
"I cannot recall any winners at all."

I think that none of us escaped, that not one of us feels whole. All our 15
choices—service in Vietnam, service at home, freedom from service altogether—failed to provide the rite of passage that every man needs. I want to
feel my own strength, worth and wholeness, and I want to belong to my
country and my generation. But history got in the way. I wonder if I will
forever be seeking something that cannot be.

REQUIEM FOR A SOLDIER

◑

LINDA BIRD FRANCKE

Linda Bird Francke is a regular contributor to the "Hers" column of the *New York Times Magazine* and a researcher on women in the military. In this piece, published in 1991, Francke contemplates the death of Major Marie T. Rossi, a soldier in the Persian Gulf war whose helicopter crashed in Saudi Arabia. Her essay asks us to think about both the benefits and the tragic drawbacks of equal opportunity in the "new military" of today.

The American flag was draped over the gunmetal-gray coffin at a funeral home in Oradell, N.J. On a table to the left of the coffin was an 8-by-10 photo of a smiling, somewhat shy-looking woman wearing a soft pastel suit and pearls. On the right was quite another photograph, of a leaner-faced woman with a cocky grin, hands on the hips of her desert camouflage uniform, an Army helicopter of the Second Battalion, 159th Aviation immediately behind her.

I drove three hours to Maj. Marie T. Rossi's wake and returned the next day for her funeral. I'd never met the chopper pilot whose helicopter had hit a microwave tower near a Saudi pipeline, the commanding officer of Company B who'd clung to civilized living in the desert by laying a "parquet" floor of half-filled sandbags in her tent, the woman who, after Sunday services, invited the chaplain back to share the Earl Grey tea her mother had sent her.

I was planning to interview Major Rossi when she returned to the States, to try to understand why she and so many other bright and thoughtful women were choosing careers in the military. Like many other civilians, I had been stunned to learn the numbers of women serving in the armed forces. If there hadn't been a war, I never would have known. Because there'd been a war, I'd now never know Major Rossi.

Watching the war on television, I'd vacillated between feelings of awe and uneasiness at women in their modern military roles. It was jolting to see young women loading missiles on planes and aching to fly fighter jets in combat. On the other hand, I admired these military women for driving six-wheel trucks and shinnying in and out of jet engine pods. A final barrier seemed to be breaking down between the sexes. But at what cost? Looking at the military funeral detachment as it wheeled Major Rossi's coffin into St.

Joseph's Church, I tried to summon up pride for a fallen soldier, but instead felt sadness for a fallen sister.

As Major Rossi's friends and relatives spoke, I recalled an August evening soon after the Iraqi invasion of Kuwait when my daughters were home on vacation and several of their male friends dropped by. The young men, juniors and seniors in college, were pale and strained, talking anxiously about the possibility of a military draft. My daughters, 19 and 21 years old, were chattering on about their hopes for interesting jobs after graduation. It hadn't seemed fair. Here were my girls—healthy, strong graduates of Outward Bound, their faces still flushed from a pre-dinner run—talking freely about the future. And here were the boys whose futures suddenly seemed threatened.

I didn't know what to think. I still don't. As a feminist and my own sort of patriot, I feel that women and men should share equally in the burdens and the opportunities of citizenship. But the new military seems to have stretched equality to the breaking point. The surreal live television hookup between a family in the States and a mother in the desert reminding them where the Christmas ornaments were stored, smacked of values gone entirely awry. Yet this woman, like the 29,000 others in the gulf, had voluntarily signed on to serve. What siren song had the military sung to them?

To ground myself in this growing phenomenon, I'd taken my younger daughter to a recruiting station in Riverhead, L.I. Each branch of the military had an office—the Army, the Navy, the Air Force, the Marines. The recruiters were very persuasive. "When you graduate, do you think any employer is going to be banging on your door in this economy?" the Marine recruiter asked her. "Think about it. You're out of college. Your Mom breaks your plate. Your Dad turns your bedroom into a den. You're on your own. Now what do you do?" He gave me a decal: "My daughter is a United States Marine."

The Air Force recruiter was easier to resist. "Have you ever had problems with the law?" he grilled my daughter. "Have you ever been arrested, ever gotten a traffic ticket? Have you ever sold, bought, trafficked, brought drugs into the country, used drugs?" Instead of a decal, he gave us a copy of "High Flight," the romantic World War II poem President Reagan had used to eulogize the crew of the Challenger. "Oh, I have slipped the surly bonds of earth and danced the skies on laughter-silvered wings" it begins. The Air Force recruiter did not mention the fact that the poem's author, John Gillespie Magee Jr., had died in the war at the age of 19.

There is no talk of death in recruiting offices, no talk of danger or war or separation from families. The operative words are "opportunity," "education," "technical skills" and "training." The Marine recruiter added another military carrot by pulling out a sheet of paper with newspaper want ads Scotch-taped to it. "Every job opening requires skills. But how do you get them? We give them to you." My daughter's face began to flush. "If we don't get out of here in 30 seconds, I'm going to sign up," she muttered.

Those in the military know about death, of course. They get on-the-job   10
training. Major Rossi's husband, Chief Warrant Officer John Anderson Cay-
ton, told the mourners at her funeral that he had prayed hard for his wife's
safety while he was serving in Kuwait. His were not the prayers that come on
Hallmark cards. "I prayed that guidance be given to her so that she could
command the company, so she could lead her troops in battle," said the tall
young man in the same dress blue Army uniform he'd worn to their wedding
just nine months before. "And I prayed to the Lord to take care of my sweet
little wife."

Habits fade away slowly, just like old soldiers. When I called Arlington   11
National Cemetery to confirm the time of Major Rossi's burial, I was told
"he" was down for 3 P.M. on March 11.

"She," I corrected the scheduler gently.   12

"His family and friends will gather at the new administration building,"   13
the scheduler continued.

"*Her* family and friends," I said more firmly. "Major Rossi is a woman."   14

"Be here at least 15 minutes early," she said. "We have a lot of burials on   15
Monday."

Hundreds of military women turned out at Arlington, wearing stripes   16
and ribbons and badges indecipherable to most civilians. I caught a ride with
three members of the Womens Auxiliary Service Pilots, the Wasps, who flew
during World War II. One was wearing her husband's shirt under her old
uniform. The shirts sold at the PX with narrow enough shoulders, she explained, don't fit over the bust.

No one knows how many women are buried in their own military right   17
under the 220,000 pristine headstones at Arlington. The cemetery's records
do not differentiate between genders or among races and religions.

"If the women were married, you could walk around and count the   18
headstones that say 'Her husband,' rather than 'His wife,'" suggested an
Arlington historian. "I've seen a few and always noticed them." Arlington is
going to run out of room by the year 2035; a columbarium will provide
100,000 niches for the ashes of 21st century soldiers. How many of them will
be women?

The military pageant of death, no doubt, will remain the same. Six black   19
horses pulled the caisson carrying Major Rossi's coffin. Seven riflemen fired
the 21-gun salute, the band softly played "America the Beautiful" and a
solitary bugler under the trees blew taps. Major Rossi's husband threw the
first spadeful of dirt on his wife's coffin, her brother, the second. It was a
scene we're going to have to get used to in this new military of ours, as we
bury our sisters, our mothers, our wives, our daughters.

THE WALL

◑

SENY NORASINGH

Seny Norasingh took this photo of the Vietnam Veteran's Memorial while on a photo assignment for the book *A Day in the Life of America*. Norasingh, who has been a staff photographer for *The Raleigh News Observer* and a contributor to *National Geographic* magazine, has twice received the North Carolina News Photographer of the Year Award. This photo appears on the cover of *The Wall: Images and Offerings from the Vietnam Veterans Memorial*, published in 1987.

The Wall © Seny Norasingh

FACING IT

YUSEF KOMUNYAKAA

Yusef Komunyakaa was honored with the Bronze Star
for his service in Vietnam, where he was a correspon-
dent and editor of *The Southern Cross*. Winner of the
1986 San Francisco Poetry Center Award, he has published three volumes of poetry: *Copacetic* (1984), *I Apologize for the Eyes in My Head* (1986), and *Dien Cai Dau*
(1988). In the following poem, taken from his last collection, Komunyakaa presents an evocative meditation
on the Vietnam Veterans War Memorial.

My black face fades,
hiding inside the black granite.
I said I wouldn't,
dammit: No tears.
I'm stone. I'm flesh.
My clouded reflection eyes me
like a bird of prey, the profile of night
slanted against morning. I turn
this way—the stone lets me go.
I turn that way—I'm inside
the Vietnam Veterans Memorial
again, depending on the light
to make a difference.
I go down the 58,022 names,
half-expecting to find
my own in letters like smoke.
I touch the name Andrew Johnson;
I see the booby trap's white flash.
Names shimmer on a woman's blouse
but when she walks away
the names stay on the wall.
Brushstrokes flash, a red bird's
wings cutting across my stare.
The sky. A plane in the sky.
A white vet's image floats
closer to me, then his pale eyes

look through mine. I'm a window.
He's lost his right arm
inside the stone. In the black mirror
a woman's trying to erase names:
No, she's brushing a boy's hair.

MAKING CONNECTIONS

1. Discuss the tensions in Atwood's poem between feeling and thinking about war. What words and images does she use to convey each, and how does she attempt to "humanize" the history of war? What has women's traditional role been in discussing and participating in war, and what is Atwood's attitude toward this past involvement? In your opinion, does Atwood capture the meaning of her subject or not? How would you paraphrase the message of the poem?

2. Compare Keen's essay to the selections on sports and masculinity in Chapter 8 and write an essay about the training of the male body. In what ways are training men for sports and for war similar? How are they different? What lessons and values do sports and war have in common? Are men the victims of injustice, as Keen and others suggest, because they are expected to subject themselves to pain and injury on the playing field or the battlefield?

3. Keen concludes his essay with the statement, "It still takes gentleness and fierceness to make a whole man." Does this idea contradict the rest of his essay? How does it correspond to Edward Tick's assessment of men of the Vietnam generation, that "not one of us feels whole"? Compare Keen's views to those of Robert Bly (Chapter 3) and write an essay on "the sword" as an image of symbolic power for men. What role does "fierceness" play in male identity? Is there a parallel formula for "the whole woman"?

4. Michalowski uses numerous quotations to construct her essay. Evaluate her choice of "speakers" in the piece. Do you feel they effectively represent the voices of men in all ranks of the military? What elements make them convincing or unconvincing spokesmen for describing life in boot camp? What might some other views be on the effect of military training? Could a defender of basic training justify the experience of Private Green? If so, how?

5. Language, specifically war rhetoric, can be effective in clarifying or obscuring the meaning of events. Gottlieb presents ways in which rhetoric can sexualize military action, but other critics have also argued that the rhetoric of war can desensitize us. They cite phrases like "collateral damage" and "surgical strike," frequently used in the Persian Gulf War, to show how language can personally distance us from the destructive realities of modern military technology. Write an essay that examines the language of modern warfare, using examples from your own experience and reading. What are the benefits and dangers of using erotic or

dispassionate metaphors to describe military action and its effects? Do you see any parallels with sexual imagery in the language of sports?

6. In Gottlieb's essay, one source quoted calls the excitement over military action "obscene." How is he using this term? Using the essays in Chapter 11 as a reference point, do you see any parallels between war and pornography, either in its images, its language, or in the connection between sexuality and violence that Gottlieb presents? What do you make of his equation of war with male sexual power? How do you explain the response of his female colleague to military videotapes? Can women participate in feelings of "male sexual power" as well?

7. Jeffords discusses the symbolic cleansing that the characters of Rambo and Braddock must undergo in the film *First Blood: Part II*. Before they can accomplish their mission, they must absolve themselves of all impurities; in particular, they must disassociate themselves from women and all that women stand for. Compare these views to those of Michalowski and Joyce Carol Oates (Chapter 8) and write an essay about the image of women portrayed in these admonitions to men. What do women symbolize as a threat to the masculine ideal in sports or in war? What obstacles might this image suggest for the growing entry of women in athletics and the military?

8. Jeffords notes in her essay that a disproportionate number of the soldiers who were in heavy combat in Vietnam were black men. Yet the popular reconstruction of the story of Vietnam creates the stereotype of a *white* male soldier in combat. Write an essay discussing this apparent contradiction between the reality and the popular image. What might this discrepancy suggest about the connections between race and war? What were the issues of race surrounding the Persian Gulf War? Can you draw any connections with Mike Messner's essay (Chapter 8) on "Sports and Inequality"?

9. How would you characterize Tick's writing style? Is it balanced? Passionate? Reasonable? Angry? Resigned? Are there any shifts in mood throughout the piece? How does he move between his own story and those of his patients, Ron and Sam? How effectively do the experiences of these three men reflect and illuminate each other? How would you summarize Tick's conclusions about the war? Do you think he is against war, for it, or neutral in his feelings?

10. Francke's essay presents one aspect of the dilemma of women in the military: On the one hand, women have long fought for equal opportunity in all areas of society. On the other hand, if we expect equal treatment for women in the military, we must also be prepared, as Francke says, to "bury our sisters, our mothers, our wives, our daughters." Take a position on women in the military. Should women be allowed to engage in active

combat alongside men, and if a draft is reinstated, should they be drafted equally? Or should exceptions be made for women, either in certain areas of combat or for certain women, like mothers of young children? What about fathers of young children? What might be the problems of a fully gender-integrated military? What discriminations might result if the military remains anything less than fully integrated?

11. Write your own brief response to Komunyakaa's poem. How does he use images of color throughout the poem? What effect is achieved by his blurring of images inside and outside the wall? What feelings do you get from the poem's final image? Using Norasingh's photograph and other photographs of the Vietnam War Memorial, or your own experience if you have visited the wall, discuss the impact of the memorial's shape, color, design, and location. During its planning stages, the memorial created controversy, with some veterans feeling that it represented shame and defeat, while others saw in its structure and color a moving tribute to the dead. What messages do you think it conveys? Does Komunyakaa's poem, both in content and style, adequately "reflect" the feel of the memorial?

12. War is a complex phenomenon involving many aspects of culture, from the language we use to describe it, to the images we create around it, to the nature of the military as a socializing agent and employer, to the realities of combat and death. Write an essay that, while it may not present any conclusions about war, lists and organizes the ways our understanding of war is shaped by society and the ways war in turn shapes our society. What are your opinions about the role that gender might play in each of these areas? Is gender a valuable tool in illuminating the issues, or does it limit our engagement with complex cultural events like war? Use examples to support and illustrate your points.

AUTHOR/TITLE INDEX

ACKNOWLEDGMENTS *(continued from p. iv)*

John Berger. From WAYS OF SEEING by John Berger. Copyright © 1972 by Penguin Books Ltd. Used by permission of Viking Penguin, a division of Penguin Books USA Inc.

Louise Bernikow. From Louise Bernikow, "Cinderella: Saturday Afternoon at the Movies," in *Among Women* (New York: Crown, 1980), pp. 17–37. Copyright © 1980 by Louise Bernikow. Reprinted with permission of the author.

Robert Bly. Robert Bly, *Iron John*, © 1990 by Robert Bly. Reprinted with permission of the publisher.

Susan Brownmiller. From Susan Brownmiller, *Femininity*, (New York: Fawcett 1984), pp. 13–17. Copyright © 1984 by Susan Brownmiller. Reprinted by permission of Linden Press, a division of Simon & Schuster, Inc. "Victims: The Setting." From Susan Brownmiller, *Against Our Will: Men, Women and Rape* (New York: Bantam, 1976), pp. 343–344. Copyright © 1975 by Susan Brownmiller. Reprinted by permission of Simon & Schuster, Inc.

Douglas Campbell. Douglas Campbell, "One Man's Pleasures: A Response to Weiss," Harper's Magazine, June 1986, pp. 74–75. Copyright © 1986 by Harper's Magazine. All rights reserved. Reprinted from the June issue by special permission.

Angela Carter. "The Company of Wolves" by permission of Angela Carter c/o Rogers, Coleridge & White Ltd. 20 Powis Mews, London W11 IJN UK. Copyright Angela Carter 1979.

Wendy Chapkis. Reprinted from *Beauty Secrets: Women and the Politics of Appearance* by Wendy Chapkis with permission from the publisher, South End Press, 116 St. Botolph St., Boston, MA 02115 U.S.A.

Sey Chassler. From "Listening," Ms. magazine, August 1984. © Sey Chassler, 1984. Reprinted with permission of the author.

Rosalind Coward. "The Body Beautiful" from FEMALE DESIRES: HOW THEY ARE SOUGHT, BOUGHT AND PACKAGED by Rosalind Coward. Copyright © 1985 by Rosalind Coward. Used by permission of Grove Press, Inc.

Robert Crosman. From Robert Crosman, "How Readers Make Meaning," *College Literature 9* (West Chester State College, 1982), pp. 207–15. Reprinted by permission of the author.

Holly Devor. From Holly Devor, "Becoming Members of Society: Learning the Social Meanings of Gender," from *Gender Blending: Confronting the Limits of Duality* (Bloomington: Indiana University Press, 1989), pp. 43–47, 49–53. Reprinted with permission.

Anthony Easthope. Anthony Easthope, "Masculine Style (2): Banter," *What A Man's Gotta Do: The Masculine Myth in Popular Culture*, Routledge 1990. Reprinted by permission of Routledge.

William Faulkner. From COLLECTED STORIES OF WILLIAM FAULKNER by William Faulkner. Coyright 1930 and renewed 1958 by William Faulkner. Reprinted by permission of Random House, Inc.

Judith Fetterley. From Judith Fetterley, "A Rose for 'A Rose for Emily,'" The Resisting Reader: A Feminist Approach to American Fiction (Bloomington: Indiana University Press, 1978), pp. 34–45. Reprinted by permission.

Elizabeth Flynn. From Elizabeth Flynn, "Gender and Reading," *College English*, vol. 35, No. 3 (March 1983), pp. 236–253. Copyright 1983 by the National Council of Teachers of English. Reprinted with permission.

Ben Fong-Torres. Ben Fong-Torres, "Why Are There No Asian Anchor*men* on TV?", adapted from *Datebook, The San Francisco Chronicle*, July 13, 1986, p. 51. © San Francisco Chronicle. Reprinted by permission.

Linda Bird Francke. Lind Bird Francke, "Requiem for a Soldier," New York Times Magazine, April 21, 1991, p. 24. Copyright © 1991 by the New York Times Company. Reprinted by permission.

Marilyn Frye. "Oppression" from THE POLITICS OF REALITY, copyright © 1983 by Marilyn Frye, published by The Crossing Press, Freedom, CA 95019. Reprinted with permisson.

Mark Gerzon. A CHOICE OF HEROES by Mark Gerzon. Copyright © 1982 by Mark Gerzon. Reprinted by permission of Houghton Mifflin Company. All rights reserved.

Walter J. Gottlieb. Walter J. Gottlieb, "The Sexual Connection," *The Progressive*, April 1991, vol. 55 (4), p. 39. Reprinted by permission of the author.

Lois Gould. © 1978 by Lois Gould, printed with permission of the Charlotte Sheedy Literary Agency, Inc.

Cynthia Hanson. Adapted from Cynthia Hanson, "The Women of China Beach," *Journal of Popular Film and Television*, Vol. 17, No. 4, pp. 155–163, Winter, 1990. Reprinted with permission of the Helen Dwight Reid Educational Foundation. Published by Heldref Publications, 1319 Eighteenth St., N.W., Washington, D.C. 20036-1802. Copyright © 1990.

Robert Hass. "A Story About the Body" from *Human Wishes*, copyright © 1989 by Robert Hass. First published by the Ecco Press in 1989 and reprinted by permission.

Ernest Hemingway. Reprinted with permission of Charles Scribner's Sons, an imprint of Macmillan Publishing Company, from MEN WITHOUT WOMEN by Ernest Hemingway. Copyright 1927 by Charles Scribner's Sons; renewal copyright 1955 by Ernest Hemingway.

Edward Hirsch. From WILD GRATITUDE by Edward Hirsch. Copyright © 1985 by Edward Hirsch. Reprinted by permission of Alfred A. Knopf, Inc.

Susan Jeffords. Susan Jeffords, "Do We Get to Win This Time," *The Remasculinization of America: Gender and the Vietnam War* (Bloomington: Indiana University Press, 1989) pp. 121–134. Reprinted by permission.

Sam Keen. From FIRE IN THE BELLY by Sam Keen. Copyright © 1991 by Sam Keen. Used by permission of Bantam Books, a division of Bantam Doubleday Dell Publishing Group, Inc.

Katherine Kersten. Excerpts from Katherine Kersten, "What Do Women Want?" *Policy Review*, No. 56, Spring 1991, pp. 4, 6–7, 10–12, 14–15. Reprinted with permission from the Spring 1991 issue of *Policy Review*, the flagship publication of The Heritage Foundation, 214 Massachusetts Ave., NE, Washington, DC 20002-4999.

Bruce Kidd. Bruce Kidd, "Sports and Masculinity," *Beyond Patriarchy*, M. Kaufman, ed. (New York: Oxford University Press, 1987), pp. 250–265. Reprinted by permission of the author.

Gary Kinsman. From Gary Kinsman, "Men Loving Men: The Challenge of Gay Liberation," in Beyond Patriarchy, M. Kaufman, ed. (New York: Oxford University Press, 1987) pp. 103–119. Reprinted by permission of the author.

Carolyn Kizer. "Pro Femina," copyright © 1965 by Carolyn Kizer, from KNOCK UPON SILENCE by Carolyn Kizer. Used by permission of Doubleday, a division of Bantam Doubleday Dell Publishing Group, Inc.

Yusef Komunyakaa. "Facing It," © 1988 by Yusef Komunyakaa. Reprinted from DIEN CAI DAU Wesleyan University Press by permission of University Press of New England.

Cheris Kramarae. From Cheris Kramer (Cheris Kramarae) "Folk Linguistics: Wishy-Washy Mommy Talk," Psychology Today, Vol. 8, No. 1, June 1974, pp. 83–85. Reprinted with permission from Psychology Today magazine. Copyright © 1974 (Sussex Publishers, Inc.)

Maxine Kumin. "The Archaeology of a Marriage," copyright © 1978 by Maxine Kumin. From THE RETRIEVAL SYSTEM by Maxine Kumin. Used by permission of Viking Penguin, a division of Penguin Books USA Inc.

Martin A. Lee and Norman Solomon. From UNRELIABLE SOURCES: A Guide to Detecting Bias in News Media by Martin A. Lee and Norman Solomon. Copyright © 1990 by Martin A. Lee and Norman Solomon. Published by arrangement with Carol Publishing Group. A Lyle Stuart Book.

Marcia K. Lieberman. From Marcia K. Lieberman, "'Someday My Prince Will Come': Female Acculturation through the Fairy Tale," College English 34 (Urbana, IL: National Council of Teachers of English, 1972) pp. 383–95. Copyright 1972 by the National Council of Teachers of English. Reprinted with permission.

John Lippert. This essay originally appeared in Brother: A Forum for Men Against Sexism, Summer 1976, and is reprinted from For Men Against Sexism: A Book of Readings, edited by Jon Snodgrass, by permission of Times Change Press, Box 1380, Ojai, CA 93024.

Hilary M. Lips. Hilary M. Lips, "Women and Power in the Workplace" by Hilary M. Lips, in Greta Hofmann Nemiroff, ed., Women and Men: Interdisciplinary Readings on Gender (Toronto: Fitzhenry and Whiteside, 1987) pp. 403–415. Reprinted by arrangement with Fitzhenry & Whiteside, publishers, Richmond Hill, Ontario.

Prudence Mackintosh. Reprinted by permission of the Wendy Weil Agency, Inc. Copyright 1977 by Prudence Mackintosh.

Pat Mainardi. From Pat Mainardi, "The Politics of Housework." Reprinted with permission from Sisterhood Is Powerful: An Anthology of Writings From The Women's Liberation Movement, compiled and edited by Robin Morgan (New York: Vintage Books, Random House, 1970); Copyright © 1970 by Robin Morgan.

Kathi Maio. Kathi Maio, "Fatal Attraction and Someone to Watch Over Me: Sex and the Single Terrorist," Feminist in the Dark: Reviewing the Movies (Freedom, CA: The Crossing Press, 1988) pp. 215–223. From FEMINIST IN THE DARK, Copyright © 1988 by Kathi Maio, published by The Crossing Press, Freedom, CA 95019. Reprinted by permission.

Sara Maitland. Sara Maitland, "The Wicked Stepmother's Tale," from More Tales I Tell My Mother, Zoe Fairbairns, Sara Maitland, Valerie Miner, Michele Roberts,

Michelene Wandor, eds. (London: Journeyman Press, 1987), pp. 157–163. Copyright Sara Maitland 1987. Reproduced by permission of Curtis Brown, London, Ltd on behalf of Sara Maitland.

Michael A. Messner. Michael A. Messner, "Sports and the Politics of Inequality," *Changing Men #17* (Winter 1986), pp. 27–28. Reprinted by permission of the author.

Helen Michalowski. Source: Helen Michalowski. "The Army Will Make a "Man" Out of You," Reweaving the Web of Life: Feminism and Non-Violence; Pam McAllister, ed. (Philadelphia: New Society Publishers, 1982), pp. 326–335. Reprinted by permission.

Joyce Carol Oates. From ON BOXING by Joyce Carol Oates. Copyright © 1987 by Ontario Review, Inc. Used by permission of Doubleday, a division of Bantam Doubleday Dell Publishing Group, Inc.

Cynthia Ozick. Reprinted by permission of Cynthia Ozick and her agents, Raines & Raines, 71 Park Ave., NY, NY 10016. Copyright © 1972 by Ms. Magazine.

Marge Piercy. "You Don't Understand Me." From STONE, PAPER, KNIFE by Marge Piercy. Copyright © 1983 by Marge Piercy. Reprinted by permission of Alfred A. Knopf Inc. "To Be of Use." From CIRCLES ON THE WATER by Marge Piercy. Copyright © 1982 by Marge Piercy. Reprinted by permission of Alfred A. Knopf, Inc.

M. Rivka Polatnick. From M. Rivka Polatnick, "Why Men Don't Rear Children: A Power Analysis," Berkeley Journal of Sociology 18 (1973–74) 45–86. Copyright © 1973, 1982 by M. Rivka Polatnick. Reprinted by permission of the author.

Adrienne Rich. "The Stranger" is reprinted from DIVING INTO THE WRECK, Poems 1971–1972, by Adrienne Rich, by permission of W. W. Norton & Company, Inc. Copyright © 1973 by W. W. Norton & Company, Inc.

Joel Roache. Reprinted from Joel Roache, "Confessions of a Househusband," Ms. No. 1, Nov. 1972, pp. 25–27, by permission of the author. Copyright 1972 by Joel Roache.

Muriel Rukeyser. Source: Muriel Rukeyser, "Myth," from *Breaking Open* (New York: Random House, 1973), p. 20. © Muriel Rukeyser, by permission of William L. Rukeyser.

Jane Rule. From Jane Rule, "Lesbian and Writer: Making the Real Visible," from *New Lesbian Writing*, Margaret Cruikshank, ed., (San Francisco: Grey Fox Press, 1984), pp. 96–99. Copyright © 1984 by Jane Rule. Reprinted by permission.

Don Sabo. Don Sabo, "The Myth of the Sexual Athlete," *Changing Men #20* (Winter 1989), pp. 38–39. Reprinted by permission of the author.

Anne Sexton. "Cinderella" from TRANSFORMATIONS by Anne Sexton. Copyright © 1971 by Anne Sexton. Reprinted by permission of Houghton Mifflin Company. All rights reserved.

Ruth Sidel. From ON HER OWN by Ruth Sidel. Copyright © 1990 by Ruth Sidel. Used by permission of Viking Penguin, a division of Penguin Books USA Inc.

Fred Small. Source: Fred Small, "Pornography and Censorship." © 1985 by *Changing Men Magazine*, 306 North Brooks St., Madison, WI 53715. All rights reserved. Used by permission. First published in *Changing Men*, 1985.

Dale Spender. From Dale Spender, "Language Studies: From the Spoken to the Written Word," *The Writing or the Sex?: Or Why You Don't Have to Read Women's*

Writing to Know It's No Good (New York: Pergamon Press, 1989), pp. 7–23. Reprinted by permission.

Gloria Steinem. Source: Gloria Steinem, "The Politics of Talking in Groups: How to Win the Game and Change the Rules." *Ms.* Vol IX, No. 11, May, 1981, pp. 43, 45, 84, 86–89. Reprinted by permission of the author. Gloria Steinem, "Erotica vs. Pornography," Outrageous Acts and Everyday Rebellions, (New York: Holt, Rinehart and Winston, 1983), pp. 219–230. From OUTRAGEOUS ACTS AND EVERYDAY REBELLIONS by Gloria Steinem. Copyright © 1983 by Gloria Steinem, © 1984 by East Toledo Productions, Inc. Reprinted by permission of Henry Holt and Company, Inc.

John Stoltenberg. John Stoltenberg, "Pornography and Freedom," *Changing Men* 15, Fall, 1985, pp. 5–6, 46–47. Reprinted by permission of John Stoltenberg. Copyright 1985, John Stoltenberg.

Meryl Streep. Meryl Streep, "When Women Were In the Movies," Screen Actor, 29 (2), Fall, 1990, pp. 15–17. © 1990, Screen Actors Guild. Reprinted with permission from *Screen Actors* and the author.

Deborah Tannen. From Deborah Tannen, "Sex, Lies and Conversations: Why Is It So Hard for Men and Women to Talk to Each Other?" *The Washington Post*, Sunday, June 14, 1990, p. C3. © 1990 by Deborah Tannen, Ph.D., author of YOU JUST DON'T UNDERSTAND.

Cooper Thompson. From Cooper Thompson, "A New Vision of Masculinity," from *Changing Men*, vol. 14 (Spring 1985), pp. 2–4, 44. Reprinted by permission of the author.

Edward Tick. Source: Edward Tick, "Apocalypse Continued," New York Times Magazine, January 13, 1985, p. 60. Reprinted by permission of the author.

Twentieth Century Fox Film Corporation. Excerpt from the screenplay of 'BUTCH CASSIDY AND THE SUNDANCE KID' written by William Goldman. "BUTCH CASSIDY AND THE SUNDANCE KID" © 1969 Twentieth Century Fox Film Corporation. All rights reserved.

Alice Walker. "In Search of Our Mothers' Gardens" from *In Search of Our Mothers' Gardens*, copyright © 1974 by Alice Walker, reprinted by permission of Harcourt Brace Jovanovich, Inc.

Alice Walker. Source: "Women" from *Revolutionary Petunias and Other Poems*, copyright © 1970 by Alice Walker, reprinted by permission of Harcourt Brace Jovanovich, Inc.

Marilyn Waring. Excerpt from IF WOMEN COUNTED: A New Feminist Economics by Marilyn Waring. Copyright © 1988 by Marilyn J. Waring. Reprinted by permission of HarperCollins Publishers Inc.

Philip Weiss. Philip Weiss, "Forbidden Pleasures," Harper's magazine, March 1986. pp. 68–72. Copyright © 1986 by Harper's Magazine. All rights reserved. Reprinted from the March issue by special permission.

Patricia J. Williams. Source: Patricia J. Williams, "On Being the Object of Property," [*Signs: Journal of Women in Culture and Society* 1988, vol. 14, no. 1]. © 1988 by The University of Chicago. All rights reserved.